Microsoft® Office Project Server 2007: The Complete Reference

About the Authors

Dave Gochberg is a senior consultant with over 12,000 hours experience as a successful project manager. In addition, he has experience as a resource manager and has a wide range of technical expertise. For the last several years and versions, he has been focused on Enterprise Project Management (EPM) using Microsoft's Project Server solution, as well as SharePoint technologies. He holds both Microsoft Certifications that are currently available for Project and Project Server 2007. He lives near Madison, Wisconsin, with his wife and two children. During the writing of this book, Dave was awarded his Third-Degree Black Belt at the USA Martial Arts Center.

Rob Stewart has been working with Project Server since before it was named Project Server. He was formerly the information technology (IT) director for a software engineering company and has provided consulting services for customers in the public, private, and government sectors. Currently, he is a solutions specialist–Microsoft for CDW Berbee in western Michigan. He lives with his better half Kelly, two monkeys, and a bald bird in Grand Rapids. His kids think he's cool, and his Mom loves him, even though she doesn't know what he does for a living.

Microsoft® Office Project Server 2007: The Complete Reference

Dave Gochberg
Rob Stewart

New York Chicago San Francisco
Lisbon London Madrid Mexico City
Milan New Delhi San Juan
Seoul Singapore Sydney Toronto

The McGraw-Hill Companies

Cataloging-in-Publication Data is on file with the Library of Congress

Microsoft® Office Project Server 2007: The Complete Reference

1 2 3 4 5 6 7 8 9 0 DOC DOC 0 1 9 8

ISBN 978-0-07-148599-9
MHID 0-07-148599-6

Sponsoring Editor
Megg Morin

Editorial Supervisor
Patty Mon

Project Manager
Vasundhara Sawhney, International Typesetting and Composition

Acquisitions Coordinator
Carly Stapleton

Technical Editor
Dan Ling

Copy Editor
Andy Saff

Proofreader
Bev Weiler

Indexer
Steve Ingle

Production Supervisor
Jean Bodeaux

Composition
International Typesetting and Composition

Illustration
International Typesetting and Composition

Art Director, Cover
Jeff Weeks

Contents at a Glance

Contents

Part III Details on the Installation and Configuration of Project Server 2007

Acknowledgments

There are many people we would like to thank for getting this book to come to pass. Without our colleague Bill Hogg, the opportunity would never have happened. In addition, we would like to thank Liz Eversoll, Paul Shain, and Greg Sliwicki for allowing us to pursue this project. In addition, we would like to thank Claus Nielsen, Jo Ellen Amato, Sonja O'Regan, and Kevin Murtha for their thoughts and mentoring. We would also like to thank the team at McGraw-Hill (Megg Morin, Carly Stapleton, Patty Mon, Vasundhara Sawhney, and Andy Saff) for helping two new authors through the publishing maze, as well as David Fugate, our literary agent for putting this in motion. In addition, we want to acknowledge Dan Ling, for editing the technical content of this work, and Gary Crich for helping toward that end. As no two Project Server implementations are ever exactly alike, helping to implement a tool to solve a wide array of real-world problems has been extremely gratifying. Meeting and working with all of the extremely intelligent and gifted people along the way has been icing on the cake.

Introduction

When we embarked on this endeavor, we knew that the tools that made up Microsoft's Enterprise Project Management (EPM) solution were large and complex. Writing a book on the topic was going to require a significant amount of work and focus. We are grateful to have been selected to add this book to the McGraw-Hill Complete Reference series. Writing a technical book where the title includes the word "complete" is a somewhat daunting task, however, especially for people who have never written anything so large. Actually, the *really complete* version would probably require thousands of pages. We did what we thought was best to cover the spectrum of topics. In some cases, we made judgment calls about features and how likely they were to provide value. Although we skipped lower-value features in some areas, we delved deeper in others. We chose to spend a good portion of effort on configuration and data flow of the systems.

Note that throughout the book, we make recommendations and discuss "best practices." We stand behind each of them based on our experiences, our discussions with other consultants, information we learned at seminars and trade shows, and so on. Keep in mind, however, that not every one of our recommendations will be the right solution for you and your organization. To succeed, make sure you identify stakeholders, analyze (with the stakeholders) your organization's needs, and make the decisions that best suit those needs.

The flow of the book follows the general process of what it takes to actually succeed with an implementation of Project Server 2007, starting with value of planning. It was written for a blended audience, from the EPM novice on one end of the spectrum, to the experienced EPM professional. Finally, we hope this can truly be a "reference" in that after your system is up and running, you may go back to a single chapter for specific and useful (through possibly obscure) information.

Part I: Consider This Before You Commit to Project Server 2007

In this section, we lay the groundwork for the deployment of Project Server 2007. First we address the things that you should consider before embarking on the journey of implementing Project Server 2007 and its associated tools. This chapter helps to set the expectation that implementing Project Server will not deliver instant results, but rather will take some time to plan and test through an iterative methodology. This section also covers the new architecture of Project Server 2007, as well as its new features.

Part II: Plan for Your Project Server 2007 Implementation

In this section, we will discuss the implementation approaches you may take and the foundations that must be in place for your implementation to have the greatest chance for success. We include some examples of specific processes that may be useful for organizations that do not already have their own methods for performing similar activities (such as requirements gathering and prioritization).

Part III: Details on the Installation and Configuration of Project Server 2007

This section covers the installation of Project Server in various environments, the configuration of your newly installed system, and some of the administrative functions, including desktop deployment. This is the largest part of the book and includes fairly deep information about critical areas such as the security of Project Server in addition to data structure and flow.

Part IV: Project Server 2007 Maintenance

In this section, we discuss migration approaches that you may encounter as well as the fine-tuning of your EPM environment, and we briefly discuss options available for integrating Project Server 2007 with other systems related to your line of business.

Part V: Project Server in Action

This section consists of numerous chapters for reference on how to complete specific tasks in the EPM system based on your role in the system. Because we cover the way that each Project Server role interacts, we had no choice but to make assumptions on the way that the system's options were configured. We based our assumptions on what we have seen in the field with Project Server 2007, as well as what we had learned from implementations of previous versions. There is also an overview chapter on resource management in Project Server.

As a bonus, an extensive chapter describes how to extend your Windows SharePoint Services (WSS) environment, which may have implications that reach beyond EPM and into the team and departmental workspaces of your organization. The section that follows our discussion of roles focuses on how to extend the collaborative area using WSS 2007 technologies. This chapter also has a section that discusses how to leverage the advanced features that are available in Microsoft Office SharePoint Server (MOSS) 2007. In our opinion, SharePoint collaborative features are too often underused in the Microsoft EPM toolset, so this chapter is pretty deep.

Part VI: Program and Portfolio Management

In this section, we discuss the different techniques used at the managerial level (and up) to understand how your organization is performing at the program level (a group of related projects). It also includes a look at using Project Server in an environment where Project Portfolio Management (PPM) is important.

Because we designed this book as described above, there will be overlap in some of the content. For example, it would be impossible to discuss the role of the resource manager without having overlap with the chapter on resource management. Likewise, Data Analysis views (reports), for example, have to come up in the chapters describing how to configure online analytical processing (OLAP) cube configuration (which data will be gathered for analysis), and when discussing the display side of that data (Manage views). The context of each chapter was used as the basis for determining how to approach this overlap, so here and there you will read very similar information. Remember that we want to support the "reference" concept—that is, to make it easy for you to go back to find information after the initial implementation.

One certainty is that every reader will have a unique experience deploying Project Server 2007, just as each one of our clients chose different paths. You must keep in mind that the success of any Project Server implementation will probably require a marriage of improvements from people, process, and technology perspectives. Organizations need to understand that a full-scale EPM implementation can touch every corner of their business. The benefits of such integration can be enormous, but the cultural change required to facilitate this integration is equally as great.

Gone are the days when your users could "prairie dog" over their cube wall to ask a coworker to complete a task. That task assignment and the communication surrounding it must now be facilitated through the EPM tools. Users must participate in the EPM system with consistency and in a standardized manner. An organizational entity should in most cases exist to create, evangelize, and enforce these organizational project management methodologies and standards. This entity is called many names—program management office, project management office, or Center of Excellence.

Typically, the success of an EPM initiative is judged by the quality of the organizational insight delivered by the reports in the EPM toolset. What is often forgotten is that the granularity and accuracy of the reports that EPM *delivers* is built by the granularity and accuracy of data that are *fed* into the EPM system. If your Project Center views (where each project is displayed at a summary level) are based on project manager *estimations*, you will have many fewer touch points into the EPM system, reducing culture change and overall complexity, but providing much less clarity and accuracy into your organization's portfolio. If, on the other hand, your Project Center views are based on direct participation by the resources doing the work, required training increases, the number of touch points into EPM increases greatly, and the culture change is significantly greater. The payoff is invaluable, providing accurate and detailed insight into your organization's capacity, load, cost, and overall health is invaluable.

Sponsorship

EPM implementation requires sponsorship at the highest levels of the organization. Thus, at a bare minimum, the sponsor of the EPM project should have the authority over every part of the organization that the EPM environment will touch. Whether through executive cheerleading, or executive mandate, this active sponsorship can drive EPM to success, and the lack of it will cause the EPM initiative to grind to a halt.

From the Authors

Thank you very much for purchasing and reading this book. For information on current hotfixes, go to http://support.microsoft.com/ph/11388/en-us/?aid=2&GSA_AC_More2.

In early December of 2007, Microsoft released Service Pack 1 for Project Server 2007. Many of the improvements are "under the hood," but especially significant from the functional perspective are improvements in the My Tasks page. We will be providing some material related to this Service Pack on the McGraw-Hill Web site, so please visit www.mhprofessional.com and select Computing and then the title of your book to find content. In addition to the Service Pack 1 updates, you'll find an installation checklist and a multitab Excel spreadsheet that has Project Planner 2007 default settings and a place to store your settings side by side. This spreadsheet includes a Table of Contents and links to specific sections of content in the spreadsheet itself.

Once again, thanks.

PART I

Consider This before You Commit to Project Server 2007

CHAPTER 1

What Your CFO Needs to Know about Project Server

At the heart of it, this is a technical book. Although this book focuses on processes and technologies, Microsoft Project Server 2007 and other tools involved in Enterprise Project Management (EPM) can touch virtually every part of an organization's business. This statement may seem daunting, but there is a wide range of project types and sizes, and EPM tools offer companies the opportunity to make significant organizational improvements in almost every case. For these improvements to occur, however, it is important to view EPM projects as not just a set of tools, but rather a marriage of people, processes, and technology. In addition, the greatest improvements come when EPM is viewed as a tool for the entire enterprise, not necessarily just a department or area such as information technology (IT).

In addition to the IT department, organizations of all types use Microsoft Project Server to deliver business value in areas such as human resources, marketing, new product development, and engineering. You can successfully implement these tools for a single department, but with a larger-scale deployment, more opportunity exists to increase both productivity and actual measurable dollars.

In project management methodologies, the *project executive sponsor* is the title designated to the person who is ultimately responsible for driving a project to a successful conclusion. This role includes advocating the project to peers, most of whom operate at the management level or higher. In EPM projects, the term *executive sponsor* should be taken literally.

If possible, the sponsor should be come from the executive level, such as the chief executive officer (CEO), chief information officer (CIO), and chief operations officer (COO). This doesn't mean that these efforts cannot be successfully completed with a director or manager as a sponsor, but the likelihood of success is greater with a sponsor who has a broader view of the organization and more ability to drive behavior.

The Value of Enterprise Project Management

There is inherent value to becoming a more project-centric organization. It is nearly certain, for example, that organizations will become more efficient in their resource allocation after a successful EPM implementation. Assuming that your EPM efforts are well planned and delivered appropriately, it is also probable that your organization will improve the quality of the projects that are delivered and the ability to execute a higher number of initiatives.

Improvements can occur in many other areas. For example, putting an EPM solution into place can often expose process inefficiencies. In some cases, such solutions can yield measurable increases in dollar savings and profits.

We know that the CFO or COO is looking for some measurable value, and we will get to that in this chapter. First, though, here are some general examples of improvements that EPM can realize:

- Reduction in manual status reporting activity
- Reduced time to create new project plans through the use of reusable enterprise project templates
- Improved accuracy of project estimates
- Role- and skills-based scheduling enabling the best use of resources
- Increased standardization and consistency of project delivery for improved quality
- Powerful reporting and analysis, including business intelligence for better visibility and insight into project and resource data
- Ability to manage project schedules across the enterprise rather than one at a time, thereby reducing incorrect output and assumptions
- Better insight into project cost information
- Improved project team collaboration
- An environment to support constant improvement
- Capacity planning to make sure that the right resources are available when required

Executives understand improvements in productivity but rarely allow the use of fuzzy productivity verbiage such as "higher efficiency" or "improved quality" as the sole justifications for green-lighting a significant effort such as Project Server 2007. They have read highly publicized information about failures of large systems such as Enterprise Resource Planning (ERP), Customer Relationship Management (CRM), and, to a lesser extent, EPM. Of course, the press tends not to report successful projects. Expect executives to look for ways to make certain that deploying EPM makes sense. They will want to see how risk will be avoided and mitigated, and they will seek actual measurable (in dollars) improvements such as new revenue, reduced cost, or new cost avoidance.

Microsoft Office Project Server 2007 can provide and has delivered substantial value and can be a fit for many sizes and types of organizations, but each of them will have a different perspective on where the value of Project Server 2007 lies. Here are some examples of how measurable value can be found:

- In larger organizations, especially those with many locations, projects often are staffed only with known local resources. In this scenario, it is quite possible that someone with the required skills may actually be available to help outside the local branch. The ability of the Project Server to support skill or role-based resource allocation could help the organization avoid unnecessary hiring and consulting costs.
- Without an EPM environment, the most common ways to share project information are via paper documents and e-mail that includes attachments. It is quite common for

multiple versions of project plans, blueprints, specifications, and change documentation to exist on an individuals' laptop or network drives, or on paper in briefcases and portfolios. Version incompatibility has often created costly problems, such as writing software code for a feature no longer required, building something incorrectly, even sending the wrong price quotes to customers. The centralized nature of Project Server and the document management features (Check-Out/Check-In, Versioning, and so on) that are provided by the base SharePoint platform can help avoid costly mistakes.

- It is often true that analyzing an organization's processes with the tools of Project Server can expose information that can be used to help make processes more efficient. In one actual case, a client was able to leverage information in Project Server to improve an internal customer-facing process substantially. This change shortened the time to invoice and payment by more than two months, greatly improving the client's financial top line.

Besides making the case for executing the deployment of Project Server, finding where your company can improve processes to achieve financial benefits will help in other ways. Understanding priorities requires understanding of both the cost and value of each specific piece of your designed solution. Later in this book, we will discuss how to decide which features to use in a specific targeted Project Server deployment, and will seek to consider and assess relative value for each possible feature.

Organizational Commitment to EPM Success

Every Project Server implementation is different, so there is no certain way to determine how much time is required. What is clear is that Project Server implementations touch people and their processes in a way that requires significant planning. Adoption and training are also considerations that are required for success. Your executive should not expect to implement Project Server in a few weeks, but rather over some number of months. The set of tools available in Project Server is complex and the broad set of features cannot be implemented in a few weeks.

The following subsections describe the key roles that groups within an organization play during the planning and execution of the EPM project.

The Executive Sponsor

The executive sponsor should expect to spend significant time in the initial envisioning and planning effort (10-20 percent of their time is a reasonable expectation), and then reduce their involvement over time. Some of this work could be delegated, but the sponsor should be available to make timely decisions during the project in case the project team needs that input.

The Project Team

The best EPM implementation projects will include a project team. This team of people represents the project stakeholders and required technical staff and is an important component of building the Project Server infrastructure in a manner that is most useful to the organization. In addition, the input that is provided to the project from this team and the resulting outcomes create a group of people who will have ownership in the project's success. This is a major asset that makes it much more likely to produce a successful project. This group should meet weekly or bi-weekly, but more frequently during the project's planning stages. More detail about the specific makeup of this team will be included in Chapter 4.

The Subject Matter Expert(s)

One or more people inside the organization will need to learn Project Server and its partner technology, Windows SharePoint Services, from the server and practical application perspective. Such experts will also require strong skills in Microsoft Project Professional and will need to develop specific expertise in the use of Project Professional with Project Server. Usually, these experts already have experience in project management. Alternatively, some organizations approach this need by training a technical employee in project management and Microsoft Project.

The perfect employee (if one actually exists) for this role is a senior project/program manager with experience managing both iterative and traditional ("waterfall") projects. In addition, he or she will have application server administration experience (tool administration) and database administration skills. Understanding complex technical security models is also important. This combination of skills is rare. This role is often filled or supplemented by consultants as the internal resource develops the necessary expertise.

You should expect this role to be very heavily involved for the life of the EPM implementation project and beyond. If you have a program management office, that is a solid place to start looking for the right person to fill this position.

Technical Services/IT

Technical resources will be needed early in the project for network, hardware, security, and installation services. This commitment will be significant for the first two-to-three weeks, but will diminish over time. In the long run, there should not be a heavy burden on this staff.

Additional technical work may be within the realm of IT, depending on how the organization applies its policies. For example, each project manager requires installation of the Project Professional client. This can be installed one desktop at a time or delivered as part of an automatically delivered "package." Also, depending on the specific level of desktop software, additional packages may be required.

Maintaining database backups and working with database logs, plans, and such are the focus of any ongoing technical work. For more detail on the technical pieces, see Chapter 9.

Active Project Sponsorship

Your Project Server 2007 deployment will probably drive substantial organizational improvement. This could require that some business processes change, and in many organizations change can be difficult. It is important for the executive sponsor to set the tone that this project is important and that the organization is expected to assist in the effort to make the project a success.

The sponsor should not be a bystander but rather an active participant in the project, at least from a decision-making perspective. That does not mean that the CFO is expected to spend many hours working deep in the process and technical weeds (which just won't happen), but rather that whomever chooses to be the sponsor show ongoing interest in the progress and outcomes.

Is the project sponsor a cheerleader or hammer? He or she can be either or both. Additionally, this role should be the final stop when the project team cannot reach decisions.

In this chapter, we have covered the potential value of Project Server and the required resource commitment. The next two chapters will cover the newly designed system architecture and the new features of the Microsoft Office Project Server 2007 solution.

CHAPTER 2

The New Architecture of the Microsoft EPM Environment

To understand what brought Project Server to where it is today, it may help to understand its origins. This chapter helps you understand the new Project Server 2007 (PS2K7) architecture, and may help to shed light on the some of the challenges that you may have experienced with earlier versions of the Enterprise Project Management (EPM) toolset. We'll briefly review the Project Server 2003 application architecture in each section, and then investigate the components of Project Server 2007 to see the inner workings of the latest version of Microsoft's Enterprise Project Management Suite.

From a high-level perspective, you might not recognize a big difference in the appearance of Project Server 2007 and Project Web Access (PWA). In this chapter, we'll discuss the core architecture of this new application and look at some different approaches to understanding these new technologies.

Authentication

Although Project Server 2003 offered two methods of authentication for access to a PWA site (Windows and Project Server authentication), implementers really only had one choice to provide seamless authentication to all of the components of Project Server 2003. That choice was Windows authentications with Active Directory Domain authentication. Some organizations attempted to configure Project Server with Windows SharePoint Services (WSS), SQL, and SQL Analysis Services on a single server in a workgroup or in a Novell or NT 4 environment, but what they won't mention are the setup headaches and astronomical support costs that they encountered. In the Project Server 2003 world, Windows SharePoint Services v2 demanded Windows authentication. This fact alone made giving users access to the documents, issues, and risk-tracking capabilities a much more administratively laborious process if the server was part of a Windows workgroup.

Project Server 2007 relies entirely on Windows SharePoint Services v3 (WSSv3) for its authentication processes, and WSSv3 now supports forms authentication. Forms authentication is the equivalent of Project Server authentication in previous versions, although it has a couple of additional advantages:

- Because the authentication information is stored at the WSSv3 farm level, forms-authenticated users can carry their authenticated state with them throughout the services on that farm (such as Office SharePoint Server sites). In previous versions, users authenticating with Project Server authentication could only access the current PWA site.
- With forms authentication, your options for the source of your directory of users are expanded greatly. Whereas with Project Server authentication users' credentials were stored in the Project Server Database, any Lightweight Directory Access Protocol (LDAP) store or SQL database can provide forms authentication.

The following steps summarize the authentication process:

1. WSS authenticates either a forms- or a Windows-authenticated user.
2. The Project Server Interface (PSI) passes an encrypted cookie to the client directly or through the PSI Forwarder if you are using a dedicated PWA Server.
3. Subsequent requests to Project Server (and the PSI) use the authentication cookie.

NOTE *If all of your intended Project Server 2007 users can use Windows domain accounts, you can disregard forms authentication altogether. There are only rare cases where a single user would require both forms-authenticated access and Windows authentication.*

NOTE *One area of the PWA 2007 user interface that requires Windows authentication is for the Data Analysis views. Aside from the software requirements and configuration that are required for users to access the online analytical processing (OLAP) data, being logged into a machine with domain credentials that the Analysis Services Server recognizes (either the same machine or a trusting Active Directory Domain) is critical. In addition, the Export to Excel function from the Data Analysis views requires this same connectivity.*

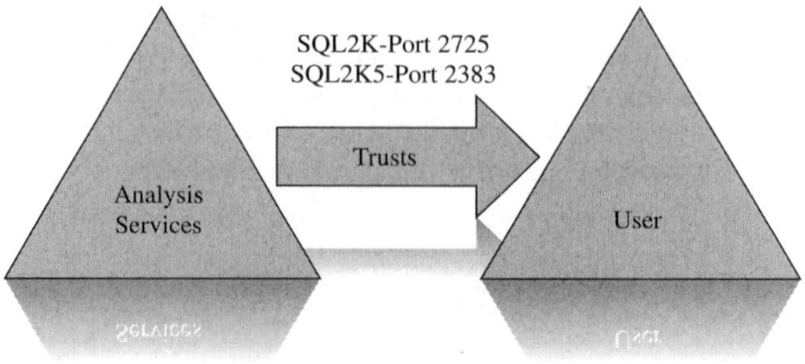

Analysis Services

Project Server 2007 supports both SQL Server 2000 Analysis Services and SQL Server 2005 Analysis Services. There are many differences between the SQL Server 2000 and 2005 Analysis Services. This section discusses the architectural changes between SQL 2000 and SQL 2005 Analysis Services working with PS 2007, including how EPM generates and consumes Analysis Services data.

NOTE *This chapter also includes details of the different requirements when running Project Server 2007 with SQL 2000 Analysis Services or SQL 2005 Analysis Services.*

Access

Prior to Project Server 2007, users needed the administrator to perform a number of steps to view Analysis Services data. Those steps included creating an OLAP administrator, giving that user rights to the Analysis Services server, possibly running the PSComPlus.exe utility on the Project Server machine to associate the OLAP administrator with the process of building the cube, and manually modifying the roles in Analysis Services to allow access to OLAP data. The Analysis Services cube role membership in Project Server 2007 is updated with each cube build or update. This membership is based on the View Data Analysis and View OLAP Data global permissions of any Project Server Security Group. When you grant the View OLAP Data permission, Project Server adds the group's members to the cube role in Analysis Services upon the next cube build; whereas View Data Analysis gives a user rights to the PWA page that houses the Data Analysis Views. As a result of the security trimming in Windows SharePoint Services v3, if this permission is not allowed (unchecked) or denied, the user will not see the Reporting section and the Data Analysis links in the quick launch bar.

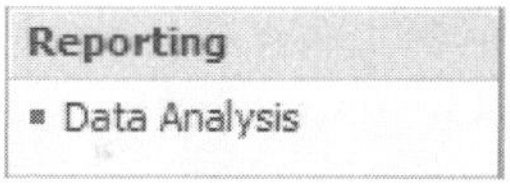

Initially, one would wonder why there are two permission settings for a single function. But when you consider that Microsoft Excel 2003 or 2007 can make connections to the Analysis Services cube independently of PWA, you see that this granularity of security is needed. The View Data Analysis permission gives rights to the PWA view, whereas the View OLAP Data permission gives rights to the data in SQL Server Analysis Services and affects the direct communication between SQL Server Analysis Services and the client machine.

TIP *The Transmission Control Protocol (TCP) port that Analysis Services uses to communicate with clients depends on the version of SQL Server Analysis Services that you are accessing. For SQL Server 2000 Analysis Services, Analysis Services uses port 2725. For SQL 2005 Analysis Services, port 2383 is used.*

Cube Generation Updating

SQL Server 2000 used a Jet database (msmdrep.mdb) file for its Analysis Services repository. Microsoft offered instructions and "best practices" for moving this repository to a more secure and scalable database within SQL Server 2000. SQL Server 2005 Analysis Services does not use a Jet database for its Analysis Services repository by default. Because the Microsoft developers had to make the solution compatible with both SQL Server 2000 and SQL Server

2005 Analysis Services, the cube building was built for SQL Server 2000 Analysis Services, with a workaround for SQL 2005 Analysis Services. Although the management of your database and Analysis Services environments will be aided by sharing a common version of SQL Server, Project Server 2007 supports using different versions for the database and Analysis Services components. For example, you can use SQL Server 2000 SP4 for your database server, and use SQL Server 2005 SP2 Analysis Services for the cube building in your environment.

Cube Capabilities

The changes in the 2007 EPM toolset as they relate to reporting and the cube-building process are vast, and include the following:

- **Dedicated Reporting Database** The cube-building process consumes data from the Reporting Database. As this database is dedicated only to reporting, it gives the administrator much more flexibility for report generation and options for achieving optimal system performance.
- **Built-in collection of cubes** Each PWA instance provides 11 cubes and 3 virtual cubes (that is, collections of these 11 cubes). In addition, the building of these cubes can be customized directly through a browser from PWA.
- **Core schemas** The cube data are layered in a way that makes finding, configuring, and exposing the data more efficient. The three core schemas are EPM, Timesheet, and Collaboration (which includes the issues and risks data from WSS).

Cube Management

In Project Server 2007, administrators are given much more information about the build settings, configuration, and build status of the Analysis Services cube. These settings are found in Server Settings, as shown in Figure 2-1.

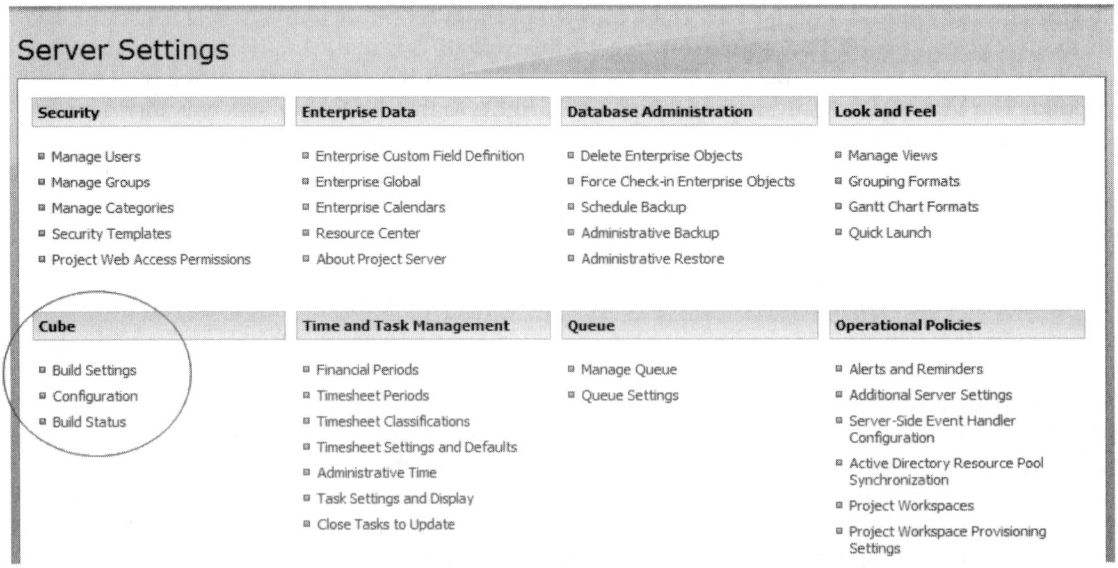

FIGURE 2-1 The cube management section of Server Settings

The entire cube-building process is now managed by the queue, with enhanced logging, configuration, and scheduling options. A more thorough discussion of the required SQL Server 2005 Analysis Services configuration steps is included in Chapter 6, whereas queue configuration settings are discussed later in this chapter.

Operating Systems

The server and workstation operating systems in your environment greatly impact your EPM deployment.

Network Operating System

When installing Project Server 2007 in a multiserver farm environment, a Windows Active Directory (2000 or above) is required. Although it is possible to install Project Server 2007 in a Windows NT4 domain and use those domain accounts for authentication, you are limited to either a stand-alone installation or a single-server small farm. The immediate obstacle is that during installation, the SharePoint Configuration Wizard looks for a dynamic global catalog and relies on the server-to-server trust infrastructure that only a Windows 2000, Windows Server 2003, or Windows Server 2008 Active Directory provides.

Client Machines

Sometimes referred to as part of the Web tier of a three-tier application, client machines are truly where the rubber meets the road—where most users will interact with the EPM system. The following are the Microsoft Office components required by the role that a user plays in the EPM 2007 system:

- **Project manager**
  - Microsoft Windows XP with Service Pack (SP) 2, Windows Server 2003 with SP1, or a later operating system with Microsoft Office Project Professional 2007.
  - Internet Explorer 6.0 or later, 32-bit browser-only Analysis Services 2005 (9.0), OLE DB Provider (if project managers require Data Analysis Views).
  - Microsoft Office Excel 2003 SP2 or later (for the Visual Reports in Project Professional 2007).
  - Microsoft Office Visio 2007 (for the Visual Reports in Project Professional 2007).
- **Executive**
  - Microsoft Windows XP with SP2 or later.
  - For Windows SharePoint Services Box/Forms Administration, the following are required: Microsoft Windows 2000 SP4 or later, Windows XP, Windows Server 2003, or Windows Vista with Internet Explorer 6.0 or later, 32-bit browser-only Analysis Services 2005 (9.0) OLE DB Provider (for Data Analysis Views).
- **Resource**
  - Microsoft Windows XP with SP2 or later. For Windows SharePoint Services Box/Forms Administration, the following are required: Microsoft Windows 2000 SP4 or later, Windows XP, Windows Server 2003, or Windows Vista with Internet Explorer 6.0 or later, 32-bit browser-only Microsoft Outlook 2003 or 2007 (for interaction with Project Server through Microsoft Outlook Calendar and Tasks).

Windows SharePoint Services

In Project Server 2003, Windows SharePoint Services v2.0 was an optional component used to facilitate the association of documents, issues, and risks with project tasks. In Project Server 2007, Windows SharePoint Services v3.0 is the foundation upon which PWA and project workspaces are created. Actually, Windows SharePoint Services v3.0 is a Microsoft Office Project Server 2007 prerequisite. This makes the Project Server 2K7 environment rich in customization possibilities, through the same tools used to customize WSS.

Ability to Scale

Many of the Project Server 2003 scalability tools actually manipulated registry settings; now these settings are maintained and stored in the WSS database. There are fewer registry entries for farmwide settings, as configuring network load balancing addresses, host headers, and management of critical services is based on the foundation of SharePoint Central Administration. These new tools allow you, as the application administrator, to change your Project Server infrastructure footprint quickly as the demand for the solution increases. It is highly recommended that you gain a firm understanding of WSS because it is a core element of installation, authentication, security, display, and integration with other Office Server products and the Project Server 2007 offering.

Tip *Microsoft has published a great deal of information regarding Windows SharePoint Services v3 and development on this platform. It can be found at http://msdn2.microsoft.com/en-us/library/aa902526.aspx.*

Networking Components

To appreciate the PS2K7 networking architecture fully, you first must understand some of the networking components of its predecessor.

Communication between Project Pro and SQL

In Office Project Server 2003, after a project manager authenticated to Project Server, his or her instance of Project Professional would make a direct connection to the SQL Server via Open Database Connectivity (ODBC) calls. Through this connection, the open, save, and publish functions would occur. From a bandwidth perspective, this required the entire version of sometimes very large project plans to cross the network every time an open, save, or publish occurred. Aside from the security aspects of opening up your SQL Server to every possible location where your project managers may be, the throughput of having multiple project managers performing this action simultaneously could bring the SQL network interface card (NIC) to its knees. Project managers would have to wait one to five minutes for their project to open across these low-bandwidth and high-latency networks. As a result, organizations would turn to terminal-emulation solutions such as Citrix and Microsoft's Terminal Services to enhance performance and security in their EPM environments.

PS2K7 solves many of these issues by implementing the Project Cache, which keeps a local copy of the project plan on the project manager's machine, and only transmits the changes to and from Project Server transparently through an incremental transaction-based save process. The process is similar to using Outlook 2003 in Cached Mode, except that instead of synchronizing mail items with an Exchange Server, you are synchronizing your project plan with Project Server. Also, instead of the ODBC connections that Project Professional 2002/2003 made to SQL Server, Project Professional 2007 now uses Web service calls over Hypertext Transfer Protocol (HTTP) and Simple Object Access Protocol (SOAP) exclusively to talk to the PSI or to the PSI Forwarder if you have a dedicated Front End Project Web Access server. The save and publish processes are now fault-tolerant, as these actions are transacted through an asynchronous process managed by the queue. Because of this architecture, all communication between Project Professional 2007 and Project Server 2007 can be secured via Secure Sockets Layer (SSL). Unlike its predecessor, PS2K7 is much more resilient to low-bandwidth, high-latency wide area network (WAN) links.

The Project Server Queue

In Project 2002/2003, there was the Views Notification service. This background service performed one of the most important functions of previous versions of Project Server: publishing the project plan. It did this by looking for Extensible Markup Language (XML) documents to be placed in the ViewDrop folder on the Project Server 2002/2003 file system for each publishing event. This process was serialized on a project and the Views Notification service was single-threaded. When the service found the document, it would then begin processing based on the contents of the XML document. This system worked well under light usage conditions. The problems arose during spike usage times, such as on Friday between 4 and 5 P.M., when all resources are scurrying to enter their time, or on Tuesday right before a weekly project management office (PMO) meeting, when all project managers are updating and publishing their projects. In Project Server 2003, these heavy usage times would result in impatient project managers publishing their project, watching the hourglass icon for an extended amount of time, thinking Project Professional had crashed, opening Task Manager on their workstation, and killing the process (You've been there, haven't you?). This could leave the project in an inconsistent state in the database, potentially leading to project corruption. An entirely new set of complications arose when you needed to scale out the view's processing service.

As an inhabitant of the application tier, the Project Server queuing system is an integral part of Project Server 2007. It's an entirely new way for Project Server 2007 to handle spikes in load gracefully, minimizing the potential for the system to quit responding under heavy stress. All core operations in Project Server 2007 go through the Project Server queue. From publishing a plan, to deleting enterprise objects, to initiating the cube-building service for your OLAP cubes, the queue manages these tasks in a linear fashion in order to maximize server resources and more efficiently handle the spikes in traffic that regularly occur.

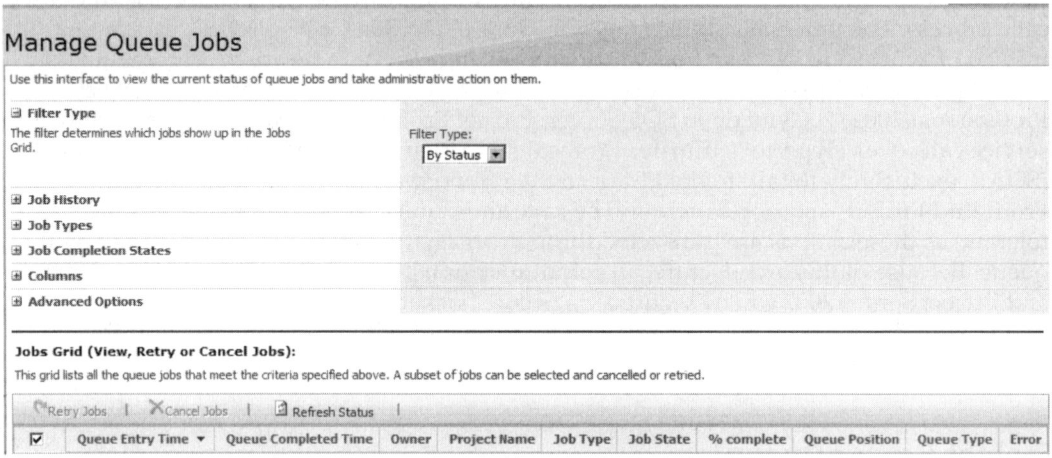

The Project Server queue provides several advantages over its predecessor:

- **Reliability** Because there is no direct file system exchange, SQL transactions can be used to help ensure data integrity. Incomplete transactions are rolled back. When an error is encountered, most jobs are rolled back in their entirety.
- **Fault tolerance** More than one queuing service can participate in an EPM environment. If one queue service instance crashes or stops, the next queuing service instance will transparently pick up remaining jobs.
- **Performance and scalability** Because the Project Server queuing service is multithreaded, it can handle several queue jobs simultaneously. If you start experiencing performance issues, you can add middle-tier application servers to spread the load. Performance of the queue can be throttled through the Queue Settings page (discussed later in this chapter).
- **Manageability** Whether it's through the PWA administrative interface, a programmatic PSI call querying the queue service, or a Performance Monitor counter, the ability to manage and the visibility to troubleshoot the queue service effectively constitute a huge improvement. The Performance Monitor, as you'll see in Chapter 14, is an administrator's friend when it comes to figuring out when it is time to scale out your EPM server environment.

Architecturally, the queue service consists of two distinct yet architecturally identical queue systems. What differentiates these queue systems is the type of information that they process and their storage location:

- **The Timesheet Queue** This queue is used primarily to process timesheet activities (such as saving and submitting timesheets). The Timesheet Queue jobs are stored in the Published database.

- **The Project Queue** This queue handles most of the project-related jobs (including Project Save, Project Publish, Reporting, Cube Building Service, and Server-Side Scheduling). The Project Queue jobs are stored in the Draft database.

The queue systems' logical architecture is represented by four different modules that work together to complete each task.

Job Storage

As new jobs are submitted to the queue, Project Queue events are stored in the Draft database, and Timesheet jobs are stored in the Published database. This is significant, as the normal SQL database backup and restore mechanisms will provide the protection and ability to recover the queue that mission-critical applications require.

Job Polling

As these new jobs arrive in the Draft and Published databases, job-polling threads look for new jobs. The Queuing NT Service (which is installed by default on every application server in the farm) creates these polling threads for the Project and Timesheet queues. Administrators can manage this polling interval through the Manage Queue user interface.

Job Processing

When the job-polling thread finds a new job, it spawns a job-processing thread to complete the job. The job-processing threads reside in the Queuing NT Service process space and run as its identity. Administrators can configure the total number of job-processing threads through the Manage Queue user interface. (Refer to Chapter 14 for information about modifying the maximum number of job-processing threads and about potential SQL deadlock issues that can result from misconfiguration.)

Job Status and Management

The fourth module of the Project Server queue provides the status of jobs active in the queue and enables administrators to manage queue settings. From the Queue Management page (found in Server Settings), you can view current queue status and retry or cancel jobs that have not completed successfully. From the Queue Settings page, you can modify how the queue performs.

NOTE *If you experience unexplained queue behavior or jobs that appear to hang, refer to Chapter 14, which provides tips for troubleshooting the queue.*

The PSI Evolution of EPM Web Services

In 2002, Microsoft added the Project Data Service (PDS) to its EPM system. It was a major step forward for developers because of the new functionality of the PDS. It was a middle-tier Component Object Model (COM)–based application program interface (API) for Project Server 2002 and 2003 written in Visual Basic 6. No longer did Project Pro users have to use Database Source Names (DSNs) to connect to the PDS. Developers enjoyed the PDS's capability as a security broker for their integration efforts, and all of the available PDS methods were exposed through SOAP.

However, the PDS's limits were quickly realized as efforts to extend the functionality of Project Server regularly ended with a frazzled developer, a frustrated business analyst, and a deflated accounting department. The problem was that the PDS, being an XML Web service, failed to provide methods by which to access all of the business objects and logic in Project Server. Developers, when tasked with extending functionality of Project Server beyond the 67 methods, were faced with a decision: write a PDS extension with event handlers, or bypass the PDS altogether and work directly with the Project Server database. Programming directly against the Project Server 2002/2003 database was a dicey notion for several reasons:

- Because different applications typically need to implement similar business logic, there can be conflicting changes to the database when these actions take place on similar data.
- Whenever developers needed to modify the schema for their applications, they had to become very familiar with the Project Server 2003 database schema (which takes considerable time).
- Applying Service Packs brought looming despair, rather than the feeling of a kid on Christmas morning anticipating new features and functionality, because of the Project Server database schema changes that Service Packs brought. (It is highly recommended to test any Service Pack or update in a test environment.)

This forced developers to write PDS extensions and their own event handlers. Creating event handlers required developers to write their own SQL triggers, then running custom code. SQL triggers had their own set of issues with regard to stability and performance of the database server. Additionally, developers had to be fairly nimble with XML; the constructed code had to include error handling and constant validation. Developers had to work with XML strings and XML DOM, and they couldn't catch compile runtime errors.

This was certainly not an ideal development environment by today's .NET coding standards.

In Project Server 2007, the developers at Microsoft went to great lengths to ensure that the application was built in line with the most current programming approaches, but they also realized that COM was out and that .NET was the new standard. Most of the COM components have now been replaced by the SharePoint configuration database components, including the introduction of the PSI. PSCOMPlus.exe is an example of this change; although it was once a tool that administrators regularly used to modify credentials to the most crucial Project Server 2003 services, it has since been eliminated from the architecture.

PSI is the new programming model used to interact with Project Server. Based on ASP.NET 2.0, the PSI and Project Server Events Service expose the functionality and data that developers require to extend the capabilities of Project Server, including external application integration. With the PSI's reusable business objects, developers can call methods based on standardized semantics regardless of the type of code they are building.

Because a complete API is provided with Project Server 2007, developers don't need to dig into and deeply understand the four Project Server databases and how each is constructed. Code is no longer written against the SQL Server databases. Rather, code can be written against the PSI, which manages all of the database abstraction and connectivity. The database machine is more secure using this tiered design, and developers can focus their efforts toward serving the Project Server infrastructure.

The PSI Forwarder

In situations where users require access outside of your network, you are presented with the dilemma of allowing access to the PSI (a middle-tier component) from the Internet or extranet. The ability to provision Project Web Access servers in a perimeter network or "demilitarized zone" (DMZ) is essential. In this case, the PSI Forwarder resides on a Front End Web server and logs on to the middle-tier Project Server computer on behalf of the user and maintains context throughout the session.

The PSI Forwarder provides a number of benefits. First, it transparently sends requests to the PSI on behalf of the end user. It employs the use of a server-based cache that works with the Project Professional Active Cache to minimize round-trips to the Project Server middle tier. It also provides a buffer between the Internet/extranet and your internal Project Server infrastructure.

TIP *If a line-of-business (LOB) application can run only on a back-end server (for the need of impersonation), it authenticates as the Project Web Access super user to call the PSI Web services without going through the PSI Forwarder.*

The Heart of the PSI

The PSI is a set of 23 Web services areas, 19 of which are designed to be accessed through the PWA address, http://ServerName/PWASiteName/_vti_bin/psi/project.asmx. The generic Web services include Admin, Archive, Calendar, CubeAdmin, Custom Fields, Events, LoginWindows, LoginForms, LookupTable, Notifications, ObjectLinkProvider, Project, QueueSystem, Resource, ResourcePlan, Security Statusing, Timesheet, and WSSInterop.

Four additional Web services can be accessed only through the SSP URL, http://servername:56737/SharedServices1/psi/authentication.asmx, where 56737 is the port for the SharedService Provider (SPP) Administration site, and SharedServices1 is the name of your SSP. These are the internal PSI Web services, and include Authentication, PWA, View, and WinProj.

CAUTION *The generic Web services differ from the internal Web services in that the internal Web services are reserved for use by Project Web Access and Project Professional. Because of changes to the internal Web services that will come with Service Packs and updates, these four internal Web services should not be used in your application development efforts.*

Where the Project Server 2003 programming model only dealt with 67 methods, the PSI in Project Server 2007 contains all Office Project Server 2007 entities. The code was written in C# and uses ADO.NET DataSets for all data transfer.

There are over 350 public methods that are accessed via SOAP over HTTP. This is a much more firewall-friendly and security-conscious model.

TIP *Solution developers and designers and application developers who wish to develop solutions with the PSI should reference the Project Server 2007 Software Development Kit (SDK) at http://msdn2.microsoft.com/en-us/library/bb226704.aspx.*

Immediate Benefits for the Developer

In all previous incarnations of EPM, Project Pro was required for scheduling updates. The data required a round-trip routing process through the client. Project Pro didn't use many of the available PDS functions, because the client connected directly via ODBC to the Project Server 2003 database. As far as Project Professional was concerned, the PDS was really only there to broker security and set up the ODBC connection to the server hosting the Project Server database. In addition to brokering security, the PSI provides the entry point for integration with and access to Project Server data, regardless of whether the user is riding in a Project Professional, Internet Explorer, or custom Web application–colored vehicle. .NET developers will appreciate and welcome Project Server 2007 to the .NET development environment family because of their ability to use the tools of a managed environment (such as C#, VB.NET, and ADO) and design-time validation (Intellisense) in Visual Studio 2005.

How Does the PSI Work?

Every request to Project Server is a SOAP call to the PSI that invokes the appropriate PSI method. If authentication succeeds, context is passed from the PSI to the user via an encrypted cookie. The cookie is then used for authentication for subsequent operations in the session.

TIP *If you are running LOB applications, they will need to run as trusted processes and use impersonation. The LOB connector sets the context and addresses of one or more of the PSI's generic Web service methods. Because the impersonation process requires avoiding the PWA site, you use the SSP URL to initialize the impersonation process.*

PSI Method Properties

Most PSI methods are synchronous. However, some that are longer running are queued to help mitigate spike situations. There are times when multiple objects are accessed in a single PSI call. If one of the dependent operations fails, the entire queue job will be rolled back. However, there are some queue functions that are not transacted. For example, one of the capabilities of Project Server is to synchronize the users of your Enterprise Resource Pool with an Active Directory group. Because you may be synchronizing thousands of users, it would be quite inconvenient if the entire synchronization process were killed because of an error occurring with one of the accounts to be synchronized. In this case, the whole job would not be rolled back; rather, the accounts that can be synchronized will be, and failures are logged.

DataSets

The Project Server 2007 PSI uses ADO.NET 2.0 typed DataSets, which are small relational databases held in memory. For performance reasons, DataSets take only small slices of data. These typed DataSets equate to the business entities in Project Server and provide a number of benefits to your .NET developers:

- They provide type safety, so that incorrect types do not compile.
- Design time is validated through Intellisense in Visual Studio 2005.

- Data are presented via an object-oriented/relational model (rows and tables).
- DataSets improve network performance over ADO.NET 1.0, primarily around binary serialization.

PSI Limitations

Even though the PSI is a monumental leap in functionality from the development and job processing perspective, it does have some limitations, including the following:

- Resource leveling cannot be done on the server.
- There can be no baselines.
- There can be no recurring tasks.
- There can be no custom local fields or local calendars.
- You cannot change between schedule-from-start and schedule-from-finish constraints on the project.
- No variance or earned value data calculations are possible.
- There are no assignment contours; you cannot change the contours programmatically.
- You cannot define the Work Breakdown Structure (WBS) code mask programmatically.
- You cannot change the cost rate tables for local resources programmatically.
- You cannot define or edit base calendars through PSI.

Project Server Events

All Project Server 2007 entities include events. Two types of events support the PSI functions: pre-events and post-events. These individual events carry no Globally Unique Identifier (GUID), nor can they be linked so that if a secondary pre-event fails, it will roll back the previous pre-event. Because there are events for every Project Server business entity, it's safe to say that events are the nervous system of this latest version of the EPM toolset.

Pre-events

Pre-events are intended to enforce constraints, conduct business rule checks, or validate data that are presented prior to Project Server database saves. Because pre-events happen prior to the work of the event, they can cancel the entire operation if something goes wrong.

Post-events

Post-events happen after transactions are committed in the database. These events are intended to perform saving and synchronization after data are presented to the database, such as exporting newly created projects to an ERP system, or triggering an alert if a new resource has been added via Active Directory synchronization and they need additional actions performed on their account. Performing additional actions on the New Resource's account is facilitated by the asynchronous communication with the Project Server queue.

PDS to PSI

Although a complete PDS-to-PSI migration manual is beyond the scope of this book, there are a few key points to consider when upgrading from Project Server 2003 to Project Server 2007:

- The PDS has been replaced by the PSI.
- All PDS methods have PSI equivalents.
- PDS extensions need to be migrated.
- Any code that directly accesses the database needs to be migrated to a PSI model.

For thorough discussions and articles related to PDS-to-PSI migration, see the article on "PDS Parity in PSI Web Services" at http://msdn2.microsoft.com/en-us/library/ms197081.aspx.

Server-Side Scheduling

This very powerful application addition enables project managers to accept updates on a plan and publish it without requiring the data to make a round-trip through Project Professional 2007. This opens many thin client options for a mobile project manager.

In Project Server 2003, all of the heavy lifting of scheduling was done from within Project Professional 2003. There was no server-side logic that could programmatically update project schedules or update resource attributes. When companies demanded to have a hands-off process to update the resource pool or update and publish a mass of projects, they resorted to some very creative workarounds to this "round-trip required" mandate. Some loaded the Project Professional client on the server and built complex macros or services that would run. Some even dedicated a workstation that had a predefined set of tasks and would fire off its opening, modifying, saving, and publishing chores in the dark of night. Needless to say, this was a clumsy and sometimes quite expensive process.

NOTE *Because the entire Project Server 2007 system relies on ASP.NET 2.0 and Windows SharePoint Services 3.0, it has been given a much larger middle-tier brain capable of performing more complex operations through a thinner client.*

The benefits of Server-Side Scheduling include the following:

- Project managers can now accept assignment updates entirely through PWA.
- Resource managers can now change Enterprise resource-level fields on resources entirely through PWA.
- Because of the preceding benefits, overall flexibility and remote access options are greatly enhanced.
- A company will save on licensing costs for resource managers and administrators.

Server-Side Events

Server-side events provide a mechanism for developers to extend Project Server by adding new business logic. Project Server calls events whenever units of data change on the server. If you associate an event handler with an event, then the handler is executed when that particular event occurs.

Businesses would rip out the guts of the Project Server 2003 application to be able to add functionality or provide new features; now these server-side events can provide the triggers for customizations, resulting in more elegant approaches to adding custom functionality. The additional flexibility enables your .NET assemblies to modify data using the PSI methods, or circumnavigate the business logic of Project Server 2007 altogether. These .NET assemblies, written in either C# or VB.Net, execute on the middle tier, so there is no custom code on your database server or on the front-end machines. If you have multiple middle-tier machines, you will need to deploy these event handlers on all of your middle-tier servers.

Where the Events Live

Although the event handlers are installed on the middle-tier machines, there is a clear separation between the Events Service and the queue and PSI middle-tier processes. This was done to provide a stability barrier; thus, if your custom event handler crashed on the middle-tier server, it would not bring down other core Project Server services.

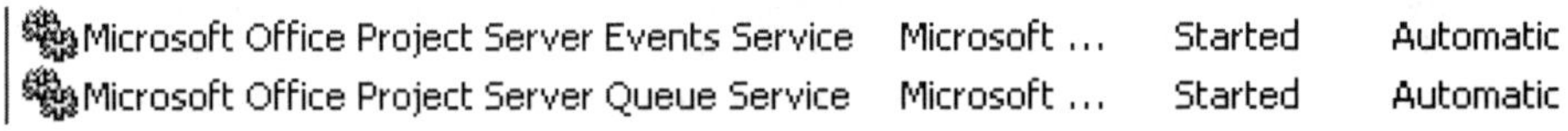

The Project Server Events Service is an NT service that is integral to server-side events. It intercepts all the PSI-called events, which can then invoke your event handlers.

Information about the Events Service is stored in the SharePoint_Config database. This information includes the event type, the PWA site to which it applies, and pointers to the event. The logical container for these events within the Config database is the Application Domain, which stores the event handlers. Upon starting, the Events Service queries the Application Domain from each PWA site and loads all event handlers into memory.

Let's examine the step-by-step process by which you rename each project as it is saved:

1. A user saves the project.
2. The PSI throws an event to the Events Service.
3. Because the event knows of an associated event handler that corresponds to the action, as well as the specific PWA site, it calls the event handler to run.
4. The event handler runs, calling the correct objects, or calling the correct PSI method, to change the project name.

There are two types of events: pre-events and post-events. Pre-events are called before data is saved to the database. These pre-events can be canceled by event handlers. Post-events cannot be canceled; they are called after the data changes are saved to the database.

Data Storage

Project Server 2002/2003 stored data in a project native file structure that was not the most efficient for data transfer or storage. All of the project information was stored in a single database, separated only by the associated tables (I.E. MSP_Projects, MSP_Web_Resources, and so on). With Project Server 2007, you have a logical database provisioning architecture that loosely maps to the actions that happen during a project's lifecycle:

- **The Draft database** This database is where your project is saved. It is the home of the Project Queue.
- **The Published database** This is where your project is published, and is also home of the Timesheet Queue. The relationship between the Draft and Published databases in Project Server 2007 is a monumental EPM data storage change, but it also contributes to the vast processing load change of your system. Much of Project Server 2003's database stress was at the NIC (setting up ODBC connections with Project Pro and sending large amounts of data); now the load is transferred to the SQL Servers because they are built for processing and memory optimization. When you publish a project from Project Professional 2007, the project data are sent from the Draft database to the Published database.
- **The Reporting database** This database continually receives data from the Published database. The Reporting database is a near real-time representation of all Published data which have been normalized with a different schema, making it perfect for reporting consumption. This is the database that is queried for views in Project Server and whose data are used to build the cubes in Analysis Services.
- **The Archive database** This database provides the in-system backup, restore, and versioning capabilities. The size of this database depends primarily on your project's size and the number of versions of each that you wish to retain.

TIP *The physical data storage and business processes implementations are masked by the business logic of the application. This makes hotfixes and Service Packs a much more pleasant proposition, because these updates often modify the database schema, which can have adverse effects on custom solutions that depend on direct database access.*

In addition, a number of other databases support the Windows SharePoint Services foundation:

- **The SharePoint_Config database** This is the configuration database for your farm. In previous versions, information about load balancing, service accounts, Project Web Access sites, Web applications (Web sites), and other administrative functions required an administrator to use a variety of tools (Internet Information Service [IIS] Manager, COMPlus.exe, registry edits) to modify. Because Windows SharePoint Services is the foundation for Project Server and Project Web Access sites, these administrative features are managed through the SharePoint configuration database instead of the IIS metabase, COM + applications, and the registry. Although you rarely would directly modify this database, there are two main methods for making changes to it: the SharePoint Central Administration Web site and the stsadm.exe utility.

NOTE *More information about the STSADM.exe utility will be provided in Chapter 14.*

- **The SharePoint AdminContent_(GUID) database** In Windows SharePoint Services, every Web application (by default) has an associated content database. So this AdminContent_(GUID) database provides the design, layout, themes, and pages of SharePoint Central Administration.
- **The WSS_Content database** This will typically be your first Web application's content database. If you follow the installation process, this is the content database for the Web application that hosts your Project Web Access sites.
- **The SharedServices1_DB** This is the database for your shared service provider. It provides information about your Project Web Access sites and their management and databases.
- **The WSS_Content_(GUID)** This can be your content database for the shared service provider Web application. Depending on how you named your databases during Web application creation, you may have several of these. The GUID exists because during Web application creation, WSS Central administration names the application's content database WSS_Content by default. During the Web application creation, the process recognizes that WSS_Content already exists as a database name and appends a GUID to the name. Having multiple _GUID named databases, although each is named uniquely, will cause your database administration many headaches and will reinforce the importance of planning and appropriately naming the database names during Web application creation.

As you can see, from this chapter of the application architecture of Project Server 2007, we're not in Kansas anymore (there's no place like home [click, click]). Because of the fundamental Windows SharePoint Server 2007 changes, the new PSI, Server-Side Scheduling, the Project Cache, and the database architecture changes, the Microsoft EPM toolset provides developers and administrators with a host of new technologies to become familiar with when installing, managing, or customizing their Microsoft EPM environment.

3

CHAPTER

New Features and Some That Have Been Retired

The previous version of Project Server (Project Server 2003) was a solid solution for organizations looking for an Enterprise Project Management (EPM) toolset. It was flexible and was usually a good choice, especially when put in context of the costs of its competition. Microsoft Office Project Server 2007 is a major leap forward from the feature and function perspective. There are a host of new features and improvements. There are also a small number of features that are no longer available. This chapter covers both.

The New Windows SharePoint Services-Based User Interface (UI)

This is not a SharePoint book. The Windows SharePoint Services (WSS) 3.0 platform that the Microsoft Office Project Server 2007 uses to provide the Project Web Access (PWA) user interface, however, provides a wealth of possibilities for powerful organizational and project team collaboration. No discussion of Project Server is complete without including SharePoint. There is an entire chapter later in this book discussing ways to get the most out of WSS in a project-focused environment. This section is just a high-level overview of WSS tools that are available in PWA as well as team-focused Project Workspaces that make up part of the EPM 2007 solution.

A Single Interface

One feature that has been available enables the user to manage each project in Project Server and to create a collaboration site automatically when a new project is published. These sites make a fantastic virtual space where the team can work together. In the 2003 version, PWA was an Active Server Pages (ASP) application, and Microsoft WSS 2003 was a .NET/ASPX application. Both offered distinct user interfaces. WSS 3.0 has a better look and feel than its predecessor and is more securable, easier to navigate, and easier to manage. Even a stand-alone WSS 3.0 system improves the look and feel of the interface and is easier to understand and to navigate than in previous versions. The fact that it is the basis not just for the Project Workspaces but for the entire environment makes this system much easier to use.

Web Parts as Part of the PWA Environment

Web Parts are discreet page components that each performs a separate function. This is a common feature in portals and collaboration environments. In other technologies, they may be called things like modules or portlets. For example, if you are on MSN.com, MSN Shopping and MSNBC News areas function like Web Parts. Web Parts can be mixed and matched to create a customized PWA that fits specific organizational needs. In Figure 3-1, you will see that the PWA (default) Home Page has areas for navigation and a page body that contains Web Parts for Reminders and Project Workspaces. You can add other Web Parts, change their respective positions, or remove them altogether. You could add a Web Part that displays information from different systems and location, even outside your company's walls. Keep in mind that this means that data from virtually any source can be part of your project environment. Even the standard Reminders section on the PWA Home Page is a Web Part. It appears in Figure 3-1 with the Project Workspaces Web Part underneath it.

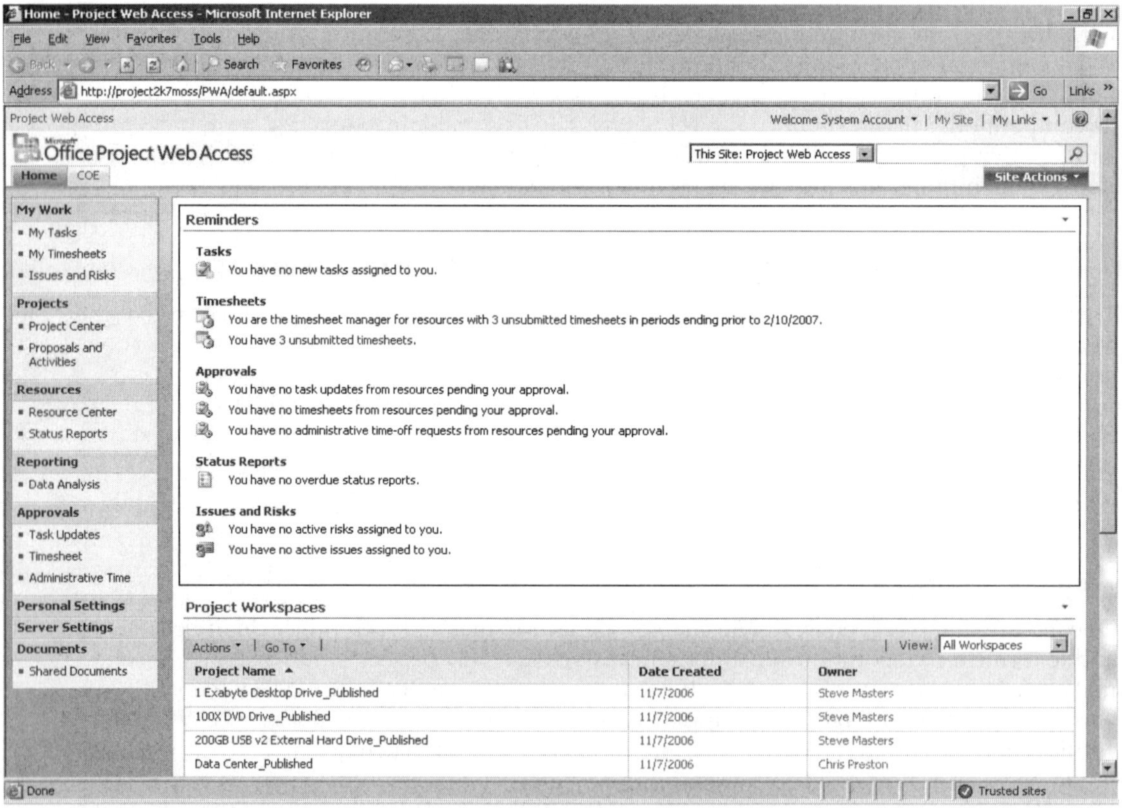

FIGURE 3-1 Reminders Web Part

UI Customization

Although customization of the look and feel was possible in the 2003 version, it was not easy or generally advisable. Customizing the UI is much easier today using a combination of templates and tools. From the time versus value perspective, this does not mean that it makes sense to make massive UI changes, but you do have greater flexibility if you so choose.

Lists

Lists are one of the great features of SharePoint. Lists are used for risks and issues out of the box, but also can be used for many other functions. Because of the divergent technologies used in the 2003 version between the project-focused PWA (Active Server Pages) and the .NET-based WSS 2003, certain views that combined areas of both tools were a bit awkward. SharePoint lists now appear directly in PWA seamlessly. Besides integration with risks, issues, and documents that were available in the 2003 version, project contacts, presence, announcements, and other functions were and continue to be available out of the box. We will discuss the new Deliverables List later in this chapter. Far deeper use is possible and will be discussed in Chapter 25. Lists items now have Version History, a new feature in the 2007 version.

Deliverables

A deliverable is a product or item that is created as part of work on a project. Deliverables is a new type of list available in the Project Workspaces that can be provisioned for each project. Deliverables have a name as well as start and finish dates and can include file attachments. As a stand-alone list, deliverables have some minimal value, but when they are actually associated with a specific project task or milestone, then there is a substantial value to be reaped for improving project management processes. Project managers can create loosely coupled cross project dependencies through the use of Deliverables. See Figure 3-2 for Deliverable item creation.

Recycle Bin

In WSS 2003, one of the greatest annoyances occurred when a user deleted and then wanted to "undelete" an item from a SharePoint list or library. A single deletion of a document (select delete and then answer affirmatively to a confirmation dialog box), for example, would delete the document and all of its Version History. The only practical way to restore it without the use of third-party tools was to recover the entire system database to another environment and grab the deleted document for a manual reposting. If you have ever had to do this, it likely wasn't one of your favorite ways to spend your time.

WSS 2007 offers a two-stage Recycle Bin that supports recovering deleted items. The Recycle Bin appears for any user who has the Delete permission. In Figure 3-3, you can see how the Recycle Bin appears in a document library. If users delete an item, they can open the Recycle Bin and restore it. Even if they delete the item from the Recycle Bin, the WSS Site Collection Administrator can restore it. Restores from the Recycle Bin are "full-fidelity," meaning that the document and all the history are restored.

Recycle Bins can be configured to delete content after a certain period of time, reducing administrative time for cleanup.

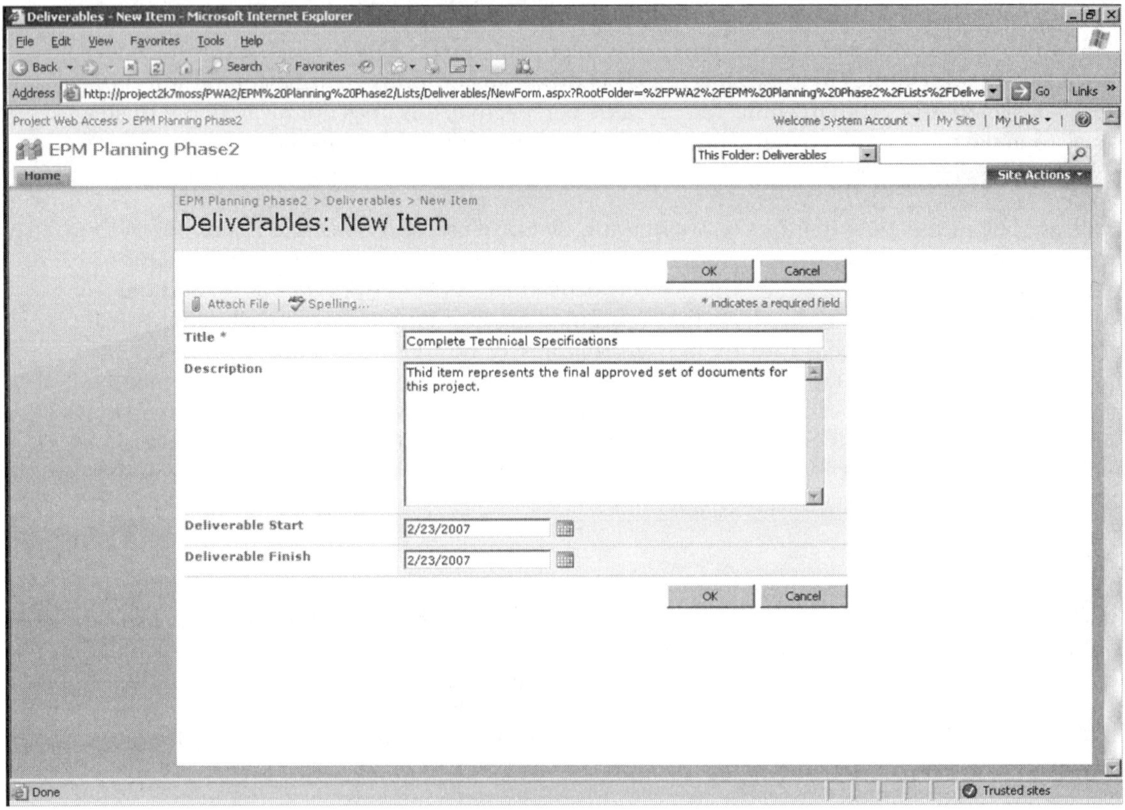

FIGURE 3-2 A deliverable

Security Trimmed User Interface

In some cases, applications will display links or buttons that, while active, take the user to "dead-ends." In WSS 2003, it was possible to select a button or link and then be rejected for permission reasons. The actual process when this occurred was fairly painful, although probably not worth describing in detail here (if you have ever experienced this process, you are already very aware of how painful it was). In WSS 2007, there is a major improvement over earlier versions of SharePoint in this area. In this version, if you don't have permission to see or do something, it will not appear at all, nor will links appear that take you to pages or items for which you have no access. This helps users avoid a significant headache and is better security practice as well.

Document Libraries and Document Management

Document libraries are a special type of list. They store documents, their history, and metadata (data about data) about the documents. In a Project Server environment, document libraries are used for project-related collateral such as Project Plan documents (such as Project Charter, Requirements, and Communications Plan). This capability was available in the 2003 version, but has been extended in several ways.

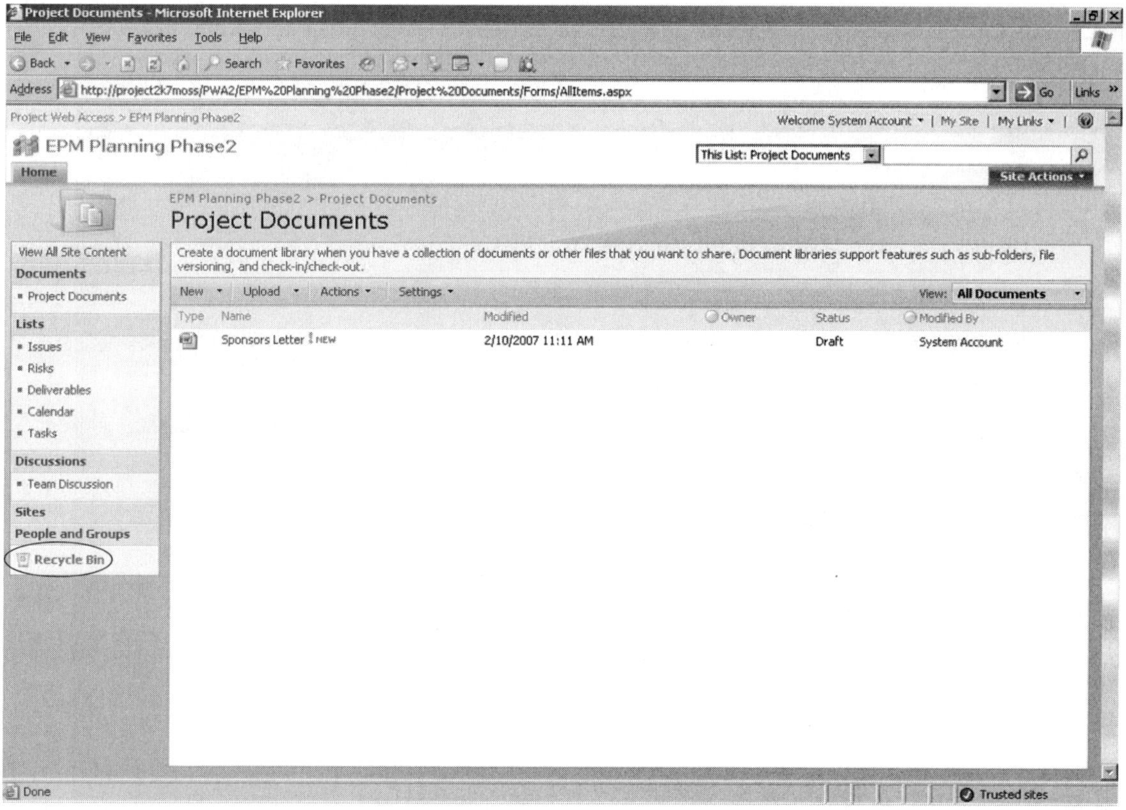

FIGURE 3-3 Document library with Recycle Bin

Document Management

The document management capability has been strengthened considerably. Included now is the ability to force check-out for editing. In the 2003 version, it was possible to select a document without using the check-out feature, make edits, and save the document back to its location without a check-in process or version number update. It is now possible to require that a document be checked out to edit it and if changes are made it must be checked back in before the edits are available to others.

In addition to improving the check-in/check-out process, WSS 3.0 has an option for Major and Minor (v1.1, 1.2, 1.3, 2.0, etc.) version numbers as opposed to the previous version, which supported only Major (1.0, 2.0, 3.0) version numbering. Minor versions can be secured from general viewing. For example, if a draft may undergo editing prior to final approval before the document is promoted to the next Major version number for a larger audience to view.

WSS presents Version History in a very usable manner, as shown in Figure 3-4.

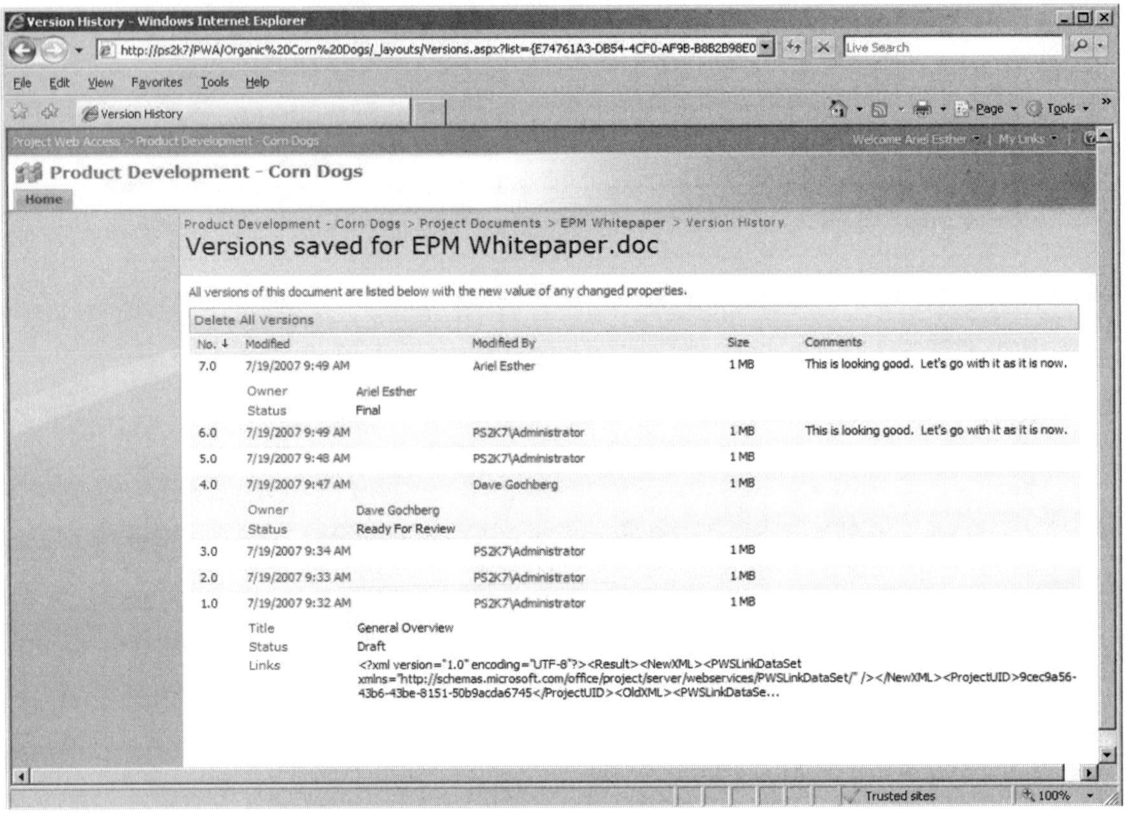

FIGURE 3-4 WSS Version History page

Bread Crumbs

As in *Hansel and Gretel*, a bread crumb is something that is left along the way to form a trail to follow your path back from where you came. On Web pages, birds don't eat the bread crumbs. They are often displayed through the use of a horizontally displayed set of links that enable users to see where they are in a site's hierarchy and a path to navigate back either all the way or part of the way through the use of links. WSS 3.0 provides this functionality as shown in Figure 3-5.

Alerts

Alerts allow individual users to be notified as they prefer for either the contents of an entire list or library or an individual item. For example, a project sponsor can set an alert for any new content in a custom-created Change Request library. Previous alert functions remain. New alerts are possible for search string results. For example, if you perform a search on issues and a certain resource, you can set an alert that tells you that the results of your string would yield a different result. The user has control over whether to be alerted to new items, changed items or both and can choose daily or weekly summaries.

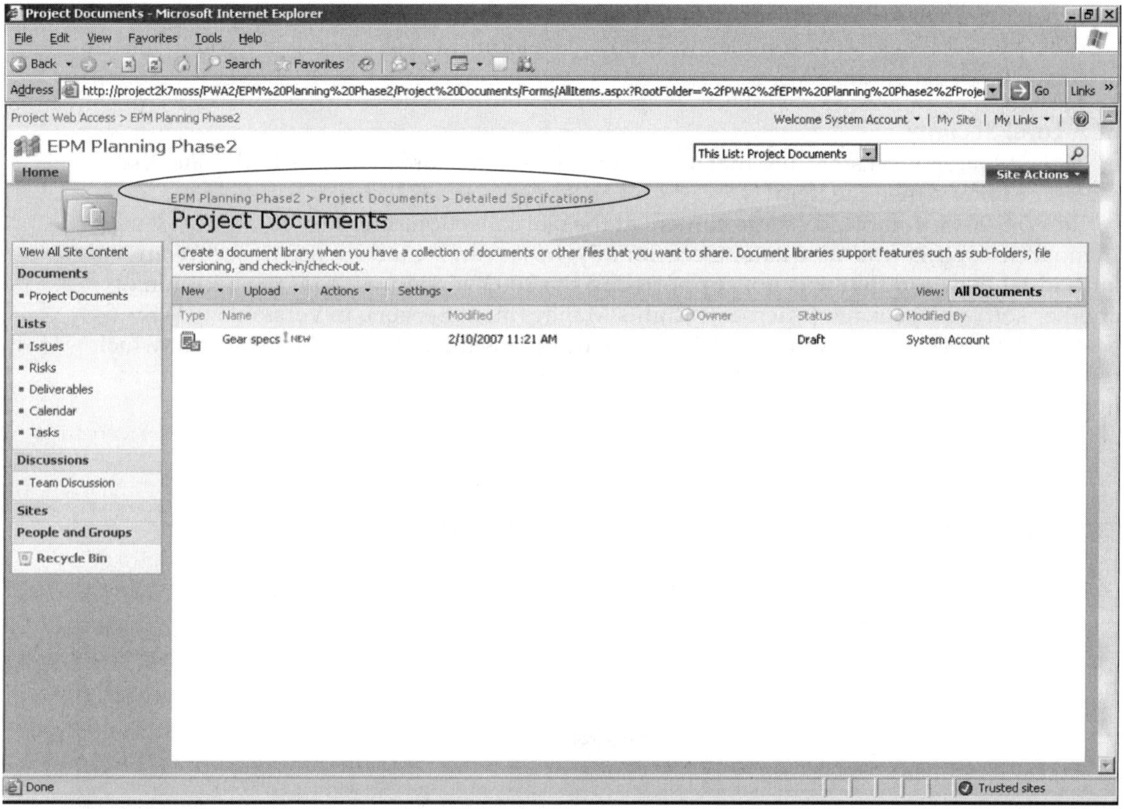

FIGURE 3-5 Bread crumbs

Workflow

There is a project workflow built into Project Server that includes the basic project management functions. At a high level, the basic workflow follows the path of building a project, staffing it, notifying the people of their assignments, and allowing for the team members to report their time and task status to their manager and project manager. The manager and project manager can then approve or reject submissions, and changes are updated into the project. The .NET 3.0 framework required to run WSS and PWA includes the Windows Workflow Foundation (remember not to call it WWF). This workflow engine allows creation of custom workflows that can be used in WSS and its PWA superset. An example of how this might be used is for routing new project requests.

More discussion about workflow, including a step-by-step custom workflow building process, is included in Chapter 25. That workflow is built using the new SharePoint

Designer 2007 (also known as "son of FrontPage"), which supports many simple-to-moderate workflow possibilities. More complex workflow development is also possible through the use of Microsoft Visual Studio 2005.

Item-Level Security

WSS has a hierarchical structure that starts at the site collection, then goes to the site, then the list or library, then the item.

In WSS 2003, you could secure content at the site collection, site, and library/list level. In most cases, this was adequate. Occasionally, however, it made sense to secure an individual item and that was not supported in the 2003 version without the addition of another software package (Microsoft Rights Management Server). In version 3.0, WSS enables you to secure an item with different permissions than the library/list within which it resides. Figure 3-6 shows how the user interface appears while the user is managing an item's security.

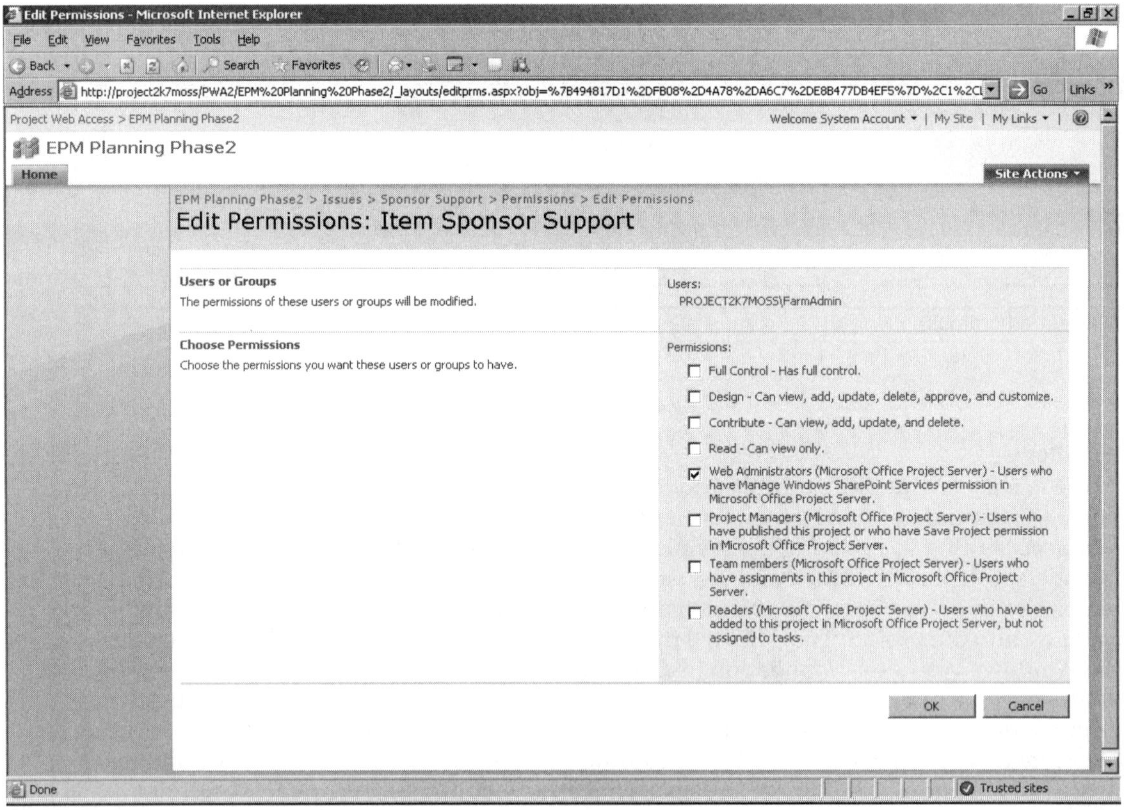

FIGURE 3-6 Item-level security

Easily Customizable Navigation

For changes in navigation elements, there is now a screen from with you can easily add sites or pages. You can use either the Quick Launch (on the left side) or Tabs (at the top) navigation, as shown in Figure 3-7. In addition, it is easy to reorganize the navigation buttons. Also, there is a feature that allows for a choice between leaving the Quick Launch bar fully expanded and expanding it only for the area of the site currently being used (see Figure 3-8).

Task List in WSS—Project Management "Light"

This feature allows the user to piece together a schedule using an out-of-the-box WSS 3.0 list and Web Part. The user can create tasks with start and end dates and assign resources, and manual fields are available for "% Complete" and task status (started, in progress, and so on). The Web Part displays the items in a bar chart (Gantt) format. There is no calculation component, nor are dependency functions included. The user can export items to the Project Professional (or Standard) client from this area as a basic starting point for a new project. Given the tools available in the rest of the EPM solution to perform similar processes with more flexible and advanced features, this WSS feature may be best used in an organization just starting to consider project management.

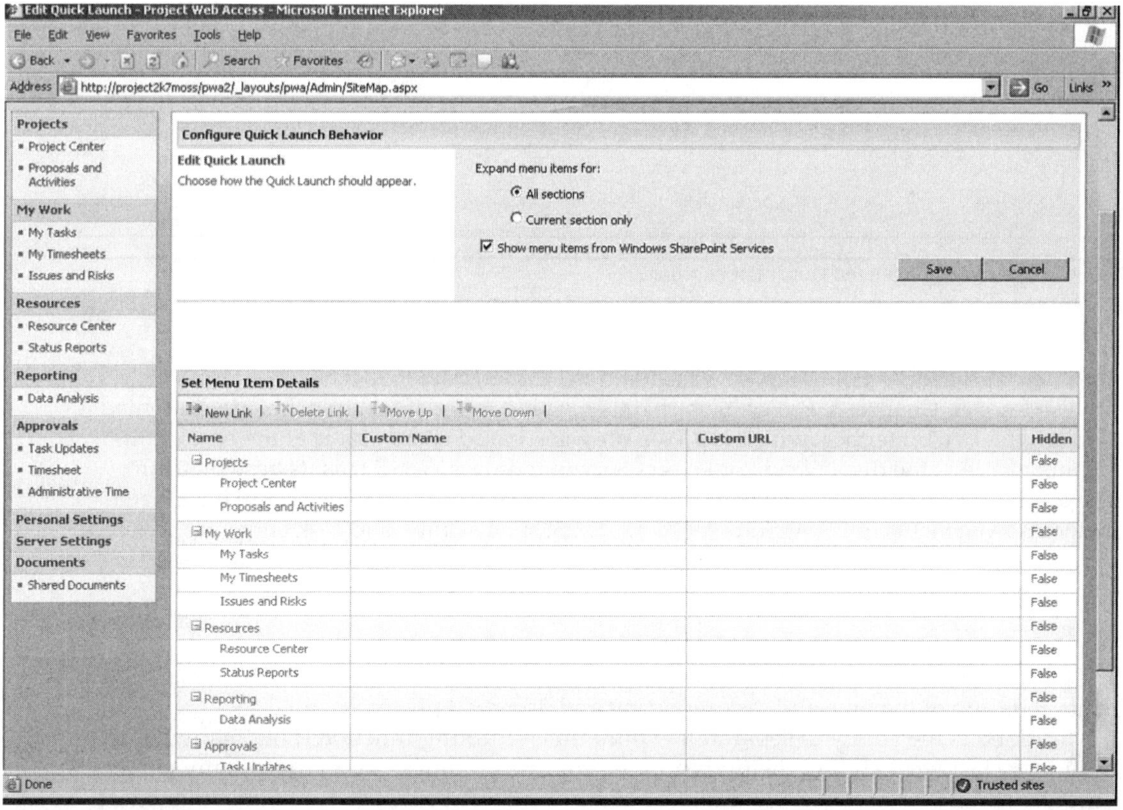

Figure 3-7 You can change navigation elements.

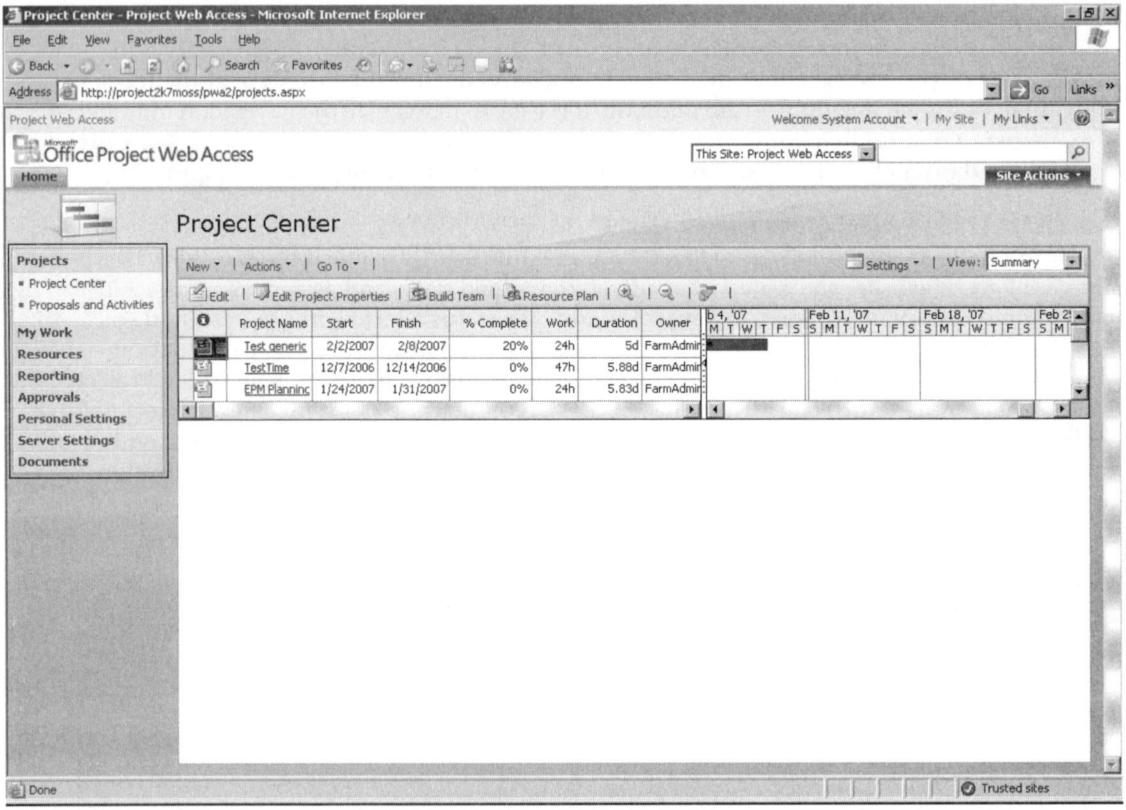

FIGURE 3-8 A customized collapsed Quick Launch bar

Project Web Access

As discussed in Chapter 3, Project Server 2007 provides a set of services that are presented through the PWA interface, which is a Web browser–based client that is at the core of this solution. PWA is the display side of Project Server and uses WSS 3.0 as its base platform. The following subsections focus on changes in the PWA-specific tools. There have been major improvements in PWA. Some of these items, such as time and task entry, are covered in more detail later in this book. Other items with a lesser profile may be discussed exclusively in this chapter.

The Completely Rearchitected and Improved Time and Task Entry

The 2003 timesheet was not bad but had limitations. In Project Server 2007, there has been a major redesign of the time and task reporting and approval process.

Included is the ability to separate the pure time reporting function (how many hours did I work last week?) from the updating of progress on project tasks (how is my task progressing and what remains for it to be completed?). Resource or functional managers now have time approval authority as most organizations prefer. Time that is reported is then imported into the area where project tasks can be updated. This new process has addressed requests that have been made by EPM customers in the past, but is not without flaws. There are some technical issues with the new time and task functions as well as functions that could have been designed differently for better overall usability. It is better than it was, but there is still much room for improvement. You will learn more on how to use these features in Chapter 18.

Time and Task Approvals

Timesheets no longer require a two-step process for someone with authority to approve their own time using automatic self-approval. In addition, comments associated with the time and task entry appear as a specific icon in the approval view's Indicator column or in a field in a view.

Ad Hoc Task and Time Reporting Support

Some organizations will create places to track all types of work, whereas others will not. One new option is just to add a line to the Tasks page (and timesheet) for something that was not preplanned for submission. As shown in Figure 3-9, the user can add a brand new task to a project plan, assuming permissions allow the user to do so.

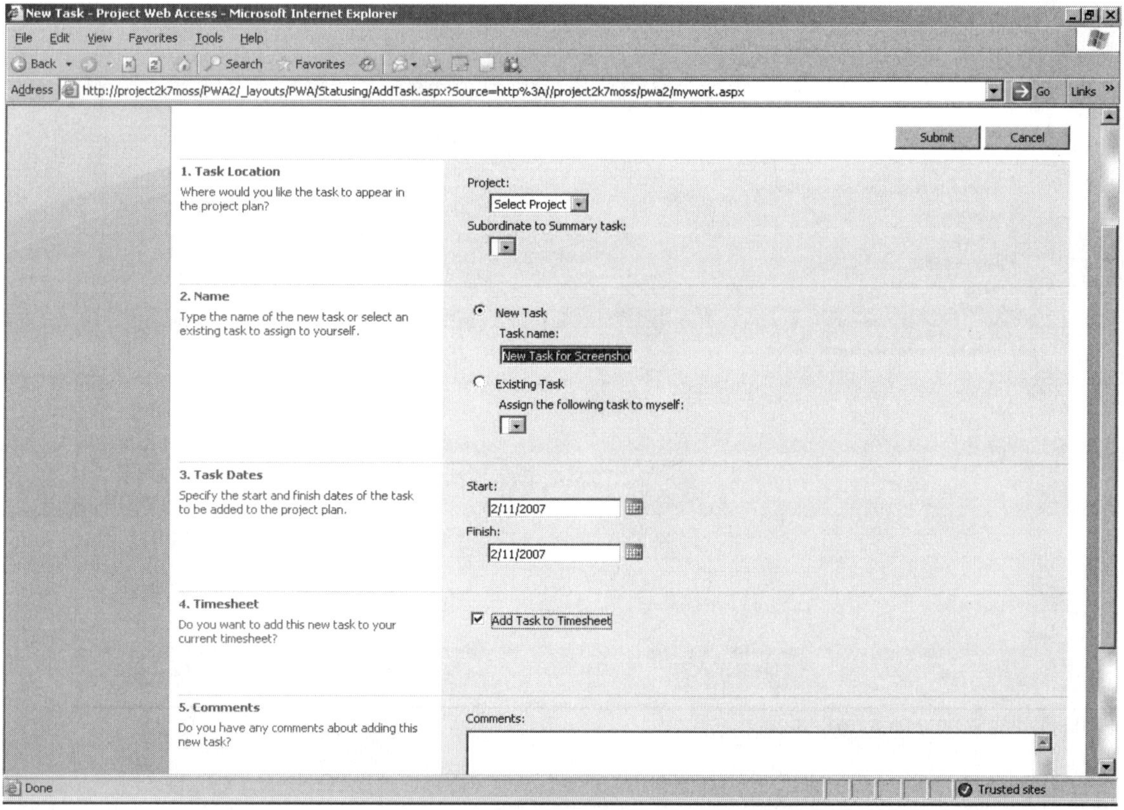

FIGURE 3-9 Add a task (with the Add Task to Timesheet checkbox).

The Task-Level Notes Field

This feature, shown in Figure 3-10, allows team members to send a note to approvers with task-level comments attached in addition to more global timesheet and task submission comments.

Team Tasks

It is now possible to assign to a project task a team rather than just an individual. When a team is assigned, each resource can see the item, and a single resource can then assign themselves, and record progress on the task.

Calendar View

Resources can now see their assignments in a calendar format (see Figure 3-11).

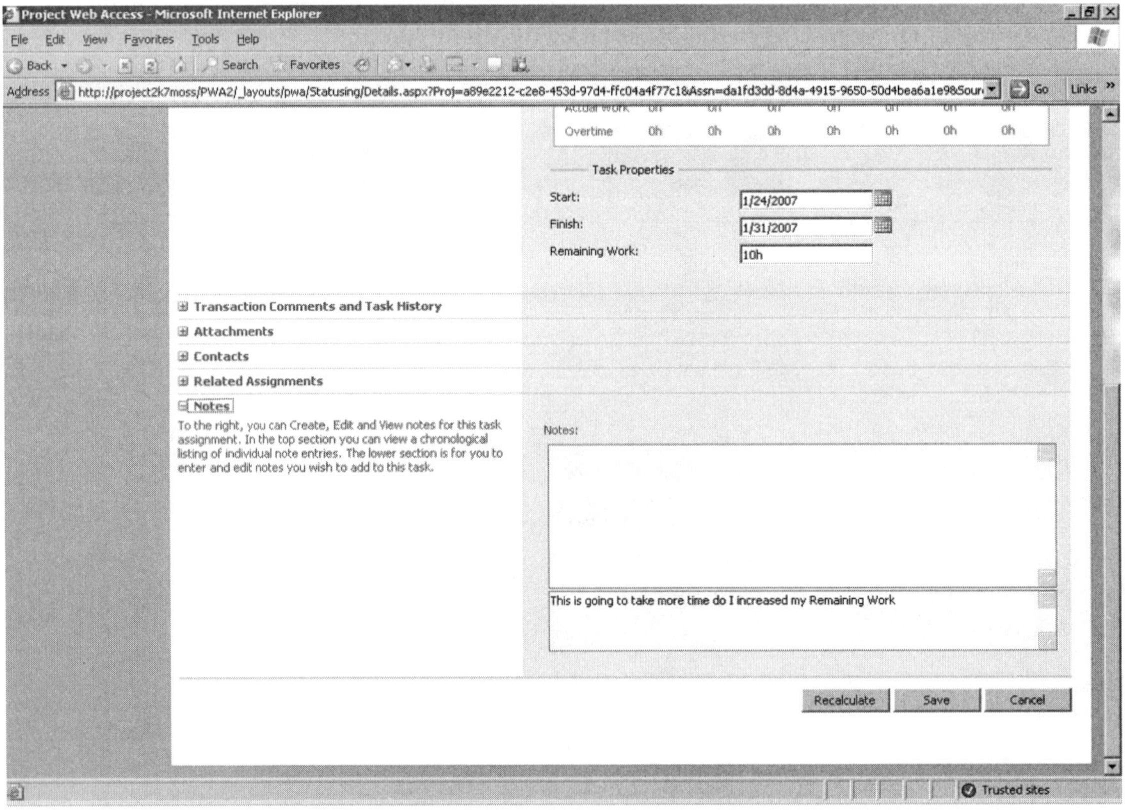

FIGURE 3-10 Adding a note to a task update

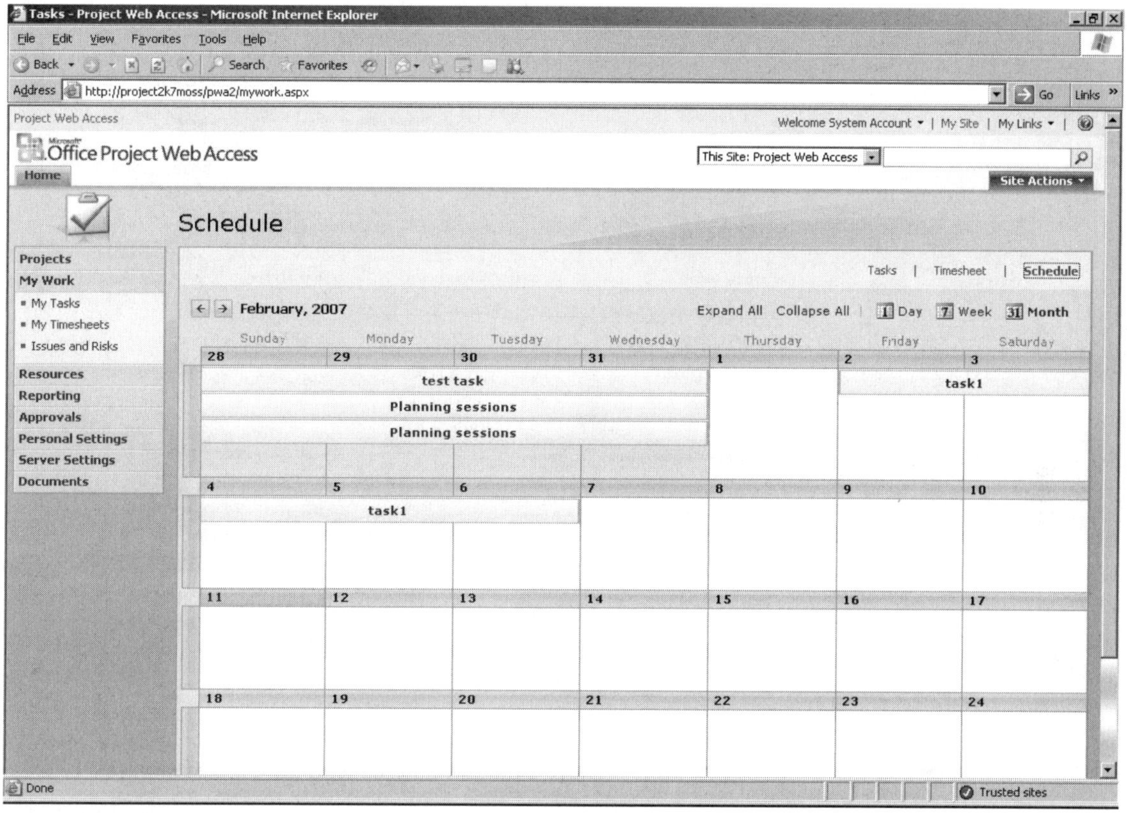

FIGURE 3-11 Calendar View

Easier and More Logical Administration Pages

Starting with the already improved SharePoint UI and redesigning the information architecture into a broader and less deep set of drill downs has made administrators' work easier and more intuitive. The PWA Administration pages are organized into eight areas, offer much better inline explanations than ever before, and are more logically subdivided. Figure 3-12 shows a high level view of the PWA Administration top screen.

WSS Administration pages for the site that hosts PWA are available on a different page and are organized using the same WSS standards (see Figure 3-13).

Task Views Color Coding and Screen Tips

Team members who are in My Task views can see which task's finish dates are imminent or late. Notice in Figure 3-14 the shading on late tasks as well as the screen tip.

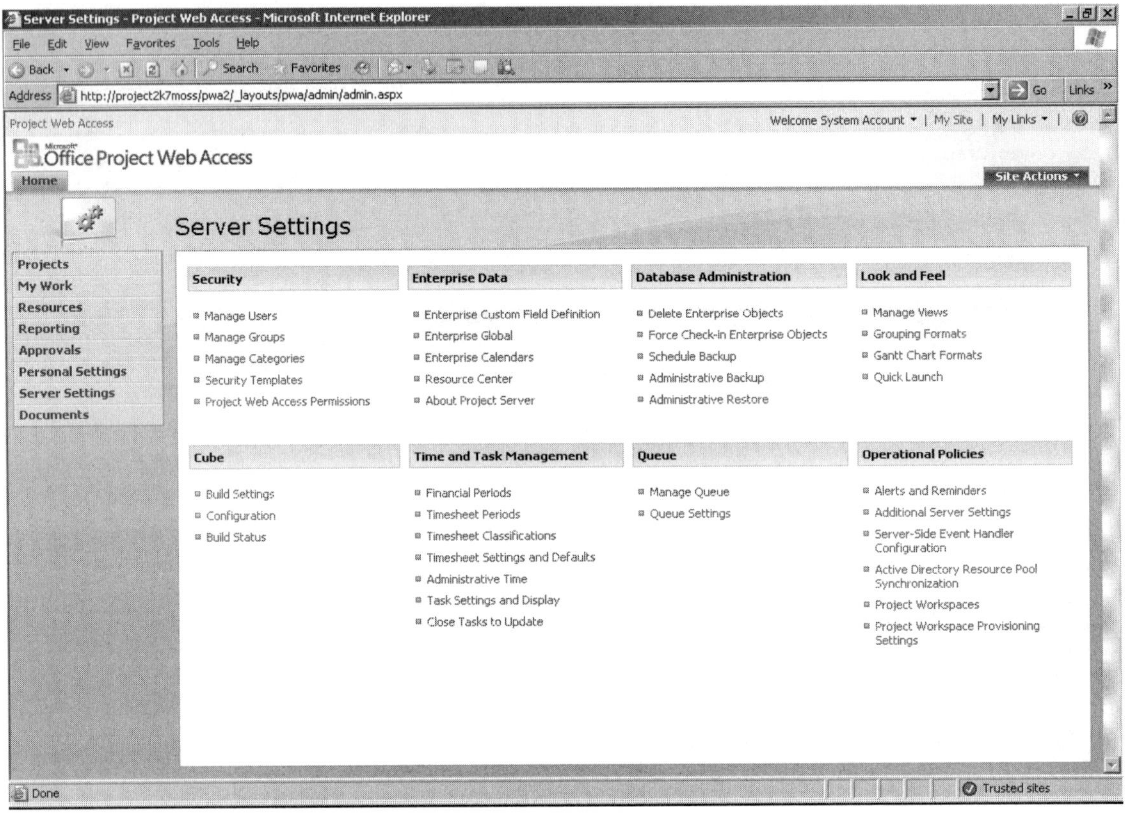

FIGURE 3-12 The main PWA Administration page

Project Workspace Subsite Provision

As mentioned before, Project Server can be set up to autoprovision a Project Workspace for project team collaboration. A new feature in 2007 allows you to create that new site either at the top level or below an existing Project Workspace. This useful feature can help support programs (a set of related projects) that might be better off with several subsites under the larger program top-level site. The new Provisioning a Sub-Site dialog box is shown in Figure 3-15.

Budget Resources

A project's Budget should be an amount of Cost and/or Work that is allocated to execute all the tasks needed to complete the project requirements. In previous versions, there really was no way to track against a budget. Instead, the "project budget" was most commonly built by completing the Work Breakdown Structure/project schedule in Project Professional, adding resources that have associated rates and sometimes including material costs. When these items were completed, Project Professional calculated a total cost that, when

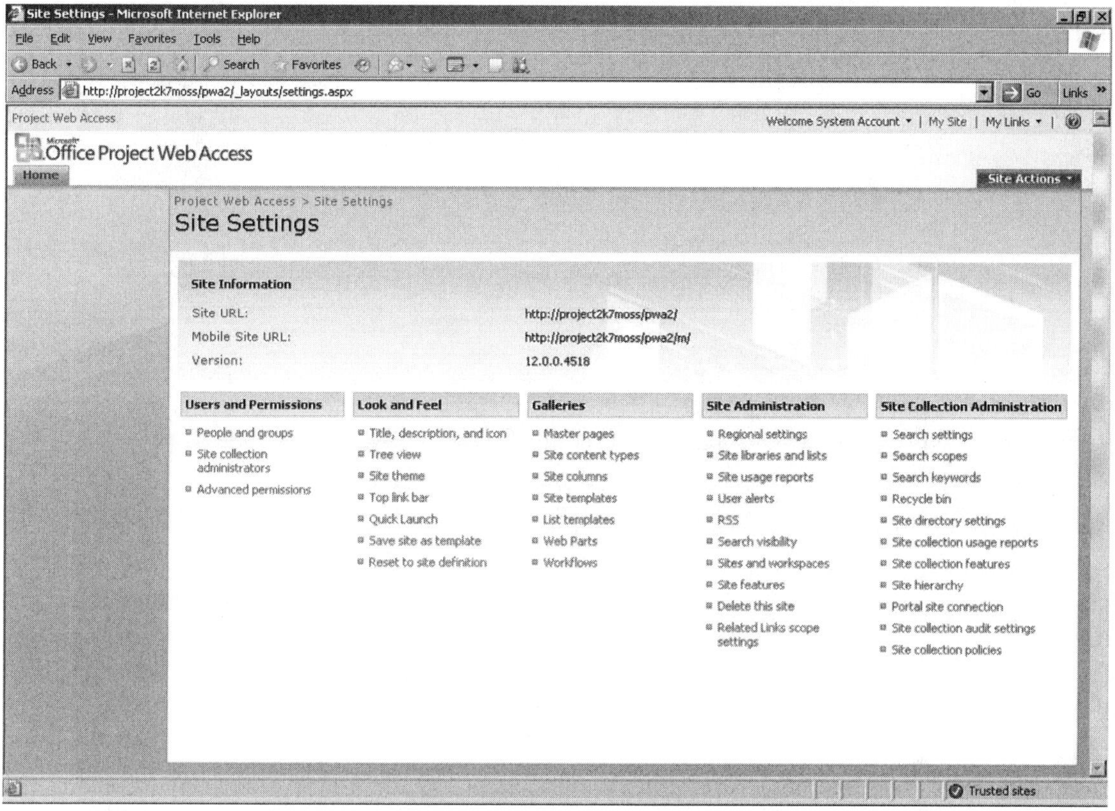

FIGURE 3-13 Site settings in PWA

baselined, represented the "budget." In the 2007 version, the user can identify budget costs and budget work separately by designating budget resources. This solves the problem with previous editions by allowing the Project Manager to assign specific Budget Resources to the project. For example, suppose that Project XYZ has budget costs of $200,000 based on budget work of 2,000 hours of work. The Project Manager can assign Budget Work and Budget Cost resources to the plan and enter the $200,000 into the Budget Cost and 2,000 hours into the plan. Thus a budget is built. The result is that these numbers can be compared to the "Estimated at Complete" cost and work or other fields. Budget resources, which can be categorized for later reporting, are associated at the project level by assignment to the Project Summary Task (Task 0).

Cost Resource Type

It was always difficult in the past to track ad hoc expenses such as project-related lodging, mileage reimbursements, and meals. The new Costs Resource Type enhances the supports for tracking these costs.

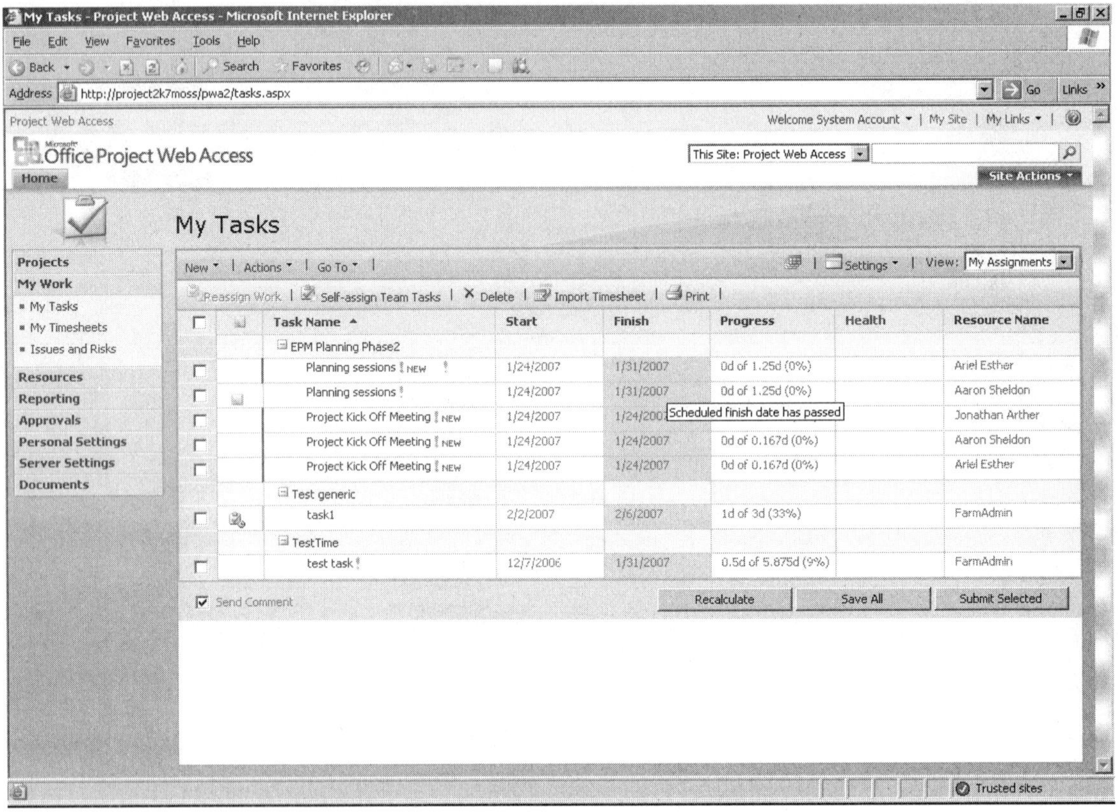

FIGURE 3-14 Onscreen hints for late and imminent tasks

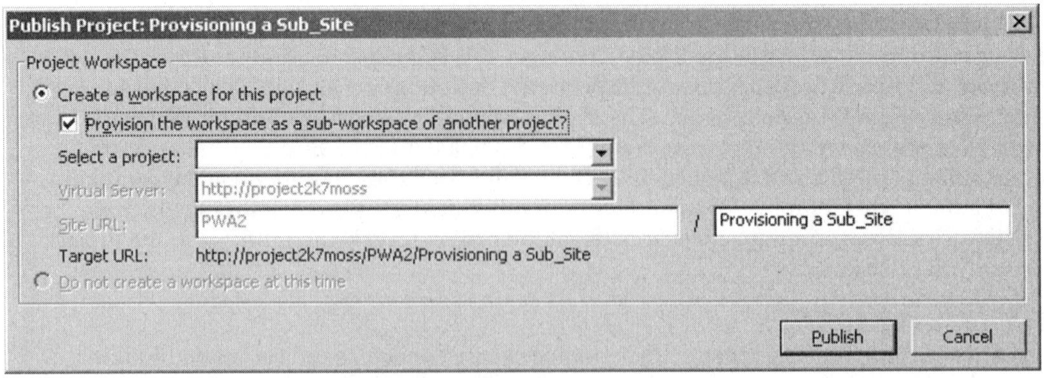

FIGURE 3-15 Provisioning a Project Workspace

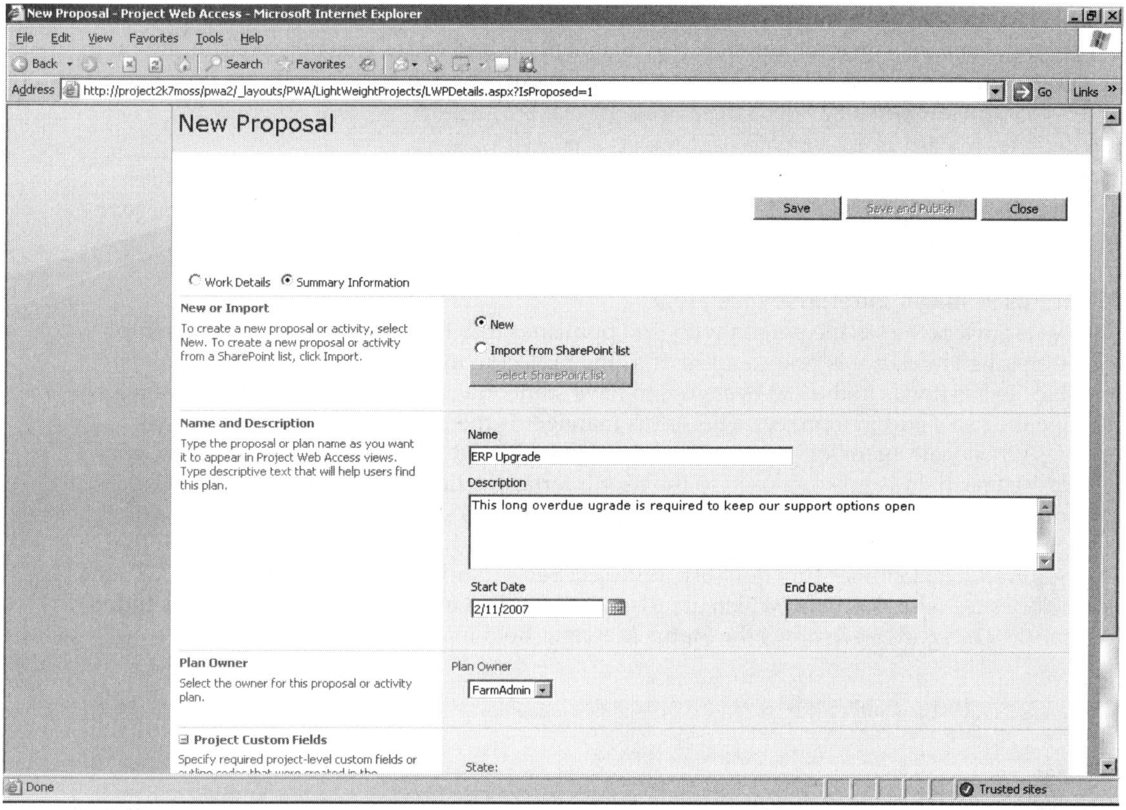

FIGURE 3-16 The New Proposal page

Proposals

Each organization might handle incoming project requests in several ways depending on how the organization approaches its Microsoft Office Project Server 2007 effort. One new way is to use a feature called Proposals (see Figure 3-16). Potential projects can be entered at a fairly high level for visibility and consideration. They can then be promoted to full project status later if appropriate.

The Proposals feature has both advantages and disadvantages over other options for project intake. Other options include using InfoPath (especially when the Forms Services feature is added with Microsoft Office SharePoint Server) a custom SharePoint list with associated workflow, or if the organization decides to also implement Microsoft Project Portfolio Server, that includes options for incoming projects. Which method is appropriate depends on the organizational needs of the individual company.

Activities

Activities replace the previous To Do lists. There are two ways to approach the use of activities. The first is to use them for managing maintenance and support type tasks. These can have a team assigned through the use of a resource plan. The second is to use them in the same way that To Do lists were used in the past: as a single user's set of items to be accomplished.

Unlimited Custom Enterprise Fields and Codes

In previous versions, the total number of available fields and codes was not an issue, although the limited number for each type of field was a problem. Those internal limits are no longer present in the 2007 version.

NOTE *In fact, there are extremely high limitations in all areas, such as the maximum number values of 9,999,999,999,999.99 and 50,000 predecessors per task. For more on limitations, go to http://office.microsoft.com/en-us/project/HP101065651033.aspx.*

The Status Manager Enterprise Task Field

The owner of a project is the person who first publishes it to Project Server. This ownership can be changed later, but is best thought of as the project manager of the entire project. It is possible, just as it was in the 2003 version, to have someone other than the project manager manage the tasks within a project. The status manager is the person who will receive task updates when team members update their tasks from PWA task pages. The Status Manager Enterprise task field is now exposed to the user interface, where the user can modify it to support multiple project managers managing tasks within a single project. This process of changing who is in charge of managing a task is more straightforward than the method that was required to get similar functionality in Project Server and Project Professional 2003. There are some issues with this field, which are discussed (and an example workaround is included) in Chapter 21. Figure 3-17 shows the Status Manager field in action.

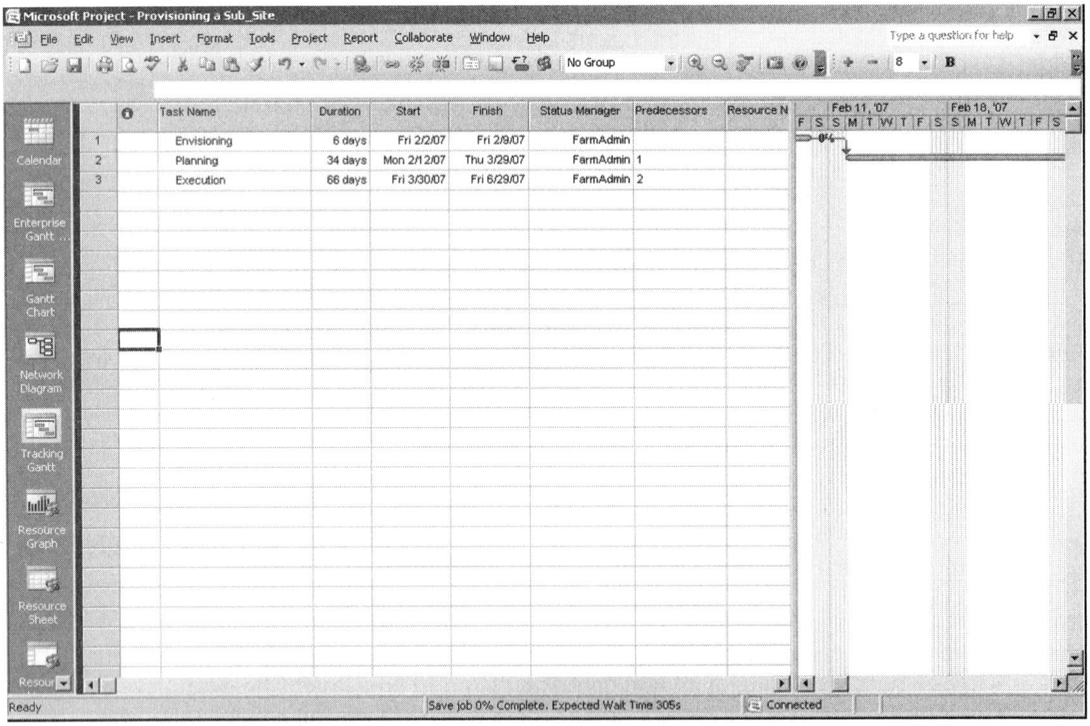

FIGURE 3-17 The Status Manager task field as shown in Microsoft Office Project Professional 2007

The Publish Enterprise Task Field

It is not until tasks are published that team members are notified of assignments, items appear in timesheets, resources become utilized, and so on. A valuable new feature is an Enterprise task field that allows the project manager to publish only portions of a project plan from Project Professional 2007 (see Figure 3-18).

Individually Targeted Issues and Risks Page

Each user can go from the Home Page to a page that includes a summary of their issues and risks across all their projects, as shown in Figure 3-19.

The Project Server Interface

The new application programming interface (API) is called the Project Server Interface (PSI). This .NET-based set of interfaces is far more broad and flexible than in any previous version of Project Server and offers a strong alternative for customizing the way that Project Server functions. There is even a page that exposes event-handler configuration in the PWA interface. There is also a Project Server 2007 Software Development Kit. At the time of the editing of this book, it was located at http://msdn2.microsoft.com/en-us/library/bb187387.aspx.

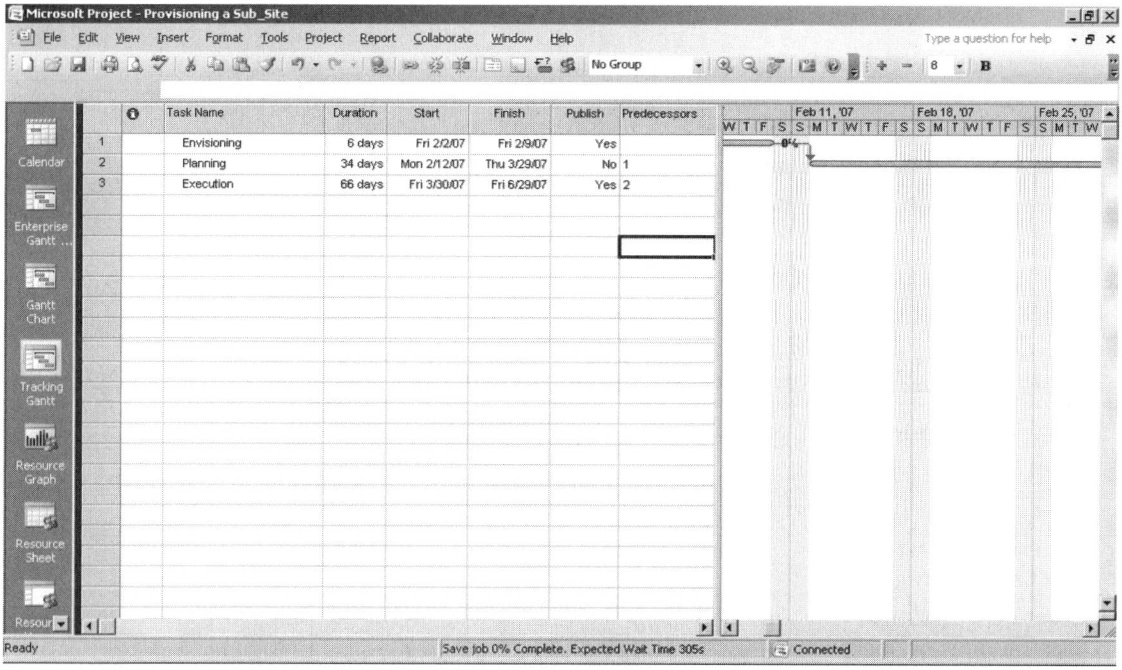

FIGURE 3-18 The Publish field

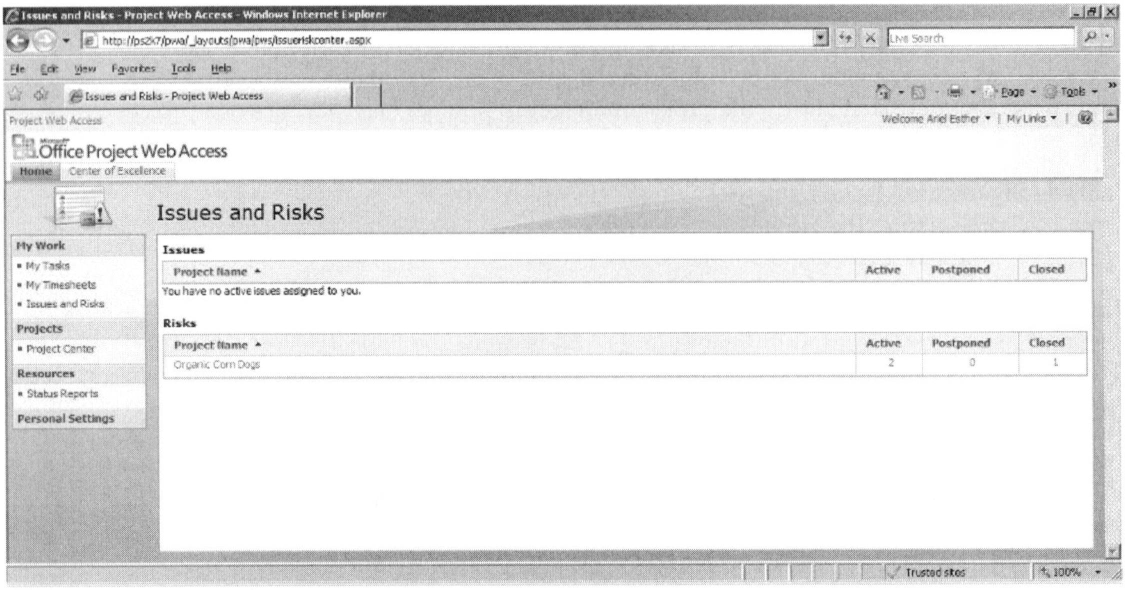

FIGURE 3-19 The Issues and Risks page

Feature	2003	2007
Activities		X
Ad Hoc Task and Time Reporting		X (not advisable)
Admin Projects with Ability to Designate Specific Team	X	
Almost Unlimited Enterprise Fields		X
Auto Self Appoval of Timesheets for Managers		X
Better Application Interface for Custom Development		X
"Bread Crumb" Navigation		X
Budget Resource		X
Calendar View of Assignments		X
Collapsible Context-Based Quick Launch Navigation		X
Color Coding and Other Graphical Hints on Tasks		X
Cost Resource (Supports One-Time Costs Such as Travel Expenses)		X

TABLE 4-1 Feature Comparison Table

Feature	2003	2007
Deliverable-Based Planning		X
Document Management	X	X
Easily Customizable Navigation		X
Filter by RBS (to Support My Resources Views)		X
Force Check-Out of Documents in Document Libraries		X
Global Administrative Time		X
Hide the Left Navigation Pane	X	
Integration with SharePoint Server (in 2003 Portal Server)		X
Item-Level Security		X
Limited Custom Enterprise Fields	X	
Major and Minor Document Versions		X
Mix and Match Web Parts in PWA and Project Workspaces		X
Multiple Options for Publishing	X	
My Risks and Issues Page		X
Office Integration	X	X-Better
Portfolio Modeler	X	
Project Management Lite		X (but of very low value)
Project Pro Multiple-Level Undo		X
Project Workspace Subsite Provisioning Option		X
Proposals		X
Publish Field (Allows Projects to Be Partially Published as in Phase One Only)		X
Reasonable Ability for Look and Feel Changes		X
Recycle Bin to Recover Documents		X
Save Link Feature for Individual Views	X	
Security Trimmed UI		X
Single Interface for PWA and Project Workspaces		X
Single Publish Process (Automated Decision Making)		X

Table 4-1 Feature Comparison Table (*Continued*)

Feature	2003	2007
Single Timesheet (to PM for Approval)	X	
Status Manager Field Exposed (Allows Changes to Individual Task Manager)		X
Support for Programs	Minimal	Better
Task Drivers		X
Task Transaction-Level Comments		X
Task Updates for PM Approval		X
Team Tasks		X
Timesheet to Resource Manager for Approval		X
To Do Lists	X	
Transparent Scheduling (Task Highlighting)		X
Two-Way Choice on Automatically Provisioned Project Workspace (Auto or by Choice)		X
Two-Way Choice on Automatically Provisioned Project Workspace (on or off)	X	
Versioning on Lists		X
Workflow without Custom Code		X

TABLE 4-1 Feature Comparison Table (*Continued*)

Project Professional 2007

The focus of this book is on Microsoft Office Project Server 2007, but just as it was important to discuss WSS 3.0, it is also crucial that we provide some level of coverage of Microsoft Office Project Professional 2007. Microsoft Project is by far the market leader in the project management tool market and acts as the main toolset for those in the project manager role in Microsoft EPM. We will not be discussing general use of Project Professional in this book, but rather focusing on the areas where Project Professional interfaces with Project Server. In Chapter 3, improvements in connectivity were discussed as well as items such as caching. This section discusses some significant changes—some directly connected to Project Server, others just worth mentioning.

Multiple-Level Undo

If there was ever a feature that people clamored for in Microsoft Project, multiple-level undo was it. Project has improved with every version, becoming more and more powerful over time. Performing more than a single undo has never been allowed until now (see Figure 3-20). The new version allows up 99 levels of undo (and redo). You probably won't need this many levels, but this is a major improvement.

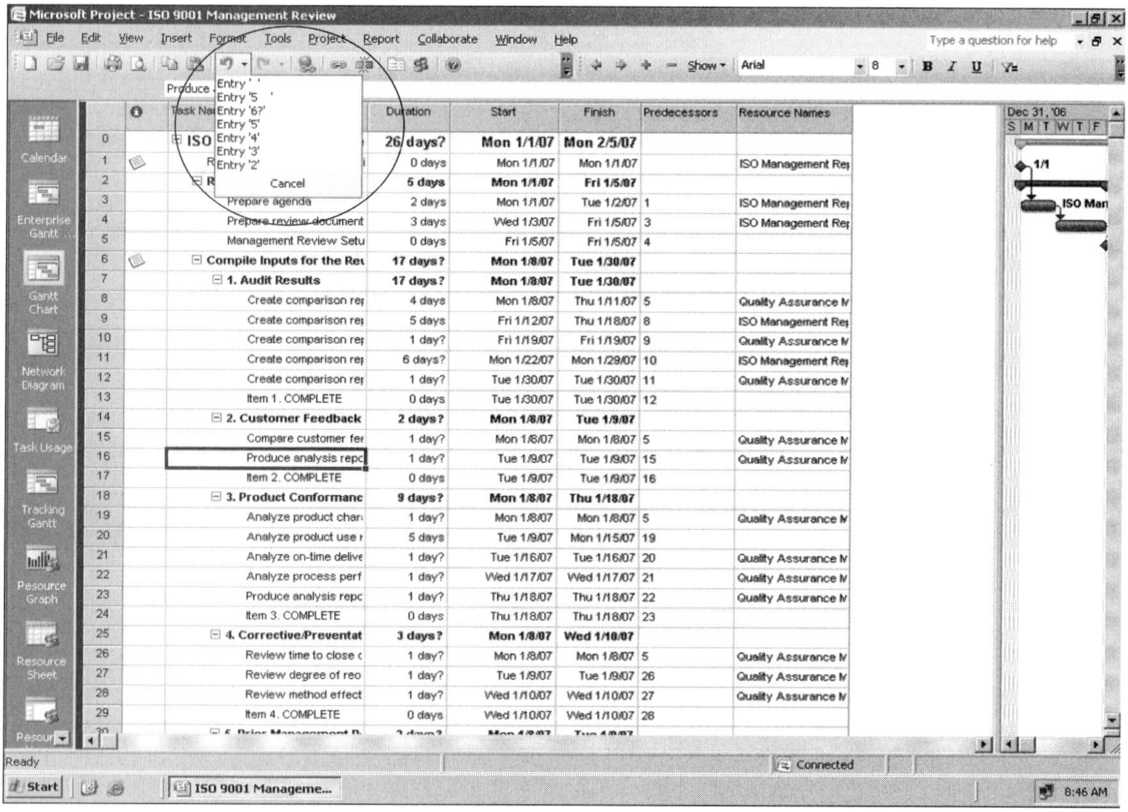

FIGURE 3-20 Multiple undo levels

Project Scheduling Improvements

The next two new functions make project scheduling more transparent and easier to manage.

Transparent Scheduling (Task Highlighting)

Successor tasks are highlighted with a color background when predecessor tasks change in a way that impacts them (see Figure 3-21). In addition, a new left-side pane (Task Drivers - next) is available if selected by the PM from the Project menu to reduce the number of clicks required to view more task-level detail (not displayed in figure).

Task Drivers

This new feature allows the project manager a view into what drives the completion of a given task. In previous versions, getting the information shown in Figure 3-22 took some additional mouse clicks as the Project Manager was forced to double-click one task at a time. Now, just scrolling through the tasks, say with the down arrow key, will expose the schedule drivers for the currently highlighted task.

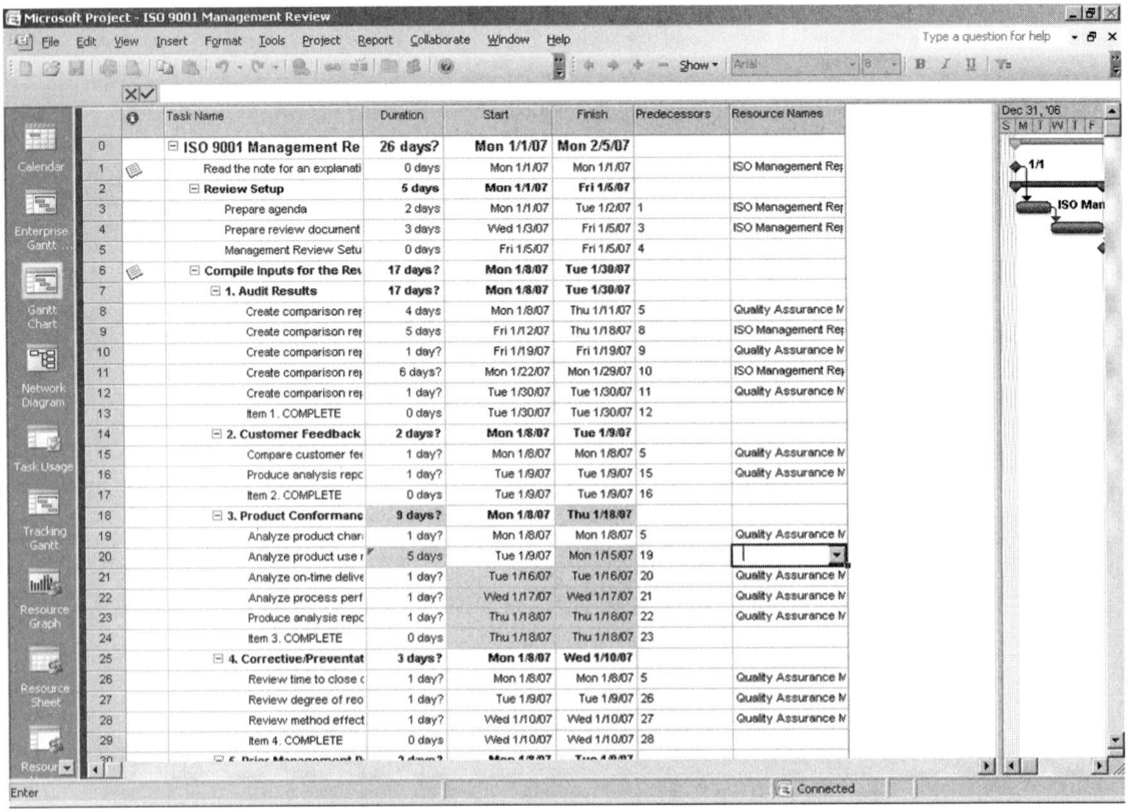

FIGURE 3-21 Transparent scheduling

A Single Publish Command

When publishing a project to Project Server 2003, you could select from one of four commands: Publish All, Publish Project Plan, Publish New and Changed Assignments, or Republish Resource Assignments. Each had its place depending on the circumstances and the need at the time. In Microsoft Office Project Server and Project Professional 2007, there is a single Publish command found in the File menu that takes care of most of the decision making for the person publishing the project.

Gantt Bars

Project Server 2007 has made a minor improvement in the appearance of Gantt bars, which now offer a three-dimensional look, as shown in Figure 3-23.

Miscellaneous Features

The following are the additional features available in Project Server 2007.

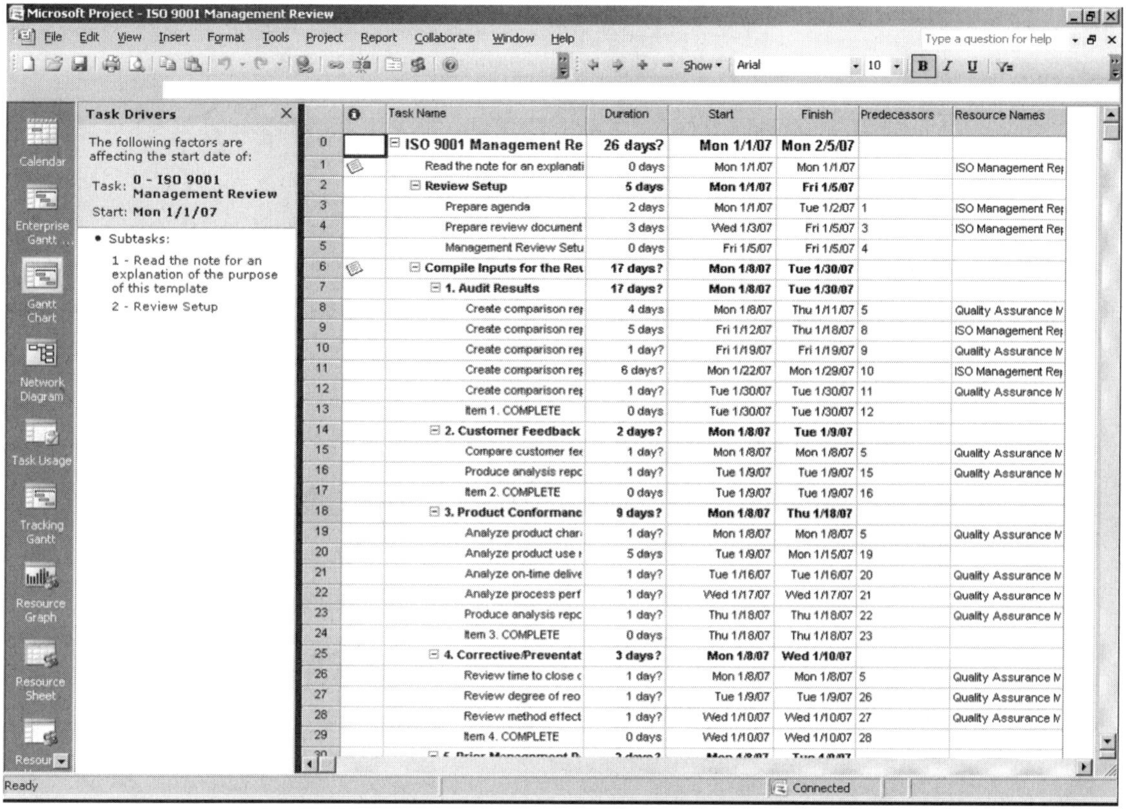

FIGURE 3-22 The Task Drivers pane

Support for Master/Sub Projects

This support enables users to manage large programs as smaller projects and to maintain them inside a single "master" plan. This support was always available in Microsoft Project when it was run as a stand-alone application, but raised serious difficulties when Project was used with Project Server. Microsoft has improved this support and it now works well. More details on this support are provided later in the book.

Deeper Office Integration with Office 2007

Microsoft Office 2007 offers better integration, whether with Excel and Visio for reporting or with Office known document types (including Word, Excel, PowerPoint, or any other document with an iFilter), for Check-In/Check-Out as well as major and minor versioning.

The key change is in the way that Project Server works with Outlook 2007. Instead of using the Outlook Calendar for tracking project tasks, Project Server now uses the Tasks feature in Outlook. Note that just as in Project Server and Outlook 2003, Outlook pulls this information from Project Server, and that Project Server has no feature that enables it to recognize existing the Outlook Calendar or tasks as a way to block available time for projects.

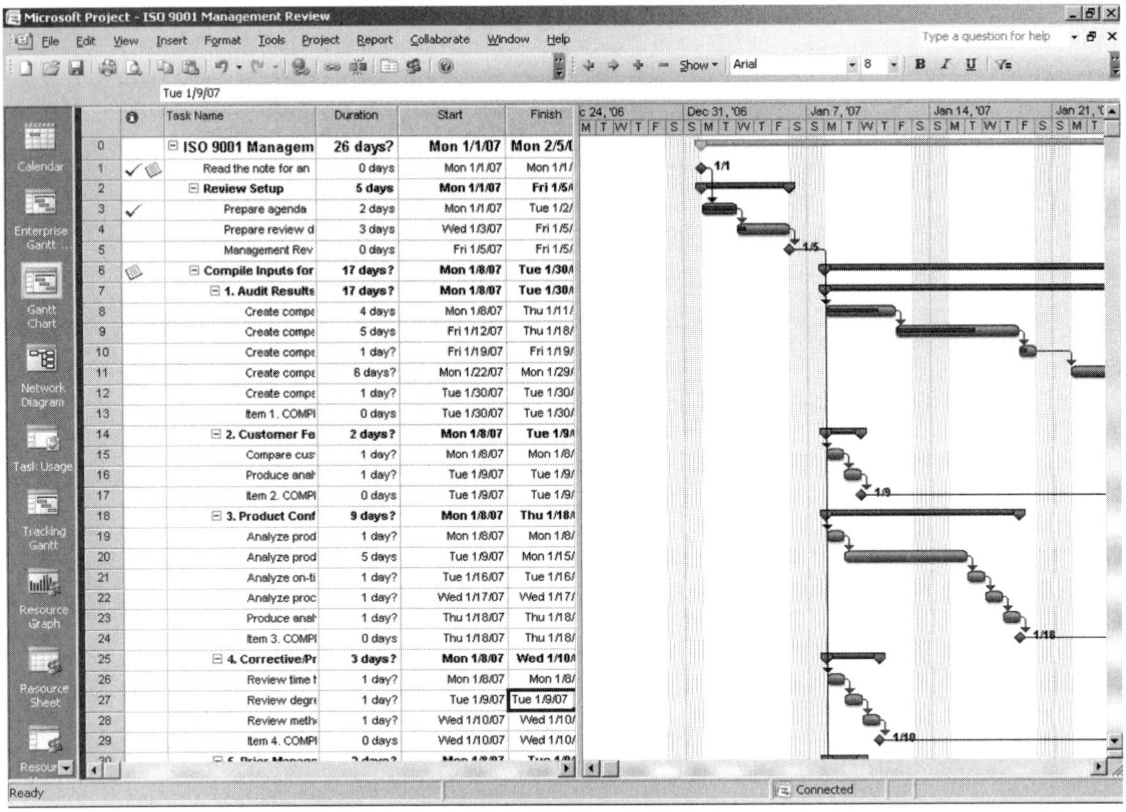

FIGURE 3-23 Gantt bars

Features No Longer Available

The following features are no longer available in Project Server 2007. Most of these are no longer needed or were not our favorites, such as the Portfolio Modeler; others we miss (such as Save Link).

Save Link

In Project Server 2003, the Save Link feature enabled users to save a view to a link after making personalized changes. Some examples include dragging a column to a different location on the page, setting a specific filter, and sorting the view differently from the default. This feature is no longer available.

Portfolio Modeler

The Portfolio Modeler was a tool that allowed for some "what-if scenario" modeling on projects. Project Server no longer includes such a function. However, a similar function that works better in any case is available in the new Microsoft Project Portfolio Server product. The Project Portfolio Server is a product that Microsoft purchased and modified somewhat and which includes a gateway to Project Server. Although the Project Portfolio Server functionality is not discussed in depth in this book, note that it is far broader and deeper than what Project Server previously offered for "what-if" processes. The tools that support Project Portfolio management are particularly strong.

To-Do Lists

To-Do lists have been replaced by activities, as discussed previously in this chapter.

Hiding of the Left Navigation Pane

The 2003 version included a feature that collapsed the PWA left navigation, freeing more screen space for the viewer. This feature is no longer present in the 2007 version.

A Word on Microsoft Office SharePoint Server (MOSS) 2007 and Project Server

In Project Server 2003 environment, SharePoint Portal Server had only the slimmest possibility of being useful. For example, you could use the SharePoint Portal Server Search feature to crawl and index the WSS 2003 team sites by identifying the Project Server WSS environment as a Content Source. Mostly, though, if you used SharePoint Portal Server 2003 for an intranet, for example, there was not really any connection to a Microsoft EPM solution environment. In fact, even WSS was not required for the use of Project Server.

As seen previously, WSS 3.0 is the base platform for PWA and is required. In 2007, the Microsoft Office SharePoint Server can be used to enhance the Project Server environment significantly. It is not required and, if chosen, it does add cost to the deployment of Project Server. However, it can be used for better business intelligence on project, resource, and financial data; better support for forms such as an InfoPath-based new project request form; better search capability; and more. This book will go deeper into this topic later.

This chapter described the extensive (and very useful) new features and improvements, as well as some features that are no longer available. In the next chapter, we move on to the processes for planning the deployment of a Microsoft Office Project Server 2007 platform with all its EPM tools.

PART II

Plan for Your Project Server 2007 Implementation

CHAPTER 4

Building Blocks for Implementation Success

Throughout this book, you'll read about the importance of planning—from planning your security, to planning your server infrastructure, to planning your project plans. There's a whole lot of planning for a solution with this many moving parts. In this chapter, we'll go back in time, to when a company was beginning to consider the introduction of Enterprise Project Management (EPM). In this way, we can look at the foundation of standardized processes upon which Microsoft Office Project Server 2007 is built. We'll look at the role of the project management office (PMO) in the organization, and look at a recognized scale for measuring project management maturity in your organization.

Implementation Approach

When considering the introduction of Microsoft Office Project Server 2007, it is critical that you consider the time it will take to implement it. If you're starting from scratch, the scope and complexity of the solution determines your timeline for complete rollout, which is usually measured in months rather than weeks. This is because an EPM solution, which has such long tentacles into the culture of an organization, is best implemented in an iterative fashion. Following the Microsoft Solutions Framework, a series of checkpoints bring your EPM environment to life by increasing functionality and audience in incremental chunks. See Figure 4-1 for a visual representation of the iterative methodology as it relates to an EPM implementation. The overall idea is to start small, with few features, then increase the user base and functionality with each successive iteration. This approach helps to minimize risk to the overall EPM implementation by accomplishing the following goals:

- The initial small team will be the core of the project server experts in your organization who will be called upon by new users for day-to-day questions. As the organization progresses from iteration to iteration, the pool of users who are familiar with the EPM environment grows, increasing organizational knowledge and overall adoption.

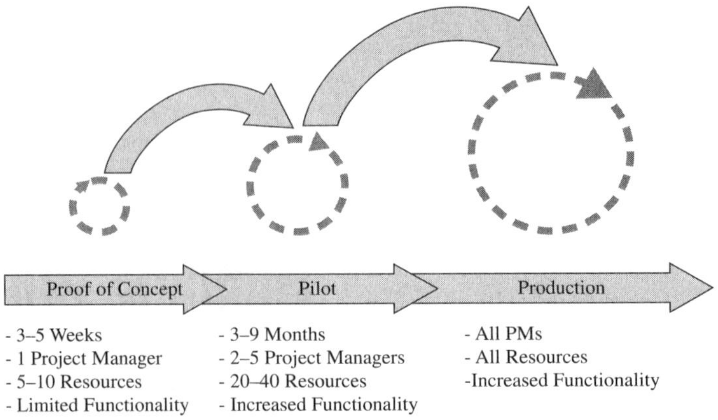

FIGURE 4-1 Implementing EPM using the iterative methodology

- By taking measured steps toward total implementation while your user base is small, you can address issues much more effectively. If the issue is one that has a large impact, the risk to the organization's operations is much smaller than if all members of the organization had been brought online at once.
- Your technical administrators and help desk team will have time to become familiar with the architecture and behavior of the application that they will help to support.
- If you are planning to integrate your data into an accounting or payroll application, you will have time through the various iterations to test your integration thoroughly for correct mapping and accuracy.

A pilot implementation could be narrowly focused with a small team (for example, a small department or PMO) but rich in features. The pilot could be broadly focused but light in features if the intended audience stretches across the organization. The breadth and depth of a pilot depend heavily on the project management (PM) maturity of the organization: An enterprise PMO could possess the process maturity to deploy a pilot to many departments with well-defined requirements; a specialized information technology (IT) PMO could do the same for a single department or functional organization.

Implementation Team

Your implementation team might include the following roles to provide organizational insight and decision making:

- **Executive sponsor** Your EPM implementation team must include at least one senior executive who is able to provide overall guidance to the team and fill the role of executive sponsor. Note that at a minimum, this person should have decision authority at least as broad as the components of the organization that will be impacted by the project. Having this person participate in various implementation meetings not only provides a communication conduit to the executive strata in an organization, but also reinforces to the rest of the team that the executives are behind this effort. Whether this sponsor provides cheerleading or executive mandates, his or her participation is crucial to keep momentum behind the EPM implementation effort. This sponsorship is a critical success factor to most significant initiatives, especially when they require process discipline and organizational change.

- **PMO representative(s)** This representative should be very closely linked with the implementation effort. The implementation's processes and standardized project management methodologies are what the PMO lives by, and they determine how users are trained and how the EPM toolset is configured. Because the PMO is generally recognized as the "owner" of the EPM system, the PMO member should have a broad understanding of the technologies involved. It is possible to succeed without a PMO, but it will be more challenging.
- **Departmental (resource) management** This role provides valuable input into the reporting requirements and cultural impact issues that the implementation effort will encounter.
- **Technical resource from the organization** Within the scope of the EPM implementation effort, this person is the conduit to the IT department to help acquire physical resources (servers, software). The technical resource also possesses a deep technical understanding of the existing network to enable him or her to make decisions and provide implementation technical support. Specific skills include database, infrastructure, and application support, as well as Information Systems security.
- **External consultant** Many companies choose to hire an EPM implementation specialist to help guide them through the technological and cultural issues that are normally encountered. The implementation specialist can also provide a fresh perspective on the organization and give frank advice while remaining independent (as much as possible) from the internal politics of the enterprise. This specialist will have deployed Project Server 2007 previously at a similar organization and will provide guidance for the successful implementation of the successive iterations of your EPM deployment.
- **Trainer** Training will play a large role in your implementation efforts. To provide EPM training for your users, you can choose from many avenues, ranging from online training, to bringing an EPM training expert to your location, to providing customized training for your users.

Many franchise training companies will offer Microsoft Project Professional training during which your beginner project managers will learn how to create a schedule and to work with the Project Professional 2007 scheduling engine. This training may provide your users with a basic understanding of one piece of the EPM toolset. However, a critical component to training your user base the right way the first time is to teach them how to accomplish tasks and manage projects based on your company's project management methodologies. One organization, Milestone Consulting, has developed an approach to EPM training called "Your Job, Tool's Job" (YJTJ). This curriculum is based on interaction with Project Professional 2007 and the information that it requires to be a truly effective scheduling tool. In addition, the curriculum can also be tailored to your company's specific project management methodologies and standards to ensure that your users are using the tool efficiently to provide the powerful reports that the executives in your organization expect.

Envisioning

The envisioning phase of your EPM implementation is typically where key members of the organization are introduced to the EPM toolset. During this phase, workshops are held that cover the EPM toolset implementation from a variety of perspectives and enable frank discussions as to how Project Server 2007 may be used in the organization. What comes out of this envisioning is a rough view of what this beast called EPM will look like once it is ultimately implemented in the organization. The following are some of the items to be realized from envisioning.

- Short/long term vision of EPM in your environment
- Functionality PMO, IT, product development, engineering, enterprise, global
- Processes and technology
- Timing
- Goals and strategy
- Challenges, pain points, and benefits

Proof of Concept

During the envisioning phase, a test server may be created to help familiarize members with the environment and the tools involved. This proof of concept (PoC) is typically the first iteration of the EPM implementation. During this time, a single project with a handful of resources begins using Project Server and Project Web Access. Feedback is captured from the PoC group in the areas of deployment/functionality of the client components, the process of entering time, the quality of the reports generated, and the overall user experience. This PoC project typically runs for three to five weeks with regular communication and feedback.

PoC Types and Descriptions

- Custom demo (very short with expert help)
- Conference room pilot (quick and dirty to demonstrate capability)
- Functional PoC
- Requirements-based PoC (show that the project can accomplish its objective, based on use cases)
- Prove concept and demonstrate value to a small group of key stakeholders only; can be done without direct user involvement for configuration and operation

Planning and the Pilot

After running the PoC, aggregating all feedback data, and defining your organization's critical success factors for EPM, you can start planning for the system that you previously envisioned. The EPM implementation team now has a clearer picture of capabilities and has begun the next iteration of an EPM implementation. In preparation for this phase, the team may enable additional features or functionality and prepare more team members to be brought into the system.

Whether a single workgroup or an entire department or business unit is being brought into the EPM system, the goal is to introduce a larger user base to EPM and potentially increase functionality as you move toward the full rollout of your envisioned environment. During this time, knowledge of and familiarity with EPM are growing organically in your organization as expertise and comfort with the toolset grow. The pilot can consist of a couple of project managers running all of their projects through the EPM system. The idea is that the selected project managers are exposed to EPM in the most pervasive manner: All of their active projects are brought into the system. The number of resources varies depending on the size of the organization and the number of resources per project, but these numbers should be kept small relative to the total number of resources envisioned.

NOTE *It is important to recognize the challenges that come when running a PoC and a pilot for EPM. Because the benefits of team member efficiency are realized when all of their tasks are accessible via Project Web Access (PWA), you should prepare your PoC and pilot team for additional work throughout the duration of the PoC, especially if the projects that they are working on are outside of the scope of the PoC or pilot.*

Full Implementation

Although you may decide that there needs to be an intermediary iteration (or several for large organizations) between your pilot and full implementation, the methodology will remain the same. Your full implementation will be a similar process of moving from your PoC to your pilot, except for this iteration, you're involving your entire organization in EPM and taking it "live." Wide-scale role-based training will have taken place, as the majority of your user base is brought into the EPM system. Additional features and functionality are implemented and refined based on the feedback and best practices learned from your previous iterations.

Role of the PMO

When it comes to the implementation of EPM in your organization, the project management office can help facilitate standardized adoption and help improve the chances of success and longevity of EPM in your organization. This group of users will define the processes and procedures that Project Server will support and give users their standard operating procedures for interacting with the environment. Being the nexus of project management wisdom in your organization, the PMO will provide the process development, mentoring, and enforcement. The importance of this is often underestimated when implementing Project Server 2007. Although a recognized PMO is not required for EPM to be successful, you increase your chances of success greatly when one is involved, or when you have a very disciplined and project-based department whose members will be the end users of the EPM toolset.

NOTE *PMOs come in many different shapes and sizes. In some organizations, the project management office is a distinct business unit whose members manage medium-to-large projects across the enterprise. In other environments, it is a subset of a business unit (such as IT) that manages the projects that originate from within the IT business unit in addition to managing the projects that originate from other business units but require IT involvement. This team of project managers does not manage resources directly; rather, they manage the approved schedules and use the resources from the required business units to complete a project. This distinction, as seen later in this chapter, provides additional challenges when describing the relationship among project managers and resource managers in your organization.*

The PMO's Place in the Enterprise

Whether you have a PMO for your business unit specifically, or share project managers across the organization, successful PMOs share some key characteristics:

- They are removed from the middle-management chain of command. This sounds like a fairly tall order, but to enable project managers to do what they do best—manage schedules—they must be separate from the chain of command. Only then can they maintain a healthy relationship with the various resource managers. After all, they will be requiring work from these managers' resources and will need to negotiate with these managers for those resources.
- After a resource manager has provided a resource to the project manager for assignment to project tasks, the project manager then has direct access rights to the resource for assignment, status, and motivation communications.

The PMO's Place in the Resource Breakdown Structure

If your organization has clear separation between resource managers and project managers, they will have to come to some agreement on assigning resources to projects. Project Server provides a framework for this process through tools such as Generic Resources, the Team Builder in PWA, and Project Professional 2007's Build Team from Enterprise tool. If project

A Word on the PMO

Project managers in an organization are typically thought of as being akin to a parental figure. You might recall why grandparents and grandchildren get along so well: It's because they have a common enemy. Of course, you should not look at your PMO as an adversarial unit of your organization; but in order to negotiate clearly and provide the brutal honesty that effective project managers sometimes must express, they are often served well by having thick skin.

Overall, the type of a PMO can vary greatly. On one end of the scale, it can provide the guidance and organizational prioritization and mapping between projects and enterprise strategy. On the other end of the scale, the PMO can consist of one or two project managers who provide planning services and mentoring for disconnected project groups. Invariably, whatever titles these people have on their business cards, they will be called on by the executive strata for executive reporting and provide process development and standardization for the organization.

managers are given free rein over assigning resources from the organization, they should be placed at a higher level in the organization's branch of the resource breakdown structure (RBS). If only resource managers have the ability to make their resources available for projects, then the PMO members' location in the RBS becomes less significant.

Project Management Maturity

Some organizations that are attracted to the powerful reports and effective tracking capabilities of Project Server 2007 believe that using EPM is simply a matter of installing the software (technology) and training people how to use it. Although these components are important, what these organizations miss is the third foundational component of EPM: processes. Normally, the mere existence of a PMO suggests that there is at least a semblance of standardized processes. These processes are what the technology is configured to support and enforce, and what your personnel are trained to use.

NOTE *Because of the flexibility of Project Server 2007 to support a wide range of usage models, implementing it without standardized methodologies (the process) ultimately ends in a GICO (garbage in, carnage out) state. When an organization reaches this point, the effectiveness of the powerful reports and tracking capabilities that was artfully demonstrated during the presales stage appears to have been exaggerated. The organization becomes convinced that the toolset is not living up to expectations because of a misrepresentation of the capabilities of the product. Its important to remember in these times that the reports generated by Project Server can only be as accurate, normalized, and granular as the data that feed Project Server.*

Having a PMO with mature processes and methodologies upon which Project Server can be built and training your personnel properly provide your best chance at harnessing the power of your EPM environment to work toward the overall improvement of your organizational efficiency. A number of frameworks are available for assessing (and possibly increasing) your organization's project management maturity. One of these is the Organizational Project Management Maturity Model (OPM3) offered by the Project Management Institute (http://www.pmi.org). These types of models provide an organizational framework by which you can assess the standardization, repeatability, and continuous improvement capacity of your organization.

Successful EPM implementations share common success factors. Although a PMO will greatly enhance the adoption of the tool from all levels of your organization, these keys to success are crucial:

- Executive management support
- Definition of scope and requirements
- End-user involvement
- Process discipline at the desired level
- Dedicated and trained users
- A planned and funded implementation
- Defined vision, objectives, and success criteria

All of these can exist without a PMO, but the existence of a PMO can reduce the overall risks associated with adoption.

Not-So-Obvious Planning Considerations

When preparing for Project Server implementation, it is easy to become immersed in the technical planning and process planning work to be done. Often peripheral processes need to be taken into consideration.

New Employee Checklist

If your organization is utilizing the Active Directory (AD) synchronization capabilities for your Project Web Access groups, you may want to consider how a new user becomes a participating member in the EPM system. The issue is that although Active Directory synchronization can add a new user to the enterprise resource pool and to PWA groups, it cannot specify values of resource-level enterprise custom fields (such as the RBS). As a result, some questions should be asked:

- Why is AD sync required and what are the driving factors for sync versus manual user administration?
- Who determines what role this new user should play in EPM?
- How does this information create a functioning user with appropriate rights and attributes in Project Server?
- Who will perform this administrative function of assigning attributes in PWA?

Because all resource-level enterprise custom fields and attributes must be set manually, a process will need to be defined that places responsibility for new user configuration. In some organizations, the new employee checklist is modified to capture this information and specify who will make these modifications to the new EPM user's PWA account. Opportunities for designing SharePoint workflows (we will discuss more on SharePoint in Chapter 25) to manage the new employee process become apparent.

Leaving Employee Checklist

Within the EPM environment, there should be an effort to establish a process for when an employee becomes an ex-employee. It is not simply a matter of deleting his or her Active Directory account and assuming that the details will work themselves out. As in previous versions of Project Server, after a resource is assigned, work cannot be deleted. This is to ensure that historical data are maintained. Organizations typically rely on the resource manager to inform the project managers that their resource is no longer available for project work.

Planning for your EPM implementation is not a trivial exercise. During the envisioning phase, you should become aware of the scope and preparation required to turn your vision into reality. Some companies, after completing an envisioning phase, realize that to achieve the levels of standardization and maturity required by the toolset, they will have to undergo a complete organizational transformation in culture and in mindset. On coming to this realization, these organizations opt to take various paths. These paths include reducing the feature set to lessen the impact on the user base, individually increasing the duration of

EPM Myths

Myth: Our IT department doesn't have a project initiation process. We expect our ability to authorize, prioritize, and communicate status to our customers to improve when we have Project Server 2007 installed.

Reality: The official project initiation process is typically owned by your PMO (whether departmental or enterprisewide). If your PMO has not created this process and had it authorized and enforced by executives at the highest level of the organization, then new project requests will certainly continue to take the path of least resistance, which is the path that they took before the implementation of Project Server.

Myth: Our entire organization will immediately see the benefits of efficiency and reporting upon installation of Microsoft Office Project Server 2007.

Reality: Although Project Server can provide dramatic enhancements in efficiency of project execution and reporting when based on standardized project management methodologies, it becomes a thoroughly useful tool when all of the members of an organization or business unit are using it to see all of their project work. Because most successful implementations are delivered in iterative phases, it is rare that immediate, widespread benefits will be realized in the short term.

each iteration, or increasing the number of iterations to make this pervasive culture and process change more palatable. Other organizations come to the realization that the change required for the EPM system is too great, and decide that they "just aren't ready yet" for a tool of this nature. For the companies that do decide to embark on an EPM initiative by doing some thoughtful planning, applying their methodologies, and embracing change, the payoff in organizational efficiency and proactive resource and portfolio planning agility will be profound.

CHAPTER 5

Requirements, Prioritization, and Project Planning for Project Server

There are many ways to implement Project Server. No matter which methodology is used, however, each requires planning. In fact, the one thing that you should remember from this part of the book is that if you don't take the planning seriously for your project, it will almost certainly fail.

This chapter discusses a process for gathering requirements for your Office Project Server 2007 implementation, prioritizing them, and building a plan for implementation. Project Server can do many things, but not all of its capabilities are important for all companies.

Let's say the organization has decided to implement Project Server to help improve the way that projects are delivered. Or perhaps the goal is to improve resource management through skills-based capacity planning. Of course, there will be a technical team that actually installs the product. Even before installation, a team should be tasked with figuring out what comes next. In addition, it is appropriate to build a plan or roadmap for the way that Project Server will be implemented in an iterative manner. Enabling all the features of Project Server at once is nearly guaranteed to result in a failed project. So how then will decisions be made about which steps are appropriate and over which timeframe?

First off, the team will have to define the requirements of the implementation; that is, which features and functions provide the most value. Requirements become the building block for how the Project Server implementation will be completed. In addition, completion of requirements gathering starts the process of mapping exactly what the correct solution will be for each specific organization.

Gathering Requirements

The process of gathering requirements generally will follow this path (details appear later in this chapter):

1. Define "requirements"—how detailed should a requirement be?
2. Gather all requirement ideas.
3. Separate requirements into "must have," "important," or "nice to have."
4. Rank or prioritize the requirements from 1 to *x* (that is, if there are 27 requirements, rank each from 1 to 27).
5. Validate prioritized requirements against technology reality.
6. Build an iterative plan with a gradually decreasing level of detail over time.

NOTE *We know, we know…we will get to the nuts and bolts soon.*

As the team sits down to decide what to include in the Project Server implementation, the first step is to review the high-level goals for the project. It may be that the organization needs a way to record hours worked on project plans. One goal of this organization might be: "Enable a system that supports the ability for all team members to record their work on project tasks into a centralized system." If the objective is to have a single location to view all ongoing projects and their current status to see how well they are tracking, make sure to keep this objective in mind. Whatever the goals are and no matter whether the goals have been generated (by the project's executive sponsor or by a team of people on a consensus basis), each organization probably has done this to some level before starting the requirements gathering process.

Requirements versus Specifications

The goal of this process is to decide, for characterization purposes, what is a requirement and what is a specification; how are they different? For the sake of this book, we'll define the difference as follows: A *requirement* is something functional, a more human view of the way the system should work. A *specification* is more defined and tends to be more technical. Another way of looking at it is that requirements define what is needed, and specifications define (without the technical design details) how it works. In either case, both should be documented. For example, the following could be a requirement for Project Server 2007:

> Executives must be able to view quickly (within 1 to 2 minutes) projects for each department at a summary level to understand overall and individual project progress.

A specification might be more like the following:

> The Marketing Executive View in the Project Server Project Center will filter 'Marketing' items from the Enterprise Custom Field 'Departments.' This Enterprise Custom Field uses the Lookup Table 'Depts' and includes each department in the

company (IT, New Product Development, Human Resources, Marketing, Production Management, Customer Support). Each view will include the following fields:

- Project Name
- BCWP (Baseline Cost of Work Projected)
- ACWP (Actual Cost of Work Performed)
- Tracking Flag
- Finish Variance %
- Project Status
- Sponsor
- ETC (Estimate to Complete)
- EAC (Estimate at Complete)
- Actual Start
- Finish

For planning purposes, it is suggested here that the Enterprise Project Management (EPM) team initially focus on functional requirements as opposed to specifications, because you have to define what the desired result is before you can get to the specifics of exactly how to implement it. It will require multiple sessions to determine requirements. It is possible to get a solid set of initial requirements, but development of requirements will continue iteratively over the life of the deployment effort as more functionality is added over time. (More on iterative project planning is discussed later in this chapter.) The next section of this chapter covers how to build requirements for your Microsoft Project Server 2007 implementation.

Building Functional Requirements

There are many ways to build a set of requirements. Initial high-level requirements can be done without specific tool knowledge. For example, the solution may be required to allow visibility into resource availability, or it may be required to include material resources (such as lumber, computers, and lease costs) in project plans and budgets. Such requirements, although generally useful, will probably not suffice for planning your actual project. Rather, the goal is to get more specific about requirements for the Project Server 2007 implementation. This can be accomplished by starting with a tool demonstration for the EPM team. A consultant commonly delivers this demo unless an organization has existing internal expertise. Don't expect a one-hour meeting to be enough time for this demo. You should plan for at least two hours, and more would be better.

> Microsoft Office Project Server 2007 and its supporting technologies are capable of a very wide and deep range of use. No organization will receive value from all of the features. In fact, it is possible to get high value from a small set of functions in certain cases.

NOTE *The process discussed is just one way to approach gathering requirements. If you have a preferred method, use it.*

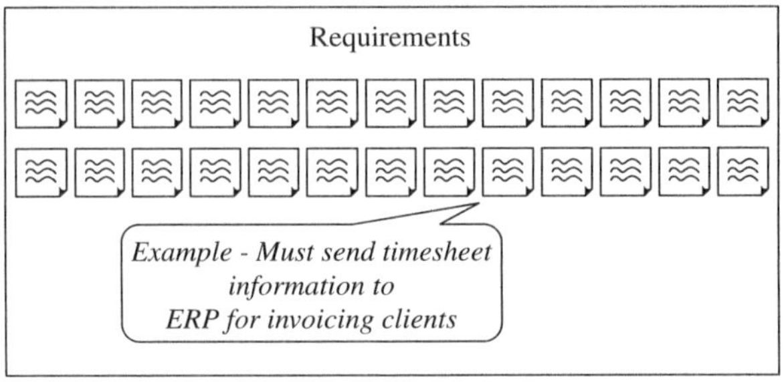

From this, the team can gain at least an overall understanding of tool capabilities.

The suggestion is to combine the understanding of the way that the specific organization functions (and wishes to function) with the knowledge of the tool to generate the output of the requirements process. Once again, this commonly involves some consulting expertise, as very few organizations have the requisite tool depth. The team then must collectively identify the specific requirements. One exercise that might be considered is a facilitated "sticky-note" session. As the team meets, members/stakeholders individually start to name requirements. The consultant or facilitator writes down each single requirement on a sticky note with a bold marker pen. The facilitator may need to probe a bit to ensure that everyone understands the meaning of the requirement. No judgment should be made on the quality of ideas at this point. Just gather everything that anyone contributes. The sticky notes can be put on a white board or even a wall, placed horizontally so as not to imply value.

The next section discusses the process of prioritization.

Requirements Prioritization

There are many methods for prioritizing, and this section describes just one. If the company has a different method in place for prioritizing needs, there is no reason to change just for this single project.

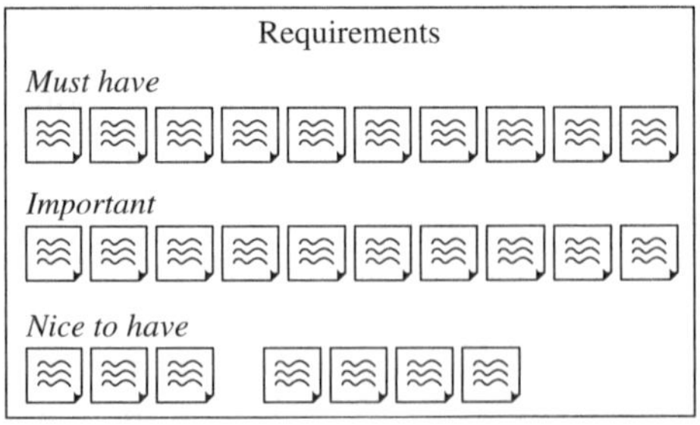

Remember that a requirement is defined as something functional—a human view of the way that the system should work. Not all requirements are created equal, so after you have gathered all the requirements, it is important to prioritize them. This isn't always easy if the EPM team is comprised of stakeholders with different agendas (as it should be). Start by asking the team to work as a group. The goal is to come to consensus on whether each specific requirement is a "Must Have," "Important," or "Nice to Have." A suggested approach for this discussion is to use a package of sticky notes and a white board or any kind of available wall space. First make a list of all the requirements and get them up on the board or wall. Then have the participants work together and decide into which category—"Must Have," "Important," or "Nice to Have"—each requirement falls. Place the sticky notes into the three different areas on the board or wall (perhaps you could place them in three different rows). You might remove the requirements from the board altogether if the group determines that an item or items are "Not Required."

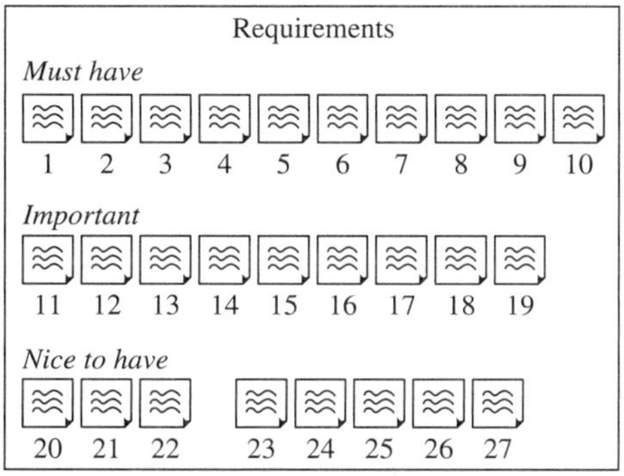

This task as described had better not be too difficult, because it gets more complicated from there. The next step is to have the group place the requirements in order by agreeing on what is the number one priority, number two priority, and so on. The idea is that if there are 27 requirements spread through the three levels of importance ("Must Have," "Important," or "Nice to Have"), there will be a ranking for each one (1 through 27). Depending on the team, this can be moderately straightforward or extremely painful. In addition to getting the team to reach a common understanding of what the project will deliver, there are additional benefits as well. For example, each participant will have a greater stake in the project, improving the likelihood of project success.

Although you have now sorted and ranked the requirements, the process is not quite complete. The next section covers how to combine knowledge of the way the tool functions with the prioritized requirements; this combination will become your project plan.

Prioritized Requirements versus Technical Reality and Cost

Following the prioritization work, there is one more step. Often, the practical realities of the way the tools function will not allow the priorities to be completed in the order they are agreed upon by the EPM team. Also, there are often areas of functionality that, when viewed against the costs of executing the project, become more or less valuable. For example, if it is the number one priority to export timesheet data to an invoicing system, there is no way that it would be logical or practical for cost reasons to build a custom time interface prior to populating the Enterprise Resource Pool (the place in Project Server where all the resources that would actually record time are together in the system). Therefore, the prioritization of requirements must be run through a "sanity check" to make sure that tool issues are considered.

Using estimated effort (cost) and business value as discussed in Chapter 1 will assist with assessing the relative worth of each prioritized requirement. This should also be considered when creating the phasing plan. Once again, this process is often done by either a consultant or someone with in-house experience with Project Server (2003 as a base, although 2007 experience is much better). The resulting output is documented for review and team approval.

There is still more to the planning process. The next section discusses the process of mapping the approved final priorities to a plan.

Use Cases

Now that there is a list of priorities that has gone through both functional and high-level technical review, some work should be done to define certain key processes that the organization requires. These vary based on the output of the work described earlier in this chapter. Plan carefully for the items that make sense for the business. A *use case* is a goal-focused set of processes that occur between users of a system and the system itself. They can vary in depth depending on the level of complexity and established rigor for each organization. An example of a use case might be the process of a project manager adding resources to a plan in Project Professional. It might look something like the high-level example as shown in Table 5-1.

There are some common items that most organizations should map with a use case for Project Server. The Time and Task entries are great examples. There are many ways to use, and therefore configure, the system for these functions. Some questions to ask include the following:

- Is it important to separate Time entry and approvals from project task updates so that the resource or functional manager approves the time, and the project manager approves task updates and applies them to the plan?
- Must all time be recorded in the system, even non-project time?
- What types of non-project time should be recorded and how should that work?
- Should vacation time planning be supported?
- Should sick time require review and approval?
- Do billable and nonbillable hours both have to be included?
- Are all employees exempt from overtime, are they all hourly, or is the workforce a combination of both?
- How should support time be handled?

Title of the Use Case	Building a Project Team—PM
Author and Date	John Cooper 03/01/2007
Version Number	V 1.2
Overview/Summary	The project manager uses "Build Team from Enterprise" tool within Project Professional to add resources to a new project.
Assumptions/Preconditions	Project managers have security access to resources within their own respective departments.
Triggers	NA
Basic Flow	The project manager opens Project Professional and logs in to Project Server. From within Project Professional, the PM selects Tools, then Build Team from Enterprise. Resources are selected from the left side (Enterprise Resources) and added to the right side (Project Resources) of the Build Team tool. The PM then selects OK and the resources are assigned.
Alternative Paths or Scenarios	The Replace function is used to replace a resource already assigned with a different resource. The Match function is used to find resources who have the same role as defined in the Custom Enterprise Resource field "Primary_Role." The assigned resources are changed from "Committed" to "Proposed."
Poststate(s) or Condition(s)	When PM views the Resource Sheet View, the resources that were just added are displayed.
Business Requirements or Rules	NA
Notes	Many other features are available within the Build Team tool, such as filtering and viewing resource availability. These other options will be covered in another use case.

TABLE 5-1 Building a Project Team Use Case

- How should maintenance time be handled?
- Should time and task information be submitted weekly, monthly, or daily?

Use cases should be written for each time and task type, such as the following:

- Regular project
- Administrative time—vacation, sick, company events, and so on

- Support—planned
- Support—incident-based

The following is a sample use case for the Time entry in Microsoft Office Project Server 2007:

Title of the Use Case	Time Entry
Author and Date	Mario Jones - 05/06/2007
Version Number	V2.0
Overview/Summary	This is the basic Time entry process that will be executed by all staff. It will include all time types and should always include a minimum of 40 hours for full-time staff.
Assumptions/Preconditions	Time periods have been created in the system. Work has been assigned to the user(s). Some administrative time categories have been enabled.
Triggers	User creates current timesheet from the My Timesheets page in Project Web Access (usually http://myservername/pwa and then navigate to My Timesheets from the Quick Launch Bar).
Basic flow	The user navigates to My Work, then Timesheet. The user enters actual hours worked for each task in the daily cell for that task. This includes at least one Administrative Time item. Upon completion of a weekly timesheet, the user makes appropriate selections to submit the timesheet for resource manager approval.
Alternative Paths or Scenarios	Full week of Admin Time (as in vacation)
Poststate(s) or Condition(s)	The timesheet manager receives the approval request and the submitter is not allowed to submit another timesheet (the option is disabled or dimmed).
Business Requirements or Rules	NA
Notes	Recalling Timesheets will be covered in another Use Case

Other related use cases might include such items as the following:

- General use cases
  - Propose a potential project
  - Review, approve, and reject a proposed project
  - View the status of a project, program, or portfolio

- View the status of issues, risks, or deliverables
- View and print reports
- Project manager–focused use cases
  - Accept and initiate a new or approved project or program
  - View resources' availability and assignments
  - Request resources
  - Build project team (if permissions allow)
  - Assignment of resources to tasks
  - Update project status (progress updates and plan maintenance)
  - Create and assign issues, risks, or deliverables
- Use cases for the resource manager
  - Add/update resource data
  - Review, approve, and reject timesheets
  - Allocate resources to a project
  - Approve administrative time
- Team member
  - View and update task progress
  - Create, update, and submit a timesheet
  - Create or update issues, risks, or deliverables
  - Request nonproject/admin time with and without approval option enabled

The use cases should include variable paths, often called *scenarios*, that could occur within each of them. Most important, the goal in the use case must have a measurable or provable component. The next section discusses how to build a Project Plan or Work Plan for the Project Server 2007 initiative.

Creating an Iterative Plan

Requirements have been prioritized and use cases have been created. In most cases, organizations that choose to implement Microsoft Office Project Server 2007 are at least somewhat mature in general project management and have had some exposure to Microsoft Project. These organizations typically expect to see a project plan document and expect the project manager to manage the EPM implementation of the plan. There are many ways to build a plan. We recommend the following approach or one that is similar.

In traditional project management methodologies, all the planning was done up front and then the project moved through its phases (such as envisioning, requirements, design, build, test, implement, and closure). Such methodologies actually worked pretty well for simple projects such as building a small computer network. They also worked pretty well for other types of projects that could be planned to a detail level with certainty that nothing major would change during the project. However, they tended to fail on large complex projects where a lot of change occurred and were especially troublesome on large software development projects. Newer thinking has espoused several different project management approaches, all falling within the "iterative" category. So the question before the organization considering a Project Server implementation is, which is the correct approach: traditional (waterfall) or iterative?

Iterative deployment is best. Project Server has a multitude of features and functions and tends to have a significant impact on companies. A successful implementation can influence the very way that an organization does business by improving project management, and therefore business processes. Don't attempt to implement everything in Project Server and all the users of Project Server at one time. The "big bang" method is usually a mistake. In addition, these projects usually go through extensive change management and control.

The preferred approach is to map the requirements to an iterative deployment process that increases functionality and audience over time. In other words, if capturing time is the most important requirement, design and build a system that meets specific time-capturing needs, and at a minimum, perform a pilot (if not a proof of concept) with a limited audience first. Then add a new set of features and expand the audience incrementally, with each iteration.

Each phase should be kept within a manageable time window (three to five weeks) and should have measurable requirements. It is very common that new ideas or opportunities will occur during an iteration (or phase). Instead of performing a complex change management process whenever a new idea comes up, document each new idea in the requirements log (such as an "Opportunities" SharePoint list) for future iterations. By setting a goal and achieving it (and not being derailed by scope change), the team establishes a win for everyone involved. The sponsor can show his or her peers, the team knows that they did what was expected of them, and the project manager also succeeds. If establishing new rigor in your project management process is part of the EPM project (an idea worth considering), the sponsor should formally sign off at the end of each iteration.

When an iteration (phase) closes with a signoff, the team and sponsor review the next set of requirements and consider whether any reprioritization should occur, and the work can begin anew. This cycle continues repeatedly until all the requirements have been realized or have fallen to a level of priority not worth the effort.

The end result of following this type of process can be a project that is more complex and longer, less complex and of shorter duration, depending on several factors. The outcome of the projects can vary considerably. Keep in mind that it is unlikely that anyone can successfully implement this tool in weeks, but rather expect the effort to take months.

The following is one example of an iterative plan at a high level:

Phase	Deliverable(s)	Audience
EPM Project Envisioning	Vision statement and high-level roadmap. PoC scope	EPM team
Proof of Concept	Successful PoC in lab	Small set of users
Detailed Planning	Prioritized requirements, pilot scope, more fleshed out phasing plan	EPM team
Pilot	Functioning Project Server in production environment with requirements met Additional function included in scope for Phase 1	Pilot team (no more than 25 users)
Phase 1	Functioning Project Server that meets Phase 1 requirements Scope for Phase 2	A single department (does not have to be IT)
Phase 2	Functioning Project Server that meets Phase 2 requirements Scope for Phase 3	Another department
Phases 3-X		Companywide
Closure		
Maintenance and Support throughout and after Closure phase		

Note that the deployment sequence from previous sections should be based on the rollout plan and process. Also note that in this example, an organization with multiple sites could choose to deploy iterations by location as opposed to department.

This chapter briefly discussed project planning for Microsoft Office Project Server 2007 deployments. For the next several chapters, the book focuses on the real "meat and potatoes" of this subject: configuration of Project Server. Although configuration of the tools is one general topic, due to the length of the discussion required, it is broken into separate chapters by subtopic.

PART III

Details on the Installation and Configuration of Project Server 2007

CHAPTER 6

Installation of Project Server 2007 and Prerequisite Software

Now that features, architecture, and planning have been touched upon, it is time to get into the meat of the book. This chapter focuses on the installation of Project Server 2007 as well as its base platform, Windows SharePoint Services 3.0.

Installation Overview

Because there are a multitude of installation scenario and configuration options, we will make several assumptions and cover the three most widely used Microsoft Office Project Server 2007 configurations:

- Stand-alone (basic)
- Small farm
- Medium farm

We'll start by assuming that Project Server 2007 is the first Office Server 2007 application that you've installed in your environment. Later in the chapter, we'll discuss options for installing it alongside Microsoft Office SharePoint Server (MOSS) 2007. As with most other aspects of the 2007 Enterprise Project Management (EPM) offering, the installation of Microsoft Office Project Server 2007 has changed greatly from previous versions. In Project Server 2003, the installation required the administrator to collect a great deal of information and then follow a serial and delicate process that often ended with rollbacks, late nights, and consecutive installation failures. In Microsoft Office Project Server 2007, the installation is separated into three components:

- Bit (binary) installation
- Windows SharePoint Service (WSS) configuration
- Project Web Access (PWA) site provisioning

Overall Considerations—Common across All Farm Sizes

Regardless of the overall size and structure of your Project Server farm, there are some common items that require consideration.

Network Operating System

The ideal and most likely situation is that you have a Microsoft Active Directory already installed and functioning in your environment. Ideally, you have Kerberos authentication established and functioning and a certificate authority in your environment able and willing to provide certificates for your users, servers, and applications, as well as administrators with plenty of time to help support and troubleshoot these services. Although Kerberos authentication is not required for a Project Server farm, it is supported.

NOTE *If your organization is still operating in a Microsoft Windows NT4 Domain, fear not: You do have an option for installation. The option is to install Project Server 2007 in a small-farm environment. When you install Project Server 2007 in a simple farm environment, all of the server components (such as SQL Server 2000–2005, SQL Analysis Services, PWA, and Project Server Application Role) are on one server. This environment will not scale, nor be able to be installed on multiple machines due to the installation routine requiring an accessible Dynamic Global catalog and the Server-to-Server trust that Microsoft Active Directory provides. However, you will be able to install Project Server 2007, WWS v3, SQL Server 2005, and Analysis Services 2005, and take advantage of most of the functionality that Project Server can offer. (You will not be able to perform any automatic group synchronization, though.)*

End-User Location Considerations

Although Microsoft Project Server 2007 allows for clients residing across a wide area network (WAN), there are some caveats to this scenario that involve the data analysis functionality of PWA. Let's first review the scenarios to which these caveats apply and which users are affected:

- **Project managers** Because all of the Project Professional 2007 to Project Server 2007 communication takes place through Simple Object Access Protocol (SOAP) calls over Hypertext Transfer Protocol (HTTP) through the active cache, project managers can work from anywhere, so long as they can resolve from their location the name of and contact for the PWA site through HTTP or HTTPS (HTTP over SSL).

NOTE *In previous versions, after a brief security brokering with the Project Data Service (PDS), Project Professional made a direct Open Database Connectivity (ODBC) connection with the SQL database. This created several challenges. First, because this ODBC connection was extremely sensitive to low-bandwidth, high-latency WAN links, Project Professional performance would suffer greatly. Second, and often a deal-breaker, most sane network/security administrators would not allow connections on port 1433 from the Internet directly into their production SQL servers. This usually led to exposing Project Server to the Internet through a new or existing implementation of Terminal Services. Although Terminal Services often solved security and networking issues of Project Professional–Project Server interaction, additional constraints arose, such as the inability to take a project offline.*

- **Executives (and data analysts)** Because the Data Analysis views utilize SQL Server Analysis Services, user instances of Internet Explorer still make direct connections and authenticate directly to the Analysis Services Server. All machines that attempt to access the Data Analysis views must do so in a way that Analysis Services understands and can authenticate. This means that the machine that the executive is logged in to must be a member of the same Microsoft Active Directory as the Project Server components, or that a domain trust is in place to accommodate this Analysis Services authentication. This can be a point of administrative angst when attempting to expose the functionality to the Internet. In view of the fact that the Analysis Services cubes often contain sensitive information about a company and its projects, it is recommended that administrators initiate a policy that forbids access to the Data Analysis views unless the end user is either physically on company premises, or has established a virtual private network (VPN) into the company network.

Secure Sockets Layer

As you will likely be using Microsoft Active Directory for authentication, the use of Secure Sockets Layer (SSL) security is a must when you expose any portion of Project Server 2007 to the Internet. Some companies enforce a policy that allows access to Project Server 2007 only when one of the following conditions is true:

- The user is physically plugged into the company network.
- The user has established a VPN connection to the company network.

Although some companies have requirements for implementing SSL on *any* Web-based application, you may find that your company does not have this particular policy.

Physical Networking Environment and Switching

Your physical networking environment may or may not affect your planned installation. Although the Project Cache will help your Project Professional users with low-bandwidth and high-latency issues, there are other aspects that are much more reliant on existing routing and switching equipment, and this reliance is due to your environment's availability and capacity plans. Although Windows Network Load Balancing is outside of the scope of this book, it is important to note that you should approach this issue with forethought and a test plan, rather than assuming that Windows Network Load Balancing will work, as there are some compatibility issues with some legacy switching equipment.

Interserver Communication

It is recommended to have a 1Gb/sec. connection between all of your Project Server 2007 server components. It is also a requirement to have all of the Project Server 2007 components configured to be members of the same Microsoft Active Directory environment.

Database

For anything other than a basic installation (where SQL 2005 Express Edition is installed automatically), either SQL Server 2000 or SQL Server 2005 is required.

Server Installation in a Stand-Alone Environment

Although Project Server 2007 can be installed in a distributed fashion with different tiers of the application residing on separate hardware, it can also be installed in a stand-alone environment. This is where the Front End Web Server (presentation tier), the Application Server (business tier), and the Database all reside on the same server instance. Installation in a stand-alone environment requires the least administrative intervention, as the installation routine automates installation of SQL 2005 Express, provisioning of SharePoint Central Administration, the SharedService Provider (SSP), their associated Web applications, and a PWA site.

Operating System

Ideally you should use Windows Server 2003 with SP1. Alternatively, you can use Windows Server 2003 R2. Windows Server 2003 Web Edition will work for a basic installation only.

Install IIS

This part of the installation may seem like a no-brainer, as Internet Information Services 6 is required for Project Server 2007. What you may not know is that ISS is required for certain components of SQL Server 2005. Although there are usually two or three ways to do anything in a Microsoft application, one of the easiest ways to install IIS is as follows:

1. Go to the Manage Your Server management window (Start | Programs | Administrative Tools).
2. Click Add a Role and specify Application Server. You are presented with two checkboxes: one for Enable Front Page Extensions, and the other for Enable ASP.NET 2.0. Enable ASP.NET 2.0 and leave Enable Front Page Extensions unchecked.

As IIS goes through its own automated installation routine, it may pause for you to look for the original installation CD of Windows Server 2003.

SQL Server Versions

The stand-alone installation is ideal for an initial proof of concept (PoC), where you need the least technical and administrative impact while allowing the core functionality of Project Server 2007 to be exposed. There are some limitations with using the stand-alone environment:

- Because it is based on SQL 2005 Express instead of SQL 2000 or SQL 2005 Standard, you are limited to 4GB maximum database size.
- The maximum amount of random access memory (RAM) that SQL 2005 Desktop can utilize is 1GB.
- If your organization is currently using SQL 2000 as its production database version, you will not be able to upgrade SQL 2005 Desktop Edition to SQL 2000 Standard or Enterprise.
- You cannot prove the capabilities of the Project Server 2007 Data Analysis views, as the supporting technology (Analysis Services) is not available.

TIP *When you are installing a server, it is often helpful to copy the I386 directory directly from the operating system media to the root of the system drive. This way, the Windows Server 2003 installation bits are always handy.*

After you receive the confirmation screen stating that your server is now an application server, you should return to Windows Update to receive critical IIS specific patches and, optionally, the .NET Framework 3.0.

Install the .NET Framework 3.0

The .NET Framework 3.0 is the managed code programming model for Microsoft Windows. It is a combination of foundational elements that Microsoft has added on to the .NET Framework 2.0. These elements include the Windows Presentation Foundation, Windows CardSpace, Windows Communication Foundation, and most relevant to Project Server 2007, the Windows Workflow Foundation. It is a relatively hands-free installation, downloadable directly from the Microsoft download site, as shown in Figure 6-1.

When you start the installation, the .NET Framework installation proceeds to download additional components. After the installation completes setting up the .NET Framework 3.0, the confirmation screen suggests that you visit Windows Update for the updates and Service Packs for the product. Do so at this time. It has become a habit during installation to reboot the server therapeutically after each major component is installed. Whether this

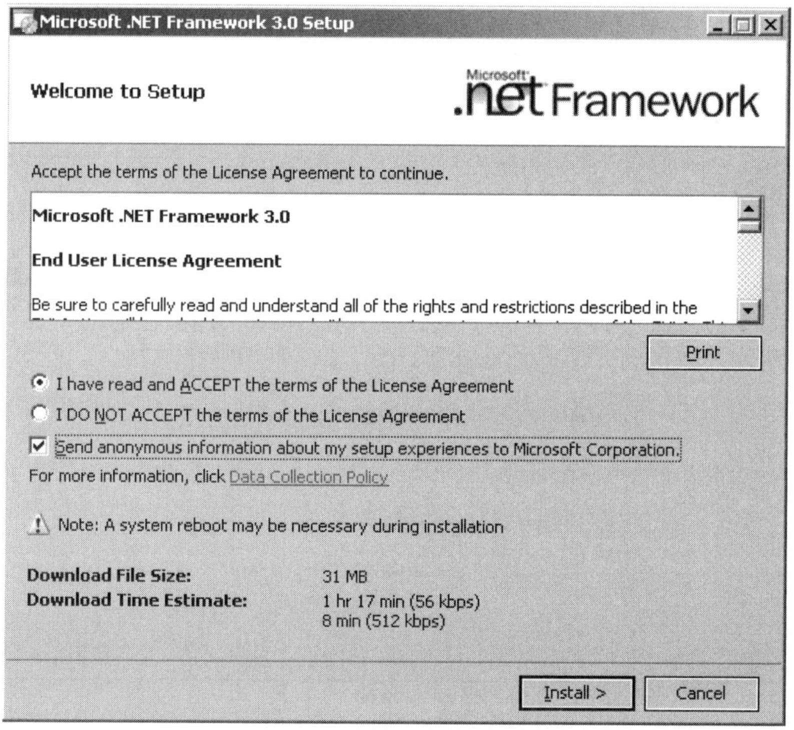

FIGURE 6-1 Installing the .NET Framework 3.0

practice is pure superstition or a valid habit carried over from installations of the past that specifically called for it, doing so helps to ensure that the system is not left in an inconsistent state through "pending file operations" messages that you may have unintentionally clicked past.

Finally, you will need to double-check that ASP.NET v2.0.50727 is allowed in your IIS Web applications.

Go to IIS Manager (Click Start | Run, and type **inetmgr**, open up the local computer, and click Web Service Extensions. Ensure that ASP.NET v2.0.50727 is set to Allowed as shown in Figure 6-2.

After you have reached this point, you are now prepared to perform the stand-alone, or basic, installation of Project Server 2007.

Put the installation media into the computer on which you have just installed IIS and the .NET Framework 3.0. (Alternatively, point to the network location for the Microsoft Office Project Server installation files.) Then run Setup.exe as follows:

1. Enter a valid license key for Microsoft Office Project Server 2007.
2. Read the Microsoft Software License Terms, smile, accept them, and click Continue.
3. On the Choose the Installation You Want page, click Basic as shown in Figure 6-3.

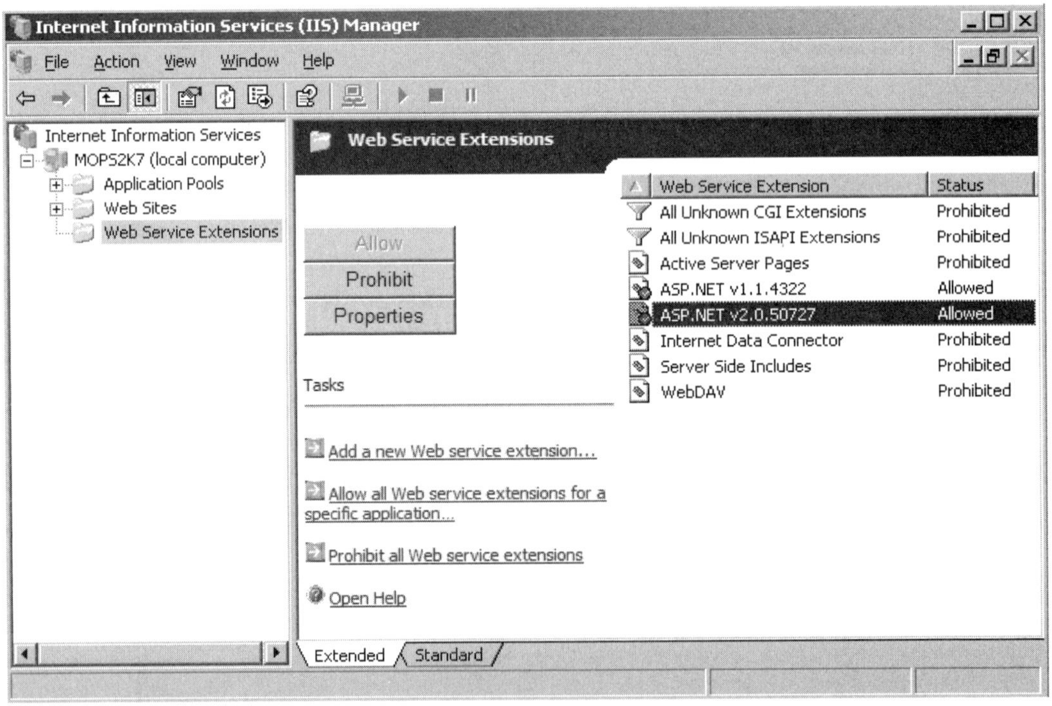

FIGURE 6-2 Ensure that ASP.NET v2.0.50727 is allowed.

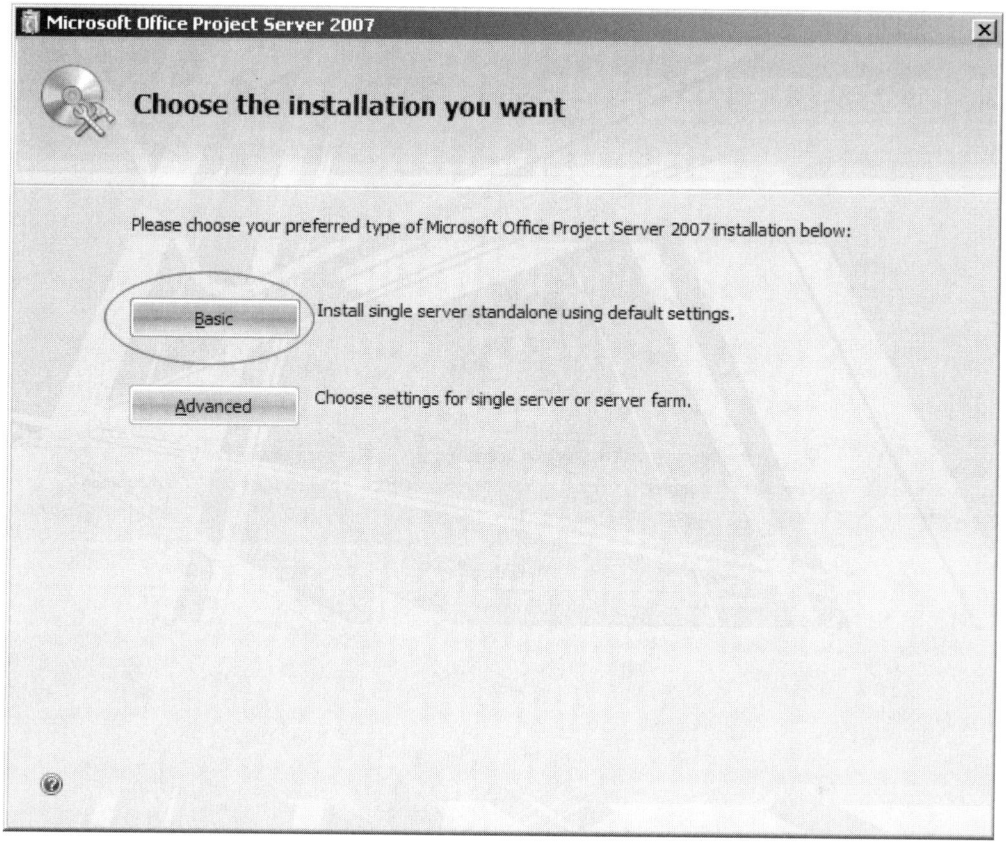

FIGURE 6-3 Choose the Basic installation type.

NOTE *If you want a stand-alone installation, but want to designate the file locations for the program files and data, click Advanced, then choose the Stand-Alone installation.*

The installation works for a few minutes installing the Project Server 2007 binaries, creating and configuring the various Web applications and the SSP and applying Updates. Be patient, as this may take several minutes.

4. At completion, the installation program prompts you to run the SharePoint Technologies Configuration Wizard. With the associated checkbox selected, click Close, as shown in Figure 6-4.

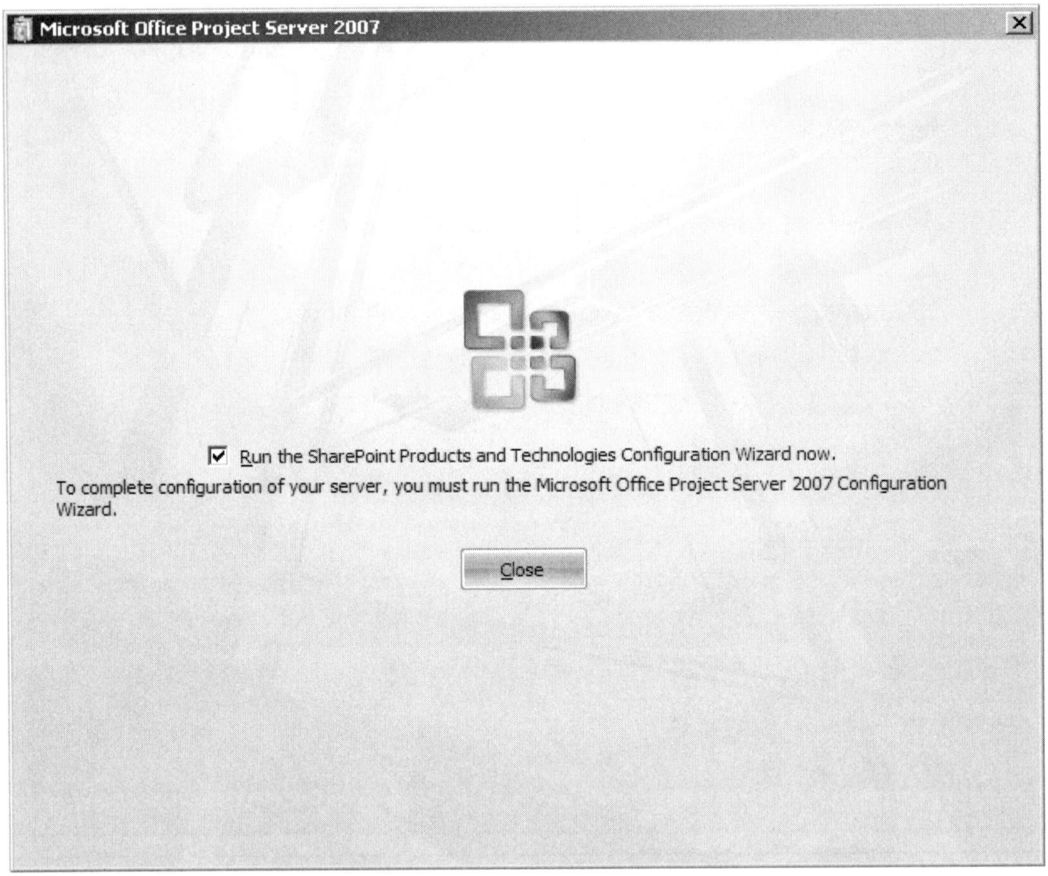

FIGURE 6-4 Post-binary installation screen

In the SharePoint Products and Technologies Configuration Wizard welcome screen, click Next. A notification window appears alerting you that a number of services must be started or reset during the process. Choose Yes, as shown in Figure 6-5.

The configuration then undertakes several tasks, which include the provisioning and configuration of the WSS configuration database. In addition, the services required on the server are configured, including the SharePoint Services, the Queueing Service, Session State Service, Windows SharePoint Service, and the Central Admin Web application.

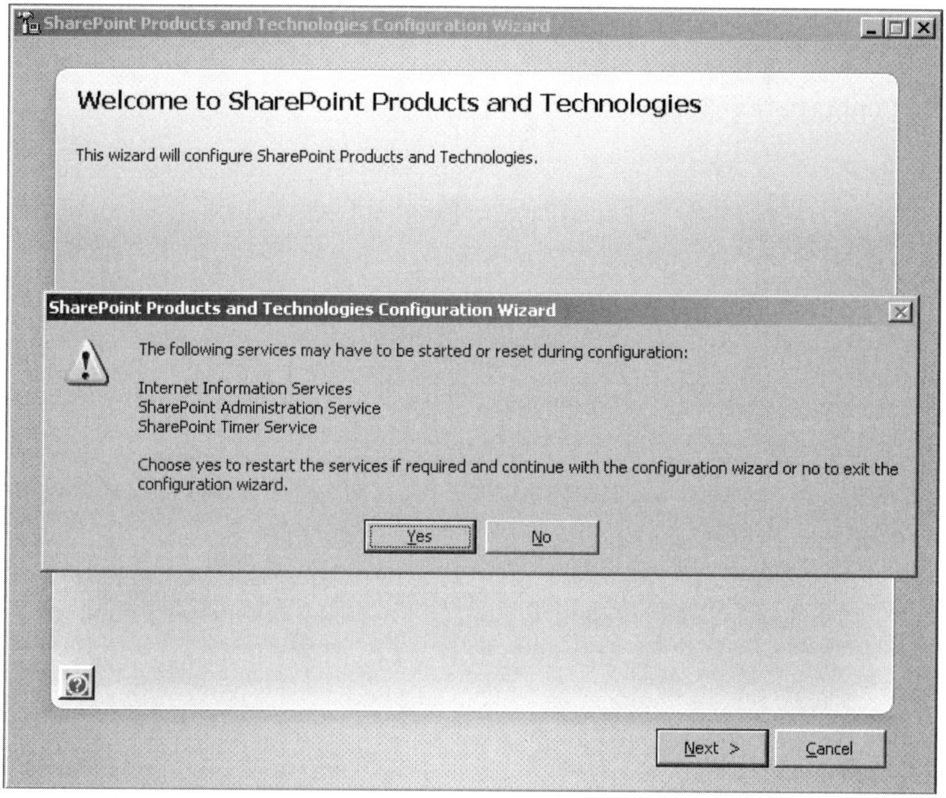

FIGURE 6-5 Notification of service interruption

After the SharePoint Configuration Wizard completes, it notifies you and instructs you to click Finish, as shown in Figure 6-6. Note that participation in the Customer Improvement Feedback Program is not available when you install the product in a stand-alone environment.

Voilà! Your PWA site has been provisioned and you are ready to move forward with your proof of concept of Project Server 2007. If your installation is a proof of concept and you are testing the base functionality or process flow of EPM, you can safely skip to the Client Components section (later in this chapter) to learn about the client components for installation.

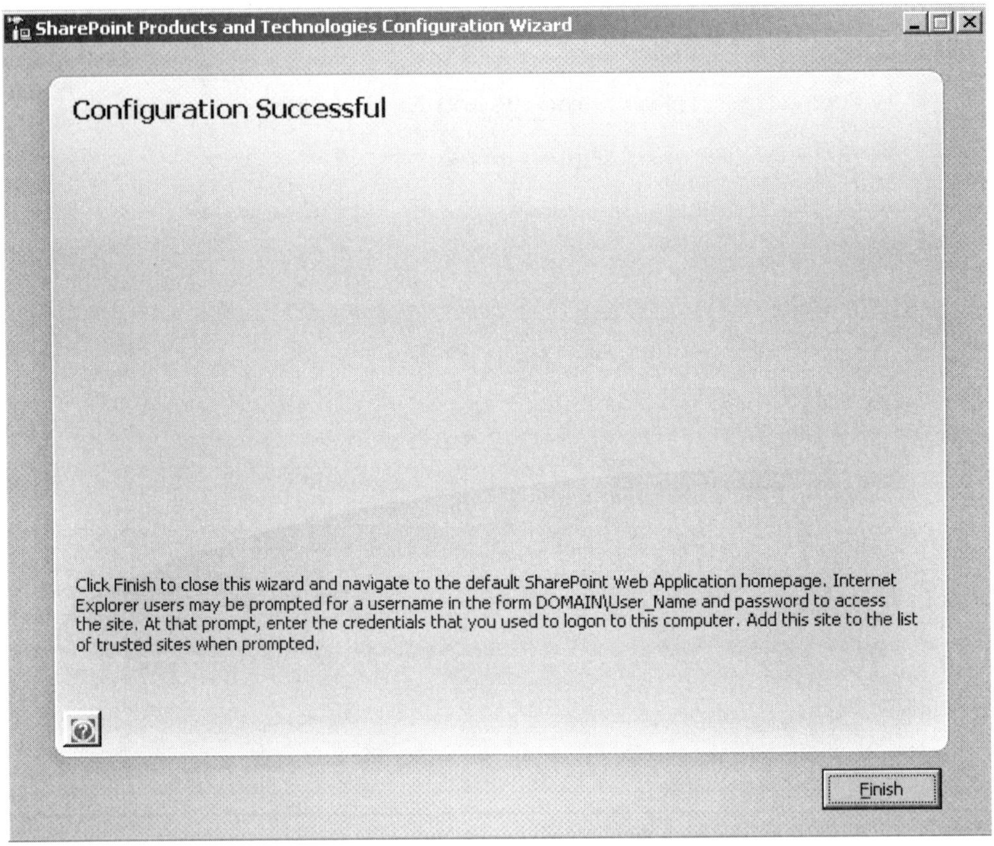

FIGURE 6-6 SharePoint configuration confirmation

Small-Farm, Single-Server Installation

The small-farm topology exists even when all of the server components reside on the same physical instance of Windows Server 2003.

The following steps assume that this is a fresh installation of Windows Server 2003 with Service Pack 1 applied, and that all updates have been installed from Windows Update. Note that a one-server small farm, as shown in Figure 6-7, is identical in setup to a two-server small farm, as shown in Figure 6-8, except that during the installation of Project Server, when you are asked for the database server name, you would specify the remote SQL Server. A printable installation checklist is provided on the accompanying CD.

The single-server small farm differs from a stand-alone installation in that the stand-alone installation automatically installs SQL Server 2005 Express Edition and creates your instance of PWA.

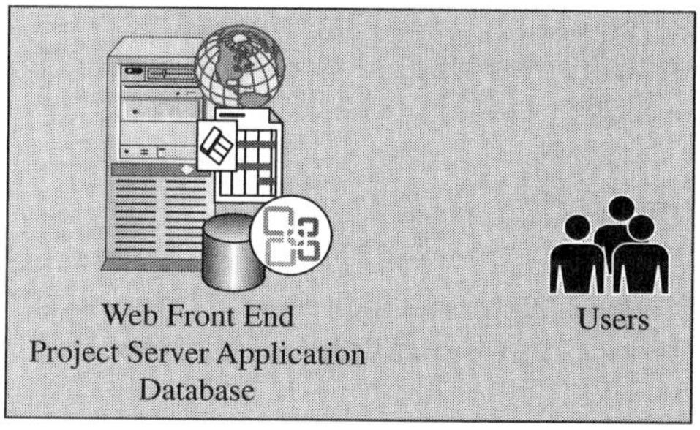

FIGURE 6-7 A single-server small farm

Installing IIS

Internet Information Services 6 is required for all servers hosting components of Project Server 2007. However, you may not be aware that in this single-server configuration, IIS is also required for certain components of SQL Server 2005, namely Reporting Services. Although there are usually two or three ways to do each thing in a Microsoft application, often the easiest way to install IIS is as follows:

1. Go to the Manage Your Server management window (click Start | Programs | Administrative Tools).
2. Click Add a Role and specify Application Server. You are presented two checkboxes: one for Enable Front Page Extensions, the other for Enable ASP.NET 2.0. Enable ASP.NET 2.0 and leave Enable Front Page Extensions unchecked.

As IIS goes through its own automated installation routine, it may pause for you to look for the original installation CD of Windows Server 2003.

TIP *When you are installing a server, it is often helpful to copy the I386 directory directly to the root of the system drive. This way, the Windows Server 2003 installation bits are always handy.*

FIGURE 6-8 A two-server small farm

After you receive the confirmation screen stating that your server is now an application server, you should return to Windows Update to receive critical IIS specific patches and, optionally, the .NET Framework 3.0.

Installing the .NET Framework 3.0

The .NET Framework 3.0 is a combination of foundational elements that Microsoft has added to the .NET Framework 2.0. These elements include the Windows Presentation Foundation, Windows CardSpace, Windows Communication Foundation, and, most relevant to Project Server 2007, the Windows Workflow Foundation. It is a relatively hands-free installation, downloadable directly from the Microsoft download site. Figure 6-9 shows the installation screen for the .NET Framework 3.0.

Accept the terms of the license agreement, decide whether you want to send information about the setup experience to Microsoft, click Install, and be happy that you aren't on a dialup connection.

After you start the installation, the .NET Framework installation proceeds to download additional components.

After you have finished setting up the .NET Framework 3.0, the confirmation screen (see Figure 6-10) suggests that you to visit Windows Update for updates and Service Packs for the product. Do so at this time. Remember to therapeutically reboot the server.

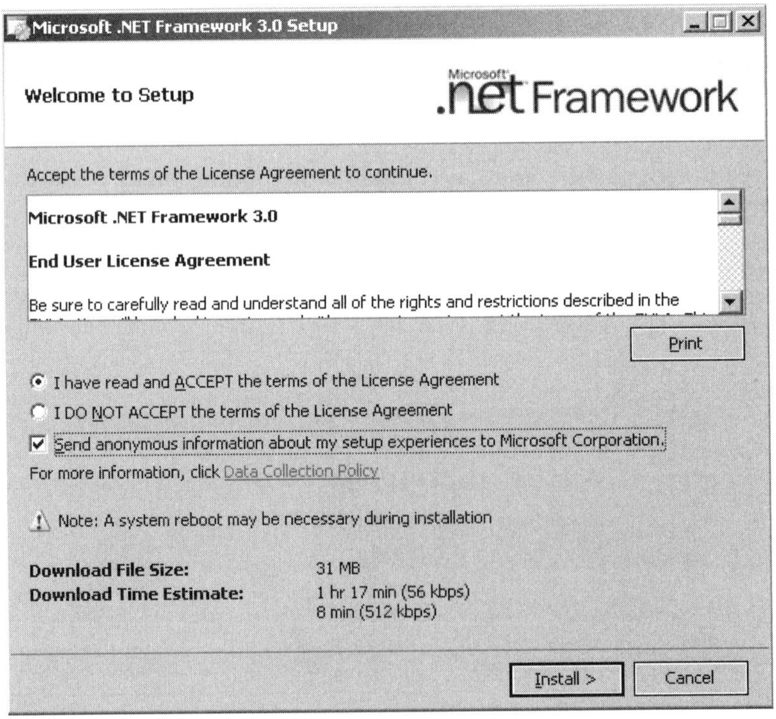

Figure 6-9 The .NET Framework 3.0 setup

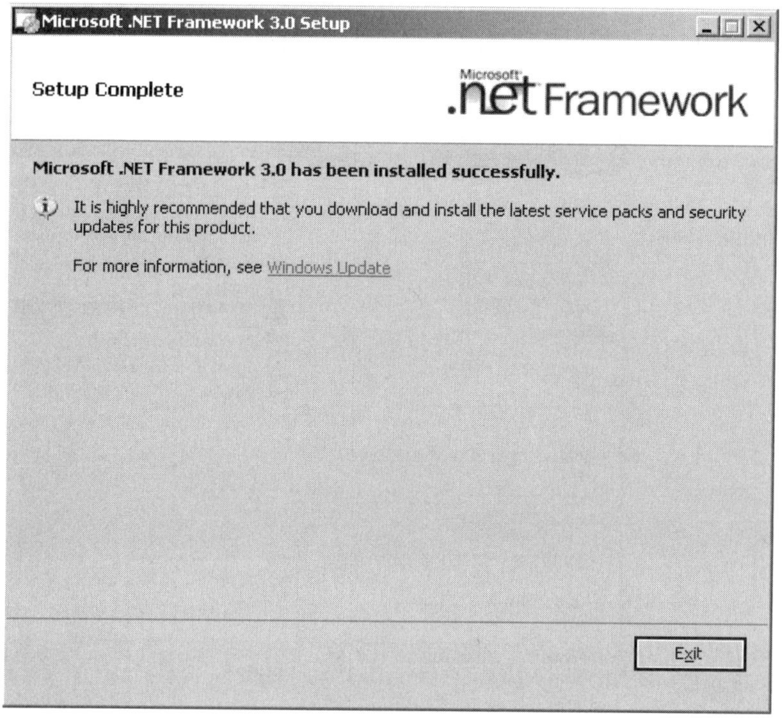

FIGURE 6-10 The Framework 3.0 installation confirmation page

Finally, you will need to double-check that ASP.NET v2.0.50727 is allowed in your IIS Web applications.

Go to IIS Manager (click Start | Run, type **inetmgr**), open up the local computer, and click Web Service Extensions. Ensure that ASP.NET v2.0.50727 is set to Allowed, as shown in Figure 6-11.

Database Server and DB Components on Other Application Web Servers

Although Project Server 2007 was designed for use with either Microsoft SQL Server 2000 (Service Pack 3a or greater) or SQL Server 2005 (Service Pack 1 or greater), this guide focuses on its installation with Microsoft SQL Server 2005 as your database engine.

During the installation of SQL Server 2005, make sure that you install the following components:

- **Analysis Services** This is the SQL Server component required for some of the most valuable reporting features of the EPM 2007 toolset. Through the cubes that are generated in Analysis Services come the data for the Data Analysis views. We are making a couple of assumptions at this stage: (1) that you will use the Data Analysis views, and (2) that you want Analysis Services to reside on the same machine as your SQL Server database engine. We'll go into further detail shortly about configuring SQL Server 2005 Analysis Services specifically for use with Project Server 2007, but for now, ensure that you select this component.

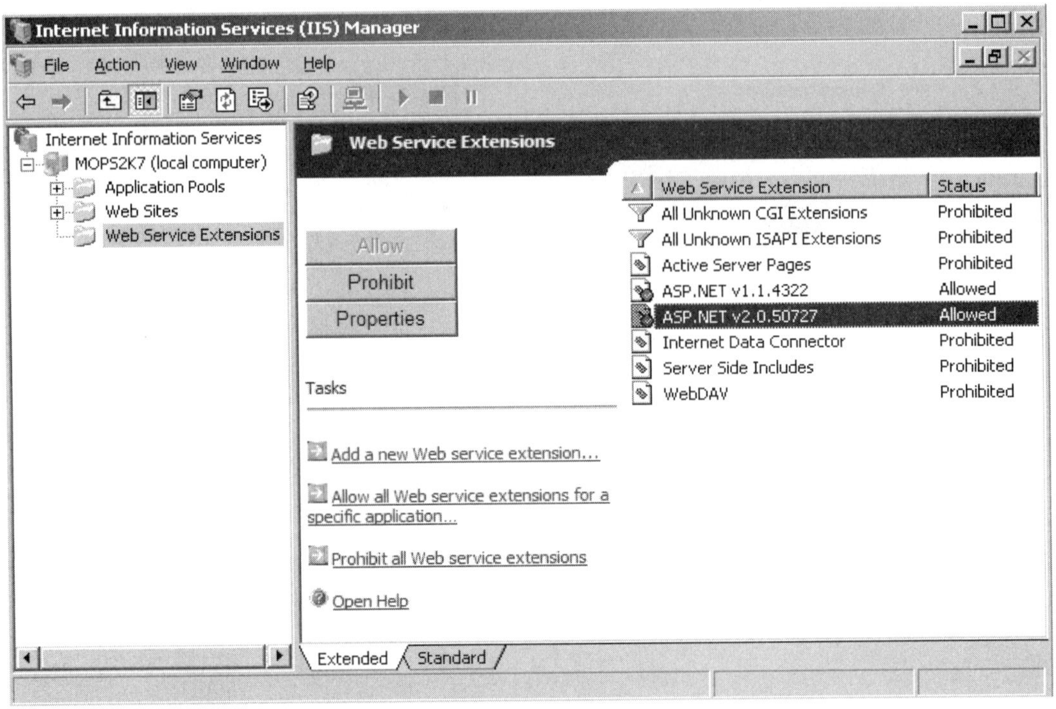

FIGURE 6-11 ASP.NET v2.0.50727 is allowed.

- **SQL Reporting Services (SRS)** This SQL Server add-on provides a platform on which to access and report on data residing in your EPM system. Although the presence of SRS on your SQL server is unlikely to give you any additional functionality in your first iteration of the implementation, it will give you and your developers more reporting options down the road.
- **Workstation components, Books Online, and development tools** This is one of the most commonly overlooked components when installing your SQL instance. Two items that you will need to keep handy for future reference are the Client Components and the SQLXML Client Features, which you can view by clicking Advanced on the screen shown in Figure 6-12.

NOTE *When you use the basic view of the installation screen shown in Figure 6-12, you install each of the components in their entirety. The advanced view, shown in Figure 6-13, allows you to specify which portions of each component to install.*

As with many Microsoft software installation routines, SQL Server 2005 enables the user to install specific application components granularly. This can be seen in the advanced view of the SQL Server installation shown in Figure 6-13.

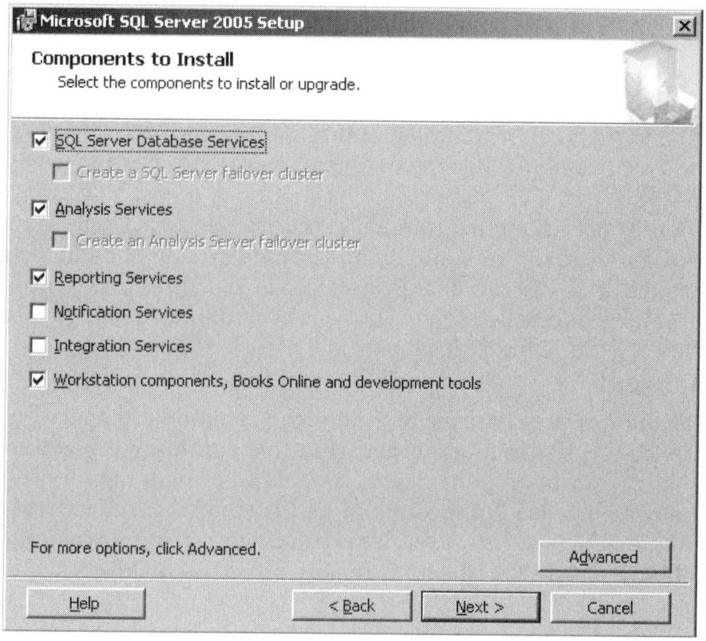

FIGURE 6-12 The basic view of SQL Server 2005 installation

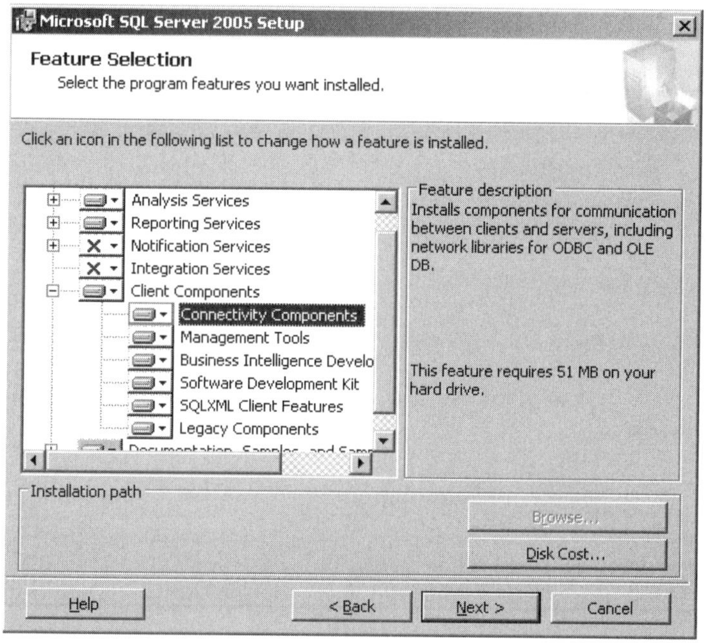

FIGURE 6-13 The advanced view of SQL Server 2005 installation

If you install SRS, you may want to install the Business Intelligence Development Studio to provide additional reporting components such as Reporting Services Report Designer, Reporting Services Model Designer, and related software development kits (SDKs).

Although SQL Books Online is not required for the installation, it may help in a pinch as a reference for your SQL database administrator (DBA).

If you want to create a named instance in SQL, you can do so at the next screen, as shown in Figure 6-14.

Named instances have been around since SQL 2000, and are a great way to compartmentalize the program files, data files, services, and overall administration of database groups. So if you want the instance of SQL Server that Project Server 2007 uses to be cordoned off to a unique administrators group, talk to your DBA about setting up a named instance of SQL.

SQL Service Account

When you are installing SQL Server, the SQL Service Account Settings screen (Figure 6-15) asks you to specify the type of account under which the various SQL services are to run. Depending on your organization's standards, you can have all of the services run as a single account, or you may have a need to specify unique accounts for each individual service.

Although changing the SQL Server service account setting from Local System to a valid Domain User will have no effect on the functionality of Microsoft Project Server 2007, for

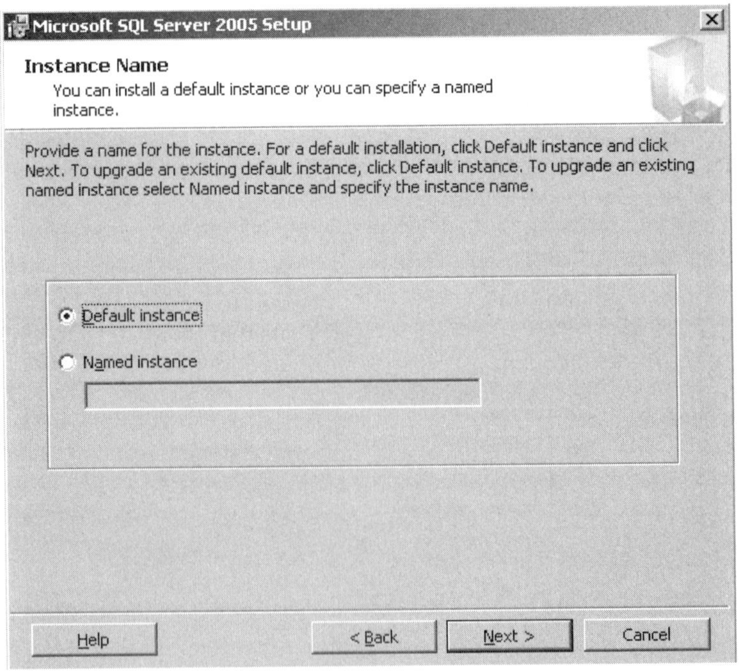

FIGURE 6-14 Choosing the instance name

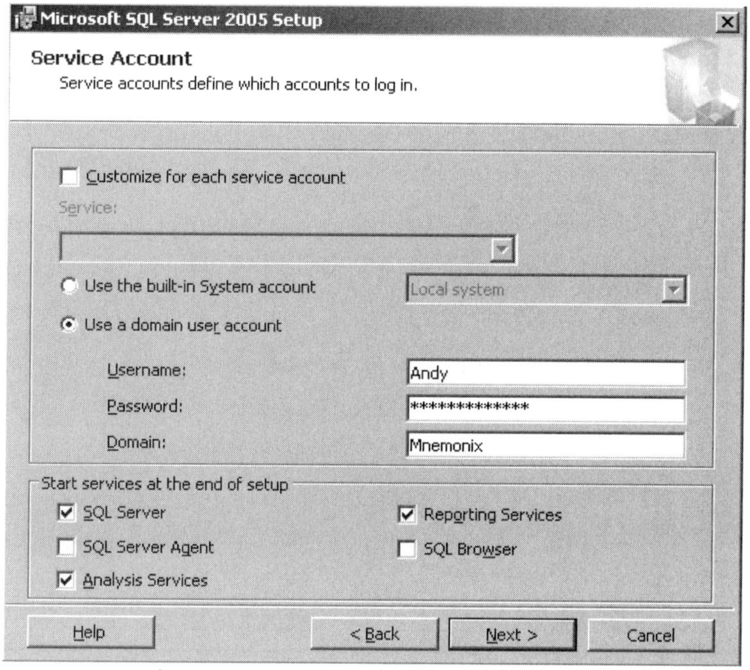

FIGURE 6-15 SQL service account settings

a number of reasons (including clustering) organizations may want to have SQL Server components run as a domain account. Your environment may require this as well. Figure 6-15 shows where you can specify the accounts under which the SQL services will run.

Authentication Mode

In previous versions of Project Server, you were required to leave SQL Server in mixed authentication mode. This was due to the SQL accounts that Project Professional and Project Server used for addressing SQL. Now it is recommended to leave SQL Server in Windows authentication mode, as shown in Figure 6-16.

Collation

Whether you plan to create your databases manually or allow Project Server Installation to do it for you, it is important to leave the default collation settings, as shown in Figure 6-17.

Report Server Configuration

If you have chosen to install Report Server, you have the option of having the installation program create the IIS Web sites and SQL databases used for Report Server and Report Manager automatically, or to install, but not configure the server, as shown in Figure 6-18.

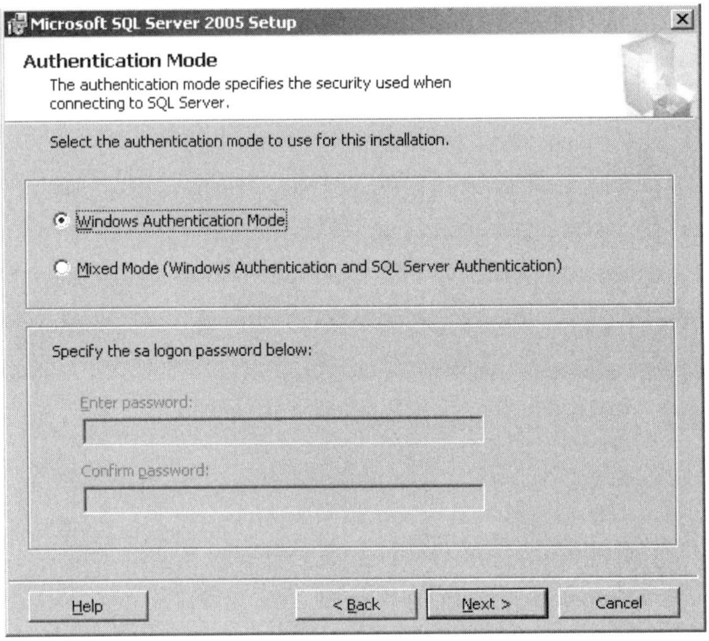

FIGURE 6-16 Choosing the SQL authentication mode

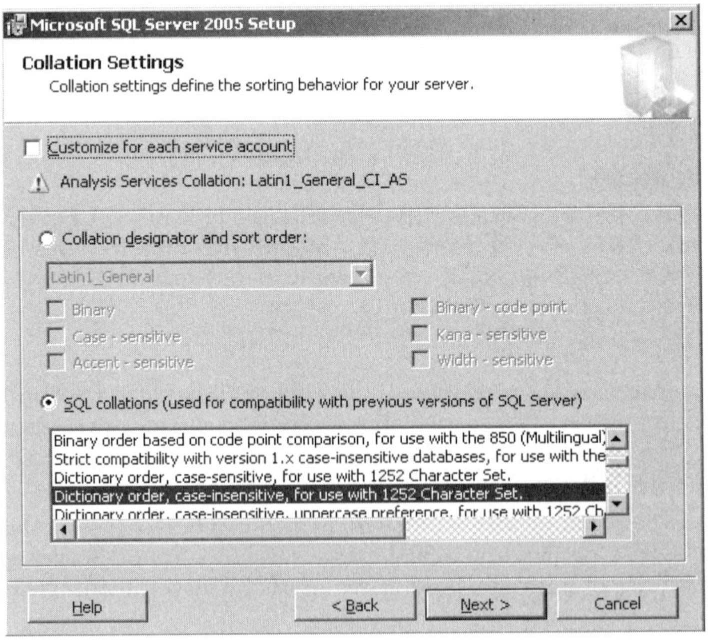

FIGURE 6-17 The SQL Collation Settings page

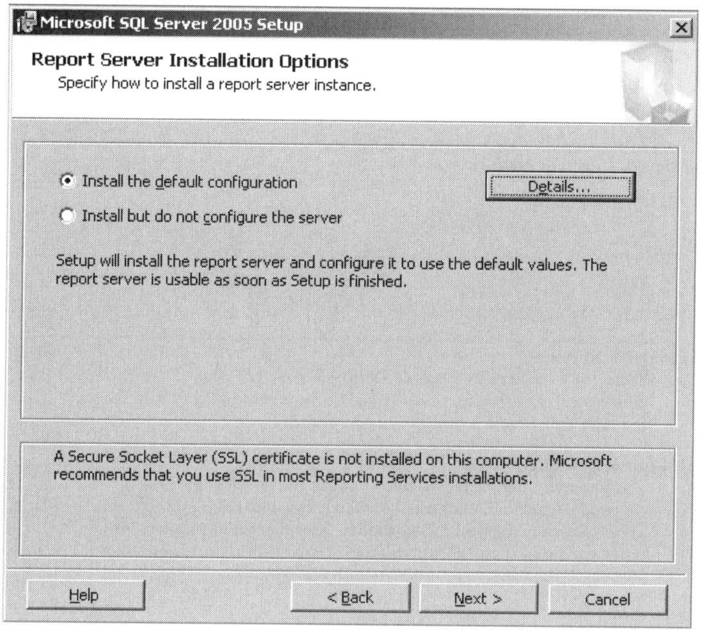

FIGURE 6-18 The Report Server Installation Options page

NOTE *If you have the setup program configure the server at this point, it uses the default Web site as the location for the Report Server and Report Manager applications. This choice is significant and will affect your decisions later on when you choose a home for your new Project Web Access site. If you do not plan on utilizing SQL Reporting Services as part of your immediate plans, you should choose to install SRS but not configure the program. If you plan to install SRS on a machine other than the one on which your SQL database engine resides, there are additional licensing requirements to consider.*

Finally, you are asked two questions: whether you want to send error reports to Microsoft for analysis, and whether you want to send feature usage to Microsoft to help it make its products more in tune with the ways that people use SQL Server 2005. When you click Next, the installation begins.

When SQL 2005 is done installing, follow the link directly to the SQL Server 2005 Surface Area Configuration tool, as shown in Figure 6-19.

The Surface Area Configuration Tool for SQL 2005

As we know from best practices in general security, convenience and security have a direct, inverse relationship. For a few years now, Microsoft has made a substantial commitment to producing software that is more secure, with fewer attack vectors out of the box. Prior to this effort, Microsoft software was installed by default with all of its features active and with instructions to turn off the features you did not use. Users would usually forget to turn

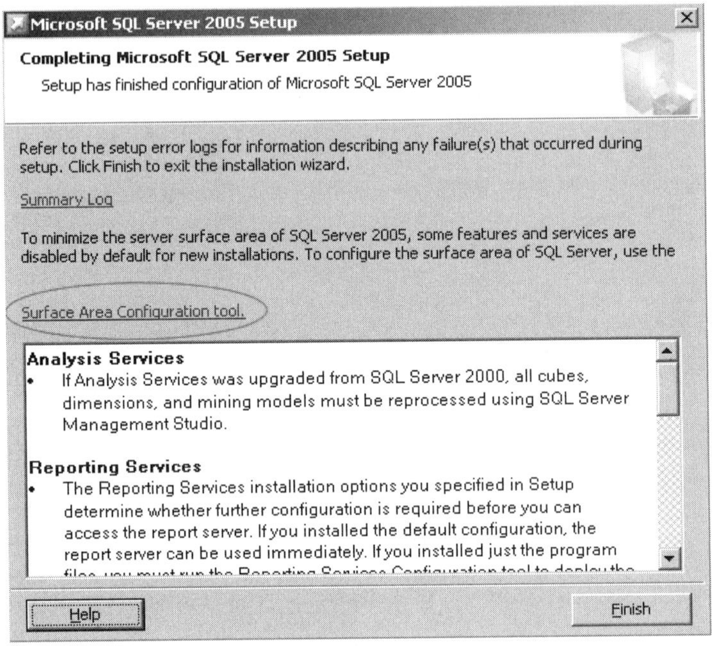

FIGURE 6-19 SQL Server installation confirmation

off unused features, leaving these unused, unwatched, and unlogged services ripe for nefarious exploitation. Now Microsoft ships software with the features disabled, providing instructions to turn them on if you need them. A manifestation of this change in approach to software can be seen in the presence of the SQL Server 2005 Surface Area Configuration tool, as shown in Figures 6-20 and 6-21.

We will be using the Surface Area Configuration tool to configure SQL Server to listen on both Transmission Control Protocol/Internet Protocol (TCP/IP) and named pipes. This configuration is a requirement for Project Server 2007.

The SQL Server Surface Area Configuration for Services and Connections tool is where you specify the "earmuff" settings for SQL Server: here, you tell SQL Server what type of connection attempt to listen to.

1. Open the SQL Server 2005 Surface Area Configuration for Services and Connections tool.
2. Expand Database Engine.
3. Click Remote Connections.
4. Under Local and remote connections, ensure that Using both TCP/IP and named pipes is selected, as shown in Figure 6-21.
5. Click OK.
6. Restart the server.

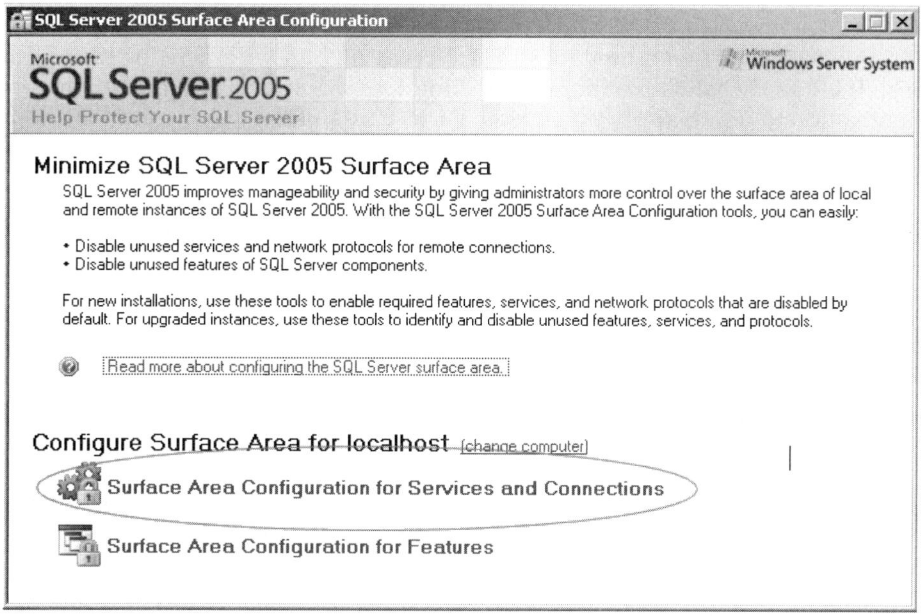

FIGURE 6-20 The SQL Server Surface Area Configuration for Services and Connections tool

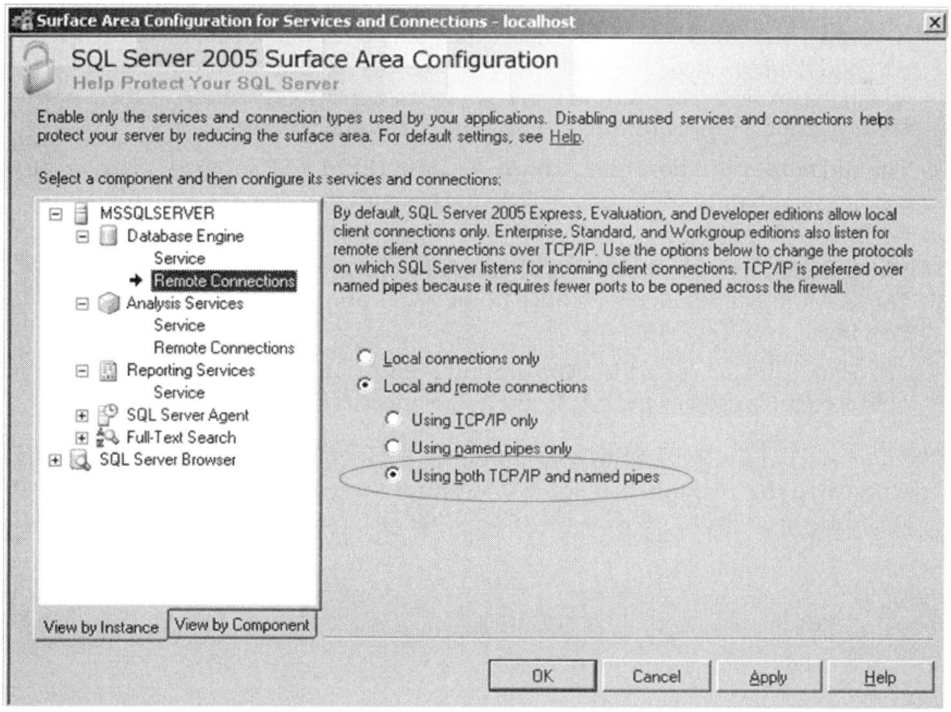

FIGURE 6-21 The SQL 2005 Surface Area Configuration screen

SQL 2005 SP1

SQL 2005 Service Pack 1 is required for Project Server 2007 and is a free download from Microsoft. It is a fairly hands-free installation, but does require that you tell it what form of authentication to use to apply the Service Pack. If you use Windows authentication, it assumes the currently logged-in user's permissions. Also, during the installation, you are prompted if any locked files must be closed for the installation to continue without a reboot, as shown in Figure 6-22. If no production databases are currently active on this instance of SQL Server, or if its purpose is dedicated to Project Server 2007, you can click Continue with the understanding that you *will* restart the server after Service Pack installation.

Service Accounts

The service accounts you'll need for your Project Server 2007 instance are critical for the security and overall smooth operation of your EPM environment. We've included suggested names for these accounts. If you must have logical separation between your various application pools, you should create separate accounts for each Shared Service Provider. Unless you are in a stand-alone environment or security is not a concern, do not attempt to have all SSP accounts run as a single user.

- **The Farm Account (EPM-FarmAdmin)** This is the first real domain account that you will need to provide (if you have used Local System for SQL installation). This account is identified initially in the SharePoint Technologies Configuration Wizard as the Farm Administrator. This is a special account, also referred to as the Database Access account. It is the Windows account that is used to create all of the Project Server databases. It is also by default the identity of the SharePoint Timer Service, which in turn is the account that is used to trigger the generation of the Analysis Services cubes. Rights for this account are set automatically.
- **The SharedService Provider Admin Account (EPM-SSPService)** This account is used as the identity of the SSP. This is the account that actually generates the Analysis Services cubes.
- **The SharedService Provider Application Pool Account (EPM-SSPAppPool)** This account is used as the identity of the application pool for the Shared Service Provider.
- **The Project Web Access Site Application Pool Account (EPM-PWAAppPool)** This account is used as the Application Pool identity for the PWA site.

Now that you have installed and configured the prerequisite software in your small farm and have prepared the accounts that you will need for the installation, you are ready—it is time to saddle up in front of your favorite keyboard, cuddle up with a frosty 20 oz.

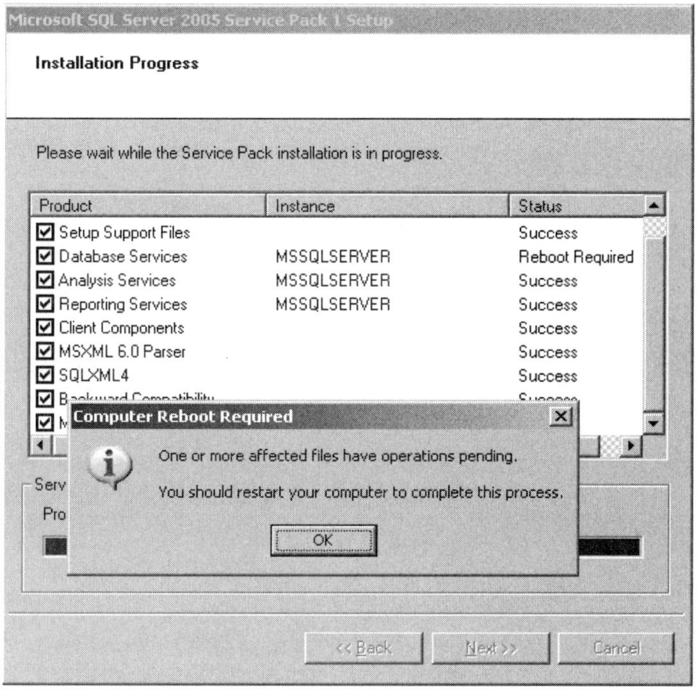

FIGURE 6-22 Plan for reboot

Mountain Dew, and bring the weight of the Microsoft Corporation to bear by aligning all of these pieces of advanced technology together in powerful harmony.

Installing the Binaries for Project Server 2007

These are the steps for installing the binaries for Project Server 2007:

1. Run Setup.exe from your installation media (or network location).
2. Enter your product key.
3. Read the license agreement fully and accept it.
4. In the Choose the Installation You Want box, select Advanced.
5. On the Server Type screen, select Complete, as shown in Figure 6-23. If you later want to add a Web server to the farm to separate the Web serving and search from your project application service, you have a number of options; see Chapter 16 for a discussion on scale-out options.

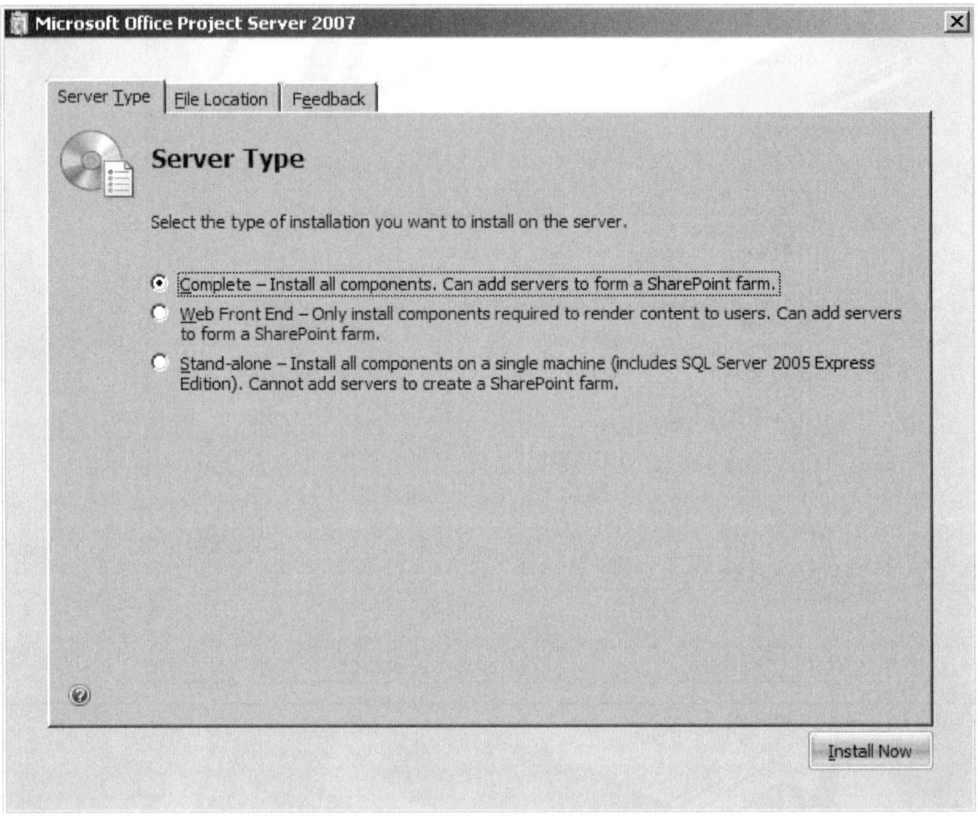

Figure 6-23 The installation Server Type screen

The Choose a File Location screen offers some important options. The first is the installation of the program files of Project Server. The second file path indicates where the search index will reside. "But wait!" you exclaim. "I didn't want to install a search server!" This serves as a clue from a couple of perspectives. First, you know that you're not in Kansas anymore, in that the search offered by WSS no longer relies on SQL Server Indexing Service, as it did in the 2003 version. Second, this search index location is for enabling users to search the WSS help file. Although you should consider ensuring data capacity for your index, do not fret. The searching service must be started and the index location can be changed later. The default file locations are shown in Figure 6-24.

By clicking Install Now, you begin the binary installation of Microsoft Office Project Server 2007. With the right tools, your superior technical abilities, and excellent decision-making skills, you have successfully completed the binary installation.

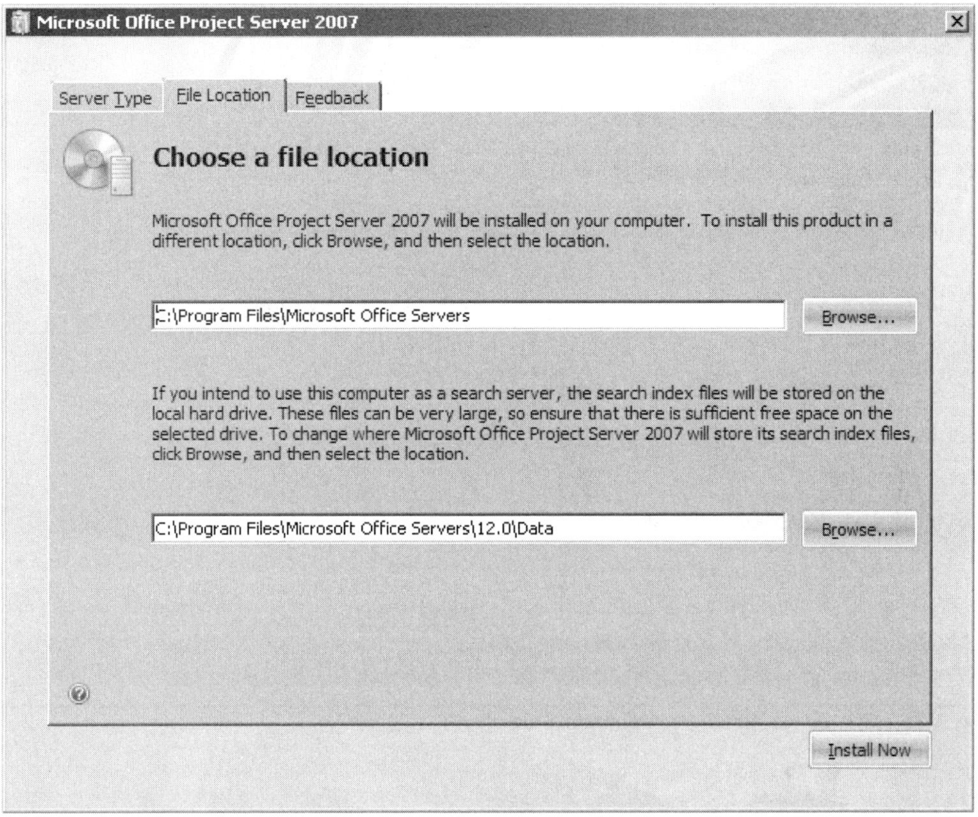

FIGURE 6-24 Installation file locations

TIP *If you must pause your installation for some reason, now would be the time to do it, as the next section involves running the SharePoint Configuration Wizard, creating the farm, configuring your Web applications, creating the SSP, and finally creating your PWA site.*

Installation Checkpoint

At this point you have only installed the binaries for Project Server 2007, so let's take a look at SQL Management Studio to get a snapshot of what your database situation looks like.

Figure 6-25 shows SQL Server Management Studio and the two databases that were created during the installation of SRS. Although these databases will have no effect on the immediate functionality of Project Server 2007, it is important to know that they're there.

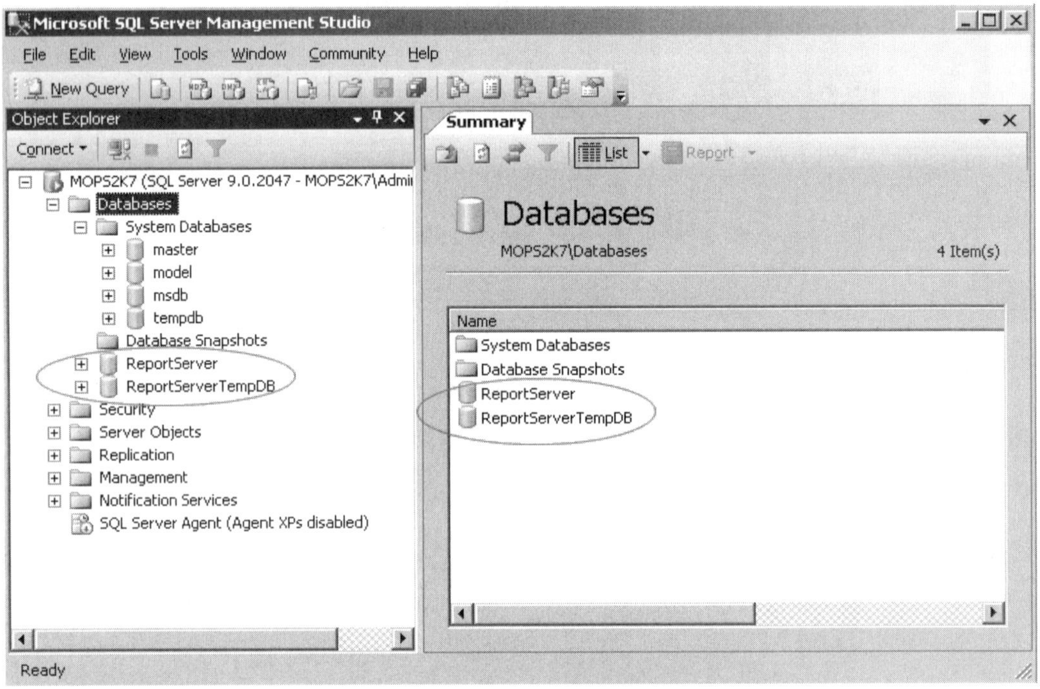

FIGURE 6-25 SQL Server 2005 Management Studio

The SharePoint Products and Technologies Configuration Wizard

Whether you used the link from the final installation screen or you navigated from the Start menu, your next task is to run the SharePoint Products and Technologies Configuration Wizard.

Use the SharePoint Products and Technologies Configuration Wizard to create your farm. Here you specify your database server and identify your EPM-FarmAdmin account credentials (see the "Service Accounts" section earlier in this chapter). When you click Next, you are alerted that you must restart some services as part of the installation process. Click Yes to acknowledge this, as shown in Figure 6-26.

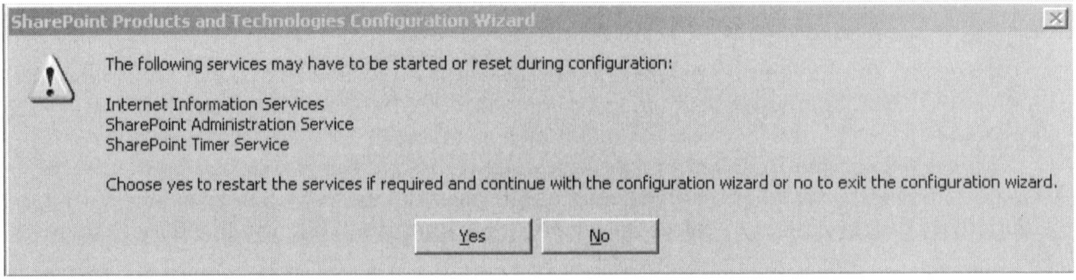

FIGURE 6-26 A warning about stopping services

On the next screen, because this will be the first server in your farm and the home of the Central Administration site, click No, I Want to Create a New Server Farm. On the screen that appears next, identify the database server that you will use to house your SharePoint Configuration database. For a single-server small farm, select the server which you are on. When asked for a Database Access Account name, provide either your Farm Account credentials, or another Windows Username/Password combination which will act as the account which constantly communicates with SQL Server.

The next screen (shown in Figure 6-27) lets you decide whether you want to use the default random high port for SharePoint Central Administration, or specify one. To make it easier to remember, we'll use port 12345. Also, if you have Kerberos configured and functioning in your environment, and you've created Service Principle Names for your service accounts, you can select Negotiate (Kerberos) here. Otherwise, choose the default of NTLM.

The next screen confirms that you are creating the Central Administration site. Click Next. If all goes well, the installation procedure runs through its various steps and you are greeted with a congratulatory screen confirming what has just been done.

Note the message given in the following screen, and refer to the "Internet Explorer" subsection of the "Client Components" section later in this chapter for instructions to follow when you are using Internet Explorer 7.

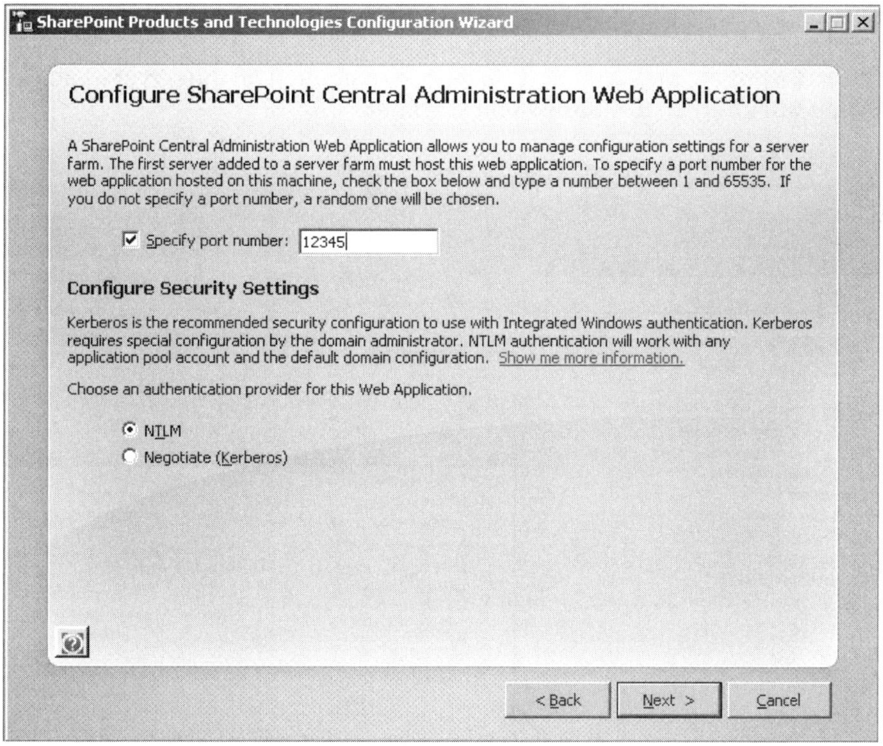

FIGURE 6-27 Configuring the SharePoint Central Administration site

Installation Checkpoint

Let's return to SQL Server Management Studio (shown in Figure 6-28) and IIS Manager (shown in Figure 6-29) to see what items have been created so far.

IIS Manager, shown in Figure 6-29, displays the default Web site on port 80 and the Central Administration Web site on port 12345.

"Now wait," you may exclaim, "We were planning on having PWA on port 80. What is with the Reporting Services application pool and associated applications squatting in my default Web site?"

There are a number of ways around this, but you can simply change the port that the default Web site uses (choose port 88 for this example) and create another site for your WSS and PWA site.

After you change the default Web site and create a new empty site called PWA to reside on port 80, IIS now resembles Figure 6-30.

At this point, you've made considerable changes to your server environment. Now would be a good time to restart the server while you proceed to check e-mail and obtain a frosty Mountain Dew replacement.

Configuring the Farm Services for a Single Server

In this small-farm installation, the next steps will be determined by our physical topology. Two farm services are relevant:

- **Project Application Service** This service is required on the server identified as the Application Server. It is turned off by default.

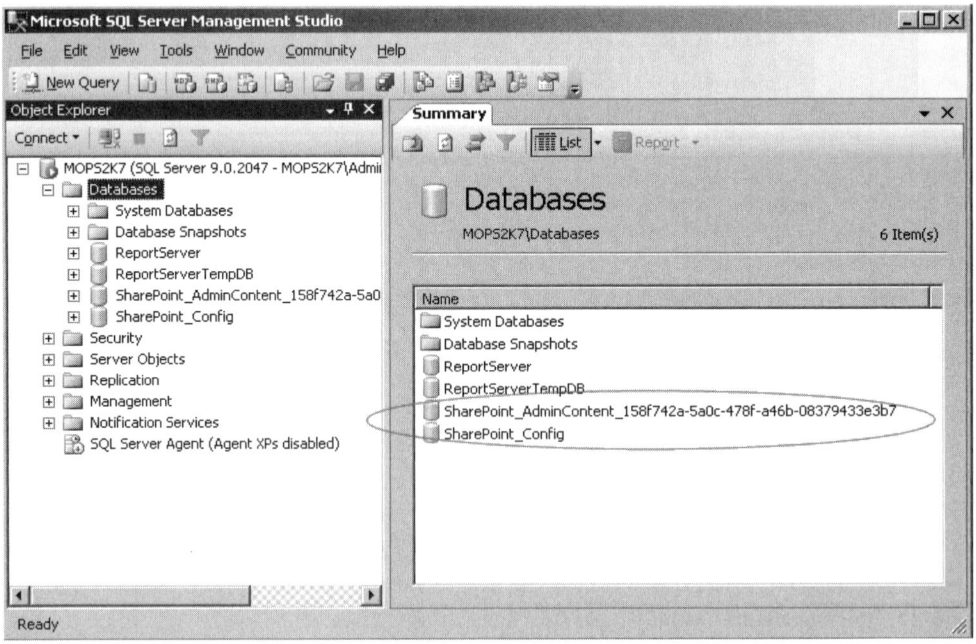

FIGURE 6-28 SQL databases for the SharePoint Central Administration

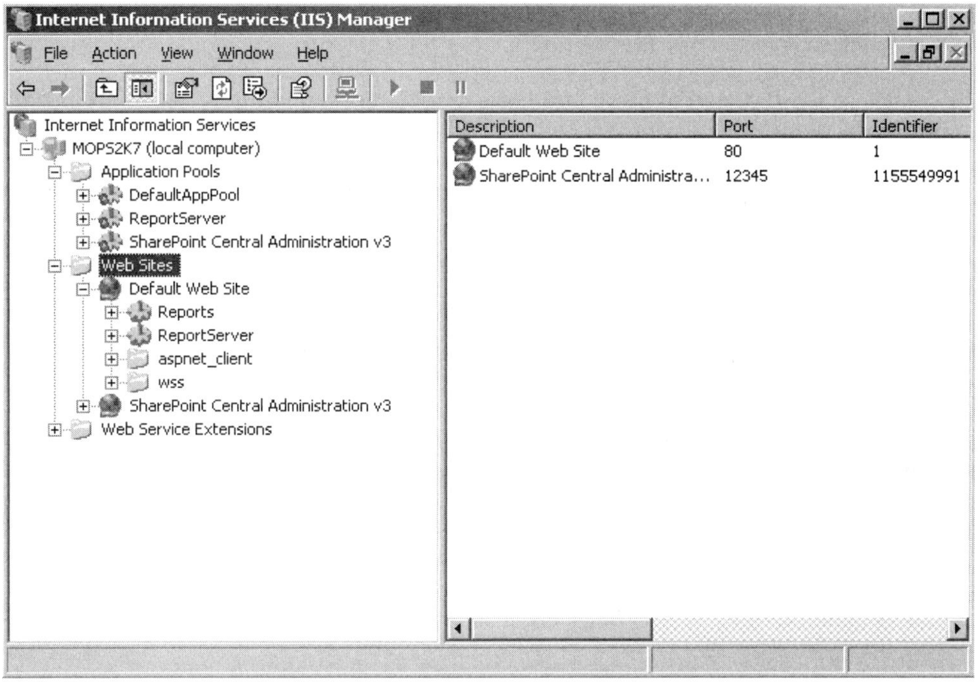

FIGURE 6-29 IIS after Central Administration installation

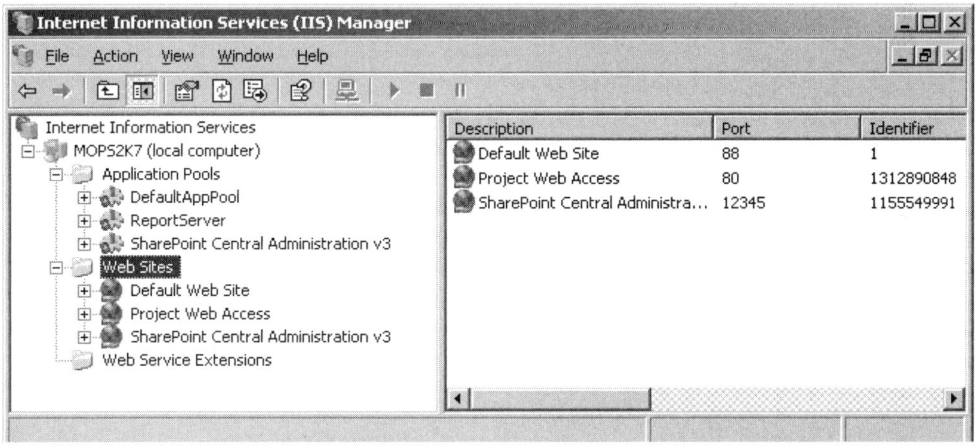

FIGURE 6-30 Modifying IIS

- **Windows SharePoint Services Web Application** Think of this service as only needing to run on your Front End Web Servers. It is turned on by default.

So, based on the function of these two farm services and knowing that you are installing all components on a single server, you'll first need to start the Project Application Service:

1. Navigate to the SharePoint Central Administration site.
2. Click the Operations tab.
3. Click Services on Server, as shown in Figure 6-31.
4. From the Services on Server page, click Custom to see all the services running on the current server.
5. Because this server will be the only machine in the farm, click Start for the Project Application, as indicated in Figure 6-32.

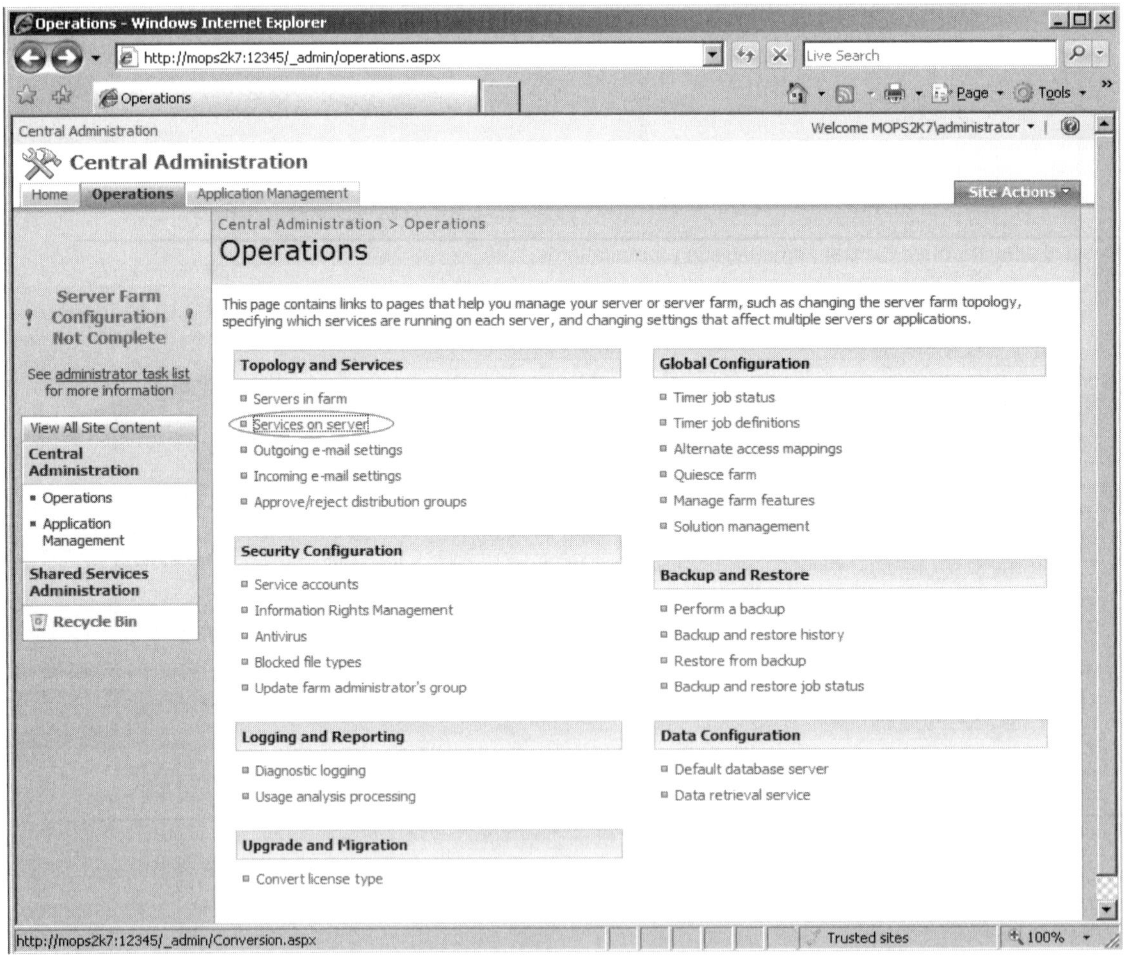

FIGURE 6-31 SharePoint Central Administration

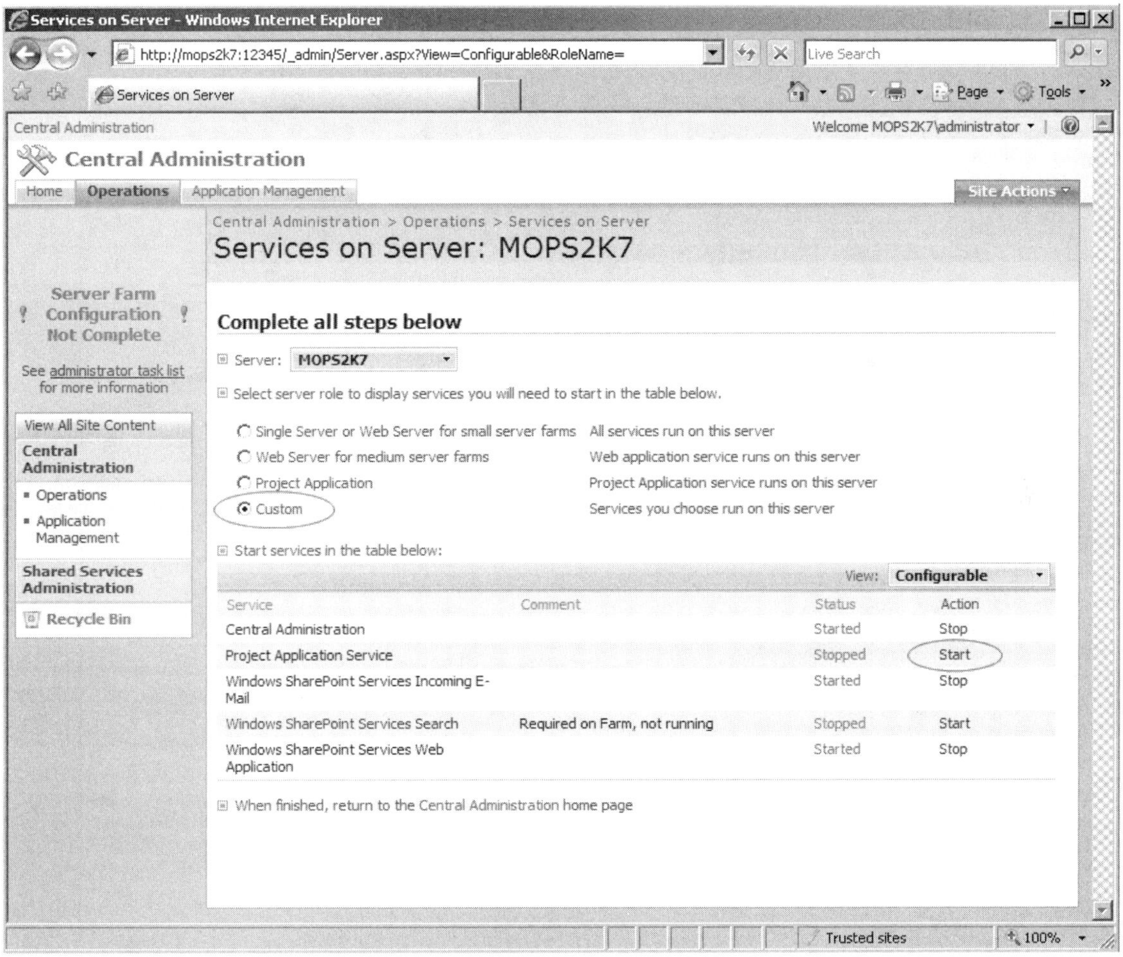

FIGURE 6-32 Start the Project Application Service.

Now you are ready to create the Web application for PWA, the Web application for the SSP, and the SSP itself.

NOTE *Although it is a challenging concept to grasp, think of the Web applications as empty houses that will soon be the homes of PWA and the SSP. You are now building the houses.*

Creating the Web Application for PWA

To create the Web application for PWA, complete the following steps:

1. Return to SharePoint Central Administration and click the Application Management tab.
2. From the Application Management page, click Create or Extend Web Application, as shown in Figure 6-33.

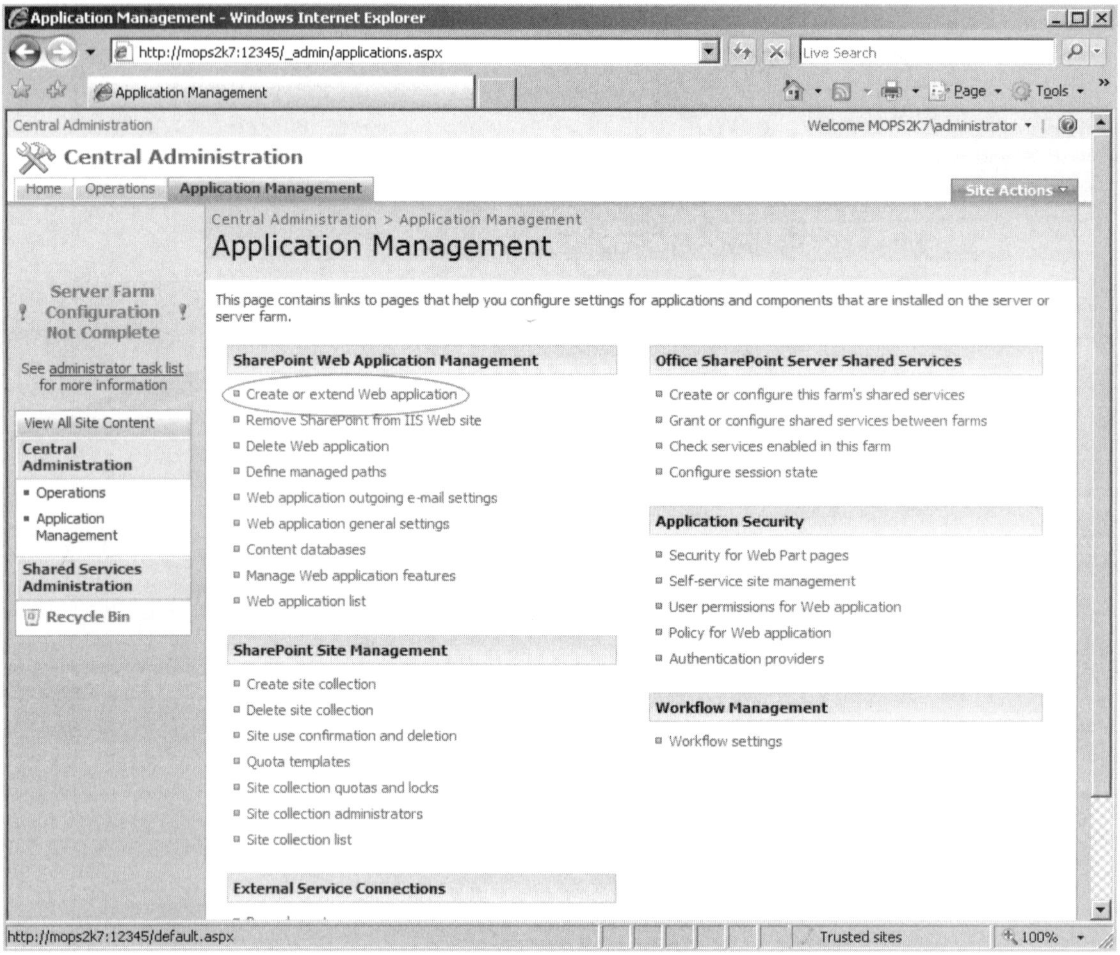

FIGURE 6-33 Creating a Web application with the SharePoint Central Administration

3. On the Create or Extend Web Application page, click Create Web Application.
4. The Create New Web Application window offers several choices. If you have followed the steps outlined previously, you can duplicate the settings displayed in Figure 6-34. The modifications to the default settings are as follows:
   a. The previously created PWA site is chosen because the Reporting Services applications are residing in the default Web site. The default setting is to create a new Web site with the name SharePoint – 80.

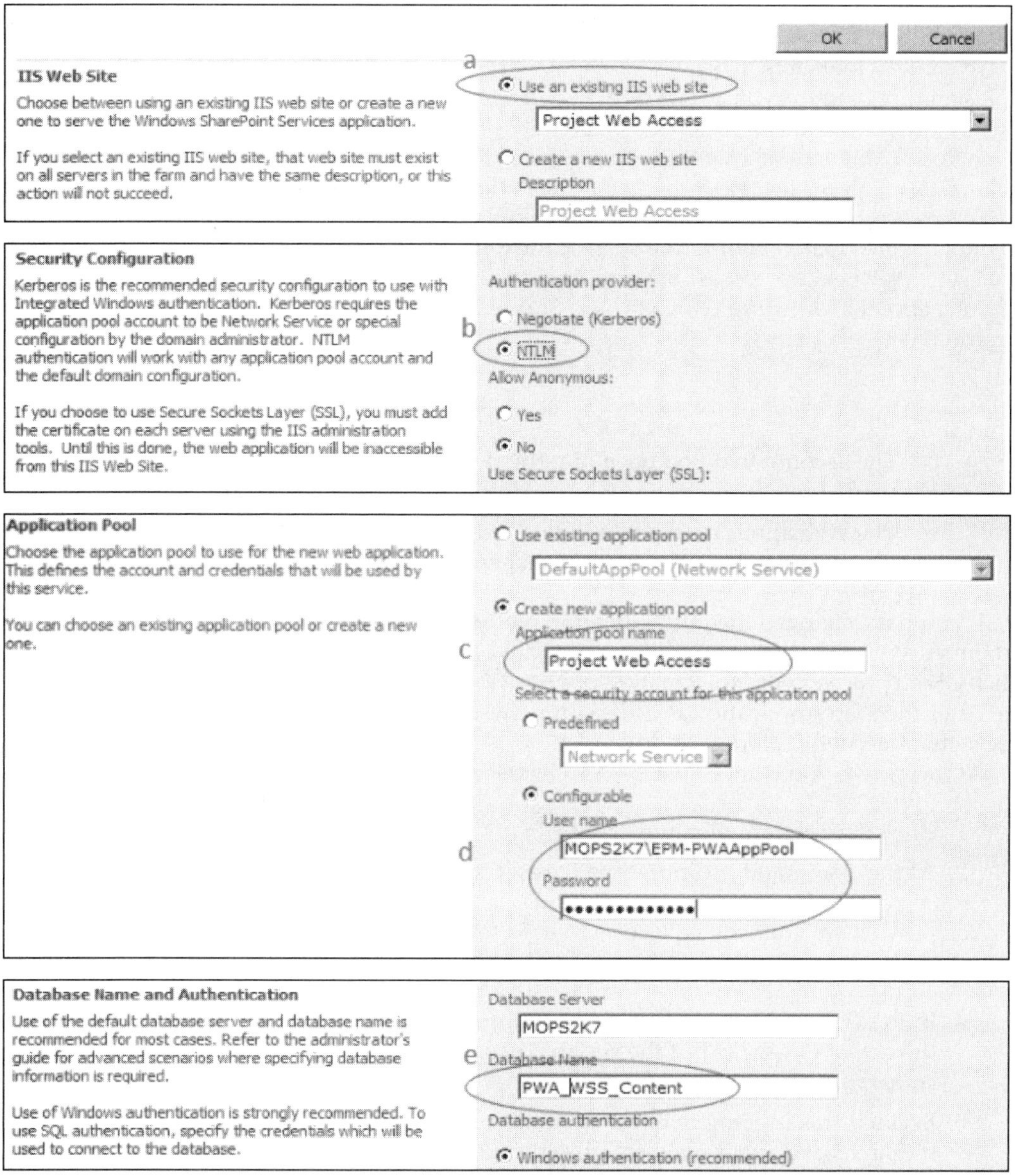

FIGURE 6-34 Create the Web Application for the PWA site.

b. Although Kerberos will provide additional security, NTLM does not require additional configuration and support by your network administrators.

c. The default name of the application pool to be created was changed from Sharepoint – 80 to match the name of the Web application.

Installation Checkpoint

Let's take a look at SQL Server Management Studio and IIS Manager at this stage of the installation. Figure 6-35 shows SQL Server Management Studio. Notice that the PWA_WSS_Content database has been created.

In IIS Manager (shown in Figure 6-36), we see the additional Web applications and application pools that were created by installation.

Yes, your PWA site and application pools were created, but a couple of other things were created behind the scenes: the OfficeServerApplicationPool and the Office Server Web Services site, shown in Figure 6-36. These were created automatically as a placeholder for future Office Project Server applications that may be added to the farm later.

d. The account that had been identified previously, EPM-PWAAppPool, is to be used.

e. The Web application content database was modified from WSS_Content for easy identification in SQL Server Management Studio.

If you have changed the authentication method from Kerberos to NTLM, you will be prompted with a dialog box making sure that you want to change authentication methods. Click OK to proceed with the creation of your Web application for the PWA site.

After the Web Application Process completes, the Application Created page appears. Leave this Internet Explorer window open.

At this point, you want to perform an iisrest /noforce command on your server:

1. Click Start | Run, then type **cmd**.
2. At the Command prompt, type **iisreset /noforce**.

You now create your site collection to hold the PWA site. You can click the Create Site Collection link from the Application Created page (see Figure 6-37). Follow these steps:

a. In the Title and Description, type a name for the top-level site. Remember, this isn't the actual PWA site, but the site that users reach if they simply type **http://*servername*** into their browser.

b. Because this is going to be above the Project Web Access site(s) in the server's hierarchy, it doesn't make much sense to apply the Microsoft Office Project Workspace template at this point. A team site will work nicely.

c. WSS v3 enhanced security enables you to have administrators compartmentalized, so you can specify administrators who need administrative access to a single site collection.

d. Click OK to create the site collection.

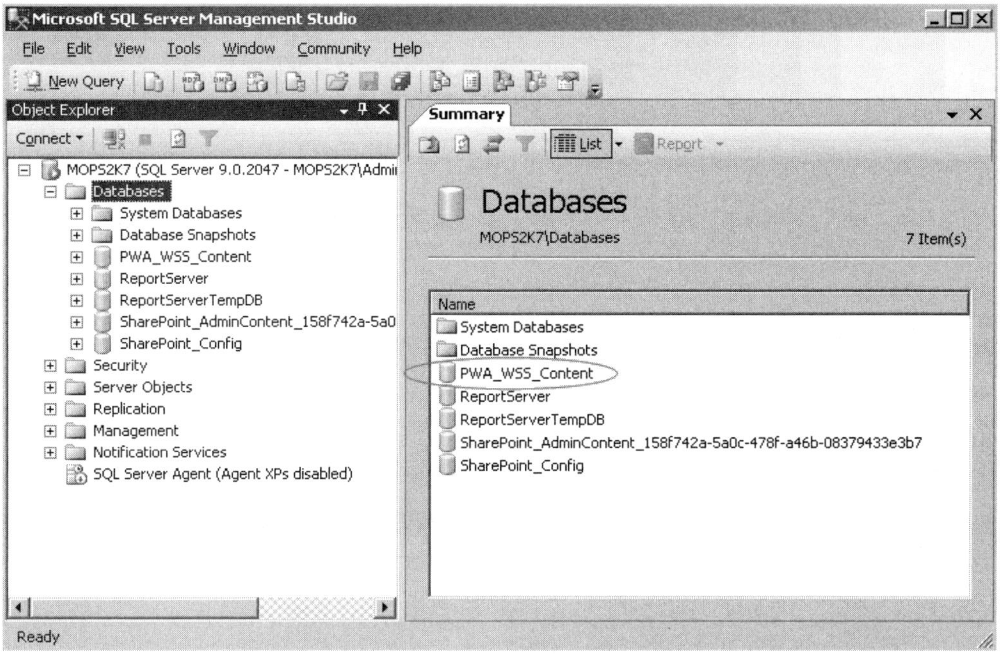

Figure 6-35 SQL Server Management Studio

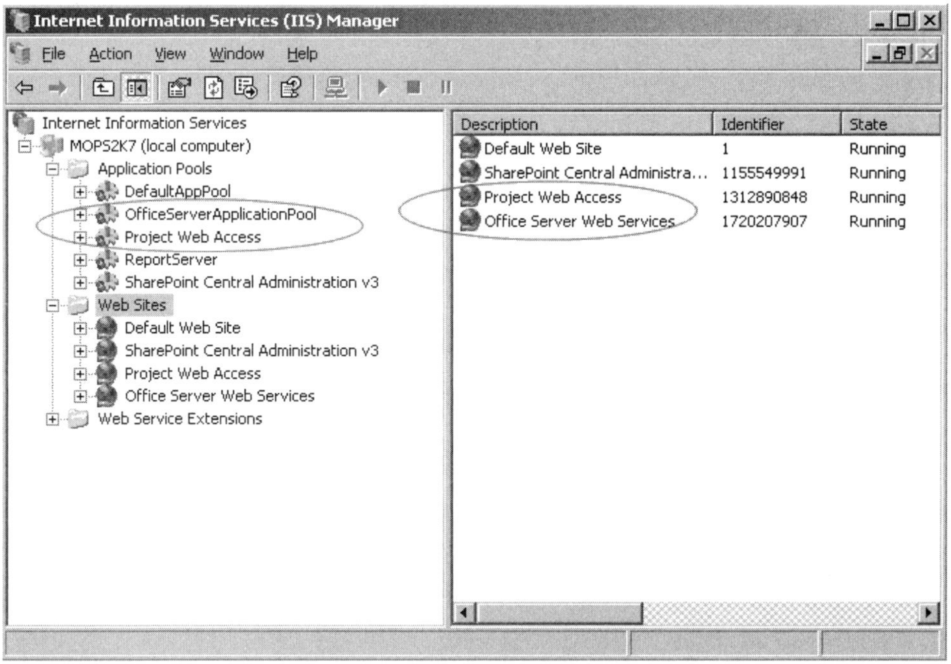

Figure 6-36 IIS Manager

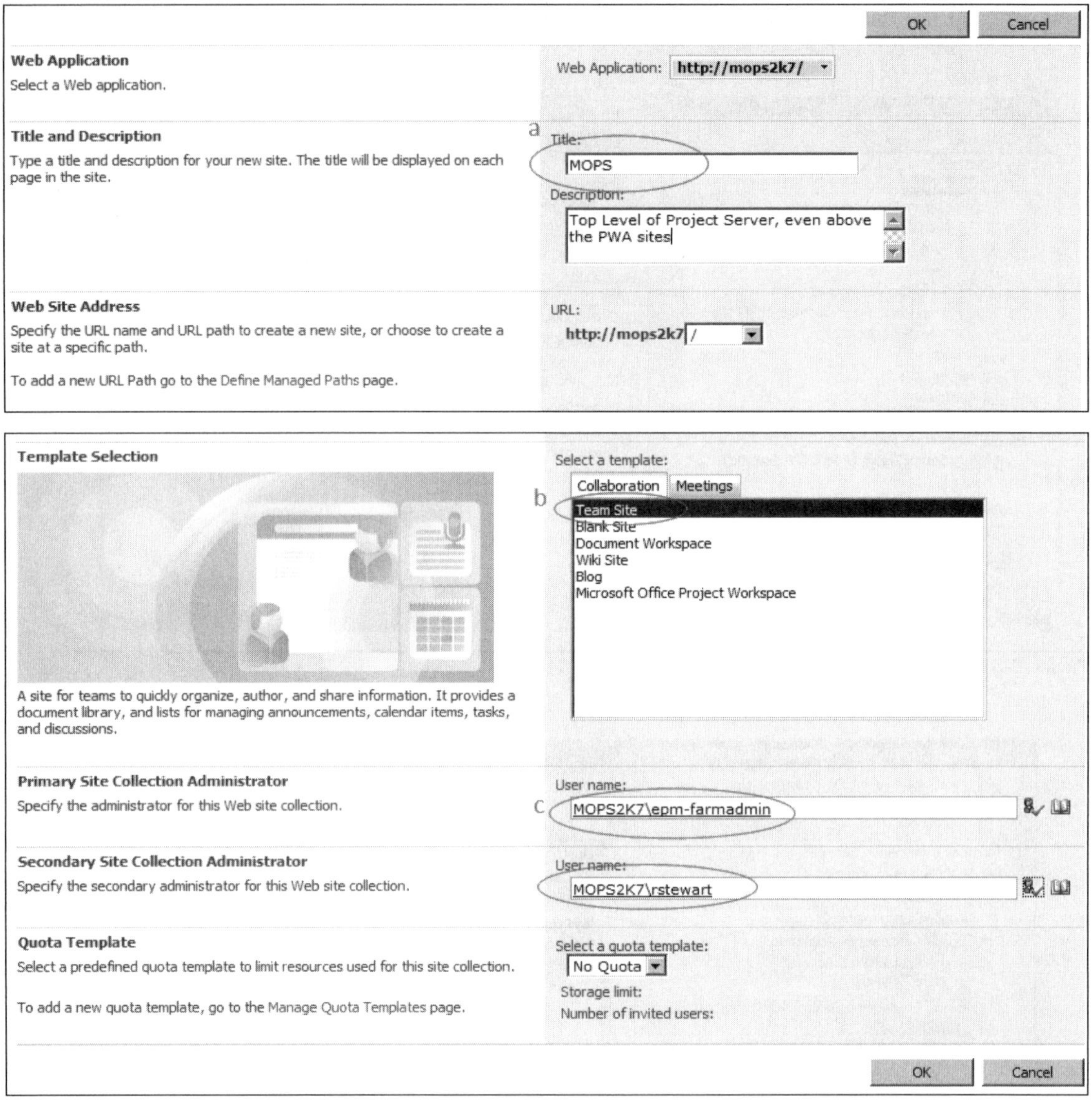

FIGURE 6-37 Creating the Site Collection to house PWA

Creating the Web Application for the Shared Services Provider

This process is very similar to creating the Web application for the PWA site:

1. From SharePoint Central Administration, click the Application Management tab.
2. Click Create or Extend Web Application.
3. On the Create or Extend Web Application page, click Create New Web Application.

4. On the Create New Application page, create a new IIS Web site, as shown in Figure 6-38. The modifications are as follows:
   a. A new IIS site was created and the description was changed to make it easy to identify when viewing the sites through IIS Manager.

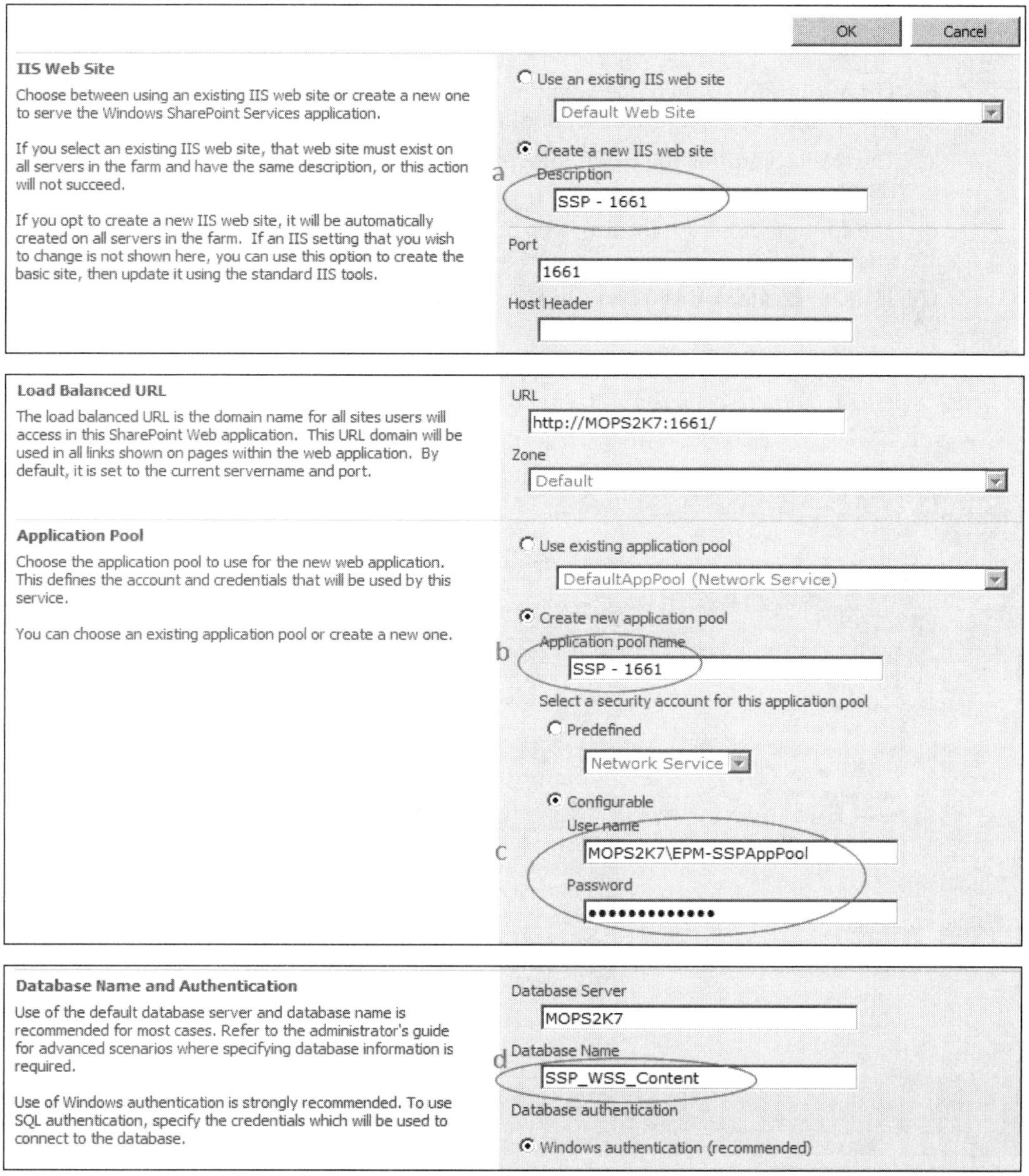

FIGURE 6-38 Creating the Web application for the SSP

Installation Checkpoint

Now that you have started the Project Application Service and created the farm, the Web application for PWA, the site collection for PWA, and the Web application for the SSP, let's look at SQL Server Management Studio in Figure 6-39 to see the results.

Figure 6-40 shows the Web site and associated application pools that were created for the SSP.

b. The application pool name was changed from the default for easy identification when viewing the application pool through IIS Manager.

c. The user account is the EPM-SSPAppPool account, described earlier in this chapter.

d. The content database for this Web application was changed to make it easier to identify in SQL 2005 Management Studio.

5. Click OK to create your Web application to host the SSP.

NOTE *Even though you do not need to create a site collection for your SSP Web application, you do need to perform an IIS reset on your server at this time.*

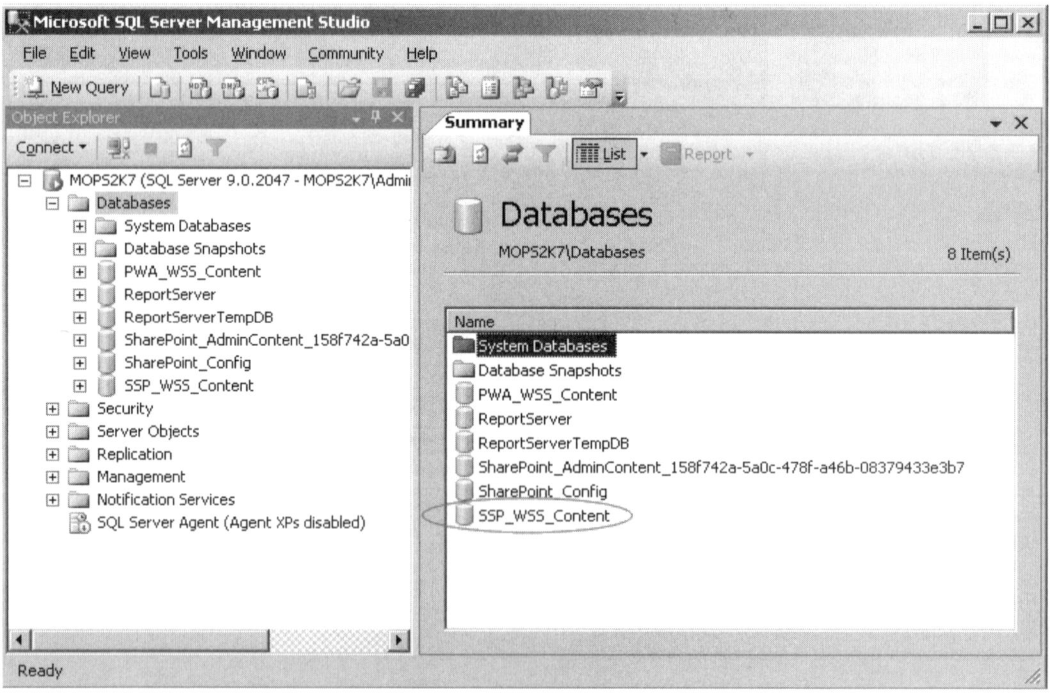

FIGURE 6-39 The SSP_WSS_Content database was created.

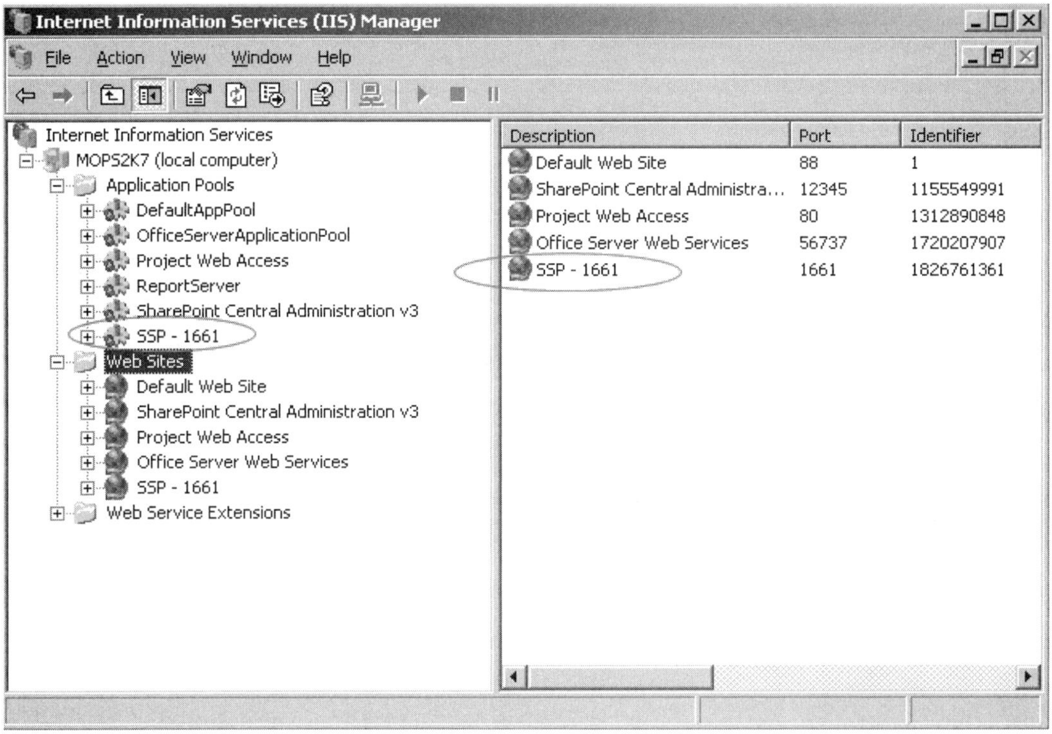

FIGURE 6-40 The IIS-SSP site and application pool

Creating the SSP

Now that you've built the house for the SSP, it's time to create the occupant and make it earn its keep. Note that the SSP Web application represents the business or middle tier of the Project Server environment.

1. From SharePoint Central Administration, Click the Application Management tab.
2. Click Create or Configure This Farm's Shared Services.
3. On the Manage This Farm's Shared Services page, click New SSP.
4. Follow these steps to configure the New Shared Services Provider page, as illustrated in Figure 6-41:
   a. Change the prepopulated name to a name that easily identifies this SSP.
   b. Change the Web application from your PWA application to your (already-created) SSP Web application.
   c. Enter the credentials of the SSP service account (that is, EPM-SSPService).
   d. Although it would be helpful to change the name of the SSP database to be similar to the name of the SSP, leave it as is; changing the name from SharedServices1_DB is not recommended.
5. After making changes to the SSP to be created, click OK.

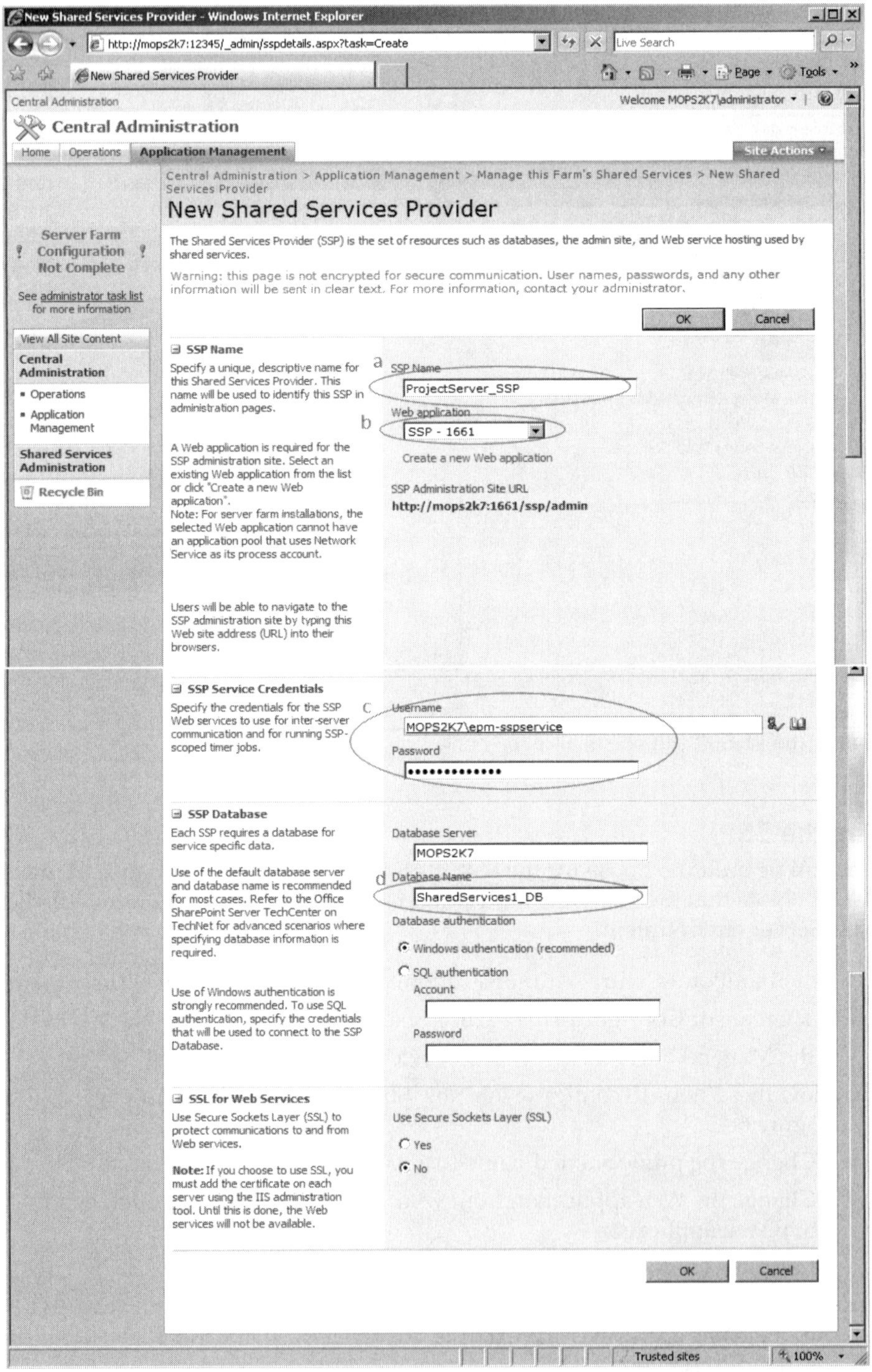

FIGURE 6-41 Create the SSP.

Installation Checkpoint

Let's take just a quick look at SQL Server Management Studio in Figure 6-42 to see what was created along with the SSP.

You now have a total of five Project Server–related databases.

After a few minutes of watching squares revolving around a circle, you should come to the congratulatory Success page.

At this point, you're in the home stretch. Now it's simply a matter of creating the PWA site.

Creating the PWA Site

You can redo this set of steps later if another distinct business unit wants its own PWA instance:

1. From SharePoint Central Administration, click the name of the SSP from the Quick Launch Bar on the left side of the screen.

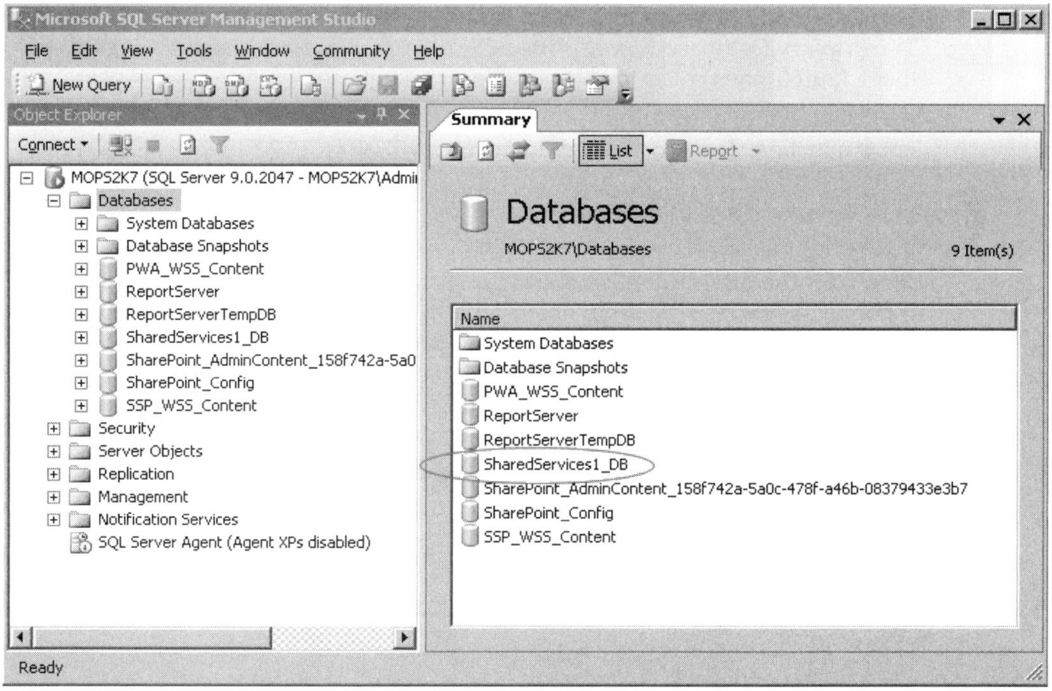

FIGURE 6-42 The SharedServices1_DB

2. From the Shared Services Administration site, click Project Web Access Sites.
3. From the Manage Project Web Access Sites page, click Create Project Web Access Site.
4. To configure the Create Project Web Access Site page (see Figure 6-43), follow these steps:
   a. The Web application that you choose is the Web application that you created to host the PWA site.
   b. The Project Web Access path is what comes after your server name in the site address. So if you are creating multiple PWA sites for multiple divisions of your organization, you can specify IS for your first site, Marketing for your second site, and so on. In this example, http://mops2k7/pwa is the URL that users will type in their browsers to access this particular PWA site.
   c. Although some minor Domain Naming Service (DNS) configuration is required for the Use Project Web Access Path as Host Header setting to function as expected, when it is enabled, users can simply type in **http://pwa** to access the site.
   d. The Administrator Account setting is prepopulated with the setup account (the current user). Note that after installation, only the administrator specified here will have access to the PWA site. This administrator will then have to grant access for other PWA users, administrators, and so on.
   e. The Primary Database Server is the SQL 2000 or SQL 2005 instance that will be the default home for the four Project Server databases.
   f. Published, Draft, and Archive Database names can be set to whatever you want, but it may be helpful to append the names with your PWA site name, as shown in Figure 6-43. This helps ensure that the database names are unique, in case you plan to create more PWA sites in the future.
   g. By default, the Reporting Database field is set to reside on the specified database server for the other three PWA site databases. If you are planning on high reporting activity, or want to ensure that frequent and heavy load on the reporting database doesn't adversely affect your production PWA database infrastructure, you can choose to have this database reside on a separate SQL 2000 or SQL 2005 instance. (You must specify machines that have the same version and Service Pack level of SQL Server.)
5. Click OK and be patient. Because it is an asynchronous process, the provisioning of the PWA databases and site will likely take several minutes.
6. When you receive the congratulatory screen indicating that the PWA site has been provisioned, you can click on the link that will take you to your first PWA Homepage, shown in Figure 6-44.

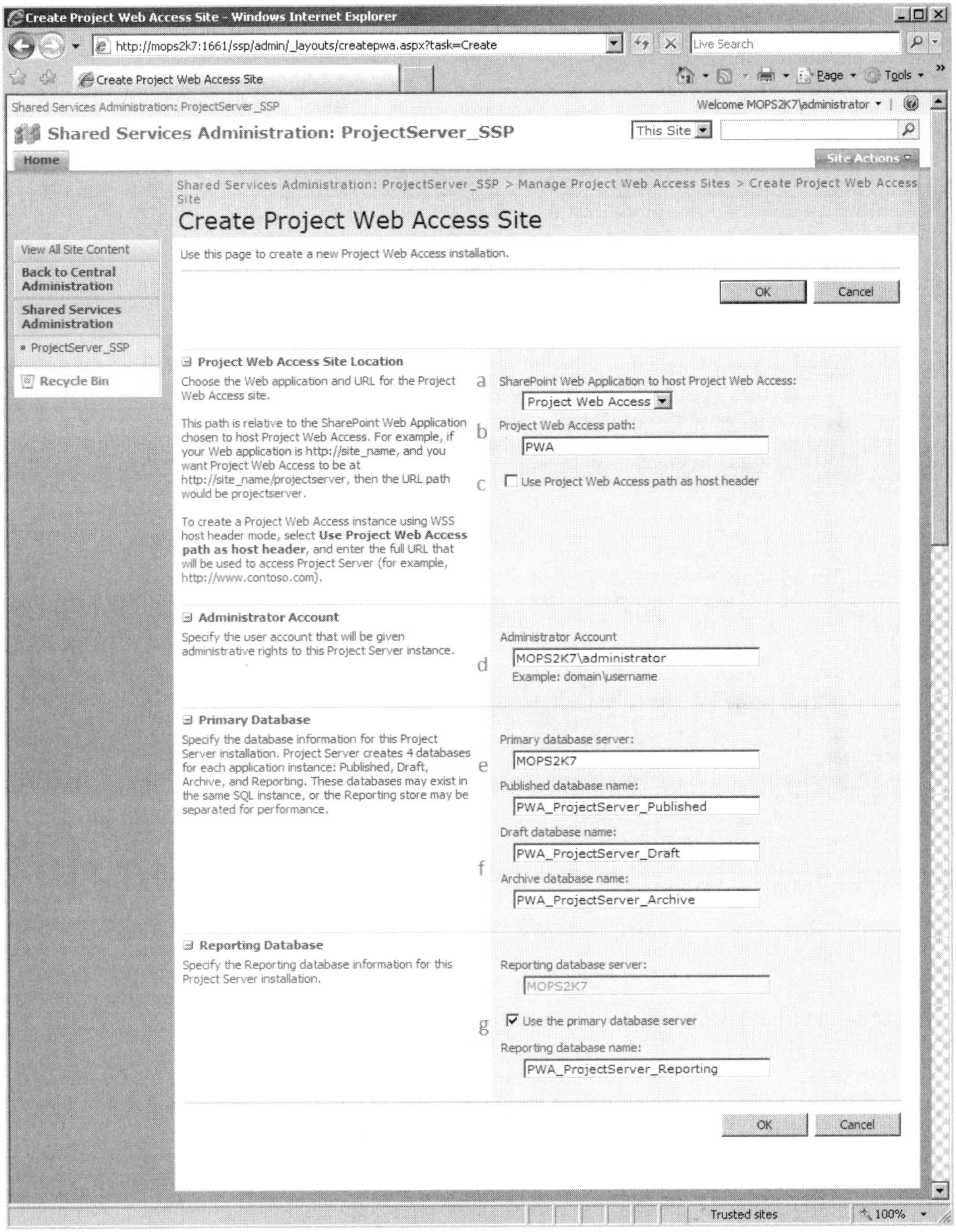

FIGURE 6-43 PWA site creation

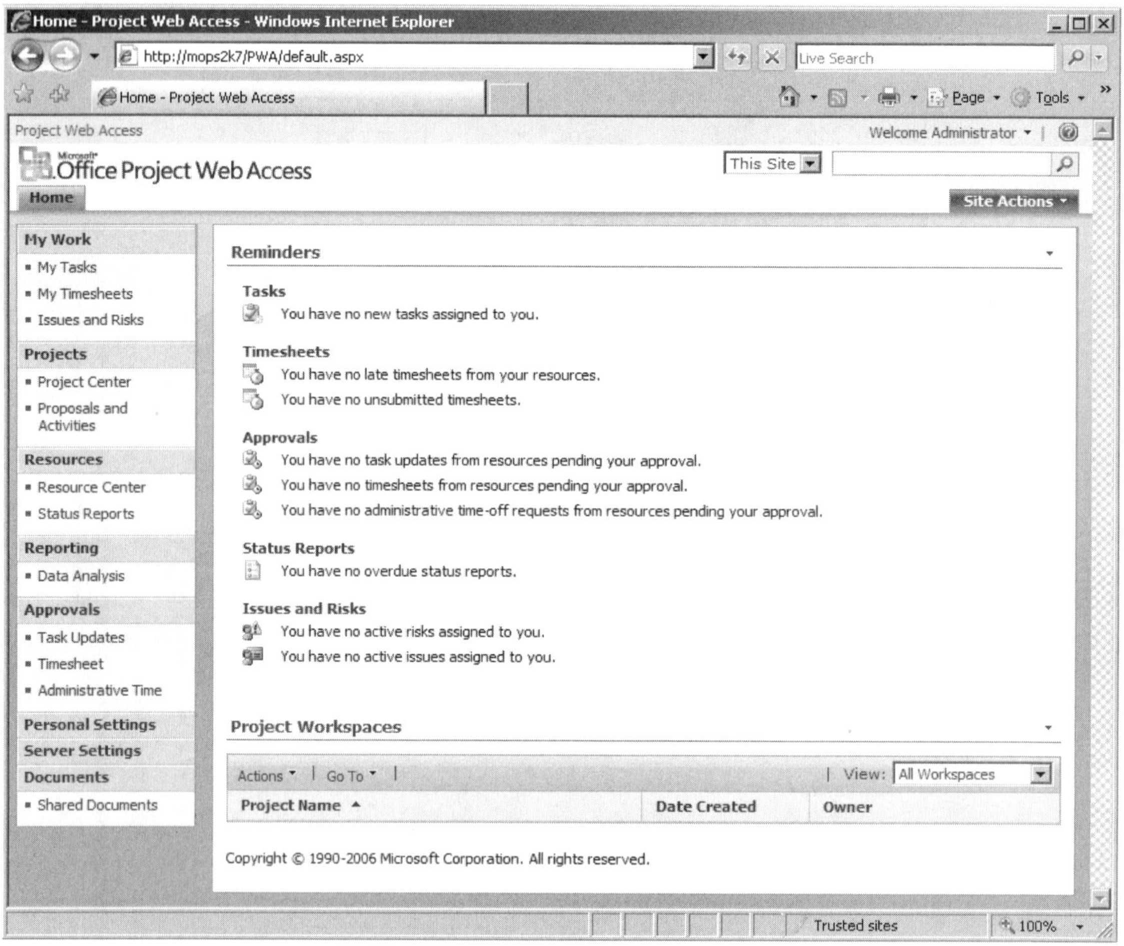

FIGURE 6-44 Your sparkly new PWA site

Installation Checkpoint: Post PWA Site Provisioning

Now that you have fully installed Project Server and created the PWA site, let's take a look at SQL Server Management Studio (see Figure 6-45).

The four new databases for the PWA instance bring the total number of databases (not including the SRS databases) to nine.

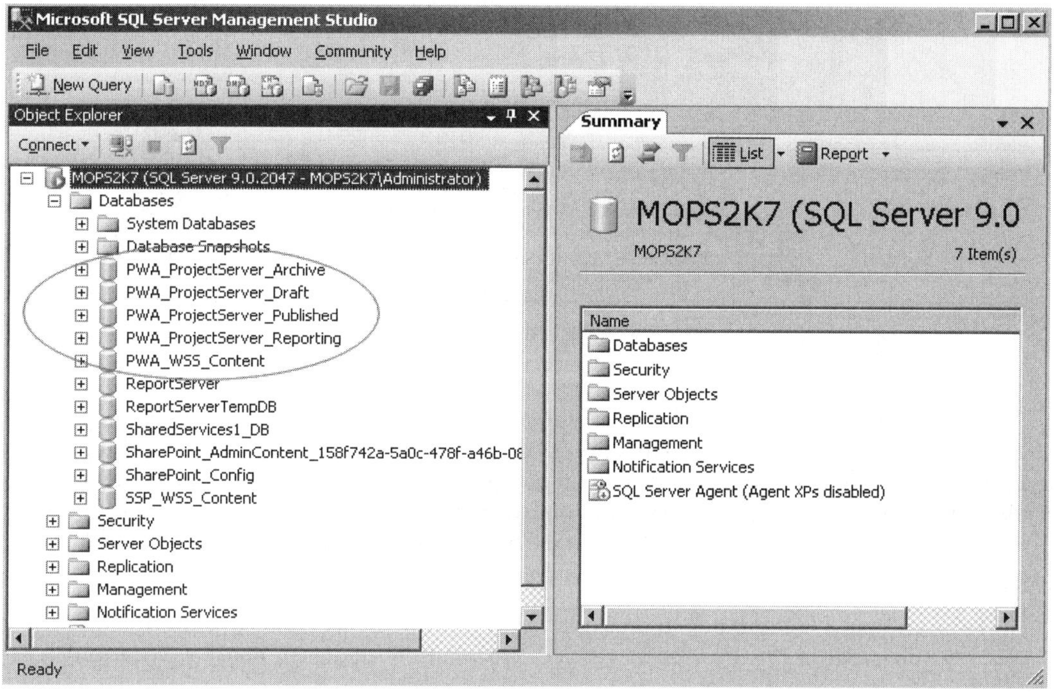

FIGURE 6-45 The four new PWA databases

Adding a Server to the Farm

Now that you've run a pilot in a single department, you may have found that word is spreading quickly among users and departmental managers that Project Server 2007 has provided a new level of work efficiency and reporting. You now have a situation where the demand for Project Server 2007 has outpaced the server infrastructure currently in place.

You are now realizing that your two-server small farm will not support the tidal wave of use that will likely come in the near future. You've weighed the options and realize that the most logical way to increase capacity is to offload the Front End Web Server duties to its own server.

At this point, it's important to take a quick refresher course on the application architecture of Project Server 2007 as it relates to the installation we just performed.

Remember that in Chapter 3 we discussed the logical tiers of the Project Server 2007 architecture. The services that are relevant to scaling your Project Server environment are the Project Application Service and the Windows SharePoint Service Web application.

As you can see in Figure 6-46, you will want the duties of the Front End Web Server to move from the existing server to the new dedicated Front End Web Server, turning Project Server 2007 into a logical and physical three-tier application.

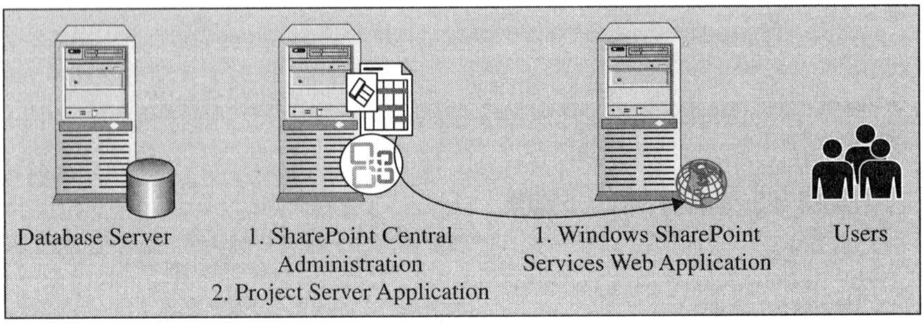

FIGURE 6-46 Adding the third tier

When adding a sparkly new Front End Web Server, it is important to consider how users have been accessing PWA to this point. Your DNS administrator will likely need to change the host record that users have been using from the server that was previously your Web Front End Server to the new Web Front End Server.

To add a Web Front End Server to your existing Project Server 2007 farm, follow these steps:

1. From your freshly patched and updated Windows Server 2003, install IIS and run Setup.exe from the Project Server 2007 installation media (or network location).
2. Insert your license key.
3. Choose Advanced from the installation type dialog.
4. Choose Web Front End from the Server Type selections.
5. Click Install Now.
6. After the binary installation completes, open the SharePoint Configuration Wizard.
7. On the Connect to a Server Farm page, indicate that you want to connect to an existing server farm.
8. On the Specify Configuration Database Settings page, indicate the server that hosts the existing farm's configuration database, as shown in Figure 6-47, and click Retrieve Databases. If you've specified the correct server, the SharePoint_Config database as well as the farm administrator username fields will be populated automatically for you, as shown in Figure 6-47. Enter the correct Active Directory Domain–based farm administrator password and click Next.

   After the SharePoint Configuration Wizard runs, your machine will be a part of the Project Server 2007 farm.
9. Next, from Central Administration on your application server (or the new middle tier), go to the Operations tab and click Services on Server.
10. In the Services on Server page, click Stop to stop the WSS Web Application Service, as shown in Figure 6-48.

As you see, adding servers to your farm has become a very straightforward process.

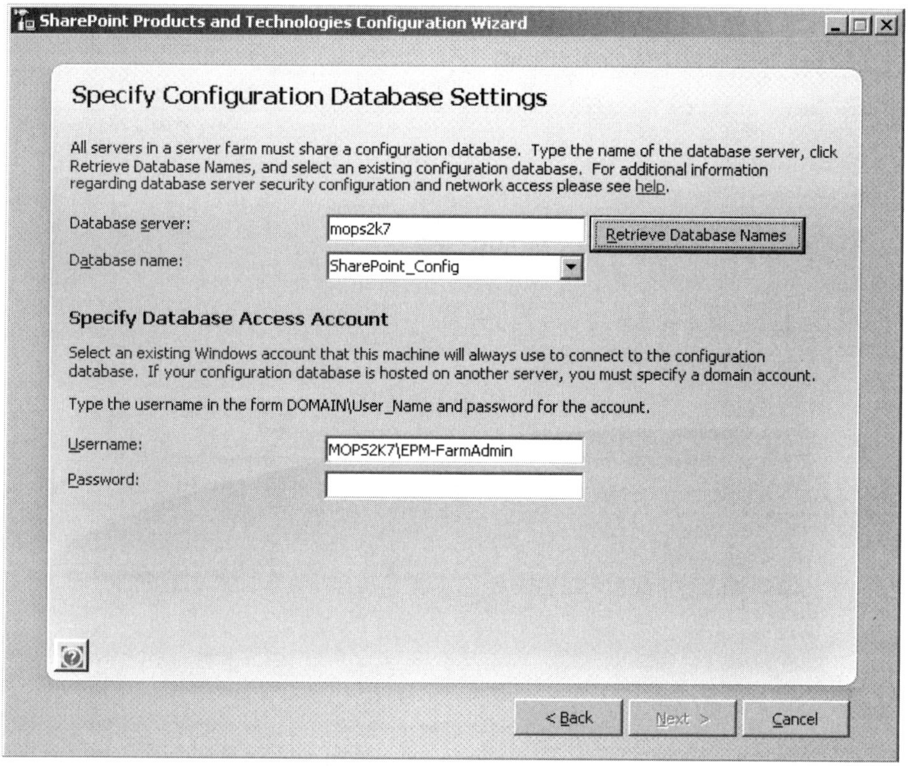

FIGURE 6-47 Connecting to the farm

Client Components

Many organizations have existing mechanisms for automated software distribution. We will focus on the minimum components required on client machines based on the EPM role that the user will fill.

The project manager will require the following components:

- Windows XP Professional (fully patched)
- Microsoft Office Project Professional 2007
- Internet Explorer 6 or Internet Explorer 7 (fully patched)
- Analysis Services 2005 (9.0) OLE DB Provider (if the project manager requires Data Analysis views)
- Microsoft Office Excel 2003 or 2007 (for the Visual Reports in Project Professional 2007)
- Microsoft Office Visio 2007 (for the Visual Reports in Project Professional 2007)

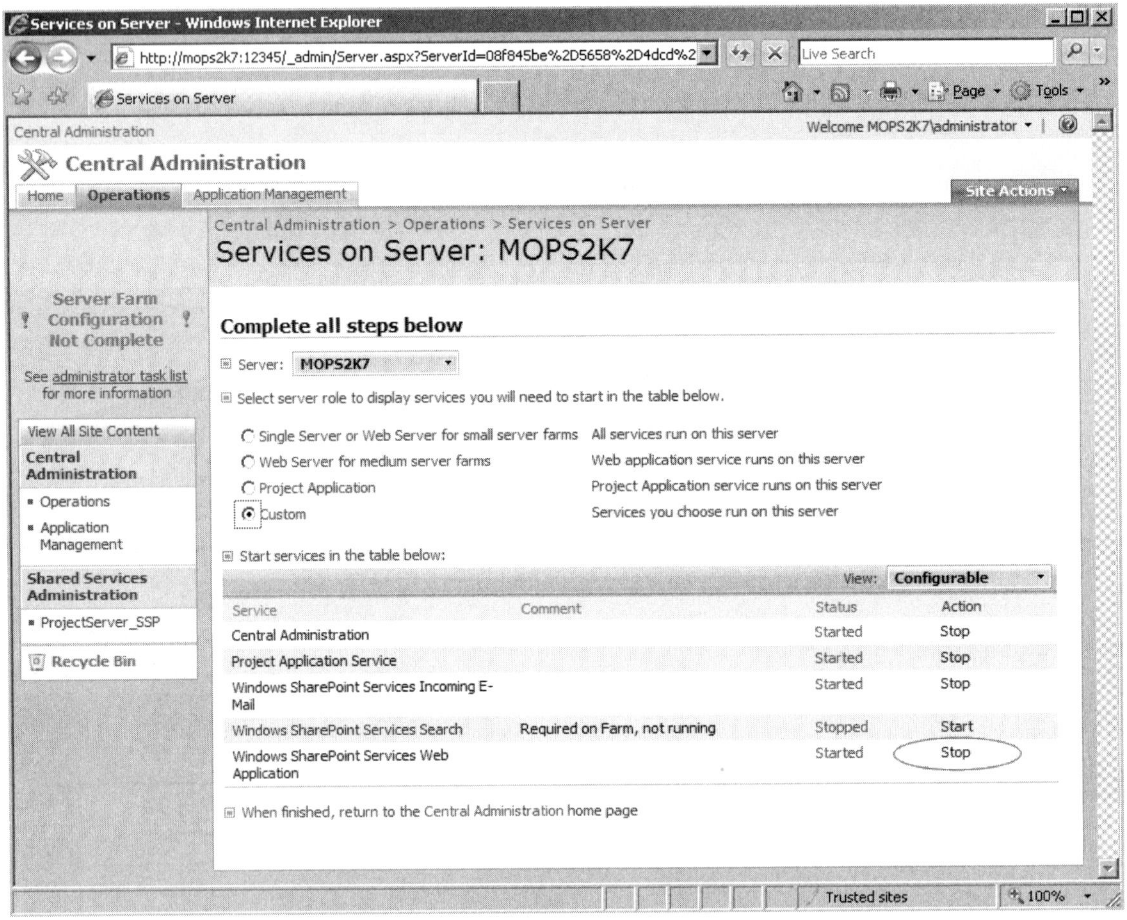

FIGURE 6-48 Stop the Web application on the middle tier.

The following components are required for the executive or other who will use the Data Analysis views:

- Windows XP Professional (fully patched)
- Internet Explorer 6 or 7 (fully patched)
- Analysis Services 2005 (9.0) OLE DB Provider (for Data Analysis views)

Resources will require the following:

- Windows XP Professional (fully patched)
- Internet Explorer 6 or Internet Explorer 7 (fully patched)
- Microsoft Outlook 2003, or 2007 (for interaction with Project Server through Microsoft Outlook Calendar and Tasks)

Internet Explorer

When you first attempt to click on the link for your PWA site, you may be confronted with an authentication box asking for your user credentials. There are two ways to enable transparent authentication, and the one that you choose depends on the version of Internet Explorer you are using:

- **IE6** If the site is added to the Trusted Sites security zone in Internet Explorer, you will be able to authenticate transparently because of the default settings of that zone.
- **IE7** If the site is added to the Trusted Sites security zone in Internet Explorer, you won't be able to authenticate transparently until you perform the following steps:
  1. From within Internet Explorer 7, click Tools | Options.
  2. Click on the Security tab.
  3. Click Trusted Sites | Custom Level.
  4. In the Security Settings—Trusted Sites Zone page, scroll to the bottom of the options window under the Authentication section and select Automatic Logon with Current Username and Password.
  5. In addition to the Logon settings, it is important to change the default behavior for Accessing Data across Domains to Enable. This setting is found in the Security Settings—Trusted Sites Zone page and shown in Figure 6-49. The reason for completing this step is to ensure that when you access the Data Analysis views, Internet Explorer behaves as expected.

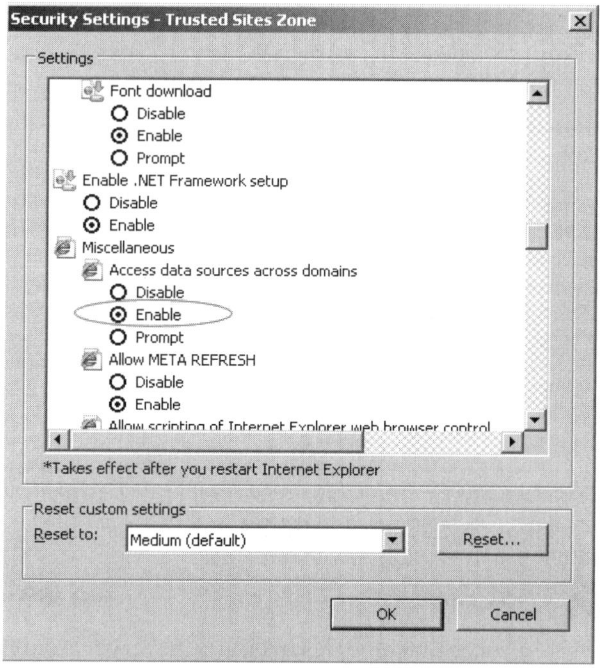

FIGURE 6-49 Modifications to the Trusted Sites Zone

SQL Server 2005 Analysis Services Configuration

Because Microsoft Office Project Server 2007 was built to be compatible with two versions of Microsoft SQL Server (2000 and 2005), you need to perform some modifications to the SQL Server 2005 Analysis Services environment to allow the automated actions and communication to occur with Project Server. In essence, following the steps in this procedure makes SQL Server 2005 Analysis Services look like SQL 2000 Analysis Services to Project Server 2007. You should perform all of the following steps from the machine running Microsoft Analysis Services 2005.

NOTE *Additional steps for configuring Analysis Services can be found in Chapter 12.*

1. In the OLAP folder (typically found in the C:\Program Files\Microsoft SQL Server\MSSQL.2\ directory), create a folder named DSO9 (with an *O* as in *Oscar).*
2. Right-click the DSO9 folder and select Sharing and Security.
3. Select to Share This Folder and enter a Share Name of **MSOLAPRepository**$.
4. Click Permissions and add the EPM-SSPService Account. Give this user read and modify permissions on the shared folder.
5. Click on the Security tab and ensure that the EPM-SSPService has modify permissions on the file.
6. Find a copy of the MSMdrep.mdb file and place it in the DSO9 folder. This MSMdrep.mdb file is the Analysis Services repository from the SQL 2000 Analysis Services world.
7. From the C:\Program Files\Microsoft SQL Server\MSSQL.2\OLAP\Config directory, open the MSMdsrv.ini file with Notepad.
8. Near the bottom of the file, replace the `DSO….` `/DSO` section with the following:

```
<DSO>
<RemoteRepositoryConnectionString>Provider=Microsoft.Jet.OLEDB.4.0;Data
Source=\\SERVERNAME\MSOLAPRepository$\msmdrep.mdb;Persist Security Info=False
</RemoteRepositoryConnectionString>
<RepositoryConnectionString>Provider=Microsoft.Jet.OLEDB.4.0;Data
Source=C:\Program Files\Microsoft SQL Server\MSSQL.2\OLAP\DSO9\msmdrep.mdb;Persist
Security Info=False</RepositoryConnectionString>
<RemoteLocksDirectory>\\SERVERNAME\MSOLAPRepository$</RemoteLocksDirectory>
<LocksDirectory>C:\Program Files\Microsoft SQL Server\MSSQL.2\OLAP\DSO9</LocksDirectory>
</DSO>
```

NOTE *Replace* `SERVERNAME` *with your analysis services machine. Also, depending on which SQL components you installed, you might need to replace* `MSSQL.2` *with the number represented in your actual installation.*

9. Save and close the MSMdsrv.ini file.
10. On the Analysis Services machine, restart the SQL Server Analysis Services Service.

NOTE *After restarting the Server Analysis Services Service, the* DSO *connection information that you just added to the MSMdsrv.ini file will be encrypted.*

Adding the SSP Service Account to Analysis Services Administration

To give the SSP service account permissions to build a cube in Analysis Services, you can take one of several paths. The easy (shotgun) approach is to make the SSP-Service Account a member of the Local Administrators group. The other and more secure method is to grant the SSP service account specific permissions on the instance of Analysis Services. Complete the following steps to accomplish this:

1. Open SQL Server 2005 Management Studio and connect to Analysis Services.
2. Right-click on the server name and select Properties.
3. Select Security from the Select a Page section on the left.
4. Click the Add button and identify the SSP service account in the format *DOMAIN\Username* and click OK.
5. Close SQL 2005 Management Studio.
6. Restart the SQL Server 2005 Analysis Services Service.

Adding the SQL Connectivity Components to Application Servers

In Project Server 2003, if you wanted to build Analysis Services cubes for your Portfolio Analyzer views, you had to ensure that the SQL Server 2000 Analysis Services Decision Support Objects (DSO) were installed on all of your Project Server servers. You also had to ensure that the Service Pack level for Analysis Services was applied and consistent across the server infrastructure.

With SQL Server 2005, this same requirement exists, but the components are named differently. Now you must install the Client Tools for SQL Server 2005 on all of the application servers in your farm. These essentially give the SSP the ability to "speak the online analytical processing (OLAP) language" with Analysis Services 2005. The Client Tools for SQL Server 2005 can be installed from the SQL Server 2005 installation media.

Installing with MOSS 2007

In previous versions, installation of Project Server on the same machine or environment as SharePoint Portal Server was something that Microsoft officially recommended against, but gave instructions for nonetheless. As anyone who has witnessed some of the odd behavior exhibited by these environments, it can be said that although it could be done, doing so did not showcase the stability, predictability, and overall normality that we've all grown to know and love from the ever-evolving EPM toolset. That said, today is a new day.

Before attempting to get these two quite impressive applications to share the same hardware, let's look at some of the reasons why you may be thinking of trying it.

1. You have used MOSS's "Project Management Light" functionality, and have gotten a sweet (but brief) taste of EPM using the MOSS Proposals feature. You have now come to the realization that this seemingly obscure feature may provide that "tipping point" application to invigorate your organization from using your SharePoint instance as

simply a collaboration/document/content management and search workhorse to a fire- breathing, PMO electrifying, project initiation–enabling, executive-delighting, infrastructure-slimming thoroughbred. You will bring together the mainstays of the Microsoft Information Worker initiative and reap the benefits as your company makes leaps in Business Productivity and is highlighted in all those neat, trendy commercials. It will be two as one. Yin and yang. The FSM smiles upon you…

Overly ambitious? Maybe, but you get points for enthusiasm and vision.

2. You know that both Server Products have the words "Microsoft Office" in them, you've got 45 minutes before your next meeting, you're wound up like an eight-day clock, and you've got a thirst for adventure and intrigue.
3. You've already been through your proof of concept with Project Server 2007, validating through use cases that the EPM toolset will definitely help to address the business challenges of resource utilization, portfolio management, and project management methodology standardization. You understand that aligning these products could save considerable amounts in hardware and administrative costs by taking advantage of common server and application infrastructure.

Because this chapter will be focusing on choices 1 and 3, let's start with our goal in sight.

Installing Microsoft Office Project Server 2007 on an Existing Instance of SharePoint Server 2007

There are a few ground rules that you need to follow when approaching this scenario.

One Server at a Time

Do not try to multitask with this process. It is very important that while you perform the farm-level actions of adding servers to the farm that you modify only one machine at a time.

Patience, Grasshopper

Many of the actions that you will be performing will happen asynchronously. If you have the desire to click refresh three times per second, then after 5 seconds perform an `iisreset`, go ahead and do it, but on a different machine. Just try to be patient.

Installing a New Instance of Project Server 2007 on an Existing Instance of SharePoint Server 2007

Although the process of getting these two server products to live side-by-side in harmony has been greatly simplified, of the two options described in this book, this is the most straightforward approach.

Installation Procedure

The next task is to install the software bits for Project Server 2007.

Installing the Binaries for Project Server 2007

During this crucial step, to reduce the chance of inconsistencies, the first thing that you should ensure is that no users are currently using the SharePoint farm. In SharePoint, the term *quiesce* means "to no longer accept new connections for long-running operations." This does not kick people out of their session, if, for example, they are in the middle of downloading a document. It will, however, prevent new connections to the servers in the farm. To quiesce your farm and install the binaries, complete the following steps:

1. From SharePoint Central Administration, click Operations | Quiesce Farm to display the screen shown in Figure 6-50.
2. After quiescing the farm, reset it by typing **iisreset** at the command prompt.
3. Install the binaries to your first Front End Server, as described previously.
4. Run the SharePoint Configuration Wizard from your first Front End Server. This can be accessed from the Windows Start button, then Microsoft Office SharePoint Server and then selecting it from the menu.
5. Continue to install the binaries and run the SharePoint Configuration Wizard for each machine serially (that is, one machine at a time).

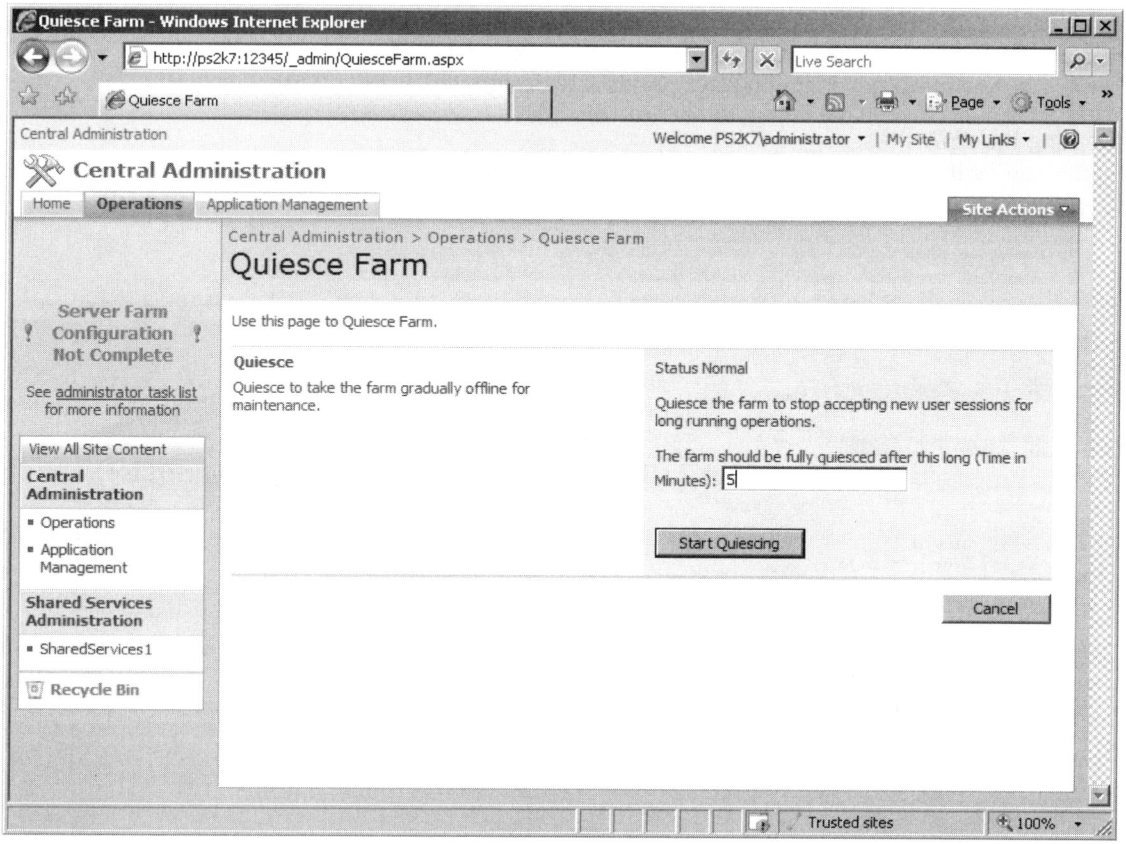

FIGURE 6-50 Quiesce the farm

Installation Checkpoint

At this point, you may be skeptically thinking, "Wow, that was easy.... Too easy." Let's take a look at Figure 6-51 for a brief tour of SQL Server 2005 Management Studio at this point in the process.

At this stage of installing Microsoft Office Project Server 2007 on an existing instance of MOSS, we see that there are seven total databases, three of which are MOSS-specific (Portal Content, MySite Content, and the Search database). The other four databases (the Central Administration content database, the SharePoint Config, the Web application for the SSP, and the SSP itself) are very similar to a fresh installation of Project Server 2007. In this instance, however, there is no Web application for the PWA sites identified. This is because you will be using the Portal Content database and Web application (the default Web site) for your PWA sites.

After you have installed the Project Server 2007 binaries and run the SharePoint Products and Technologies Configuration Wizard on all machines in your farm, you'll need to return to the Central Administration Operations area and start the Project Application Service on any machines that you have previously designated as the middle tier.

Creating the PWA sites

So far, you've installed the Project Server binaries to the MOSS servers and started the Project Application Service. Figure 6-52 shows the Shared Services Administration page of

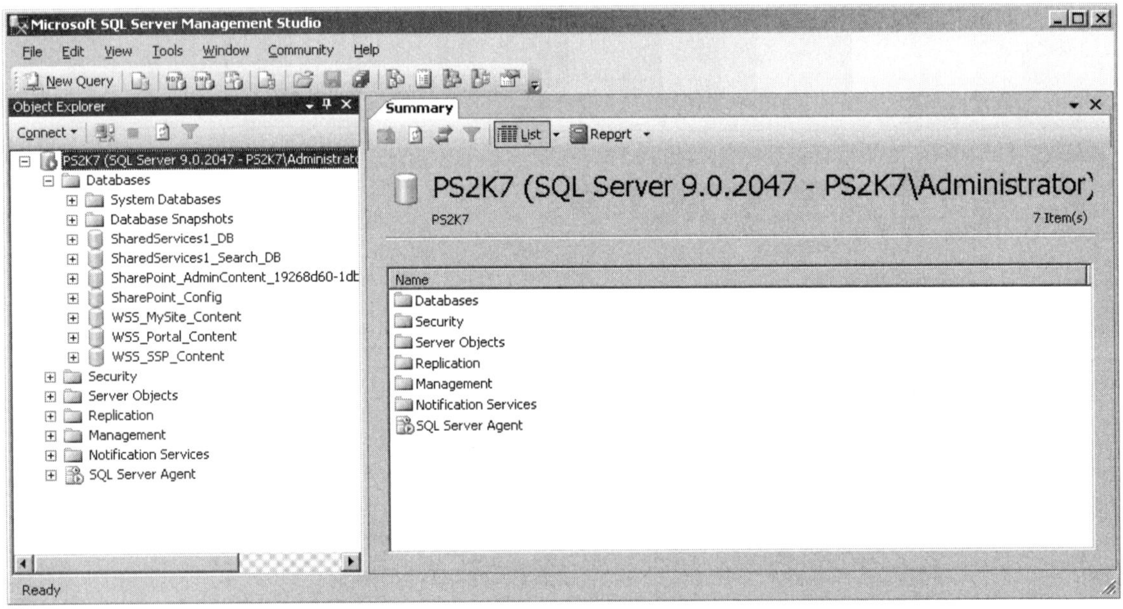

FIGURE 6-51 SQL 2005 Management Studio showing the MOSS-specific databases

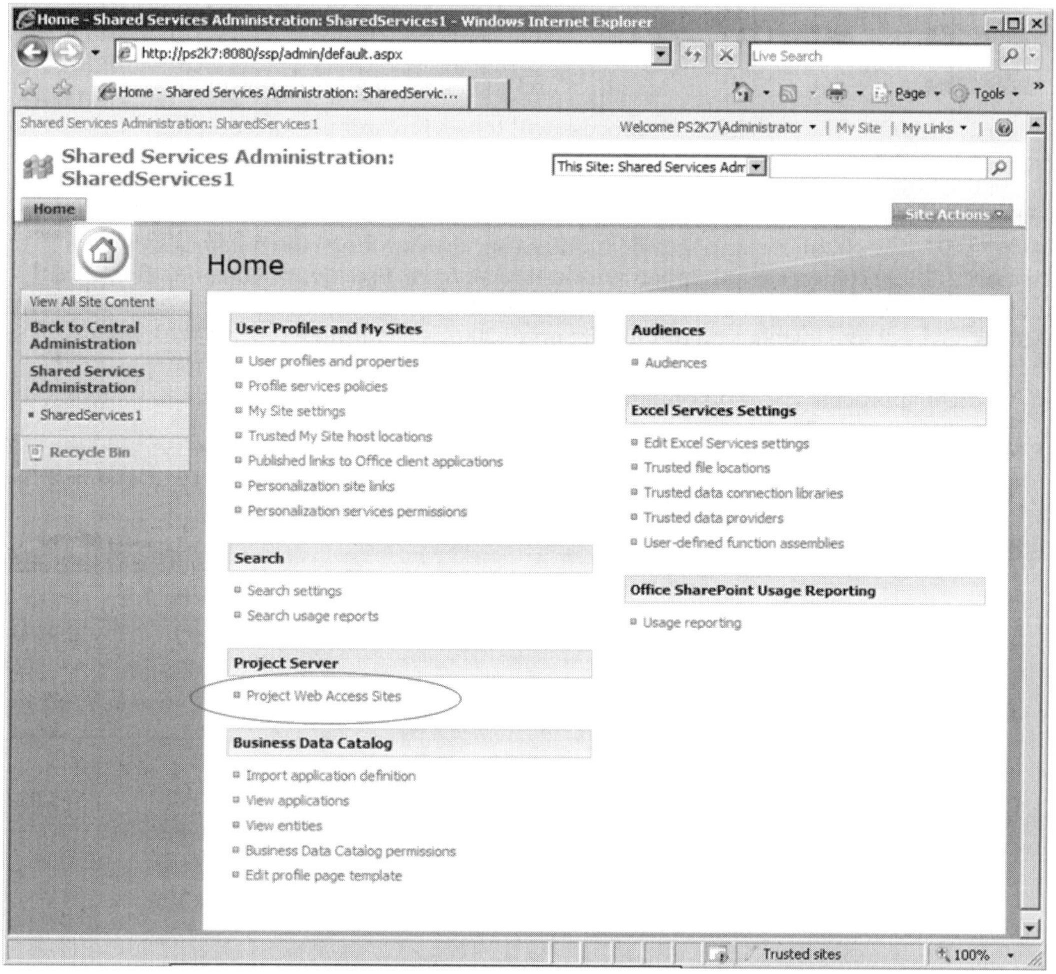

FIGURE 6-52 The Shared Services Administration page with Project Server and SharePoint Server

the SharedServices1 SSP. Notice all of the MOSS-specific SSP modules. From within the Create Project Web Access Site page, complete the following steps:

1. Decide which SharePoint Web application you will use to host the PWA sites. In this scenario, where you want to host it within the Web application used for MOSS, use the default Web site.
2. Choose the path. The default is PWA.
3. Choose your Project Web Access instance administrator. The default is the Setup User account.

4. Identify the database server to host and the names for your Draft, Published, and Archive databases.
5. Identify the database server to host and the name of your Reporting Database.
6. Click OK. The provisioning process will take a few minutes to complete.

In this chapter, we have looked at several Project Server 2007 installation scenarios, from a stand-alone installation, to a small farm, to installing Project Server 2007 on an instance of MOSS 2007. The chapter examined the required service accounts, the databases that are created, and the changes that happen within IIS. We have also identified components that must be installed on the client machines based on the role that the user will play in the EPM system. Overall, the installation of Project Server 2007 is a complex process with many moving parts. However, with a firm understanding of the underlying components, a methodical approach, and a bit of patience, you will end up with a finely-tuned system that will reliably support your users into the future.

7 CHAPTER

SharePoint Central Administration in a Project Server Environment

When you install Project Server 2007, the installation program also installs Windows SharePoint Services (WSS). At the end of that process, when you run the SharePoint Products and Technologies Configuration Wizard, the Central Administration site is first created. As described in the previous chapter, you then open the SharePoint Central Administration tool, create the Site Collection, a SharedService Provider (SSP), and a Project Web Access (PWA) site. The Central Administration tool also acts as the foundational administrative element in terms of managing a Project Server environment. Project Server administrators need to access Central Admin only occasionally, as the items configured there affect the infrastructure of your Project Server 2007 environment.

If you want to start "turning the knobs" by actually configuring the Project Server application, skip this chapter for now. If the goal is to understand the foundational elements on which Project Server 2007 is built, then stay here.

The SharePoint Central Administration application is used by WSS, as well as the Microsoft Office SharePoint Server (MOSS) if it is installed. Project Server requires only WSS, and many organizations use this standard/base configuration. From a pure Project Server perspective, MOSS is not required and its settings are not included in this discussion.

NOTE *MOSS can be valuable in some organizations and is a very powerful collaboration solution. To learn more about the features possible with MOSS and Project Server, see Chapter 25.*

SharePoint can be used to support a wide range of purposes outside of traditional Enterprise Project Management (EPM). The material in this chapter is intended to provide the information most useful to the administrative staff of Project Server 2007, rather than complete details on every possible setting for a SharePoint environment (this is after all, a Project Server book). SharePoint Central Administration is a powerful and complex tool.

Because the settings in Central Admin work well out of the box in most cases, however, significant interaction is rarely required for Project Server after a solid environment has been established. For in-depth information on SharePoint 3.0 Central Administration, you will need to seek material in addition to what is provided here (we know of at least one entire book that has been published that covers this topic).

Central Admin Home Page

The main page in Central Admin acts primarily as a launching point. To start SharePoint 3.0 Central Administration, the user must be on the server console, either by actually physically being logged on to the server where it is installed, or by connecting via a remote tool such as Microsoft's Remote Desktop Connection tool. You find the link to Central Administration by selecting the Windows Start button, then All Programs | Microsoft Office Server | SharePoint 3.0 Central Administration. Figure 7-1 shows the Home Page.

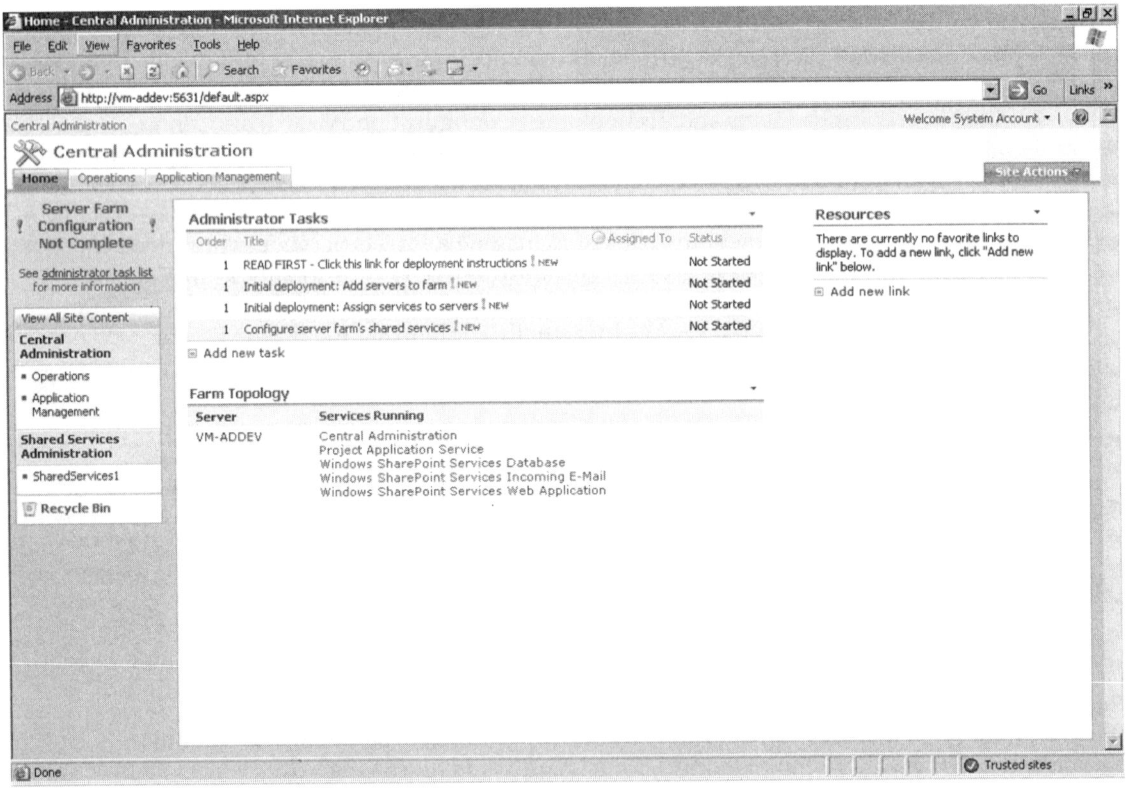

FIGURE 7-1 Central Admin Home Page

On this page, items are primarily used for viewing and navigation only. Action requires moving into the Operations, Application Management, or Shared Services areas of the tool. On the Home Page are the following items:

- **Administrative Tasks** On the top of the Home Page body is a Web Part called Administrator Tasks. It acts as a "to-do" list for administrators and is not automated. To read the details of any single item, select it. You can then edit it by selecting Edit Item from the next page, as shown in Figure 7-2. To view the entire list behind the Web Part, just navigate from the Home Page by selecting the words Administrator Tasks at the top of the Administrator Tasks Web Part.
- **Farm Topology** This Web Part simply displays the components that have been included in the farm. In many cases, a Project Server farm includes only a few items (including Central Administration, Project Application Service, Windows SharePoint Services Web Application, Windows SharePoint Services Database, Windows SharePoint Services Incoming E-Mail, and Windows SharePoint Services Search if it has been enabled). Selecting the server name to the left of the listed services navigates the user to the Operations, Services on Server page, which is covered in the next section, "Operations."
- **Resources** This unpopulated Web Part allows the administrator to add links. The administrator can use this Web Part's link list to link to administrative resources.

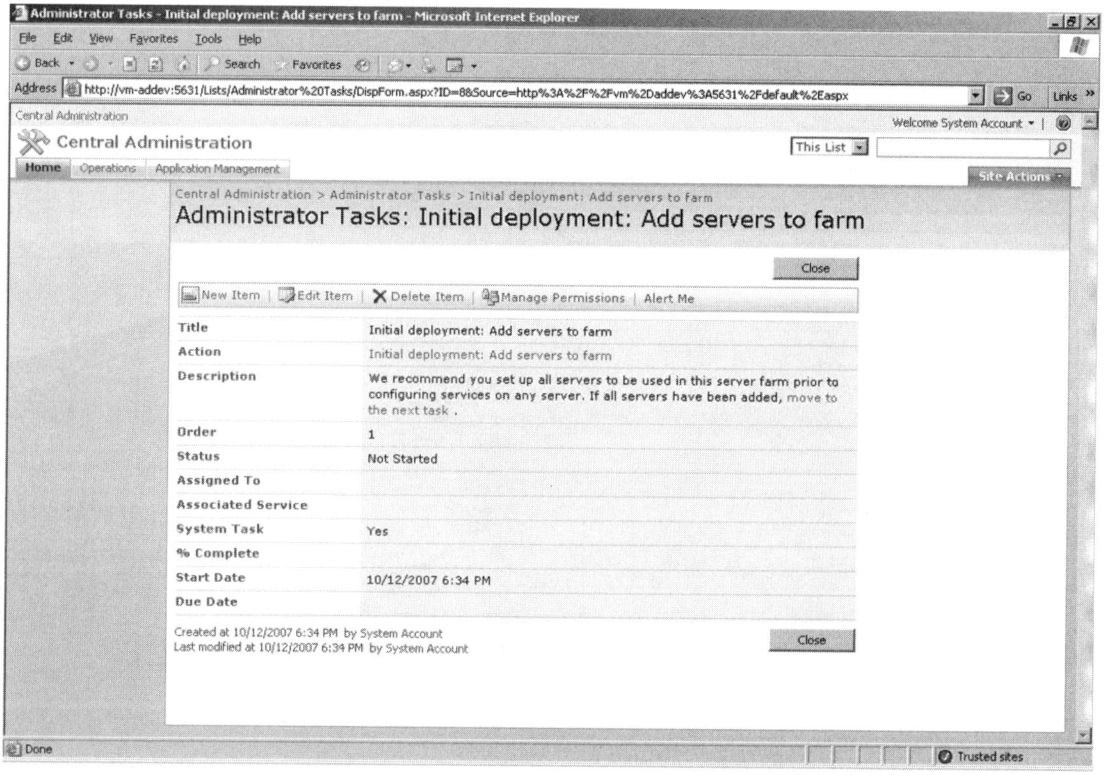

FIGURE 7-2 Administrator Tasks view

Operations

To find the Operations page, just select Operations from either the top tab or the left navigation (called the Quick Launch Bar). Figure 7-3 shows the items listed in the Operations page. The page is organized by sections and we will follow the way the page is organized when getting into the details here.

Topology and Services

This section covers the Topology and Services areas within the Central Administration tools. Within this page area are some of the core settings for configuring the SharePoint farm. The following are the available options:

- **Servers in Farm** This page displays the basic farm information. The only action that you can take on this page is to remove the server from the farm.
- **Services on Server** On this important page, you can stop and start services. Selecting the Custom radio button displays all the services, as shown in Figure 7-4. The other options narrow the display. Services can be started or stopped as needed from this page. For example, it is recommended that you stop the Project Application Service before performing a farm backup (you will learn more about farm backups in the "Backup and Restore" section later in this chapter).

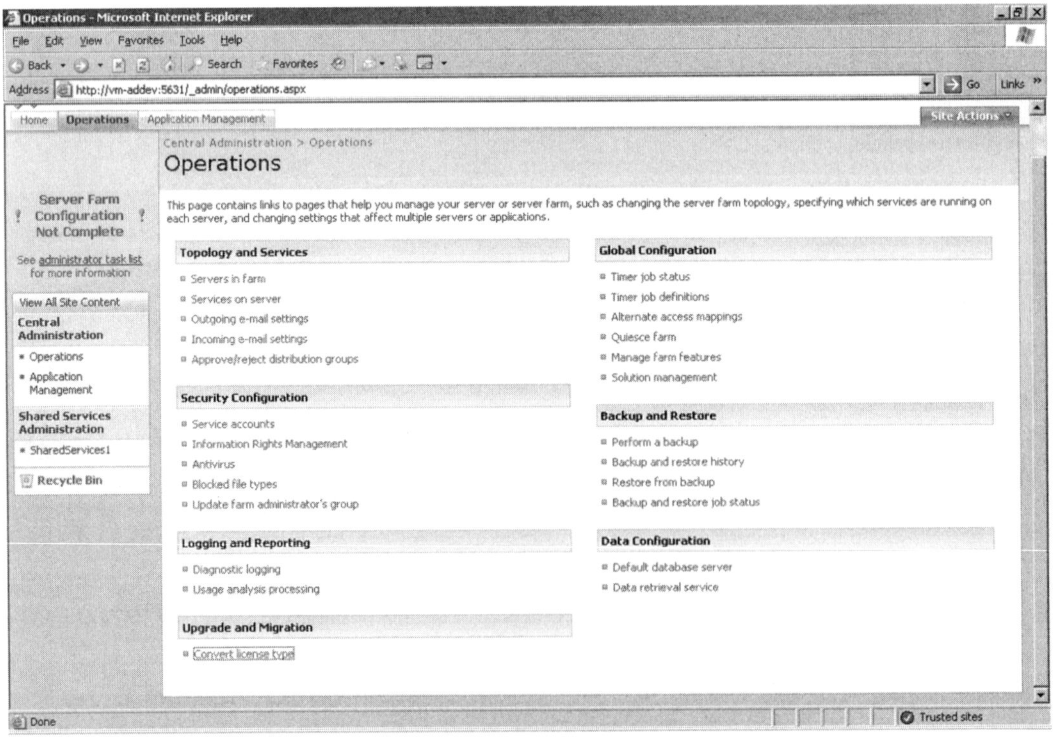

FIGURE 7-3 Operations page items

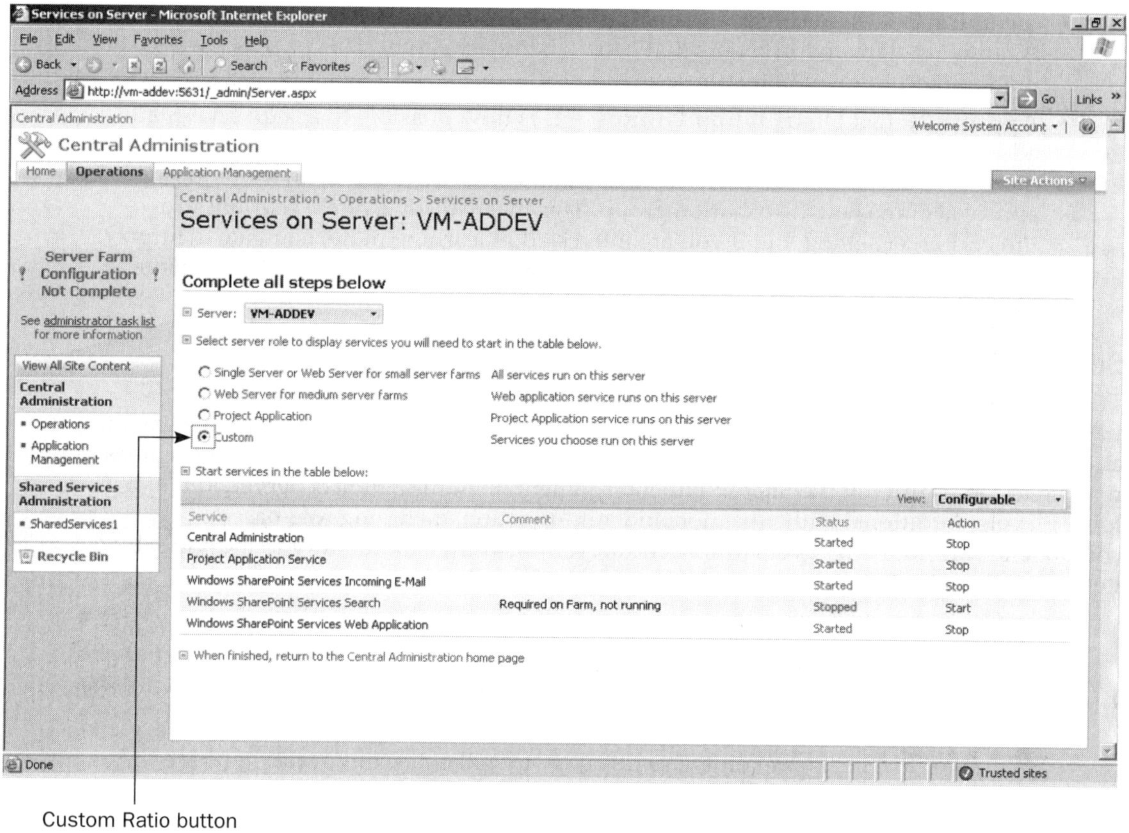

FIGURE 7-4 Custom radio button

- **Outgoing E-Mail Settings** Most organizations want to use outgoing e-mails to notify Project Server users. Examples include notifying team members of assignments, project managers of task updates from team members, or teams about requested status reports. For e-mail notification to function, you must make a connection to a mail server from this page (there is another location to enter this information in the PWA Server Settings as well). Project Server/SharePoint can send mail to any Simple Mail Transfer Protocol (SMTP) mail system, and it is on this page that the SMTP server address, the From address, the Sender Name, and the character set can be configured. Note that to enable the mail features, you must first install the SMTP service in Internet Information Services (IIS).

Install the SMTP Service

To install SMTP, navigate to Control Panel and select Add/Remove Programs | Add/Remove Windows Components. In the wizard that starts, select Application Server inside the components box, then click the Details button. In the Application Server dialog, select Subcomponents of Application Server | IIS, then click the Details button. In the IIS dialog, select the SMTP checkbox. Select OK twice, then Next. After SMTP is installed, select Finish.

- **Incoming E-Mail Settings** SharePoint 3.0/2007 can receive e-mail. This capability is rarely used in environments that focus on Project Server. This page is used to set up these incoming mail features.
- **Approve/Reject Distribution Groups** It is now possible to assign an e-mail address to a site group upon site creation in WSS. It can even create new distribution groups in Active Directory. This feature adds a security mechanism for requiring the approval of the new distribution group. This mechanism is rarely relevant in a Project Server setting, but if you are interested in learning more, navigate to http://technet2.microsoft.com/windowsserver/WSS/en/library/445dd72e-a63b-46d0-b92d-bcf0aa9d8d061033.mspx?mfr=true.

Security Configuration

The Security Configuration area is used for settings related to security from a broad perspective, not just authentication and authorization. It also includes rights management, antivirus protection, and more. For the traditional access security, this section covers areas relating to the security of the SharePoint environment, including Project Server, at the lowest levels. Additional authentication and authorization, including role-based components, are added in layers from Central Administration all the way to individual items. The Security Configuration settings include the following:

- **Service Accounts** This page is used to manage the SharePoint Service account credentials. For example, if your security policy requires password expiration and/or changes, you can use this page to map the service accounts to the new passwords.
- **Information Rights Management Services (RMS)** It is possible to integrate Windows RMS to SharePoint. Use this page to make the configuration needed from the SharePoint perspective to connect to and enable RMS.
- **Antivirus** It is possible to integrate compatible antivirus solutions to SharePoint. The antivirus software must be installed on all Web Front End Servers in the farm. After it is installed, this feature supports configuration.
- **Blocked File Types** SharePoint comes preconfigured to block file extensions that could create security issues with the server or content. For example, .EXE files cannot be stored in SharePoint to prevent them from running what could be dangerous code. This feature allows addition and/or removal of blocked file types.
- **Update Farm Administrator's Group** This feature enables you to manage who is included in the farm administrator's group. This list should be limited to a small number of people, typically domain administrators.

Logging and Reporting

There are several functions available in Project Server 2007 for logging and reporting user activity and errors:

- **Diagnostic Logging** Included in this page are tools for the management of the Customer Experience Improvement Program (which sends errors to Microsoft), error reports, event throttling (which sets the level of severity logged by category of error), and trace logging. Event throttling settings can be useful for troubleshooting by "dialing up" the logging. These logs can be categorized and levels can be set for both the Windows and trace logs and include the following levels:

The Windows event log includes the following:

- None
- Error
- Warning
- Audit Failure
- Audit Success
- Information

The trace log includes these levels:

- None
- Unexpected
- Monitorable
- High
- Medium
- Verbose

As previously noted, the trace logs can be useful for troubleshooting, but the output of these logs can be cryptic in the case of a Windows event log, or very deep and complex in the case of the trace log, and thus require experts for deciphering.

- **Usage Analysis Processing** This feature is for tracking usage such as top users in last 30 days, average number of requests per day, number of queries per day, total hits, and bandwidth. For more on usage analysis processing, see http://www.microsoft.com/technet/windowsserver/sharepoint/V2/reskit/c2961881x.mspx.

Convert License Type

This area has a single interface in which you can upgrade the license by entering a product key. It is used to upgrade SharePoint Client Access License (CAL) versions.

Global Configuration

The SharePoint Central Administration interface has organized several setting topics into this area. Each focuses on a topic that affects the entire SharePoint farm, rather than more narrow topics.

- **Timer Job Status** The SharePoint Timer service is used to manage timed jobs and is a very important component in the Project Server 2007 environment. If this service is not running, Project Server is effectively not functional (e.g., the Project Queue will not process). This page is used to display the status of SharePoint Timer jobs. Although you can filter the view of these jobs, you cannot take action here.
- **Timer Job Definitions** This page displays the timer jobs and enables you to take action. One common example (especially when you are first configuring the backup), is if a farm backup fails, it displays in its failed state on this page. (You will learn more

about farm backups in the following section.) To attempt another farm backup after a failure (when making configuration changes to the backup destination SHARE, for example), you first must remove it from the existing list of timer jobs.

- **Alternate Access Mappings** This page is for the management of a feature that SharePoint uses to make sure that Web requests map correctly to the appropriate Web application. This feature is useful in load-balancing and reverse-proxy network environments. In a Project Server environment, this feature could come into play if you are granting access to the Project Server from outside the internal network (for example, from an extranet). Note that adding external access requires other, non-SharePoint changes. Granting external access here will not work without network access already in place.
- **Manage Farm Features** This page can be used to view installed features as well as to turn them on and off, as shown in Figure 7-5, where it can be viewed in a Project Server/MOSS environment.
- **Solution Management** SharePoint solutions are custom applications that are developed for inclusion in the SharePoint environment. A commonly-known

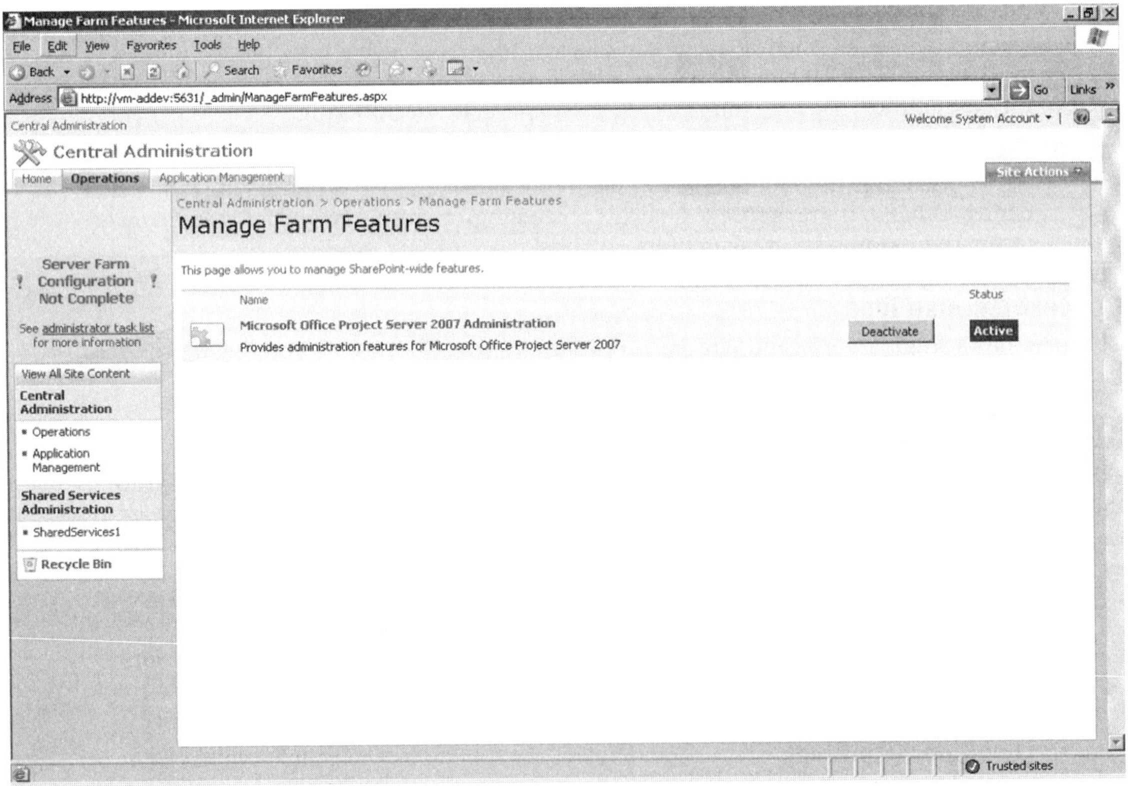

FIGURE 7-5 Manage Farm Features page

solution can be downloaded from Microsoft that enables the user to add the Microsoft site templates. However, this feature is highly unlikely to be used in a Project Server environment. A more likely alternative would be a Project-specific application that could be developed as a solution.

Backup and Restore

This area is used for configuration of the farm backup tools. This is a critical area for Project Server and SharePoint administrators to understand and use. The following are the specific links and the tasks that each performs:

- **Perform a Backup** The new Farm Backup feature that is executed from this page can be leveraged as part of a disaster recovery plan. Basically, it backs up the entire SharePoint farm to a network location. To perform this backup, make sure that a network drive is shared to the farm administrative account that is used to execute the backup. From the Perform a Backup page, select the checkbox to select the entire farm, as shown in Figure 7-6.

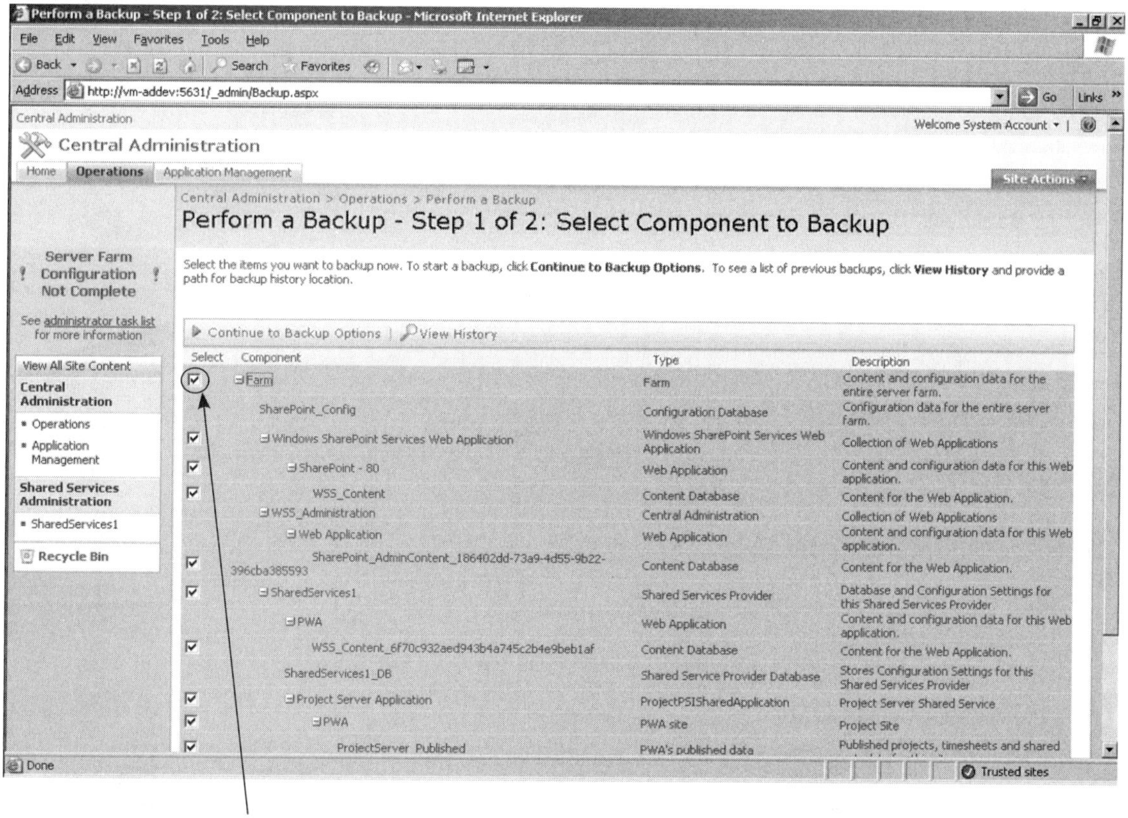

FIGURE 7-6 Selecting the farm to back up

Next select the Continue to Backup Options button. From the next page, select Full or Differential for the backup type and type in the name of the network location destination. Next click OK. A page appears to show the backup status as shown in Figure 7-7. Be patient when this is running.

Once complete, the entire farm can be restored to a specific point in time.

NOTE *The backup solution provided from this page is not a complete one that can be used in most disaster recovery models. It can be useful as part of a more complete backup solution, however, and it has saved a few rear ends of people supporting Project Server. In most cases, additional backup components should be employed, including SQL Server database backups and possibly more. For a more comprehensive look at disaster recovery read the Microsoft SharePoint Team's white paper "Data Protection and Recovery for Microsoft Office SharePoint Server 2007 in Small to Medium-Sized Deployments," at http://technet2.microsoft.com/Office/en-us/library/288fecfb-53fb-4988-89d7-b7888f82bf961033.mspx?mfr=true.*

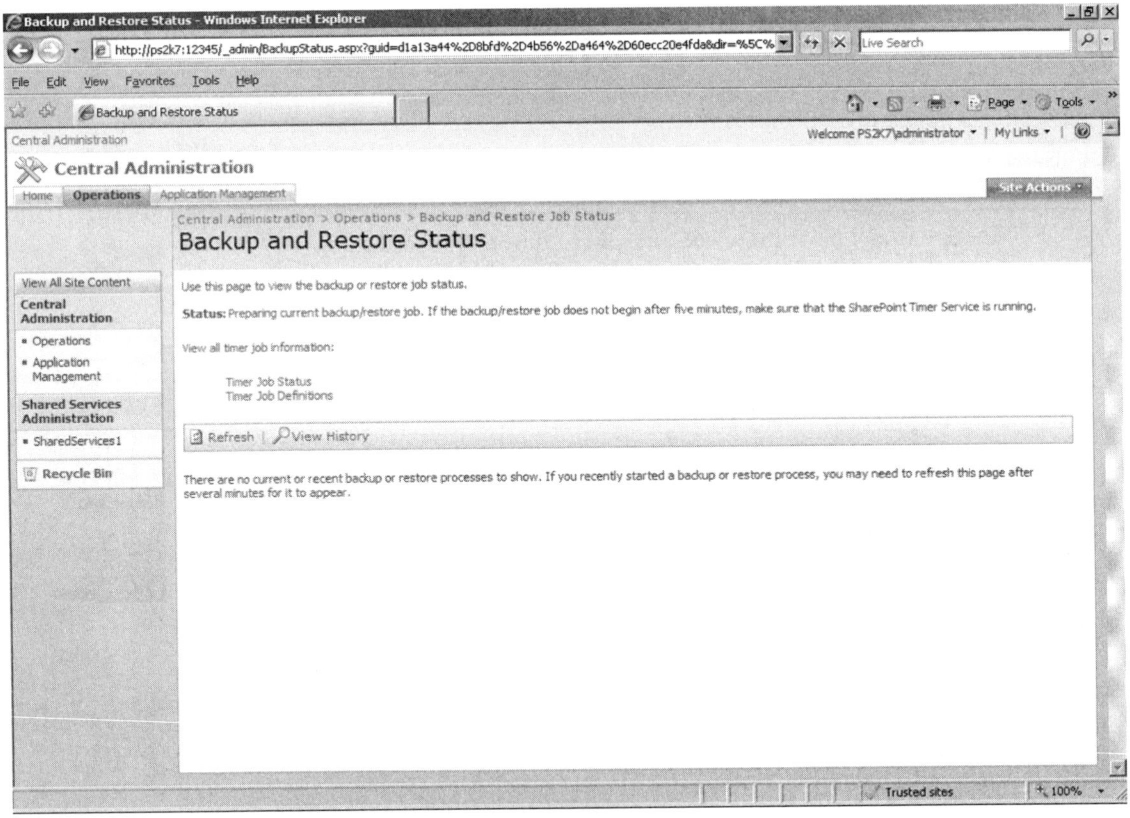

FIGURE 7-7 Backup and Restore Status page

- **Backup and Restore History** This page displays the entire history of backups and includes any failed backups, as shown in Figure 7-8. Selecting from the history then starts a process that is the reverse of that of the backup described previously. Select the farm or portion of the farm to restore and continue process to restore.
- **Restore from Backup** Use this page to set the file location of the specific backup needing restoration.
- **Backup and Restore Job Status** This page displays the status page, as shown previously in Figure 7-7.

Data Configuration

The Data Configuration area focuses on areas relating to how SharePoint (and therefore Project Server) interact with the data. Changes in the database server name are also managed in this area.

- **Default Database Server** This page is used when modifying the default database server name in the farm. Usually it requires changes to have been made previously in the Application Management area (discussed in the next section). Its use is not likely to be necessary in most Project Server environments.

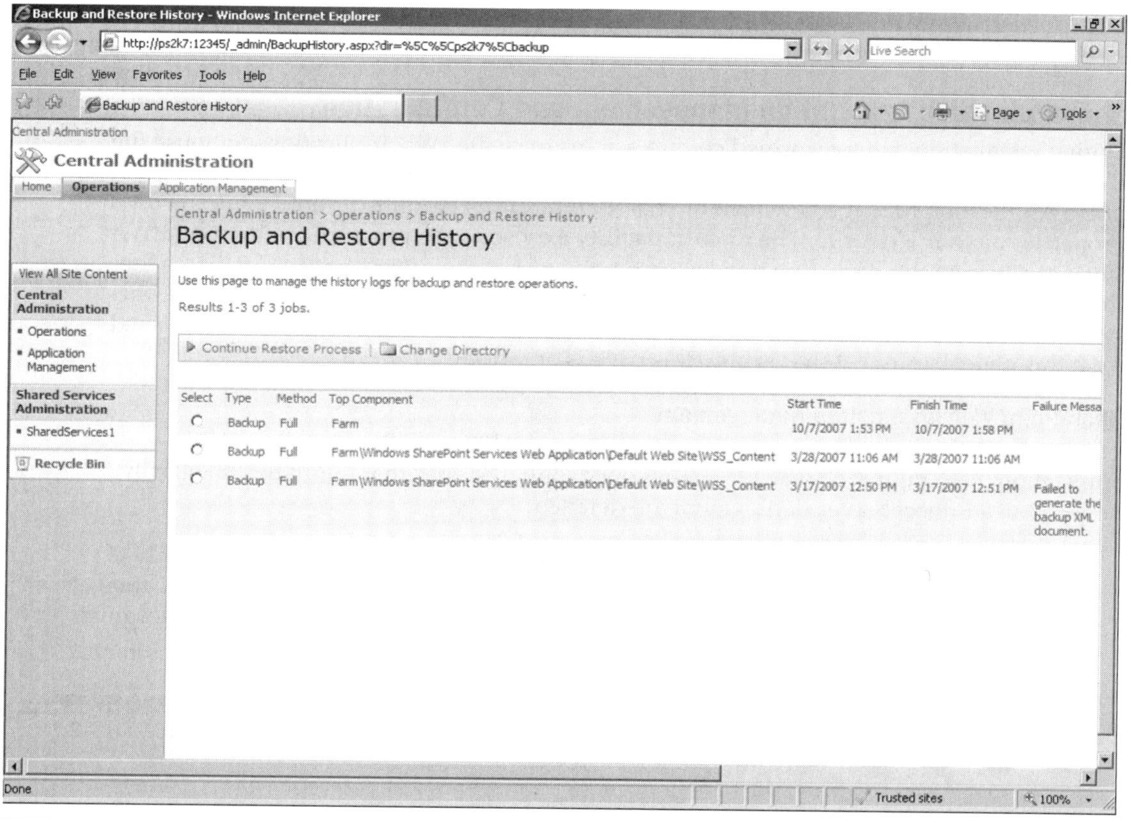

FIGURE 7-8 Backup and Restore History page

- **Data Retrieval Service** This page is used to manage data retrieval services in the farm. Examples of data retrieval services include Windows SharePoint Services and Object Linking and Embedding Database (OLEDB).
- **SOAP Passthrough and XML-URL** It would be rare that a Project Server administrator would ever need to access this feature.

Application Management

The Application Management section of SharePoint Central Administration is where specific modifications can be made to the installed applications and components in your farm. If a component or application is not installed in your farm, then the associated section in Central Administration's Application Management section will not be found.

In this section of Central Administration, you can create new SharePoint Web applications, remove SharePoint from an IIS Web site, Remove Web applications, and define managed paths (that is, URL paths that SharePoint recognizes and that are managed through SharePoint rather than directly through IIS Manager).

Through the Application Management section of SharePoint Central Administration, an administrator can manage individual Web application settings, manage the content databases of a SharePoint site, or manage the features that individual sites have enabled. This section focuses primarily on the aspects of the Application Management section of SharePoint Central Administration that are relevant to Project Server 2007.

SharePoint Web Application Management and Configuration

During installation, you performed certain actions to create Web applications to house the PWA site and the SharedService Provider. In addition, in the SharedService Provider section of the Application Management area of SharePoint Central Administration, you can edit the properties of your PWA site. The main capability exposed when you edit an existing PWA site is to separate the Reporting database from the rest of the Project Server databases for that PWA site. Cues as to when this might be necessary are discussed in Chapter 14. Other tasks, including creating additional PWA sites or deleting PWA sites, can be accomplished from this page. Figure 7-9 shows how this page is organized.

SharePoint Web Application Management

This page area includes links to feature management relating to the SharePoint Web application. Although each feature is mentioned, only the ones that might be realistically accessed in a Project Server deployment are detailed:

- **Create or Extend Web Application** This feature would normally be used only to create an additional SharePoint application. This additional SharePoint application could be used when you are sharing the environment with a non-PWA collaborative space, or when you have a parallel test environment.
- **Remove SharePoint from IIS Web Site** This feature is unlikely to be used.
- **Delete Web Application** This feature is also unlikely to be used.

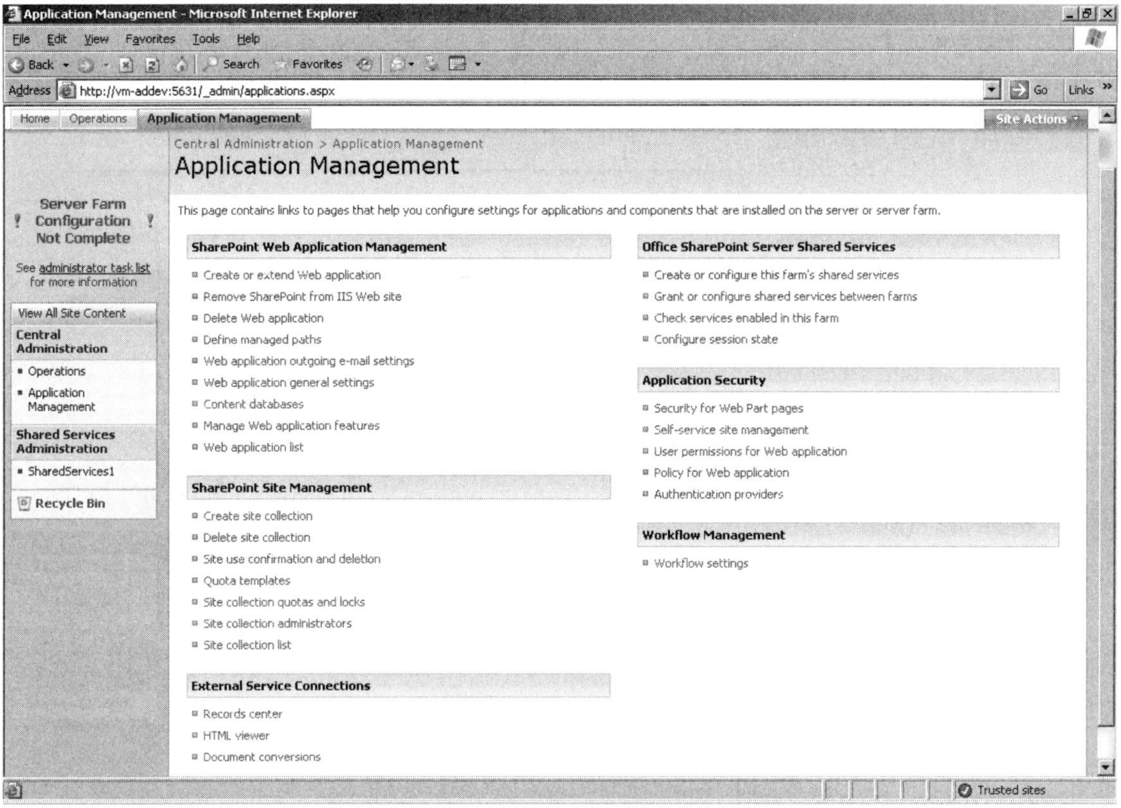

FIGURE 7-9 Application Management page

- **Define Managed Paths** This too is unlikely to be used.
- **Web Application Outgoing E-Mail Settings** This link destination is the same as the one described in the "Operations" section earlier in this chapter.
- **Web Application General Settings** There are several items that you may wish to configure in this area, but typically few of them require changes. Possible candidates for change include the maximum upload size (defaults to 50MB), page security timeout duration (defaults to 30 minutes without activity), and Recycle Bin options.
- **Content Databases** This feature is unlikely to be used.
- **Manage Web Application Features** This feature also is unlikely to be used.
- **Web Application List** This feature is just a list of all the Web applications that have been created. It contains only navigation links.

SharePoint Site Management

There is almost never a need to modify the items in this section, which include the following. They are configured appropriately out of the box in nearly all cases.

- **Create Site Collection** This is another area that would be touched only when you are creating a parallel environment for collaboration, or a second PWA site (such as for testing).
- **Delete Site Collection** This feature is unlikely to be used.
- **Site Use Confirmation and Deletion** This is another feature that is unlikely to be used.
- **Quota Templates** This also is a feature that is unlikely to be used.
- **Site Collection Quotas and Locks** This feature also is unlikely to be used.
- **Site Collection Administrators** Site collections each have a primary and a secondary administrator. You can define or modify these from this page. If more than one site collection has been defined, the tool allows navigation so that you can manage them all.
- **Site Collection List** This page displays information on a single site collection. In an environment with multiple site collections, you can view each by selecting the specific collection from a popup window. To display this window (shown in Figure 7-10), select the Web Application dropdown list from the blue bar in the body of the page.

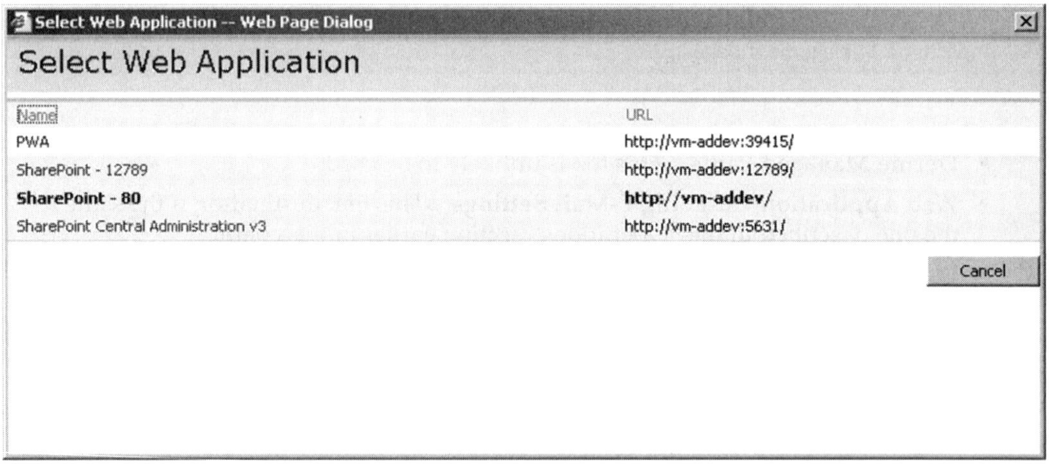

FIGURE 7-10 Select a site collection.

External Service Connections

The External Service Connections links would most likely be used in a document management–focused environment (External Service Connections supports a new SharePoint feature focused on document lifecycle management), and the authors have never seen this feature used for PWA. Therefore, although the components are listed, no detail will be provided here.

- **Records Center** This feature is unlikely to be used.
- **HTML Viewer** This is another feature that is unlikely to be used.
- **Document Conversions** This also is unlikely to be used.

Office SharePoint Shared Services

The Office SharePoint Shared Services area is rarely accessed after installation (once again because its settings are generally set appropriately out of the box) and contains the following items:

- **Create or Configure This Farm's Shared Services** This feature could be used to add new SharedService Providers, something that is rarely required in the base Project Server environment. The ability to create of configure shared services is more likely to come into play if the Microsoft Office SharePoint Server is installed.
- **Grant or Configure Shared Services between Farms** If services are to be shared across multiple farms, this area is where settings are configured. Configuring these settings is unlikely to be necessary if you are not using MOSS.
- **Check Services Enabled in This Farm** These settings are rarely used without MOSS in a PWA environment.
- **Configure Session State** The session state stores specific user information for the user's SharePoint session. The timeout length for the session is set to 60 minutes by default and can be modified here.

Application Security

The Application Security management tools are collected in this page area. They focus on security-related items at the level of the SharePoint application.

- **Security for Web Part Pages** These general settings include those for Web-Part-to-Web-Part connectivity and access to the Online Web Part Gallery. They rarely come into play in a PWA environment.
- **Self-Service Site Management** This feature, which is turned off by default, can be used to enable users with appropriate permissions to create sites and subsites in the PWA/WSS environment. This feature can be useful. For example, a large project might require an extensive, well-planned closure meeting with the project team and the customer. In such a situation, a WSS Meeting Workspace can be a great place to present agendas, associated documents, meeting minutes and notes, and so on.

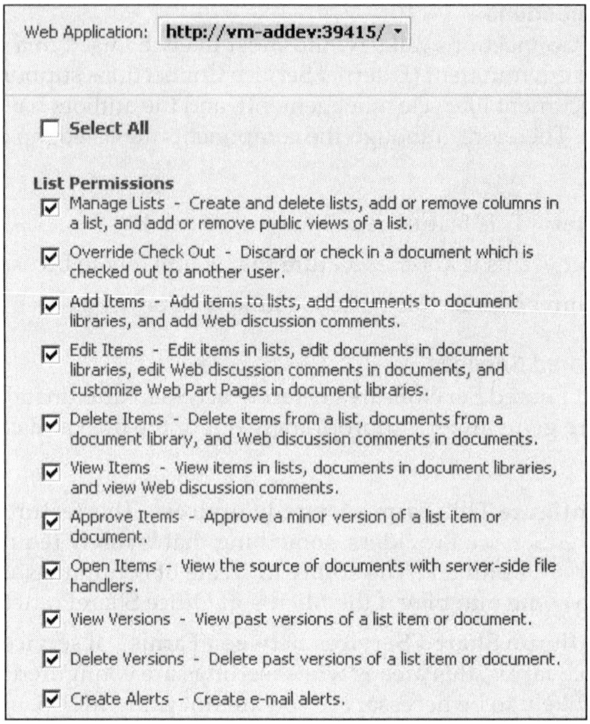

FIGURE 7-11 User Permissions for Web Application Management page (top)

- **User Permissions for Web Application** This page lists all the items where permissions can be granted (see Figures 7-11 to 7-13). It is used to disable permissions on a global level and is rarely modified, as modifications are usually done at a lower level in the system. If you wanted to restrict all users from creating their own customized views, for example, deselecting the checkbox on this page would disable the feature globally.
- **Policy for Web Application** These settings are rarely relevant for PWA.
- **Authentication Providers** This feature is used to manage the types of authentication in play in the environment. Most PWA deployments use Windows authentication. Some may also include forms authentication. For Windows authentication, the default settings are usually adequate. Forms authentication makes sense if nonlocal Windows users are to access the system (by extranet, for example). This area will also come into play if you are deploying PWA in an environment where a Web single sign-on (SSO) system is in place to map SharePoint to the SSO provider.

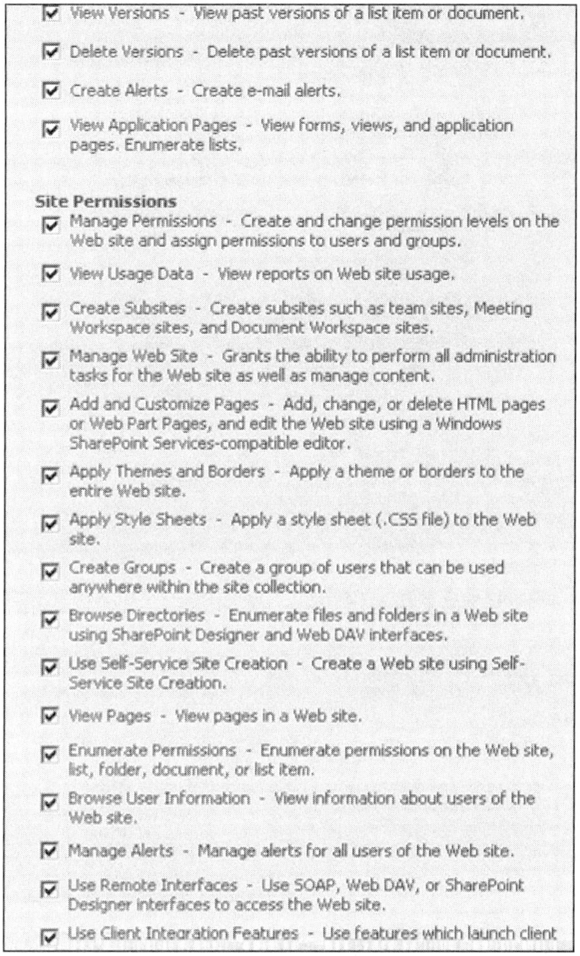

FIGURE 7-12 User Permissions for Web Application Management page (middle)

Shared Services

The Shared Services area of the Central Administration tool is for the management of shared services. In most Project Server environments, there is a single SSP, and after installation, no activity is required. To drill down to the SSP, you usually select SharedServices1.

The Shared Services management item from the Quick Launch Bar is just a link that allows the user to configure a single SSP with the same destination described in the Web application general settings earlier in this chapter in the section "SharePoint Web Application Management," such as maximum upload size and timeout settings.

After you have selected the Shared Services Administration option from the Quick Launch Bar, in most Project Server/WSS environments, the only item inside this area is a link to one or more PWA sites (more in the case of multiple instances). Far more features

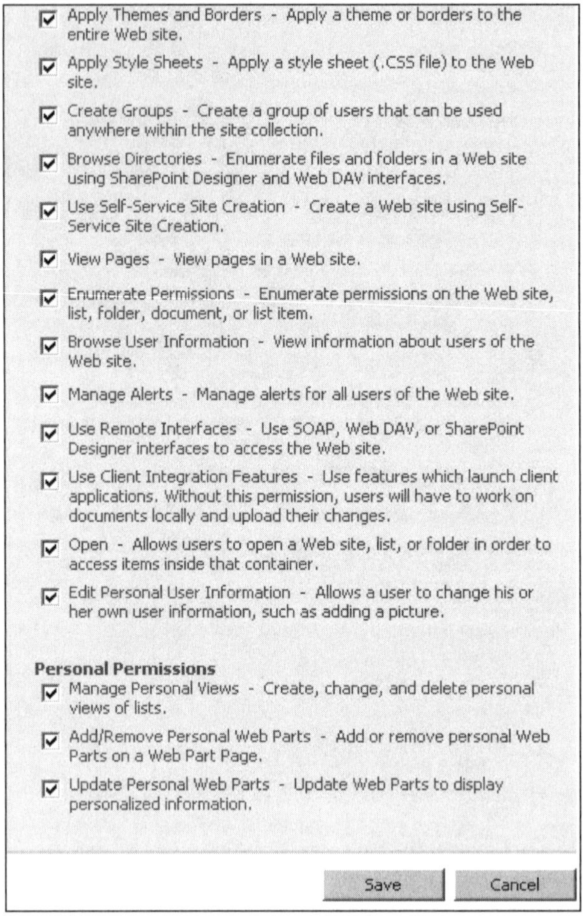

FIGURE 7-13 User Permissions for Web Application Management page (bottom)

appear inside the Shared Services Administration area if you are deploying Project Server in a MOSS environment, but for the base installation of Project Server and WSS, this link is all that the area contains.

The SharePoint Central Administration tools are part of the foundation of a SharePoint/Project Server environment. After initial configuration, minimal administration is required. In addition, most features are ready to use and are set appropriately out of the box. However, critical items reside within the tools, especially the Farm Backup feature.

The SharePoint Central Administration area is not a place for regular users to loiter. As a result, a user must have elevated privileges even to access the site, because misconfiguration of the components of this site can have catastrophic results. For most environments, you configure the items in the SharePoint Central Administration only when installing server products, changing the farm size or structure, or attempting to troubleshoot an infrastructure component of your SharePoint farm.

8

CHAPTER

Configuring Security in Your EPM Environment

Configuring security, like configuring the Enterprise Project Management (EPM) toolset, is much more than just a technology issue. Security is a process that when is made repeatable and unobtrusive becomes a foundation for good habits and safer computing. The problem is that security as a practice is often perceived to have a direct, inverse relationship with convenience. And when this practice is viewed as an impediment to productivity, it is usually avoided. The overall goal is to balance the value of the thing being protected with the resources spent to secure it.

Throughout this chapter, keep in mind the concept of balanced security to refer to the middle ground between these extremes. In this chapter, we'll explain the security concepts that Project Server lives by, and along the way provide examples of how some companies implement security in their EPM environment. We'll categorize this chapter by the context in which the security is applied, working from the high level (including Internet Information Services [IIS], Kerberos, and Secure Sockets Layer [SSL]) and working down to the tactical level of Project Web Access (PWA) permissions (such as explaining why you can't see a particular project).

Balancing Your Security

When securing something, whether it's a bicycle or a building, you must always take a few things into consideration. What happens if the security is breached? Will it matter if a user in the Marketing Department sees a project in the Information Services (IS) department? If someone breaks into your bank vault, is it a problem? The point is that it doesn't make much sense to spend $1,000 on a bike lock to secure a bike worth $30. Likewise, you wouldn't tie a rope around your brand new $1,000 mountain bike and leave it unattended on the rough side of town overnight. The key is to balance the worth of the item that you are protecting with the cost it takes to secure it.

IIS Security

There are several areas of Internet Information Services 6 where you can configure the system for a more secure EPM environment.

Setup

With a little extra planning, coordination with your network administrator, and balancing of your overall security, you can realize an environment that your users will access securely and efficiently.

Application Pools

In the Installation chapter, we set up an environment where the application pools created their individual boundaries of security. We did so by indicating unique accounts under which each of the application pools were to run (for example, the farm administrator is the Windows account that is used as the identity of the SharePoint Central Administration application pool, but was not the identity of the application pool to host the Shared Services Provider). Creating these boundaries helps isolate your Web sites to keep overly ambitious users, hackers, and associated processes contained. It also helps improve server resiliency; if a single application pool hangs, the other applications on the server can continue with their tasks.

TIP *Microsoft has published a great deal of information on different secure farm deployment topologies for Project Server 2007. You can find them at http://technet.microsoft.com/en-us/projectserver.*

User Accounts

During setup, you are tasked with providing Windows accounts for various Windows SharePoint Services (WSS), SQL Server, and Project Server service accounts. We will categorize them by their scope in your EPM environment.

Farm Accounts

The Farm Accounts are crucial to the installation, and continuing functionality of your Project Server instance.

- **SQL Server service account** If your instance of SQL Server is running as a LocalSystem or NetworkService account, you will not need to provide a Windows account for this item. If it is running as a domain account, it is likely maintained by your database administrator (DBA) and is used only during the installation of SQL Server.
- **Server farm account** This account is referred to as the Database Access account because it is the account under which all farm-level communication with SQL Server occurs. It is also the account under which the application pool for SharePoint Central Administration runs, as well as the identity of the WSS Timer Service. This account has a great deal of power in the macro sense, adding servers to the farm, adding or deleting Shared Service Providers (SSPs), or provisioning additional SharePoint sites. This account will also be granted the SQL Server role's of Security Admin and DB Creator for the databases it creates.

- **Setup user account** This account is used to perform the installation steps. This account must be a local administrator on all of the servers involved during setup. The account will automatically have full access to the PWA root site and the SSP site.

SSP Accounts

The Shared Service Provider accounts allow finer granularity of administrative access.

- **SSP application pool security account** As the name implies, this is the account under which the SSP's application pool runs.
- **The SSP service account** This account is used by the SSP Web services for interfarm communication and intra-SSP database communication. In addition, it is the identity of the SSP Timer Service that performs such tasks as Analysis Services cube building. Because it is from the SSP administration pages, this account provisions and deletes individual PWA sites and their databases.

NOTE *Although the accounts referenced so far in this section are powerful at the farm, server, and service level, as far as the PWA site is concerned they are simply users that must be given explicit rights to the PWA instance.*

WSS Accounts

With a much narrower scope of administrative access, the WSS accounts must be defined.

- **WSS application pool account** As the name implies, this is the account under which the WSS site that hosts the Project Web Access site runs.
- **WSS search accounts** There are two accounts that relate to WSS Search: the service account and the content access account. These accounts and the services they provide do not affect core Project Server 2007 features or functionality and can be ignored at this stage.

SSL

Configuring Secure Sockets Layer in IIS 6 affects the communication channel between clients and your Front End Web Server(s). Using encryption for your EPM environment is critical in the following scenarios:

- You've exposed Project Server (or a PWA Front End Web Server) to the Internet and want to give your users access to PWA through Internet Explorer and Project Professional 2007.
- You have implemented forms-based authentication.

To enable SSL on a Front End Web Server, complete the following tasks from its console:

1. Navigate to IIS Manager on your Front End Web Server by clicking Start | Run and entering **inetmgr**.
2. Click the plus sign (+) until you see all of the Web sites on the server.
3. Right-click on the Web site used to host your PWA site(s).
4. On the Directory Security tab, click Server Certificate…

PART III

TIP *If your organization has an established internal public key infrastructure (PKI), the following steps will vary. See your network's security administrator for information about the process that you should use to create a valid certificate for your PWA servers.*

5. Click Next on the Welcome to the Web Server Certificate Wizard.
6. Ensure that Create a New Certificate is enabled and click Next.
7. Ensure that Prepare the Request Now…. is selected and click Next.
8. On the Name and Security Settings page, type a friendly name for this certificate, choose 1024 for the bit length, and click Next.
9. On the Organization Information page, provide your company name as it will be verified by a third party and click Next.

NOTE *Most public certificate authorities check to ensure that you are who you say you are through a Dunn and Bradstreet check or other mechanism. It's the idea of third-party trust that makes the implementation of security certificates work. (For example, if you trust a well-known company such as Thawte, and Thawte trusts the Web server to which you are connecting, then you can have a bit more trust in the Web server.) Luckily, this process usually happens transparently, and we just see a little padlock on the bottom of our browser as we go about our business. Well-known certificate authorities include Verisign and Thawte.*

10. On the Your Site's Common Name page, provide the fully qualified domain name for the site (such as projects.mnemonix.com) and click Next.
11. Provide your geographical information, noting that if you are in the United States, you must spell out your state's full name without abbreviation.
12. For the Certificate Request File name, provide a name and a location where you will be able to find it, ideally leaving it in the .txt format.
13. Verify that your information is correct and click Next.
14. Next traverse to a well-known registrar to begin the process of purchasing your certificate. (Expect to pay anywhere from $450 to $700 for a two-year certificate for your site.) Follow the steps provided by the individual company to complete the process.

Application Pools

IIS 6 brought the concept of application pools into mainstream use within the Microsoft Web Server. Among the benefits that they bring to the security landscape is the ability to isolate processes and Web sites to the confines of the application pool, essentially creating a boundary between one application and others running on the server. This isolation allows for the remaining sites and associated application pools on the server to continue running even if one application pool hangs or crashes. When installing Microsoft Office Project Server 2007, you really only need to worry about three Web sites and four application pools:

- The site and application pool for SharePoint Central Administration
- The site and application pool that contains the Shared Services Provider

- The application pool for the Shared Services Provider (named SharedServices1 by default)
- The site and application pool for the site to host your PWA sites, typically the default Web site

Now there is a fourth Web site and fifth application pool: the Office Server Web Services Web site. This site is created when the Project Application Service is started from WSS Central Administration. This site is used as a communication channel among Web servers and application servers, as well as a common location for Web services that are installed when Microsoft Office Server products coexist on the same server. It uses a preinstalled SSL certificate to secure communications with this site. For example, if Microsoft Office SharePoint Server (MOSS) is installed, the Excel Calculation services, the Document Conversion services, and the SharePoint Search service reside here. When Project Server is installed, the Project Application Service resides in this location as well.

NTLM and Kerberos Authentication

There are two main forms of communication security as they relate to the IIS components of a Project Server 2007 environment: New Technology LAN Manager (NTLM) and Kerberos. Kerberos is an authentication protocol initially developed at the Massachusetts Institute of Technology (MIT). It uses encryption and a trusted third party to provide secure authentication. Kerberos employs a cryptographic ticket-granting process to avoid transmitting passwords over the wire in plain text. Kerberos features, such as delegation, help provide secure, transparent access to services in a distributed server networking architecture. Although Kerberos is a more secure and capable authentication protocol, you may find that NTLM is the ideal authentication protocol for your EPM environment.

Times That You Might Favor NTLM Authentication

NTLM authentication is often selected. Typically, NTLM is selected for one or more of the following reasons:

- You have a single-server environment.
- You want no additional setup steps.
- You do not have an existing Kerberos PKI infrastructure in place.

In contrast, times that you might favor Kerberos authentication include the following:

- Security is a top concern.
- Having secure, transparent authentication to distributed server infrastructure is critical.
- Use of "multiple hops" is required in the SharePoint environment; for example, if there is data in a "back-end" system that is imported into an Excel Calculation Services spreadsheet for formatting and then is displayed in a Web Part. Any two-hop solution that uses .NET requires Kerberos.

The primary issue that must be resolved when configuring Kerberos authentication is the creation of a service principal name (SPN) for the account under which the WSS site's application pool will run. This is done by using the `setspn` utility, which is part of the

Windows Server 2003 SP1 support tools. Instructions for enabling Kerberos authentication for a WSS site can be found in the Microsoft Knowledgebase (KB) article found at http://support.microsoft.com/?kbid=832769.

TIP *For most installations, you should choose NTLM authentication. Note that if you do specify Kerberos authentication and do not configure an SPN, only server administrators will be able to authenticate to the IIS site where your Project Web Access site resides.*

Project Server 2007 Permissions

Having looked at some components of the operating system and IIS 6, you are now entering the realm where WSS and Project Server security come into play. We'll assume that you are at the point where you have just installed Project Server and provisioned your PWA site. The account that was specified as the PWA administrator during PWA site provisioning is the only user who can access your PWA site.

NOTE *Project Server requires that users be specifically named. Thus a user who happens to be a local administrator of a Project Server machine must be given permission to enter the PWA site.*

PWA Security Fundamentals

Although the security model for Project Server is extremely robust and can provide intricate and extremely sophisticated access rules, the best advice for new PWA implementers and administrators is to keep your configuration simple. While the permissions model in Project Server 2007 has not changed dramatically from that in Project Server 2003, there are fundamental elements of PWA security that warrant review.

Principals

No, this doesn't refer to the school administrators who thwarted your greatest, most evil plans or the "dignity" that you claimed to have in high school. Rather, a principal in the realm of Project Server refers to users or groups. You are a principal. The Resource Managers group is a principal. Principals have permissions granted to them directly through their global permissions. You can modify what actions are available to all users of the PWA site through the Project Web Access Permissions link in the Security section of the Server Settings page. You can modify individual principals' global permissions from the properties of a user in the Manage Users page (which is not recommended), and you can modify a group's global permissions from the properties of the group from the Manage Groups page (which is recommended).

Objects and Categories

An *object* is a resource, a project, or a view. Think of them as things on which a principal can perform an action (permission). *Categories* are groups of objects. You define which objects comprise a category (for example, resources beneath the viewer in the RBS (Resource Breakdown Structure), all projects in Project Server, and so on) through the category's properties from the Manage Categories page.

Permissions

Permissions are the act that can be performed. "Manage Notifications and Reminders" is a permission, as is "Build Team on Project." It is the act that can be performed. Who performs the act is determined by the group or user. Who or what the act can be performed on is determined by the category.

Manage Users

There are three primary ways to give users access to PWA: by using the Resource Center, by using the Manage Users portion of the Server Settings page, or by having Project Server synchronize with groups in your Active Directory. This section focuses on the Manage Users function. Although these are the primary ways to grant access, you may find that your organization requires additional functionality, such as having an external interface to activate or deactivate users.

On the Server Settings page, click on Manage Users under the Security section. From the Manage Users page, shown in Figure 8-1, you have three options: Create a New User, Modify an Existing User (click on the User's name), and Deactivate a User. You can also see the users' e-mail addresses and logon accounts, their position in the RBS, whether they are active or inactive, and when they last connected to PWA or used Project Professional to connect to PWA. When creating or modifying a user, you will have a number of options to set from within the user's properties.

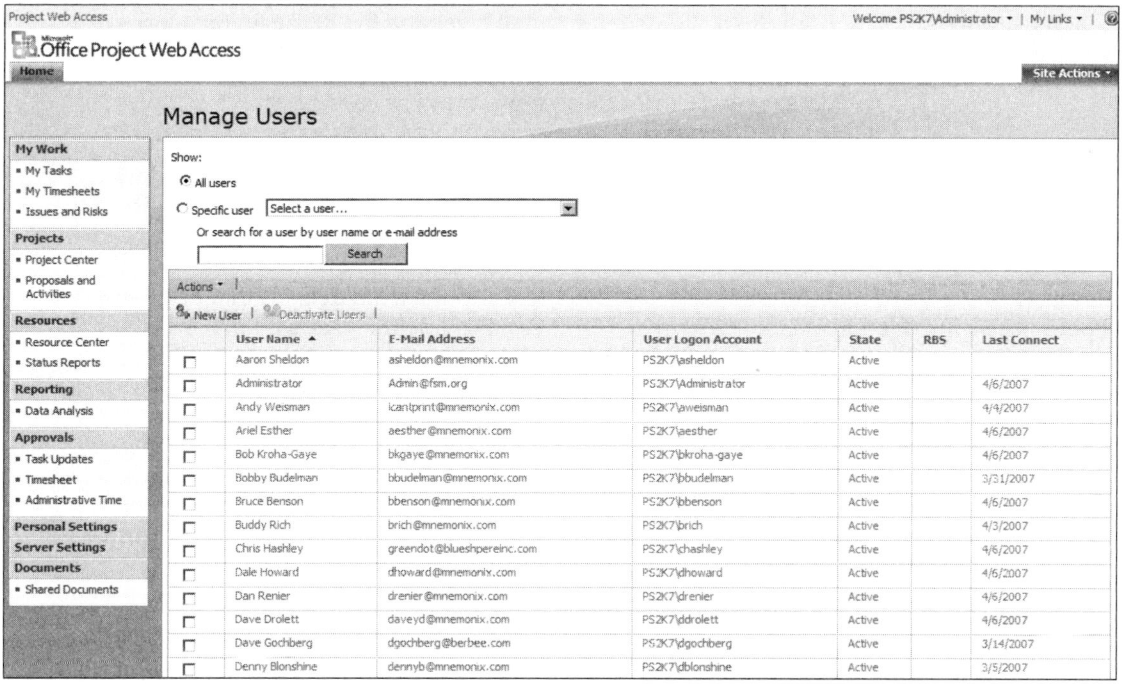

FIGURE 8-1 The Manage Users page

Recommendation for Project Server Beginners

Because Project Server has several security entities (such as users, categories, and groups), it is recommended that you use a model where a new user is simply added to a group or groups. The group members are assigned the group's global permissions, as well as permissions on a category (of projects, resources, and views). If this is your first exposure to PWA and its security concepts, you should consider implementing a scenario where you have a one-to-one relationship between PWA groups and categories. This achieves three important goals during your initial proof of concept or pilot:

- It simplifies your security model so you can use the Active Directory synchronization to its fullest extent.
- It reduces the amount of time it takes to create a new user manually because you might only need to provide authentication, Enterprise field, and PWA group membership. This scenario bypasses the specification of the individual user's category permissions and global permissions.
- As you become familiar with the toolset, such a model will help you reduce the variables of multiple category permissions when troubleshooting issues related to an individual user's access.

The View Effective Rights tool for Project Server 2003 helped you troubleshoot the effective rights of users. This tool helped an administrator better understand overall user access by pinpointing the specific permissions that are affecting the projects, resources, and features that a user can access. It is rumored that a version for 2007 is in the works.

Identification Information

If you were to select the name of a User from the Manage Users page, the first item listed when the next page appears is User Can Be Assigned as a Resource, which is a new capability within Project Server 2007. It toggles automatically when changing a user from inactive to active. One case where this setting may be of use is when a manager or executive has mistakenly become part of the enterprise resource pool and the team decides that he or she should not be included in a list of enterprise resources. Provide the user's display name, e-mail address, location in the RBS, initials, hyperlink information for the team Web site, and whether they are an active PWA user or not. Figure 8-1 displays these fields.

User Authentication

If you have forms authentication configured in this environment, make the selection and provide the username in the format *MembershipProvider:UserAccount*. If you are using Windows authentication, provide the username in the format *DOMAIN\Username*. (Note that the format is critical for forms authentication to function properly.)

TIP *Unlike previous versions of Project Server, authentication information and encrypted passwords are no longer stored in the Project Server database. Authentication relies on the standard authentication mechanism provided by ASP.NET 2.0 and WSS. Although configuring forms authentication in WSS is beyond the scope of this book, there is a wealth of information regarding its creation, configuration, and maintenance. Refer to http://technet.microsoft.com/en-us/projectserver for a detailed walkthrough to enable this feature.*

Assignment Attributes

The Assignment Attributes section defines how a particular resource can be used as a resource in your EPM environment. Items in this section include whether the Enterprise resource can be leveled or not, the user's base calendar (which is not the same thing as a resource calendar), and their default booking type. The default booking type defines whether the resource is committed (assignments take away the resource's availability and the user is notified) or proposed (the resource is used for planning purposes, without committing the resource nor providing notification about the assignment). Here you specify the user's timesheet manager and default assignment owner. The user's earliest and latest available dates would be modified if the user were on a fixed-length contract, or if the resource had recently won the lottery and would not be available for their assigned tasks after a certain point in time.

Resource Custom Fields

If you have defined enterprise resource custom fields, you have the ability to set or modify them here. Examples of resource custom fields are Resource Location and Resource Role. There is much more on custom fields in Chapter 9.

Security Groups

By default, Project Server provides eight security groups from which you can choose. Select the group to which the user belongs and then click the minus sign (–) next to Security Categories and the minus sign next to Global Permissions to collapse both of these sections

The Timesheet Manager and Default Assignment Owner

The timesheet manager is a new concept in Project Server 2007. Whereas in previous versions the information associated with the timesheet manager was derived from the RBS, now it is set at the user level. The timesheet manager is typically set to the resource's functional manager, or the person who ensures that the resource comes to work every day, approves their vacation, and gives the resource an occasional managerial pat on the back (optional). By default, the user will be set as his or her own timesheet manager. This implies that there is self-approval (no approval process) for their timesheets and associated administrative time. The default assignment owner is a resource who is responsible for entering the progress information. So if the user is a subcontractor who does not have access to PWA, another user could be identified to be responsible for relaying the progress information back to the project manager.

without modifying them. That's right, ignore the Security Categories and User's Global Permissions for now and skip down to the "Group Fields" section.

Security Categories

Ignore this field.

Global Permissions

Ignore this field.

Group Fields

If you have created codes for grouping and cost categorization of resources, type their group, code, and cost center in the available text boxes. Cost Type, a predefined enterprise resource field, can be selected from a list if you have specified values for it in the Cost Type lookup table in the Enterprise Fields (details in Chapter 9) section of the Administration pages.

Team Details

If you have identified a lookup table that is to be associated with your team enterprise field, you can assign this resource to a team resource pool. One example of a situation in which this capability is useful is when you have a team of users who can complete a task and you want the first available member to complete it. The project manager would assign the team

Securing the Individual User

You may be clearing your throat to prepare for your best Desi Arnaz impersonation: "Lucy, you got some 'splainin' to do!" So let's start with a broad statement. Barring any extreme situations, you should not modify an individual user's global permissions or permissions that the individual has on a category (security categories). By obeying this rule, you will avoid many of the headaches that the Project Server security model can inflict upon you. The reasoning is that because your users are added to groups, those groups already have category permissions and global permission applied to them. You should usually not apply global permissions, category permissions, or a security template for either global or category permissions, to the user individually. If you need to change a user's access, you can always add the user to (or remove them from) additional groups. Of course, as soon as you finish reading this paragraph, you will be summoned to a meeting where a single person in your organization will require such unique access to your environment that it will force you to modify the user's access individually, resulting in a higher level of security complexity in your EPM environment. In this case, investigate whether others in the organization have these unique security needs.

Global Permissions, Categories, and Category Permissions

The relationship between global permissions and category permissions is one of the most challenging concepts to grasp within the EPM environment. The problem is that it is one of the most important concepts for you, as an administrator, to understand. Begin by thinking of the group global permissions as determining what overall functions (which are commonly associated with the ability to create new things) you or your group can do. The category permissions determine what the user or group can do to the category's objects (which are commonly associated with ability to view or modify existing things). The global permissions for groups are identical to the user global permissions in action and similar to the PWA permissions, except these permissions are applied only to members of the specified group and have no capacity to be contextually sensitive (unlike category permissions, which are contextually sensitive).

resource to the task in the project. The task is available when the resource selects Self Assign Team Tasks from his or her My Tasks page.

System Identification Data

In the System Identification Data section, you will find relevant information about the user's account. These items include creation date, modified date, checked-out date, and the user to whom the user checked out the item. The section also presents a field for users' external ID. If you are integrating your users' accounts with external applications, you can use this field to link the users to an ID in the remote application. You can also use this field to extend your reporting capabilities for an external reporting service.

PWA Permissions

For your users to have been granted access to the PWA site, you would have either added a resource through the Resource Center, added the user through the Manage Users page (described in the previous section), or synchronized with an Active Directory group. The Project Web Access Permissions page is where the administrator determines what actions can be performed throughout the entire PWA site. The settings on this page differ from other pages where global permissions are applied in that, on the Project Web Access Permissions page, the only checkbox next to each item is labeled Enable to indicate whether the feature or action is available or not. These permissions are divided into categories of usage.

Many of the settings on this page determine whether or not the associated link appears in the Server Settings page or associated PWA pages. If you notice a grayed-out button while using PWA, it may indicate that the setting has been disabled through this page or has been disallowed or denied to you.

As these permissions are described, we'll note whether they are shared among the three types of permissions in PWA. The first is global permissions (*global*), meaning that they are found in the Global Permissions section of both the properties of an individual user and in the properties of a Project Server group. Category permissions (*category*) refer to the permissions that are contextually sensitive and are applied on the object defined in an associated category. PWA permissions (*PWA*) refer to the permissions that affect the overall capabilities of the entire PWA site.

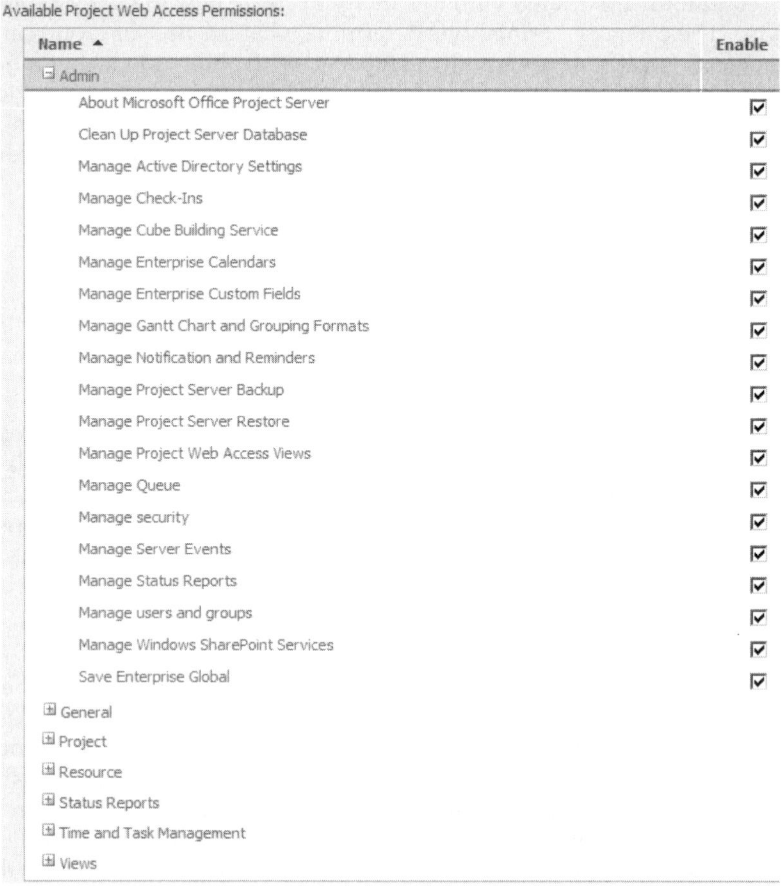

Admin: About Microsoft Office Project Server (Global, PWA)

This setting gives an administrator the ability to check how many Active Project Server users and how many Project Professional users have been associated with this PWA instance. This may be helpful in determining your licensing of PWA and Project Professional users. Disabling this setting will remove the link "About Project Server" from the Enterprise Data Section of the Server Settings page.

Admin: Clean Up Project Server Database (Global, PWA)

Disabling this permission removes the Delete Enterprise Objects link from the Database Administration section of the Server Settings page. (More information on database administration can be found in Chapter 12.)

Admin: Manage Active Directory Settings (Global, PWA)

This setting removes the Active Directory Resource Pool Synchronization link from the Organizational Policies section of the Server Settings page. It also removes the Active Directory Group to Synchronize settings in each group's properties.

Admin: Manage Check-Ins (Global, PWA)

This setting removes the Force Check-in Enterprise Objects link from the Database Administration section of the Server Settings page. (More information on database administration can be found in Chapter 12.)

Admin: Manage Cube Building Service (Global, PWA)

This setting removes the entire cube section of the Server Settings page. (More information on the Analysis Services cubes and the associated Data Analysis views can be found in Chapter 12.)

Admin: Manage Enterprise Calendars (Global, PWA)

This setting removes the Enterprise Calendars link from the Enterprise Data section of the Server Settings page. (More information can be found in Chapter 9.)

Admin: Manage Enterprise Custom Fields (Global, PWA)

This setting removes the Enterprise Custom Field Definition link from the Enterprise Data section of the Server Settings page. (More information can be found in Chapter 9.)

Admin: Manage Gantt Chart and Grouping Formats (Global, PWA)

This setting removes the Grouping Formats and Gantt Chart Formats links from the Look and Feel section of the Server Settings page.

Admin: Manage Notifications and Reminders (Global, PWA)

This setting removes the Alerts and Reminders link from the Operational Policies section of the Server Settings page.

TIP *Although unchecking this setting removes the link to manage the Alerts and Reminders, it will not enable or disable the alert and reminder functionality or settings you might have made previously. Disabling this setting after configuring your mail server settings is a good way to reduce the clutter of the Server Settings page and can potentially help avoid an unintentional misconfiguration.*

Admin: Manage Project Server Backup (Global, PWA)

This setting removes the Schedule Backup and Administrative Backup options from the Database Administration section of the Server Settings page. It does not enable or disable the backup schedules that you may have already set; rather, it disallows you from managing them. (More information on Database Administration can be found in Chapter 12.)

Admin: Manage Project Server Restore (Global, PWA)
This setting removes the Administrative Restore link from the Database Administration section of the Server Settings page. (More information on Database Administration can be found in Chapter 12.)

Admin: Manage Project Web Access Views (Global, PWA)
This setting removes the Manage Views link under the Look and Feel section of the Server Settings page. This setting has no effect on the actual views, but simply enables you to modify, add, or remove them.

Admin: Manage Queue (Global, PWA)
This setting removes the entire Queue section, including the Manage Queue and Queue Settings links from the Server Settings page.

Admin: Manage Security (Global, PWA)
This setting, although oddly named, removes the Manage Categories and Security Templates links in the Security section of the Server Settings page. This setting does not restrict the ability to change the permissions that your groups have on categories; rather, it restricts you from defining new categories or modifying existing ones.

Admin: Manage Server Configuration (Global)
This setting is intended for administrator access, and allows custom menu creation, and the enabling/disabling of enterprise features.

Admin: Manage Server Events (Global, PWA)
This setting removes the Server-Side Event Handler Configuration link from the Operational Policies section of the Server Settings page. (More information about the Operational Policies section can be found in Chapter 12.)

Admin: Manage Status Reports (Global, PWA)
In the current version of Project Server 2007, this checkbox does not appear to have any effect. There likely will be a hotfix or Service Pack that resolves this issue by the time this book is published.

Admin: Manage Users and Groups (Global, PWA)
Disabling this setting removes the Manage Users and Manage Groups links from the Security section of the Server Settings page. It also removes the Identification Information section from the Resource Properties in Resource Center. This setting does not affect any of your Active Directory synchronization settings.

Admin: Manage Windows SharePoint Services (Global, PWA)
This setting removes the Project Workspaces and Project Workspace Provisioning Settings links from the Operational Policies section of the Server Settings page. Enabling or disabling this setting has no effect on existing workspaces or the ability to provision them.

Admin: Save Enterprise Global (Global, PWA)
This setting removes the Enterprise Global link from the Enterprise Data section of the Server Settings page. This setting also prevents any user, including an administrator, from editing the Enterprise Global from within Project Professional 2007.

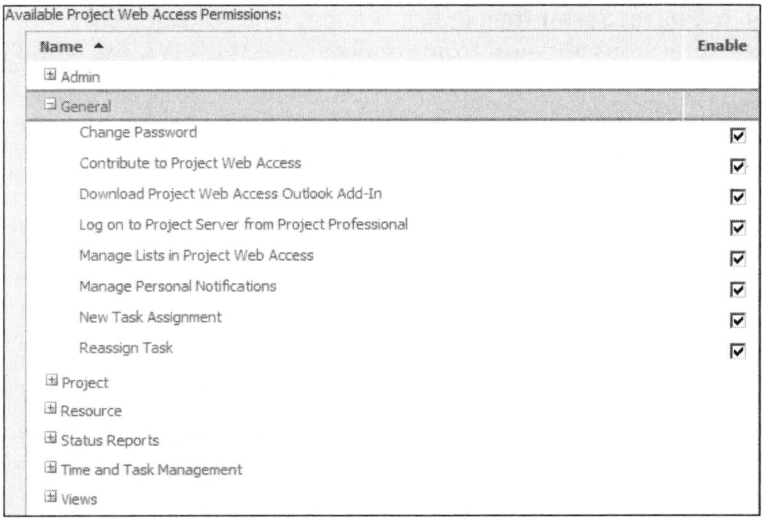

General: Change Password (Global, PWA)

This setting allows users to change their forms-authenticated user account password from PWA. If you have implemented forms-based authentication, you must check with the person who set it up to ensure that this setting is allowed.

General: Contribute to Project Web Access (Global, PWA)

Disabling this setting prevents users from editing items within lists in the PWA WSS site.

General: Download Project Web Access Outlook Add-In (Global, PWA)

Disabling this setting grays out the Set up Outlook Sync link within the My Tasks page. Although this link may not be grayed out from the timesheet, clicking the link takes you to an error page indicating that you do not have sufficient permissions. Disabling this item will have no effect on users who have downloaded the Outlook add-in. This setting is checked if your organization requires that the add-in be deployed through another mechanism.

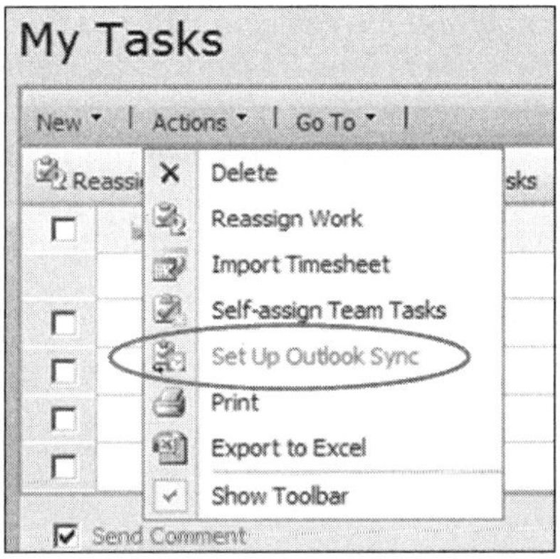

General: Logon to Project Server from Project Professional (Global, PWA)

Disabling this setting stops any user from connecting to this PWA site with Project Professional 2007.

General: Logon (Global)

This permission resides only in the user or group's global permissions. Disabling this permission on the user or group would prevent it from authenticating in any manner to PWA. This setting is not available from PWA permissions, because disabling it would prevent any user, including the administrator, from logging on.

General: Manage Lists in Project Web Access (Global, PWA)

This setting enables users to create, modify, and delete lists within the Project Workspaces in WSS. It is used when synchronizing (either manually or automatically) users with the Project Workspaces.

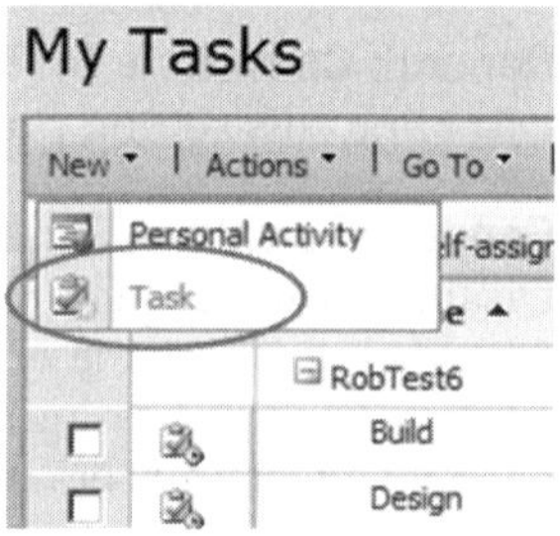

General: Manage Personal Notifications (Global, PWA)

Disabling this setting removes the Manage My Alerts and Reminders link from the Personal Settings page, found on the Quick Launch Bar on the PWA Home Page.

General: New Task Assignment (Global, PWA)

Disabling this setting grays out the New Task option through all users' My Tasks page.

TIP *Reassigning work can be an important piece of your EPM puzzle. If your project managers are managing extremely large projects where team leaders are managing their portions of work, you may gain efficiency by having the project manager assign tasks directly to the team leader. The team leader then reassigns the tasks to the individuals who are actually completing the work. Although this potentially adds another layer of task approval, you may find that it simplifies resource allocation and reduces the load on the project manager for large projects.*

General: Reassign Task (Global, PWA)

Disabling this permission grays out the Reassign Work option from the Actions menu on all users' My Task page.

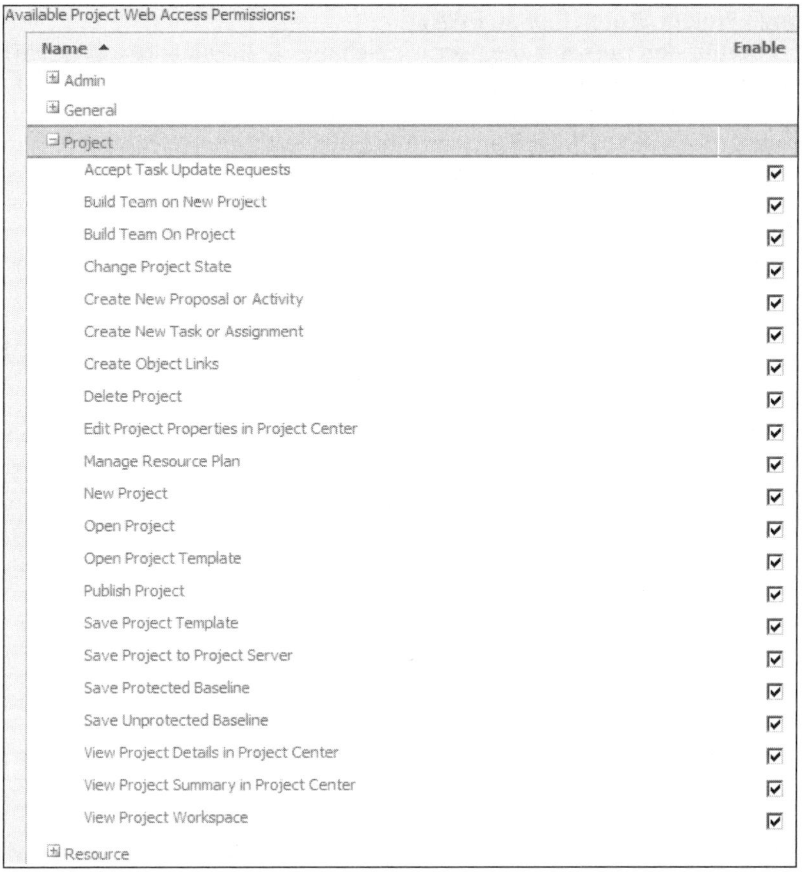

Project: Accept Task Update Requests (Category, PWA)

Allows a user to accept updates on projects without that user having the Save Project permission.

Project: Build Team on New Project (Global, PWA)

Disabling this permission prevents anyone from using the Build Team from Enterprise functionality in Project Professional 2007. This does not, however, prevent a user with the appropriate permissions (Assign Resources and View Enterprise Resource Data) from performing the Build Team function from the Project Center on an existing project.

Project: Build Team on Project (Category, PWA)

Disabling this permission from the PWA Permissions page prevents anyone from using the Build Team functionality on an existing project through Project Center or Project Professional 2007. An existing project is classified as a project that has been saved and published to Project Server. When the permission is set on the category to which the user or group has access, it determines whether the user or group member can perform the Build Team function on the category object (in this case, Project).

Project: Change Project State (Global, PWA)

Disabling this permission prevents the user from changing the state of a project (Proposed, Approved, or Rejected) manually from PWA. If the Project State section of the Additional Server Settings page is set to Yes, then the field is rendered read-only as it will rely on an external workflow process (powered by MOSS or a custom built workflow) to control it. See Chapter 12 for more information about the Operational Policies section of the Server Settings page.

Project: Create New Proposal or Activity (Global, PWA)

When this permission is disabled, clicking the Proposals and Activities link in the Quick Launch Bar of the PWA Home Page raises an error.

TIP *When the built-in security trimming of Windows SharePoint Services does not take effect on a feature that you want to remove from the home page, you can always modify the Quick Launch Bar by clicking the Quick Launch link from the Look and Feel section of the Server Settings page, as shown in Figure 8-2.*

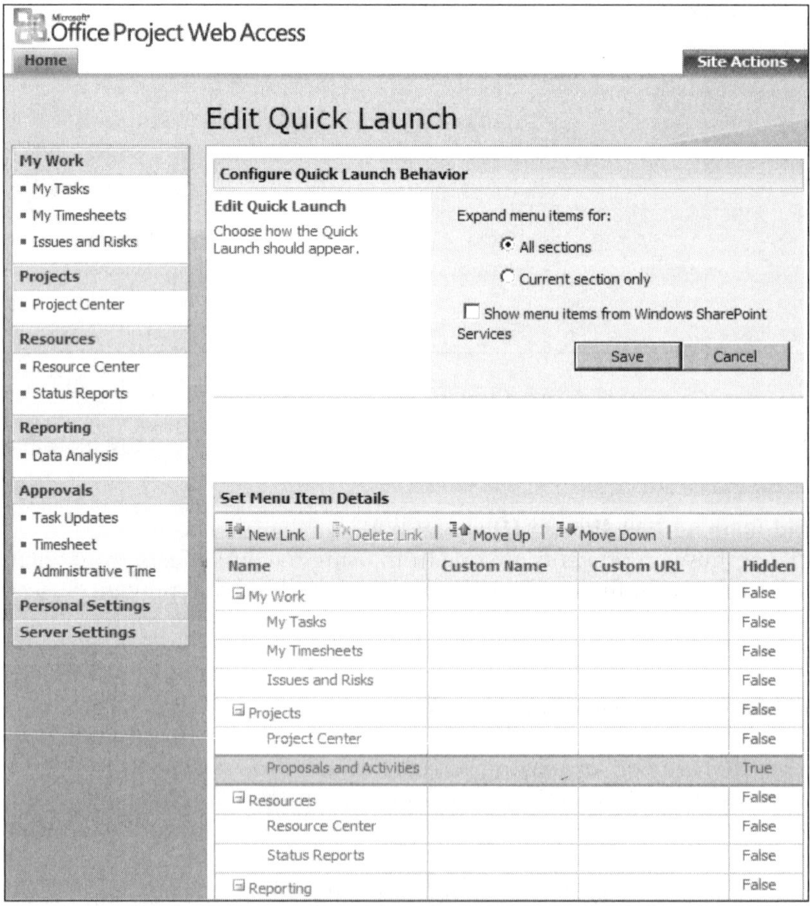

FIGURE 8-2 Editing the Quick Launch Bar

Project: Create New Task or Assignment (Category, PWA)

If this feature is disabled from the PWA Permissions page, users will be unable to create any new tasks via PWA. When the permission is set on the category to which the user or group has access, it determines whether the user or group member can create a new task or assignment in the category object (in this case, Project).

Project: Create Object Links (Category, PWA)

Disabling this setting from the Project Web Access Permissions page prevents users from Linking their tasks with Documents, Issues, or Risks. When the permission is set on the Category which the User or Group has access to, it determines whether the User or Group member can Create Object Links in the Category Object (in this case, Project).

Project: Delete Project (Category, PWA)

Disabling this setting from the PWA Permissions Page prevents Project Professional users from deleting projects in the instance of Project Server. This includes attempts to delete projects from within the Project Professional Open Project dialog box. When the permission is set on the category to which the user or group has access, it determines whether the user or group member can delete the category object (in this case, Project).

Project: Edit Project Properties in Project Center (Category, PWA)

Disabling this permission from PWA Permissions prevents users from modifying the project name, project owner, and project custom fields by raising an error message when users select a project and then click the Edit Project Properties button from within Project Center. When the permission is set on the category to which the user or group has access, it determines whether the user or group member can edit the project properties the category object (in this case, Project) from within Project Center.

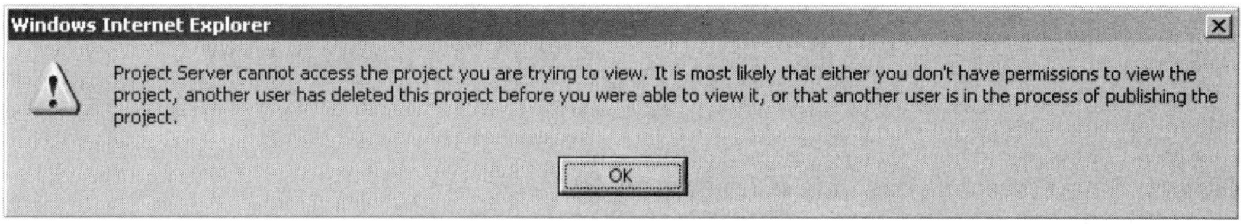

Project: Manage Resource Plan (Category, PWA)

Disabling this setting prevents users from creating or editing a resource plan. If they attempt to do so, they receive an error message indicating that they do not have sufficient permissions to check out or update the resource plan. When the permission is set on the category to which the user or group has access, it determines whether the user or group member can manage the category object (in this case, Resource Plan).

Project: New Project (Global, PWA)

Disabling this setting prevents users from adding a new project using Project Professional 2007, using the Import Projects Wizard, or adding a project through the Project Server interface.

Project: Open Project (Category, PWA)
Disabling this permission from the PWA Permissions page prevents all users from opening a project that is stored in Project Server through Project Professional 2007. Disabling this permission also prevents users from opening a project in Project Professional by clicking the link from Project Center. When the permission is set on the category to which the user or group has access, it determines whether the user or group member can open the category object (in this case, Project) with Project Professional 2007.

Project: Open Project Template (Global, PWA)
Disabling this permission prevents users in your organization from opening enterprise templates that are stored in your Project Server instance. (Disabling this permission removes the Enterprise Templates tab from the Template Selection dialog box within Project Professional.) When the permission is set on the user or group, it determines whether the user or group member can open an enterprise project template.

Project: Publish Project (Category, PWA)
Disabling this permission from the PWA Permissions page prevents all users from publishing projects through Project Professional or publishing projects and proposals through PWA. When the permission is set on the category to which the user or group has access, it determines whether the user or group member can publish the category object (in this case, Project or Proposal).

Project: Save Project Template (Global, PWA)
Disabling this permission disables the user from saving enterprise templates in the PWA instance.

Project: Save Project to Project Server (Category, PWA)
Disabling this permission from the PWA Permissions page prevents all users from saving projects to Project Server. When the permission is set on the category to which the user or group has access, it determines whether the user or group member can save the category object (in this case, Project).

Project: Save Protected Baseline (Category, PWA)
Disabling this permission in the PWA Permissions page prevents all Project Professional users from saving or clearing baselines 0 through 5. When the permission is set on the category to which the user or group has access, it determines whether the user or group member can save or clear baselines 0 through 5 on the category object (in this case, Project) using Project Professional 2007.

Project: Save Unprotected Baseline (Global, PWA)
Disabling this permission prevents Project Professional users from saving or clearing baselines 6 through 10.

Project: View Project Details in Project Center (Category, PWA)
Disabling this permission from the PWA Permissions page prevents users from seeing the project information for a specific project through either Project Professional or PWA. When the permission is set on the category to which the user or group has access,

it determines whether the user or group member can view the project details of the category object (in this case, Project) from Project Center.

Project: View Project Summary in Project Center (Category, PWA)

Disabling this permission from the PWA Permissions page prevents all users from viewing project summaries in the Project Center. It is highly recommended not to disable this permission. When the permission is set on the category to which the user or group has access, it determines whether the user or group member can view the category object (in this case, Project) summary in Project Center.

Project: View Project Workspace (Category, PWA)

Disabling this permission from the PWA Permission page prevents users from viewing projects' workspaces where associated documents, issues, and risks are tracked and stored. When the permission is set on the category to which the user or group has access, it determines whether the user or group member can view the category object's (in this case, Project's) WSS workspace.

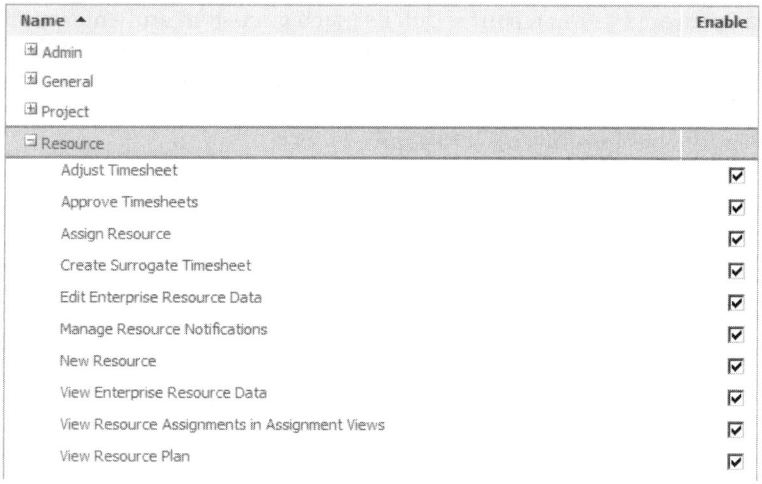

Resource: Adjust Timesheet (Category, PWA)

Disabling this permission from the PWA Permissions page prevents all PWA users from modifying any team members' submitted timesheets. When the permission is set on the category to which the user or group has access, it determines whether the user or group member can adjust the category object's (in this case, Resource's) timesheet.

Resource: Approve Timesheet (Category, PWA)

Disabling this permission prevents any user (typically the timesheet approver) from approving a team member's submitted timesheet. When the permission is set on the category to which the user or group has access, it determines whether the user or group member can approve the category object's (in this case, Resource's) timesheet.

Resource: Assign Resource (Category, PWA)

Disabling this permission from the PWA Permissions page prevents any resources from being assigned to tasks in your instance of PWA. Because assigning resources is a fundamental function of Project Server 2007, If you disable this PWA permission, you should consider throwing away the calculator that sits on your desk, quitting your job, and moving to a resort area high in the mountains to get a job as a snow cat driver. When the permission is set on the category to which the user or group has access, it determines whether the user or group member can assign the category object (in this case, Resource) to a task.

Resource: Create Surrogate Timesheet (Category, PWA)

Disabling this permission from the PWA Permissions page prevents users from creating and filling out timesheets for other users. When the permission is set on the category to which the user or group has access, it determines whether the user or group member can create the category object's (in this case, Resource's) surrogate timesheet.

Resource: Edit Enterprise Resource Data (Category, PWA)

Disabling this permission from the PWA Permissions page prevents project managers and resource managers from editing resource details (such as custom and enterprise field data) either from the Resource Center in PWA or through opening the Enterprise Resource Pool through Project Professional. When the permission is set on the category to which the user or group has access, it determines whether the user or group member can edit the enterprise data of the category object (in this case, Resource).

Resource: Manage Resource Notifications (Global, PWA)

Disabling this permission prevents users (typically project managers and resource managers) from changing how their resources are notified about their project tasks.

Resource: New Resource (Global, PWA)

Disabling this permission prevents nonadministrators (project managers or resource managers) from adding new resources to the Enterprise Resource Pool from either Project Professional or the Resource Center. This does not prevent Active Directory synchronization.

Resource: View Enterprise Resource Data (Category, PWA)

Disabling this permission from the PWA Permissions page prevents all users from viewing resource details by clicking the resource's name and selecting Edit Details from within Resource Center. When the permission is set on the category to which the user or group has access, it determines whether the user or group member can view the category object's (in this case, Resource's) enterprise data.

Resource: View Resource Assignments in Assignment Views (Category, PWA)

Disabling this permission in the PWA Permissions page prevents users from viewing any resource's assignment details in the assignment views of the Resource Center. When the permission is set on the category to which the user or group has access, it determines whether the user or group member can view the category object's (in this case, Resource's) assignments in Assignment views.

Resource: View Resource Plan (Global, PWA)

Disabling this setting prevents users from accessing the PWA Resource Plan page.

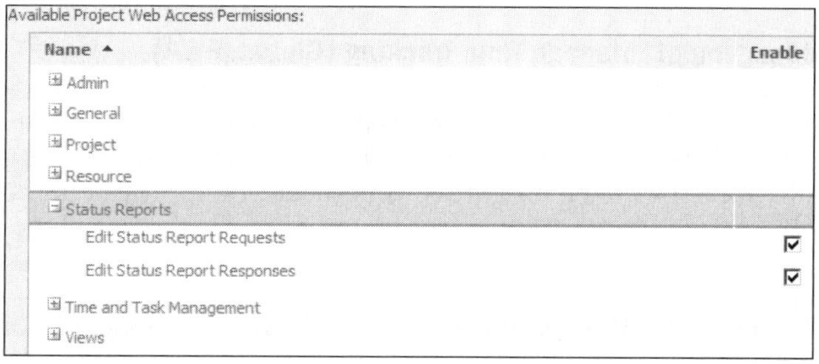

Status Reports: Edit Status Report Requests (Global, PWA)

Disabling this permission prevents any user from requesting a status report or viewing status reports from their team. Unrequested status reports are the only ones that would be used in this environment.

Status Reports: Edit Status Report Responses (Global, PWA)

Disabling this permission prevents any user from submitting a status report.

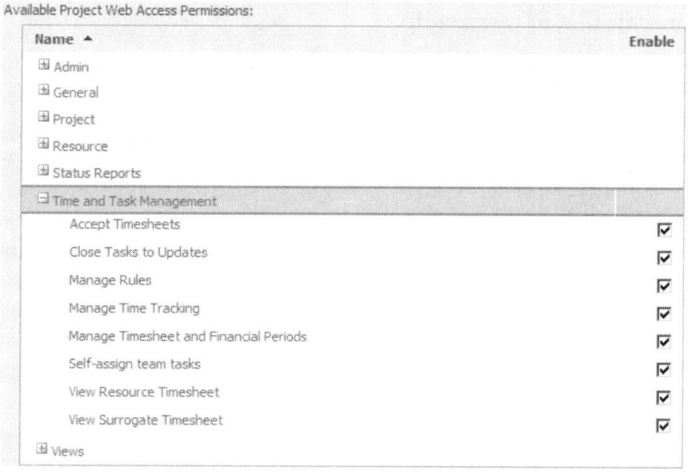

Time and Task Management: Accept Timesheets (Global, PWA)

Disabling this permission prevents a user from accepting or approving timesheets from users by sending an error message when a user attempts to go to the Timesheet Approval page.

Time and Task Management: Close Tasks to Update (Global, PWA)

Disabling this permission grays out the Close Tasks to Update action from Project Center and removes the associated link from the Time and Task Management section of the Server Settings page.

Time and Task Management: Manage Rules (Global, PWA)

Disabling this permission restricts project managers from defining rules for automatic approvals for Task Status updates.

Time and Task Management: Manage Time Tracking (Global, PWA)

Disabling this permission removes the Timesheet Classifications, Timesheet Settings and Defaults, Administrative Time, and Task Settings and Display links from the Time and Task Management section of the Server Settings page. The category permission is different, as it relates to the ability for a user to be forwarded timesheets for approval. In the practice, users who have this permission on a category can be chosen as the timesheet approver when users submit their timesheets.

Time and Task Management: Manage Timesheet and Financial Periods (Global, PWA)

Disabling this permission removes the Timesheet Periods and Financial Periods links from the Time and Task Management section of the Server Settings page and restricts users from creating and defining timesheet and fiscal periods.

Time and Task Management: Self-Assign Team Tasks (Global, PWA)

Disabling this permission grays out the Self-Assign Team Tasks button from the My Tasks page, resulting in the user losing this functionality.

Time and Task Management: View Resource Timesheet (Global, PWA)

Disabling this permission restricts PWA users from viewing other resources' timesheets, regardless of approval state or ownership.

Time and Task Management: View Surrogate Timesheet (Global, PWA)

Disabling this permission prevents a user from accessing the View Surrogate Timesheet page in PWA. (The timesheet owner must have the Create Surrogate Timesheet permission for this permission to be active.)

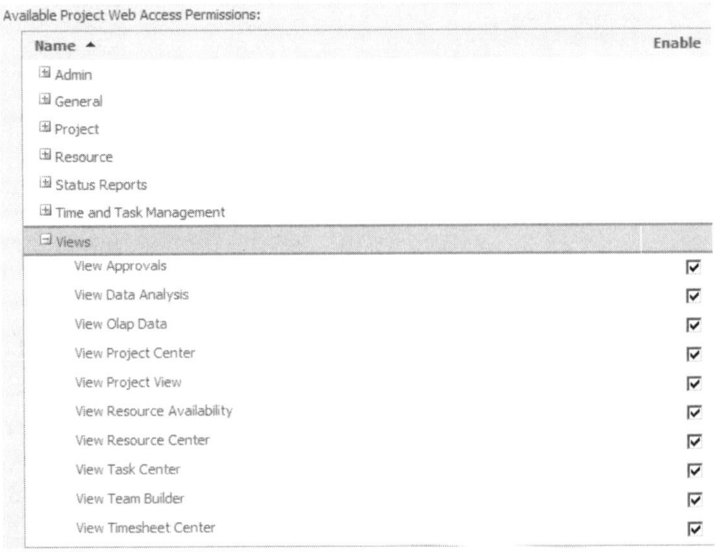

Views: View Approvals (Global, PWA)
Disabling this permission prevents all users from viewing the Task Updates and Administrative Time Approval pages of PWA.

Views: View Data Analysis (Global, PWA)
Disabling this permission prevents all users from viewing the Data Analysis page and all the views contained within it.

Views: View OLAP Data (Global, PWA)
Disabling this permission prevents all users from being added to cube roles in Analysis Services, resulting in the inability to feed the Data Analysis views with cube data. This setting takes effect the next time the cube is built.

Views: View Project Center (Global, PWA)
Disabling this permission prevents all users from viewing projects in Project Center. Users who attempt to do so receive an error message indicating that they do not have sufficient permissions to perform this action. This permission affects both users of PWA and Project Professional when they click the Project Center link from the Collaborate menu.

Views: View Project View (Global, PWA)
Disabling this permission prevents all users from viewing the Project Details views when drilling down on a project name from within Project Center or Project Professional.

Views: View Resource Availability (Global, PWA)
Disabling this view prevents users from seeing resource availability information in the Resource Center page. (This does not prevent users of Project Professional or PWA from viewing the information when using the Build Team from Enterprise tool.)

Views: View Resource Center (Global, PWA)
Disabling this permission prevents users from accessing the Resource Center pages from within PWA.

View Data Analysis and View OLAP Data
The View Data Analysis and View OLAP Data permissions seem naturally tied together, and through normal PWA reporting, they will both either be enabled or disabled for users in PWA. There are reasons why these permissions are split. Because SQL Server Analysis Services can reside on a different server than your primary databases, authentication for this cube data happens directly between the end user's machine and SQL Analysis Services. In addition, the ability to use Microsoft Office Excel independently of Project Server allows users to bypass Project Server security and access the cube data independently. This is another reason why it is imperative that Windows Domain Authentication is used and that users are logged in to their workstations with their domain accounts when working with PWA. (Additional software is required to use the Data Analysis views. Refer to Chapter 6 for more details.)

Views: View Task Center (Global, PWA)

Disabling this permission prevents users from accessing the My Work top-level navigation from the Quick Launch Bar. (This does not stop a user from navigating to the My Tasks and My Timesheets pages, which contain similar data.)

Views: View Team Builder (Global, PWA)

Disabling this permission prevents users from using the Team Builder tool by graying out the Build Team button from within Project Center and the Project Details views. (This permission has no effect on the Build Team from Enterprise tool from within Project Professional.)

Views: View Timesheet Center (Global, PWA)

Disabling this permission prevents all users from accessing their Timesheet Center. Users can, however, create, modify, recall, and submit their timesheet using the My Work page as shown in Figure 8-3.

Manage Groups

If you are just beginning the process of understanding the security mechanisms in Project Server 2007, you should focus most of your efforts on managing groups in your EPM environment.

When editing a group in PWA, you will see some similarities among the properties of individual users, except that within a group you have the additional setting to synchronize with an Active Directory group.

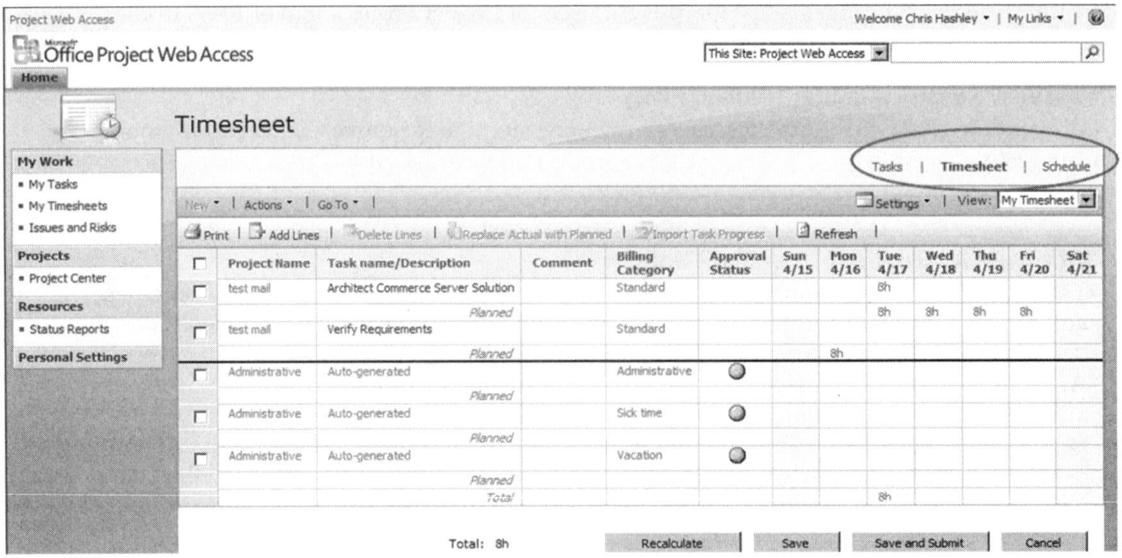

FIGURE 8-3 My Work page can be used to expose timesheets to users when the Timesheet Center is disabled.

AD Synchronization Considerations

Giving the vast majority of your users access to Project Server 2007 should be a matter of simply adding them to preexisting PWA groups. The groups will have global permissions applied to them and have predefined permissions on categories. Microsoft helps with this approach by providing the Active Directory Group Synchronization. Although this approach requires more planning and integration with your human resources department and information service (IS) new employee checklist, it can greatly reduce the account management and administration overhead when a large and dynamic user base is involved. Figure 8-4 provides a flow chart of the new user creation process. This chart may help you to simplify the management of user security. Also, it is recommended to have a one-to-one ratio of groups to categories for your initial iteration of your EPM implementation. If need be, you can add additional categories (and associated category permissions) to achieve your desired results.

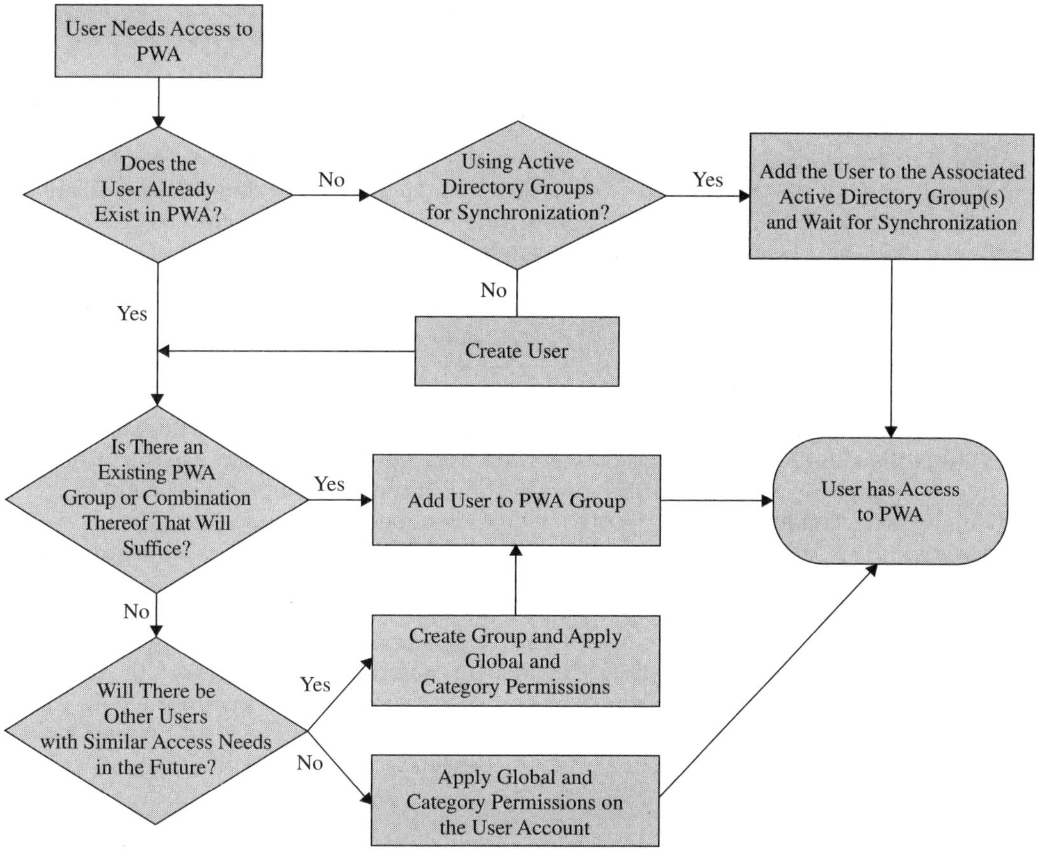

FIGURE 8-4 Giving a user access to PWA

Administration Pages

The Manage Groups page provides general information about the existing PWA groups, including the group name, description, identification of the Active Directory group with which the PWA group synchronizes, and the results of the most recent synchronization attempt. This page also includes an Active Directory Sync Options button. This setting should not be confused with the Active Directory Enterprise Resource Pool Synchronization functionality that is found in the Operational Policies section of the Server Settings page. There are two distinct Active Directory synchronization schedules within each instance of PWA:

- **Groups synchronization** With this schedule, PWA looks at the membership of the specified Active Directory groups and duplicates the membership in the designated PWA access groups.
- **Active Directory Enterprise Resource Pool synchronization** PWA looks at the membership of a specified Active Directory group and duplicates the membership in the Enterprise Resource Pool.

NOTE *In previous versions of Project Server and Project Web Access, the ability to "synchronize now" was available only if you were viewing PWA from the console of the Project Server. Otherwise, you were only able to set the time for the synchronization and wait.*

Group Management

The global permissions for groups are identical to the individual user's global permissions in action, and similar to the PWA permissions, except that global permissions for groups are applied only to members of the specified group and they have no capacity to be contextually sensitive (as opposed to category permissions, which are contextually sensitive).

Three-State Permission Model

When you specify the PWA permissions, you use only a single checkbox to enable (checked) or disable (unchecked) that capability for all users for a specific permission in PWA. With a three-state permission model, there are two checkboxes: Allow and Deny. The three states that this model supports are allowed, denied, and not allowed. You specify not allowed by selecting neither the Allow nor Deny boxes. You may find that you can use the built-in groups and categories with very little modification. If the Allow box is checked for a particular permission for a single group to which a user belongs, that user will be allowed that permission, as long as the Deny permission is not checked for that same permission in any other group to which the user belongs.

It is highly recommended that you exercise caution when applying the Deny state, because Project Server security works on the most restrictive permission model. In other words, Deny on a permission will override any Allow state that you might have specified with the user's individual settings or for groups to which a user belongs. If there are situations where you cannot achieve your desired results through the Not Allow state and you must use the Deny state on a permission, do so on the smallest entity possible, ideally the individual.

Manage Categories

Whereas PWA permissions determine what capabilities are available to the whole PWA site, global permissions determine what remaining capabilities are available to a user or a group.

Understanding Group-Category Relationships

To illustrate how groups and categories relate, let's focus for a moment on the Project Managers group in PWA. When you look at the group's default settings, you see the group information, active directory group partner, and group membership (users) information. The interesting part is when you look at the next two sections: categories and global permissions. Only when you click on the category name do you see the permissions that the Project Managers group has on that category. If you click on the My Projects Category and then click on the My Organization category, you will see the permissions change as you click from one to the other. For example, because you know that project managers have the ability to view and open their own projects but are not allowed to see other project managers' projects, you can see how this result is achieved. When you click the My Projects category, you see all of the permissions that the Project Managers group (Principal) has on the projects (objects) defined by the My Projects category. (Whether you are viewing the group's permissions by clicking on categories from the Add or Edit Group page, or you are clicking on the various groups that have access to the category from the Add or Edit Category page, you are looking at the same permissions. They are simply displayed in reverse order to allow you to view the categories to which a group has access or the groups that have access to the category, respectively.)

Category permissions put contextually sensitive permissions on objects that are defined by the category.

Custom categories can be used to help facilitate special circumstances where organizations require nonstandard access to groups of projects. For example, suppose that your organization has a "supersecret" project that only a handful of users can access and view. You could accomplish this by completing the following tasks:

1. Create a group and add the users who will need to see this project. (You need not apply any global or category permissions at this point.)
2. Create a category that includes this project.

Contextually Sensitive Permissions—the RBS Connection

When the RBS is used as a representation of your organizational reporting hierarchy, it is one aspect that is considered when we refer to the categories as being contextually sensitive. The RBS is used to represent relationships between users in your organization and can be used to determine what objects (resources and projects) a user can see. When defining categories for your organization, you are defining what members of the category can see. This causes some Project Server administrators grief, because they may have two users who have identical individual and group global permissions and identical permissions on categories, but these two users, when viewing Project Center or Resource Center views, see different sets of projects and resources. This is commonly attributed to the fact that the two users are located at different branches of the RBS.

3. Ensure that the supersecret project is not exposed through another category—that is, modify the My Organization category to show only projects specified by specific criteria rather than all current and future projects in the Project Server database. Ideally, the project manager of the supersecret project will be dedicated to these types of projects, be at the top level of the RBS, or not be part of the RBS at all. This is dependent on how your RBS was planned and how selective you were with members who reside at the highest levels.
4. There is no way to restrict PWA administrators from seeing these supersecret projects or granting themselves access. In other words, it is very important to grant access only to the administrator group that absolutely needs access to this group. Another option is to reassess whether the project should reside in PWA at all.
5. From the properties of the group that you created in step 1, add the category (as in step 2) and apply the permissions that the group has on the category.

Category Properties

When creating a new category or editing an existing one, you have multiple options to determine what objects comprise that category:

- **Name and description of the category**
- **Users and groups** Select the users and groups that you want to have permissions on this category. (When you add the users and groups, you will then see which permissions they have on the category.) Although you can grant individual users permissions on a category, it is recommended to use groups whenever possible.
- **Projects** The two main choices are All Current and Future Projects in the Project Server Database or Only the Projects Indicated. If you want to be selective with the projects to be included in this category, you can select each project for inclusion individually, or you can use the five contextually sensitive checkboxes to determine which projects (objects) to display to the users or groups (principals) with permissions on the category.
- **Resources** The two main choices are All Current and Future Resources in Project Server Database or Only the Resources Indicated. If you want to be selective with the resources to be included in the category, you can select each resource for inclusion individually, or you can use the five contextually sensitive checkboxes to determine which resources (objects) will be displayed to the users or groups (principals) with permissions on the category.
- **Views** You can specify which views are made available to the members (principals) of this category. This page includes information indicating which views are included in the category, and you can check the properties of a particular view (from the Manage Views page) to see the categories to which the view belongs.

Security Templates

Security templates provide an administrator a way to apply predefined permissions to users and groups. Although such templates can help expedite the creation of new groups, if you rely on them for new users, you can quickly lose control of the security in your EPM environment. Security templates are intended to allow an administrator to give principal predefined rights quickly, but they often become a crutch and a shortcut too often relied on because of poor planning. If you as an administrator thoroughly plan for the required levels of access that your users require, you will rarely need to apply templates to individual users.

CAUTION *Modifying the security templates from the Manage Templates page, as shown in Figure 8-5, does not change the group's permissions. It modifies only the template from which permissions can be applied.*

Client Security

Client or workstation security typically applies to the applications that connect to Project Server 2007 and the communication channels that link them.

Project Professional 2007 Security

Project Professional 2007, being the primary tool for the project manager's access to the EPM environment, has multiple aspects of security that need to be considered. As with the previous version of the EPM toolset, Project Professional 2007 has a very close relationship with Internet Explorer. As a matter of fact, many of the options within the Collaborate menu

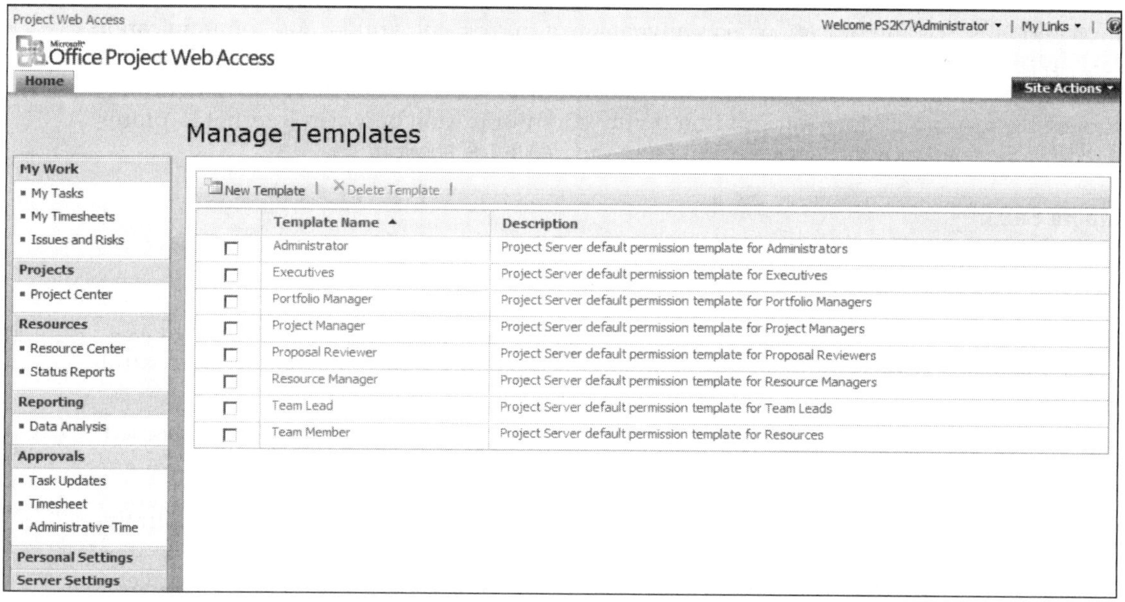

FIGURE 8-5 The Manage Templates page

in Project Professional display PWA information in the main frame of Project Professional. In these cases, Project Professional is a wrapper for Internet Explorer.

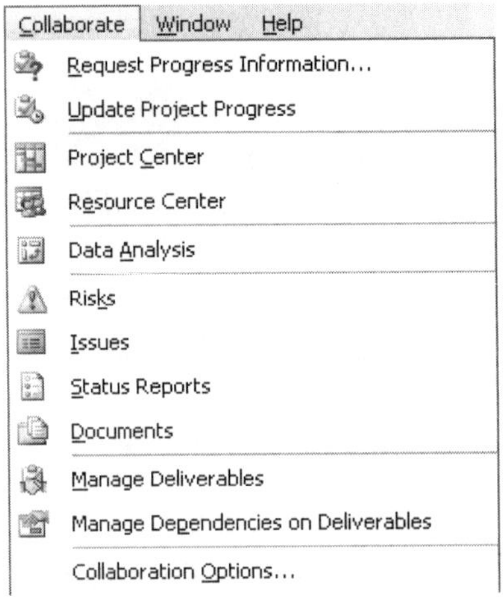

Communication with Project Server

By default, communication between Project Professional and the Project Server Interface (PSI) (or PSI Forwarder in certain topologies) happens through Simple Object Access Protocol (SOAP) calls over Hypertext Transfer Protocol (HTTP) (port 80). If you have installed an SSL certificate on your Front End Web Server for use by your PWA site(s), this Project Professional–PSI communication takes advantage of the SSL encryption, and communication takes place through HTTPS (HTTP over SSL) (port 443).

The only exception to this is when you attempt to access the Data Analysis views through Project Professional. More information on the communication between Internet Explorer and SQL Server Analysis Services is given in the following section.

Macro Security

If at some point you want to implement a macro for your Project Professional users, you have two options for doing so:

- Obtain a digital certificate for your macro so that Project Professional treats it as a signed macro. (This is an ideal method for larger organizations that tightly control and restrict macro use.)
- Lower the security settings in Project Professional so that users can run unsigned macros.

These solutions can be implemented on each workstation or via various administrative package deployment applications.

If you fail to implement macro security, a security warning message will appear every time users run Project Professional 2007.

Internet Explorer

Because Internet Explorer is the client application that enables all interaction with PWA, its role is very important in your EPM implementation.

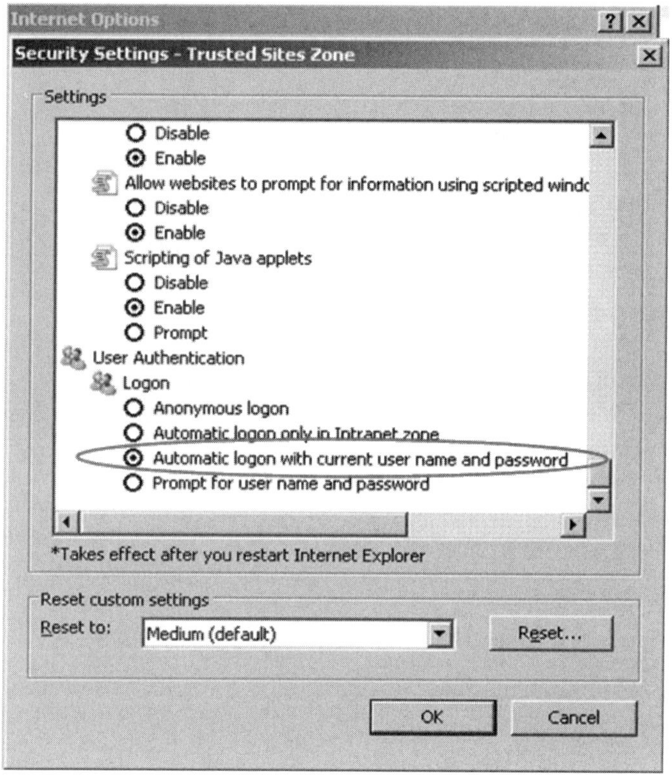

User Authentication

In past versions of Project Server, modification of your Trusted Sites security zone in Internet Explorer was required. This allowed for transparent authentication, because for sites in the Trusted Sites Zone, Internet Explorer would allow automatic login with the current username and password. Placing the PWA site in the Trusted Sites Zone also facilitated the ActiveX control installation and the interaction of Project Professional and Internet Explorer. The same Internet Explorer settings can be used for Project Server 2007. Early releases of Internet Explorer 7 switched the settings of the Trusted Sites Zone so that automatic and transparent authentication did not work. Complying with your company's policy for patch management, if you are using Internet Explorer 7, verify that your PWA site is listed in Trusted Sites Zone, and the zone has the User Authentication setting Automatic Login with

Current User Name and Password selected. (PWA 2003 can be run in parallel with PWA 2007, as the ActiveX controls are versioned differently for both products and can coexist.)

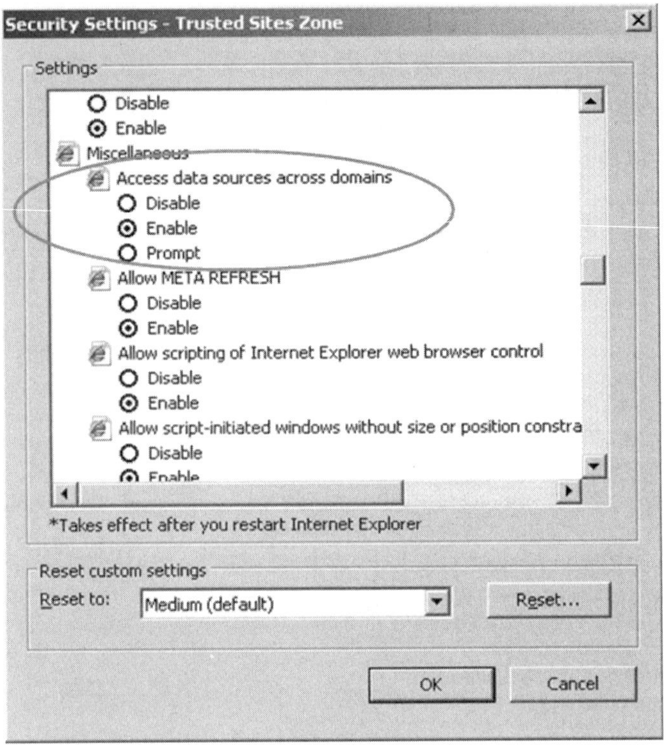

Data Analysis

As was noted earlier, the vast majority of client-server PWA communication happens over either HTTP or HTTPS. However, there is an exception, and that is when a user creates or accesses a Data Analysis view. When this happens, Internet Explorer uses the existing connection to the Front End Web Server for the view definition date and also makes a direct connection with SQL Analysis Services as shown in Figure 8-6. This has several implications for Internet Explorer. First, because the workstation is connecting to SQL Analysis Services, the user who is logged on to the workstation will be authenticating to it. For this reason, the workstation must be a member of the same Active Directory domain or a trusted one. The user must be logged in to the machine with his or her domain credentials as well. In addition, the Enable Access across Domains field must be set to at least Prompt for Internet Explorer to connect to Analysis Services for the online analytical processing (OLAP) data.

NOTE *Because each of the Data Analysis views can include the ability to export to Excel, when a user clicks on the Export for Excel button, Microsoft Office Excel opens, the connection to SQL Analysis Services is set up, and Microsoft Excel makes a direct connection with the SQL Server Analysis Services server to work with the cube data independently of Internet Explorer and PWA.*

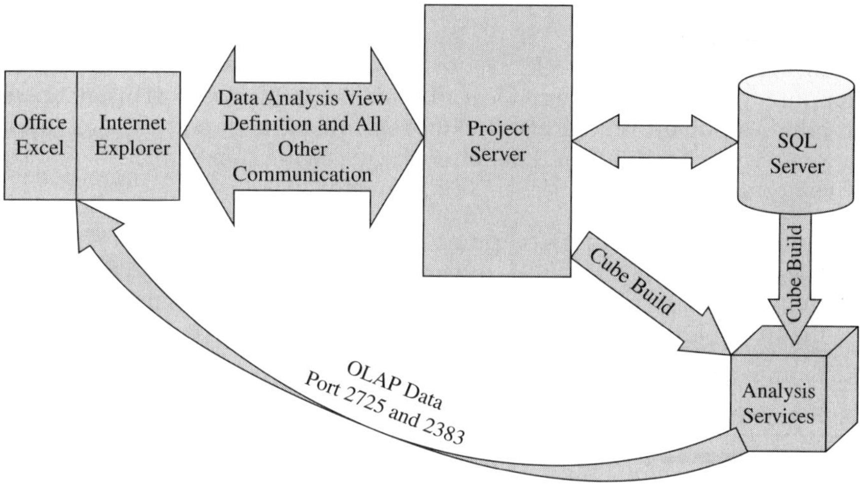

Figure 8-6 Data Analysis view data flow

ActiveX Controls Security

ActiveX controls were used in Project Server even before it was called Project Server. These controls allow for a wide variety of functionality within PWA, including views where a grid and Gantt chart are displayed (like Project Center), actions where you can export a view to another Microsoft Office application, and when you click a link to open Project Professional (and perhaps populate it with data) from within Internet Explorer. The problem is that many organizations have very tight restrictions on ActiveX controls. This stems from several years ago when someone first thought it was OK to build an ActiveX control for nefarious purposes. As a result, medium-to-large organizations restrict the installation of all ActiveX controls and install them administratively as needed.

Note *The 1033 folder is language-specific. Because there are many languages for Project Server, this number may be different for the language that has been installed.*

Outlook Plug-In

The PWA plug-in for Microsoft Office Outlook can help increase the efficiency of your resources by enabling them to work with their PWA tasks through the Outlook Calendar or Task List. This creates a temporary direct link between PWA and the Outlook client. This link between Outlook and PWA is optimized for Windows authentication, and because it deals with Windows and Outlook profiles, it does not provide the smooth "log on as different user" functionality that is available with PWA and WSS. If you do not use the credentials of the user who is logged in to the machine, any other authentication is assumed to be Project Server (or forms) authentication. Likewise, the PWA plug-in for Microsoft Office Outlook can support no more than one PWA site at any given time.

Active X Controls

Because most organizations are reluctant to allow users to perform day-to-day tasks on their computer while logged in as a local administrator, they want to install the ActiveX controls administratively onto users' desktops. Administrative software deployment applications vary in capability and detail, so the following steps can be taken to install the ActiveX controls for Project Server 2007 manually:

1. From the Project Server Computer, navigate to the C:\Program Files\Common Files\Microsoft Shared\web server extensions\12\TEMPLATE\LAYOUTS\PWA\Objects\ folder, copy the PJClient.cab file to the desktop, then go into the 1033 folder and copy pjcintl.cab file to your desktop.
2. From your desktop, open the pjcintl.cab file.
3. Right-click pj12ENUc.dll and click Extract.
4. On the Select a Destination page, select C:\Windows\Downloaded Program Files. (You don't need to extract the langcabENU12.inf file.)
5. From your desktop, open the PJClient.cab file.
6. Select all the files, right-click, and choose Extract.
7. On the Select a Destination page, select C:\Windows\Downloaded Program Files as the destination for the files. (After you've extracted both cab files, you can safely remove them from your desktop.)
8. Register all of the .dll and .ocx files that you've just placed in the Downloaded Programs folder:
    a. Open a command prompt and traverse to the C:\Windows\Downloaded Program Files directory.
    b. Type **for %i in (pj*.dll) do regsvr32 %i** and press Enter. In the windows that appear, click OK to confirm registration of the .dll files.
    c. Type **for %i in (pj*.ocx) do regsvr32 %i** and press Enter. In the windows that appear, click OK to confirm registration of the .ocx files.

Several administrative software distribution tools are available that can automate this process. One such tool, Microsoft Systems Center Configuration Manager 2007, can be used to deploy the ActiveX control to many desktops in a locked-down environment. You can download the product from the following site: http://support.microsoft.com/default.aspx?scid=KB;EN-US;818046.

In this chapter, we reviewed security in your EPM environment from a number of different perspectives. At the Web server level, we discussed the application pools, service accounts, and the use of SSL encryption. From the PWA instance level, we discussed the different levels of permissions, including the PWA (environment) permissions, global (principal) permissions, and the rights that principals have on collections of resources or groups, which are the category permissions. We also reviewed the client-side components of Internet Explorer, Microsoft Office Project Professional 2007, and the ActiveX components within the EPM toolset.

As you see, security is a pervasive topic when configuring your EPM environment. Implementing it in a way that is effective yet not overly burdensome to your users or Project Server administrators requires thorough planning and acclimation. Complexity is the enemy of security, in that the more complicated your security approach is, the more complicated it will be to understand, maintain, and troubleshoot. In addition, with the highest levels of complexity, it will become much easier to make a mistake in configuration. This can open up a hole in the security framework, and make the security applied much more time consuming to test and validate. So, in conclusion, keep it simple. Plan your RBS wisely. Keep your users in groups and apply category permissions to the groups. This will be your best shot at obtaining and maintaining balanced security in your EPM environment.

CHAPTER 9

Configuring Enterprise Data Settings

The Enterprise Data area is found within the Server Settings of Project Server 2007. To navigate there from the Project Web Access Home Page, select Server Settings from the Quick Launch Bar (left navigation) (see Figure 9-1). Keep in mind that access to this area, and even portions of this area, are controlled by the security model. In the SharePoint security trimmed user interface, that means that if access is disallowed, links and functions will not even be visible.

As you can see in Figure 9-2, the Enterprise Data area includes five subheadings. These subareas are the topic of this chapter. They are as follows:

- **Enterprise Custom Field Definition** This definition is a critical component for building a solution that meets specific organizational needs for reporting, filtering, grouping, and sorting information. No "complete reference" would be thorough without a discussion of project fields in general. These fields are used without any customization, but are also important building blocks for custom fields (by dividing one by another, for example), so this subarea includes a general section for fields. Fields and enterprise custom fields are a key topic and take up the major part of this chapter.
- **Enterprise Global** This is the place where Project Professional settings are established that affect all projects, including configuration of what columns are used, filtering, and views.
- **Enterprise Calendars** Organizational base calendars are configured for what is working and nonworking time for groups of people.
- **Resource Center** This is a rich and powerful environment for configuring settings for individual project resources. In addition, Resource Center is the launching pad for critical resource views such as Resource Availability by Project.
- **About Project Server** This tool helps track user information to support licensing decisions for the environment.

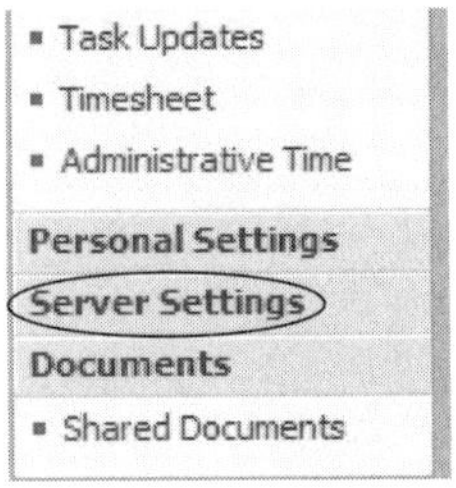

Figure 9-1 Server Settings button on the Quick Launch Bar

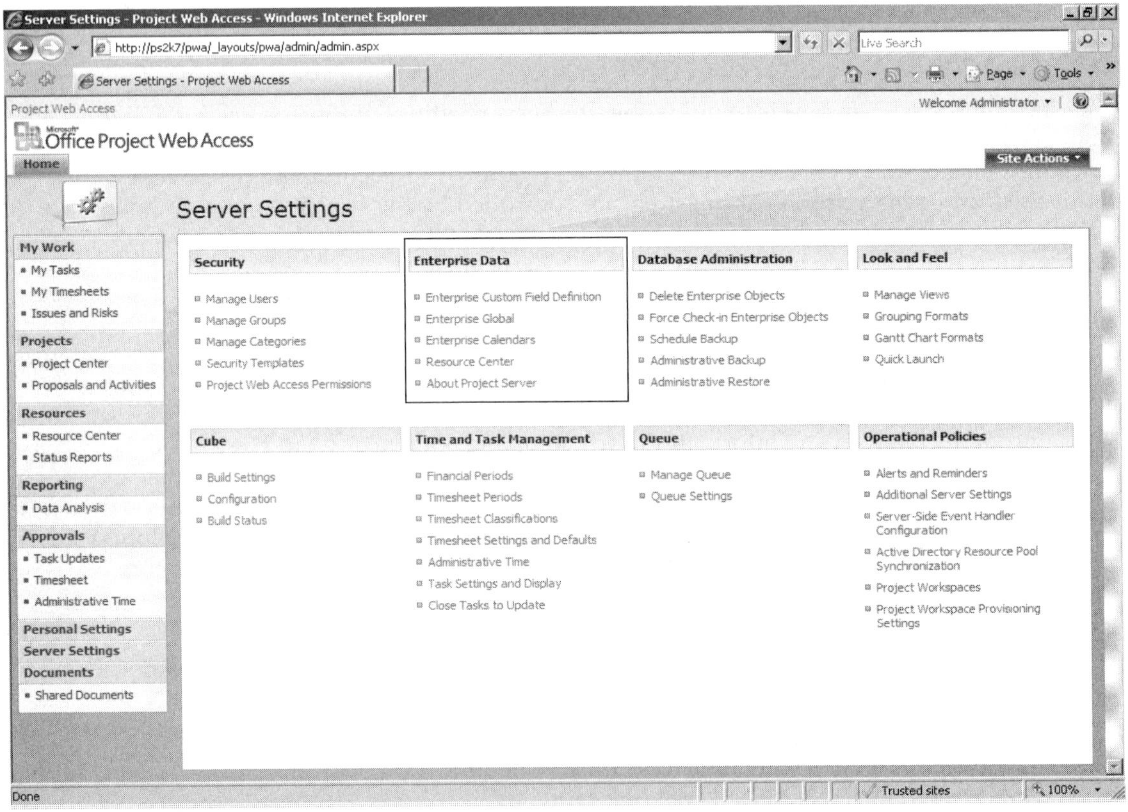

Figure 9-2 Server Settings page

Enterprise Custom Field Definition

Within Project Server, there is a set of tools that enable you to create custom attributes for application to different parts of the system. These attributes, called *enterprise custom fields*, are used to sort, filter, report, group, and manage data in the system in ways that are logical to an organization. Before starting down the path of building custom fields, however, note that there are many built-in fields within the Project Server and Project Professional environment. These fields can provide a wealth of possibilities for how data are used as information in the system. Keep in mind that fields that may be hidden from the Project Professional user, normally the project manager, are still calculated and available on the server. These built-in fields can be mixed and matched in views (covered in detail in Chapter 11) to get exactly the right set of data to the targeted audience. In addition, these built-in fields can be used to develop new custom fields. For example, you can create a new custom enterprise field by comparing two of the existing fields.

Before embarking on a discussion of enterprise custom fields, it makes sense to give an overview of Project Professional and Project Server fields. More detailed information about out-of-the-box fields will come later in this chapter.

Entities

Entities are the three areas where fields (attributes) are associated. Each has different characteristics, particularly in the way the output can be displayed in views. Understanding how each entity works is important in deciding which fields to use, and then later what enterprise custom fields to build.

Projects

Project-level fields are used to distinguish projects at a summary level. In other words, the project fields are at the level of the entire project, not at the detail level. These fields are used to filter, sort, and group data in Project Center views, where each project is displayed in a single row as part of a collective of projects. These fields can also be used in Data Analysis views, where the viewer can display and even perform on-the-fly modification of complex pivot tables and charts.

Resources

Resource fields are used to associate attributes to resources. Resources can be work (people), generic resources, material resources (such as board feet or computers), or cost resources. Resource fields are displayed in Resource views and Data Analysis views. Selection of attributes in Resource views are commonly set by either an administrator or by resource managers for their resources.

Tasks

Task fields are used at the detailed task level. In our experience, these are the least commonly used. Task-level fields can be displayed in the Project views of PWA. Project views show only one project and include the details of the tasks in the project. Task Name is a task field.

Types

There are six field types. In general, these types are self-explanatory, so the following descriptions are brief.

Cost
The values in this field are displayed as the currency of choice (e.g., $4,353.00 for USD).

Date
Values in this field are displayed as dates depending on date options chosen (Mon 3/19/07, for example).

Duration
Duration measures the number of hours, days, weeks, etc. from start to finish of a Task, Assignment, or Project. Duration is typically displayed in days.

Flag
The flag field type is used to display information such as whether some type of action is required for other types of classification.

Number
Number fields are one of the most commonly used field types. You should use them in any case where the displayed data can include only numeric characters such as the number of days or hours of work. Number fields can be used for comparison purposes as well, such as when you compare the number of hours of baseline work with the number of hours of actual work.

Text
Text is an option for several solutions, but is frequently used for displaying items from a dropdown list such as Project Status or Project Sponsor.

Field Categories
The built-in fields in Microsoft Office Project Professional are, for the most part, available to Project Server and are organized by the following categories:

- **Assignment** An assignment is the task plus the resource performing the task. Assignment fields can be displayed in the Usage views in Project Professional, or in many areas of PWA.
- **Assignment Timephased** This field category is used for resource assignments throughout the duration of the project.
- **Resource** This field shows information about resources, including rolled-up totals for the resources' task information.
- **Resource Timephased** This field holds information about the resource as spread throughout that resource's availability during a project.
- **Task** Task fields can be displayed anywhere that task information is used in either Project Professional or PWA. These fields are commonly displayed in project Gantt Chart views and task sheets.
- **Task Timephased** Timephased task fields hold information on the allocation of time throughout the duration of a task. In other words, this field shows when the work is occurring within the task itself.

NOTE *Timephasing is a way to spread work, cost, resources, or assignments over time. For example, if a staff member is assigned a 40-hour task spread over five days, the spreading of the assignment over the five days can be viewed as timephased data. From within Project Professional, the Usage views are where timephased data can be viewed. Resource usage is for timephased information by resource, and task usage is likewise viewed by the task.*

Field Types and What They Each Contain (More Detail)

For the next several pages, this section breaks down the high-level field types with lists of the detailed field types that each contains, as well as their most common usage (where appropriate). To understand each detailed field, it is important to keep in mind the previous section on field categories. This section attempts to be more (and less) than just a standard field reference in the sense that items such as how a field is calculated are included only where they add value. In addition, concepts that are detailed early on, such as how each field category changes the usage of the field, are less detailed as you delve further into the chapter. Author comments on fields, such as whether they are of high value or not, are scattered about as makes sense from the authors' perspective. The most commonly utilized field types are marked with an asterisk(*):

- **Currency fields** These display results as currency.
  - **Actual Cost fields*** These fields display actual cost, which is determined by multiplying the work times the rate of the resource plus fixed or pre-use costs. Rate is based on the rates set for resources in the Enterprise Resource Pool.
    - **Actual Cost (Task field)** Most common usage is when a person applies hours to a task; those hours are multiplied by the resources rate per hour and displayed in the Actual Cost field. The Task field associates the actual cost with the project task itself and can be rolled up to display the total actual cost for the project.
    - **Actual Cost (Resource field)** Most common usage is to display the costs associated with a resource in Resource views. This field can also be rolled up to show the summary actual cost by resource for the entire project.
    - **Actual Cost (Assignment field)** Most common usage is for display in Task Usage or Resource Usage views. An assignment is a combination of a task and a resource. This perspective looks at cost per assignment.
    - **Actual Cost (Task Timephased Field)** Most common usage is for display in Task Usage views. The field is used to display task-level actual cost, but in a way that allows for understanding when the costs were incurred over time.
    - **Actual Cost (Resource Timephased field)** Most common usage is to display this data in Resource Usage view(s). This view shows actual cost by resource and when that cost was incurred.
    - **Actual Cost (Assignment Timephased field)** Most common usage is to display the data in Task Usage or Resource Usage views. This category of the Actual Cost field holds these costs by assignment and when they were incurred.

- **Actual Fixed Cost (Task Timephased field)** This field is used to display actual fixed costs for a non-human resource on a task. For example, if there is a meal per diem, that number (currency) can be entered in the field. Depending on how accrual is handled, this cost may be spread out over a period of time.
- **Actual Overtime Cost fields** These fields show the cost of work performed by resources that are classified as overtime and can be seen from the three different perspectives:
  - Actual Overtime Cost (Task field)
  - Actual Overtime Cost (Resource field)
  - Actual Overtime Cost (Assignment field)
- **ACWP (Actual Cost of Work Performed) fields*** These are earned value fields as well as currency fields and are generally used when compared to BCWP (Budgeted Cost of Work Performed) fields. These can be displayed individually or used in calculated fields (which you will learn more about later). Note that this comparison is frequently done at a project level by rolling up the information to be viewed at the summary level. Rollups will also be discussed later in this chapter.

NOTE *Some handy existing field types—CPI (Cost Performance Index), CV (Cost Variance), and CV% (Cost Variance Percentage)—compare ACWP and BCWP.*

  - **ACWP (Task field)** Most common use is to compare to BCWP to show how a task is tracking.
  - **ACWP (Resource field)** Compare this data with BCWP data in Resource views.
  - **ACWP (Assignment field)** Compare this data with BCWP data in Assignment views.
  - **ACWP (Task Timephased field)** Compare this data with BCWP data in Task Usage or Resource Usage views.
  - **ACWP (Resource Timephased field)** Use this in Resource Usage views.
  - **ACWP (Assignment Timephased field)** Use in the timephased portions of Resource Usage or Task Usage views.
- **Baseline Cost fields*** These fields hold the total cost expected for the task, resource, assignments, and so on. These fields are also known as Budget at Completion or Baseline at Completion (BAC), which are earned value fields. These are often compared to Actual Cost fields. When used in this manner, Baseline Cost fields enable the viewer to see the burn rate (how much the project has cost so far compared to the total budget).
  - **Baseline Cost (Task field)** This field is used for tracking the task budget.
  - **Baseline Cost (Resource field)** This tracks the resource budget.
  - **Baseline Cost (Assignment field)** This tracks the assignment budget.

- **Baseline Cost (Task Timephased field)** This tracks the timephased task budget.
- **Baseline Cost (Resource Timephased field)** This tracks the timephased resource budget.
- **Baseline Cost (Assignment Timephased field)** This tracks the timephased assignment budget.

- **Baseline1–10 Cost fields** These fields are used for calculations when multiple baselines are used in a project. They act the same way that Baseline Costs fields function except that the data are not based on the original baseline, but rather a later baseline (1, 2, 3, 4, and so on).
- **BCWP fields (Budgeted Cost of Work Performed)*** This highly useful set of fields can be used to display how much of the budget should have been used by the current date. As mentioned in the ACWP discussion previously, these fields are often used to compare against the ACWP fields in order to track the earned value of the task, resource, assignment, and so on. You can also compare these fields with their counterpart BCWS fields (discussed next) to see whether the item is tracking to schedule.
  - BCWP (Task field)
  - BCWP (Resource field)
  - BCWP (Assignment field)
  - BCWP (Task Timephased field)
  - BCWP (Resource Timephased field)
  - BCWP (Assignment Timephased field)
- **BCWS fields (Budgeted Cost of Work Scheduled)*** These are fields that represent planned value for tasks, resources, and so on. They are used to see how much of the budget has been used to date and, as discussed previously, as a way to see how the item is tracking (by comparing this field to BCWP fields).
  - BCWS (Task field)
  - BCWS (Resource field)
  - BCWS (Assignment field)
  - BCWS (Task Timephased field)
  - BCWS (Resource Timephased field)
  - BCWS (Assignment Timephased field)
- **Cost fields*** These fields combine the cost for work actually performed and the remaining scheduled work to display what is basically a project total cost. In other words, unlike the Baseline Cost fields, which do not move based on the input of actual data, these fields change as projects are executed.
  - Cost (Task field)
  - Cost (Resource field)
  - Cost (Assignment field)

  - Cost (Task Timephased field)
  - Cost (Resource Timephased field)
  - Cost (Assignment Timephased field)
- **Cost per Use (Resource field)** This field is used for a work resource, both people and things like hardware and other equipment, where a set fee is required. For example, if there is a single warehouse fee associated with the storage of items on a project (PCs, for example), this fee can be entered in the Cost per Use field.
- **Cost Variance fields*** These fields are used to hold and display information by subtracting actual cost from baseline cost to view whether the project is within, under, or over budget. Although these fields can be valuable, the authors prefer the use of Earned Value variance fields. The fields include the following perspectives:
  - Cost Variance (Task field)
  - Cost Variance (Resource field)
  - Cost Variance (Assignment field)

NOTE *Variance fields require that a baseline is set for the project. Using baselines is a best practice and demarcates the set of values in the project at the time the baseline is set. Eventually, most mature organizations learn to use earned value (EV) fields or to compare EV fields them to each other for project tracking. Establishing baselines, and therefore having something by which Variance fields can be driven, is a good starting point for organizations that are early on the road to project management maturity.*

- **Cost1–10 fields** These fields are primarily for use in Project Professional 2007. They are used to develop custom fields for Project 2007 and can be pushed to the server as enterprise fields, but custom enterprise fields are more commonly created from the PWA interface.
- **Cumulative Cost fields** These fields add costs already reported to the cost of the remaining work and can be viewed in all three timephased perspectives:
  - Cumulative Cost (Task Timephased field)
  - Cumulative Cost (Assignment Timephased field)
  - Cumulative Cost (Resource Timephased field)
- **CV (Cost Variance) fields** These fields display the result of subtracting ACWP from BCWP and are very useful in the Project and Project Server environment.
  - **CV (Task field)** Use this in either a project task sheet or in a project view in PWA to see how a task is tracking to budget.
  - **CV (Resource field)** View budgetary variance by resource.
  - **CV (Assignment field)** This is the assignment perspective.
  - **CV (Task Timephased field)** All the timephased versions enable the user to track costs to budget spread over time.
  - **CV (Resource Timephased field)** See the Task Timesphased field description.

- CV (Assignment Timephased field) See the Task Timesphased field description.
- **EAC (Task field)*** The formula for this field is EAC = ACWP + (Baseline cost X - BCWP) / CPI. This is a change from previous versions. Use this field to understand the predicted final cost of a task based on previous history (you will learn more about CPI later). Note that this is also an earned value field.
- **Fixed Cost fields** This type can be used for Task and Task Timephased views and displays expenses not related to a specific resource or resources. Examples include travel expenses, shipping charges, and postage.
- **Overtime Cost fields** These fields are used to display totals for overtime expenses and use a summary of actual incurred overtime cost and planned remaining overtime cost.
  - Overtime Cost (Task field)
  - Overtime Cost (Resource field)
  - Overtime Cost (Assignment field)
- **Overtime Rate (Resource field)** This field is set in the Enterprise Resource Pool to establish, by individual, the hourly rate for overtime work.
- **Remaining Cost fields*** These display the cost that is left to complete a task and includes cost and overtime cost.
  - Remaining Cost (Task field)
  - Remaining Cost (Resource field)
  - Remaining Cost (Assignment field)
- **Remaining Overtime Cost fields** These are the same as Remaining Cost fields, but they cover just the remaining work to be done at the overtime rate.
- **Standard Rate (Resource field)*** This is the rate that is set for each resource in the Project Server Enterprise Resource Pool. It is a critical field, in that all cost and earned value calculations are based on this rate. Note that most organizations choose not to display the actual cost for each person in the organization, as this information is exposed to too many people inappropriately. Rather, they use either a global blended rate or a rate schedule depending on general job responsibilities. One of the authors' clients decided to set this rate at $1.00 per hour just to calculate cost and value relatively. Note that it is critically important in almost every environment to set this rate.
- **SV (Schedule Variance) fields*** This is an earned value field that compares two other EV fields (Budgeted Cost of Work Projected and Budgeted Cost of Work Scheduled) to display the current project cost with the baseline plan. Note that using a value type formula such as this is often a better way to gauge how well things are tracking than, for example, duration comparisons.
  - SV (Task field)
  - SV (Resource field)
  - SV (Assignment field)
  - SV (Task Timephased field)

    - SV (Resource Timephased field)
    - SV (Assignment Timephased field)
- **VAC (Variance at Complete) fields*** Used to compare Estimate at Completion (EAC) and Budgeted at Completion (BAC) fields. This field type can be a task, resource, or assignment category item and is useful for tracking how things are going from a budget perspective.
- **Custom fields** These fields are primarily for use in Project Professional 2007. They are used to develop custom fields for Project 2007 and can be pushed (or in some cases just displayed) to the server as enterprise fields, but custom enterprise fields are more commonly created from the PWA interface.
    - **Cost1–10 fields** These can be used to hold whatever cost information is required.
    - **Date1–10 fields** These fields can be used to display whatever cost information is desired.
    - **Duration1–10 fields** These are the same as the Date1–10 fields.
    - **Enterprise fields** You might find these fields in other material for Project (especially older versions), but enterprise fields are now generally created on the server and there are no internal limits (such as a maximum of 10 enterprise cost fields as follows). Therefore, you will not see any of these in Project Server or Project 2007.
        - ~~Enterprise Cost1-10 fields~~
        - ~~Enterprise Date1-30 fields~~
        - ~~Enterprise Duration1-10 fields~~
        - ~~Enterprise Flag1-20 fields~~
        - ~~Enterprise Number1-40 fields~~
        - ~~Enterprise Project Cost1-10 (project fields)~~
        - ~~Enterprise Project Date1-30 (project fields)~~
        - ~~Enterprise Project Duration1-10 (project fields)~~
        - ~~Enterprise Project Flag1-20 (project fields)~~
        - ~~Enterprise Project Number1-40 (project fields)~~
        - ~~Enterprise Project Outline Code 1-30 (project fields)~~
        - ~~Enterprise Project Text1-40 (project fields)~~
        - ~~Enterprise Resource Outline Code1-29 fields~~
        - ~~Enterprise Task Outline Code1-30 (task fields)~~
        - ~~Enterprise Text1-40 fields~~
- **Finish1–10 fields** As mentioned previously, these numbered fields are more for Project-only use, as opposed to Project Server and Enterprise Project Management (EPM). They can, however, be used to hold whatever Finish fields might meet requirements and can be displayed in PWA.
- **Flag1–20 fields** See the description for Finish 1–10 fields.

- **Number1–20 fields** See the description for Finish 1–10 fields.
- **Outline Code1–10 fields** Outline codes allow a hierarchical, nested set of selections. For example, a products-related field could allow for the following choices:

  Food

  Food.Cheese

  Food.Pretzels

  Food.Brats

  Food.Beer

  COMMENT**:** In Wisconsin, beer is a food

  NonFood

  NonFood.Packers_Gear

  NonFood.Packers_Gear.SuperBowl31Clothing

  These are rarely used in Project Server as this functionality is replaced with Lookup Tables with a Code Mask.
- **Start1–10 fields** These fields can be used in any way that makes sense to the user.
- **Text1–30 fields** These fields can be used in any way that makes sense to the user.

- **Date fields***
  - **Actual Finish fields*** These fields display the date that a completion is reached. In other words, when a task, resource, or assignment has zero remaining work, this date is set. In the Project Server environment, it is the date that the task updating process results in a 100 percent complete result.
    - Actual Finish (Task field)
    - Actual Finish (Resource field)
    - Actual Finish (Assignment field)
  - **Actual Start fields*** As with Actual Finish, these fields are driven by what actually occurs in a project. When a user enters a task update and it goes through the approval process, the date that the work begins is set as the Actual Start.
    - Actual Start (Task field)
    - Actual Start (Resource field)
    - Actual Start (Assignment field)
  - **Available From (Resource field)** This field and the next are used to set parameters limiting when a resource will be available for work. To set these fields, use the Resource Details dialog from within the Enterprise Resource Pool. Select Tools | Enterprise Options | Open Enterprise Resource Pool. Next select the resource(s) you want to edit by using the checkboxes and select the Open button. This should open the Enterprise Resource Pool for editing in Project Professional. From there, double-click the resource and use the tools shown in Figure 9-3.

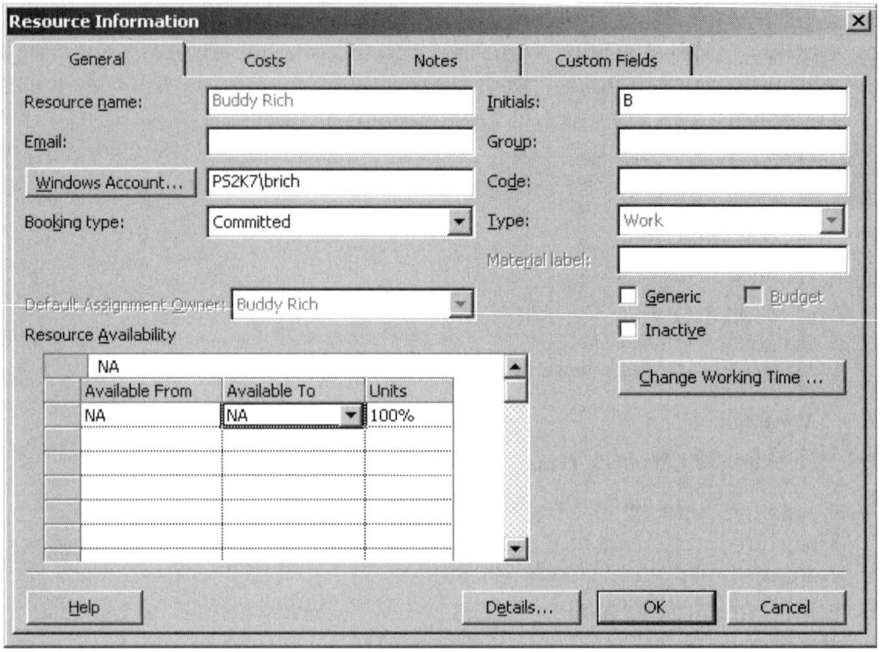

FIGURE 9-3 Using Project Professional to set Available To and Available From options

- **Available To (Resource field)** See the preceding description for Available From.
- **Baseline Finish fields*** These are dates set when the project has its baseline set. These fields are often compared against Finish (projected actual finish) or, after completion, compared to Actual Finish (to determine how accurate the estimate was). Note that these fields can roll up to the project level for summary information.
  - Baseline Finish (Task field)
  - Baseline Finish (Resource field) This field does not display any data, but is used only for supporting the Assignment field.
  - Baseline Finish (Assignment field)
- **Baseline Start fields** As with Baseline Finish, this field is set at the time that the project baseline is established. It is more commonly used to check whether tasks or assignments are starting when expected.
  - Baseline Start (Task field)
  - Baseline Start (Resource field) As with Baseline Finish, this field does not display any data, but is used only for supporting the Assignment field.
  - Baseline Start (Assignment field)
- **Baseline1–10 Finish fields** Project and Project Server support up to 10 baselines. These are represented by these fields.

NOTE *We don't generally recommend the use of multiple baselines in any but the most mature Project "shops." Using them adds a level of unneeded complexity in our opinion.*

- **Baseline1–10 Start fields** See the description for Baseline 1–10 Finish fields.
- **Complete Through (Task field)** This field is used to display a date that represents the last update to the task. In Project Server, it is the date that the status manager for the task (usually the project manager) has accepted an update from the person performing the task.
- **Constraint Date (Task field)** This is a Project-only field that is not available for Project Detail views in PWA. It relates to the constraint type, such as Must Finish On, which can be set from within the Advanced tab or the Task Information dialog in Project.
- **Created (Task field)** This Project-only field is the date that a task was entered in the project.
- **Date1–10 fields** These fields can be used to hold dates for whatever you want and can be displayed in PWA.
  - Date1–0 (Task field)
  - Date1-10 (Resource field)
  - Date1-10 (Assignment field)
- **Deadline (Task field)** This is a fantastic field that almost no one uses. To set it, you must go to the Advanced tab in the Task Information dialog in Project. Unfortunately, the actual deadline image does not display in PWA Gantt Charts.
- **Early Finish (Task field)** This field displays the earliest possible finish date for a task based on whatever constraints have been set on the task itself or on task relationships (predecessors and successors).
- **Early Start (Task field)** This fields is the same as Early Finish, except it displays the earliest possible start date.
- **Finish fields***
  - **Finish Task** This is a useful field for seeing projected task completion dates.
  - **Finish Assignment** This field shows the projected finish for an assignment. It reflects changes in the execution of the project and therefore is not a fixed date.
  - **Finish Resource** The date projects when resources will complete tasks to which they are assigned.
- **Finish1–10 fields** These fields can hold whatever date information you want and can be displayed in PWA views.
  - Finish1–10 (Task field)
  - Finish1–10 (Resource field)
  - Finish1–10 (Assignment field)
- **Late Finish (Task field)** This field displays the latest date that a task can complete without causing the project to run over. It is affected by whatever constraints are in place in the task, as well as other related tasks and constraints.

- **Late Start (Task field)** Similar to the preceding Late Finish field, this field displays the latest date that a task can start without making the project run long.
- **Preleveled Finish (Task field)** This field displays the date that a task was expected to complete prior to the use of the resource leveling function. The leveling function in Project is quite a complex topic that is beyond the scope of this book.
- **Preleveled Start (Task field)** This is similar to the Preleveled Finish field except it shows the start date.
- **Resume (Task field)** This field is used to set a date when a task is targeted to resume. The project manager can use it manually to set a date for a task that is on hold, for example.
- **Start fields*** These fields display the scheduled start for a resource or task. Note that these fields are dynamic based on predecessor activity.
  - Start (Resource field)
  - Start (Task field)
- **Start1–10 fields** These can be used for whatever is needed and can be used in PWA views.
  - Start1–10 (Task field)
  - Start1–10 (Resource field)
  - Start1–10 (Assignment field)
- **Stop (Task field)** This field allows the project manager to set a stop date during a task (the Resume field would be the restart date).

- **Duration fields**
  - **Actual Duration (Task field)** This field shows result of durations multiplied by the percentage complete. It is not a commonly used field.
  - **Actual Overtime Work fields** Available in all five field categories, these fields display the actually recorded overtime work.
  - **Actual Work fields*** All five field categories are available in this commonly used field, which displays work that has actually been done. The field is often compared to Baseline Work.
  - **Assignment Delay fields** These Project-only fields are used just to display task and assignment delays in usage views.
  - **Baseline Duration (Task field)*** This field holds the established duration that was in place at the time the task baseline was set.
  - **Baseline Work fields*** These fields hold work (hours of effort) as set when the baseline is established.
    - Baseline Work (Task field)
    - Baseline Work (Resource field)
    - Baseline Work (Assignment field)

- **Baseline1–10 Duration (Task fields)** If you are using multiple baselines, this field holds the appropriate duration numbers.
- **Baseline1–10 Work fields** If you are using multiple baselines, this field holds the appropriate effort numbers.
- **Cumulative Work fields** These Project-only timephased fields hold summary information on effort and can be viewed across time.
    - Cumulative Work (Task Timephased field)
    - Cumulative Work (Resource Timephased field)
    - Cumulative Work (Assignment Timephased field)
- **Duration (Task field)*** This is the projected duration that a task is expected to take. It is dynamic, so changes in constraints can change the data.
- **Duration Variance (Task field)*** This field displays the difference in days between the baseline duration and the current projected duration. If the number is greater than zero, then the task will take longer than the baseline; if the number is negative, then it projects a shorter duration.
- **Duration1–10 fields** These fields can be used to hold any duration information that might be useful and can be implemented as task, assignment, or resource category fields.
- **Finish Slack (Task field)** This field holds the difference between the Early Finish and Late Finish fields.
- **Finish Variance fields*** These fields hold the difference between the Baseline Finish and Finish fields and are commonly used to track whether completion will occur on time. Note that this field is commonly rolled up to display at the project level.
    - Finish Variance (Task field)
    - Finish Variance (Assignment field)
- **Free Slack (Task field)** This represents the amount of time that a task could slip before having an effect on successors.
- **Leveling Delay fields** These fields show the amount of delay due to the use of the Resource Leveling function.
    - Leveling Delay (Task field)
    - Leveling Delay (Resource field)
    - Leveling Delay (Assignment field)
- **Negative Slack (Task field)** This field shows that there is not enough time left to complete the task on time, and the amount to the negative that it would take to make up in previous tasks to get back on track.
- **Overallocation fields** These fields show cumulative information on resource overallocation spread over time.
    - Overallocation (Task Timephased field)
    - Overallocation (Resource Timephased field)
    - Overallocation (Assignment Timephased field)

- **Overtime Work fields** This is available in all five field categories and shows the scheduled work where the overtime rate applies either cumulatively or spread over time.
- **Regular Work fields** These fields are similar to Overtime Work fields for hours at the regular rate.
- **Remaining Availability fields*** These fields are useful for understanding how much resource time is available and when.
  - Remaining Availability (Task Timephased field)
  - Remaining Availability (Resource Timephased field)
- **Remaining Duration (Task field)** This dynamic field holds the projected amount of time remaining for a task to be completed.
- **Remaining Overtime Work fields** These fields display overtime work that is scheduled and has not been completed.
  - Remaining Overtime Work (Task field)
  - Remaining Overtime Work (Resource field)
  - Remaining Overtime Work (Assignment field)
- **Remaining Work field*** One of the most commonly used fields, the Remaining Work field displays the projected amount of work remaining on a task, resource, or assignment. It is often used side by side with Work and Actual Work and is also commonly used with Baseline Work and Actual Work for comparison purposes.
- **Start Slack (Task field)** This is the duration between the Early and Late Slack fields.
- **Start Variance fields** For tasks or assignments, these fields show the difference between the Baseline Start and Start (Start mean that the date is scheduled to start on the day displayed until the task actually has work recorded against it and at that time, the Start date changes to match the Actual Start date).
- **Total Slack (Task field)** This field looks at slack at a task level and determines how long is available for a finish date before it affects the project's finish.
- **Work Availability (Resource Timephased field)** This field holds the amount of time that a resource can work in a specific time period. It is affected by the resource's individual calendar (Enterprise Resource Pool).
- **Work fields*** These are among the most commonly used and valuable fields. At the core, work is what projects are about. In some less mature organizations, duration is the driving force and work is less important. Most experienced project-focused organizations, however, do not favor the duration-focused model. Work is about the scheduled amount of work for a task, resource, or assignment and can be viewed over time. It is dynamic, changing as the project is executed.
  - Work (Task field)
  - Work (Resource field)
  - Work (Assignment field)

- Work (Task Timephased field)
- Work (Resource Timephased field)
- Work (Assignment Timephased field)
- **Work Variance fields** From the task, resource, or assignment perspective, Work Variance compares the work (scheduled) with the baseline work and displays the difference.

- **Earned value fields***
  - **ACWP fields*** These were discussed earlier in this chapter.
  - **Baseline Cost (BAC) fields** These were also discussed earlier in this chapter.
  - **BCWP fields*** These also were discussed earlier in this chapter.
  - **BCWS fields*** These fields were covered earlier in the chapter.
  - **CPI (Cost Performance Indicator) fields*** These can be task or task timephased and is BCWP divided by ACWP.
  - **CV fields*** Covered previously.
  - **CV% fields*** Covered previously.
  - **EAC (Task field)*** Covered previously.
  - **Earned Value Method (Task field)** There are two methods available (based on effort represented by % Work Complete or real accomplished work [Physical Percent Complete]) for calculating earned value, and this field is available to set and view which method is in use for a task.
  - **Physical Percent (%) Complete (Task field)** This method is used when measurements are done based on a specific measure as opposed to work effort. For example, if you are being paid for washing the windows on a three-story building and each floor has the same number of windows, the first floor will take the least time because no ladders or scaffold are needed (adding time to build and time to move). If payment is being made using $*X* per floor, this method allows payment for the first floor when it is completed, even though the work performed on the first floor will not account for a third of the work required for all three.
  - **Schedule Performance Index (SPI) fields** These fields (Task and Task Timephased) are used often to project completion dates by value. The formula is [BCWP] / [BCWS] = SPI.
  - **SV fields** These fields were covered earlier in the chapter.
  - **SV Percent (%) fields*** These are the same as the SV fields, only via a ratio. You can use these fields for a Task or a Task Timephased field to view schedule variance as a percentage. The formula for this is ([SV] / [BCWS]) * 100 = SV%.
  - **TCPI (Task field)** This field is the "To Complete Performance Index." It is used to show the work/funds ratio for what work is remaining to be completed. It is a good way to see the ratio of your budget to the remaining need of funds.
  - **VAC fields** These fields were covered previously.

PART III

- **Enumerated fields**
  - **Accrue At (Resource field)** This field enables you to set the method for accruing time for overtime purposes. The options are Start, End, and Accrual. This setting is done through Project Professional with the Enterprise Resource Pool open as shown in Figure 9-4.
  - **Base Calendar (Resource field)*** The Base Calendar is a setting that is done by resource that selects a calendar to use for that resource as the base. In most organizations, the Standard Calendar holds the company holidays and that is the only Base Calendar (an easy choice). In global organizations, multiple Base Calendars can be created for different parts of the world and for different cultural reasons. If there is more than one, this field holds which calendar is correct for the resource. There are other uses for Base Calendars, such as 4-day work weeks, three shift environments, and more.
  - **Constraint Type (Task field)*** This field is where the project manager sets whether a task is fixed work, fixed units, or fixed duration, and can be exposed in PWA Project Detail (Task) views. Project managers must understand the concept of this setting, as it is crucial to successful project management. There is a deeper discussion of this topic later in the book when we cover the project manager's role.

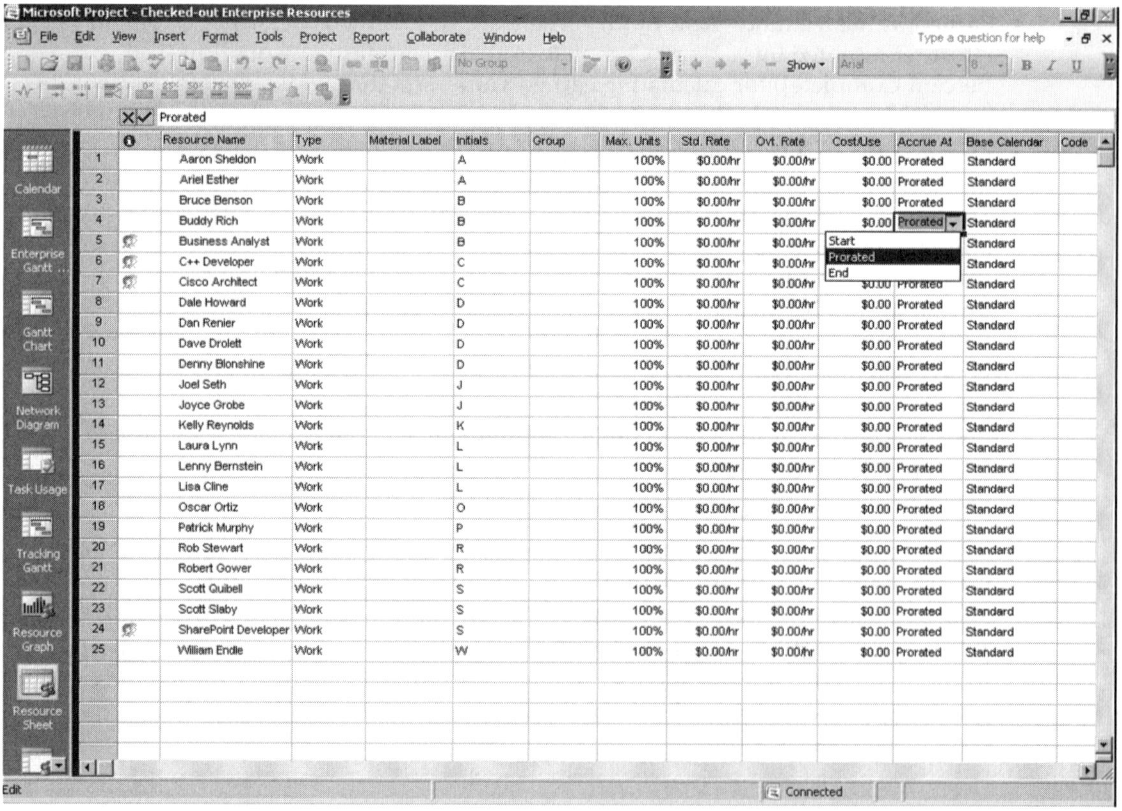

FIGURE 9-4 Setting the accrual method

  - **Cost Rate Table fields** This Project-only field allows a view into the costs for a task based on the rate of the assigned resources.
  - **Earned Value Method (Task field)** This field was covered previously.
  - **Priority fields** These fields (Task and Assignment) are used to set the priority primarily for the purposes of resource leveling.
  - **Resource Type fields*** These fields are used for information on whether a resource is a work or material resource and apply to the Task and Assignment categories.
  - **Status (Task field)** This Project-only field shows whether a task is complete, on schedule, late, or a future task.
  - **Task Calendar (Task field)** This field shows all the calendars that can be applied to a task. It can be displayed in PWA, although it is difficult to see why it would ever be chosen for display.
  - **Type fields** These fields were covered earlier in the chapter.
  - **Work Contour fields** These Project-only fields are one of the more obscure features (see Figure 9-5). They allow the project manager to establish when work will be performed on a task based on prebuild (Microsoft) forms. Each type is graphically represented in the Indicator column (usually the leftmost column in Project Professional views). If none of these match what is required, then manually timephasing the work is necessary. There options are as follows:
    - Flat (no graphic)
    - Back-Loaded (five bars going uphill)
    - Front-Loaded (five bars going downhill)
    - Double Peak (low, high, low, high, low)
    - Early Peak (low, high, then downhill)
    - Late Peak (uphill for four bars, then low)
    - Bell (peaks in the middle)
    - Turtle (shaped like a turtle)
- **Indicator fields** All of these fields have been covered previously:
  - Accrue At (Resource field)
  - Base Calendar (Resource field)
  - Constraint Type (Task field)
  - Cost Rate Table fields
  - Earned Value Method (Task field)

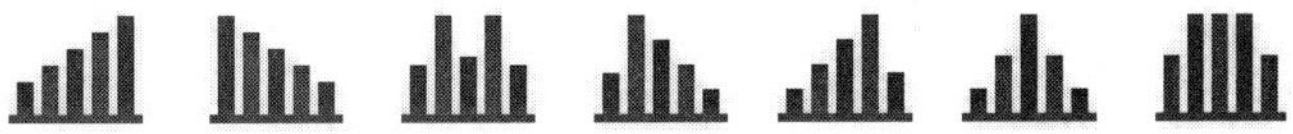

FIGURE 9-5 Work Contours

    - Priority fields
    - Resource Type fields
    - Status (Task field)
    - Task Calendar (Task field)
    - Type fields
- **Integer fields**
    - **Enterprise Unique ID (Resource field)** Project Server generates this field for each resource, and it stays with the resource. Note that this is also a unique ID in the form of a Globally Unique Identifier (GUID) that is sometimes useful for deep troubleshooting.
    - **ID fields** This Project-generated field can be displayed in PWA and is unique. If you are using this field, however, take care because it is dynamic based on the relationships in the plan. In other words, if a project manager adds a task before another task within the same work breakdown structure (WBS) level, this number will change.
    - **Outline Level fields** These Task and Assignment fields hold information on where an item is in the outline or WBS. If it is a top-level item, it is Level 1, then Level 2, and so on. Figure 9-6 shows an example.
    - **Predecessors (Task field)*** Predecessors are tasks that occur prior to the task where the field is applied. If, for example, you must open the garage door before you can pull the car in, then Open Garage Door is a predecessor task to Pull in Car. There are several methods for setting predecessors and they are displayed as the Task ID field (a number). Note that it is possible to have predecessor-successor relationships that are Start to Finish, Start to Start, and Finish to Finish. In addition, lag time can be included. For example, if you can't mow the lawn in the spring until after you mow it in the fall (and after the snow melts), that could be a Finish to Start field with lag. The field might look like the following:

      FS+75d (Finish to Start plus 75 days)

    - **Resource ID (Assignment field)** This is the ID field (covered previously) as applied to an assignment.
    - **Successors (Task field)** This is the opposite of the Predecessors field. Successors are tasks that are dependent on a previous task.
    - **Task ID (Assignment field)** This is the Task ID field as associated with an assignment.
    - **Unique ID fields** These are ID fields as applied to tasks, resources, and assignments.
    - **Unique ID Predecessors (Task field)**
    - **Unique ID Successors (Task field)**

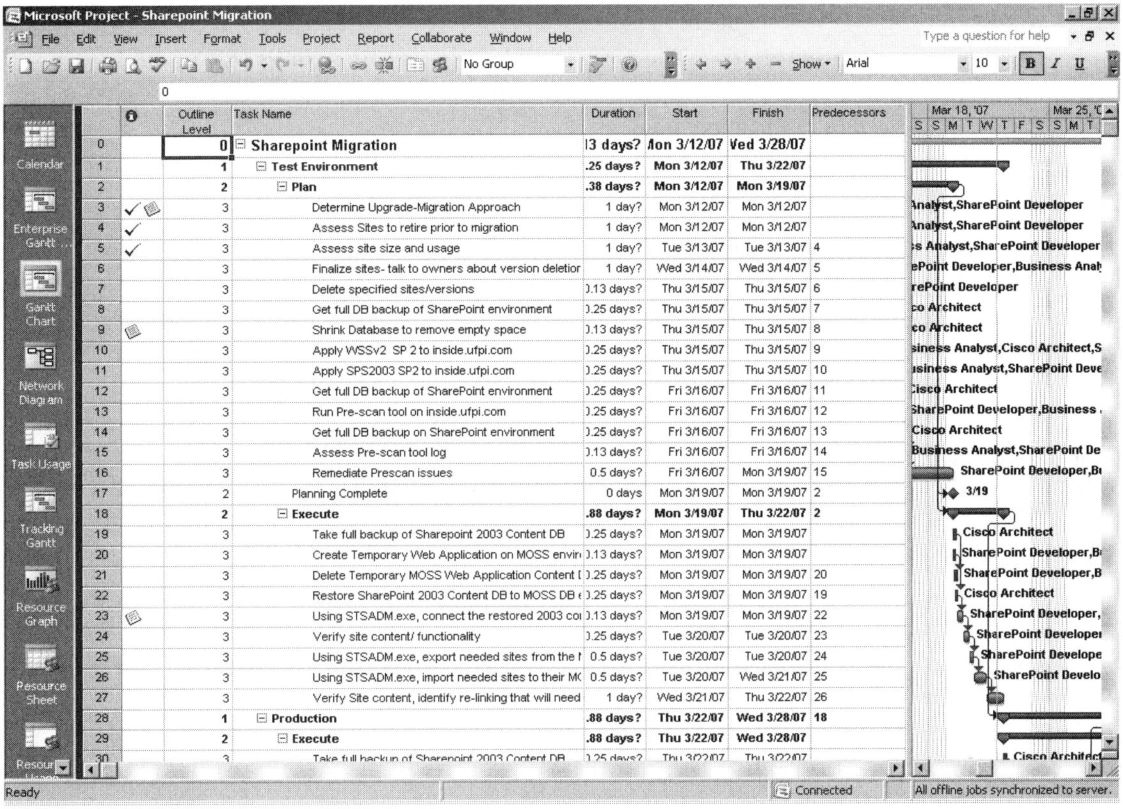

FIGURE 9-6 Outline Levels

- **WBS Predecessors (Task field)** The WBS is a key part of using Project and Project Server. It is a hierarchical view of the project's major phases broken down into more detail. If following good project management practices, when building plans you should always produce a WBS rather than simply creating a list of things to do. If displayed, the WBS field appears as *number.number.number*, like an outline. It does change dynamically when tasks are added or moved around. Find additional Project resources to learn about the use of WBS. This field displays the WBS number of the predecessor(s).
- **WBS Successors (Task field)** This is similar to the WBS Predecessors field, except that it displays the WBS number of the successor(s).

- **Outline code fields** Outline codes have been replaced in Project Server 2007 with the use of custom enterprise fields that have an associated lookup table (you will learn more of this later in this chapter).

- **Percentage and number fields**
  - **Assignment Units fields** These are used to show resource units (the percentage of their workday available) at the assignment level.
    - Assignment Units (Task field)
    - Assignment Units (Resource field)
    - Assignment Units (Assignment field)
  - **CPI fields** These fields were covered previously.
  - **Cumulative Percent (%) Complete (Task Timephased field)** This is a Project-only field where you can display total percent complete (percent of duration complete) and view it over time up to the current day. This duration data show how a task is running from that perspective.
  - **CV% fields*** These fields were covered earlier in this chapter.
  - **Max Units (Resource field)*** This field is set per resource and represents the largest amount of time that a resource can be scheduled before becoming overallocated. This is used in most Project Server deployments as part of the total perspective of resource management and capacity planning.
  - **Number1–20 fields** These can be used to hold whatever number information is needed and can be displayed in PWA.
  - **Objects fields** This is a Project-only field that can be used to display a count of objects associated with a task or resource. This field is rarely if ever used.
  - **Peak fields** This is a Project-only field, but has a functional equivalent in PWA when using the resource assignments and Availability views from within the Resource Center.
  - **Peak Units fields** These fields are the same as the Peak fields.
  - **Percent (%) Allocation fields** These fields show the percentage of a resource's total capacity that is booked. They apply to resource and assignment timephased allocation.
  - **Percent (%) Complete fields** This set of fields (task and timephased task) show the percentage of the task completion from the duration perspective. The Percent Work Complete fields (discussed next) are more likely to provide a better understanding of task progress. Note that these fields are often mistakenly used by project managers who believe that they represent a work-based calculation.
  - **Percent (%) Work Complete fields*** These fields apply for task, resource, and assignment categories and display the percentage of effort (work) that has been expended on a task as compared to the Work field.
  - **Physical Percent (%) Complete (Task field)** This field was covered previously.
  - **SPI fields** These were described earlier in the chapter.
  - **SV Percent (%) fields*** These fields were covered previously in the chapter.
  - **Task Outline Number (Assignment field)*** This is the autogenerated number in the WBS field at the task level. Remember that these numbers change if additional tasks above them are inserted or deleted.

- **TCPI (Task field)** This field was covered previously.
- **Unit Availability (Resource Timephased field)** This resource timephased field displays the percentage of a resource's availability based on previously defined units (percentage or the day, week, and so on) as spread out over time.

- **Text fields**
  - **Code (Resource field)** This field allows assignment to a resource of any type of code desired.
  - **Contact (Task field)** This field is used to display the name of a resource that is responsible for a task if the resource is different from the person or people assigned. This field is rarely used.
  - **E-mail Address (Resource field)** This field is the resource's actual e-mail address. It can be populated manually in the Enterprise Resource Pool or by importing the information through synchronization with Microsoft Active Directory (AD).
  - **Group (Resource field)** This field is used to associate a resource to a group. For example, the resources might be associated to a group for reporting purposes.
  - **Hyperlink fields** Hyperlinks can be added manually. This field displays a common language version (for example, MyLink) followed by the actual URL.
  - **Hyperlink Address fields** This field shows the actual link.
  - **Hyperlink Href fields** This field allows use of the HTML Href technique inside of a local Project plan, but is not for use in Project Server.
  - **Hyperlink SubAddress fields** This Project-only field is for linking the actual item in a linked location such as a network Share. This field does not work for linking to any object stored in a database, so it can't be used to link to documents in a SharePoint site, for example.
  - **Initials (Resource field)** This is used to hold the initials of a resource. It is most commonly used for display in Project Professional as it uses less space whether displayed as a column or as a label by a Gantt bar chart.
  - **Material Label (Resource field)*** This is used for material resources and would normally hold the unit of measure such as board feet, lbs, and so on, for calculation of costs.
  - **Name fields*** This field holds the name of a task or a resource.
  - **Notes fields** Notes can be associated with a task in Project and are displayed in the MyTasks View in PWA, which can be viewed by each resource. This is a helpful new feature, as previously it was only available to the project manager. In addition, task-level notes can be associated from PWA with a task's history. They can provide a way to display both the task update information (hours reported, remaining work, date of update, and so on) and the hand-entered notes.
  - **Outline Number (Task field)** This field was covered previously.

    - **Phonetics (Resource field)** This field can hold the phonetic version of a name if necessary.
    - **Project fields** These fields are Project only, but have a parallel in the Project Server world called Enterprise Project fields. Read more about them in the next section on custom enterprise fields.
    - **Resource Group fields** These are just like Group fields but for resources. They are used primarily in Project. Project Server uses several other methods for group information at the resource level.
    - **Resource Initials fields** These fields provide the initials for Resource views.
    - **Resource Name (Assignment or Task fields)** These fields are equivalent to the name of the resource on an assignment or task.
    - **Resource Phonetics (Task field)** This field is equivalent to the Phonetics field but is displayed for tasks.
    - **Subproject File (Task field)** If there is a subproject included in a Master project, a feature that finally works in an EPM environment, this field displays the link to the subproject.
    - **Task Name (Assignment field)** This field was covered previously.
    - **Task Summary Name fields** This field holds the name of the summary task in the case where viewers are looking at assignments.
    - **Text1–30 fields** These fields can be used to hold whatever test information is required and can be displayed in PWA.
    - **WBS fields** There are three fields: WBS, WBS Predecessors, and WBS Successors. These are represented in Outline Code form (3.21.34.2.3…).
    - **Windows User Account (Resource field)** This holds the actual Windows login account for each user (in the format *DOMAIN\loginname*).
- **Yes/No fields**
    - **Assignment fields** These Project-only fields display whether a row is an assignment. They have very little practical value.
    - **Can Level (Resource field)** This displays whether or not a resource can be leveled. This field is set in the Enterprise Resource Pool of Project Server.
    - **Confirmed fields** These fields can be used to display whether there has been a response (for example, if the assigned resource submits a task update) to a new task or an updated task. It is useful for determining whether a resource may need to be replaced (if there has been no response for a while). This could be valuable in large organizations. In smaller organizations, picking up the phone or walking to the resource's cube would be better.
        - Confirmed (Task field)
        - Confirmed (Resource field)
        - Confirmed (Assignment field)

- **Critical fields** These display whether a task or assignment is on the critical path and can be used in PWA for task and assignment Project views in PWA.
- **Effort Driven (Task field)** Effort-driven scheduling is used for maintaining the work on a task as resources are added or removed. For example, if an additional resource is added, the work hours do not increase, but rather either units or duration are decreased depending on task type settings. Usually, this is the recommended approach to scheduling.
- **Enterprise Base Calendar (Resource field)** This field displays which base calendar is being used by a resource. The field is usually useful only in larger organizations where it makes sense to use multiple enterprise calendars.
- **Enterprise Required Values (Resource field)** This Project-only field is used to display whether all required fields are completed. The field is used primarily for custom coding in Visual Basic for Applications (VBA). In most circumstances, the field is of little value.
- **Estimated (Task field)** This field indicates whether the task this estimated or not. The field can be displayed in PWA and is a useful replacement for the question mark (?) in Project for display on task duration.
- **External Task (Task field)** Project tasks can be linked between projects. This field displays whether or not a task has a predecessor or successor relationship with a task in another project. This field can be displayed in PWA Project views, and can be useful especially when running a set of related projects (often called a Program).
- **Flag1–20 fields** These fields are usually used to identify or mark (flag) something and can be used in PWA views. These can be used in any way that makes sense for a particular organization.
- **Generic (Resource field)** This field displays whether or not a user is a generic resource. You will learn more on generic resources later in the book as resource management is discussed.
- **Group by Summary fields** This Project-only field indicates a yes or no for grouping.
- **Hide Bar (Task field)** This low use and value Project-only field displays whether a Gantt bar is hidden.
- **Ignore Resource Calendar (Task field)** This is used to display whether a resource's calendar is ignored. Normally the field displays No, but there is occasional use for this field. For example, if you know that an all-nighter is required to migrate a large amount of files, setting this field to Yes will allow the tools' calculations to schedule in the way this scenario would require. Specifically, setting the field to Yes would allow work to be scheduled during what is normally considered non-working time overnight.
- **Inactive (Resource field)** This Project-only field displays whether a resource is set to inactive. Project Server handles this differently.
- **Level Assignments (Task field)** This Project-only field is used to set whether a task can be split or incur a delay if autoleveling is used.

- **Leveling Can Split (Task field)** This Project-only field is used to set whether a task can be split when leveling. When a task is split, it can start, then have a gap, then resume again later when the leveling calculation allows the work to complete. Unless you are something of a Project guru, you should set this to No.
- **Linked Fields fields** In Project, this setting shows whether there are any OLE links inside the plan. In Project Server, there is a similar function to display whether a task in a project has any issues, risks, or documents associated and provides the viewer a direct link to that material.
- **Marked (Task field)** From Project, the project manager can set this field to note that the task is identified as needing some action or for any other Yes/No function. In Project Server, this field can be displayed.
- **Milestone (Task field)*** This type of task item in a project plan represents an event that has no duration or work associated. It is usually used to mark the end of something or a date when something is delivered. For example, a milestone may be used to mark the end of a project phase.
- **Overallocated fields** These fields display whether or not there is an overallocation. Take care with these settings, however, as the context is critical and the fields cannot be used to display global overallocation (for example, that Bob is overallocated across all his projects). There are other ways to find out global overallocation in Project Server.
    - Overallocated (Task field)
    - Overallocated (Resource field)
- **Recurring (Task field)** This displays whether a task is part of a series. This can be displayed in Project Server. Usually there are many more reasons not to use recurring tasks than there are reasons to use them. It may be easy to set the Friday status meeting as a recurring meeting, but doing so raises some issues. For example, if a project team of 10 is scheduled for one hour each every Friday and only seven folks show up, the three hours remaining will stay scheduled in the past and require manual PM intervention to keep the plan current. Although there are exceptions, generally you should not use recurring tasks.
- **Request/Demand (Assignment field)** This field in Project's Resource Substitution Wizard sets whether a resource must be used or would be used if it were not overallocated.
- **Response Pending fields** The project manager manually sets these Project-only fields, which are not particularly useful.
- **Rollup (Task field)** This field is rarely used. When it is used, it is most likely just for reporting. It is used to set whether a task should roll up to a summary task. It is set automatically to Yes and should almost always remain that way.
- **Subproject ReadOnly (Task field)** This field is used to display whether any subproject in a Master project relationship is set as read-only.
- **Summary (Task field)** This field displays whether a task is a summary task.

- **TeamStatus Pending fields** A feature in Project allows the project manager to request a project update. This field displays whether the team has fully responded. This field can be displayed in PWA.
- **Text Above (Task field)** This Project-only field sets whether subtask text displays by summary task roll up Gantt bars.
- **Update Needed fields** This field displays whether a project in the Project Server environment should be republished to notify team members of changes in the plan.

Project Server Built-In "Custom" Fields

In addition to the fields from Project Professional, there are Project Server–specific fields. Project Server 2007 has a series of five fields that are built in for enterprise use. They appear as custom enterprise fields. The following is a list of those fields as well as a description of what they are used for in the 2007 Project Server environment:

- Cost Type
- RBS (Resource Breakdown Structure)
- Health
- State
- Team Name

Cost Type is mapped to the Cost Type Lookup Table but holds no actual types when first installed. If a company is looking for reports that used categories of cost, then this field would be useful.

RBS is mapped to the RBS Lookup Table and also starts empty. The RBS is a critical Project Server field. It is most commonly used to build an outline-style format (*name.name .name…*) that represents your organization as it works functionally. A more detailed discussion about the RBS appears in Chapter 20.

Health is mapped to the Health Lookup Table and is prepopulated with the following:

- Not specified
- On schedule
- Late
- Early
- Blocked
- Completed

State comes mapped to the State field and is prepopulated with the following:

- Proposed
- Approved
- Rejected

NOTE *Do not change these as they are part of the approval workflow that can be used with proposals.*

CAUTION *Please read the next section carefully. Don't modify this field until you are sure that you know how to make modifications correctly. A detailed process for this is located later in the section "Correctly Connecting the Team Name Field" of this chapter.*

Team Name, for some reason, does not come with a lookup table, although one is required to use the Resource Plans and Team Tasks features in Project Server 2007. A custom lookup table is required that includes the names of the teams that will be used by an organization. Take care not to save this field until after you have a lookup table; otherwise, SQL Server field–level modifications will be required to recover this functionality.

Custom Fields

Even with all the built-in fields, most organizations will find value in creating some custom fields. As mentioned previously, existing fields could be compared. In other cases, a completely new field may be the appropriate choice. For example, if you want to see data by the department of the resource, it is necessary to create an enterprise custom resource field called Department.

In previous versions, there was a predetermined set of fields by type. For example, you could have only 30 enterprise custom resource fields with one field reserved. This type of internal limit by specific type is no longer in place, allowing more flexibility.

Each field must be associated with an entity and a type (more information on entities and types is provided later in this chapter). Each field also can be constructed in several formatting models, some simple to develop and others more complex. Finally, fields can be configured to require information to be in place.

Project fields are for the entire project, not just a single task. Once created, enterprise custom project fields are populated from within Microsoft Office Project Professional 2007. To find the place to choose and/or populate enterprise custom project fields, open Project, then select Project from the main menu across the top, then select Project Information. Figure 9-7 shows the Project Information dialog that appears.

CAUTION *Enterprise custom project fields appear for each project manager within the Project Information dialog in Project Professional. Keep in mind that the more of these fields you create, the more cluttered and less usable the interface becomes. They also each add a small amount of performance overhead. These fields are valuable—just don't overuse them.*

These fields can also be configured from PWA by using the Edit Project Properties feature in Project Center. Figure 9-8 shows how the configuration page appears after selection. There is one way to get there. If you are in detailed Project Views, you select the button as well, as shown in Figure 9-9.

Resource fields are set from the Enterprise Resource Pool, from Resource Center views in PWA, or from the User area under Security in the Server Settings area. You can open the Enterprise Resource Pool from within Project Professional by selecting Tools | Enterprise Options | Open Enterprise Resource Pool. The PWA Enterprise Resource Pool opens within Project Professional to allow selection of specific resources. After selection, as shown in Figure 9-10, the selected enterprise resources are ready to be edited from within Project Professional. Resource Center (shown in Figure 9-11) within PWA can also be the starting point. Select users and then click the Open button. Figure 9-12 displays the editing page from within the Manage Users section in PWA.

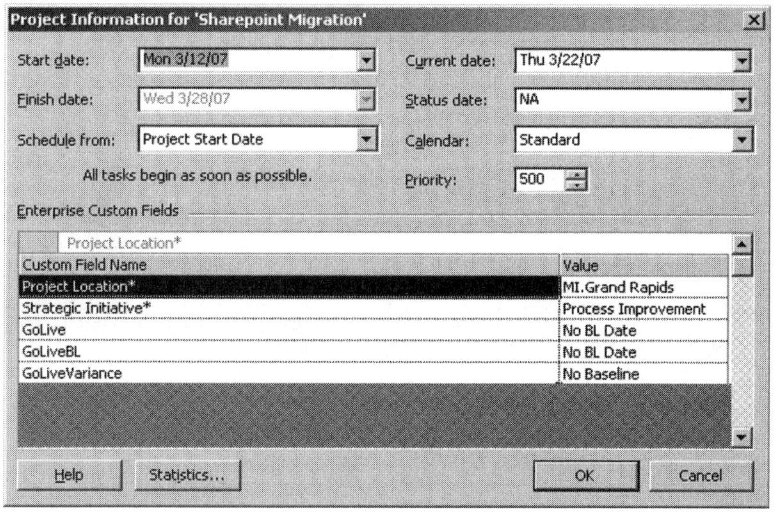

Figure 9-7 Project Information dialog

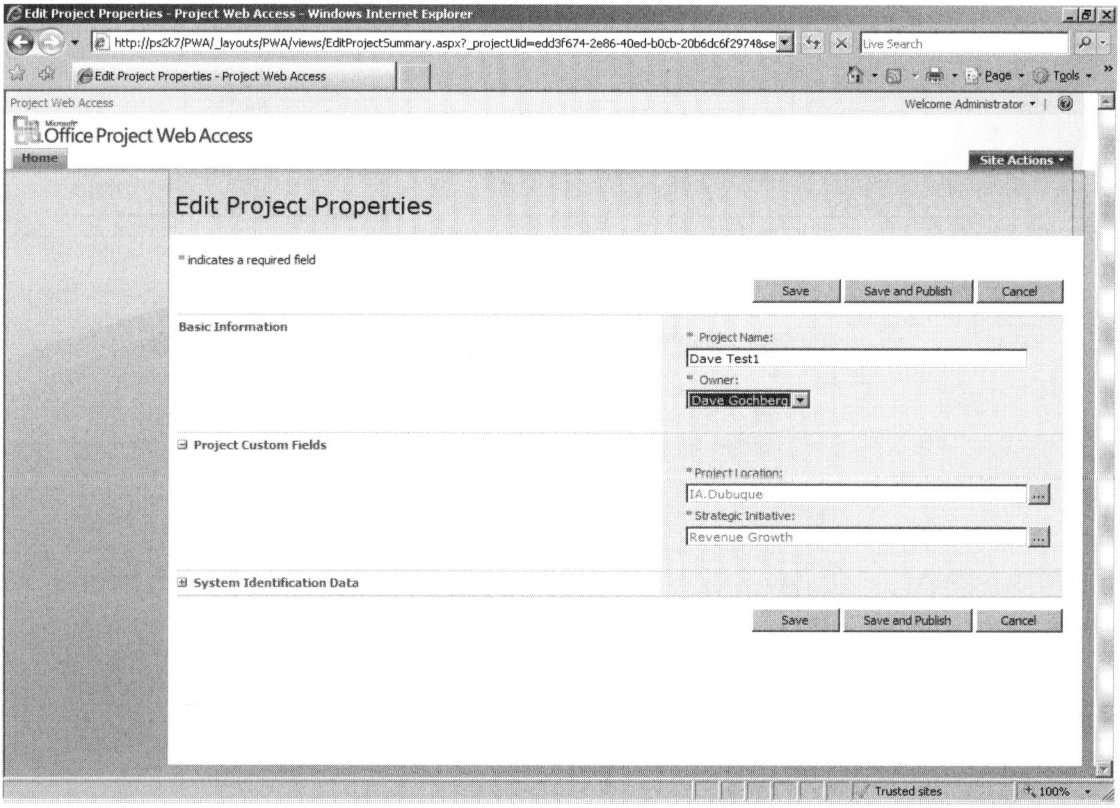

Figure 9-8 Edit Project Properties in Project Center

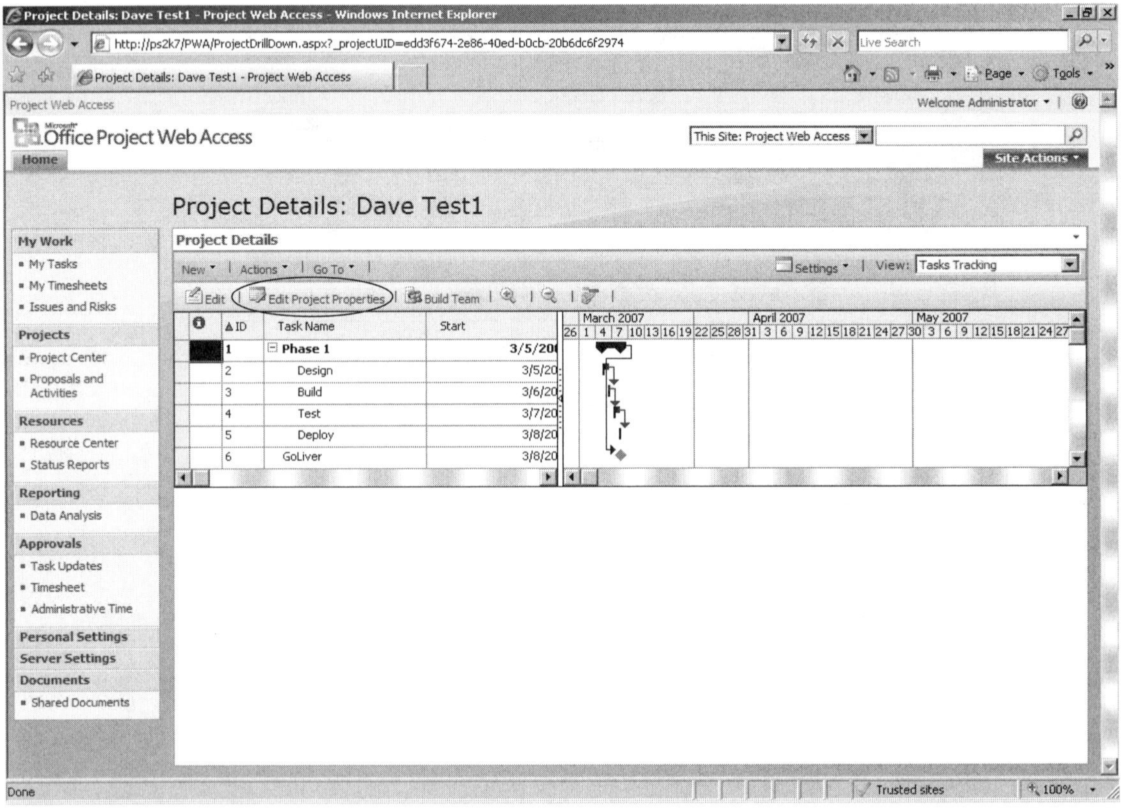

FIGURE 9-9 Edit Project Properties in Project views

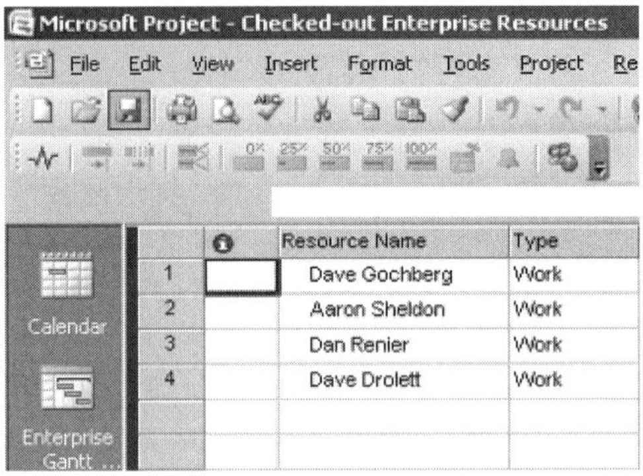

FIGURE 9-10 Editing Enterprise Resources from within Project Professional

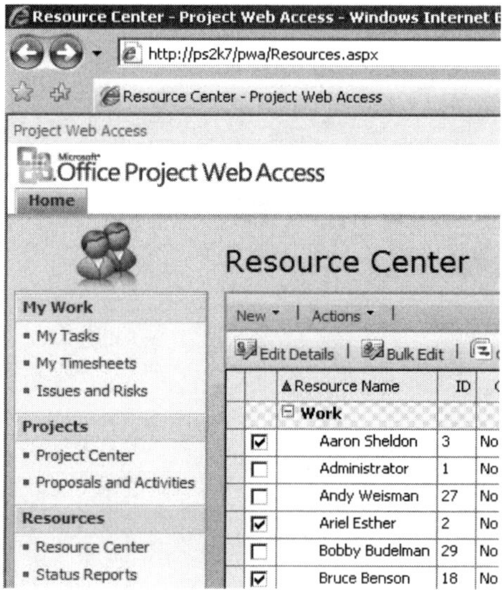

Figure 9-11 Selecting resources to edit from Resource Center

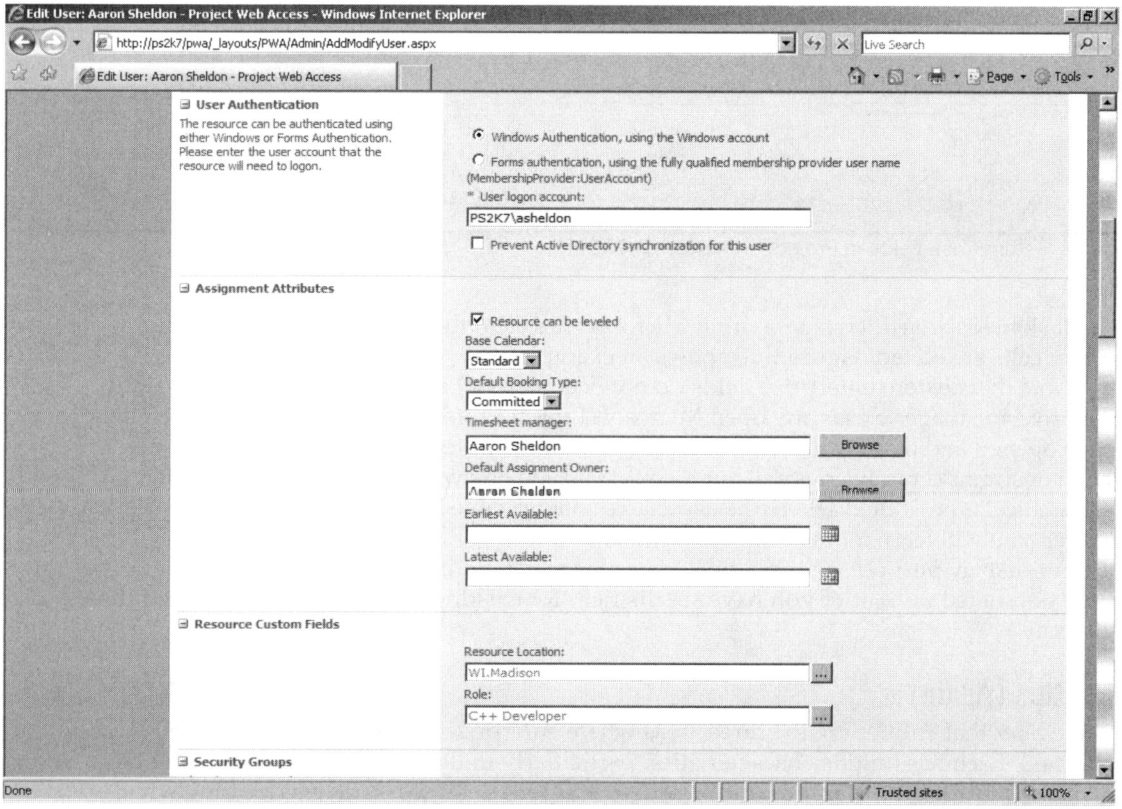

Figure 9-12 Setting Resource fields from the User settings

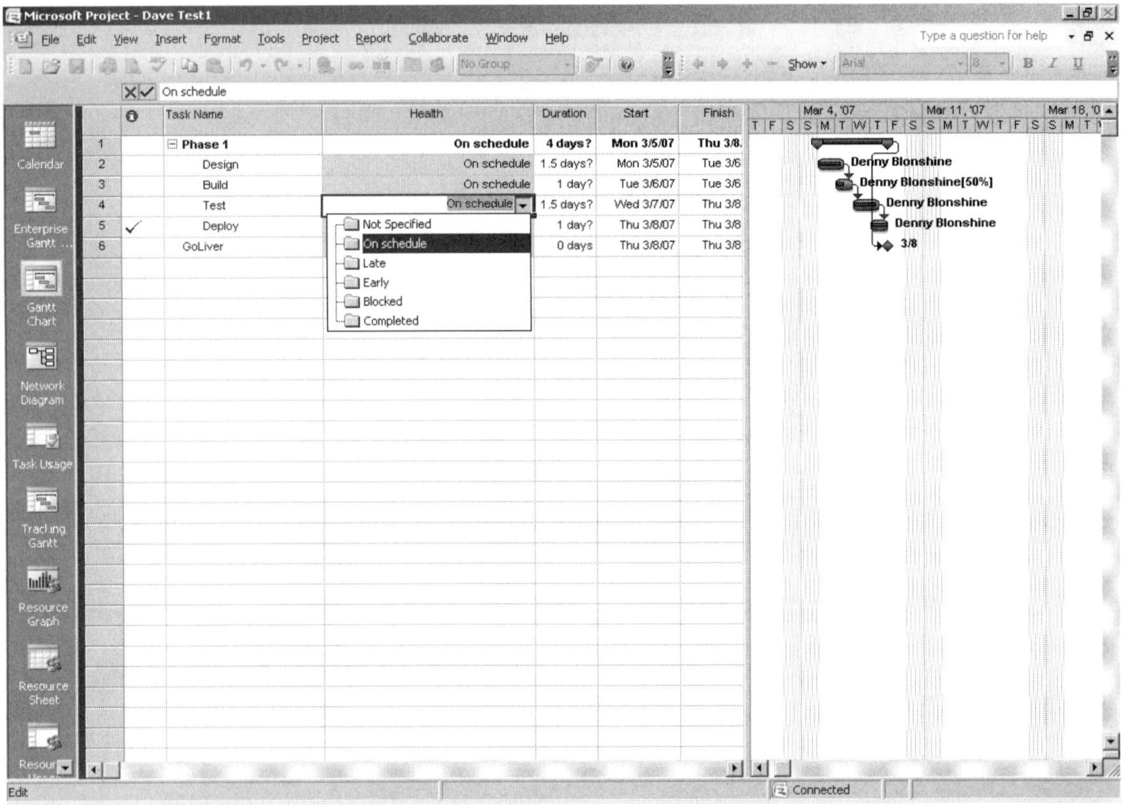

FIGURE 9-13 Setting Task fields in Project Professional 2007

Task fields are edited from within Microsoft Project only through the use of a column where cells are edited. Figure 9-13 shows an example.

Note that custom enterprise fields do not become available for project managers until the project manager closes any open Microsoft Project Professional sessions that they might have opened and restarts Project. Fields are generally limited to a total of 255 characters. This constraint is rarely an issue, but it could become one when you are dealing with a hierarchical type of field where the associated lookup table has what is called a *Code Mask* (which you will learn more about later in this chapter).

For display purposes, it is possible to use the new field in a view, but the data will not be fully populated until after you have set the field for existing projects and republished those projects.

Entities (Again)

Remember that entities are the three areas where enterprise custom fields (attributes) can be attached. Each has unique characteristics, particularly in the way that the output can be displayed in views. It is important to understand how each works when deciding what enterprise custom fields to build.

Projects

Project-level attributes are used to distinguish projects at a summary level. Enterprise custom project fields are commonly set by the project manager. The following are some example custom enterprise project fields:

- **Project Status** This field includes such options as Request Pending, Started, Postponed, Cancelled, and Completed.
- **Capital or Expense**
- **Project Sponsor** This field displays names from a dropdown menu.
- **Regulatory** This field displays either Yes or No or a list of possible regulatory types such as HIPAA and Sarbanes-Oxley.
- **Priority** This field displays High, Medium, or Low, or 1, 2, 3, 4, 5, or some similar rating.
- **Tracking Cost** This field tracks cost by variance or by actual dollars.
- **Tracking Work** This field tracks work by variance or by actual hour differentials.
- **Tracking Finish** This field tracks the finish of a project by using date differences as numeric or percentage data.
- **Tracking Value** This field tracks value by using earned value or comparing fields.
- **Overall Health** This field presents either calculated or subjective criteria.
- **Other Project Level Comparisons** These types of fields evaluate the project level by using multiple fields and comparing them.
- **Strategic Initiative** This field presents a pick list of company strategies.
- **Level of Risk**

Resources

As mentioned earlier, enterprise custom resource fields are used to apply attributes to resources. Resource fields are commonly set by either an administrator or by resource managers for their resources. Some common uses for Resource fields include the following:

- **Exempt or Not Exempt** Indicate whether the employee is exempt or not.
- **Location** Choose the location from a dropdown list.
- **Department** Select the employee's department from a dropdown list.
- **Cost Center** Enter the cost center code.
- **Employee Type** Examples of employee types include full-time employee (FTE), consultant, and subcontractor.
- **Resource Breakdown Structure (RBS)** Indicate where the resource fits in the organizational or location structure. (This field is available out of the box and can be highly useful for reporting and security purposes; see Chapter 8.) Note that although this field exists out of the box, it must be customized to be useful.

Task

As described earlier, enterprise custom task fields are used for attributes at the detailed task level. Examples might include the following:

- **Cost Center**
- **Capitol or Expense**

NOTE *For tax purposes, when working on a capital project, some tasks cannot be legally capitalized.*

- **Key Milestone** Note that it is possible to use task fields such as a milestone to form the basis for project fields that roll up the task fields from underneath. A discussion of that will come later in this chapter in the "Building and Formatting Custom Enterprise Fields" section.

Types (Again)

As mentioned earlier, there are six field types. In general, these types are self-explanatory, so the descriptions that follow are brief.

Cost

The values in this field are displayed as the currency of choice (e.g., $2,343.00 for USD).

Date

Values in this field are displayed as dates depending on date formatting options chosen (as in Mon 3/19/2007, for example).

Duration

Duration is the time between Start and Finish of a task, project or assignment.

Flag

The flag field type is used to display information such as whether some type of action is required for other types of classification.

Number

Number fields should be used in any case where the displayed information can include only numeric characters.

Text

Text is an option for several solutions, but is frequently used for displaying items from a dropdown list such as project status or project sponsor.

Building and Formatting Custom Enterprise Fields

Several formats can be used for enterprise custom fields. To build any of the following fields, follow these steps:

1. Navigate to the Server Settings from the PWA Home Page (see Figure 9-14).
2. In the Enterprise Data area, select Enterprise Custom Field Definition. The Custom Fields and Lookup Tables screen appears as shown in Figure 9-15.

FIGURE 9-14 The Server Settings button from Quick Launch Bar

Notice that the screen is divided into two areas. The top area, Enterprise Custom Fields is always used for creation of the actual fields. The bottom section, Lookup Tables for Custom Fields, is frequently but not always used. Note that the field names must follow certain rules. Names cannot use any existing field names. In addition, no "illegal characters" should be used. The only characters that should be used are uppercase and lowercase letters, (*A* through *Z* and *a* through *z*), numbers (0 through 9), and underscores (_). Although creation of fields with illegal characters is allowed, they will create significant database issues.

Enterprise Custom Field (Free Entry)

At the most basic level, an enterprise custom field can be used for open entry. One real-world example is one that we encountered for a project description. Due to the number of

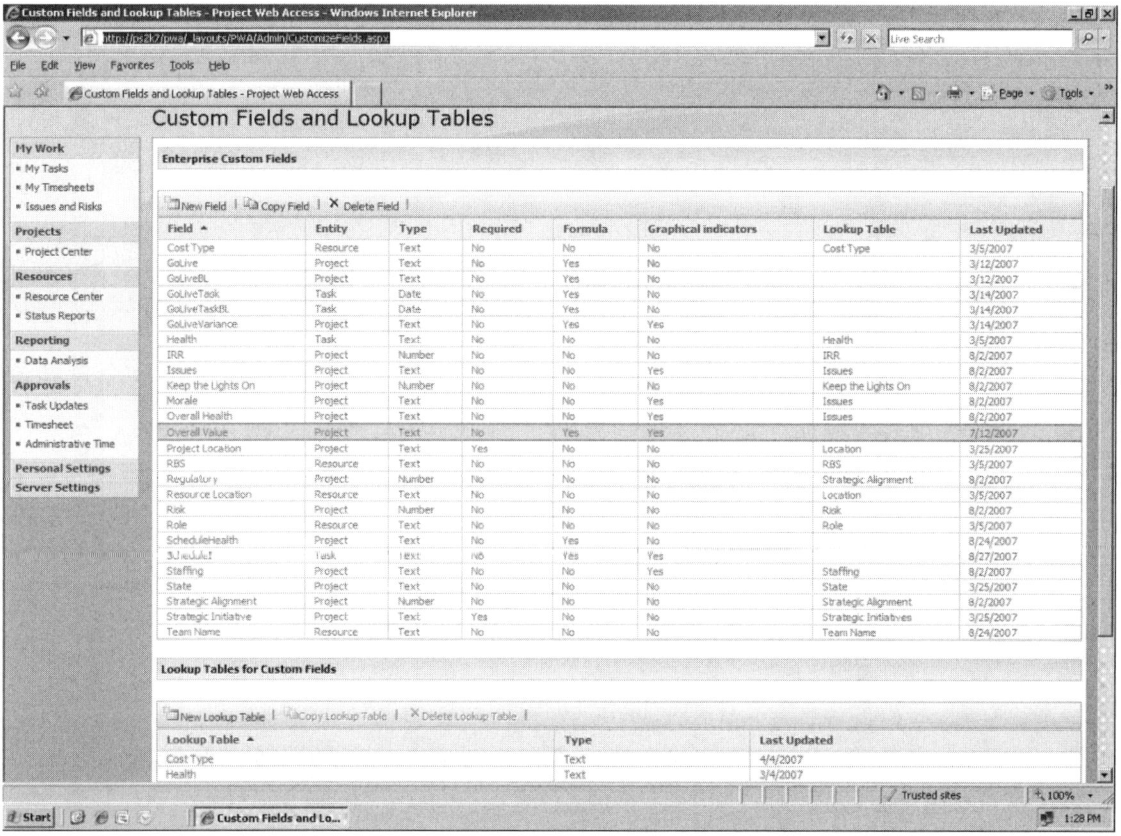

FIGURE 9-15 The Enterprise Custom Fields and Lookup Tables screen

fields displayed, we had to limit the built-in Project Name field in character length to avoid horizontal scrolling in Project Center views. This field allowed for a longer description, but was placed all the way to the right in the view so that scrolling was used only occasionally when the user did not understand the shorter project name. To build a field of this type, we used only the top section, as follows:

1. From within the Custom Fields and Lookup Tables page, select the New Field button. The form shown in Figure 9-16 appears.
2. Enter a name the Name field, then select the entity (Project, Resource, or Task) in the Entity field and select the type in the Type field, as shown in Figure 9-17.
3. In the Custom Attributes area, select None. In the Values to Display area, select Data. In the Required area, choose whether you want the field to be required.
4. Select Save.

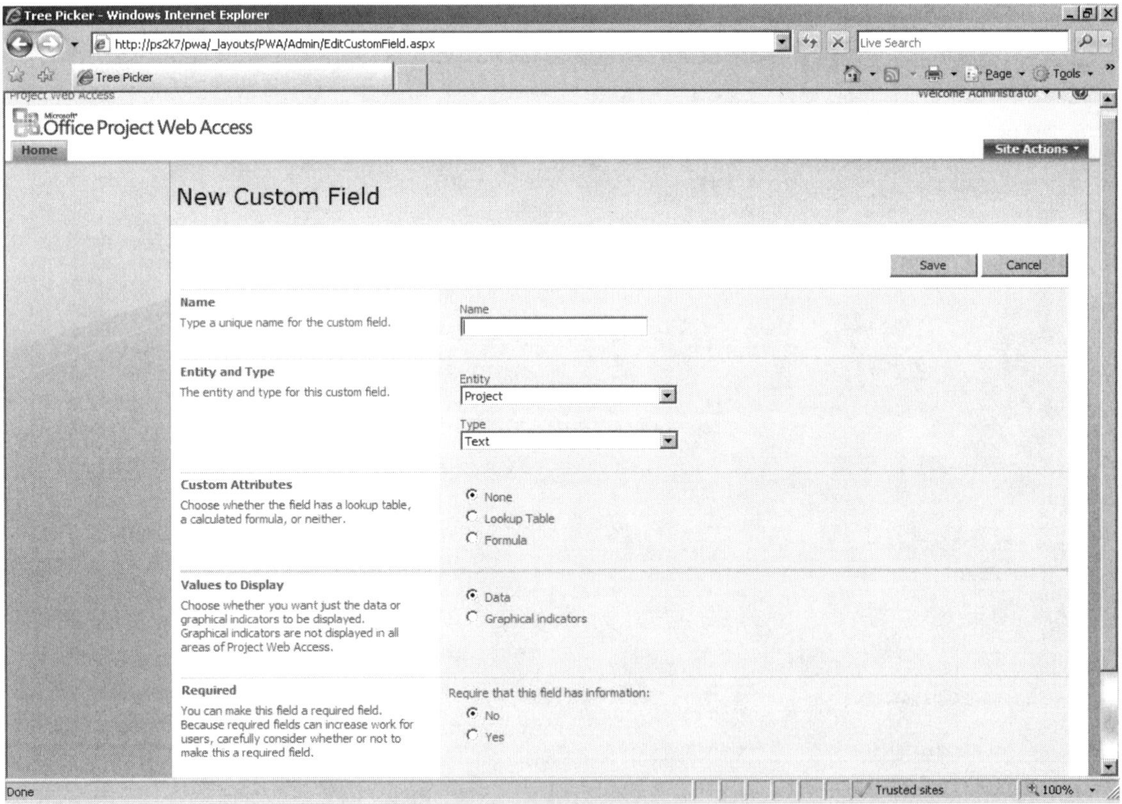

FIGURE 9-16 New Custom Field form

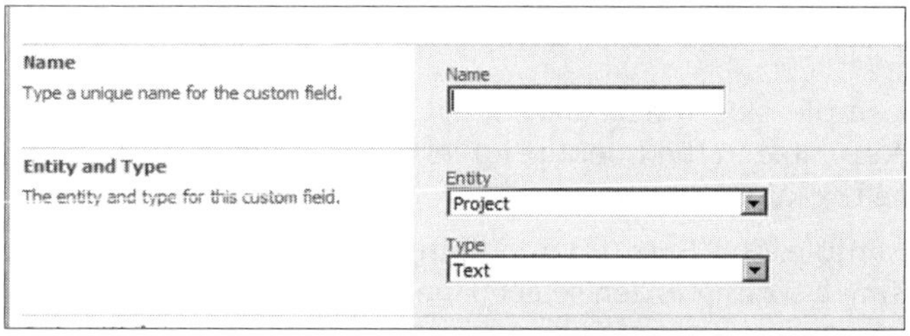

Figure 9-17 Specifying the new custom field

Enterprise Custom Field with Lookup Table

This kind of field is often used to create pick lists. Note that lookup tables can be shared among enterprise custom fields but should not be shared when using any of the built-in lookup tables. In this case, start with creation of a Lookup Table:

1. Select New from the Lookup Table section on the bottom of the page as shown in Figure 9-18.
2. Name the Lookup Table in the Name field and select the type.

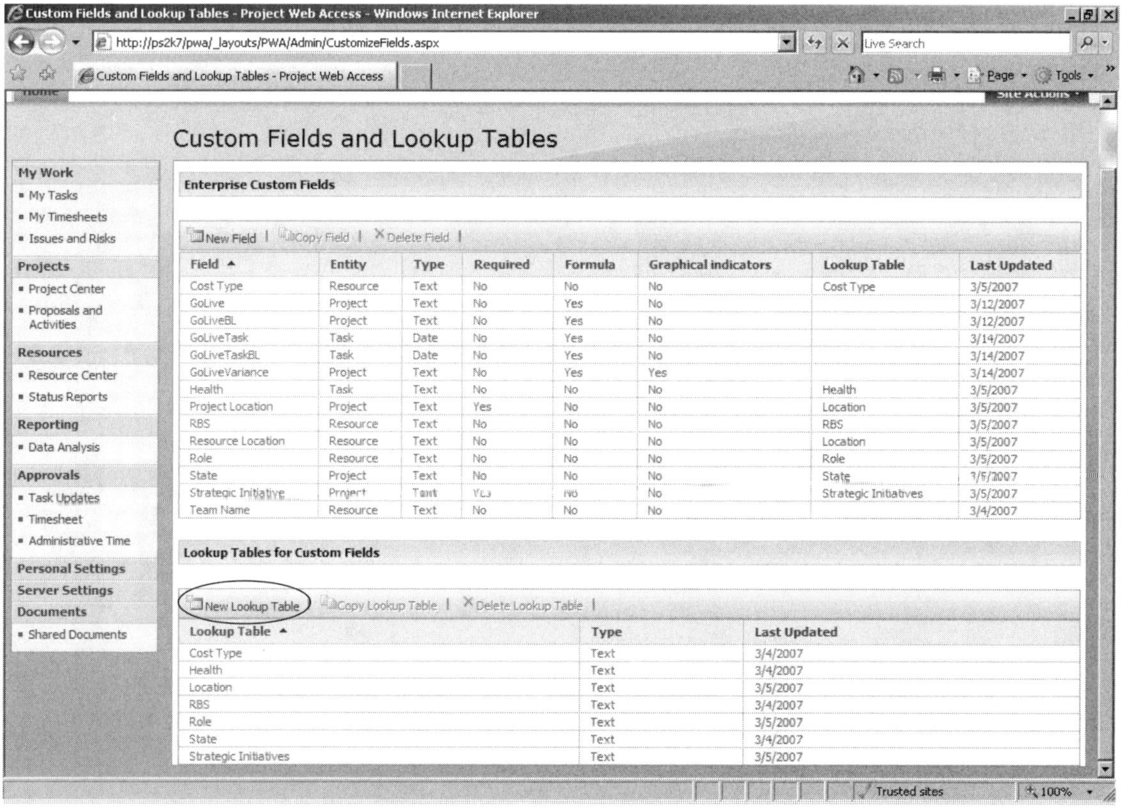

Figure 9-18 Selecting to create a new lookup table

NOTE *It is a best practice to name the field the same as the associated Lookup Table.*

3. For this example, skip the next section, Code Mask. Type in the data for the contents of the lookup table in the Lookup Table area (see Figure 9-19). Figure 9-20 shows the tools in the Lookup Table area.
4. For this example, don't use any indenting features. After populating the field values and choosing a sorting order, select Save.
5. Navigate to the Enterprise Custom Field area on top of the page and select New Field. Name your field and then select the entity. In the Custom Attributes area, select Lookup Table. The page now changes to display a dropdown list of existing lookup tables, as shown in Figure 9-21.
6. Select the lookup table that you just built. Decide whether there should be a default value for the field. If you decide to do so, then make the appropriate selection. Leave unselected the checkboxes Only Allow Codes with No Subordinate Values and Allow Multiple Values to Be Selected from Lookup Table. Values to display should be set to data. In the Required area. decide whether to make the field required.
7. Select Save.

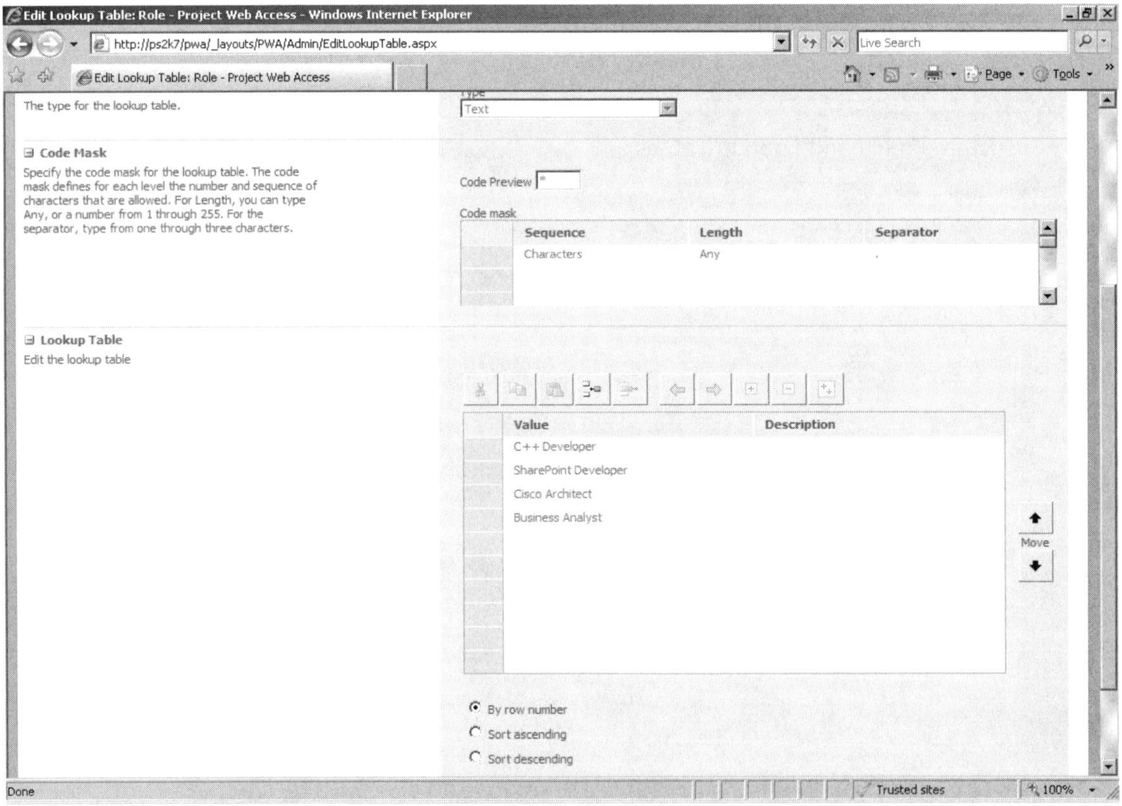

FIGURE 9-19 The Edit Lookup Table area

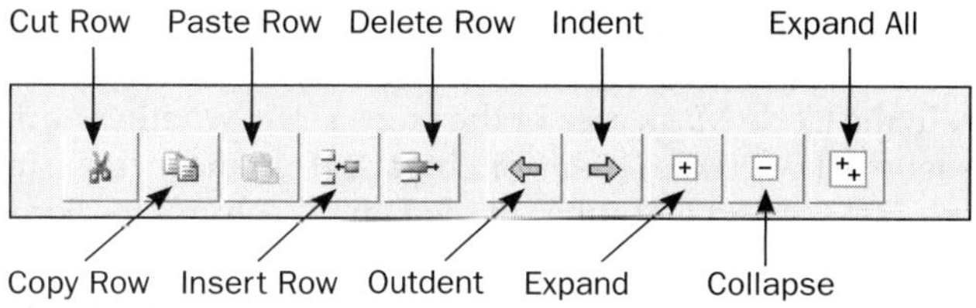

FIGURE 9-20 Functional tools available in the Lookup Table area

Enterprise Custom Field with Lookup Table with Code Mask

In previous versions of the tools, this type of field was called an enterprise custom outline code. This kind of field is similar to the previous one with the major exception that the lookup table is hierarchical. In other words, it is possible to build a drill-down lookup table. For example, if the organization wanted to have a Primary Skill field, it could go through a drill-down such as InformationTech.Developer.C.Expert or Language.Chinese.Cantonese.Fluent.

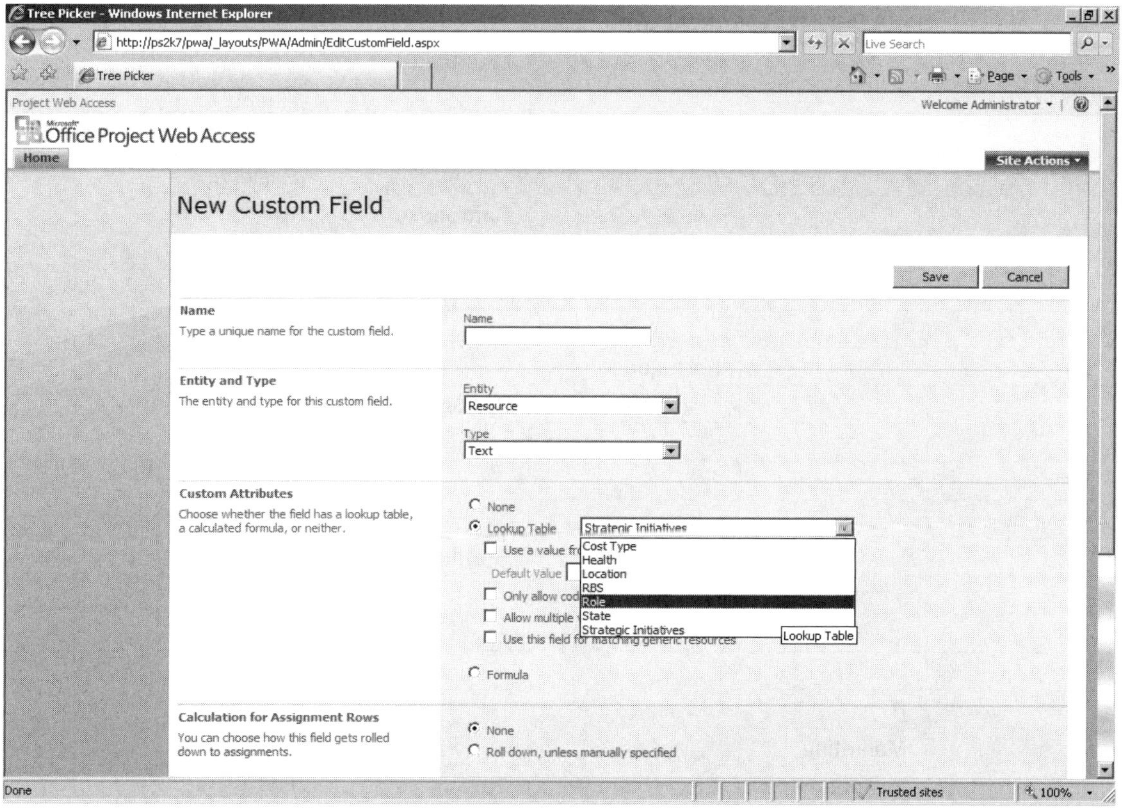

FIGURE 9-21 Dropdown list for lookup tables

To build a field that includes a Code Mask from the Enterprise Custom Field Definition page, start with a new lookup table as described previously. After naming your new lookup table, select the type. In the Code Mask area of the page, select whether you want to use numbers, uppercase letters, lowercase letters, or characters. In most cases, it makes sense to use numbers or characters. Next, insert a number in the Length column to represent the maximum length of the top level, or leave it set to Any. Normally, there is no compelling reason to restrict this length unless there is an expectation of a very long cumulative string (maximum total of 255). Finally, if the separator field type is acceptable (as it usually is), then go to the next row.

In the next row, follow the same procedure and continue until you have created enough rows to cover the deepest mask needed. If you are using the two previous examples, the first example of the C developer needs five levels and the Chinese skill would need four levels.

The next step is to navigate down to the lookup table. Enter the top of the hierarchy first. Consider something very inclusive such as the company name or Skills. Then, using the Indent and Outdent buttons, create the outline. Once again using the Language example, the outline might be something like that shown in Table 9-1.

Company				
	Language			
		Chinese		
			Mandarin	
				Fluent
				Acceptable
				Beginner
			Cantonese	
				Fluent
				Acceptable
				Beginner
		Portuguese		
			Portugal	
				Fluent
				Acceptable
				Beginner
			Brazilian	
				Fluent
				Acceptable
				Beginner
	IT			
	Marketing			
	Engineering	Etc.	Etc.	Etc.

Table 9-1 Outline Created for the Language Example

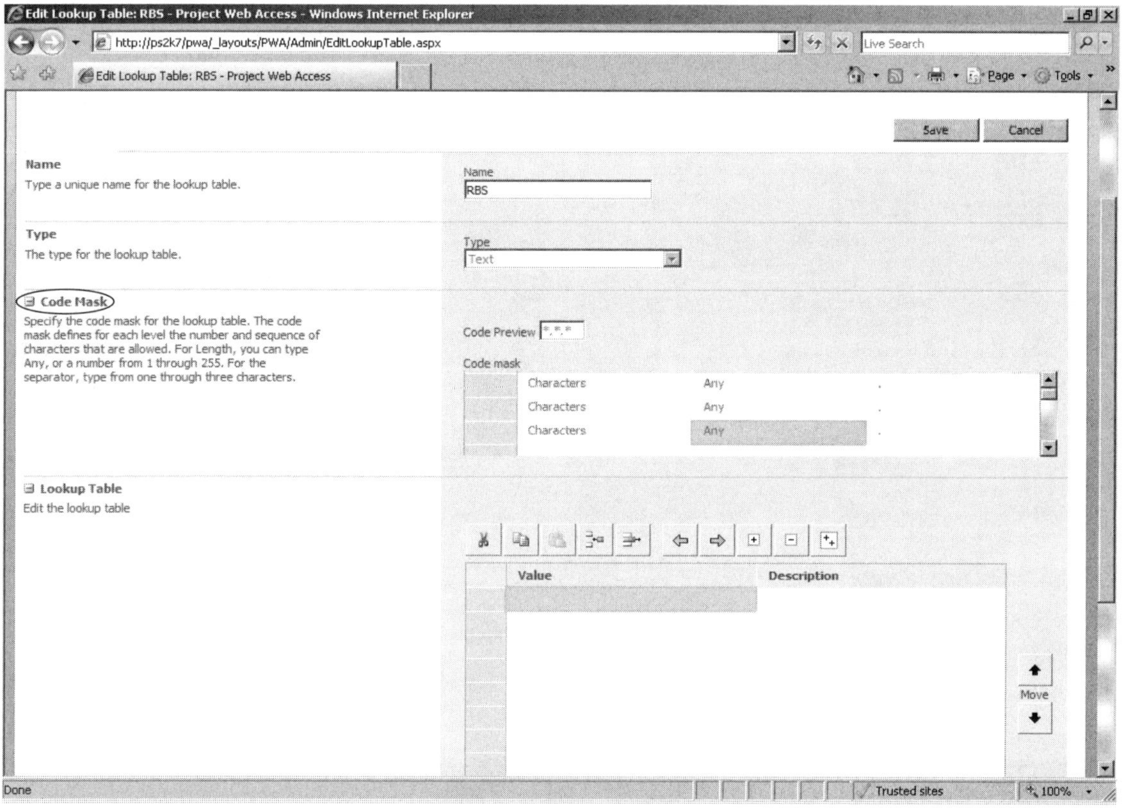

FIGURE 9-22 Code Mask

Figure 9-22 shows a constructed Code Mask.

Once the Lookup Table is ready to go, select the sort order and click Save. Figure 9-23 shows a completed Code Mask and Lookup Table.

From there, go to the Enterprise Custom Fields area on the top of the page and follow the process outlined previously.

Multiple Values

If a field uses a Lookup Table with a Code Mask, it is possible to build an enterprise custom field that allows multiple values. This is commonly used for skills as opposed to the Primary Skill field described above. There are advantages and disadvantages to using multivalue fields. Advantages include the ability to associate more than a single value to a project, task, or resource from a single field. Once again, the example of skills is ideal as people all have more than a single skill. For example, you could have someone who is a fluent Spanish speaker and a mid-level architect with excellent customer service and communications skills.

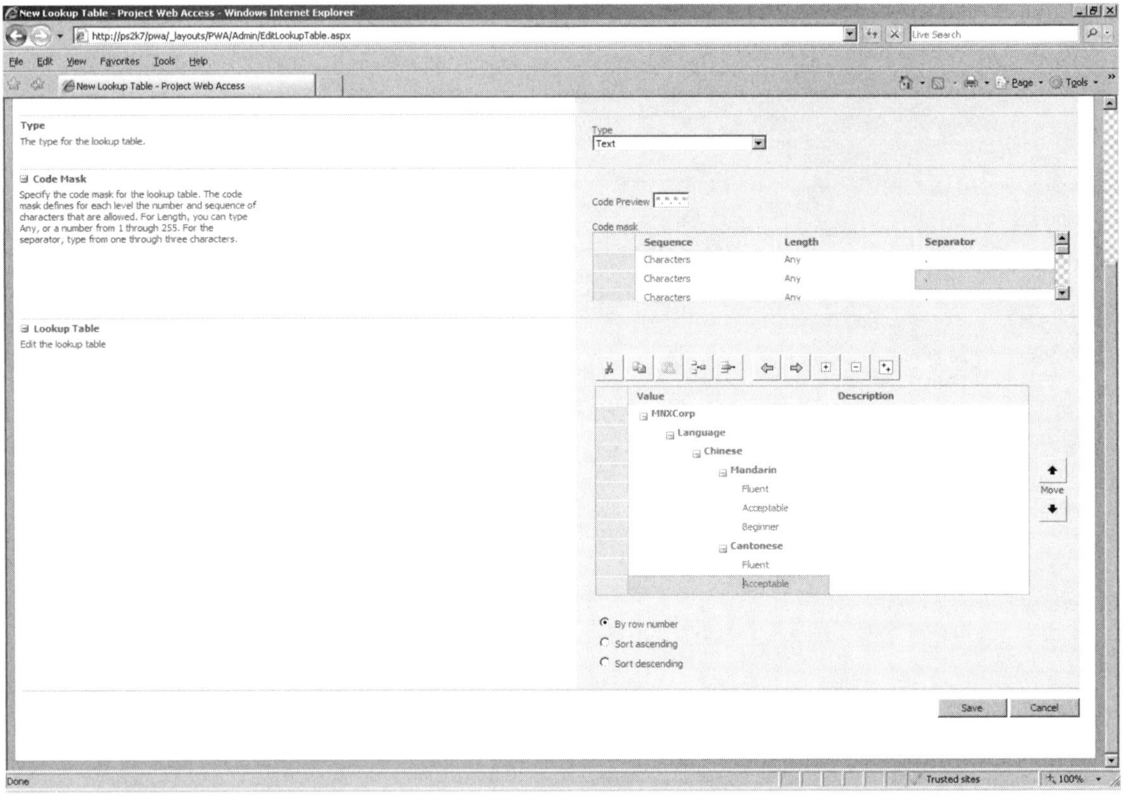

FIGURE 9-23 Code Mask and Lookup Table

Using an Enterprise Custom Resource text field could allow you to assign all these skills to the single individual. This can be very useful for skills-based planning.

Using multivalue fields can have some downsides. Any function where an exact match is required, such as the Match feature in the Build Team from Enterprise tool, will be difficult. Because an exact match is required, finding a resource can become difficult if you are using a skills multivalue field and choose to use that field for resource matching. In addition, these fields can present maintenance issues, as they become large and unwieldy if not carefully planned.

To build a multivalue field, create a lookup table with a code mask as described in the previous section. Then create an enterprise custom field as before, select the lookup table, and select the checkbox Allow Multiple Values to Be Selected from Lookup Table as shown in Figure 9-24. Once again, decide whether the field is required and click Save. Allowing multiple values is useful for Roles, Skills or other similar fields.

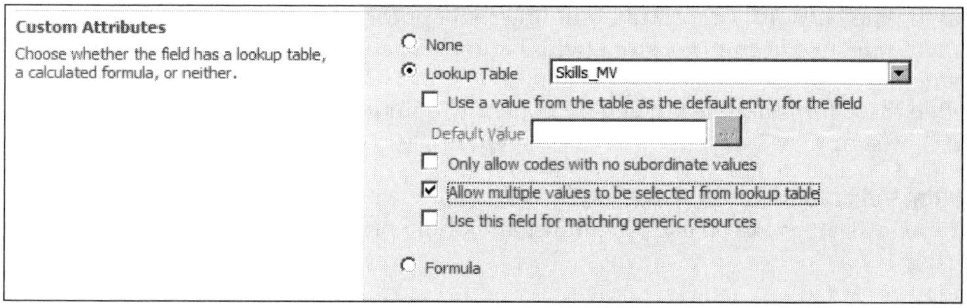

FIGURE 9-24 Allowing multiple values to be selected from a lookup table

Rollup

If there is interest in associating an attribute and then rolling up the task to the project level (Task0 or Summary Project Task) to display the rolled-up output in Project Center or other views, the process is as follows. Once again, navigate to PWA's Server Settings, then to Enterprise Custom Field Definition. You can use a formula (which you'll learn more about later in this chapter) or just manually enter data for this field. You cannot use a lookup table for this field. From the Enterprise Custom Fields section of the page, select New, name the field, and select the task entity. The screen shown in Figure 9-25 appears.

Next select the type (note that text fields cannot roll up). In the Custom Attributes area, select whether to use a formula or not.

In Calculation for Summary Rows, select Rollup. Decide whether to make the field required, then leave the rest of the fields at their default settings and click Save.

Formulas

Formulas can provide some additional power to your environment, but building and validating them in Project Server 2007 can be somewhat difficult. Note that formulas cannot be validated without access to the Project Professional client, which opens to validate a formula each time it is saved. Therefore, formulas cannot be created with only PWA access. Formulas can be applied to project, resource, or task entities. The output can be displayed as data or with graphical indicators (which you'll learn more about later in this chapter).

Formulas can be simple or very complex. A simple formula might use an existing built-in field and just display a graphical output based on value. A complex formula could compare multiple fields, use mathematical components, and include multiple thresholds for

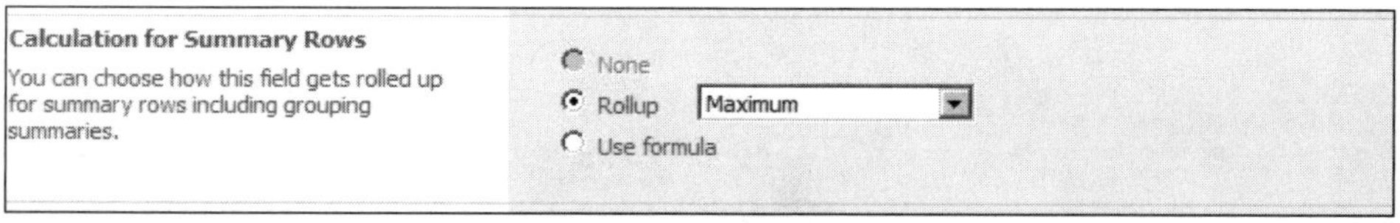

FIGURE 9-25 Selecting rollup

displaying the output. The formula-building tool appears whenever you select a formula when building an enterprise custom field. Figure 9-26 shows the function-building component.

Often these formulas are created by manually entering Visual Basic for Applications (VBA) type script.

Graphical Indicators

Graphical indicators can be used in almost any of the preceding examples. They include the following:

- Thirteen colored balls that are commonly used for the classic stoplights
- Eight flags of many colors
- Five colored squares
- Five plus signs
- Five minus signs

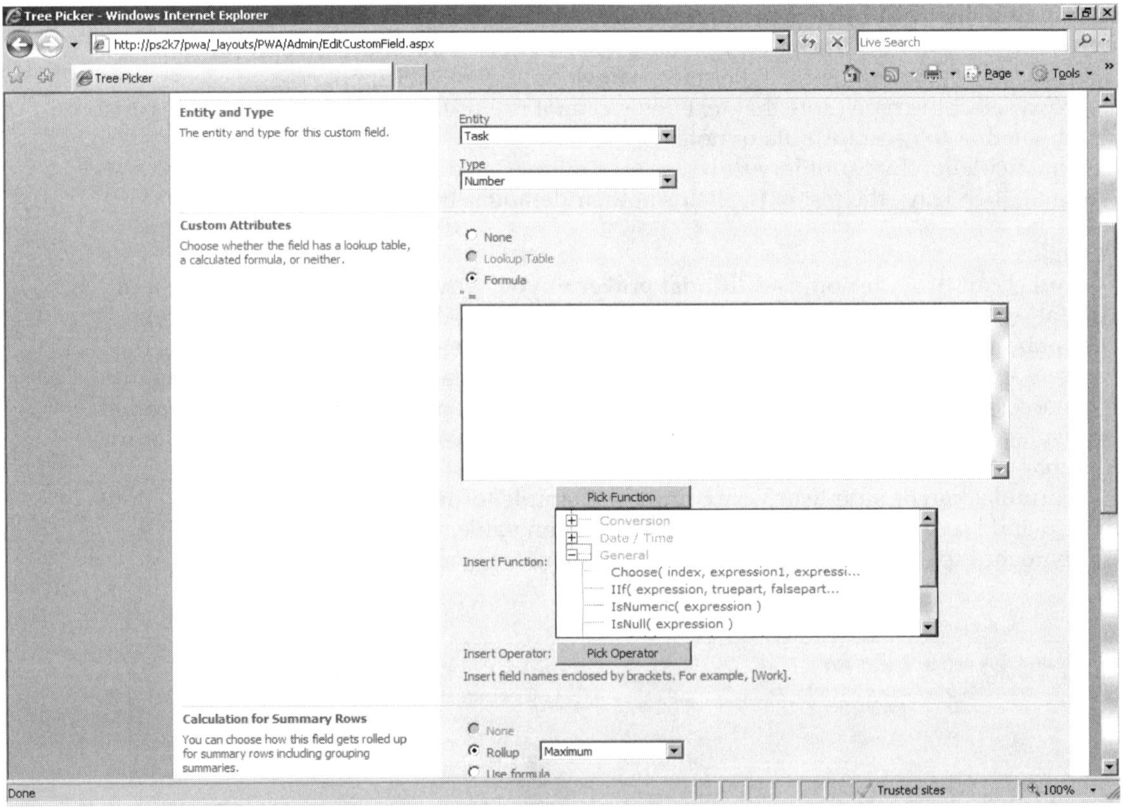

FIGURE 9-26 The function building tool

- Diamonds (red, green, or yellow)
- Five types of arrows
- Black and white (empty, full, or partially full) circles
- White and yellow light bulbs
- A checkmark
- A stylized *X*
- A question mark
- A clock face
- Five smiley faces and one red frowning face
- A dash

NOTE *As much as you may want to, you cannot import other graphics. We always wanted to add a few such as party favors, skull and crossbones, a tombstone, happy fireworks, and more.*

Some Notes on Required Fields

Limit the required fields to those that really count. They do have impact.

Requiring enterprise custom project fields will keep projects from being saved to the Project Server until these fields are populated. This can be a headache for the project manager as it is common that a draft plan could be saved or even published and the project never actually is executed. If the field has a default value, that issue goes away. Fields can be populated from within Project Professional in two ways.

- Inside the Project Menu under Project Information
- While Saving the Project

If there is not a preset default value, required task fields can be painful for the project managers, as each task within a project will need to be set.

Enterprise custom resource fields set to be required present an interesting side-effect. Under an Active Directory syncing model (highly recommended for maintenance purposes in a large organization), if a resource field is required and the field is not part of the users' Active Directory profile, the synchronization for that user will fail. This is a serious problem, as often that field does not even exist in Active Directory. Therefore, as a rule of thumb, stay away from making resource custom fields required.

Example Formulas

This section presents some examples of formulae that might be built and applied.

Example 1 The following is a simple formula with graphical indicators (stoplights) for date slippage using the following thresholds:

- The project Start Variance is equal to or less than zero over the Baseline Start—Green (OK) (note that the divide by 480 makes it days as opposed to minutes).

- The project is more than 10 days over the baseline Start Date—Red (Late).
- The project is greater than Green and is not Red—Yellow (Caution).

If a text ToolTip is required while hovering over the stoplights, start by creating a new enterprise custom task (with no lookup table). Next name the field (don't use special characters in the field names). Select Project | Text. Next set the radio buttons in the Custom Attributes area to Formula.

In the formula box, enter the following:

```
IIf([Start Variance]/480<=0,"OK",IIf([Start Variance]/480>10,"Late","Caution"))
```

Next, in the Values to Display area, select Graphical Indicators. In the first row in the Test column, select equals, and in the Value(s) column, type **OK**. In the Image column, select the green stoplight. Move to the next row and in the Test column, select equals; then in the Value(s) column enter **Late**, and in the Image column select the red stoplight. In the third row, select equals, Caution, and Yellow. Select Show Data Values in ToolTips (see Figure 9-27).

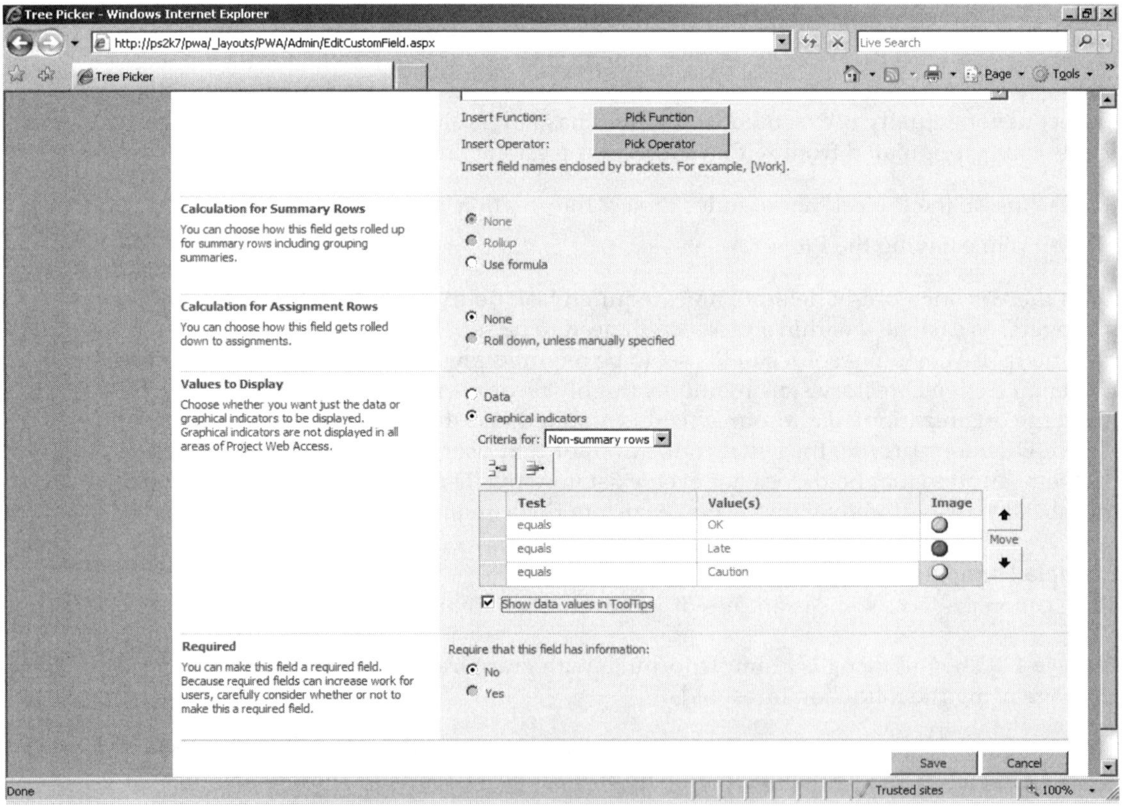

FIGURE 9-27 Data values and ToolTips

NOTE *The preceding formula will not work without the project manager setting a baseline (which is a best practice). You might be able to work further with the formula to add a way for the system to handle a situation in which no baseline has been set.*

Example 2 In this example, if the finish variance is greater than or equal to 10 days (note that this field displays in minutes, hence the division by 480), then it will be result in a 3 (red stoplight). If the variance is less than 10 but greater than or equal to 5 days, then it will result in a 2 (yellow stoplight). If it is less than 5 days, then it will be assigned a 1, which should be set to a green stoplight.

```
IIf([Finish Variance]/480>=10,3,IIf([Finish Variance]/480>=5,2,1))
```

Keep in mind that as soon as a condition is met, the formula stops. Thus the stoplight indicators would be:

- The output of 3 results in the display of a red stoplight.
- The output of 2 results in the display of a yellow stoplight.
- The output of 1 results in the display of a green stoplight.

In other words, it is really late, a little late, or OK.

Example 3 The following formula is an example of a pretty complex enterprise custom task field that was also rolled up to the Project Center:

```
IIf([Finish Variance]>120,"Late",IIf([% Complete]=100,"Complete",IIf(ProjDateDiff
([Current Date],[Baseline Start])/480>0 And [% Complete]=0,"NotStarted",IIf(ProjDateDiff
([Baseline Start],[Current Date])/480>0,"LateStart","OnTime"))))
```

This formula is then mapped to Graphical Indicators, so that the end result is the following:

- If a task is late (a very small cushion included), then it goes red.
- If a task is complete, then it goes green.
- If a task has not started, but is not late, then it goes white.
- If a task was supposed to start, but has no actual work has been recorded, it goes yellow.
- If a task has started on time, then blue.

Note that on the day a task is supposed to start, it goes blue. If no actual work is applied by the next day, it goes yellow.

The tasks roll up to a summary task, which is what shows up in the Project Center.

Example 4 This is an example that was recently used in the case where each project needed a milestone to be tracked and exposed in a Project Center view for comparison with other projects. This "GoLive" milestone did not mark the end of the project as a whole. This date was the key reporting event that needed to be viewed across Projects in a Project Center View. Here is how this task level field was exposed at the project level:

Two custom task fields and three custom project fields were created. The custom task fields are designed to test for the name of the milestone, and were designed as follows:

- `GoLiveTask` (Formula driven task-level date field) set to roll up the maximum value
  - `IIf([Name]="GoLive",[Finish],"1/1/1998"`
- `GoLiveTaskBL` (Formula driven task-level date fiels) set to roll up the maximum value
  - `IIf([Name]="GoLive",[Baseline Finish],"1/1/1998"`

The custom project fields were as follows:

- `GoLiveBL` This project level text field displays the rollup of the GoLiveTaskBL date field.
  - `IIf([Baseline Finish]>99999, "No BL Date",(GoLiveTaskBL))`
- `GoLive` This Project Level text field displays the rollup from the GoLiveTask task level date field.
  - `IIf([Baseline Finish]>99999, "No BL Date",(GoLiveTask))`
- `GoLiveVariance` This project level text field uses a formula and a graphical indicator to display one of a set of colored flags based on how the GoLive task is tracking.

Construction of the `GoLiveVariance` field required the four other fields and consists of the following formula:

- `IIf([Baseline Finish]>99999,"No Baseline", IIF(right[GoLive],2)=88,"No GoLive Milestone",(ProjDateValue ([GoLive])-ProjDateValue ([GoLiveBL]))))`

  This field used graphical indicators (see Figure 9-28) represented by fields in the formula as follows:

  - No baseline: question mark
  - No GoLive milestone: hyphen
  - Is less than or equal to 2 (days late): green smiley
  - Is within 2-10 (days late) yellow smiley (straight mouth)
  - Is greater than or equal to 10 (days late): red smiley (frown)

  Finally, The "GoLive Variance" Project Level field must be exposed in a Project Center View. This is done by creating or modifying a Project Center View, and adding the GoLive Variance field to it.

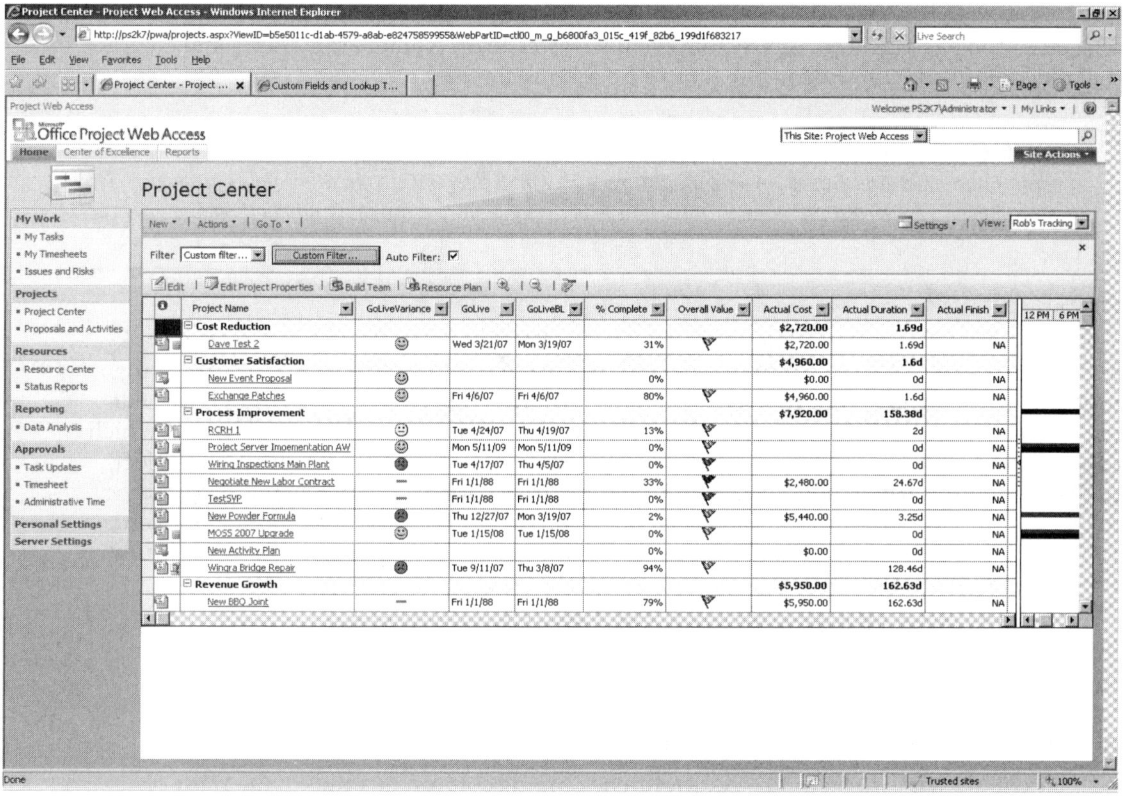

FIGURE 9-28 View with GoLiveVariance indicators

Correctly Connecting the Team Name Field

Before moving on to the next section, we added the next few words to help you avoid mistakes when configuring the Team Name field. From the Custom Fields and Lookup Tables page, the first task is to go to the bottom half and select Create New Lookup Table. Name the lookup table Team Name. Leave the type set to Text. The Code Mask can be left in its default setting. In the bottom section, Lookup Table, select Edit the Lookup Table and add the names of the teams that are going to be used in the organization.

Remember that each resource can be assigned to only a single team in this field. The actual team names could require significant planning, but if you need to change them later, that is not a major consideration. In fact, if the company is not ready to complete the required planning (for example, in an early iteration), only a single entry is required. When ready, save the lookup table.

This action takes you back to the Custom Fields and Lookup Tables page. From the top portion of the page (Enterprise Custom Fields), select Team Name. From there, make sure that the lookup table in Custom Attributes is set to Team Name.

CAUTION *Do not save this field with a field name other than the one just mentioned. This is a common mistake and causes some very real repair pain. Select options in other fields as appropriate (don't make it required if AD synchronization is being used for resources) and click Save.*

Enterprise Global

The Enterprise Global template is *the* base project template for how projects will look and work in the EPM environment. It contains settings information, such as groupings, toolbars, forms, and so on. It also contains information such as the specific views that are in the Project Professional client, such as the Enterprise Gantt Chart View, and which columns appear in the view. Changes in the Enterprise Global template affect all project plans following a save and check-in of the Enterprise Global, as long as the project managers shut down Project Professional and then restart the Project Professional client. From within the Server Settings page, select Enterprise Global. Then select Configure Project Professional.

Microsoft Office Project Professional then launches with the Enterprise Global "checked out." Following are some commonly used adjustments that you might consider when modifying the Enterprise Global template.

Adding a Column Displayed in a View

Navigate to the view to be modified. Right-click on the column heading to the right of where you want to place the new column. Then, from the Column Definition dialog (see Figure 9-29), select the column to be displayed.

You can use this dialog to make other modifications that affect how the display looks. After the settings are ready to go, select OK. After the Enterprise Global is saved and checked in and Project Professional is restarted, the new column appears in any new Plans.

Removing a Column from the View

To remove a column from a view, right-click on the column heading and then select Hide Column.

Creating a New View (Single)

From the View Bar (which you can display by clicking Views | View Bar), click View | More Views to display the More Views dialog shown in Figure 9-30. Select New.

Name the view (the name must be unique) and then set up any options from the Screen, Table, Group, and Filter dropdown menus. Select the Show in Menu option if you want to display the item in the menu and as a button in the View Bar, as shown in Figure 9-31.

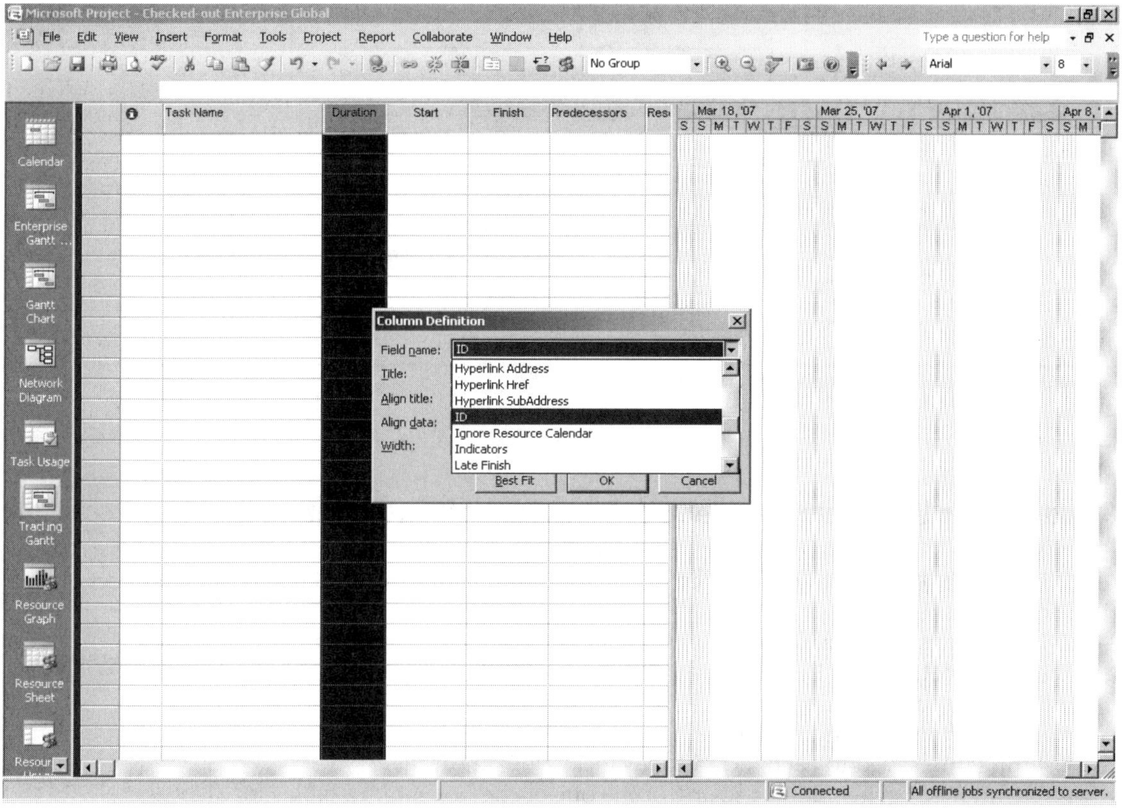

FIGURE 9-29 Add a column

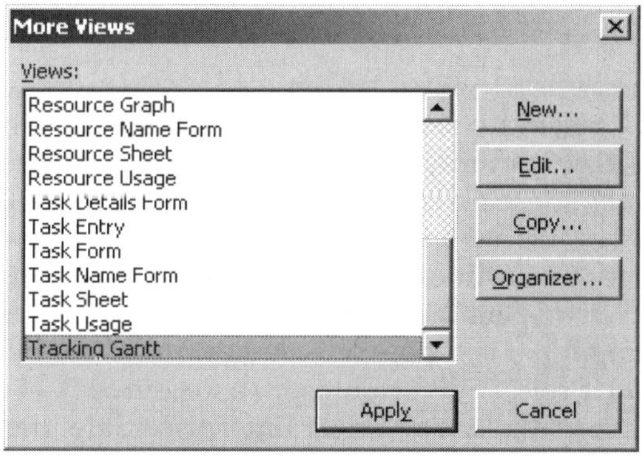

FIGURE 9-30 More Views dialog

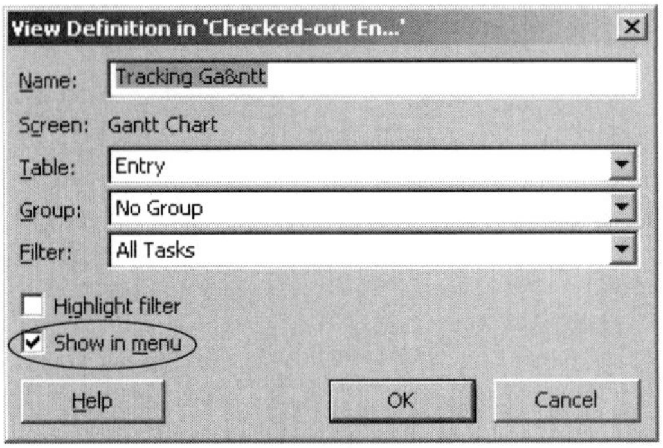

FIGURE 9-31 Show in Menu option in the View Definition dialog

Removing the View from the Menu or View Bar Without Deleting It

From the More Views dialog, either in the View Bar or from the View menu, select the view to modify. Next select Edit,which takes you to the View Definition screen and then deselect the Show in Menu option.

Other settings can be associated with the Enterprise Global template, such as macros and toolbars. Note that in Project Server 2003, many of the items under the Tools and Options menus could be set in the EGlobal. These included things like date format. calculation settings, and more. This is no longer the case in Project Server 2007. Instead, these settings are saved to each individual's local global.mpt file.

As mentioned earlier, don't use any of the out-of-the-box lookup tables for sharing.

NOTE *Once a new version of the Enterprise Global template is saved, each project manager must restart Project Professional before the changes are applied.*

Enterprise Calendars

The standard calendar is generally used by organizations that want to block out holidays for everyone. In global organizations, it could make sense to use multiple base calendars for this purpose. Typically, these calendars are edited annually and reflect the entire year's holidays and those occuring early into the next year as organizations make the official holidays available. An additional possibility is to create an additional seven-day calendar to allow project managers the ability to set this special option at the task level and allow for work during what is typically non-working time (like nights or weekends). Each work resource in the Project Server Enterprise Resource Pool is assigned to one base calendar. To edit an enterprise calendar, select Enterprise Calendars from with the Enterprise Data area on the Server Settings page, as shown in Figure 9-32.

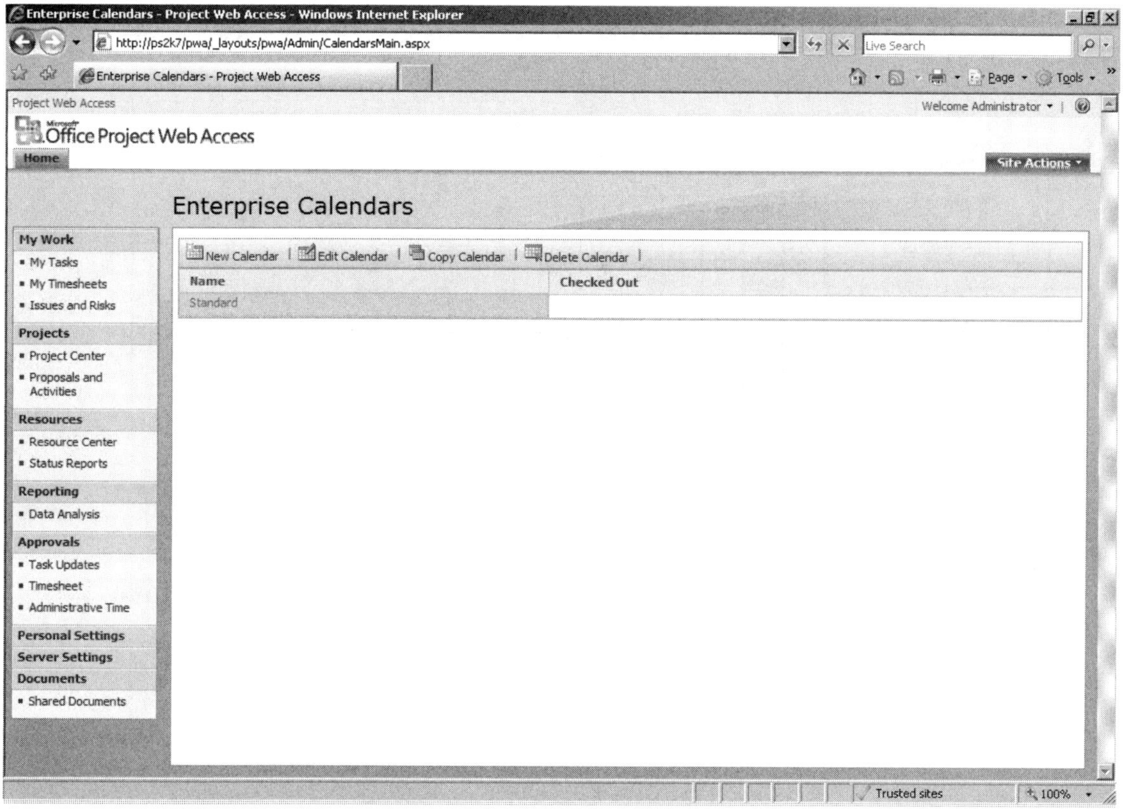

FIGURE 9-32 Enterprise Calendars page

Select the name of the calendar. When you start, there is only one calendar, the standard calendar. Select Edit Calendar (see Figure 9-33).

To add a holiday (or other global nonworking time), navigate to a day that should be set to Non-Working, such as September 3. Click the Exceptions tab (see Figure 9-34) and enter the name (Labor Day); then, when you navigate to the next cell or press ENTER, the date selected will fill in automatically.

FIGURE 9-33 Edit Calendar button

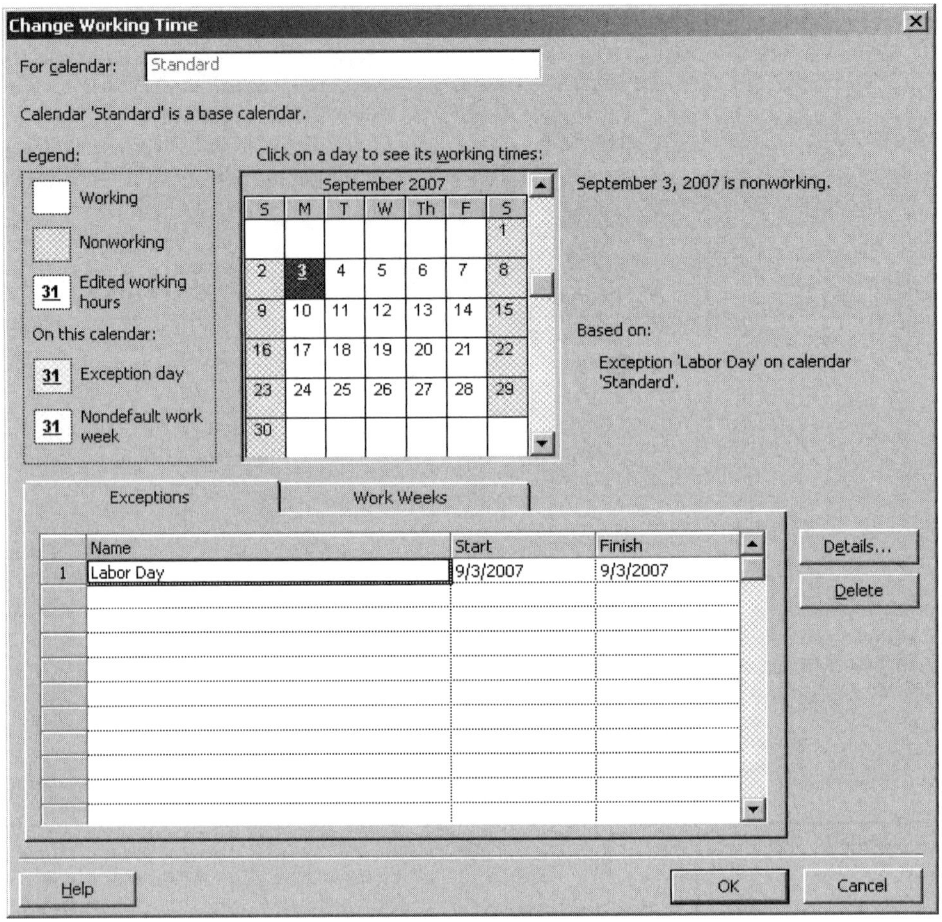

FIGURE 9-34 Exceptions tab

The same process can be done for entire weeks from the Weeks tab. Many companies can get by with a single enterprise calendar, but not all. When multiple enterprise calendars are created, perhaps for different global office locations, each individual can be assigned to only one enterprise calendar. This is done at the resource level from either the Enterprise Resource Pool or the Resource Center (see the next section). Other calendar options are available at the project and resource level. To change working time within a day, select the name of the day from the Set Working Times for These Exceptions area of the Details dialog , then select the Details button. Modify the time as seen in the example shown in Figure 9-35, where there is only a half day of work.

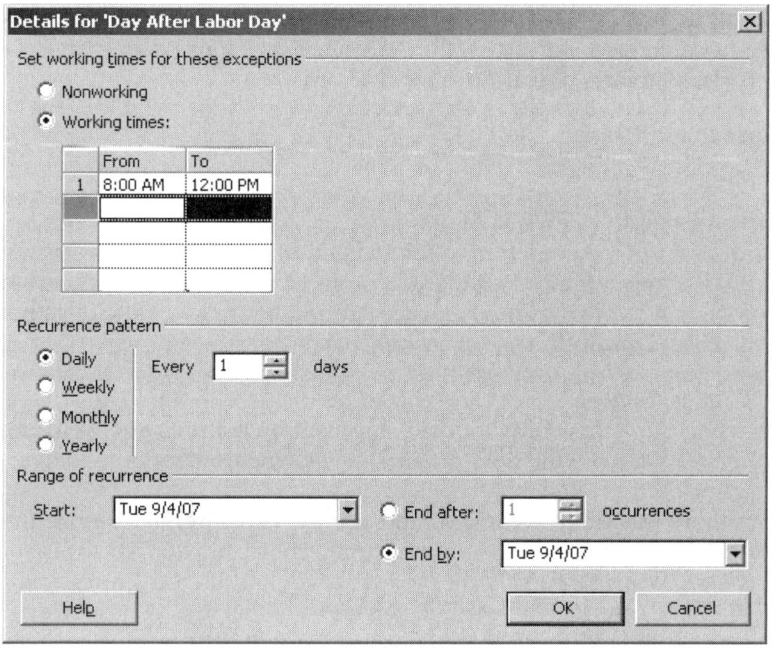

FIGURE 9-35 Change working time

PART III

Resource Center

Resource Center is just a link from the Server Settings page and does not have any settings that you can access without actually going to the Resource Center views. After navigating to the Resource Center (which you can do from anywhere the Quick Launch Bar [left navigation] is available), you can accomplish many tasks.

The resources in the Resource Center include all the resources in the Enterprise Resource Pool, including generic resources, material resources, cost resources, or human resources (work). In many organizations, the Enterprise Resource Pool is populated through a synchronization process with Microsoft Active Directory. This process is discussed in Chapters 8 and 12.

Note that significant overlap is possible between what can be configured in the Enterprise Resource Pool, the Resource Center, and the Security Administration pages. All of these options are controlled by the security model.

Resource Center Settings

Resource Center provides the following settings for you to configure.

Editing the Resource Type

Set the resource a person (work), a cost (for example, for expenses), or material (lumber, servers, lease costs, software, power poles, and so on).

Setting the Resource as Generic

This is a checkbox.

Setting Whether a Login from PWA Is Allowed

Usually resources are allowed to log in to the system, but not always. For example, an outside vendor on a project may be added to a project for tracking purposes, but not be allowed on the system. Note that if a resource cannot log in, he or she does not require a client access license. This option is a checkbox.

Changing the Display Name

When you are using the Active Directory synchronization features, this field is pulled in to the system. You can overwrite the field manually, but synchronization will overwrite the field with what is in Active Directory.

No matter where this field is viewed (and it is everywhere), if you use the naming convention of *Last_Name, First_Name*, a very common choice in your AD for Display Name, this displays as *Last_Name; First_Name* in Project Server and Project Professional. In other words, they replace the comma with a semicolon and a space. Project has always reserved the comma for other use, and although we are not thrilled with this result, you get used to it quickly and the advantages of a *Last_Name* first Display Name would be our recommendation for sorting reasons. The AD Display Name field affects many other Windows-based applications, such as Exchange/Outlook, so we would not expect you to make this decision without considering the larger impact to your organization.

Populating or Editing E-Mail Addresses

This field also can be populated either by AD synchronization or manually.

Assigning Resources in RBS

The RBS is a custom enterprise resource field with a Code Mask that is generally used to filter, sort, and group resources. It can be configured in several ways, but the most common is in a structure that is similar to an organization chart. Some Project Server categories use the RBS for access purposes. The access role of the RBS is discussed in Chapter 8, as well as in Chapter 20. The RBS displays as a hierarchical drilldown list. Select from this field the group to which the resource belongs.

Setting Initials

This field is self-explanatory.

Associating a Hyperlink Name and URL

An example of a situation in which you might use this setting is when a resume is on the intranet or connected to a Microsoft Office SharePoint Server (MOSS) 2007 MySite. (MySite is a feature in MOSS 2007 that supports each individual in an organization having his or her own personal portal site with both a private and public view.)

Activating or Deactivating the Account

You can activate or deactivate an account manually in this field. If the account is removed from Active Directory, the resource is removed from Project Server if AD synchronization is being used.

Setting the Authentication Type (Windows or Forms)

Although this field is available here, the authentication type is normally set as part of your configuration in the Security area.

Preventing Active Directory Synchronization for the User

This checkbox is used for making this resource an exception to AD synchronization.

Setting the Timesheet Manager

This field is used to determine where a resource's timesheet is sent for approval. In the new 2007 model, timesheet approval can be separated from Project Task updates and the timesheet manager is usually the functional/resource manager of the user. Timesheet managers available from this field are those generally included in the Resource Managers group.

Setting the Default Assignment Owner

By default, these owners are the resource themselves. You should almost always leave this setting unchanged. Occasionally this field might be used when someone other than the assigned resource needs to update tasks.

Setting Earliest Available and Latest Available Dates

If a new employee is expected to start on a certain day, or if a consultant is coming in for some work, the earliest available date can be set. Conversely, if a consultant must leave on a certain day, if an employee is leaving, or if for other reasons the resource will become unavailable, the latest available date field can be set. For most resources, this field is not used.

Setting Any Enterprise Custom Resource Fields

In addition to the RBS, any enterprise custom resource fields created in the system can be set from Resource Center.

Adding or Deleting the User from Security Groups and Categories, Setting Category Permissions, and Setting Global Permissions

These settings can be changed from Resource Center, discussed in Chapter 8.

Setting Group Fields

Use these fields to add or delete the individual from Project Server 2007 security groups. There was more about this task in Chapter 8.

Setting Team Details

If you are using assignment teams, this field is used to set the resource to a team relationship.

Viewing System-Unique IDs and Setting External IDs

Each user has a unique ID. This can be used for deep troubleshooting. An external ID is used to relate a user to an external system. For example, you might set an external ID if the user has a different ID in the company's Enterprise Resource Planning (ERP) system.

Features of Resource Center

In addition to the preceding settings, Resource Center offers several useful features and functions.

Creating a New Resource

To create a new resource, select New, then Resource from just under the Resource Center heading on the blue horizontal toolbar. Populate the fields as appropriate and then select Save.

Selecting Resources for Editing

To select resources individually, use the checkboxes to the left of the resource names. In addition, selecting and clearing all resources' checkboxes are functions available under the Actions button (see Figure 9-36).

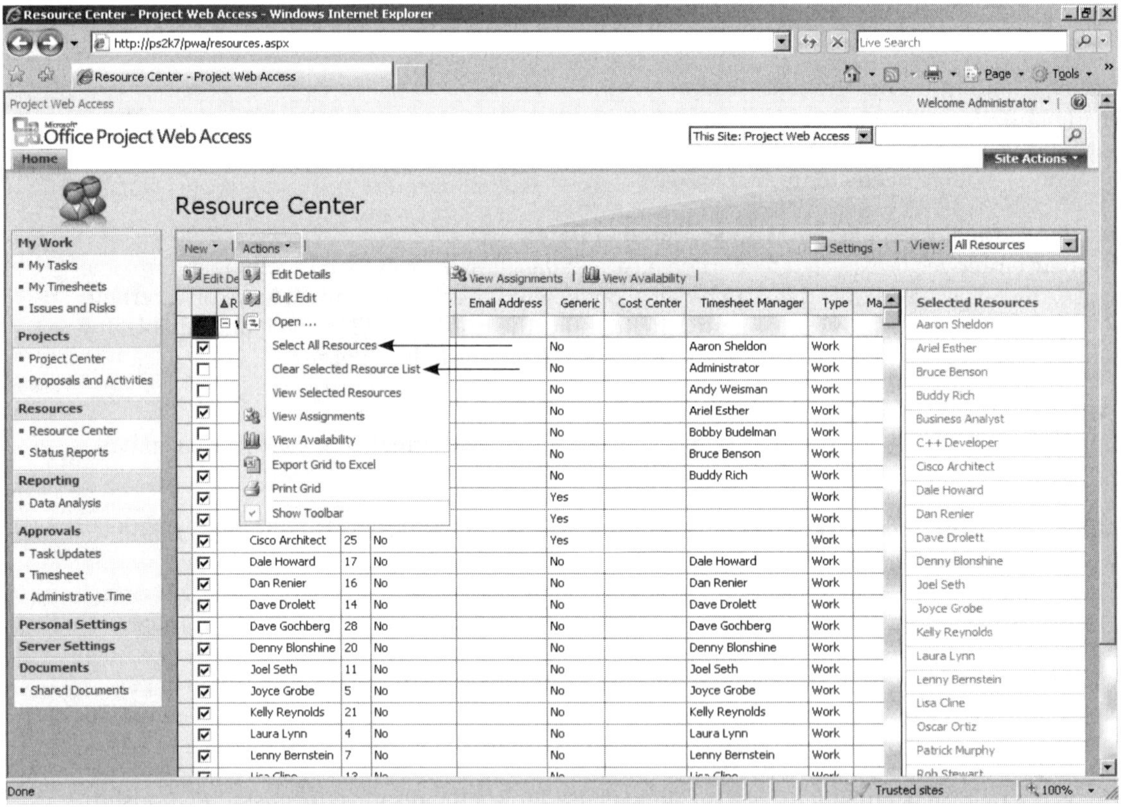

FIGURE 9-36 Resource Actions options

Whatever resources you select display along the Resource Center page's right side in the Selected Resources column.

Editing Details

Whether you have selected a single resource or more than one, the Edit Details feature enables you to edit individual resources. If you select multiple resources, then a serial process ensues.

Start by selecting the resources for editing. Then select Edit Details from either the Edit Details button or from the Actions button menu (see Figure 9-37). Edit the first resource as appropriate, then select from the three buttons on the top or bottom of the page: Save and Continue, Continue without Saving, or Cancel Remaining. If you do not select Cancel Remaining, once you have made the edits to the first resource, the next selected resource's details page displays for editing, then the next, and so on.

Bulk Editing

The Bulk Edit feature can be accessed from a button or from an item in the Actions button menu. This feature opens with certain features in edit mode for the selected resources from the Resource Center main page. As shown in Figure 9-38, there are fields for Assignment Attributes (Timesheet Manager and Default Assignment Owner). There are also fields for the Built-In Custom Fields (RBS, Team Name, and Cost Type). Any enterprise custom resource fields can be edited as well. Note that for changes to be applied, the Apply Changes checkbox for any given field must be selected and then a Save action will make the changes to all the selected users.

Editing the Enterprise Resource Pool in Project Professional You can open selected resources for editing in Microsoft Office Project Professional 2007 by selecting the Open button (see Figure 9-39).

This feature opens the resources for editing in the enterprise resource pool, giving you more flexibility for which fields can be edited. For example, this interface enables you to edit the resource's hourly rate or "Max. Units." Note that changes must be saved in Project to take effect. Be careful to check in the enterprise resource pool when you finish editing.

Viewing Assignments

You can view assignments for the selected resources by selecting the View Assignments feature from either the Actions button menu or the View Assignments button. There is a single view that comes out of the box, as shown in Figure 9-40.

FIGURE 9-37 Edit Details options

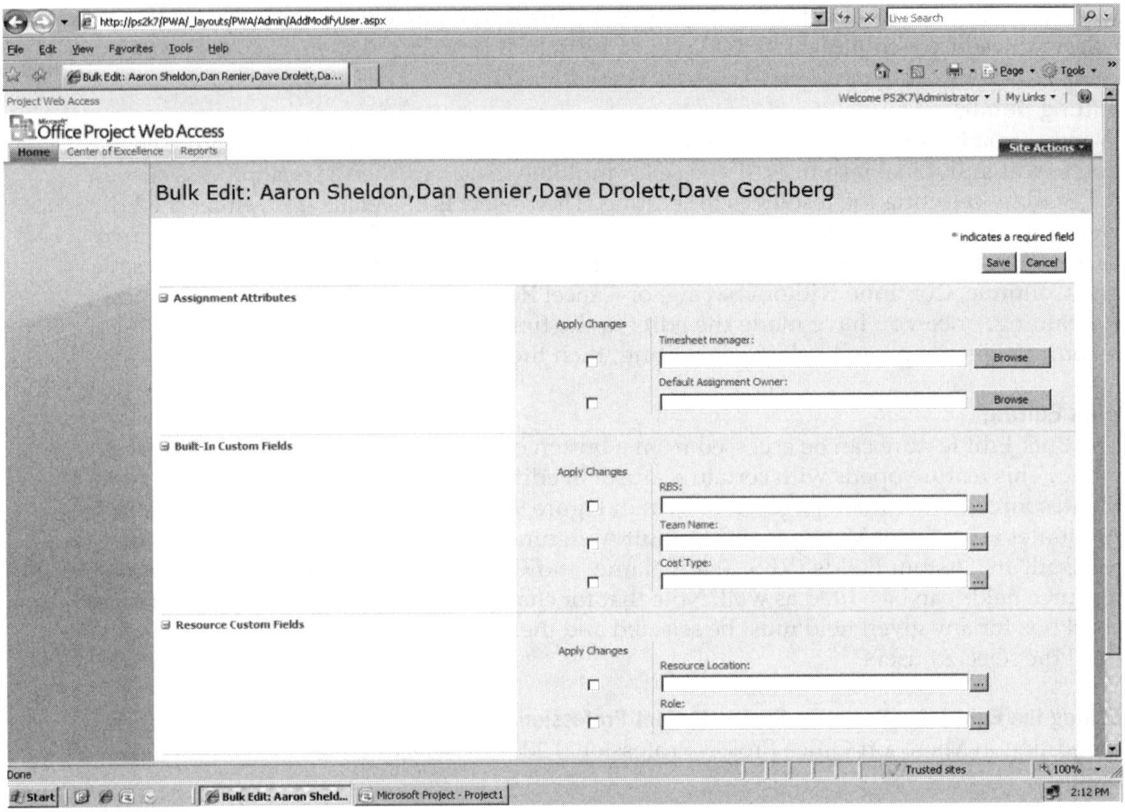

FIGURE 9-38 Bulk Edit page

The Actions button includes zooming, scroll to task, and other miscellaneous functions. The Go To button allows easy navigation to the Availability Views (see the following section) and back to Resource Center.

Clicking the Settings button presents the following options:

- **View Options** This presents outline levels (rollup to project, summary task, or detail levels), checkboxes that enable you to display summary tasks and summary rollup, and an option to display the date and time as opposed to just the date.

FIGURE 9-39 Open button

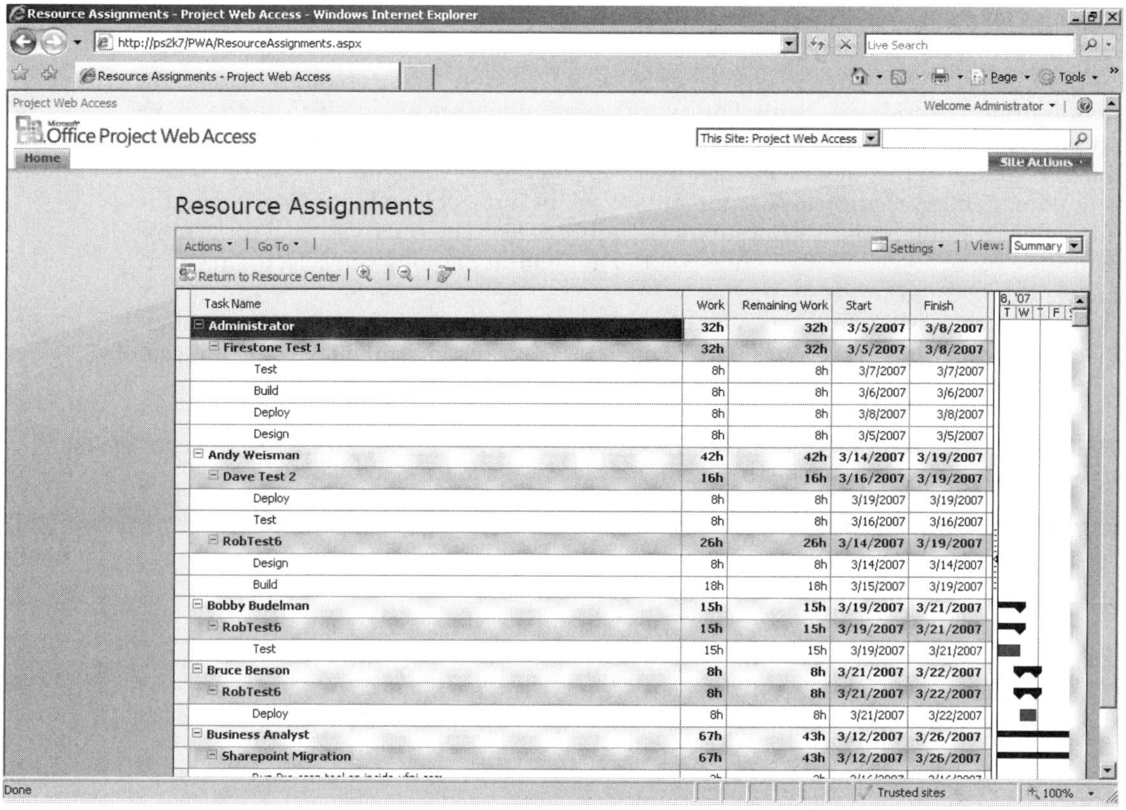

FIGURE 9-40 Resource Assignment view

- **Filter** The Auto Filter checkbox adds a filtering dropdown arrow to every column. These can be very useful in this context. For example, to view only assignments with a finish date of today, select Custom Filter, then enter Finish, equals, and the type in the current date. Then click OK.
- **Group** This option uses the grouping format as defined in the Manage Views item for this view.
- **Search** This option opens a search pane for the page.

Viewing Availability

Availability of the selected resources can be viewed in a combination of chart and table views with this feature, which can be accessed from a button or an item on the Action Button dropdown menu. Four very useful views are available from the Views dropdown list at the top-right of the page. The next view, Assignment Work by Resource, is the default. Note that these views are fixed, as you can see in Figure 9-41. No customization is possible. The next view is Assignments Work by Project (see Figure 9-42), and the third view is Remaining Availability (see Figure 9-43). The final view is Work (see Figure 9-44). As you can see, there is a lot of availability among the selected resources during the selected time window.

Note that in each of these views, View Options are available by selecting Settings | View Options. When the settings pane is opened, you can manipulate the date range and

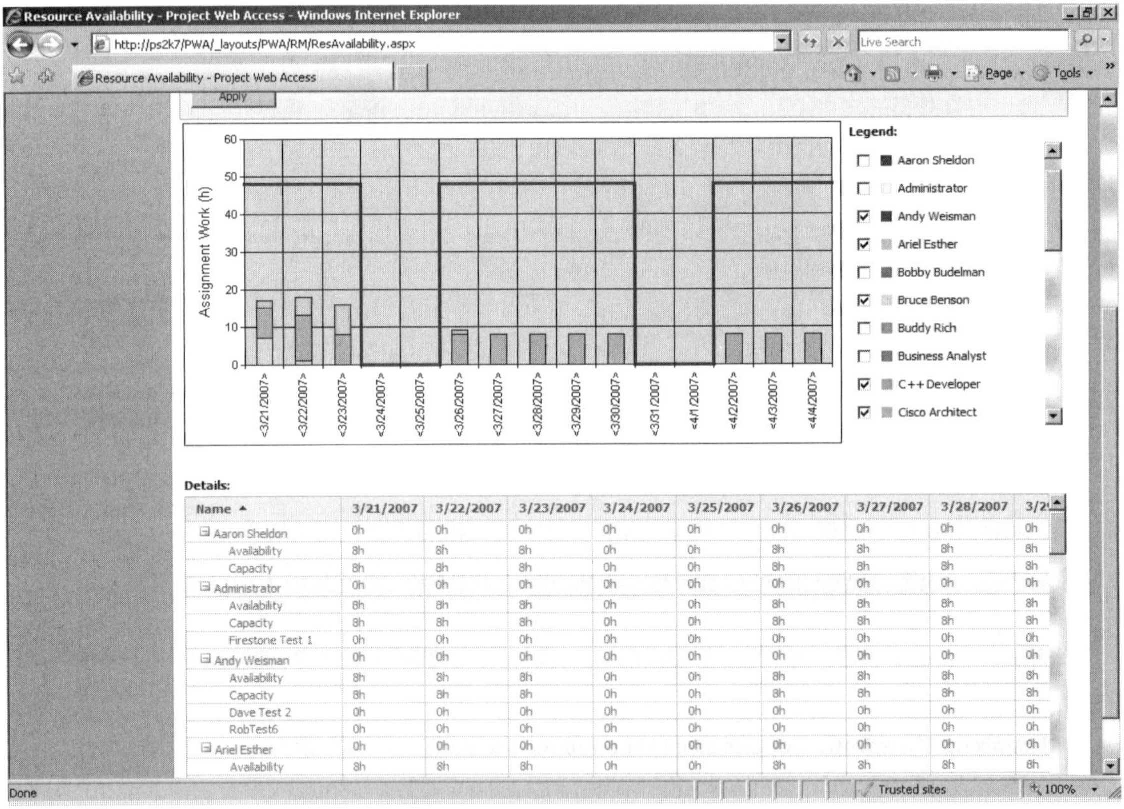

FIGURE 9-41 Assignments Work by Resources view

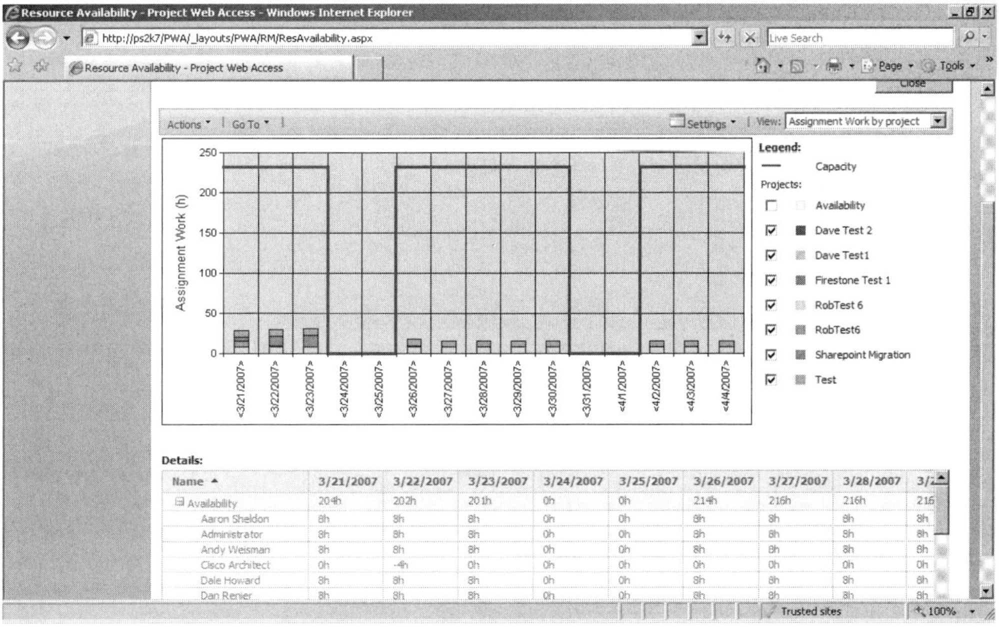

FIGURE 9-42 Assignments Work by Project view

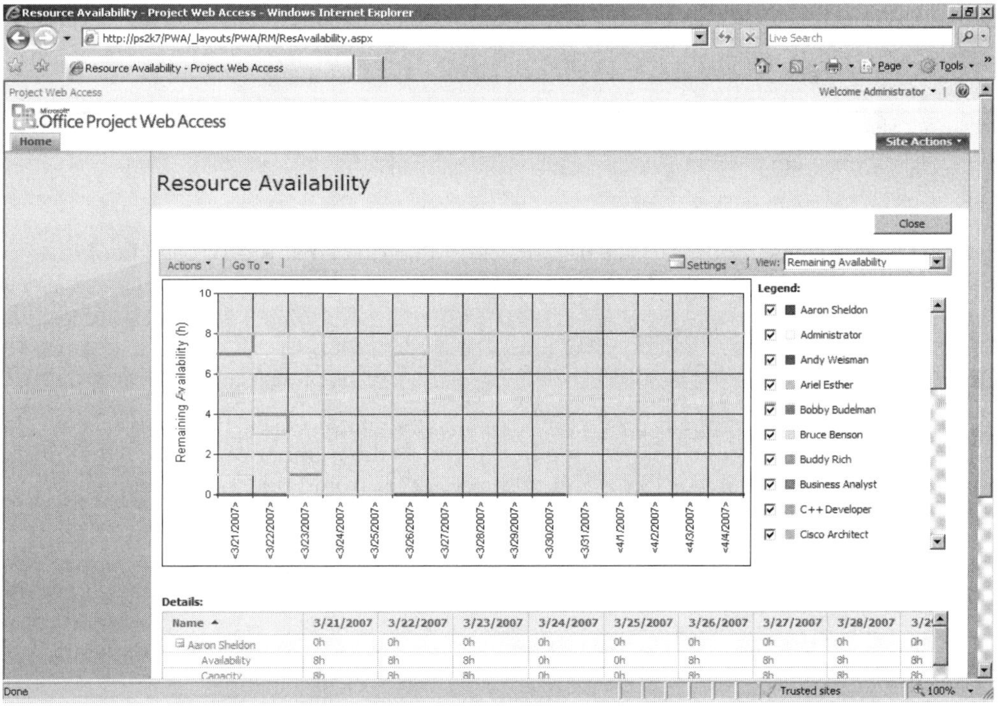

FIGURE 9-43 Remaining Availability view

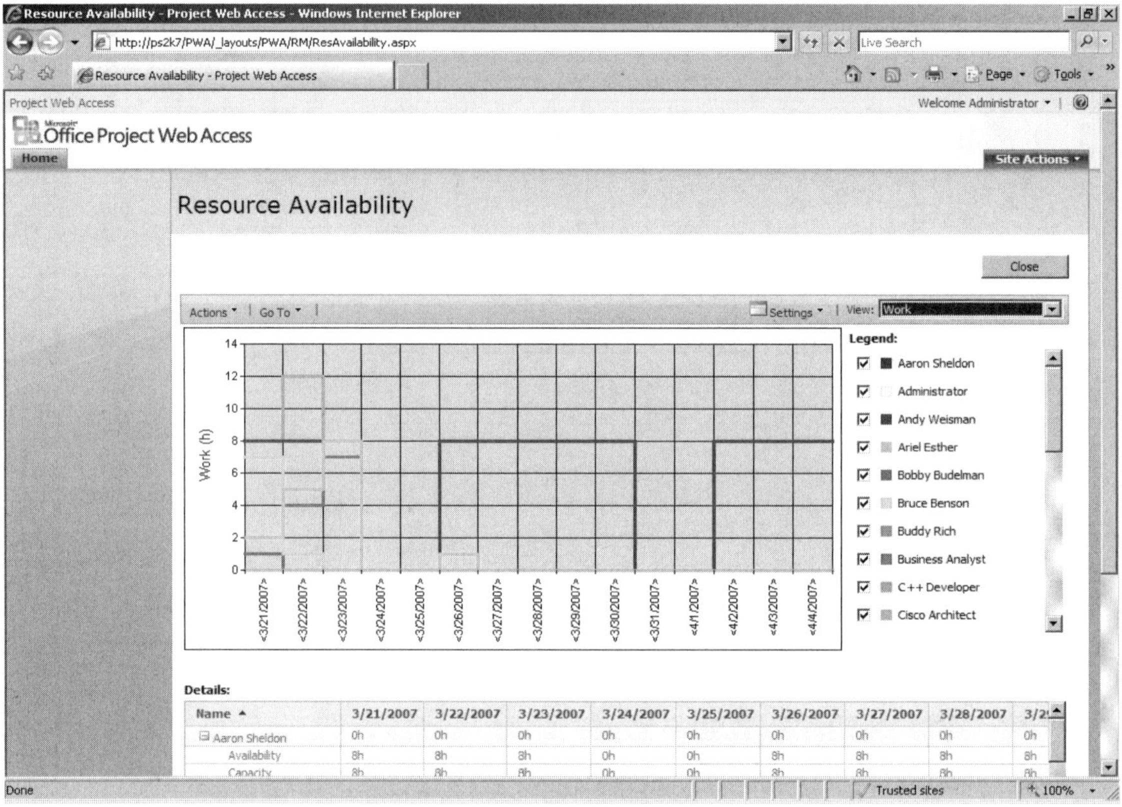

FIGURE 9-44 Work view

the units (days, weeks, months, or years). In addition, you can add proposed bookings to the view data by selecting a checkbox. See the Settings pane in Figure 9-45.

About Project Server

The About Project Server page is used primarily for tracking licenses. It displays a count of PWA accounts that have permission to log in, as well as the number of accounts that have the project manager permission "Log on to Project Server from Project Professional to Microsoft Office Project Server 2007."

FIGURE 9-45 The Date Range setting

Although this page does not guarantee perfect licensing information, keep in mind that at the time of writing this book, all Project Professional client licenses include a single Project Server Client Access License (CAL). This means that under most circumstances, licenses are actually based on the number of project managers (each with a Project Professional license) and PWA users minus the number of project managers.

The Enterprise Data area in Project Server and Server Settings administrative areas are used to handle some of the most important components of the EPM solution. This is an area that should be given special attention during the planning processes. It also is one of the areas that require organizational knowledge for ongoing maintenance of the system. While this chapter is relatively deep, many organizations will need consulting assistance from a Microsoft EPM partner to get its internal staff ready to support the Enterprise Data areas of the system. An experienced partner should be selected.

CHAPTER 10

Configuring Time and Task Management

Understanding time and task management within Project Server 2007 and Project Web Access (PWA) is critical to extracting the data that your organization needs. Because of the flexibility of the settings that will be covered, it is critical to know specifically what data you need to report and how you require it to be presented. For example, if you wish to implement a timesheet system in your organization, you would need to understand the following items:

- How often are resources required to submit timesheets? (What is the period length in which your users have to enter and submit time? Every day? Every week? Every month?)
- When does this set of periods start? (Today? January 1? Should they line up to your company's fiscal calendar?)
- How far into the future do you want users to be able to enter their time? (Consider vacation requests.)
- Is there another accounting application used in your organization that has specific periods defined?

There is more to defining time and task management than simply making guesses and hoping your choices won't break anything. The choices you make in defining the properties in this section can possibly save you tens of thousands of dollars in development costs when you want to align project costs across your enterprise with your company's fiscal calendar year, or integrate Project Server 2007 timesheet data with a third-party system. It also reinforces the notion of taking an iterative approach to implementing Enterprise Project Management (EPM). If you implement the timesheet periods or financial periods incorrectly in a proof of concept or a pilot, there is a much greater chance that you will recognize the problem before you roll out Project Server 2007 to your entire organization. A discussion of the iterative approach can be found in Chapter 5.

Task Updates vs. Timesheets

Of the overarching themes of this chapter, understanding the difference between task management and timesheet management, and specifically the fact that they are now two distinct processes in Project Server 2007, is crucial. Whereas timesheet management deals with the creation and the exposing of timesheets, the rules governing timesheets, and the relationship between the *resource manager* and resource, task updates and management deals with the tasks that are assigned through Project Professional 2007 and the relationship between *project manager* and the resource.

Because successful implementation of EPM depends on organizational project management methodology standardization, this tool, like its predecessor, works within the GICO (Garbage-In, Carnage-Out) framework.

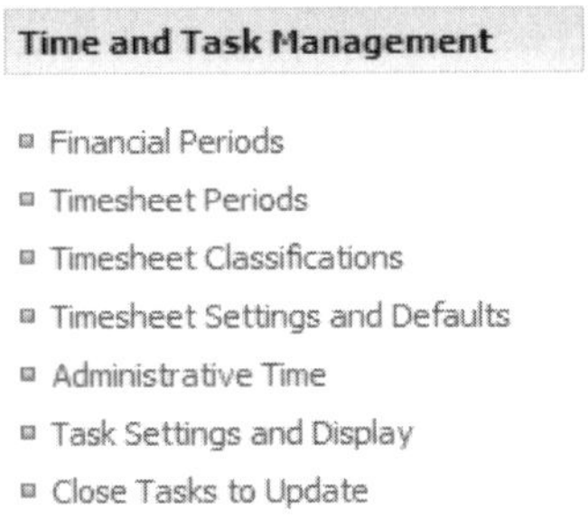

Financial Periods

You must define your organization's fiscal periods before you can track fiscal years in contrast to the normal calendar year. This contrast provides a different timescale (fiscal time) for reporting and integration efforts. If you plan on integrating Project Server 2007 with an external financial application, it is critical that these fiscal periods are in sync. For reporting, the PWA Data Analysis views can include a Fiscal_Time dimension in order to show how your totals (work, money, and so on) fall according to this nonstandard timeframe.

NOTE *Although many companies will require the ability to track project or program work using Fiscal_Time as the time dimension, if you do not currently have this requirement but may in the future, do not fret. You can set up financial periods at any time and apply them to the project the next time a project is opened and published. In the case of the Data Analysis views, after the project is published, when the cube is built, you will be able to use the new Fiscal_Time dimension with standard time or as an alternative to standard time.*

Prior to defining your fiscal periods, you'll need to talk to your accounting department to discover how it needs fiscal time defined. Ideally, a representative would be present during the initial planning meetings for your EPM implementation where a visual representation could be provided. Some questions you may ask the accounting representative might include the following:

- When does the fiscal year start?
- How are the fiscal years defined?
- Is there a naming convention that is preferred?

After you have discovered the needed information from your accounting department, it's time to configure the settings for your fiscal periods. Complete the following steps to do so:

1. From Server Settings, under the Time and Task Management section, click Financial Periods.
2. From the dropdown list of available years, define last year's fiscal period. (For example, if the current standard year is 2008, the first fiscal year you want to define is 2007.)
3. In the Define Fiscal Year Parameters page, as shown in Figure 10-1, using the date that your accounting department representative gave you, specify the date on which the fiscal year begins.

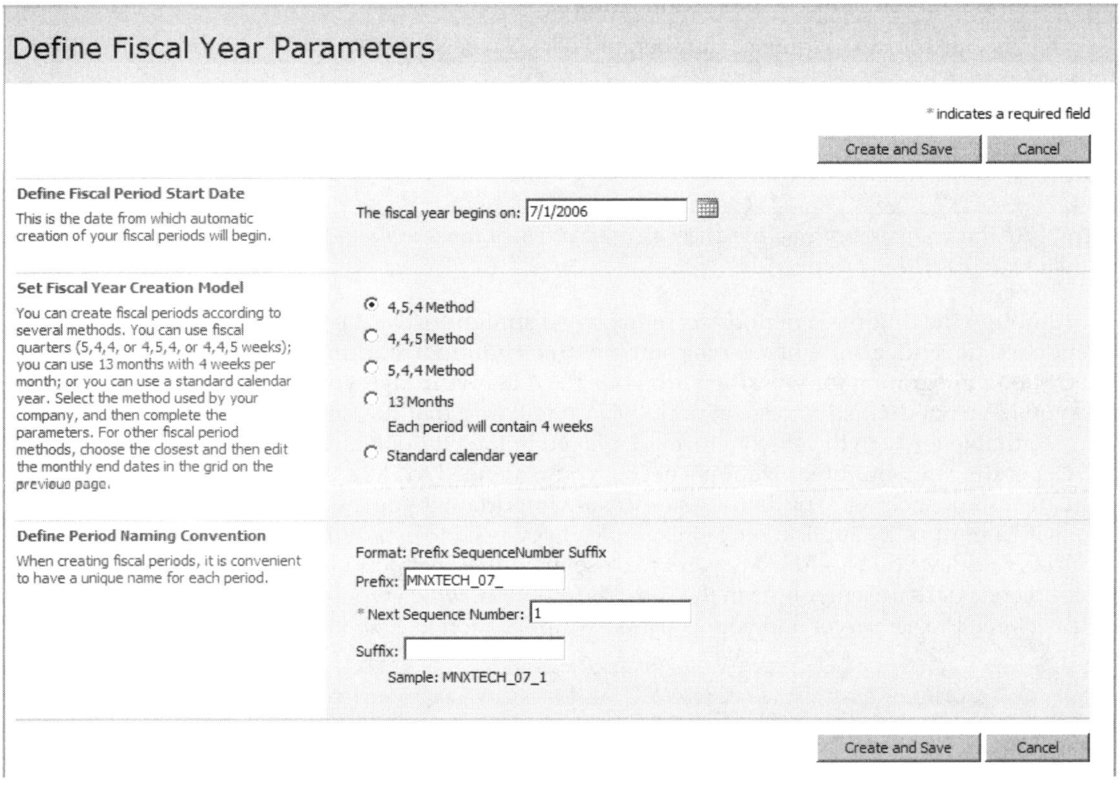

FIGURE 10-1 Define your fiscal periods.

4. Using the input from your accounting department, identify the fiscal year creation model.
5. Using the input from your accounting department, identify the preferred naming model with the prefix and, if needed, the suffix.
6. Click Create and Save.

Timesheet Periods

If your EPM implementation includes the use of timesheets, setting up your timesheet periods is critical. Doing so provides general guidelines about timesheet usage, such as what day of the week your timesheet should begin, how you want to name your organization's timesheets, what numbering sequence you should use, and how far into the future you want your resources to be able to enter time in the timesheet. To define your timesheets, complete the following steps:

1. From Server Settings, under Time and Task Management, click Timesheet Periods.
2. Type a number of periods to be created.
3. Provide a date for the commencement of the first period.
4. Provide a standard timesheet period length in days.
5. Optionally provide the prefix and suffix.
6. Provide the next sequence number and click Save.

If you have previously created a batch of timesheets and you are now creating another batch, it is important to modify the setting for Next Sequence Number so that your timesheet periods are named in a logically ascending manner.

NOTE *After a user has created a timesheet associated with a timesheet period, that timesheet period cannot be deleted.*

Although the timesheet periods seem to have a straightforward purpose, a commonly overlooked dependency involves integration with the Outlook add-in. If you attempt to use the Outlook integration for working with your PWA tasks through your Outlook task list and you have not defined timesheet periods, you will find that the timephased actuals will not be editable through the custom form displayed in the Outlook task.

Depending on your organization's needs, you may need to close timesheet periods regularly as time goes on. This becomes especially important if you are integrating timesheet data with a third-party application. For example, if you need to export timesheet data from last week on Tuesday, you would likely want to close that timesheet period after export to ensure that someone does not enter time in that timesheet period, which would result in inconsistent data between Project Server and your third-party application (e.g. an invoicing application).

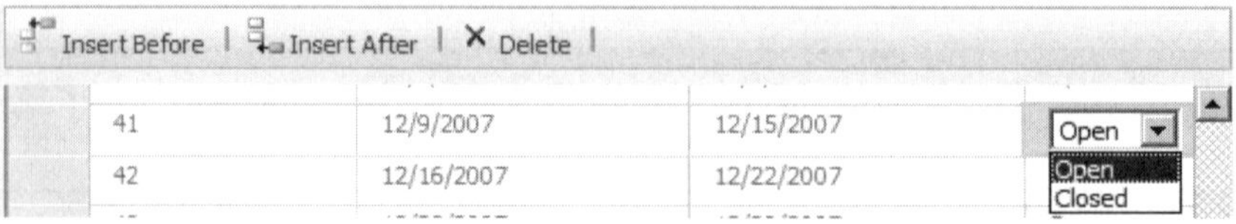

Timesheet Classifications

Timesheet classifications are categories that your organization defines for the work that you do. If you have Travel Time or other time classifications that you are required to capture in relation to timesheet tasks, the Timesheet Classifications section is where you would specify these categories. These classifications show up under the column Billing Category in a user's timesheet and are available when users click Add Lines when working in their timesheet. The decision to create additional timesheet line classifications depends on a number of factors, including whether you will be billing the time that the timesheets capture back to another entity or organization, how that time is organized, and whether you will be utilizing timesheets in your organization at all. After you have the required information about your company's plans for timesheet use, setting up the timesheet classifications is a straightforward process:

1. From Server Settings, under Time and Task Management, click Timesheet Classifications.
2. On the Edit or Create Line Classifications page, click New Classification.
3. Type a name for the new line classification and optionally a description.
4. Ensure that its status is set to Active.
5. Click Save.

CAUTION *Creating or changing the status of the line classification from Active to Inactive is done from the Edit or Create Line Classifications page and the changes take effect immediately on all active timesheets upon saving the page.*

Timesheet Settings and Defaults

You may find through feedback sessions with users during your proof of concept or pilot phase that the default method for viewing tasks doesn't fit with the time reporting method dictated by your organization. From the Timesheet Settings and Defaults page, you can change the way that users interact with their timesheets.

CAUTION *It is recommended that if you do not have rigid plans for displaying timesheets, make sure during your proof of concept that you address this issue after users have had a chance to experience the Outlook integration and timesheets. This feedback from your small focus group will be invaluable for you to assess how users in your organization use the tool, and will give you the best chance of providing a solution that is agreeable to and increases the efficiency of all.*

From within the Timesheet Settings and Defaults page, there are a number of sections for you to consider, as described in the following subsections.

Outlook Display

This setting assumes that you are using the Microsoft Outlook integration capabilities and are using Outlook for your timesheet functionality. The setting modifies the fields that users have available through the Outlook interface.

Project Web Access Display

If you are tracking billable time versus overtime or non-billable time, you must leave this checkbox checked. If you uncheck this box, your users will not have the Non-billable or Overtime fields available to them in their timesheets.

Default Timesheet Creation Mode

When users create their timesheet for each period (week or month), the administrator can determine whether the timesheets are prepopulated with their current task assignments, with only the projects to which they are assigned, or left blank. The default value, Current Task Assignments, brings in the assignments that are supposed to happen during the time that the timesheet covers.

Timesheet Grid Column Units

Timesheets can capture work completed daily or as a single entry for work on a task for the whole week. This setting allows you to define the unit (days or weeks) in which users enter their time.

NOTE *It is important to ensure that the task tracking method is using the same method for entry, to avoid user confusion and keep consistency across your EPM system.*

Default Reporting Units

Here you can specify whether time units within each reporting period are reported in hours or days. To specify how many hours a timesheet considers is one day, type the hours in the "Number of Hours in a Standard Timesheet Day Is" box (the default setting is 8). Likewise, if you are using weeks as the Timesheet Grid Column Units described in the preceding subsection, you will want to enter a figure in the "Number of Hours in a Standard Timesheet Work Week Is" box (the default is 40).

Hourly Reporting Limits

Depending on the consumers of the data that are captured in timesheets, you may need to restrict how users can enter time. In the Hourly Reporting Limits section, you can limit the total number of hours per timesheet and the maximum hours per day. In addition, if your company requires that your resources account for a minimum number of hours per time period, you can set this limit here. If resources report time beyond these limits, errors will appear on their timesheets when they submit them.

Timesheet Policies

If your organization requires that users can enter time only for current work, you can set this by deselecting the Allow Future Time Reporting checkbox. If you select Allow Unverified Timesheet Line Items, this option setting enables users to create line items in their timesheet that have no relation to existing projects or tasks in Project Server.

NOTE *You must select Allow Unverified Timesheet Line Items if you are using only the timesheet and are not tracking project tasks through the My Tasks task status pages.*

Auditing

Project Server 2007 allows for robust timesheet logging and, if enabled, allows you to view all changes that were saved to a timesheet during creation, approval, and later modification.

Although this log is not exposed through the PWA user interface, it is stored in the dbo.MSP_TIMESHEET_ACTUAL_AUDIT table of the published database and is retrieved through Project Server Interface (PSI) Web service calls. The log and associated table in the published database can be purged using the Purge Log button in this section.

Approval Routing

When users create their timesheet and select Settings | View Header Data, they can view and potentially change relevant information about that particular timesheet. Among other things, the Approval Routing setting determines whether users can change who approves their timesheet when they submit it.

NOTE *The Approval Routing setting helps make timesheet functionality more flexible. It provides an elegant method to handle situations such as when a resource's default timesheet manager is unavailable and the resource needs another resource manager to approve the time. However, only users with the Accept Timesheets global permission are presented as available users to whom timesheets can be redirected. By default, this permission is assigned to the resource manager's Project Server security group.*

Administrative Time

Defining administrative time enables you to track calendar exceptions or time that differs from the project calendar. Administrative time in Project Server 2007 is implemented quite differently than in previous versions of the EPM toolset. In previous versions, a resource manager would create administrative projects and assign resources to the tasks within them. If one of these administrative project tasks was, for example, vacation (where the resource will not be working on any company-related tasks), the resource manager would need to open the Enterprise Resource Pool, open the user, find the time in the resource's calendar that was approved for vacation, and block off that time as non-working (see the subsection "Work Type"). In Project Server 2007, administrative time is implemented much more logically and performs much of the calendar manipulation automatically. The administrative time is now exposed as Administrative Time categories, and each category has four settings that determine its behavior. Note that the settings on this page apply to all users of timesheets in your PWA instance.

Status

The Status field determines whether users' timesheets display the Administrative Time category. Because Administrative Time categories cannot be deleted after you save them, this field is in essence the on/off switch for the specified Administrative Time category.

Work Type

The Work Type field determines whether a calendar exception will be created for the time applied to this item. If the time category is Meetings or Training, this is typically considered Working Time, whereas Vacation or Sick Time are typically considered non-working time demanding a calendar exception. If this field is set to Non Work, when a user successfully submits time against it (for a vacation, for example), the next time that a project manager opens his or her project, the manager will see that planned work has split around the non-working calendar exception.

Approve

This toggle setting simply determines whether the user's timesheet manager must approve the time applied to the Administrative Time category prior to submittal. Scheduling a future vacation is an example of an instance where this setting may be applicable.

Always Display

When this checkbox is selected, this Administrative Time category is always displayed near the bottom of every user's timesheet. When it is not checked (and as long as the category's status is Open), it will not display by default, but the user will be able to select it when inserting lines in their timesheet.

Task Settings and Display

Whereas many of the settings in the previous sections of this chapter deal with the timesheet functionality, the Task Settings and Display section enables you to define how resources interact with the My Tasks section of PWA. This section also allows you to define (and potentially enforce) the default tracking method that project managers use in managing their schedules.

Tracking Method

Of all of the settings you will configure in Project Server, this setting is one of the most weighty and will have far-reaching effects into resource user experience, project manager scheduling, and executive reporting. It is very important to gather input from your project management office (PMO) prior to implementing this setting for your project managers. What is even more important is that you understand the importance of consistent data.

The methods available include the following:

- **Percent of Work Complete** This method assumes that the task starts on the scheduled date, and users simply enter a percentage (from 0 to 100) of completed work. Project Server will calculate the actual work based on the percentage complete of planned work.
- **Actual Work Done and Work Remaining** Regardless of the calendar time, the resource enters overall actual work and remaining work for a task.
- **Hours of Work Done per Period** Resources are expected to enter their actual work over a given time period. They can enter remaining work on the task to indicate variance from the planned work. This is the preferred option for a best practices approach.

Tip *It is highly recommended to select the checkbox Force Project Managers to Use the Progress Reporting Method Specified Above for All Projects. By doing so, you will take a major step toward ensuring that your data are consistent when reporting on organization-wide data. If you allow project managers to change their tracking method, resources may end up with task sheets that are inconsistent among projects, potentially leading to confusion. By forcing a tracking method on all project managers in your EPM system, you can help avoid this inconsistency and confusion. Doing so will prevent your project managers from changing the progress reporting options within Project Professional 2007 on the Collaborate tab.*

Reporting Display

If you are using the Hours of Work Done per Period tracking method (described in the preceding section), this is where you define how you want users to report their hours—either every day or with a total for the week.

Protect User Updates

By selecting the Restrict Updates to Project Web Access checkbox, you prevent the project manager from manually changing the resource's reported actual work done. By selecting the checkbox Time Entry by Timesheet Only…, you are requiring your users to use only the timesheet. This can help to ensure that timesheet data and task status data on tasks are consistent.

Define Current Tasks

This setting enables an administrator to define what "current" is. The user's My Tasks page displays not only the tasks that the user has started but has not completed, but also the tasks that have been rejected. The number that you specify in days will determine the time window into the past and into the future in which unstarted tasks will appear.

Enable Team Member Gantt View

This setting enables users to view their personal Gantt view of their project work. From their My Tasks page, they can click GoTo | My Task Gantt View. The reason that there is a control for this view is that it is powered by an ActiveX control, and some organizations have specific policies regarding such controls.

Close Tasks to Update

If at some point you wish to prevent your resources from updating specific tasks in your project, the Close Tasks to Update page is where you perform this action.

NOTE *The Close Tasks to Update page is one of the only Server Settings options available to members of the default Project Managers group. Once there, a project manager may only have access to see his or her projects. As an administrator, you may have access to all projects in the PWA instance.*

Giving Users a Single Point of Entry

The Time Entry by Timesheet Only option is an important concept and decision point for defining how resources interact with PWA. The option may be attractive, because it can be the connecting thread between the timesheet data and the task status data to give users a single place to enter their time. It is important to note, however, that once you make this connection by checking this box, your users will be unable to enter remaining work for any of their tasks. This may be the deciding point for whether or not to create this link.

To close tasks from being updated further, complete the following steps:

1. Select the project to which you have access.
2. Check the box(es) next to the tasks that you wish to close.
3. Click Submit if you want to just save the changes, or click Publish to have the changes take effect immediately.

Because time and task management in Project Server is your users' most frequent interface for day-to-day interaction with PWA, it will have a large impact on the overall perception that users have of the EPM system. This is another reason that it is so important to take an iterative approach to implementing Project Server 2007. If your resources consistently provide feedback indicating their dislike for a particular aspect of time entry, or your billing department informs you that the time period naming convention is not compatible with its accounting software, these are spectacularly good things, because you are discovering them during your proof of concept or pilot, when you can modify your environment with the lowest risk possible. By thorough planning and regular feedback from your users during your initial phases, you'll have the best chance of implementing time and task management in a way that provides immediate benefits for your new users.

CHAPTER 11

Configuring Look and Feel Settings

The place to configure the Project Server look and feel is within one section on the Server Settings page. Once again, Project Server permissions control who has access to these items. To provide an easier path for the reader, this chapter approaches the subheadings in the reverse order from that in which the Project Web Access (PWA)/Server Settings list is displayed. The contents of this chapter are broken down as follows:

- Quick Launch
- Gantt chart formats
- Grouping formats
- Managing views

Quick Launch

The Quick Launch Bar is the leftmost navigation provided to PWA by the Windows SharePoint Services (WSS) 3.0 platform in which PWA is hosted. In traditional Web sites, the "left nav" was either the main navigation element or sometimes it was used for context-sensitive menus. For example, all areas of a Web site might have the same top-level tabs no matter where the viewer navigated, whereas the left side would have navigation only for the area where users found themselves.

PWA offers a lot of flexibility is determining what will appear in the Quick Launch Bar (as well as the top-level tabs). Keep in mind that only areas of the site to which the user has permission access will display.

To navigate to this location, select Server Settings and then under the Look and Feel section, select Quick Launch. The top section of the Edit Quick Launch page allows the person doing this configuration (usually the Project Server administrator) the chance to edit a couple of behaviors. The first option, All Sections, results in the display of the Quick Launch Bar as fully expanded no matter the page or feature to which the user has navigated, as shown in Figure 11-1.

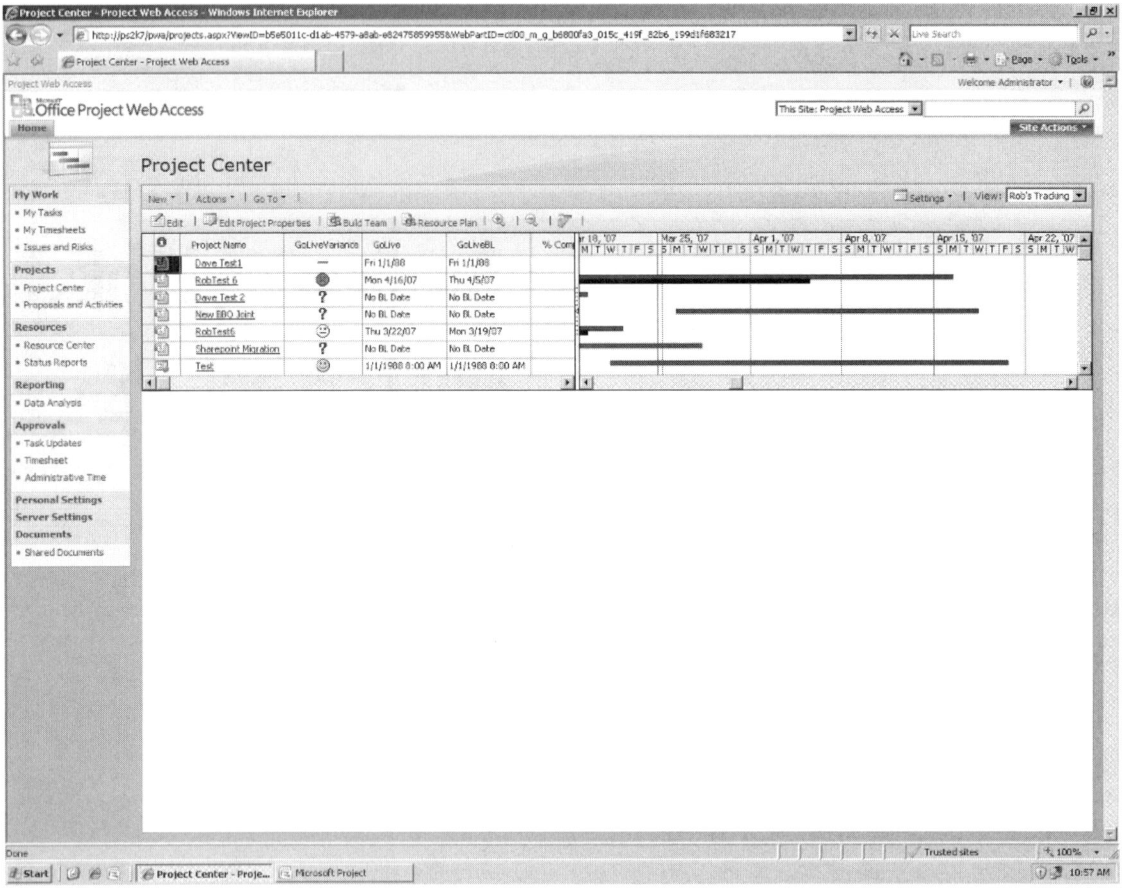

FIGURE 11-1 Quick Launch Bar in its expanded state

The section option, Current Section Only, reduces the size of the Quick Launch Bar by collapsing it so that only the area that is currently being viewed is expanded. See an example of the same PWA view with the collapsed version in Figure 11-2.

Usually there is no reason to collapse this view unless large amounts of new pages are added with the PWA environment. This is possible in some cases, but not common. The recommendation is that unless users cannot see all the items without scrolling vertically, leave it set at the default, All Sections.

There is an additional setting in the top section of the page, the check box Show Menu Items from Windows SharePoint Services. Minimal classic WSS content is in PWA when it is first installed—only a single Shared Documents library. If it is not needed or if there is no

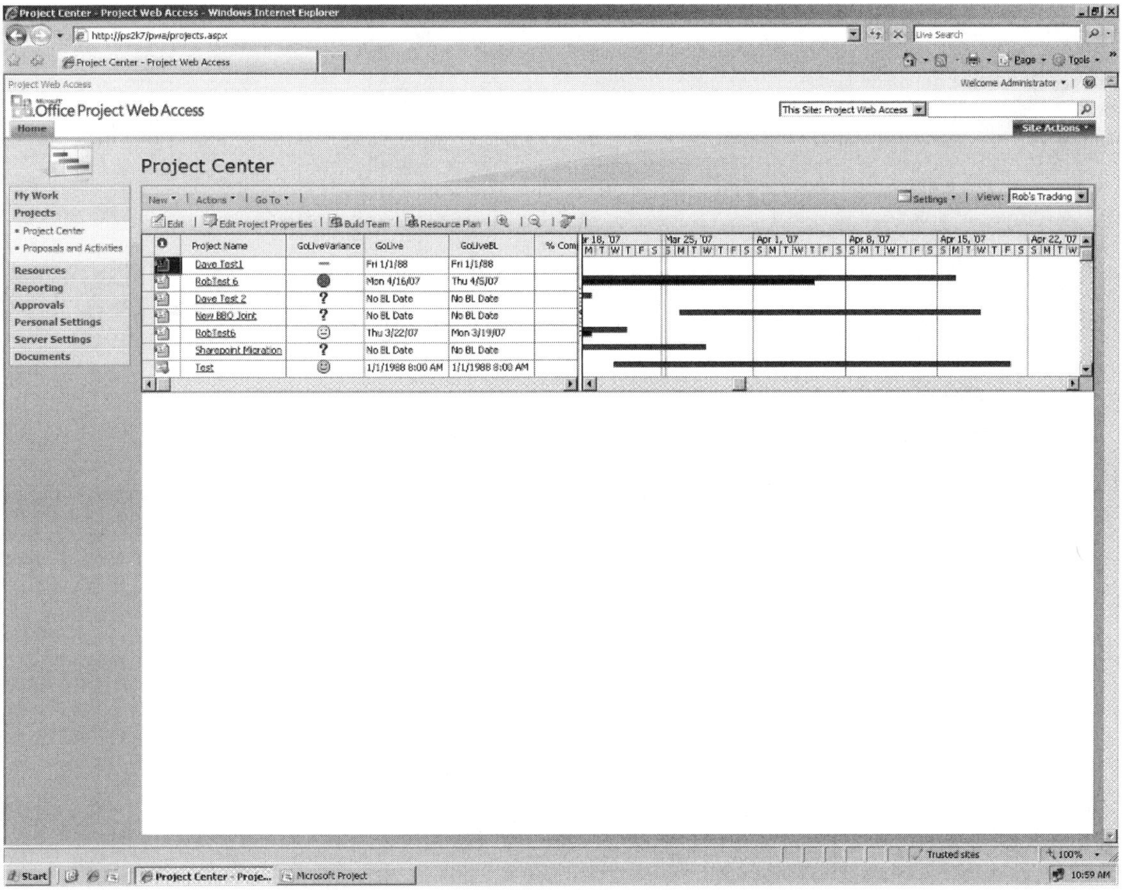

FIGURE 11-2 Quick Launch Bar in its Current Section Only state

intent to add much new WSS content in PWA, you can deselect this checkbox to hide even the initial document library. WSS is rarely used from the PWA main area; however, in the 2007 versions of WSS and Project Server, there is far more potential for using this area to support than in previous versions.

The bottom portion of the Edit Quick Launch page is Set Menu Item Details. This area enables the administrator to add, delete, or move items for the Quick Launch Bar display.

Move an Item

Microsoft did a great job of placing the buttons in an appropriate order, but you can move them if you like. To move an item, highlight the row that you want to move, as shown in Figure 11-3.

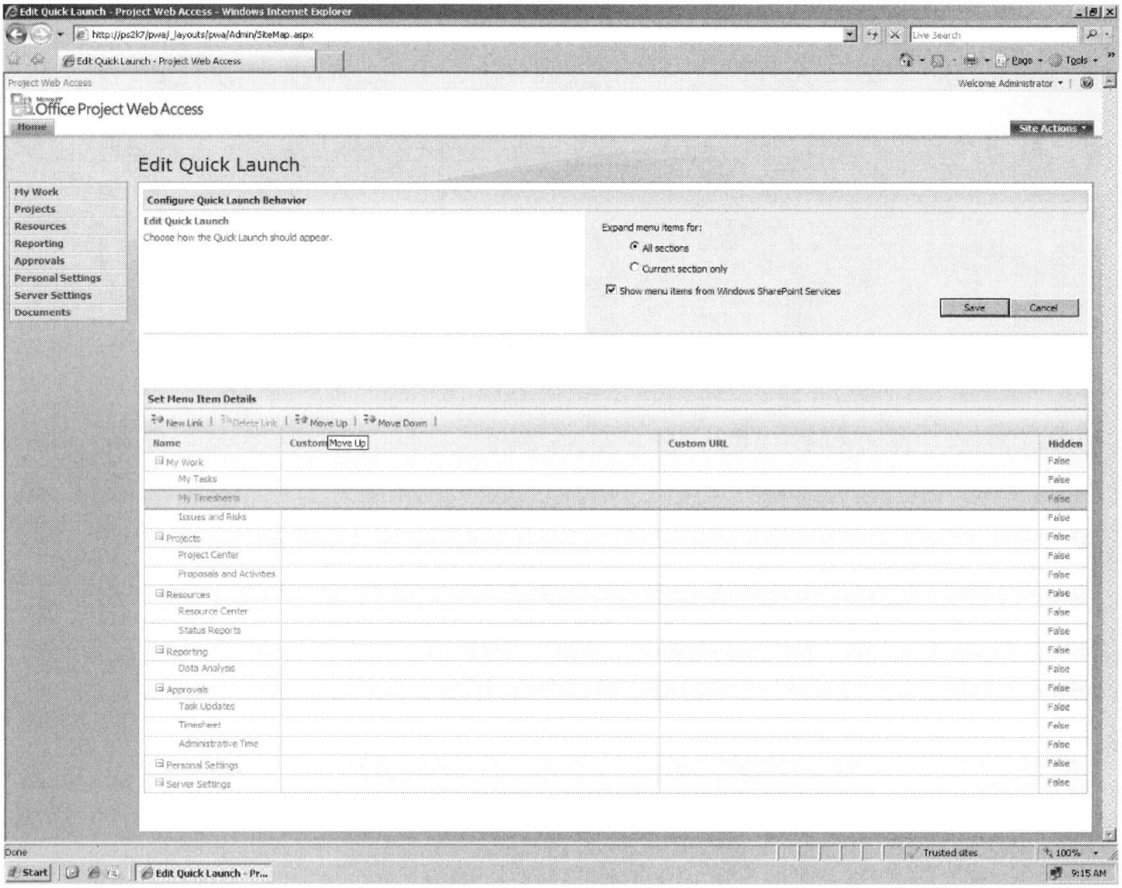

FIGURE 11-3 Highlighted menu item

Then use the Move Up or Move Down buttons to relocate the item(s) where required for the organization (see Figure 11-4). The primary goal should be to make these system menus as easy for users to navigate as possible.

Adding a New Link to the Quick Launch Bar

It can be handy to add a new link to the Quick Launch Bar, even one that is outside the normal PWA functions. Here is an example. The Project Workspaces Web Part on the PWA Home Page can grow quite long as projects are added to the EPM environment. Why not create a new Web Part page just for the large Project Workspaces Web Part and add a link to it on the Quick Launch Bar? To create a new link, select the New Link button. The Add or Edit Link dialog appears as shown in Figure 11-5. Next add a common language name for the link (keep it brief). Then enter in the uniform resource locator (URL) address and decide whether to include it under an existing heading or have it be a new top-level heading. (Don't change the dropdown for display.) Finally, select OK. Figure 11-6 shows the newly edited Quick Launch Bar.

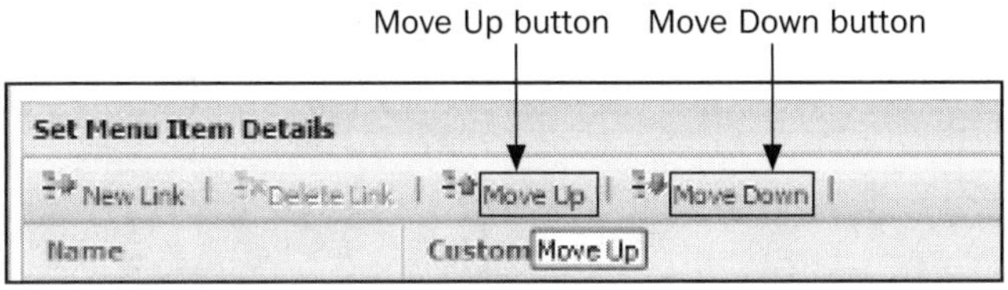

FIGURE 11-4 Move Up and Move Down controls

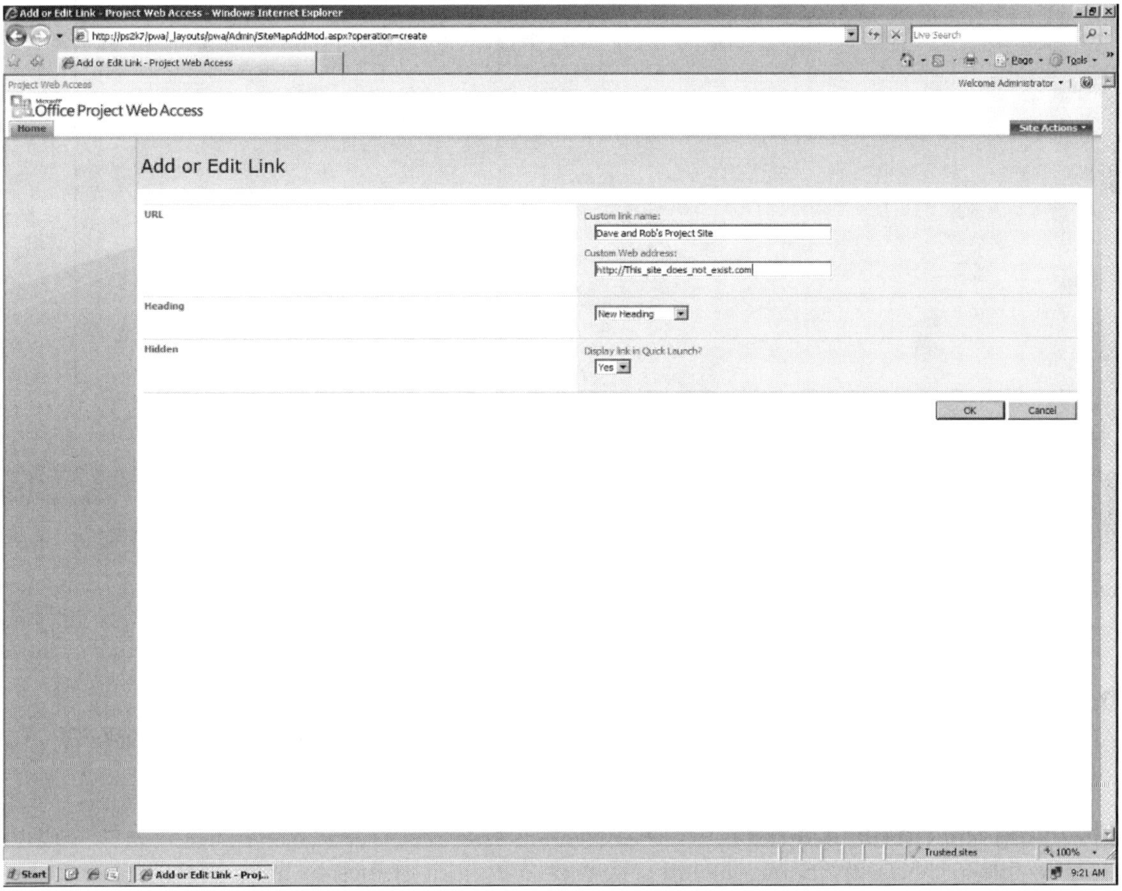

FIGURE 11-5 Add or Edit Link dialog

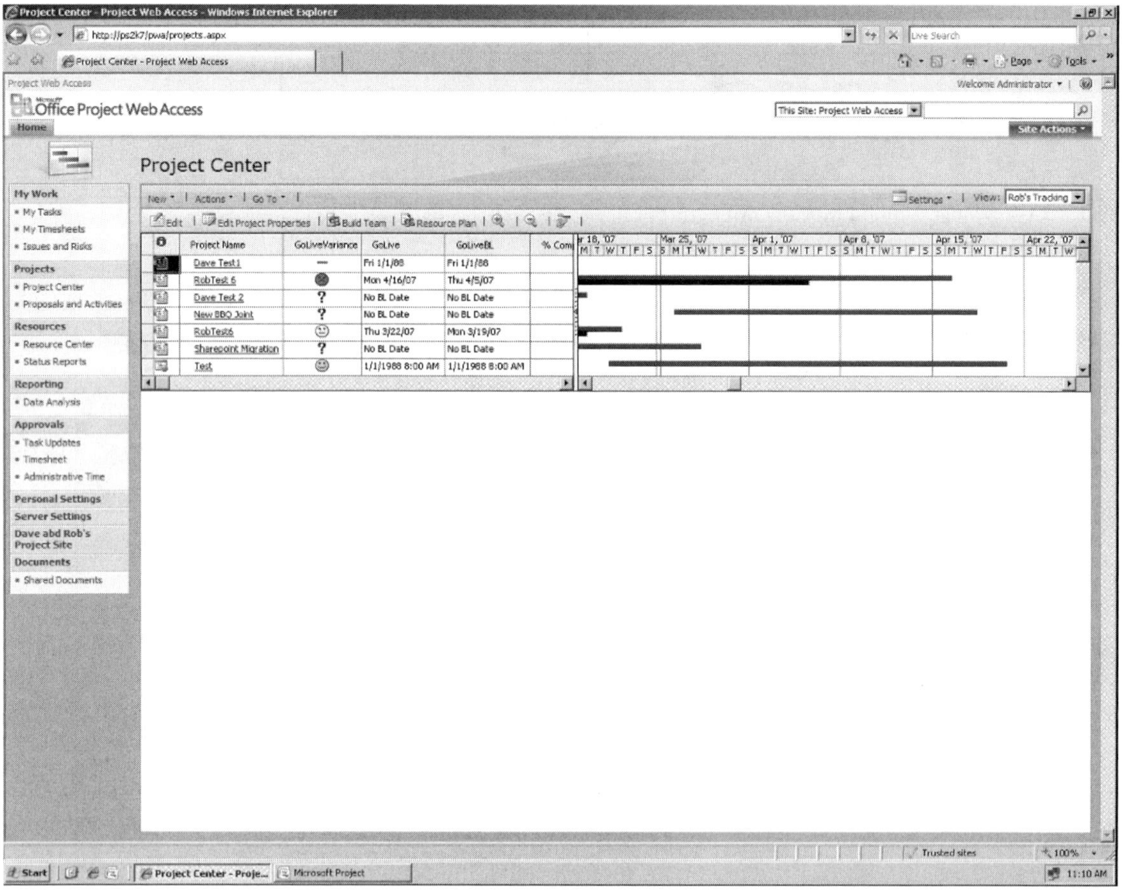

FIGURE 11-6 Edited Quick Launch Bar

Deleting a Link

As shown in Figure 11-7, deleting a link is easy. Just highlight the row and select the Delete button.

Changing the Name of a Link

It is possible to change the name of a link, even one of the out-of-the-box links. Feel free to edit any links to meet the organization's specific needs. However, there is no need to change those that come with PWA that point to pages with the same names as the links.

The next section discusses the look and feel of the PWA Gantt charts.

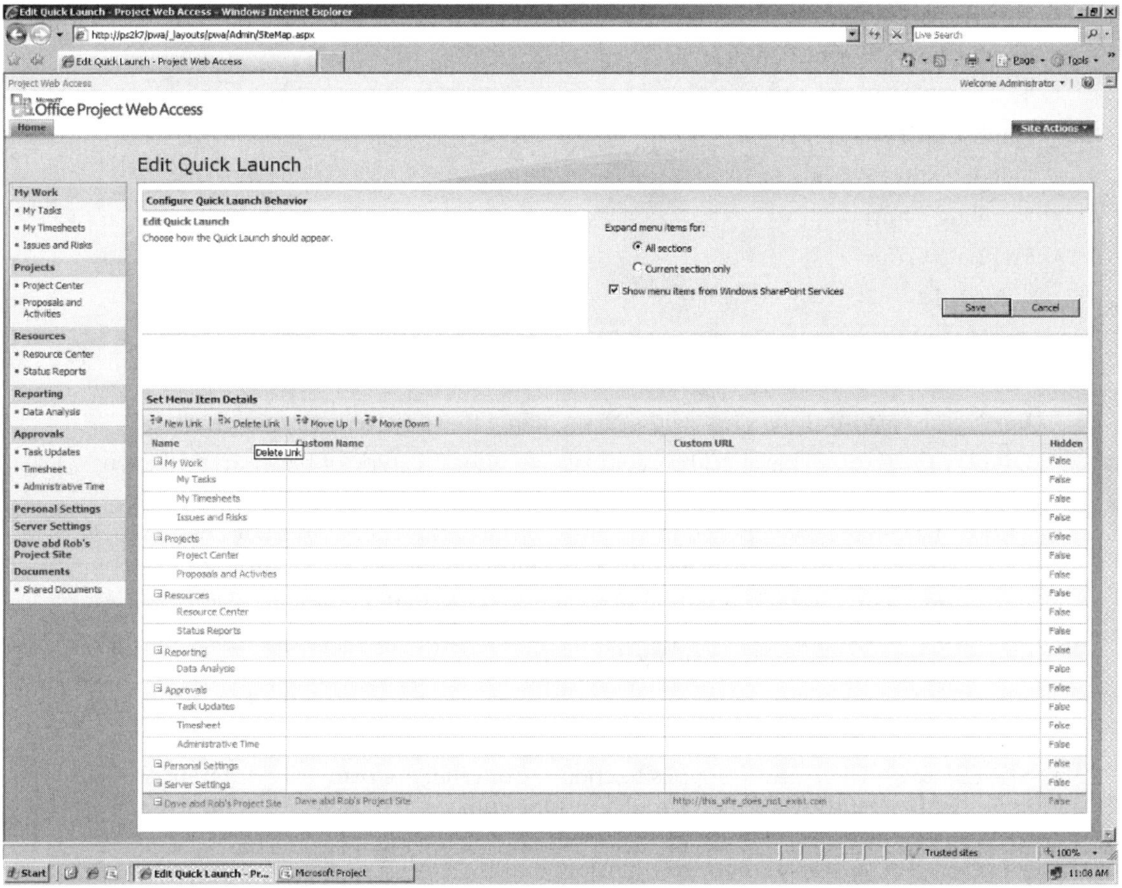

FIGURE 11-7 Deleting a Link from the Quick Launch Bar

Gantt Chart Formats

Gantt chart formats and the next section, "Grouping Formats," make the authors pine for a color version of this book (which is sadly not going to happen). When installed, Project Server provides 27 different Gantt charts that can be associated with different views in PWA (you will learn more about views later in this chapter). The following categories of Gantt charts are available, each with different attributes:

- Personal Gantt (Tasks)
- Gantt Assign Info

- Approvals Gantt
- Gantt Chart (Project Center)
- Tracking (Project Center)
- Gantt Chart (Views)
- Detail Gantt (Views)
- Leveling Gantt
- Tracking Gantt
- Gantt1–10

In each of these Gantt chart formats, the following settings can be modified:

- **Bar Name (read-only)** This field sets the name that appears for your chart.
- **Display (yes/no)** This checkbox controls whether this type of bar chart will even be displayed at all.
- **Middle Bar Shape (as opposed to the ends of the bar)** The Middle Bar Shape allows the setting of narrow and wide bars as well as top, middle, or low vertical justification.
- **Bar Color** This allows the setting of the middle bar to the following vast array of color possibilities. They are Black, Red, Yellow, Lime, Aqua, Blue, Fuchsia, White, Maroon, Green, Olive, Navy, Purple, Teal, Gray, and Silver.
- **Bar Pattern** This setting allows a pattern overlay if desired for the middle bar and includes grids, lines, and more.
- **Start Shape** There are 20 shapes to choose from that are primarily different arrow styles with a handful of other WingDing-type choices.
- **Start Color** These can be set to one of the same set of colors as the bar.
- **End Shape** These are the same 20 shapes mentioned for Start Shape.
- **End Color** These are the same colors mentioned for Start Color.

Although it is possible to edit these bars to create an explosion of color, you shouldn't do so. Keep in mind that usability is paramount. The team members will not appreciate a lime Gantt bar with a fuchsia start and a purple end if they have to view the chart daily. This is not to say that changing these settings is always a bad idea. It can be a good idea if done with discretion.

To edit the bar styles, select Gantt Chart Formats in the Look and Feel area on the Server Settings page in PWA. Navigate to the Gantt chart type that you want to modify. Next select the bar name that needs modification. From there, go right into the table and make the changes, as shown in Figure 11-8.

Notice that as you make changes, the Gantt chart area to the right side of the page displays the results so that you can view their effect before you commit to the change. When you are certain that the settings are ready, select Save.

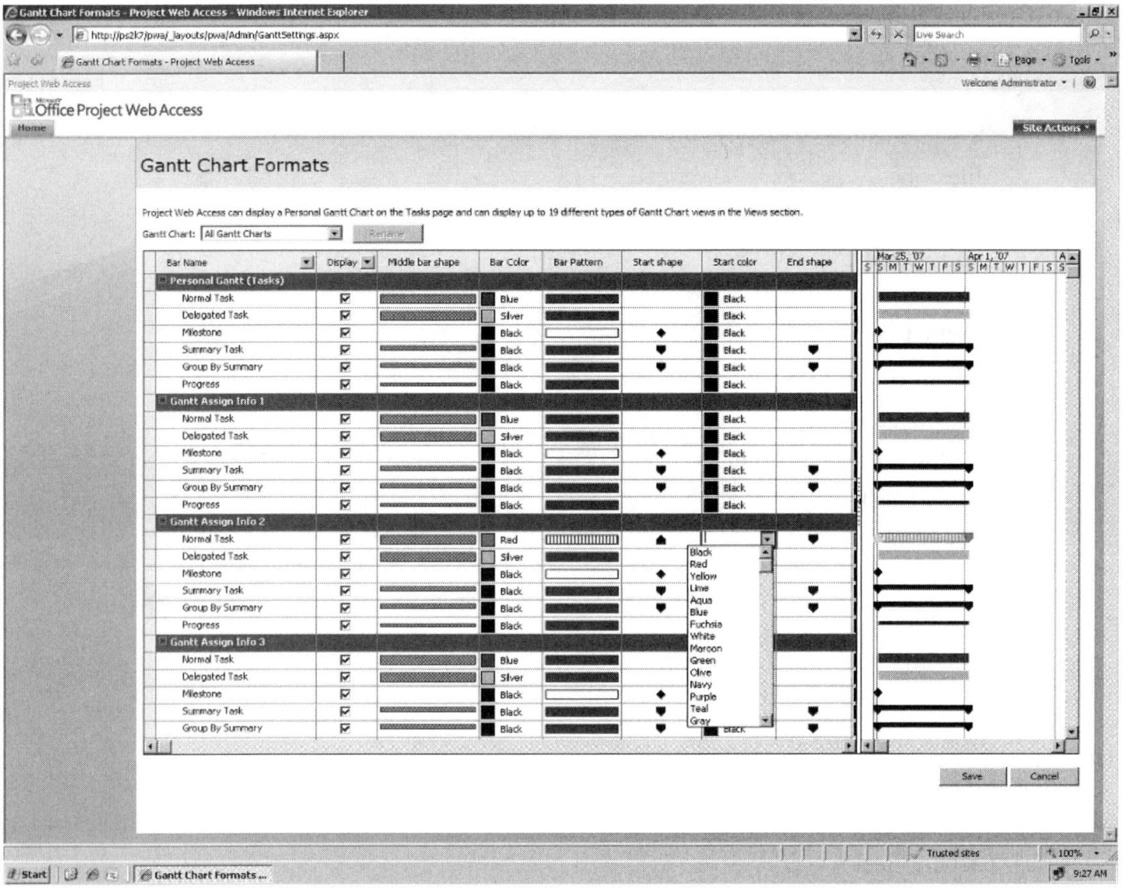

FIGURE 11-8 Editing the Gantt chart format

The available Gantt bars change depending on the context. The following is a breakdown of what bars can be set when formatting based on context for each Gantt Chart option.

- Personal Gantt (Tasks)
  - Normal Task
  - Delegated Task
  - Milestone
  - Group by Summary
  - Progress

- Gantt Assign Info – Same as Personal Gantt
- Approvals Gantt
  - Normal Task
  - Delegated Task
  - Milestone
  - Summary Task
  - Group by Summary
  - Progress
  - Old Task
  - Old Summary
  - Old Milestone
- Gantt Chart (Project Center)
  - Normal Task
  - Critical Task
  - External Task
  - Milestone
  - Summary Task
  - Project Summary
  - Group by Summary
  - Progress
  - Summary Progress
  - Baseline Task
  - Baseline Summary
  - Baseline Milestone
  - Preleveled Task
  - Preleveled Summary
  - Deadline
  - Slippage
  - Delay
  - Custom Duration 1–10
  - Early Schedule
  - Late Schedule
  - External Milestone
  - Project Summary Version 1–5
- Tracking (Project Center)—Same as Gantt Chart (Project Center) listed above
- Gantt Chart (Views)—Same as Gantt Chart (Project Center) listed above

- Detail Gantt (Views)—Same as Gantt Chart (Project Center) listed on the previous page
- Leveling Gantt—Same as Gantt Chart (Project Center) listed on the previous page
- Tracking Gantt—Same as Gantt Chart (Project Center) listed on the previous page
- Gantt1-10—Same as Gantt Chart (Project Center) listed on the previous page

Note that although many of the Gantt chart formats include the same available fields, they can all be used differently. In fact, when the initial installation is performed of Microsoft Office Project Server 2007, many of these fields are preconfigured for different use with different fields displayed, different bar styles, and so on. For example, red is commonly used to notate the critical path tasks.

Following are some examples of how different Gantt chart formats can be used within common views. There are many more out-of-the-box combinations and they can be modified extensively as needed. The first one uses the standard Gantt Chart (Views) format with the Assignment Costs View (see Figure 11-9).

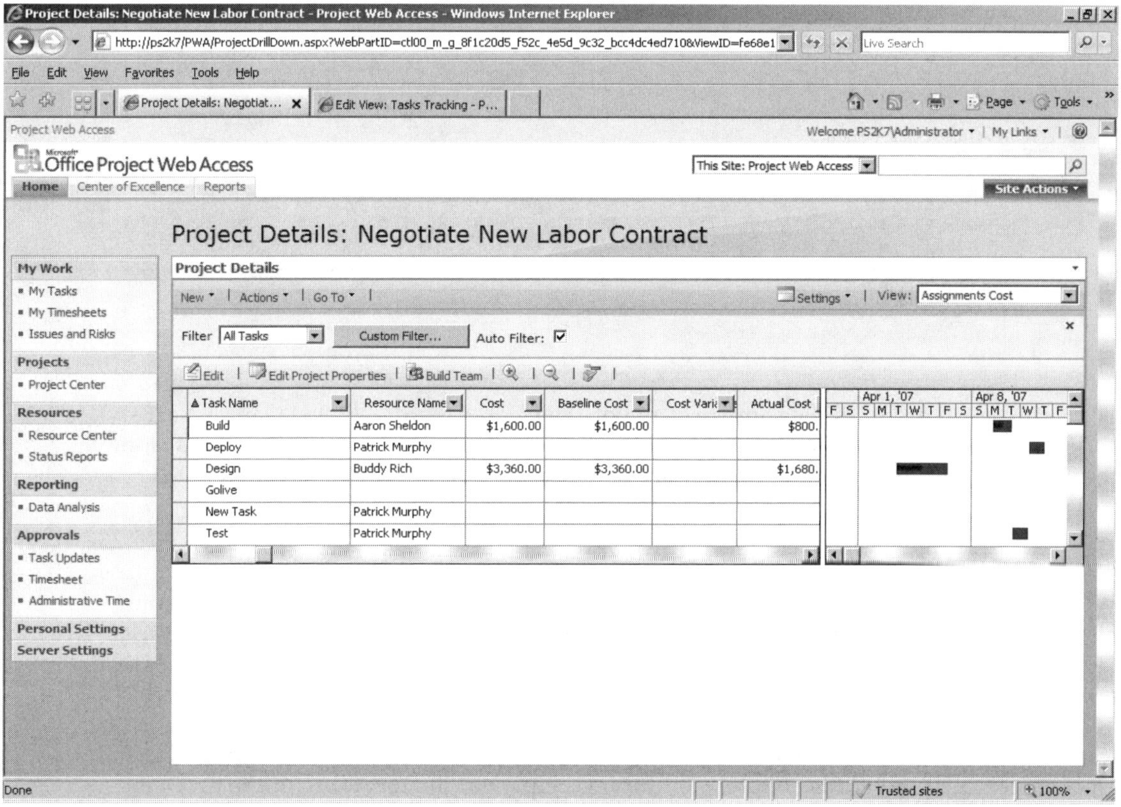

FIGURE 11-9 Gantt Chart (Views)

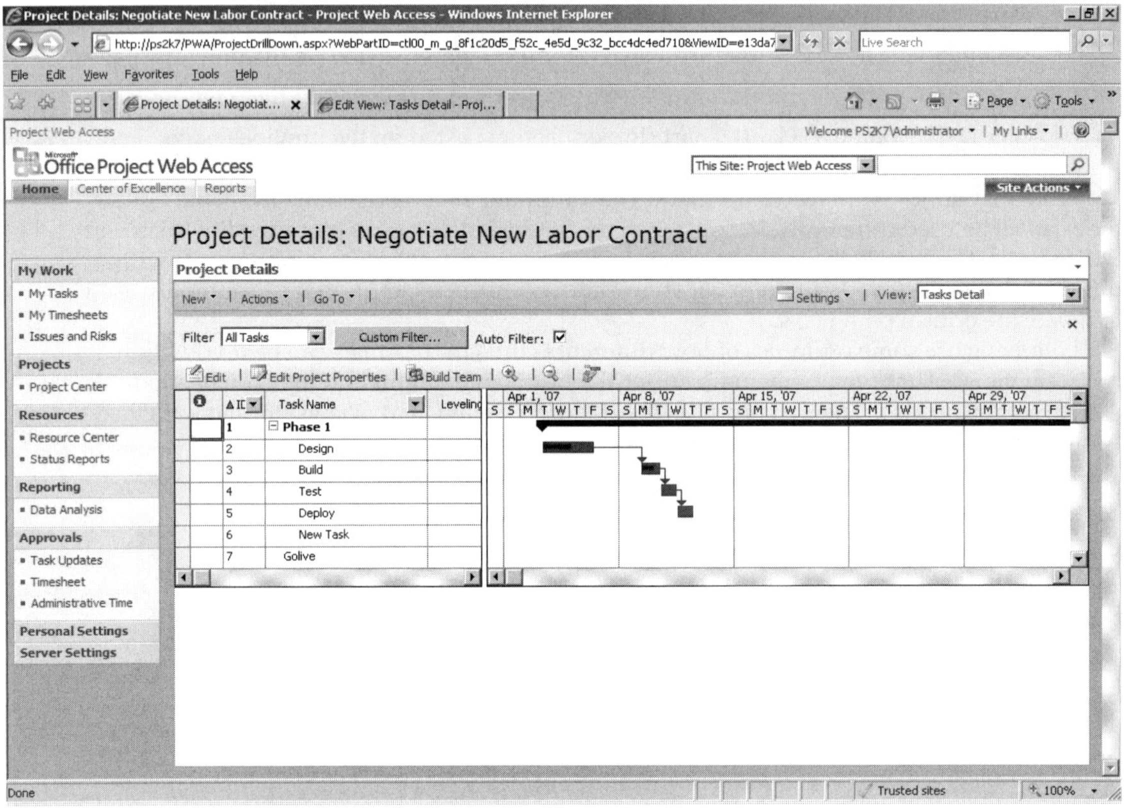

FIGURE 11-10 Detail Gantt (Views)

Figure 11-10 displays the same project with the Detail Gantt (Views) Gantt Chart style.

Finally, Figure 11-11 displays the Tracking Gantt style. Note the multiple entries along the same task row that mark the difference between the baseline and actual dates.

Grouping Formats

When you are looking at large amounts of data, it is difficult to sort through the meaning of all of that information. Grouping the information is a way to view data in a way that uses certain types of information as the basis for how the data are displayed. For example, if data are to be viewed by project name and then by the team that is responsible for the project and then by task names, the data would be easier to understand than if they were just a long list of tasks with resources next to them. You can set grouping with Manage views (see the next section of this chapter). Grouping helps, but if everything in the grouping hierarchy has the same look and feel, it would be difficult to readily understand the key

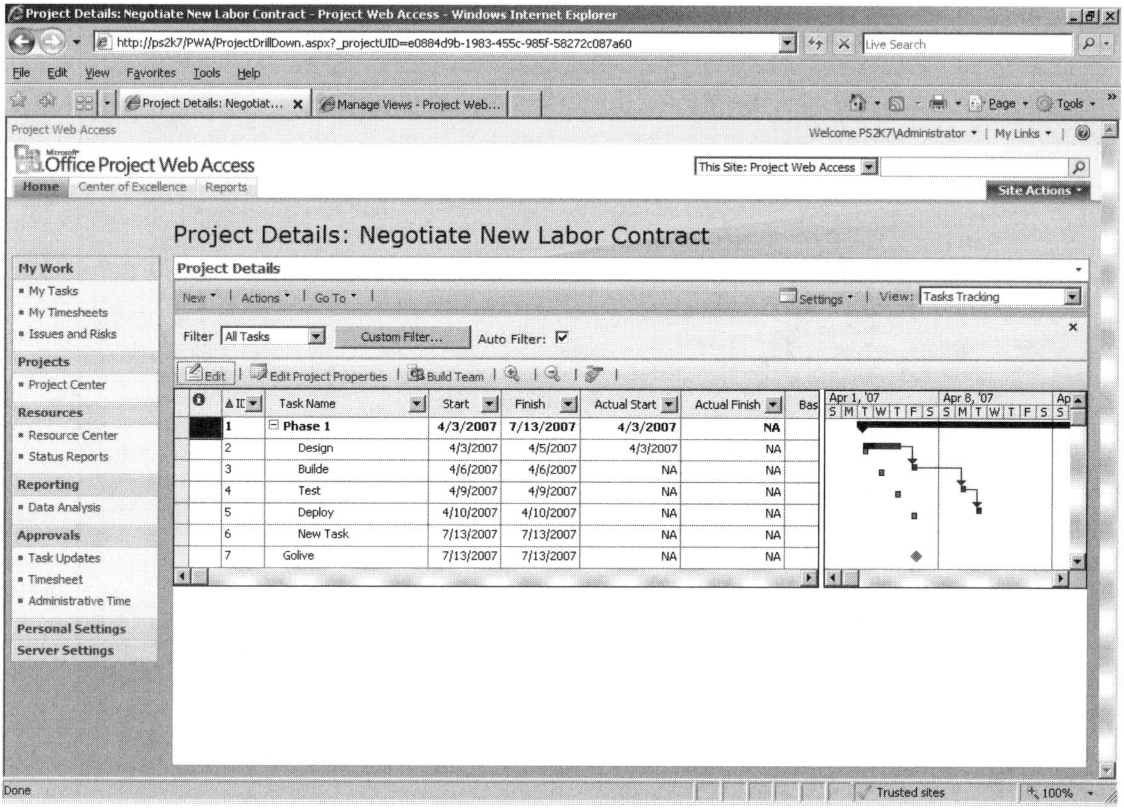

FIGURE 11-11 Tracking Gantt (Views)

pieces of information that the user is seeking. If the projects were shown in yellow, the resources in green, and the tasks in light blue, the user viewing this information will more readily understand it. Grouping formats are used to make it easier to understand views that use grouping.

There are nine grouping formats available: One is Timesheet, one is Views, and the rest are Grouping 1–9. It is possible to edit cell color, cell pattern, and font color (all using the same colors listed previously), or the font style (using regular, italic, bold, and bold italic).

To edit the grouping formats, navigate to Grouping Formats from within the Look and Feel area of the Server Settings page. Select the grouping format and grouping level for editing, as shown in Figure 11-12.

The process is similar to that of editing Gantt chart styles. Select the combination of colors, patterns, fonts, and font styles required and select Save when you are ready. In the next section, you will use much of what you have learned about formatting groups and Gantt charts, as well as much more.

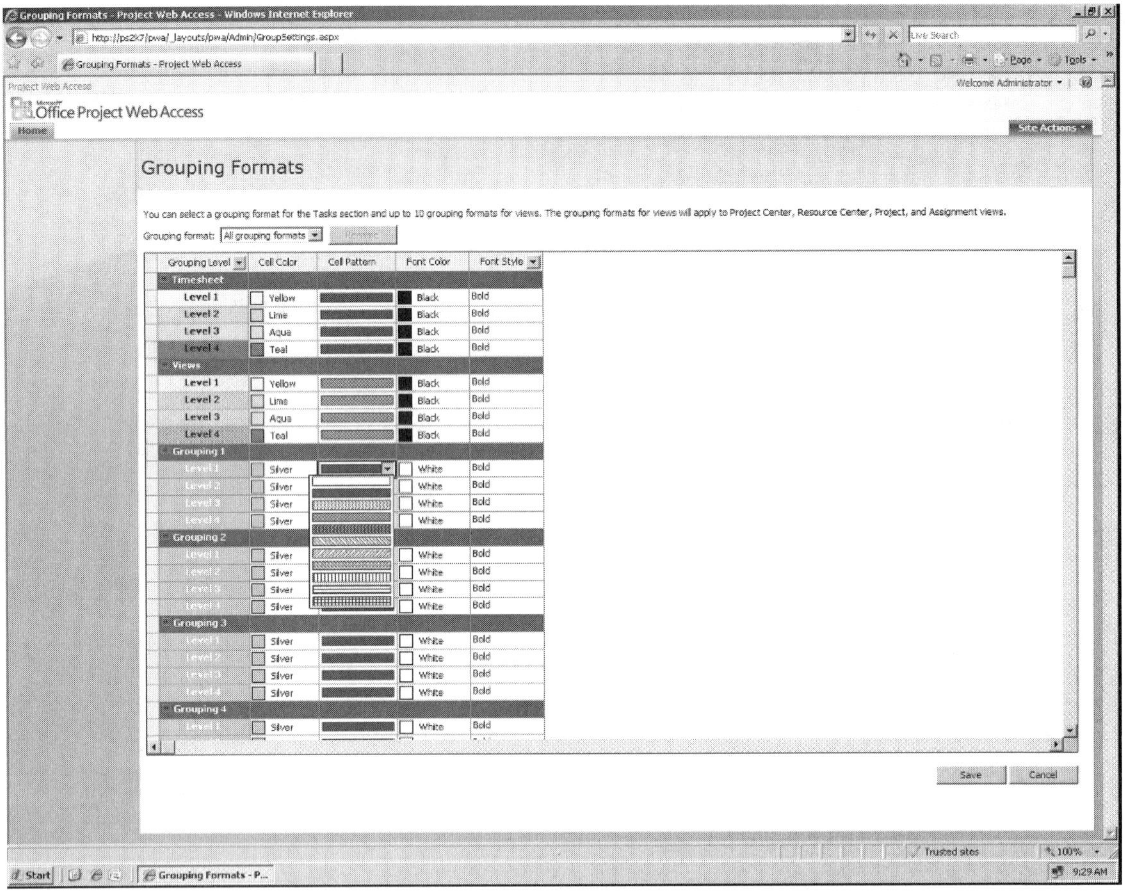

FIGURE 11-12 Editing grouping

Managing Views

Views are collections of data/information from within the Project Server databases. They act as the user interface for interacting with the system, such as when the user is recording time and project task progress. They are also used to view resource availability, project progress, detailed task information, and assignments, and to utilize powerful analysis features.

View Types

Project Server 2007 offers 10 view types, more than in previous versions, to enable new features such as proposals. Most view types offer great flexibility and control for configuration, although there are some that are limited. The view types are as follows:

- **Project views** Project views are used to display data at the detailed project level and can include tasks, assignments, and task/resource information. These views usually are shown in a view that is similar to what the project manager can see in the Microsoft Project Professional client, except that Project views are in read-only mode. This is one of the most commonly modified view types. Most Project views include a table and a Gantt chart, although Project Resource views do not include a Gantt. Note that there are many built-in Project views in Project Server, actually too many to allow them all to be available for all people, as these views, when seen as a collective, offer too many choices for almost any environment. Pick and choose the appropriate out-of-the-box views, modify them as needed, and build your own if like. It is not recommended that you delete views, as they may come in handy later. Figure 11-13 shows an example Project view.

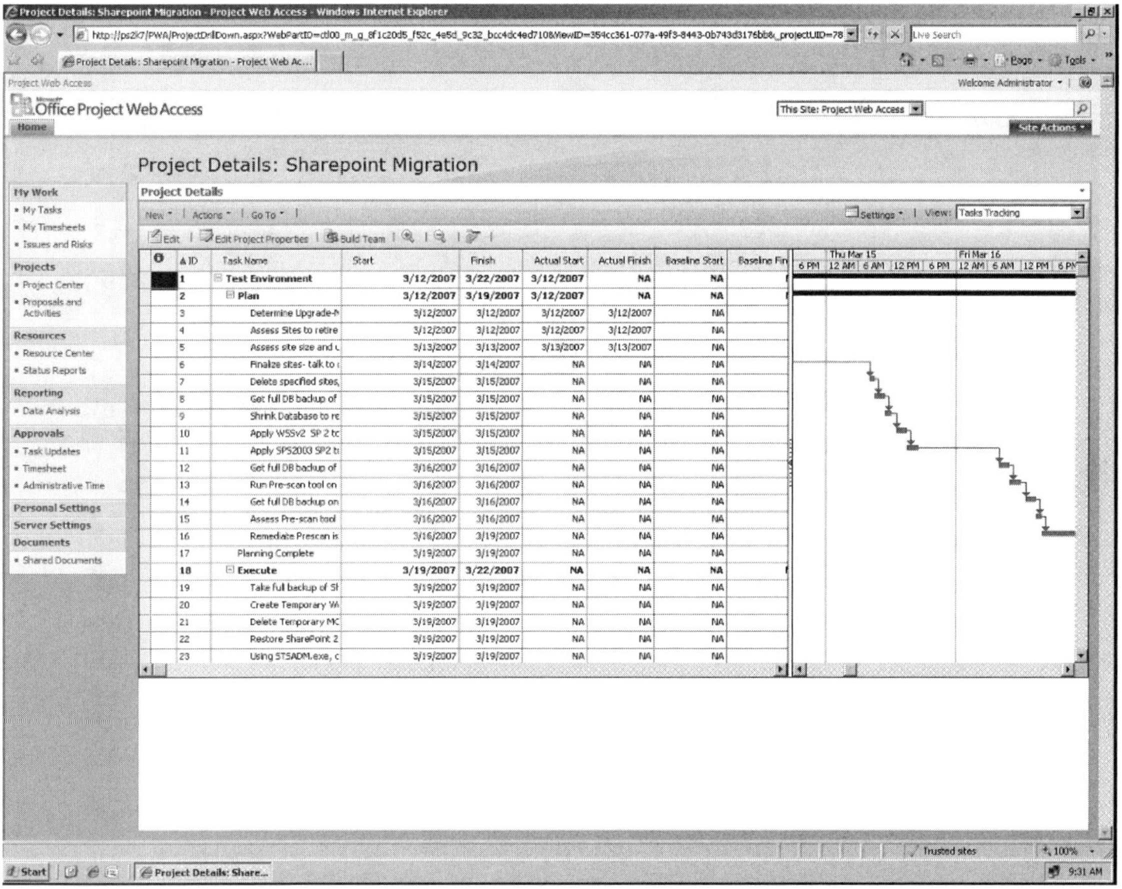

Figure 11-13 Project Tracking view

- **Project Center views** The Project Center is where projects are aggregated at the summary level. Each project is allocated only a single row that represents the collective information about the project. These views are used to display all the projects, projects that make up a program, projects by department, projects by project manager, or any other way that makes sense for a particular organization. These views share a single common element: one row per project that displays the summary of the each project. Each row includes a cell that displays the project name as a link that takes permitted viewers to the Project views of that project (a process known as *drilling down*). Project Center views are often used to display project-level "stoplight indicators" for work, schedule, cost, or earned value. These views are one place where you might create special executive views. Figure 11-14 shows an example Project Center view.

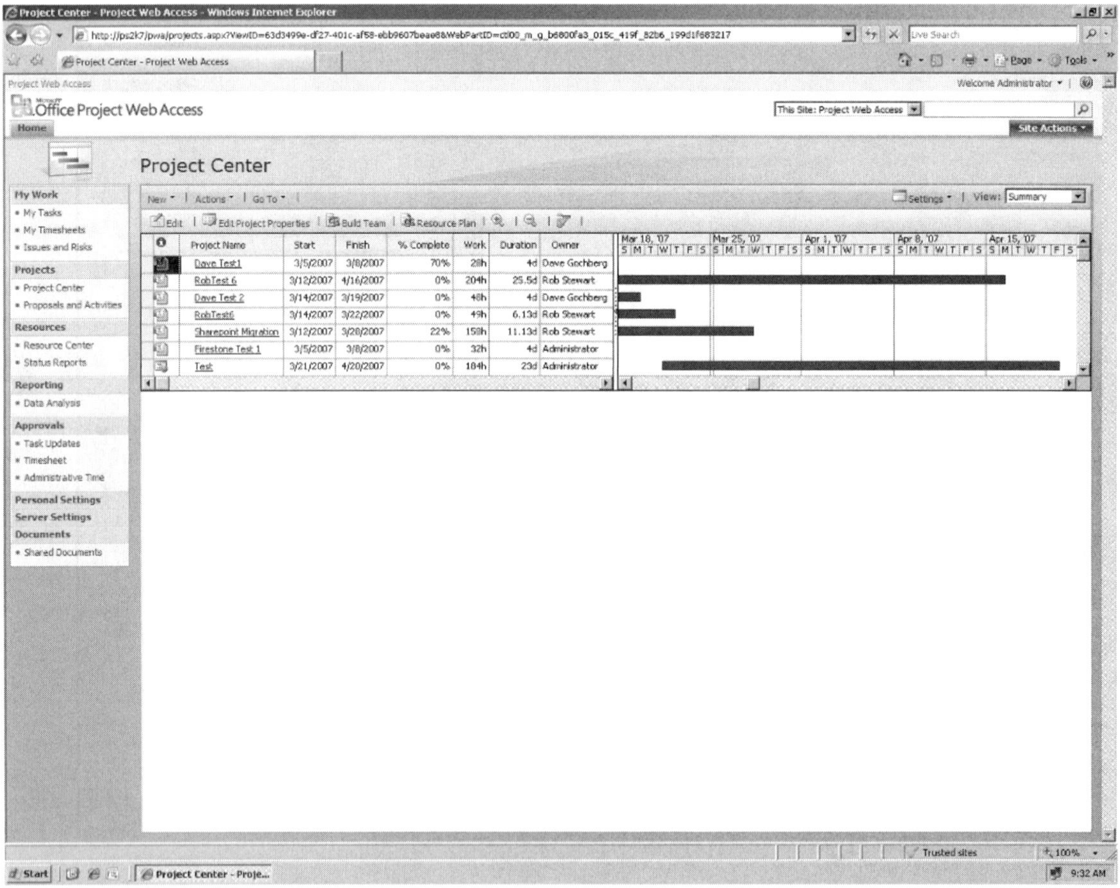

FIGURE 11-14 Project Center summary view

- **Resource Assignments views** There is only a single Summary View out of the box in this category. This type of view displays when a user with appropriate permission (such as a resource manager) selects View Assignments from within the Resource Center. It displays the assignment information only for the resources that were previously selected in Resource Center, as shown in Figure 11-15.
- **Resource Center views** The Resource Center views display table-based information about resources. This information includes all resource types and can include any resource fields available in the system. Figure 11-16 shows an example.

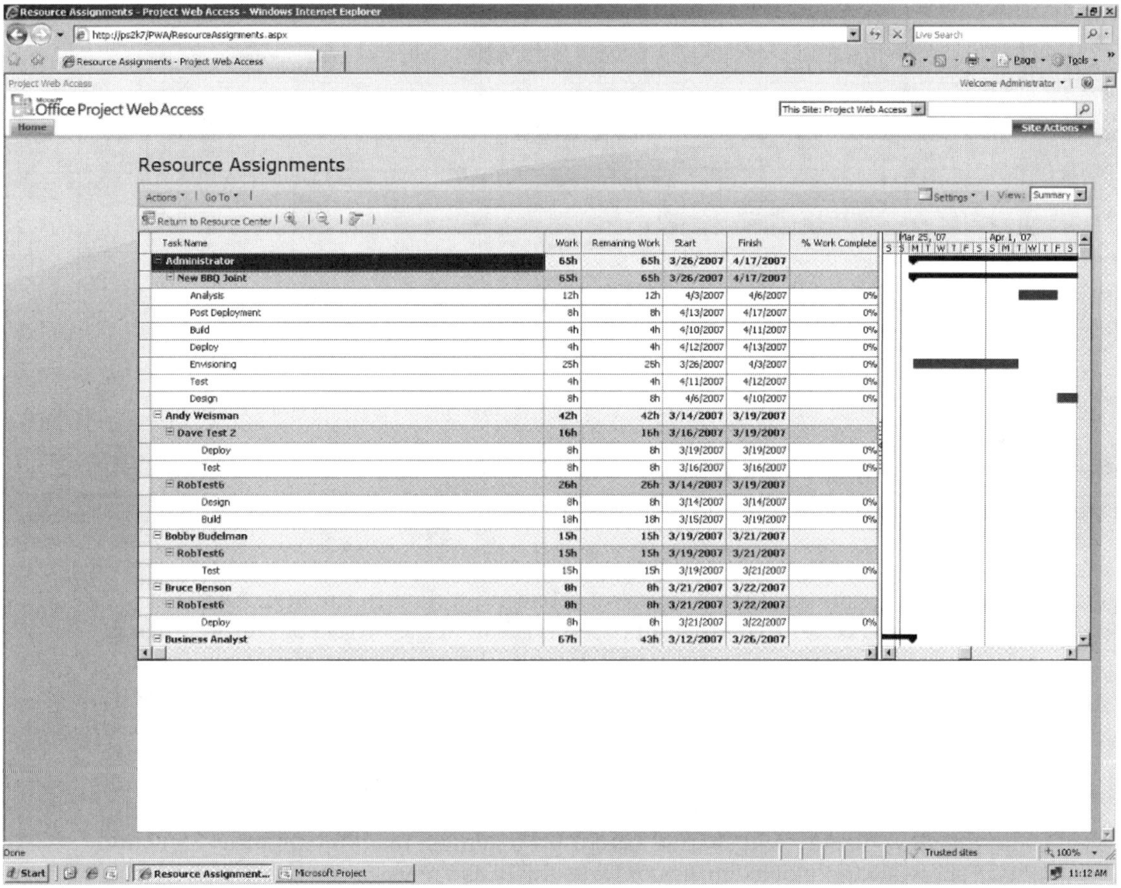

FIGURE 11-15 Resource Assignments summary view

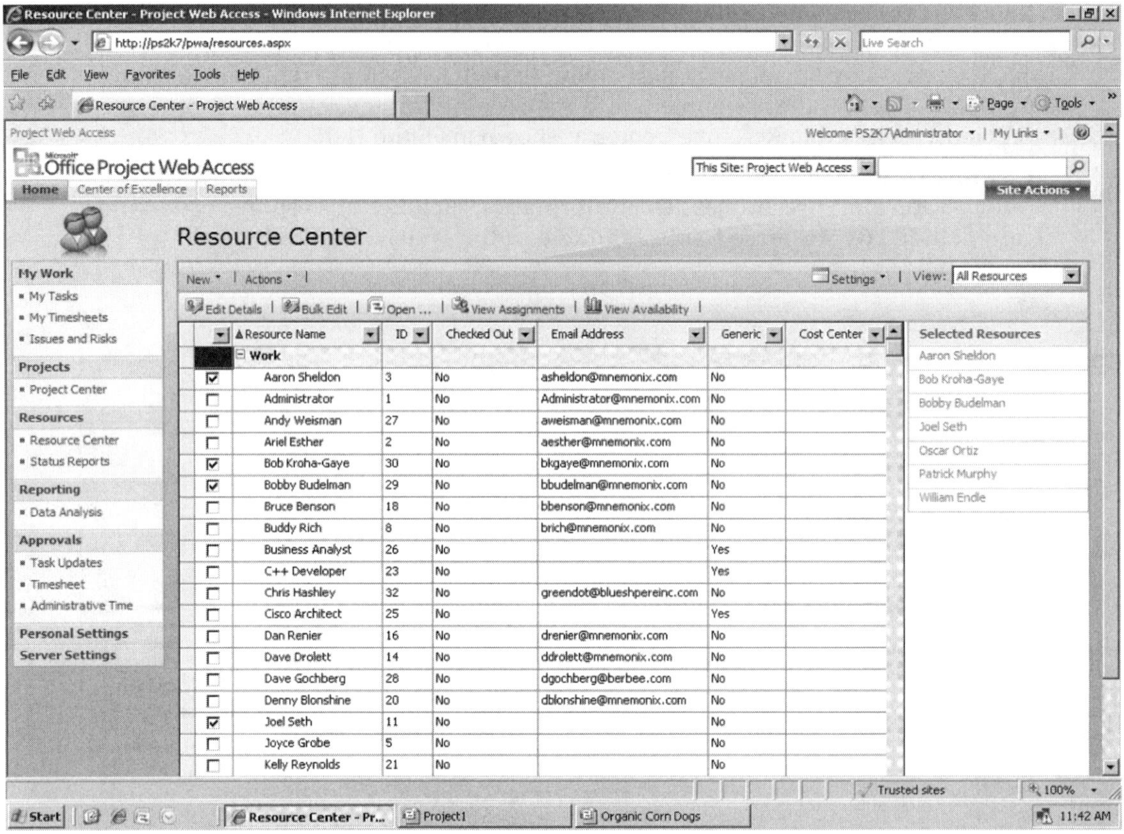

FIGURE 11-16 Resource Center All Resources view

- **Data Analysis views** These views are based on data in the SQL Analysis Services–based cubes that are built based on data in the Project Server Reporting database (ProjectServer_Reporting by default). There is enormous flexibility in what can be displayed in these views based on the way that the cube settings are configured. Keep in mind that for read access, cube data security is basically all or nothing. These views can contain pivot tables and charts, and can actually be pivoted on the fly by permitted users in the system. For example, if a view is built that includes baseline work and actual work, the viewer can add work on the fly and the view display will change as a result in almost real time. Figures 11-17 and 11-18 show a couple of examples of Data Analysis views.
- **My Work views** There are two views in My Work; one is a summary of My Assignments and the other a more detailed view. You can modify these views to a certain degree, but be careful as there are some fields that would not make sense to change. For example, don't remove the Task Name field as it will be needed.

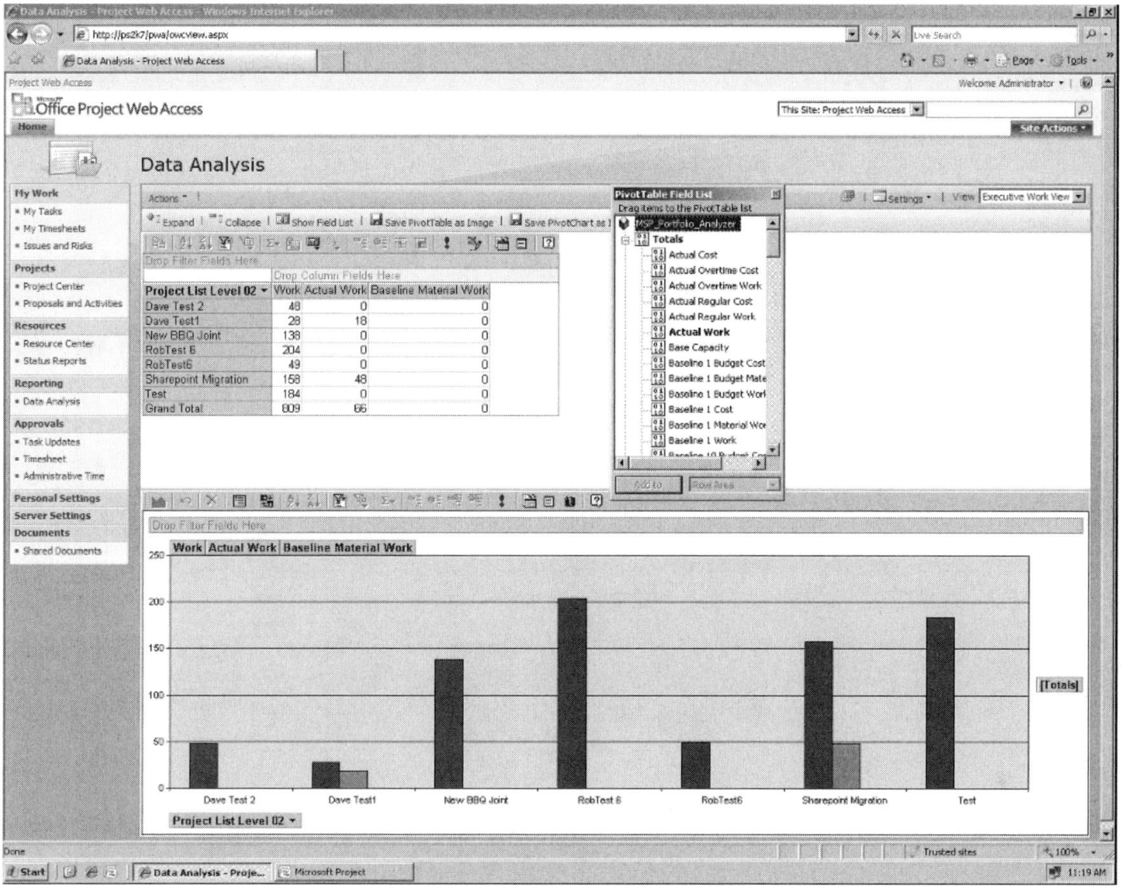

FIGURE 11-17 Data Analysis Executive Work (Custom) view

Note that for some inexplicable reason, if the Remaining Work field is added to the Summary View (a very reasonable thing to do), it displays in days rather than hours. The same field is displayed in hours if the user looks at the detailed level. Note that this is a unique view in that items presented are both task and assignment field types.

- **Resource Plans views** There is a single out-of-the-box view to support this new Project Server 2007 feature. It can be modified (adding fields primarily) if the organization decides to use Resource Plans. Resource Plans allow a less granular view of resources for purposes such as planning, support, and maintenance. The tools for managing this view type offer one interesting setting that enables you to restrict the resources displayed to the users' resource breakdown structure (RBS) branch. If this is enabled, it effectively results in a display of only those resources in one part of the RBS structure.

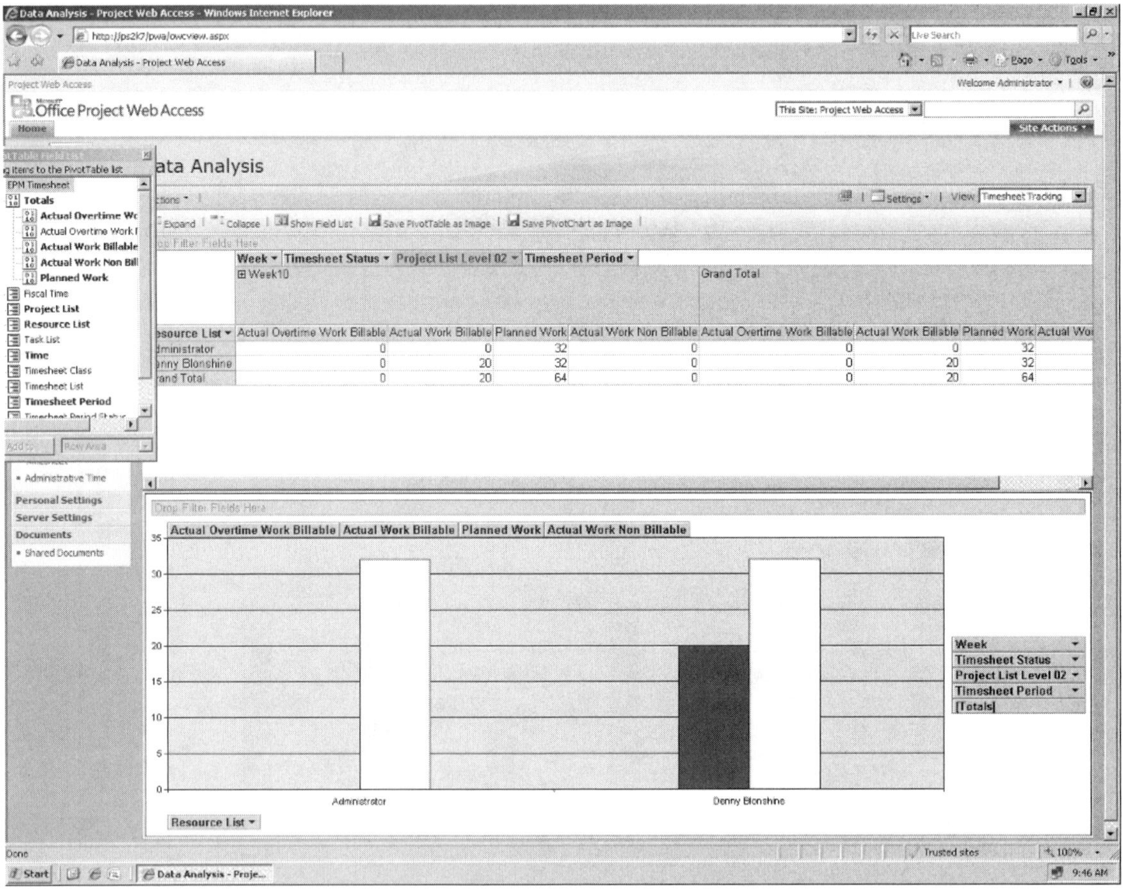

FIGURE 11-18 Data Analysis Timesheet Tracking (Custom) view

- **Team Tasks views** This is another new feature. Team Tasks are tasks that have a team assigned as opposed to a particular individual, allowing resources to self-assign to an existing task. The feature would be most commonly used for support and/or maintenance work. These views display assignments for team resources based on teams that the administrator has defined.
- **Team Builder views** Although in most organizations the project manager builds his or her project teams, some companies prefer to assign this job to resource managers, the project management office (PMO), or a "master resource controller." The PWA-based Team Builder views support the ability for project teams to be built from the Web and can include whatever resource data make sense. Note that people permitted to use Team Builder views do not need to use Microsoft Project if they don't actually build project plans but instead just populate the team. If, however,

the goal is not just to assign people to a team but also to assign them to the tasks in the project, this task must be done from Project Professional.

- **Timesheet views** Practically speaking, there really is only one timesheet and there is very limited ability to modify the view. What displays in the timesheet is mostly based on decisions made administratively about how resources will work (weeks or days, overtime, billable time, and so on). There is very little configuration available to the Timesheet view or views (too little, actually). Keep this in mind: The Project Name field and the Task Name/Description field autogrow and do not wrap. If project names and task names are too verbose, users will have to scroll horizontally to complete their timesheet, which is definitely a usability drawback. Figure 11-19 shows a Timesheet view.

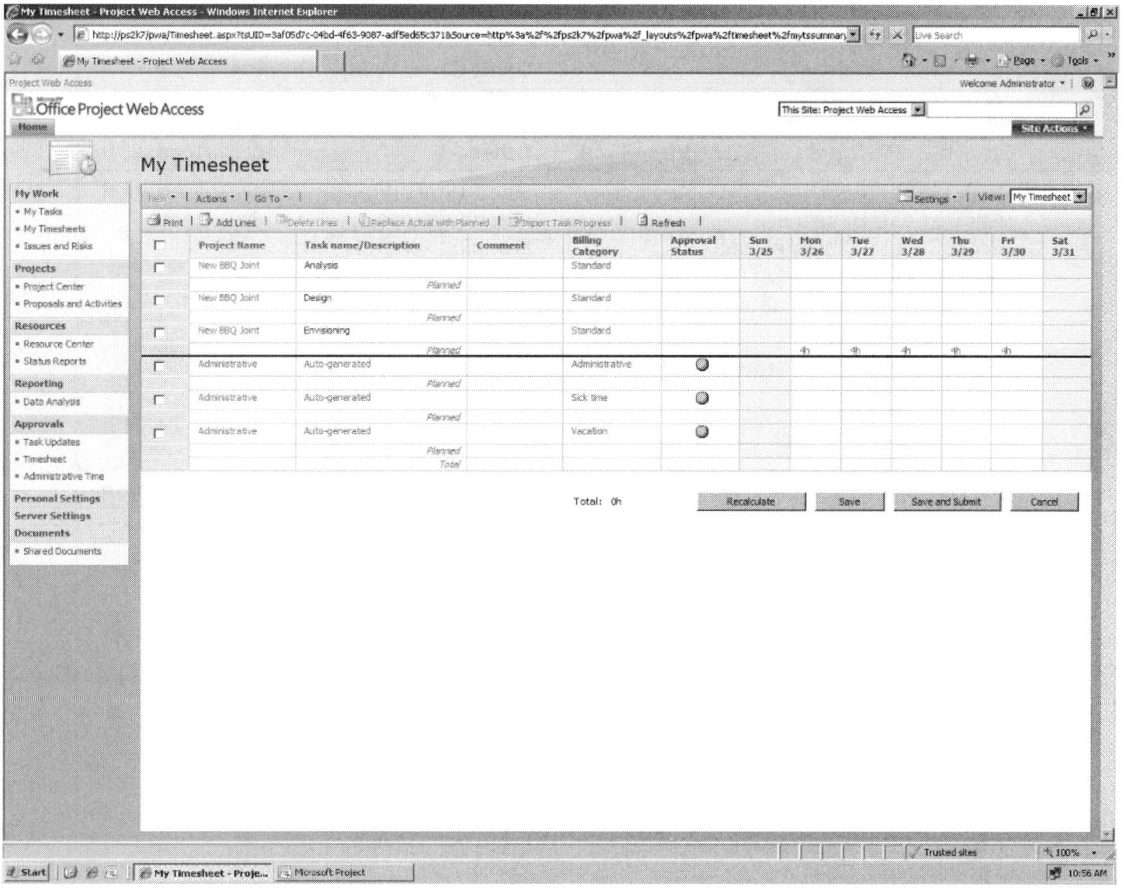

Figure 11-19 Timesheet view

Views from Microsoft

Out of the box, Microsoft Office Project Server 2007 comes with a pretty large set of prebuilt views. Keep in mind that the views in Project Server do not map directly to views available within Project Professional, nor should they. For example, there is no Network Diagram view in PWA. The Network Diagram view as well as other views make more sense from a usage perspective as part of the Project Professional client, rather than as part of the server.

Before an organization begins building new views, it should first become familiar with what is already available. Each table represents a single view type.

Many views require horizontal scrolling (assuming a reasonable screen resolution of 1,024 × 768) to display all the columns (fields), so showing them all in screenshots here is not possible or practical. However, Tables 11-1 through 11-9 describe the contents of each view to provide a more complete set of information.

View Name	Fields Included in View in Left-Right Order	View Type	Gantt Chart Type, Outline Level, Grouping Format, Other	Categories That Have Access
Assignments Cost	Task Name, Resource Name, Cost, Baseline Cost, Cost Variance, Actual Cost, Remaining Cost, Start, Finish, Work	Assignment	Gantt Chart (Views), all outline levels, grouping—Views, sort by task name (ascending)	My Organization, My Projects
Assignments Detail	Task Name, Resource Name, Delay, Work, Start, Finish	Assignment	Detail Gantt (Views), all outline levels, grouping—Views, sort by task name (ascending)	My Organization, My Projects
Assignments Earned Value	Task Name, Resource Name, BCWS, BCWP, ACWP, SV, CV, Cost, Baseline Cost, VAC, Start, Finish	Assignment	Gantt Chart (Views), all outline levels, grouping—Views, sort by task name (ascending)	My Organization, My Projects
Assignments Summary	Task Name, Resource Name, Assignment Owner, Work, Start, Finish, % Work Complete	Assignment	Gantt Chart (Views), all outline levels, grouping—Timesheet, sort by task name (ascending)	My Organization, My Projects
Assignments Tracking	Task Name, Resource Name, Assignment Owner, Start, Finish, Actual Start, Actual Finish, Baseline Start, Baseline Finish, % Work Complete, Actual Cost, Actual Work	Assignment	Tracking Gantt, all outline levels, grouping—Views, sort by task name (ascending)	Organization, My Projects

Table 11-1 Project Views—Views from the Project Detail Perspective

View Name	Fields Included in View in Left-Right Order	View Type	Gantt Chart Type, Outline Level, Grouping Format, Other	Categories That Have Access
Assignments Work	Task Name, Resource Name, Work, Baseline Work, Work Variance, Actual Work, Remaining Work, % Work Complete, Start, Finish	Assignment	Gantt Chart (Views), all outline levels, grouping—Views, sort by task name (ascending)	Organization, My Projects
Resources Cost	Unique ID, Resource Name, Cost, Baseline Cost, Cost Variance, Baseline Cost, Actual Cost, Remaining Cost, Start, Finish	Resource	All outline levels, grouping—Views	Organization, My Projects
Resources Earned Value	Unique ID, Resource Name, BCWS, BCWP, ACWP, SV, CV, Baseline Cost, VAC, Start, Finish	Resource	All outline levels, grouping—Views	Organization, My Projects
Resources Summary	Unique ID, Resource Name, Group, Max Units, Peak, Standard Rate, Overtime Rate, Cost, Work, Start, Finish	Resource	All outline levels, grouping—Views	Organization, My Projects
Resources Work	Unique ID, Resource Name, % Work Complete, Work, Overtime Work, Baseline Work, Work Variance, Actual Work, Remaining Work, Start, Finish	Resource	All outline levels, grouping—Views	Organization, My Projects
Tasks Cost	ID, Task Name, Fixed Cost, Fixed Cost Accrual, Cost, Baseline Cost, Cost Variance, Actual Cost, Remaining Cost, Start, Finish	Task	Gantt Chart (Views), all outline levels, grouping—Views, sort by ID (ascending)	Organization, My Projects
Tasks Detail	ID, Task Name, Leveling Delay, Duration, Start, Finish, Successors	Task	Detail Gantt, all outline levels, grouping—Views, sort by ID (ascending)	Organization, My Projects

Table 11-1 Project Views—Views from the Project Detail Perspective (*continued*)

PART III

View Name	Fields Included in View in Left-Right Order	View Type	Gantt Chart Type, Outline Level, Grouping Format, Other	Categories That Have Access
Tasks Earned Value	ID, Task name, BCWS, BCWP, ACWP, SV, CV, Cost, Baseline Cost, VAC, Start, Finish	Task	Gantt Chart (Views), all outline levels, grouping—Views, sort by ID (ascending)	Organization, My Projects
Tasks Leveling	ID, Task Name, Leveling Delay, Durations, Start, Finish, Successors, Preleveled Start, Preleveled Finish, Early Start	Task	Detail Gantt, all outline levels, grouping—Views, sort by ID (ascending)	Organization, My Projects
Tasks Schedule	ID, Task Name, Start, Finish, Late Start, Late Finish, Free Slack, Total Slack	Task	Leveling Gantt, all outline levels, grouping—Views, sort by ID (ascending)	Organization, My Projects
Tasks Summary	ID, Task Name, Duration, Start, Finish, % Complete, Work,	Task	Gantt Chart (Views), all outline levels, grouping—Views, sort by ID (ascending)	Organization, My Projects, My Tasks
Tasks Top-Level	ID, Task Name, Duration, Start, Finish, % Complete, Work	Task	Gantt Chart (Views), all outline levels, grouping—Views, sort by ID (ascending) Filter—outline level is less than or equal to 1	Organization, My Projects
Tasks Tracking	ID, Task Name, Start, Finish, Actual Start, Actual Finish, Baseline Start, Baseline Finish, % Complete, Duration, Actual Duration, Remaining Duration, Actual Cost, Actual Work	Task	Tracking Gantt, all outline levels, grouping—Views, sort by ID (ascending)	Organization, My Projects
Tasks Work	ID, Task Name, Work, Baseline Work, Work Variance, Actual Work, Remaining Work, % Work Complete, Start, Finish	Task	Gantt Chart (Views), all outline levels, grouping—Views, sort by ID (ascending)	Organization, My Projects

TABLE 11-1 Project Views—Views from the Project Detail Perspective *(continued)*

View Name	Fields Included in View in Left-Right Order	Gantt Chart Type, Grouping Format	Categories That Have Access
Cost	Project Name, Finish, Start, Cost, Baseline Cost, Actual Cost, Fixed Cost, Cost Variance, Remaining Cost	Tracking (Project Center), all outline levels, grouping—Views	Organization, My Projects
Earned Value	Project Name, Finish, Start, Cost, Baseline Cost, Budgeted Cost of Work Performed (BCWP), Budgeted Cost of Work Scheduled (BCWS), Schedule Variance (SV), Cost Variance (CV), Actual Cost of Work Performed (ACWP), VAC(Variance at Completion)	Tracking (Project Center), all outline levels, grouping—Views	Organization, My Projects
Summary	Project Name, Start, Finish, % Complete, Work, Duration, Owner	Gantt Chart (Project Center), all outline levels, grouping—Views	Organization, My Projects, My Tasks
Tracking	Project Name, % Complete, Actual Cost, Actual Duration, Actual Finish, Actual Start, Actual Work, Baseline Finish, Baseline Start, Duration, Remaining Duration, Finish, Start	Tracking (Project Center), all outline levels, grouping—Views	Organization, My Projects
Work	Project Name, % Work Complete, Finish, Remaining Work, Start, Work, Baseline Work, Actual Work, Work Variance	Tracking (Project Center), all outline levels, grouping—Views	Organization, My Projects

TABLE 11-2 Project Center Views—Global-Level Information about Multiple Projects

View Name	Fields Included in View in Left-Right Order	Gantt Chart Type, Grouping Format	Categories That Have Access
Summary	Task Name, Work, Remaining Work, Start, Finish, % Work Complete, Comments, Resource Name, Project Name, Actual Work	Personal Gantt (Tasks), all outline levels, grouping—Views, group by resource name, then project name, sort by resource name (ascending)	Organization, My Projects, My Tasks

TABLE 11-3 Resource Assignments after Resources Have Been Selected in Resource Center and the View Assignments Button Has Been Clicked

PART III

View Name	Fields Included in View in Left-Right Order	Outline Level, Grouping Format, Other	Categories That Have Access
All Resources	Resource Name, Email Address, Timesheet Manager, RBS, Checked Out, Windows User Account, Initials, Last Modified, Type, Material Label, Standard Rate	All outline levels, grouping—Views, sort by resource name (ascending), RBS filter off	My Organization, My Projects, My Resources
Cost Resources	Resource Name, Standard Rate, ID, Checked Out, Generic, Cost Center, Timesheet Manager, Earliest Available, Accrue At, Booking Type, Can Level, Windows User Account, Initials, Group, Code, Phonetics, Hyperlink, Hyperlink Address, Hyperlink HRef, Default Assignment Owner, Unique ID, Last Modified	All outline levels, grouping—Views, sort by resource name (ascending), RBS filter off, filter—type equals 2	My Organization, My Projects, My Resources
Material Resources	Resource Name, ID, Checked Out, Material Label, Generic, Cost Center, Timesheet Manager, Earliest Available, Latest Available, Accrue At, Booking Type, Can Level, Windows User Account, Initials, Group, Code, Phonetics, Hyperlink, Hyperlink Address, Hyperlink Href, Default Assignment Owner, Unique ID, Last Modified	All outline levels, grouping—Views, sort by resource name (ascending), RBS filter off, filter—type equals 2	My Organization, My Projects, My Resources
Resources by Team	Resource Name, ID, Checked Out, Email Address, Generic, Cost Center, Timesheet Manager, Earliest Available, Latest Available, Accrue At, Booking Type, Can Level, Windows User Account, Initials, Group, Code, Phonetics, Hyperlink, Hyperlink Address, Hyperlink Href, Default Assignment Owner, Unique ID, Last Modified, Team Assignment Pool, Team Name	All outline levels, grouping—Views, group by team name, sort by resource name (ascending), RBS filter off, filter—team name does not equal 00000000-0000-0000-0000-000000000000*	My Organization, My Projects, My Resources

TABLE 11-4 Resource Center—Information about Resources

View Name	Fields Included in View in Left-Right Order	Outline Level, Grouping Format, Other	Categories That Have Access
Work Resources	Resource Name, ID, Checked Out, Email Address, Generic, Cost Center, Timesheet Manager, Earliest Available, Latest Available, Accrue At, Booking Type, Can Level, Windows User Account, Initials, Group, Code, Phonetics, Hyperlink, Hyperlink Address, Hyperlink Href, Default Assignment Owner, Unique Id, Last Modified	All outline levels, grouping—Views, sort by resource name (ascending), RBS filter off, filter type equals 0	My Organization, My Projects, My Resources

*This effectively means that if the resource is not associated with a team name, then the resource will not display

TABLE 11-4 Resource Center—Information about Resources (*continued*)

Data Analysis—No included Views out of the box			
View Name	**Fields Included in View in Left-Right Order**	**Gantt Chart Type, Grouping Format**	**Categories That Have Access**
Details	Start, Finish, Remaining Work	N/A	N/A
My Assignments	Task Name [Task], Start [Assignment], Finish [Assignment], Progress [Assignment], Health [Task], Resource Name [Assignment]		My Organization, My Projects, My Tasks

TABLE 11-5 My Work Views

View Name	Fields Included in View in Left-Right Order	RBS Filter	Categories That Have Access
Resource Plans	Resource Name, Booking Type	Off	My Organization, My Projects, My Resources

*Note that the RBS filter is set to off by default.

TABLE 11-6 Resource Plans View

PART III

View Name	Fields Included in View in Left-Right Order	Categories That Have Access
Resource Team	Resource Name, Booking Type*	My Organization, My Projects, My Tasks

*Note also RBS field is deselected.

TABLE 11-7 Team Tasks View

View Name	Fields Included in View in Left-Right Order	Outline Level, Grouping Format	Categories That Have Access
All Resources	Resource Name, Type, Generic, Cost Center, Timesheet Manager, Default Assignment Owner, Earliest Available, Latest Available, Booking Type	All outline levels, grouping—Views, group by type, sort by resource name (ascending) RBS filter off	My Organization, My Projects, My Resources
Cost Resources	Resource name, Type, Generic, Cost Center, Timesheet Manager, Default Assignment Owner, Earliest Available, Latest Availible, Booking Type	All outline levels, grouping—Views, sort by resource name (ascending) Filter type equals 2 RBS filter off	My Organization, My Projects, My Resources
Material Resources	Resource Name, Type, Generic, Cost Center, Timesheet Manager, Default Assignment Owner, Earliest Available, Latest Available, Booking Type	All outline levels, grouping—Views, sort by resource name (ascending) Filter type equals 1 RBS filter off	My Organization, My Projects, My Resources
Work Resources	Resource Name, Type, Generic, Cost Center, Timesheet Manager, Default Assignment Owner, Earliest Available, Latest Available, Booking Type	All outline levels, grouping—Views, sort by resource name (ascending), Filter type equals 0 RBS filter off	My Organization, My Projects, My Resources

TABLE 11-8 Team Builder Views

View Name	Fields Included in View in Left-Right Order*
My Timesheet	Project Name, Task Name/Description, Comment, Billing Category, Approval Status

*Note that all these fields are preset and can be changed only slightly depending primarily on settings in the Time and Task Management section of Server Settings.

Table 11-9 Timesheet View

Note *For resource views, if there is a filter set for type, that refers to whether the resource is a Work Resource (Type 0), a Material Resource (1), or a Cost Resource (2).*

Given the 40 out-of-the-box views and the scrolling issue noted previously, we cannot possibly show all the available views. However, the single screen shot shown in Figure 11-20 is provided as a representative view.

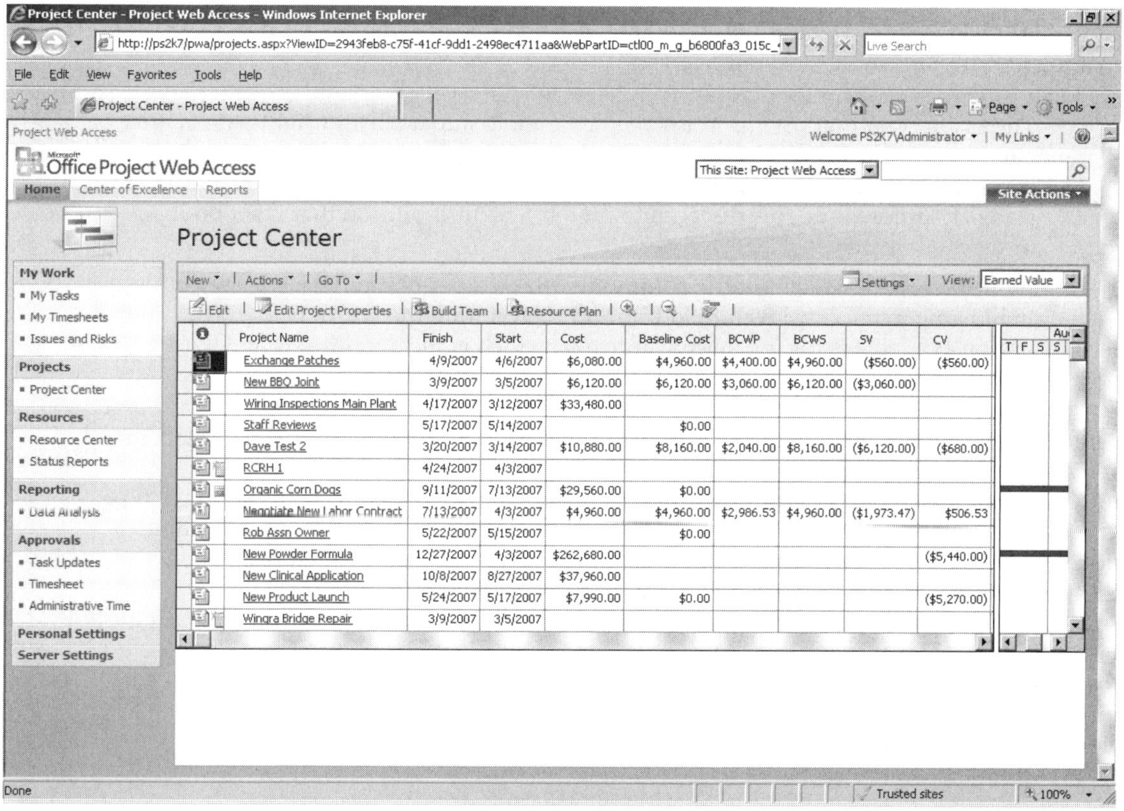

Figure 11-20 Example view: Project Center Earned Value view

Some Guidelines on Views

In Project Server, making views fit specific organizational requirements is essential for success. In the big picture, for example, views that focus on duration and finish dates are probably not the ideal approach for a company where cost is the primary focus. More specifically, the goal should be to define a set of views that cover exactly what the company needs for each view type. In some cases, some view types won't be used at all. Views should be honed to include the right fields, and security categories should be used to make sure that data are presented to people who should have access.

Security is not the only concern when considering which views to present. If, for example, the organization decides that project managers should have access to project views for their own projects, that does not mean that all of the many views should be presented. Providing all the views would be confusing. This is especially true for folks in the team member group (probably My Tasks category). If the goal is to get them the information that they need to perform their tasks, record their time and task updates, and get an overview of the big picture, don't present them with large sets of views from which to choose. Get them what they need with a set of targeted specific views.

Creating and Modifying Views

Now it is "meat and potatoes" time. There are just a couple of things to keep in mind when creating, modifying, and examining views:

- The splitter bar that divides the screen into a left-side table and right-side Gantt chart in most views can be set to a default starting position based on the number of pixels from the left of the page. Keep in mind that this position will mean different things to different people depending on the screen resolution that is set on their individual display.
- In most views, you can set the column width on a per-column basis by selecting the field name in the displayed field box and then setting the width below. The other option available is for the field to autosize, which is the default setting.

Navigate to Manage Views from the first item in the Look and Feel section of the Server Settings page. To modify an existing view from the page shown in Figure 11-21, select the view by clicking on the View Name.

Changing the view type of an existing view is not allowed, so if it is a project task type, you cannot convert it to a resource assignments type, for example. To change the name or description, just enter the changes. Use the Add and Remove buttons that reside between the Available Fields and Displayed Fields boxes as desired (see Figure 11-22).

As fields in the Displayed Fields box are highlighted, you can change the width in the Field Width box or set the field to Automatically Fit This Field to Width. From there, select the Gantt chart format. As discussed earlier in this chapter, these formats can also be modified. The next box contains the pixel count for how far the splitter bar is from the left side. Make changes as appropriate.

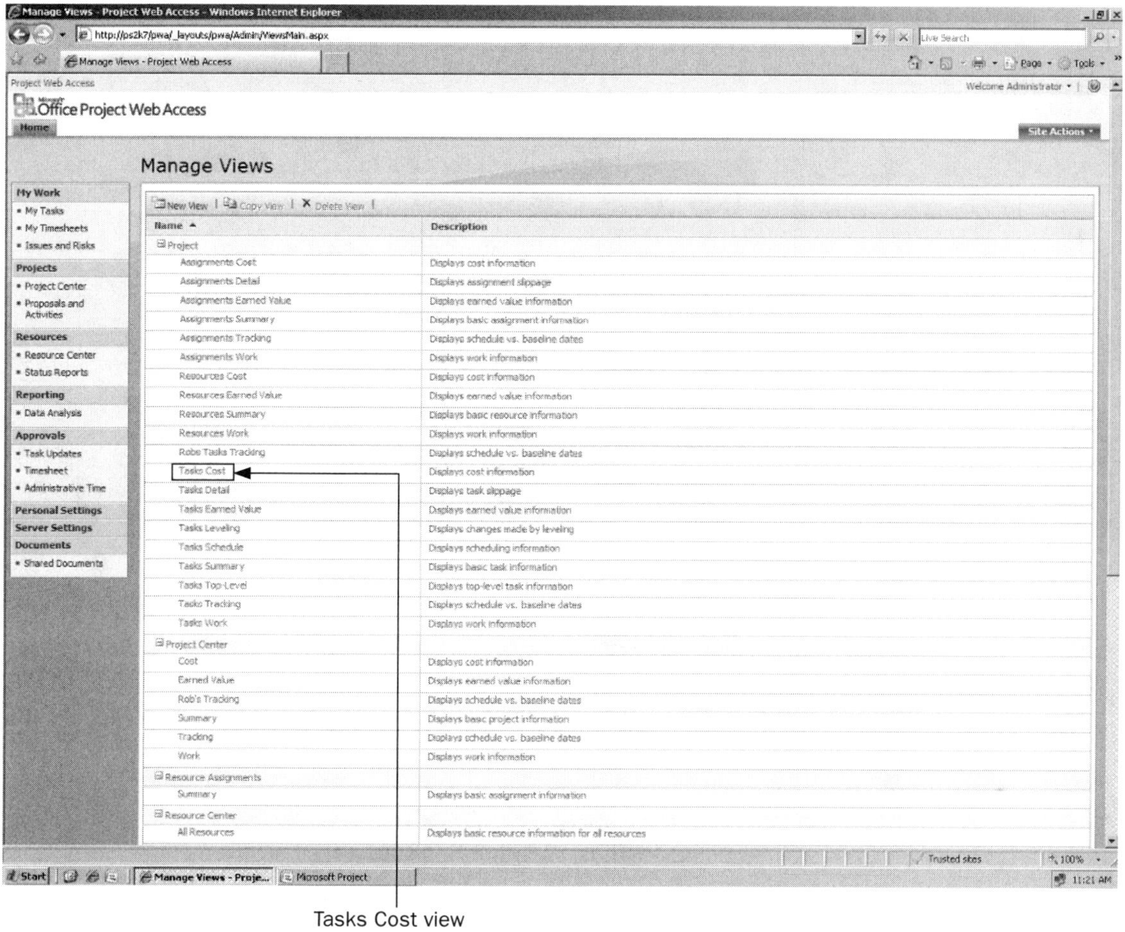

FIGURE 11-21 Modifying the existing view

From the Show dropdown list, select the outline level. Figures 11-23 through 11-26 show the results of different outline level selections (up to Level 3).

Keeping in mind the grouping formats discussed earlier in this chapter, select the grouping format desired. After that, you can choose custom grouping, using up to three grouping levels (Group by X, then by Y, then by Z). Sorting can be set as well on any fields that are displayed in the view by using the Sort By feature as shown in Figure 11-27.

You can add, modify, and delete custom filters in the Define Custom Filter dialog. To access this dialog, select the Filter button. To work with filters, first select the field

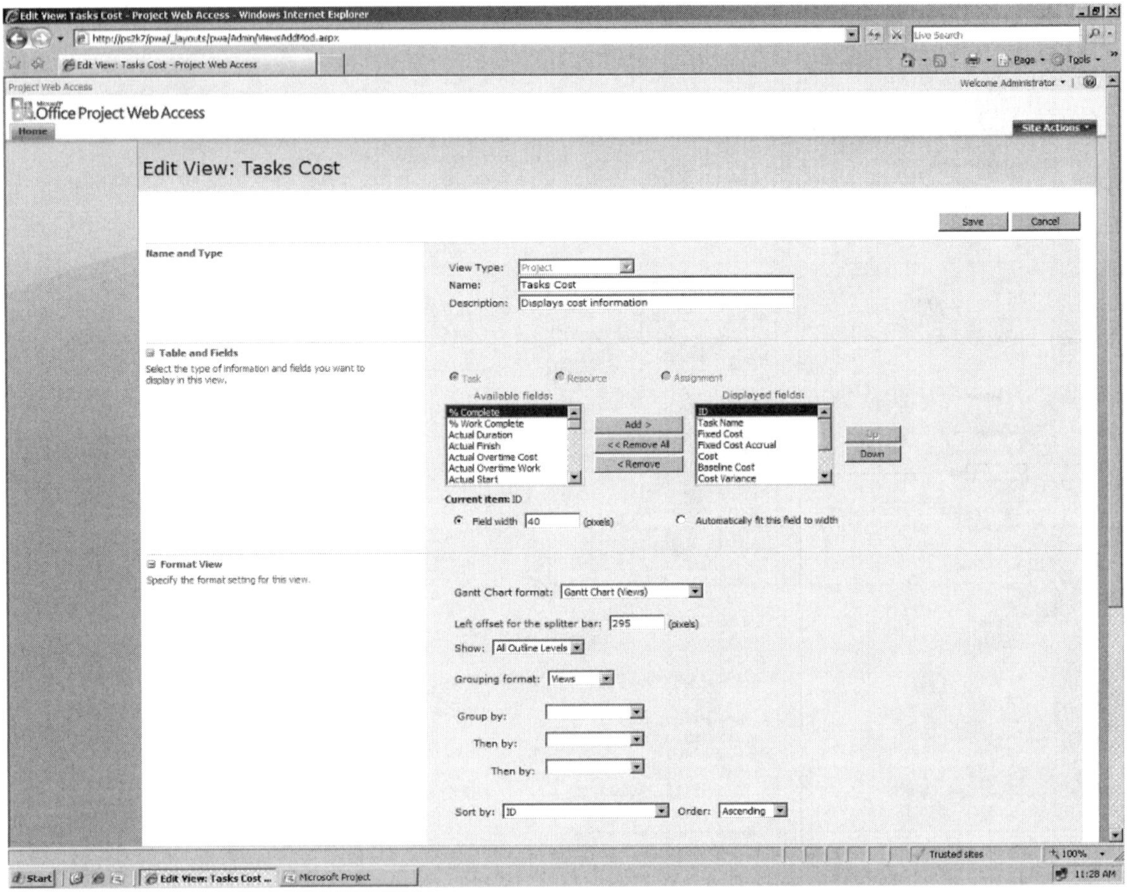

FIGURE 11-22 Available and Displayed field boxes

name desired for the filtering from the context-based Field Name dropdown list shown in Figure 11-28. Then select an option from the Test dropdown list, also shown in Figure 11-28. Then enter the value for filtering. From there, it is possible to add additional layers of filtering using the And/Or box, which will add a row if selected. Note that you can validate filters by selecting the Validate Filters button shown in Figure 11-28.

When ready, select Save on the view modification.

Deleting a View

It is easy to delete a view. To delete the view, highlight it in the Manage Views page (remember not to select the actual name of the field, as that is a link). Next select Delete View. If you are certain that you want to proceed, select OK from the dialog that asks, "Are you sure that you want to delete this view?"

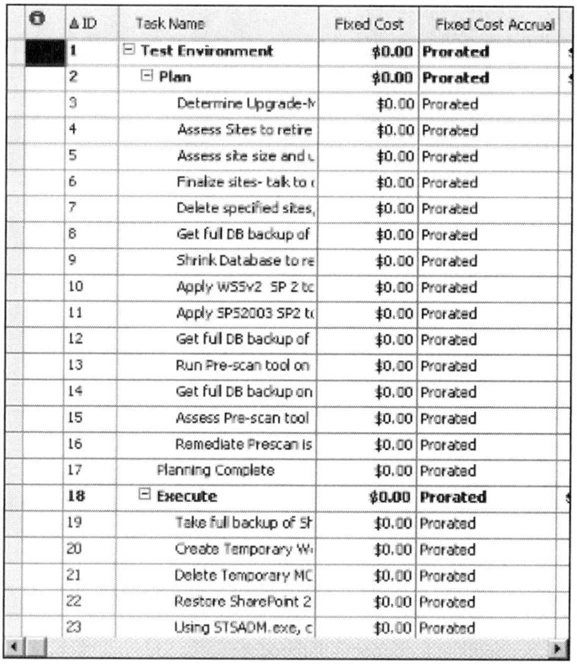

ID	Task Name	Fixed Cost	Fixed Cost Accrual
1	**⊟ Test Environment**	**$0.00**	**Prorated**
2	**⊟ Plan**	**$0.00**	**Prorated**
3	Determine Upgrade-M	$0.00	Prorated
4	Assess Sites to retire	$0.00	Prorated
5	Assess site size and u	$0.00	Prorated
6	Finalize sites- talk to (	$0.00	Prorated
7	Delete specified sites,	$0.00	Prorated
8	Get full DB backup of	$0.00	Prorated
9	Shrink Database to re	$0.00	Prorated
10	Apply WSSv2 SP 2 tc	$0.00	Prorated
11	Apply SPS2003 SP2 t(	$0.00	Prorated
12	Get full DB backup of	$0.00	Prorated
13	Run Pre-scan tool on	$0.00	Prorated
14	Get full DB backup on	$0.00	Prorated
15	Assess Pre-scan tool	$0.00	Prorated
16	Remediate Prescan Is	$0.00	Prorated
17	Planning Complete	$0.00	Prorated
18	**⊟ Execute**	**$0.00**	**Prorated**
19	Take full backup of SI	$0.00	Prorated
20	Create Temporary W	$0.00	Prorated
21	Delete Temporary MC	$0.00	Prorated
22	Restore SharePoint 2	$0.00	Prorated
23	Using STSADM.exe, c	$0.00	Prorated

FIGURE 11-23 View that appears when you select the All Outline Levels option

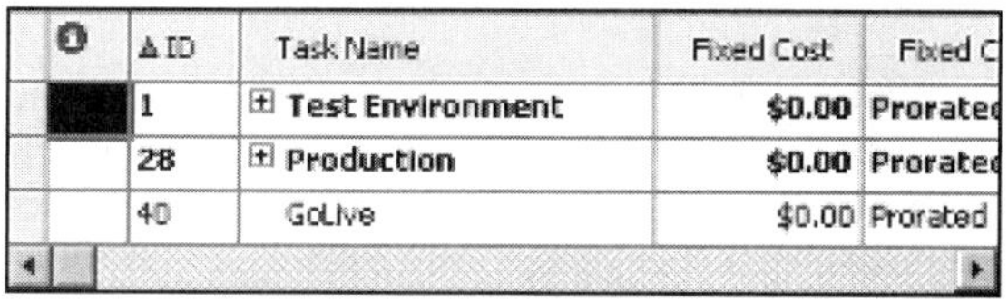

ID	Task Name	Fixed Cost	Fixed C
1	**⊞ Test Environment**	**$0.00**	**Prorate**
28	**⊞ Production**	**$0.00**	**Prorate**
40	GoLive	$0.00	Prorated

FIGURE 11-24 View that appears when you select Outline Level 1

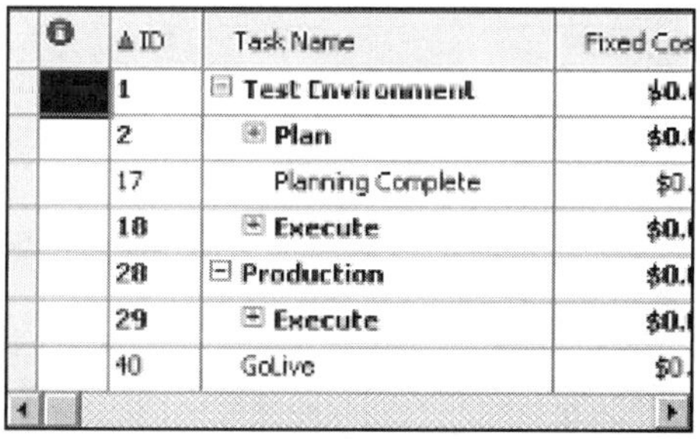

ID	Task Name	Fixed Cos
1	**⊟ Test Environment**	**$0.**
2	**⊞ Plan**	**$0.**
17	Planning Complete	$0.
18	**⊞ Execute**	**$0.**
28	**⊟ Production**	**$0.**
29	**⊞ Execute**	**$0.**
40	GoLive	$0.

FIGURE 11-25 View that appears when you select Outline Level 2

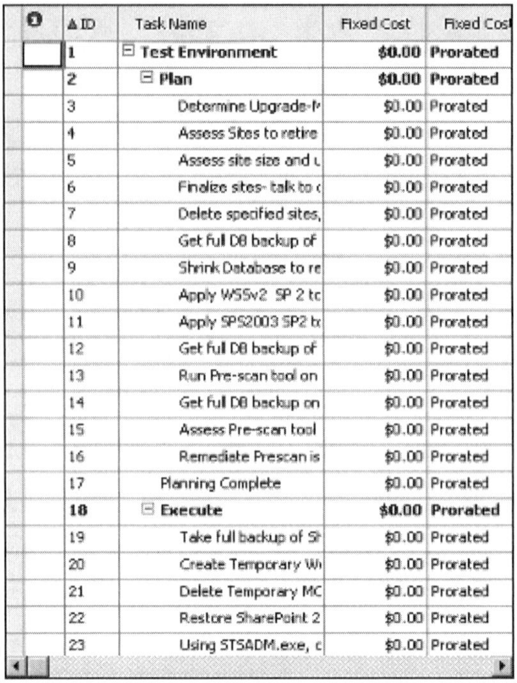

	ID	Task Name	Fixed Cost	Fixed Cos
	1	**Test Environment**	**$0.00**	**Prorated**
	2	**Plan**	**$0.00**	**Prorated**
	3	Determine Upgrade-f	$0.00	Prorated
	4	Assess Sites to retire	$0.00	Prorated
	5	Assess site size and u	$0.00	Prorated
	6	Finalize sites- talk to c	$0.00	Prorated
	7	Delete specified sites,	$0.00	Prorated
	8	Get full DB backup of	$0.00	Prorated
	9	Shrink Database to re	$0.00	Prorated
	10	Apply WSSv2 SP 2 tc	$0.00	Prorated
	11	Apply SPS2003 SP2 tc	$0.00	Prorated
	12	Get full DB backup of	$0.00	Prorated
	13	Run Pre-scan tool on	$0.00	Prorated
	14	Get full DB backup on	$0.00	Prorated
	15	Assess Pre-scan tool	$0.00	Prorated
	16	Remediate Prescan is	$0.00	Prorated
	17	Planning Complete	$0.00	Prorated
	18	**Execute**	**$0.00**	**Prorated**
	19	Take full backup of Sh	$0.00	Prorated
	20	Create Temporary Wi	$0.00	Prorated
	21	Delete Temporary MC	$0.00	Prorated
	22	Restore SharePoint 2	$0.00	Prorated
	23	Using STSADM.exe, c	$0.00	Prorated

FIGURE 11-26 View that appears when you select Outline Level 3

Copying a View

Often a great way to start a new view is to copy one that already exists to a new name and make modifications under that new name. To copy a view, just highlight the source view and select the Copy View button. A dialog then appears in which you can type the new name. From that point, the new view, based on an existing one, can be modified as previously discussed.

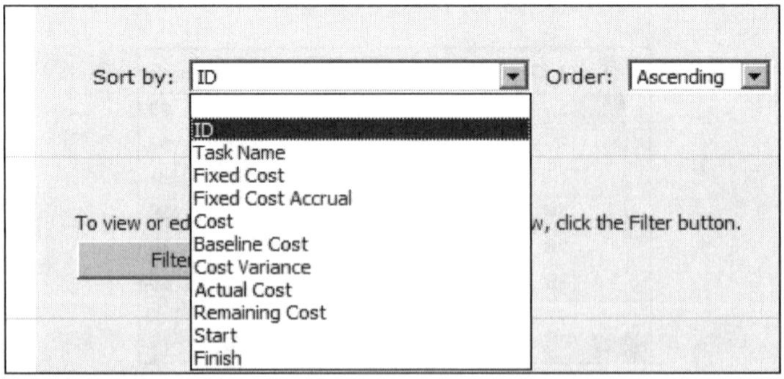

FIGURE 11-27 Using the Sort By feature

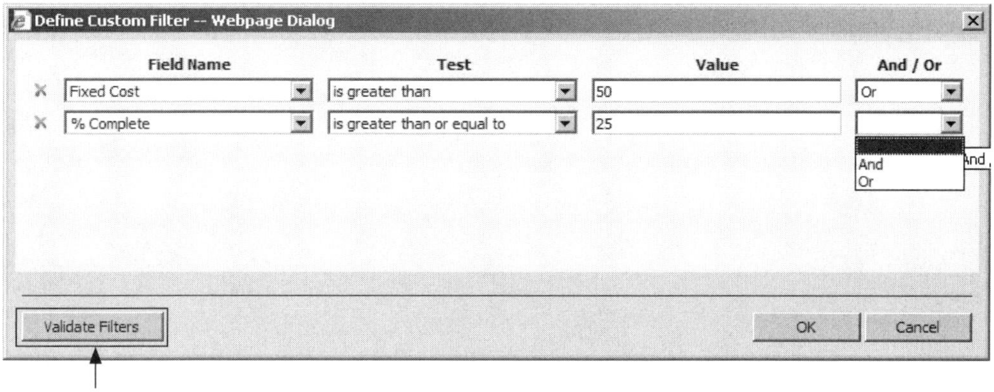

FIGURE 11-28 Field Name dropdown list

Creating a New View

From the Manage Views page, select the New View button. From the View Type dropdown list, select the type of view to be built. This selection redraws the screen as items such as Available Field will change based on this first selection. Next, name the field (the name must be unique) and add a description if you like (the description is not required).

From that point, move fields from left to right as appropriate, set widths, Gantt chart formats, groupings, outline levels, and so on as described previously. Add a filter if doing so makes sense. Select the categories to which the new view belongs. Finally, when all of these items are set, select Save and (voilá) a new view is created.

A Few Last Words about Classic "Look and Feel"

The material discussed in this chapter is based on Project Server Look and Feel settings, which are in most cases set from within the Look and Feel area in the Server Settings page in PWA. Additional Look and Feel items, such as colors, fonts, and styles, are handled from within the Windows SharePoint Services base platform and are covered at a high level in Chapter 25 of this book.

The ability to modify the look and feel of the Project Web Access interface allows for both cosmetic and functional changes to enhance the specific solution based on organizational requirements. The tools described in this chapter can be used as appropriate to give your solution the finishing visual touches and make the application as usable as possible for your company's business users.

CHAPTER 12

Configure the Remaining Server Settings

The mindset that a Project Server administrator must possess ranges from the curious, very technical, freewheeling Ubergeek, to the focused, measured, process-oriented business analyst. When these personality traits are found in the same person, it sometimes involves a big leather couch and expensive medication. Other times, an organization recognizes the person with this combined skill set is ideal for Enterprise Project Management (EPM) administration, and understands that paying one salary is better than paying two. It is in this blended (shaken, not stirred) spirit that this chapter has been written. In it, we'll discuss some of the technically mysterious aspects of the EPM toolset and the process considerations that you'll take into account when configuring them. Although several of the topics discussed may not be relevant to your installation, of the topics that are, it is hoped that the discussions provided give you a multifaceted view of these remaining Project Server 2007 settings.

Database Administration Section of Server Settings

The Database Administration section of the Server Settings page enables you to perform administration functions on the content of your EPM system. Whether you need to delete a swath of timesheets from the distant past, or restore your Enterprise Global template to a previous state, the Database Administration section of the Server Settings page can help you. We'll cover the five areas of this Database Administration section, starting with the item that the Project Server administrator should approach first in a freshly installed Project Web Access (PWA) instance.

Schedule Backup

Configuring the Backup Schedule is one of the first tasks that an administrator should complete on a freshly installed PWA site. From this page, you can set independent schedules for backing up the following items. The backup schedules that you choose should be based on the anticipated frequency of restore requests that you will receive. The frequency options you have for scheduling these backups are either never or daily.

NOTE *Because never backing up components of your PWA site is a foolhardy option for the astute Project Server administrator, we'll discuss manually backing up some items in the "Administrative Backup" section shortly.*

Recommended Scheduled Backup Approach

The following is a recommended approach for scheduling your backups:

- **Projects** This is the most commonly restored item. Its backup should be scheduled. Note that multiple versions of projects can be backed up (see below).
- **Enterprise Resource Pool and calendars** These are infrequently restored. They are backed up manually.
- **Enterprise custom fields** These fields are infrequently restored. The process is manual.
- **Enterprise Global template** This template is infrequently restored.
- **View definitions** These are infrequently restored. They are backed up manually.
- **System settings** These settings are infrequently restored.
- **Category and group settings** These are infrequently restored.

Versions

The Project Retention Policy (versions) box only affects projects and is populated with the number of versions to be retained. There is some confusion among users about this because this box is on the same page as the scheduled backups listed above (Server Settings | Schedule Backup). Versions can be an administrative friend and nightmare all in a single number box. On one end of the scale, you want to be able to provide your users a respectable cushion for when (not if) they inadvertently corrupt, mangle, or delete their project plans. On the other end, you don't want to have to blow your budget wad on a new storage area network (SAN) just to support your archived database and the 32,767 versions of all of your organization's projects that it can theoretically house. You will have to strike a balance and be comforted that this is a semi-intelligent backup mechanism that recognizes that if a project has not changed since the last backup date, it will not create a new version. If multiple versions of a project are published on a single day, only the last version prior to the scheduled backup will be saved to the archive. Our clients have chosen from two versions to eight. We have never seen a project going back more than four versions that was required for restoration.

Administrative Backup

Administratively backing up items in your PWA site is typically done immediately before making major changes to the items. As an administrator, you will want to perform an administrative backup of your Enterprise Global template prior to adding macros or radically changing the views and tables intended for distribution to your Project Professional users.

Performing an administrative backup of the custom field definitions, view definitions, category and group settings, and system settings should be completed as soon as your fresh PWA site is active, again after you have reached a stable environment, and immediately before making any major changes to these settings.

Forced Check-in Enterprise Objects

Occasionally, when attempting to edit an item, you'll receive an error indicating that the item is currently checked out and thus you can only view the item. This may indicate that another user is editing the item. Other times, enterprise objects will be closed ungracefully and the item(s) may be left in a checked-out state. This can be triggered by a number of actions, including the following:

- While a user is working on an enterprise project, Project Professional appears to lock up. The user opens Task Manager and kills the WinProj application, leaving the project in a checked-out state.
- If a user is serially editing multiple resources and forcibly closes his or her Internet Explorer window, this action leaves resources in a checked-out state.
- If a user is editing a custom enterprise field and forcibly closes his or her Internet Explorer window, this action leaves the enterprise field in a checked-out state.

To resolve the issue of an item being stuck in a checked-out state, from the Database Administration section of the Server Settings page, click Force Check-in Enterprise Objects. Select the type of object that you want to check in forcibly, then click Check In. Click OK in the acknowledgment box to confirm that you want to check in the specified items forcibly. You'll see the job state change to Processing, and when you refresh the page, you should no longer see the object, indicating that it is no longer checked out. Note, that by forcing the check-in of a project, you check in the last saved version of the item, not the last checked-out version.

Delete Enterprise Objects

From time to time, you may be confronted with the necessity to delete objects from your PWA instance. For instance, if you find that your users are complaining about the huge list of status reports, or if a resource has become permanently unavailable and you have already reassigned their work, you will likely use the Delete Enterprise Objects area of the Database Administration section to clear out old information from your environment.

Administrative Restore

If you have administratively backed up or set a backup schedule for the projects in your PWA instance, but have not deleted the project from the Archived database, you can restore the project to the Draft database through the Administrative Restore page. Although this process may restore the project to its most recent backed-up state, there are some additional factors to consider. If there were documents, issues, risks, or deliverables associated with

> **Project Archival**
>
> It is in this section where we again expose the function of the Archived database. By having the capability to specify from which database(s) the project is deleted, it lends itself to a process where you can have different levels of deletion.
>
> If, for example, a project manager is drafting a project and mistakenly publishes it, you could delete the project from the Published database, yet allow the project manager to open it up from Project Professional to continue to work with it from the Draft database. Because the Reporting database is continually kept in sync with the Published database, if a project is deleted from the Published database only, it will be deleted from the Reporting database, keeping this project from being viewed through any reports or any online analytical processing (OLAP) cubes that will be built in the future. (The project will still be viewable in existing Data Analysis views until the next time that the cube is updated.) Additionally, when the project is deleted from the Published database, resources will no longer be allowed to enter time against the project.
>
> If the decision has been made to delete a project completely and permanently from the PWA site, consideration needs to be taken as to whether the associated Windows SharePoint Services (WSS) project team site is to be deleted as well. If your WSS site is deleted when you delete a project, all of the documents, issues, risks, and deliverables associated with that project will be lost. There is no capability within PWA to restore a deleted WSS site. Recovery of these items will be left to a SharePoint administrator at best, and a database administrator at worst (assuming a well-designed disaster recovery plan).

this project that you need to retain, the best-case scenario would be not to delete the WSS site during the initial project deletion. In this situation, you will need to reassociate the WSS site with the project, then reassociate all of the documents, issues, risks, and deliverables with the tasks within the project, as follows:

1. From the Administrative Restore page, select the project that you want to restore and click Restore.
2. Have the project manager open Project Professional and open his or her newly restored project from the Draft database, save it, and publish it. The project manager may need to save the workspace under a different name if the original was not deleted during the initial deletion process.
3. As administrator, go to the Project Workspaces page, found in the Operational Policies section of the Server Settings screen, select the newly created project workspace (for the restored project), and click Edit Site Address.

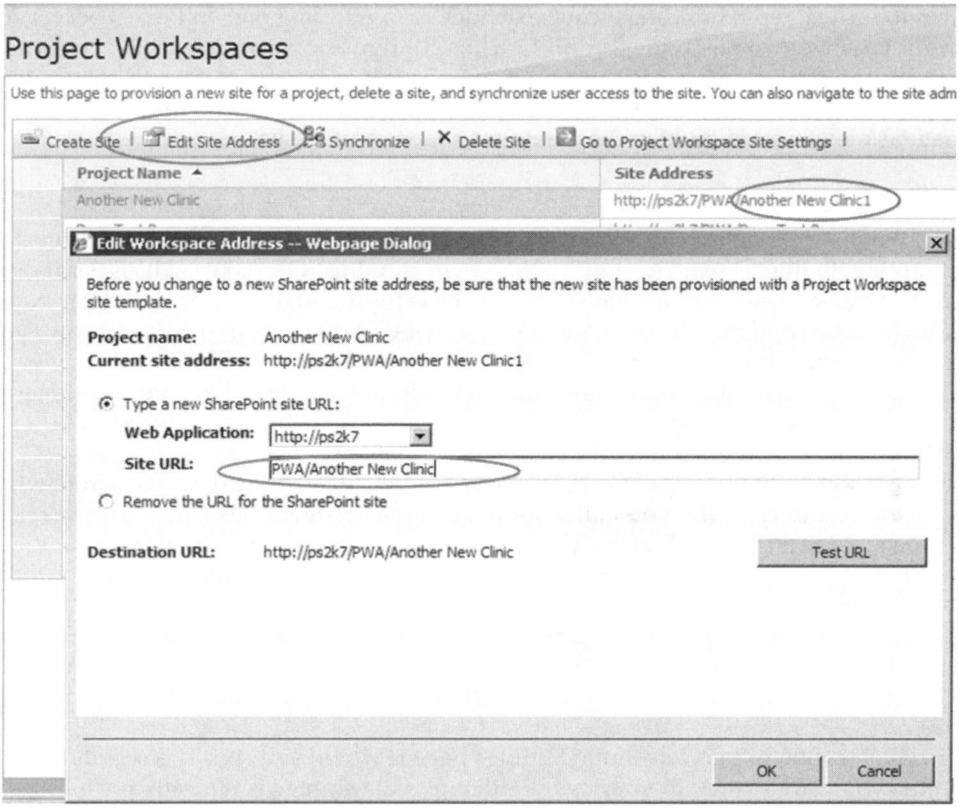

4. In the Edit Workspace Address window, modify the workspace name to match the name of the workspace that was created the first time that the project was published.
5. With the project selected, click Synchronize to enable the project participants to access the new site immediately.
6. Either from the project itself or from the project workspace, relink the individual WSS items with their tasks.

Cube Section of the Server Settings Page

Previous versions of the EPM toolset didn't have much out-of-the-box capability to modify the way that the Analysis Services cubes were built. For example, all of your project-level enterprise outline codes would be included in the cube, but to include any task-level fields you had to turn either to building a cube extender or purchasing one. In Project Server 2007, Microsoft has given you extreme flexibility when configuring how your OLAP cubes are to be built. The package even includes built-in cube extensions (such as a "Weeks" time dimension) and the ability to drill from the project, to the summary, to the subtask, for detailed task-level information in these extremely powerful views.

Cube Build Settings

In the Cube Build Settings page, you can define broad administrative configurations for cube building. In this screen, you specify the server running SQL 2000 Analysis Services or SQL 2005 Analysis Services, the name that you chose for the Analysis Services database to be created, and an optional description. The Extranet URL field is optional and allows you to identify an extranet URL for your Analysis Services server if your Data Analysis views' consumers will be accessing those views from a nonlocal location. (There are additional port requirements and security topics to consider in this scenario, which are addressed in Chapter 8.)

The next section of this page allows you to specify the date range of projects from which to build your cube. Typically you will want to keep this setting as Use the Earliest Project Start Date and Latest Project Finish Date to give the view's user the maximum amount of data to analyze. At some point in the future, compelling business or technical reasons to limit the data for the cube build may arise. An acquisition, where project data before a certain point in time would skew the overall Data Analysis View, may be a business reason. If your cube building process is taking hours to complete because of the massive quantity of project data, this may provide the compelling technical reason to limit the date range of projects to be analyzed.

The final section of the Cube Build Settings page is where you specify a schedule for how often you want to rebuild your cube. Although data storage is typically not a factor in this setting (because your cube is overwritten each time it is built), usage patterns, executive reporting needs, and cube build elapsed time are very important factors.

Usage Patterns

In many cases, an organization will place its four Project Server databases (including the Reporting database) on a single instance of SQL Server. Installing SQL Server Analysis Services on this SQL Server is very common as well. In these cases, when the cube-building process is running, a great percentage of system resources is devoted to building the Analysis Services cube from the Reporting database. These SQL Server system resources, as a result, will be competed for by a user of PWA who is attempting to submit a timesheet or a project manager attempting to publish his or her project.

Executive Reporting Needs

If every Thursday at 2 P.M. your executives have a meeting during which they review the Data Analysis views, it doesn't make much sense to update your cube every Friday at 10 P.M. (Although it might make sense if your executives were on a six-day time lag, which has been known to happen.) Ideally, these executives will have a freshly built cube waiting for them Thursday morning, when they can view it in preparation for, and during their meeting.

Cube Build Elapsed Time

As mentioned earlier, the time that it takes to build your cube may oblige you to modify the date range of your project data to limit the cube size. Likewise, if you find that the elapsed time to complete your cube build process is longer than the interval you set, you will likely not get to use the new capability of having your cube built every so many number of hours, and will instead have to resort to a nightly or weekly cube build.

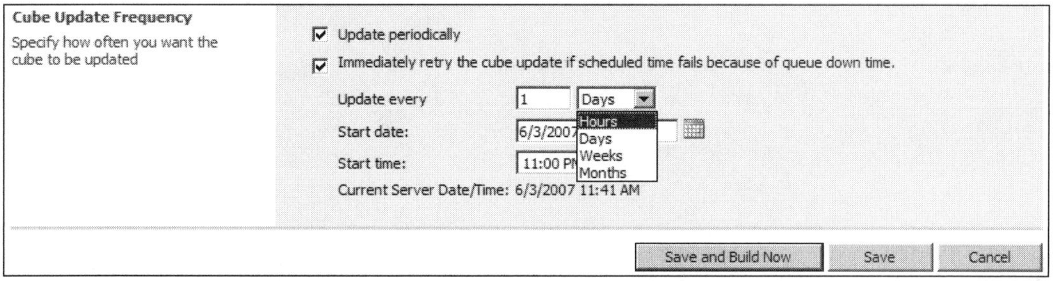

NOTE *As you have probably noticed, there are few if any places that you'll find information about backing up your OLAP data. The reason is that these data are generated from your Reporting database each time the cube-building service runs. So, if your OLAP data are deleted for some reason, do not fret; simply rebuild them.*

Cube Configuration

To add custom fields to your OLAP cubes, you must specify which of these fields you wish to add as dimensions to be available in your cube. To get started quickly, in the Cube Dimensions section, specify the Assignment Cube from the available dropdown list and add all available fields to the list of dimensions. Saving these settings and then performing a cube build will make all of your specified dimensions available to the MSP_Portfolio_Analyzer cube. You can now create Data Analysis views, built from the MSP_Portfolio_Analyzer cube, which contain your custom fields. Try adding different combinations of available fields to your cube to achieve your specific reporting goals.

NOTE *If you have created custom fields that allow the user to select multiple values from the lookup table, when you attempt to add the table as a selected dimension in the Cube Configuration page you receive an error message. This is by design. The reason for it becomes clear when you consider a Data Analysis view that you might use to view all work grouped by project location. If each project could have multiple location values, the view would skew actual work by potentially double-counting totals.*

If you have specified custom fields that you want brought into your Data Analysis views as measures, you will see your available custom fields and can bring them in as selected measures the same way that you brought available fields in as dimensions in the previous section.

Calculated Measures

If you want to perform calculations on an existing field that is in your cube, you can write Multidirectional Expressions (MDX) to perform the calculation. These formulas are structured identically to the formulas that you would write for your custom fields and are similar to the calculated totals from within the Data Analysis view itself, except this calculated measure will be available to all of the views for which the cube supplies information and can be used as any other measure would be.

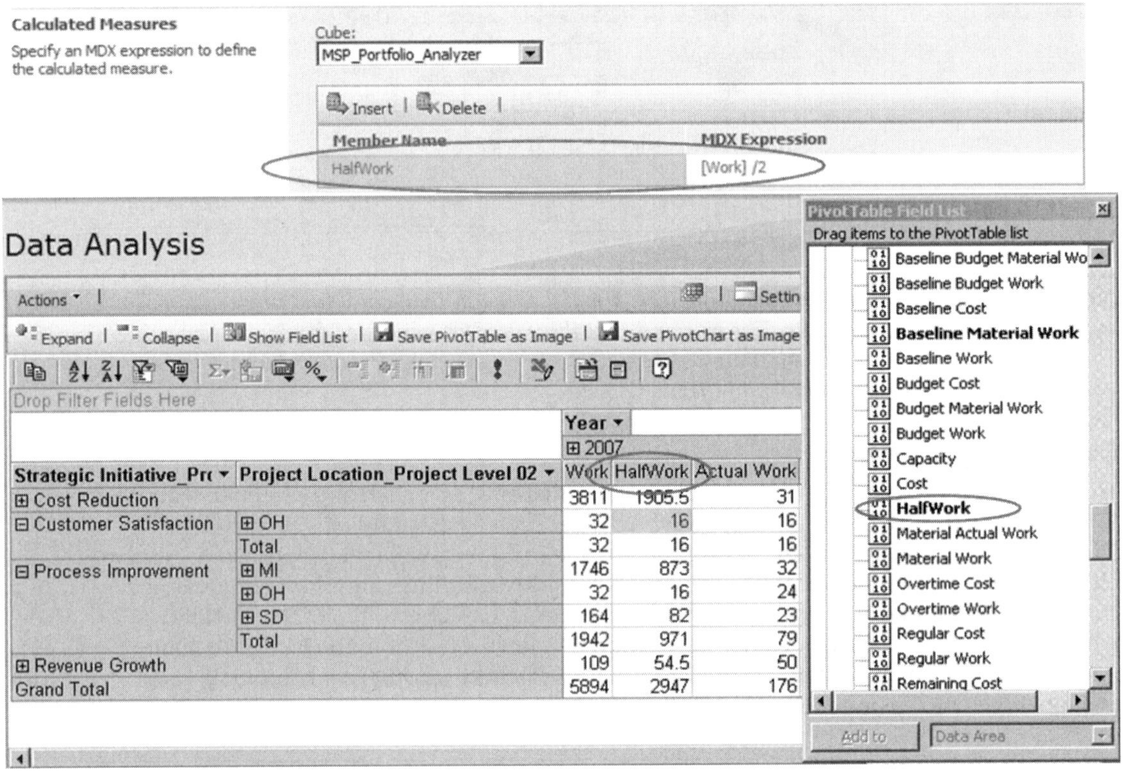

Cube Build Status

Previous versions of Project Server did not expose to the casual observer the cube building process and its status. Troubleshooting was much more of a burdensome process, as different logs needed to be found and analyzed. In Project Server 2007, the decision was made to make this process much more transparent, enabling the administrator to assess information quickly about the overall cube building process, including its elapsed time to complete. The three sections of this page show information about the cube build settings, the build stages of the most recent run, and a detailed log of the steps the Cube Building Service completed to create the OLAP data.

Database Server Modifications

Because Project Server 2007 supports both SQL Server 2000 and 2005 as its database store, there are modifications that administrators need to make depending on the version of SQL Server they are using. Most of the configuration differences are noticed when implementing the Analysis Services component of the different SQL Server versions.

Enabling SQL Server 2000 Analysis Services for Use with Project Server 2007

When implementing Project Server 2007 with SQL Server 2000, there are a number of configuration tasks that the database administrator will need to complete:

- Ensure that both SQL Server 2000 and Analysis Services 2000 are at Service Pack 4.
- Ensure that you have installed the Decision Support Objects (DSO) for SQL Server 2000 Analysis Services on your middle-tier (PWA) servers. Apply SQL Server 2000 Analysis Services Service Pack 4 to these middle-tier servers where the DSOs have been installed.

NOTE *The DSOs are installed with the advanced installation of SQL Server 2000 Analysis Services. The only two components needed on the middle-tier machines are the client components and the DSOs.*

- Add the Project Server Queue Service account to the OLAP Administrators group. This account (domain account in a small or medium farm installation) was specified during the SharedService Provider (SSP) creation when Project Server 2007 was first installed, and can be identified by observing the Log On credentials of the Microsoft Office Project Server Queue Service NT service. Add this account to the OLAP Administrators group on the server running SQL 2000 Analysis Services.
- Ensure that the OLAP Administrators group has full control on the Analysis Services \bin folder. You perform this step from the server running SQL Analysis Services. This action enables the OLAP administrators to perform needed functions within Analysis Services.
- Grant read access to the Reporting database for the account under which Analysis Services is running. If during installation of Analysis Services a domain account was specified as the service to run as, grant the db_datareader right on the PWA Reporting database. (If the service is running as Local System, you need to specify *Domain\MachineName$* with these rights.)
- Optionally, you can migrate the SQL Server repository.

If you need to increase the security of your Analysis Services environment, you can migrate the Analysis Services repository to a SQL 2000 database, by following these steps:

1. In SQL Enterprise Manager, create a new database and name it Analysis Services Repository.
2. In the Security section of Enterprise Manager, create a new login, click the ellipses, and select the OLAP Administrators group from the local computer.

3. In the Database Access tab, select the Analysis Services Repository database and give it the db_owner role.
4. Open SQL Server Analysis Manager and connect to the Analysis Services server.
5. Right-click the name of the server, select Migrate Repository, and specify the Analysis Services Repository database that you created in step 1.

Enabling SQL Server 2005 Analysis Services for Use with Project Server 2007

When the developers at Microsoft set out to create the next version of the advanced Analysis Services–based reporting in the EPM toolset, they had a choice: Either design the tool from the ground up to work seamlessly with SQL 2005 Analysis Services, or design the tool to work seamlessly with SQL 2000 Analysis Services. Because of the installed user base of SQL 2000 and the ability to modify SQL 2005 Analysis Services to work like the 2000 version, the developers targeted the older version. As a result, organizations that implement Project Server 2007 with SQL Server 2005 Analysis Services are required to perform some extra steps to enable the advanced reporting features offered through the Data Analysis views. Although a philosophical discussion of *why* an administrator needs to "dumb down" SQL Server 2005 Analysis Services to work with Project Server 2007 is beyond the scope of this book, we will focus on *how to do it*. The installation and configuration steps for Analysis Services 2005 can be found in Chapter 7, but they are summarized here:

1. Ensure that SQL 2005 and SQL Server 2005 Analysis Services are at identical Service Packs, and at least Service Pack 1.
2. Install the DSOs on each Project Server Application Server (this step is not required in a single-server small farm).
3. Create the Analysis Services Repository.
4. Grant the Analysis Services Service account db_datareader access to the Project Server Reporting database.
5. Ensure that client components are installed (see Chapter 13).

Forms Authentication

Forms authentication is very similar to the Project Server authentication in previous versions of EPM. Users first must enter a username and password into a Web page, and those credentials are then compared against a user directory for authentication. In Project Server 2003 and earlier versions, these credentials were stored in the Project Server database and were valid only in the PWA site. With forms authentication, the credentials can be stored in Active Directory, an external Lightweight Directory Access Protocol (LDAP) directory, or a separate SQL database. Alternatively, if you have Windows Server 2003 Release 2 or above, you can use the Web Single Sign on with Active Directory Federation Services (ADFS). These credentials can be used throughout the Project Server farm. For a complete discussion about configuring forms authentication specifically to meet your needs, see the Project Server deployment section relating to forms authentication in TechNet, located at the following URL: http://technet2.microsoft.com/Office/en-us/library/5f4e1169-f1bd-40fe-a1e9-25d31e93a2db1033.mspx?mfr=true.

Configuring Project Server with Excel Services

While most of the book focuses on just the features available with the base Project Server and Windows SharePoint Services features, the Excel Services is a very compelling feature from the Microsoft Office SharePoint Server Enterprise Edition. This section covers that MOSS-only feature from a settings perspective. There is more on MOSS features in Chapter 25.

When we think of the benefits of installing Project Server 2007 in the same farm as Microsoft Office SharePoint Server (MOSS) 2007, the usual decision points involve the proposals workflow or administration and server consolidation. However, if the stars align correctly and your software acquisition process had an infusion of luck (that is, good planning), then you will be able to take advantage of another impressive capability that fits in with one of Microsoft's long-term strategies.

The Microsoft Office Web Components (OWC) feature has been around for several Office versions and has been the vehicle through which the Resource Availability and Data Analysis views (as well as the Portfolio Analyzer views before them) are exposed. At some point during Office 12 and SharePoint Server development, the decision was made to quit upgrading the OWC as part of a paradigm shift toward server-based control, calculation, and display, thus reducing the footprint on local machines. Excel Calculation Services (ECS) was the result and is a component of the Enterprise version of MOSS.

ECS allows an author to publish his or her Excel workbooks to the Web for viewing through a Web browser while enabling the author to restrict which parts of the workbook are exposed. In regard to Project Server 2007, ECS provides a mechanism to expose the Data Analysis views without forcing users to install the Office Web Components or have Microsoft Excel installed on their system.

Prerequisites for using Project Server 2007 with ECS include the following:

- **MOSS Enterprise** The Enterprise version of MOSS Server must be installed in the same farm as Project Server 2007. It provides two important and related components: the Excel Calculation Services itself, and the capability to create a data connection library. If you install MOSS Enterprise after installing and configuring your PWA site, then you'll likely have to enable the associated site and site collection features, as described later in this section.
- **Office 2007 Ultimate, Office 2007 Professional Plus, Office 2007 Enterprise, or stand-alone Office Excel 2007** Versions of Excel that derive from those of Microsoft Office other than those listed here (such as Office 2007 Professional) cannot save a self-updating spreadsheet to a server running ECS. Although you can still create a spreadsheet that has the connection to an OLAP cube that displays a modified pivot table and pivot chart through ECS, you will not have the granular control over which portions of the spreadsheet are exposed, and the user may be forced to open the Excel Web Access page and refresh the data to display updated cube data through ECS.

The instructions given are intended for a user with moderate-to-advanced technical knowledge of their environment's MOSS and Project Server architecture and functions. Although security can be locked down around the functions performed, it is assumed that the user setting up this relationship between Project Server and MOSS has all required administrative rights.

Steps to Enable ECS for Use with Data Analysis Views

Although the set up of Excel Calculation Services and connecting them to your OLAP cube can involve many detailed steps, highlights of this configuration are as follows:

1. From within a SharePoint site, create a document library whose document template is based on the Microsoft Office Excel spreadsheet.
2. Add this document library as an ECS trusted file location. From the Administration pages of the SharedService Provider, specify this document library as an ECS trusted file location. Be sure to specify the Automatic Workbook Calculation Mode, allow external trusted data connection libraries, and disable the refresh warning.
3. Create the data connection library (DCL). If this option does not exist, ensure that the Office SharePoint Server Enterprise site collection features are activated.

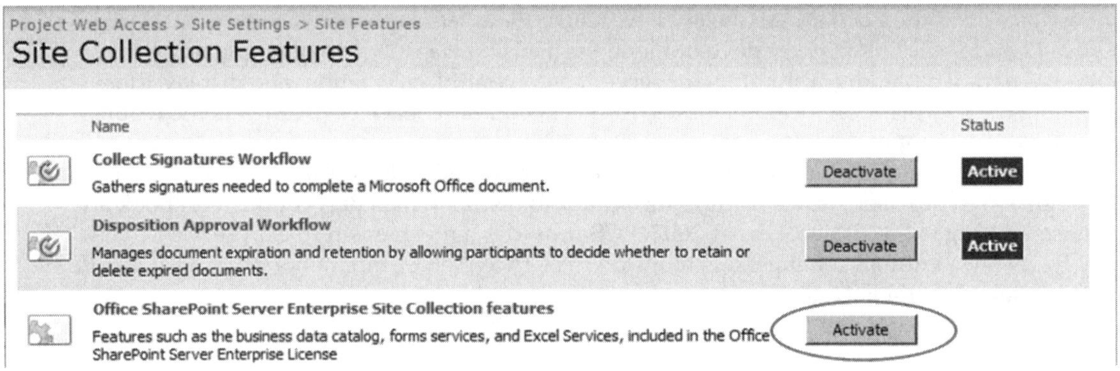

4. Add this DCL to the list of ECS trusted data connection libraries from within the SSP Administration page.
5. Run `stsadm -o set-ecssecurity -ssp` *`YourSSPName`* `-Accessmodel Delegation` (where *`YourSSPName`* is the name of the SSP—by default, the SSP's name is SharedServices1). Perform an `IISRESET` command.
6. From within a new Microsoft Office Excel workbook, click Publish | Excel Calculation Services. Publish the Excel worksheet to the document library created in step 1.
7. From within the open spreadsheet, click the Data ribbon, then select From Other Sources | From Analysis Services.
8. Type the name of the server that performs the SQL Server Analysis Services duties for your PWA site.
9. Select the existing cube that contains your PWA data.
10. When prompted to save this data connection file (.odc), add the Web address of the DCL created in step 3 (that is, http://ps2k7/pwa/ExcelConnectionTemplateLibrary/PS2K7 ProjectCube MSP_Portfolio_Analyzer.odc). Modify the pivot table and pivot chart until you are satisfied with it. Save the file, then close Office Excel.
11. From within a PWA or SharePoint site where you want to display the ECS sheet powered by the OLAP data in your Data Analysis views, click Site Actions | Edit Page.

12. In the Web part zone in which you want to display the OLAP data, click Add a Web Part and select the checkbox to add the Excel Web Access Web part.

13. Open the Tool pane and specify the URL of the workbook created in step 6, then click Apply | OK. You can exit the edit mode of the SharePoint page that you are editing.
14. Depending on the version of Excel 2007 and the settings you used to create the workbook, you may have to click Update–Refresh All Connections to see the most recent version of the data. Your users can now view and enjoy one of the most advanced integrated reporting features available, all through a browser, without the need for the OWC or Microsoft Excel on their desktops.

NOTE *More information about customizing the SharePoint environment can be found in Chapter 25.*

Project Server 2007 Report Pack for SQL Server 2005 Reporting Services

If you have identified a reporting requirement that cannot be provided by the out-of-the-box reporting capabilities of PWA and integration with the Microsoft Office client tools, you may want to look at the Project Server 2007 Report Pack for SQL Server 2005 Reporting Services, which is provided by Microsoft as part of the Project 2007 software development kit (SDK). It contains seven sample reports, along with sample queries for correctly extracting data from the Project Server Reporting database. (The Project 2007 SDK can be found at http://msdn2.microsoft.com/en-us/library/ms512767.aspx.) There are certain requirements for using and customizing the seven sample reports provided. Aside from the obvious requirements for modifying the reports, such as the Business Intelligence Development Studio for Microsoft SQL Server Reporting Services (SSRS), you will need to create some custom fields, lookup tables, and data in order to supply the information that the sample reports consume and expose. These reports include the following:

- **Cost Center Availability Report** The main page of this report provides a graph and table of your resources' availability and capacity over time. Subsequent pages of this report enable the user to view individual resources' capacity, availability, and assignments over time.
- **Project Deliverable Gives/Gets Report** Intended for the project manager, this report shows the deliverables that originate from the project (gives), and the deliverables on which the project depends (gets).
- **Project Portfolio Trend Report** Intended as a mechanism of oversight, this report provides manually entered status information about the project over time. Requirements include the creation of two custom fields, association with a single lookup table, and the process by which the project manager regularly updates these fields.

- **Project Proposals Listing Report** Based on the current proposal state of a project, this view is targeted to a regular project management office (PMO) status meeting where all of the proposed and approved projects are evaluated. This report identifies proposals created in the last seven days as "New."
- **Project Review Report** Intended as a mechanism of oversight, this report provides summary information about the project, actual versus scheduled work, and cost. It also includes information about milestones, issues, deliverables, and risks possessed by the project.
- **Timesheet Audit Report** A timesheet manager uses this report to get the status of timesheet submissions in PWA. Aside from showing the number of hours reported during a given period, the report shows whether the resource has created the timesheet, has submitted and gotten his or her timesheet approved, or has had that timesheet rejected.
- **Work versus Effort Audit Report** As an oversight function, this report allows a manager to audit what a resource enters in his or her timesheet and compare it with the project task status updates that the resource has provided.

As an administrator of your Microsoft Office Project Server 2007 environment, you must consider many factors before making each of your decisions. For example, the decision to have Project Server 2007 coexist in the same farm as MOSS is one that requires many ancillary considerations. These considerations range from server and application administrative ownership and maintenance to the version of the client software needed to take advantage of the features and capabilities exposed through this cohabitation. A single book could never account for all of the situations, software configurations, administration models, and user requirements of all potential readers. Still, we hope that the importance of the iterative implementation model becomes apparent, and that you use it to help ensure end-user expectations are set appropriately and an overall successful implementation is achieved.

CHAPTER 13

Roll Out the Desktop

Implementing Project Server 2007 without planning for the desktop components is like christening a pirate ship without the grog: You'll end up with a surly gaggle of participants who can't do the job expected of them during a pivotal moment of new tool adoption. As discussed in various sections of this book, positive overall perception of the Enterprise Project Management (EPM) environment is a critical step toward the adoption of the processes required to make it all work. In this chapter, we will discuss the configuration requirements for two of the client interfaces to Project Server 2007, and we'll cover the not-so-obvious client components to be installed that enable Project Web Access (PWA) functionality.

Internet Explorer

As the primary interface with PWA for a majority of your users, Internet Explorer is a critical component of your Project Server 2007 implementation. Because this tool is pervasive throughout your user base, we will discuss the required configuration settings of the browser and the additional components that are required for functionality based on the user's role within the EPM system.

Trusted Sites Zone

The Trusted Sites Zone in Internet Explorer has a number of modifications that you must make in order to realize all of the functionality in PWA. Although there are some differences in the default security settings of Internet Explorer 6 and Internet Explorer 7, we will focus on the default configuration settings of the latter. To reach the configuration settings discussed in this section, from Internet Explorer click Tools | Options. Most of the settings are located on the Security tab. In addition, you can apply group policies to make these settings for large groups of users.

Sites

Either by establishing a group policy, or by manually modifying the sites included in the Trusted Sites Zone, you must identify the PWA site as a member of this zone. (If you installed your PWA site on a port other than port 80, you will need to specify it when identifying the site to the Trusted Sites Zone [that is, http://ps2k7:81]).

Custom Level

Now that the PWA site is a member of the Trusted Sites Zone in Internet Explorer, you must make some modifications to this zone to allow for the transparent authentication and functionality provided by the PWA ActiveX controls. In Internet Explorer's Trusted Sites Zone, you should modify the following settings from the Trusted Sites Zone Settings page (these changes assume that you've started from the default level of Medium):

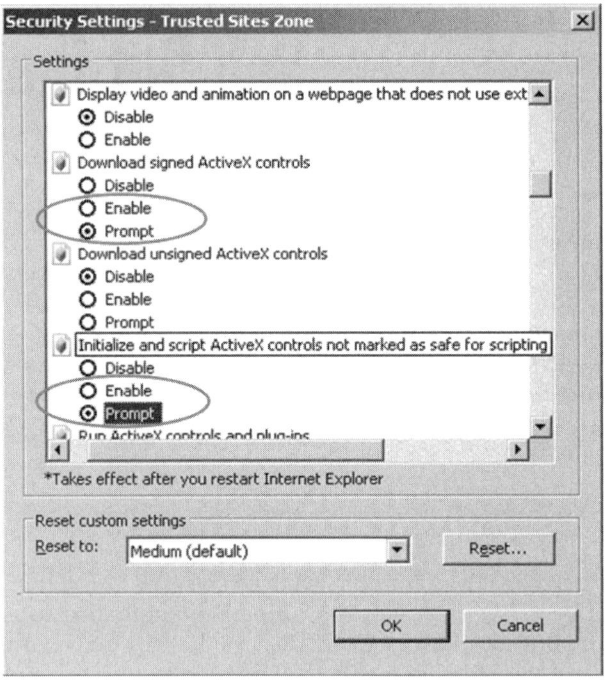

- **Download Signed ActiveX Controls** This portion of the custom-level security settings determines whether users can download the ActiveX controls. These controls perform a wide variety of functions in PWA, including displaying the grids and Gantt charts that comprise Project/Resource Center views, as well as enabling functionality between PWA and other Microsoft Office applications. The action of downloading and installing ActiveX controls happens only once per machine, although it may need to happen again if a machine becomes corrupted or a future Project Server 2007 Service Pack requires it. If your organization has a policy that prevents users from installing these controls on their machines, refer to the "ActiveX Controls" section of this chapter. Otherwise, ensure that this parameter is set to either Enable or Prompt.
- **Initialize and Script ActiveX Controls Not Marked as Safe for Scripting** Leaving this setting disabled prevents functionality where you need to export to Excel or to Microsoft Word, open enterprise projects by clicking an Edit Project link in PWA, or view status report responses through Microsoft Word. Whereas the Download Signed ActiveX Controls setting enables the downloading and installation of the

ActiveX controls, this setting allows the initialization of the controls when certain actions are requested. You must change this setting to either Enable or Prompt to achieve this functionality.

- **Enable Data Access across Domains** Although wording of this setting could potentially have URL, Active Directory, and firewall implications, in the context of PWA, it applies specifically to Internet Explorer accessing data stored in SQL Server Analysis Services. Because these online analytical processing (OLAP) data bypass the PWA server en route to Internet Explorer, the browser treats these as data that are in "another domain." This setting dictates how Internet Explorer responds when this type of access is attempted. To provide users of the Data Analysis views access to the data that the views use, you must modify the setting to Enable or Prompt.
- **User Authentication** As of this writing, in Internet Explorer 7 the default (Medium) security settings for the Trusted Sites Zone define that transparent authentication takes place only for those sites identified in the local intranet sites zone. To enable transparent authentication for the PWA site that has been added to the Trusted Sites Zone, you must change this setting to Automatic Logon with Current User Name and Password. (You have probably experienced the effects of this setting shortly after you created the SharePoint Central Administration Site, navigated to it, and were confronted with a logon box. At that point, you probably canceled the navigation, went into the options of Internet Explorer, modified the sites membership of the local intranet or Trusted Sites Zone, and refreshed your browser to experience transparent authentication.)

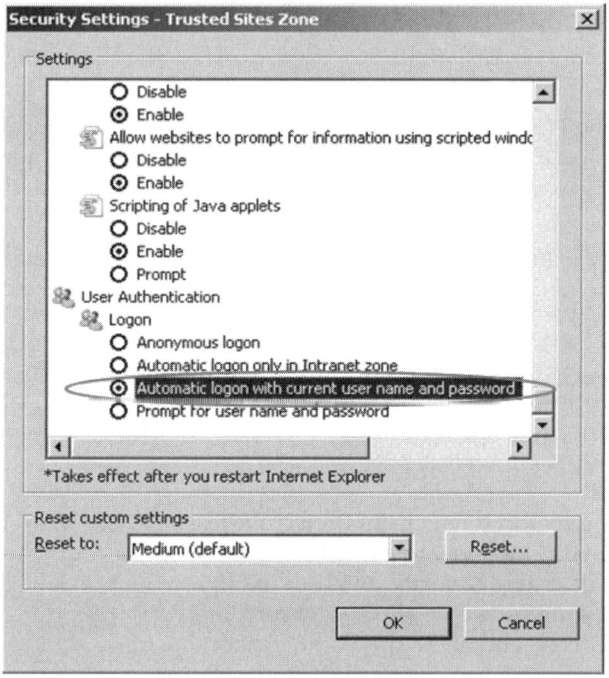

Project Professional

If you are in a mid- to large-size organization, it is likely that your information technology (IT) department uses some sort of administrative software packaging and distribution system. These organizations frequently have policies restricting users from installing software on their company-owned machines. Project Professional can present a gray area for companies that "push" software to their users, primarily because of the fact that relatively few users will require the Project Professional 2007 client on their machines, making it questionable whether the small number who do require it justifies package development, testing, and deployment. Although there are relatively few settings in Project Professional that the Enterprise Global template won't overwrite, there are some guidelines for features that you can distribute through administrative installations.

Project Server Accounts

If your PWA environment is using Windows for user authentication, an administrator can predefine Project Server accounts during distribution package development. The end result is that once the package is deployed to the desktop, the user can open Project Professional and automatically connect to the correct instance of PWA based on the package configuration. To create a Project Server account, a user performs the following steps:

1. Open Project Professional 2007.
2. Click Tools | Enterprise Options | Project Server Accounts.
3. Click Add to begin adding a Project Server account.
4. In the Account Name field, specify a user-friendly name for this account.
5. In the Project Server URL field, specify the URL to the PWA site (that is, http://ps2k7/pwa).
6. From the When Connecting radio button selection, select Windows or forms authentication. (If you intend to package Project Professional administratively for more than one user, you should not create a forms-authenticated Project Server account.)
7. Check the Available box to indicate whether the account that you are now creating should be the default account.
8. Click OK.
9. On the Project Server Accounts page, if you have more than one account listed and want the user to be able to select which account to use, make sure the Manually Control Connection State radio button is selected. Click OK.

Macro Security Level

If you are distributing required macros to Project Professional users through the Enterprise Global template, then each workstation must be able to run the code. Project Professional 2007 by default has its macro security level set to High, which means that only signed macros from trusted sources will be allowed to run. The Project Server administrator has a number of options. On one end of the spectrum, the administrator could acquire the certificate and append the trusted publishers list to allow Project Professional to run the specified signed and trusted macro. On the other end, he or she could simply lower the macro security level on each Project Professional client to Low. It is important to recognize that there are security versus administration trade-off considerations and potentially mitigating factors involved when introducing macros to your EPM environment.

The Project Cache

The Project Cache is an integral part of the communication between Project Professional and PWA, namely, the Project Server Interface (PSI). Users of Project Professional 2007 have the ability to manage this local cache, including the ability to delete projects individually or en masse. Two registry parameters help you manage the size and location of the Project Cache (HKEY_CURRENT_USER\Software\Microsoft\Office\12.0\MS Project\Settings):

- `CacheLocation`
- `CacheSizePerProfile`

These parameters are also accessible from Project Professional's Tools menu; click Tools | Local Project Cache | Cache Settings. You can control these two parameters via Group Policy Object (GPO), especially when Project Professional is deployed in a Terminal Server/ Citrix environment.

Additional Client Components

The additional components that can be installed on the client machines in the EPM environment are not the most obvious, in that they are not the first thing to come to mind when one thinks of Enterprise Project Management. Although seemingly at the periphery, these components will be a weighty factor when it comes to user perception of the overall EPM system.

ActiveX Controls

The ActiveX controls included with Project Server 2007 provide grid and Gantt chart rendering services to views such as the Project Center and Resource Center views, as well as the ability to open other Microsoft Office applications and populate them with current data (for example, exporting to Excel). Within PWA, all users can download the provided ActiveX controls. The settings defined in individual users' Internet Explorer Trusted Sites Zone (described earlier in this chapter) dictate whether these controls can be downloaded and initialized. The issue is that ActiveX controls have gotten a bad name in years past, and as a result, numerous organizational IT departments have implemented strict control over software installation, and ActiveX control installation in particular. To increase control over its IT assets, organizations can implement administrative software deployment solutions that come in a variety of flavors. Because these administrative software deployment applications vary in capability and detail, the following steps can be taken to install the ActiveX controls for Project Server 2007 manually.

1. From the Project Server computer, navigate to the C:\Program Files\Common Files\Microsoft Shared\web server extensions\12\TEMPLATE\LAYOUTS\PWA\Objects\ folder and copy the Pjclient.cab file to your desktop, then go into the 1033 folder and copy the Pjcintl.cab file to your workstation's desktop. From your desktop, open the Pjcintl.cab file to see the compressed files.
2. Right-click on pj12ENUc.dll and click Extract.
3. On the Select a Destination page, select C:\Windows\Downloaded Program Files. (You don't need to extract the langcabENU12.inf file.)
4. From your desktop, open the Pjclient.cab file.
5. Select all the files, right-click, and choose Extract.
6. On the Select a Destination page, select C:\Windows\Downloaded Program Files as the destination for the files. (After you've extracted both cab files, you can safely remove them from your desktop.)
7. Register all of the .dll and .ocx files that you've just placed in the Downloaded Programs folder.
   a. Open a command prompt and traverse to the C:\Windows\Downloaded Program Files directory.
   b. Type **for %i in (pj*.dll) do regsvr32 %i** and press Enter. Click OK in the windows that appear to confirm registration of the .dll files.
   c. Type **for %i in (pj*.ocx) do regsvr32 %i** and press Enter. Click OK in the windows that appear to confirm registration of the .ocx files.

NOTE *Depending on your environment, you may be required to have administrator access to complete the preceding tasks.*

Office Web Components

The Office Web Components (OWC), as they relate to Project Server 2007, provide Web-based Excel PivotChart and PivotTable functionality to the Data Analysis views. In other words, these controls are required only by users who access the Data Analyzer views (that is generally, only by Executives or Analysts). They can be downloaded and installed directly from the PWA site, and the installation happens only once per machine. If the current user has the right permissions on the workstation, installation is transparent and takes only a minute or two. Often, users face an obstacle if their IT policy prevents them from installing software on their client machines. In this case, the user needs to be given (temporary) administrative access to his or her machine, an administrator needs to log on and install the components, or the OWC must be installed administratively. The following steps describe the manual installation of the OWC:

1. From the server, find the owc11.exe file (located by default in the folder C:\Program Files\Common Files\Microsoft Shared\web server extensions\12\TEMPLATE\LAYOUTS\PWA\DOWNLOAD\en-us\).
2. Copy the owc11.exe file to the client machine and run the executable.

NOTE *You might wonder why the file is named owc11. Version 11 refers to the 2003 version of all things Microsoft Office. Where is the 2007 Version, owc12? The reason that you are not using owc12 (even if you did a complete installation of Office 2007) is that there isn't a version of the OWC for Office 2007, nor will there ever be. It's not hidden in a service release somewhere, and it's not tucked away in the recesses of Microsoft's download cavern. The file owc12.exe simply does not exist. Microsoft has decided to make the 2003 version of the OWC the last version and ship it with Project Server 2007. Finding the reasons that Microsoft decided to drop the OWC involves exploring the benefits of Excel Calculation Services, which is currently available in Microsoft Office SharePoint Server 2007. These benefits include server-side calculation and control, as well as less software required on client workstations. So close that Goo-er Windows Live search window, rest your frenzied fingers, and rest easy knowing that the Office 2003 OWC is the most recent version and will work just fine with your Project Server 2007 installation.*

Analysis Services 2005 (9.0) OLE DB Provider (If Using Analysis Services 2005)

If the database (DB) infrastructure for your EPM environment is based on Microsoft SQL Server 2005, there is an additional component that you will need to install on the client workstations that access the Data Analysis views. This component allows the workstations to "speak the 2005 Analysis Services language." A prerequisite for the Analysis Services 2005 (9.0) OLE DB Provider is Microsoft Core XML Services (MSXML) 6.0. Only viewers of the Data Analysis views require these components. If users have the appropriate permissions, they can find the components among the items available in the SQL Server 2005 Feature Pack, found at http://www.microsoft.com/downloads/details.aspx?familyid=50b97994-8453-4998-8226-fa42ec403d17&displaylang=en. Both of the downloads are provided in .msi format, which makes for convenient distribution to a select group via a group policy.

NOTE *There are additional components from the SQL 2005 Feature Pack that you will need for the server(s) running the Project Application Service in your environment. More information about these server components and the configuration of your EPM environment with SQL 2005 as your database provider can be found in Chapter 12.*

Microsoft Office Client Applications

Microsoft Outlook 2003 SP2 or greater, Microsoft Excel 2003 SP2 or greater, Microsoft Word 2003 SP2, and Microsoft Visio 2007 are applications that provide additional functionality to your EPM system. Although none of these Microsoft Office components are required for EPM use, having them installed on the client workstations offers a degree of flexibility for time reporting, additional functionality, and options for reporting not possible through Internet Explorer or Project Professional 2007 alone.

Microsoft Excel 2003 SP2 or Greater

There are three primary uses for Microsoft Excel as it relates to your EPM environment:

- **Export list/grid views** From practically all views where you see a list of items (including Project Center and Resource Center views), the Actions menu provides an Export to Excel option. (ActiveX control initialization is required for this action to complete successfully.)
- **Data Analysis views** With Microsoft Office Excel 2003 SP2 or greater, you can work directly with the OLAP data contained in the Data Analysis views.
- **Visual Reports in Project Professional 2007** Excel provides additional report templates for the Visual Reports functionality.

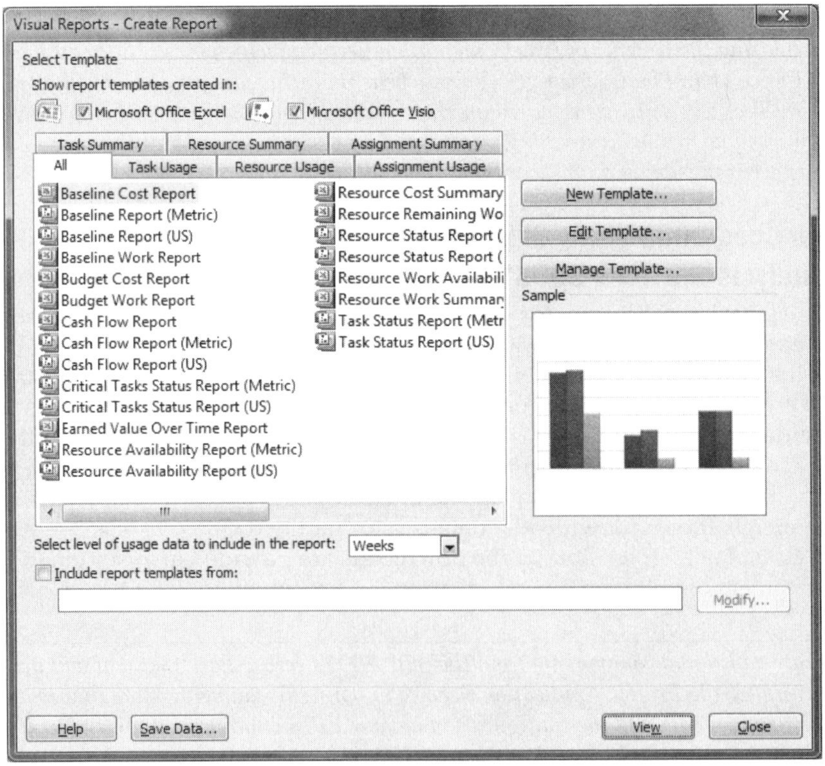

Microsoft Office Visio 2007

Visio 2007, when installed with Project Professional 2007, adds reporting templates and styles for the Visual Reports feature found in Project Professional. The reporting capability that Visio adds to Project Professional is not dependent on connectivity to Project Server 2007.

Microsoft Outlook 2003 SP2 or Greater

The purpose of having Microsoft Outlook to increase functionality in your EPM environment is to enable task status and timesheet submittal directly through a user's Outlook Calendar or Task List. This functionality is enabled by the PWA add-in for Outlook, which must be installed and is described later in this chapter. Although any mail client can receive the alerts and reminders that Project Server 2007 may frequently send, version 2003 SP2 or greater is required to install the PWA plug-in for Outlook.

The Microsoft Office Project 2007 Add-In for Outlook

This Outlook add-in enables resources to interact with their task updates and timesheets directly through their Outlook Calendars or Task Lists. It is provided in .exe format and downloaded directly from Project Server. Because companies often restrict users' ability to run executable files on their workstations, you may be forced to install this component administratively. It can be found on any machine where the Project Server binaries have been installed. By default, it is located in the C:\Program Files\Common Files\Microsoft Shared\Web Server Extensions\12\TEMPLATE\LAYOUTS\PWA\DOWNLOAD\en-us directory. This directory is shared with the installation file of the OWC. When installed via PWA, the add-in is automatically configured for the PWA site from which it was installed.

PART III

NOTE *Regardless of whether you intend to implement timesheets in your EPM environment, the establishment of timesheet periods is required to allow full grid functionality in your tasks imported from the PWA site.*

Configuring the Outlook Add-In

The Outlook add-in is installed with the default settings to interact with the current user's Outlook Task List, as well as to import and update PWA manually. Although each user has the option to have this add-in interact with Outlook's Calendar, you may find that user perception and efficiency are improved through the integration with the Outlook Task List. You can modify these settings from Outlook Options.

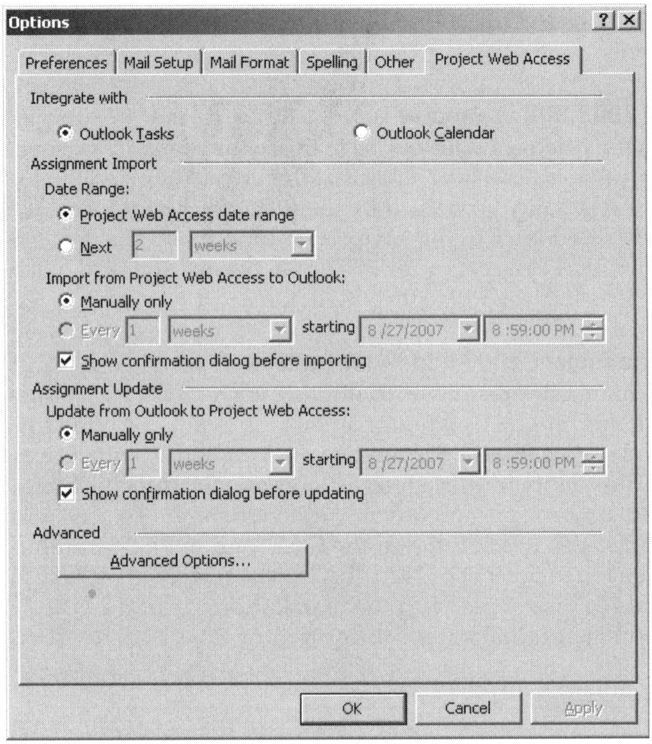

NOTE *Most of the time, installation of this add-in will provide your team members seamless integration with your EPM environment. Occasionally, though, a user who has installed the Outlook add-in will open a task that was imported from PWA and find that he or she has opened a regular task, as if the user had just opened a new task from a fresh install of Office 2003. These symptoms are more frequent when the Outlook add-in is administratively installed. You can correct the problem by deleting or renaming the Frmcache.dat and the UserClass.dat files from the user's Windows Profile. Because Windows typically has a lock on the UserClass.dat file in the profile of the active user, an administrator will need to log in to the machine to delete the following files for the default user on a Windows XP machine.*

- *Delete Frmcache.dat from c:\documents and settings\USERNAME\local settings\application data\microsoft\FORMS*
- *Delete UserClass.dat from c:\documents and settings\USERNAME\local settings\appilication data\microsoft\windows*

Planning for and implementing the desktop components of your system are crucial steps in ensuring the overall success of your EPM implementation. In this chapter, we discussed the main desktop components that are used when interacting with the EPM environment based on the tool and the role of the user who uses them. It's very important that an administrator test these desktop settings (ideally during the proof of concept), because if your users have problems with the desktop components, you will have problems with user participation and adoption. Participation and adoption provide the data and reporting that justify most EPM implementations. Unfortunately, when implementations start to lose momentum, organizational fingers start pointing at the captain of the EPM boat. By planning and testing the desktop components of your EPM system, you will help ensure that your users "Arrgh, Loaded to the Gunwhales" with enthusiasm and positive momentum when embarking on your maiden voyage of Project Server 2007.

PART IV

Project Server 2007 Maintenance

CHAPTER 14

Performance of Your EPM System

When users assess a system's performance, they usually do so through subjective sensing devices, with very few standardized measures by which to compare the results over time. Administrators frequently become aware of performance issues when end users complain that the server is slow or that a certain action that they have performed in the past is not functioning to their expectations. Because end users' positive perception of performance is crucial to the overall success of your EPM implementation, as an administrator you need to know where to look when different observations or reports of system sluggishness cross your desk, and be able to respond quickly. In this chapter, we will discuss the primary performance-impacting components of your EPM system, look at the tools and tactics to assess the components objectively, and address any issues proactively before they escalate.

Tools from the Past

In Project Server 2003, Microsoft made a number of tools available to assess the overall environment performance of your EPM system. Among the most useful tools for capturing and analyzing trends in performance was the Project Server Smoke Test. This was a client-side tool that ran through a set procedure of opening, saving, and publishing a project, as well as performing normal tasks such as logging on and displaying various views. The Smoke Test tool captured the time that it took to perform each task in an XML file that was built upon during each subsequent test. The result was that you would have a performance profile of your EPM 2003 environment at a given point in time. By running this tool periodically, an administrator had visibility into the performance trends of the EPM environment, providing objective performance data that could be used as justification to scale up, scale out, or modify the EPM environment.

> **Capacity versus Availability**
>
> Performance, as it is discussed in this chapter, is related to a system's capacity rather than its availability. Whereas *capacity* is the ability to service more users, *availability* is the ability for the EPM system to be consistently available by reducing single points of failure. For example, if it is determined that SQL Server processing or memory is the culprit when performance degradation occurs, adding the hardware and software to create an active/passive (failover) SQL cluster will not help the performance of your system. It may increase the availability of your environment, but it will not inherently increase the SQL performance of it.

Identifying Potential Performance Degradation Areas

Because the EPM toolset can be scaled out to include several Project Server machines, it can be difficult to determine what exactly is causing your performance problems. Often, it is a combination of issues that affect the user's experience. Overall, there can be a total of five areas where misconfiguration or other variables can impact performance.

Client

Client performance issues are typically pretty straightforward to diagnose. As long as the client machines exceed the minimum hardware and software requirements, the Project Professional 2007 client is quite resilient to system faults or unexpected shutdowns. There are times when the Project Cache becomes corrupted and you might subsequently hear the following complaints:

- "My project is stuck in a 'Check-in Pending' state, and I cannot edit it."
- "My custom fields' lookup tables are scrambled."

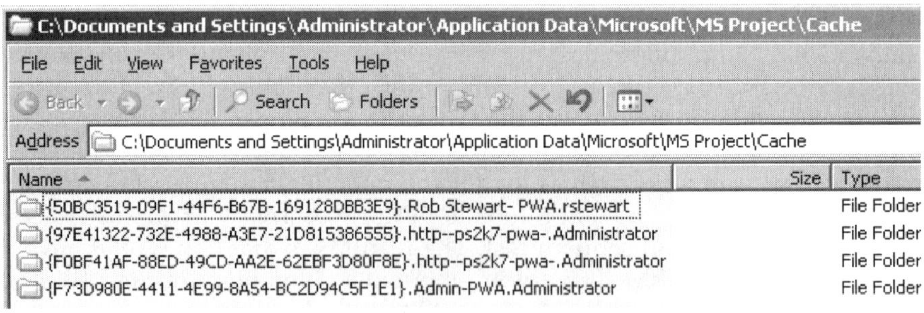

For the first complaint, this problem is typically caused by a project manager publishing his or her project, then closing the project before Project Professional 2007 completes the publish operation. It can also occur if a project is closed and an attempt is made to reopen it prior to the completion of the initial close process. The problem behind the second complaint has been attributed to when there are multiple Project Server accounts on a machine, the Enterprise Global template is undergoing frequent modification, and the cached version of the Enterprise Global template becomes corrupted. You can resolve both issues by taking one of two approaches: performing a Project Cache cleanup operation from within Project Professional, or deleting all of the folders that reside under the folder C:\Documents and Settings*USERNAME*\Application Data\Microsoft\MS Project\Cache. (You should close Project Professional before performing this operation.) By doing so, you bypass the benefits of performing only an incremental open of the project, and force Project Professional to transfer the full project file (Full Open) the next time it is opened.

Internet Explorer can be adversely affected by additional popup blockers or accessory toolbars that users frequently install on their machines. Because of the tight integration with the Project Professional client, performance degradation, and the potential security ramifications, it is recommended that you not use these Internet Explorer add-on products in your EPM environment.

Front End Web Server

The performance of your Front End Web Servers plays a large role in the overall performance of your EPM system. Where the majority of users interact with the system, the Front End Web Servers perform the page-displaying and security functions for users of Internet Explorer. For Project Professional 2007, your Front End Web Servers act as a proxy for the Project Server Interface (PSI) (PSI Forwarder) to help handle the load in a multitiered environment. If you've acquired and installed an SSL certificate for your PWA site, it is here where data are encrypted to and from the clients, decrypted, and sent on to the other EPM back-end farm members. As a result, overall system responsiveness and performance will be affected when SSL is employed.

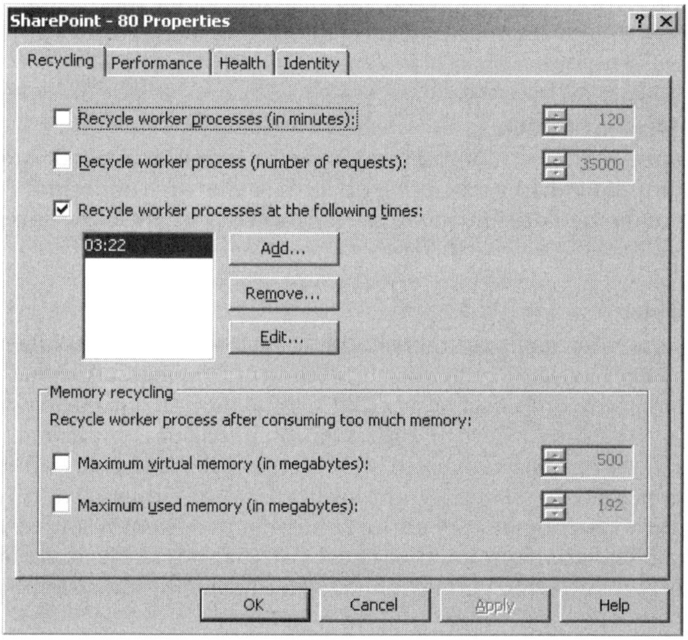

NOTE *As you may know from using SharePoint technologies sites (PWA included), the first time that a user accesses the site after its Internet Information Services (IIS) application pool worker process is restarted (such as after a system reboot), the initial page can take an agonizingly long time to load. This delay is understandable after you reboot the server, or if you are performing an administrative* `iisreset`*. But often, even after long periods of time during which neither of these events occur, a particular site page still may take a very long time to load. This delay may be caused by the application pool that is associated with the site having been recycled. You can check the recycling settings on your application pool by opening IIS Manager, expanding the Application Pools folder, right-clicking on the application pool associated with the site that hosts your PWA site, choosing Properties, and then observing the worker process recycling settings. You might consider setting the worker process recycle thresholds to be based on maximum memory instead of based on an arbitrary time.*

Application Server

Whereas your Front End Web Server performs the majority of the client communication duties in your EPM environment, the Application Server handles a number of heavy processing chores that comprise much of the business logic of the EPM system. As a result, this tier is heavily reliant on processing power and network interface card (NIC) speed, and can benefit most from the processing and memory advantages of a 64-bit operating system and multiple NICs. In addition, if you plan to integrate other Office Server products, such as Microsoft Office SharePoint Server (MOSS) 2007, additional services (such as Excel Calculation Services and MOSS Search) will rely on the capabilities that this system can provide and should be accounted for when identifying the physical specifications of your Application Server(s). Because the Application Server will be facilitating the server-to-server communication, it is recommended that this system uses gigabit-speed NICs.

SharePoint Central Administration

The SharePoint Central Administration site is where the farm is managed. Any changes to the farm topology or frequent administrative operations that are run from this tier (such as `stsadm`) will have an immediate impact on the performance of the other services that this server provides.

SharedService Provider

The SharedService Provider (SSP) uses considerable system resources while managing a number of Project Server–specific business objects and NT Services. Although a single SSP will suffice for the majority of Project Server 2007 installations, configuring additional SSPs may be required in situations where an organization needs to compartmentalize its multiple PWA instances administratively. Although this will not create additional Project Server queue NT Services, the load on your application tier will rise sharply with each additional SSP, as the Project Queuing Service contends for system resources. Additionally, if MOSS 2007 were installed, items such as Excel Calculation Services, Forms Services, Audiences, and Enterprise Search will be managed and contend for system resources from this entity.

The PSI

The Project Server Interface is a core server component enabling users to interact and exchange data with Project Server. Opening, saving, and publishing projects, as well as creating and submitting timesheets, are among the actions that involve the PSI. Performance counters (discussed later in this chapter) are the ideal way to see trends of usage and identify when your project or timesheet queues are the culprit of system performance degradation.

Database Server

Because the database tier of the EPM application was completely redesigned in this version of Project Server, this server depends heavily on processor and memory in addition to the NIC and disk speed. Because much of the processing and memory needs are related to moving data between the databases, this tier benefits from the processing and memory capabilities that a 64-bit operating system provides.

Troubleshooting the Project Server 2007 Queue

As the Project Server Queue is one of the more complex parts of your EPM environment, troubleshooting it often requires administrative access to all items in your EPM environment. For example, one of the best troubleshooting methods for the Queue requires that you look at the Manage Queue page from within the PWA site and then compare the Queue failures with events exposed in the Windows event log. A variety of Project Server Consultants and experts give advice and guidance in the day-to-day operation of an EPM environment. One of these experts, Christophe Fiessinger, provides a wealth of up-to-date information and advice. You can find his blog at http://blogs.msdn.com/chrisfie.

Analysis Services and the Reporting Database

When you think about the process of generating or updating the online analytical processing (OLAP) cube, it will become clear why Microsoft enables you to place the Reporting database on a separate database instance altogether. During this process, data are heavily read from the Reporting database, which is transformed according to your cube configuration settings; then these data are sent to Analysis Services and are used to build the 11 cubes, and 3 virtual cubes in Analysis Services. If both the Reporting database and Analysis Services reside on your primary database server, you will want to be specific about when the cubes are built, ensuring that the building occurs during low-use times.

Network

Your networking infrastructure is the circulatory system of the EPM environment. In the 2003 version of the EPM toolset, the performance of Project Professional experienced serious performance degradation when the network link to Project Server passed mildly low bandwidth (<10MB/sec) or mildly high latency (>30 ms) thresholds. Although most of these issues have been resolved through the use of the Project Cache and the queuing processes, network connectivity is still a very important factor in the communication within your EPM server infrastructure. (If you are implementing a load-balanced Front End Web Server architecture, consider the use of secondary NICs that are dedicated to the interserver communication traffic. In such a setup, each NIC can have a dedicated purpose. For a dual-homed Web server, one NIC is part of a network load-balanced "cluster" that serves requests from the Web, whereas the other NIC is dedicated to communication with the other servers in the Project Server 2007 farm, thus reducing the load on the individual NICs and increasing throughput and performance for each.

Tools to Diagnose Your System Objectively

Although subjective assessments of your EPM system's performance will happen every day when users are in the environment, it is important for administrators to have access to tools to periodically take objective snapshots of the infrastructure's load and performance profile. In addition, you can use the tools listed in this section with other application and operations management software (including Microsoft System Center Operations Manager) to centralize and automate this performance and health data collection.

Best Practice Analyzer

The Best Practices Analyzer for Windows SharePoint Services (WSS) v3 is an administrative tool that is used to assess the configuration of your EPM environment. The output of the

Microsoft Best Practices Analyzer

The Microsoft Best Practices Analyzer for WSS 3.0 and the 2007 Microsoft Office system can be downloaded from http://www.microsoft.com/downloads/details.aspx?FamilyID=cb944b27-9d6b-4a1f-b3e1-778efda07df8&DisplayLang=en.

After downloading the software, complete the following steps:

1. Double-click the BestPracticeAnalyzer.exe file and extract it to a location that you can easily navigate to via a Command Prompt command (for example, C:\BPA).
2. Open a Command Prompt and change the directory to the location to which you extracted the file in step 1.
3. Type **sharepointbpa.exe -cmd analyze -substitutions** ***SERVER_NAME yourservername*** and press Enter. Replace *`yourservername`* with the actual name of a server in your farm running SharePoint Central Administration. *`SERVER_NAME`* is case-sensitive, as the *`-substitutions`* parameter will by default look to the rule file (sharepointbpa.config.xml) for this variable, and use *`yourservername`* in it. If you work within a larger environment and want to script or collect health information from multiple SharePoint farms to a central location, this technique will be useful.
4. From the the directory into which you extracted the original file, open the sharepointbpa(x).config.xml file to review the issues that this tool has found.

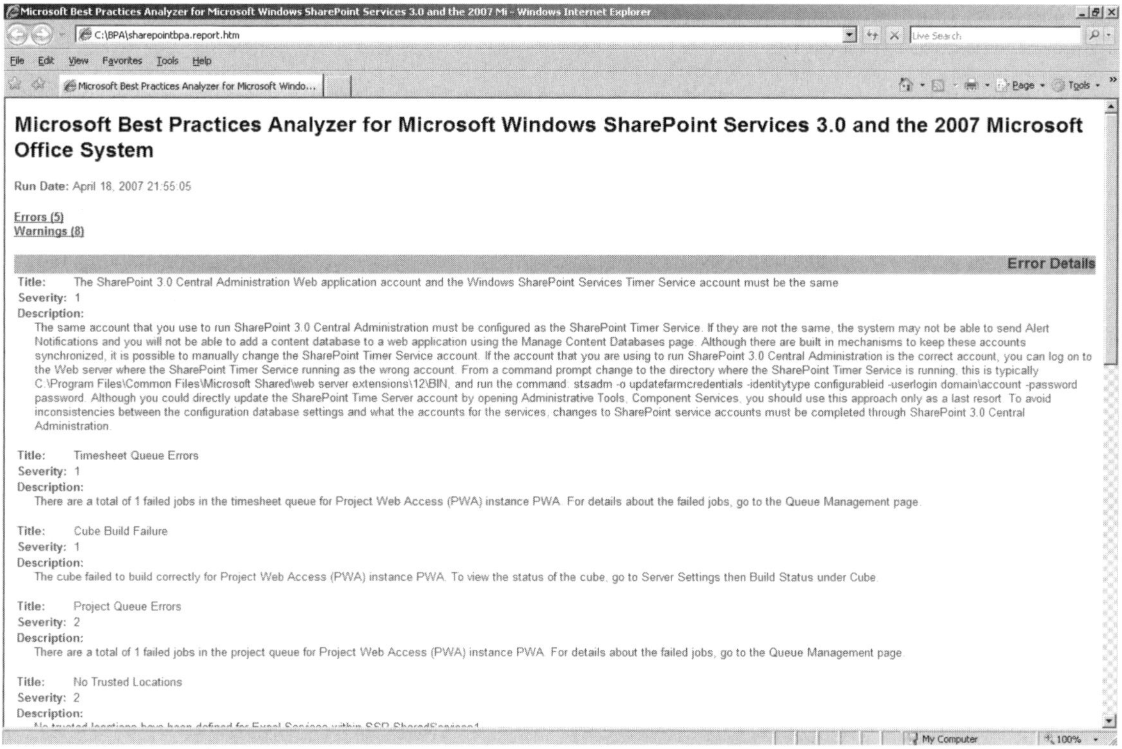

FIGURE 14-1 Microsoft Best Practices Analyzer for Windows SharePoint Services v3.0 and the 2007 Microsoft Office system

tool is an .htm document (shown in Figure 14-1) that includes errors and warnings concerning issues that the tool discovered in your environment. The .htm document also provides possible remediation steps for the errors and warnings that it generates.

Performance Monitor

Microsoft Windows 2003 comes with an administrative tool that can capture performance information from a wide variety of Windows Server's core subsystems. Among these are processor, memory, and disk counters. When the Project Server 2007 binaries are installed on this server, additional Performance Monitor counters are made available to this tool (and the diligent administrator). These counters are grouped according to the relevant Project Server core components.

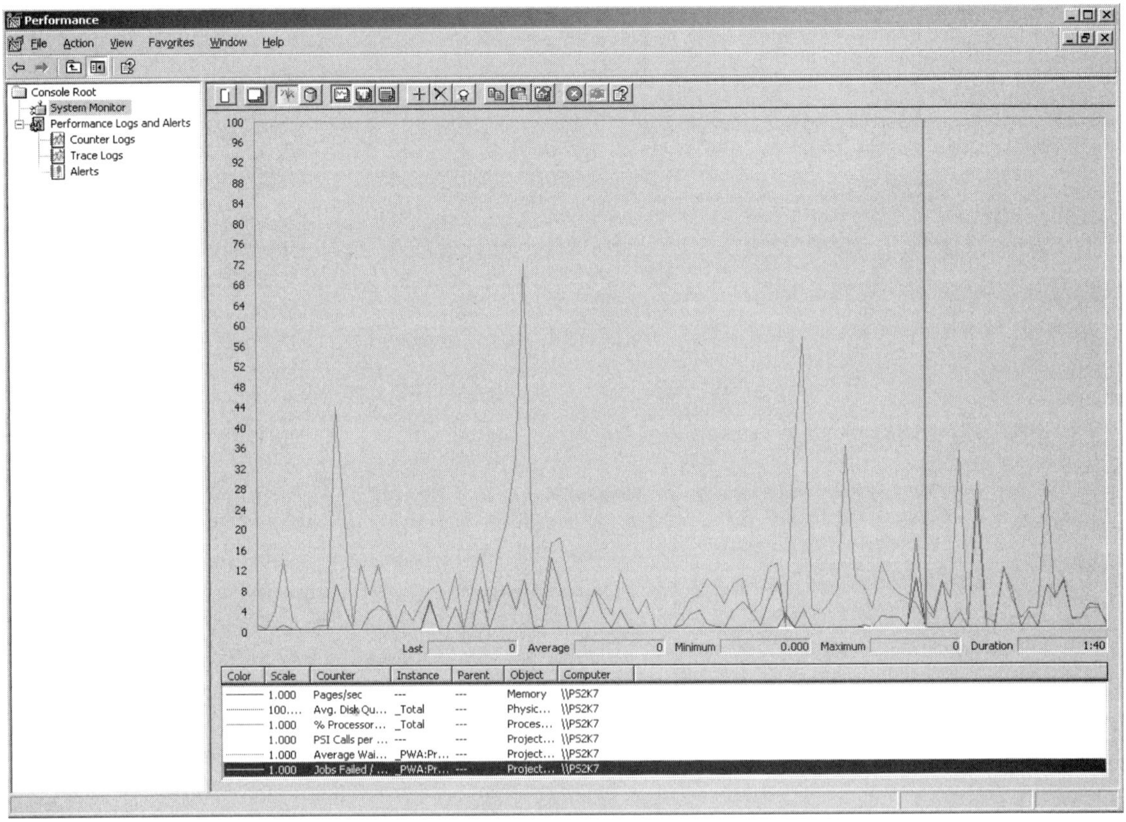

Table 14-1 describes the Project Server–specific Performance Monitor counters available. Ideal counters for monitoring overall health trends include the following:

- Overall time taken for project open
- Jobs failed per day
- Percentage of incremental saves to full saves

Ideal counters for assessing peak usage times are as follows:

- PSI calls per second
- Current unprocessed jobs
- Average wait time per minute
- Jobs processed per hour per day

Project Server: Queue General	Project Server: Queue Jobs	Project Server: User Activity	Project Server: WinProj
% SQL retries/day	% jobs failed/day	PSI calls per sec	Average time taken for project open
% SQL retries/hour	% jobs failed/hour		Percentage of incremental save to full save
Active job processing threads	% jobs retried/day		WinProj full open count in the last hour
Average unprocessed jobs/day	% jobs retried/hour		WinProj full save count in the last hour
Current unprocessed jobs	Average processing time/day		WinProj incremental open count in the last hour
New jobs/min	Average processing time/min		Winproj incremental save count in the last hour
SQL calls/hour/day	Average wait time/ day		
SQL calls/min	Average wait time/ min		
SQL retries/min	Jobs failed/min		
	Jobs processed/ hour/day		
	Jobs processed/min		
	Jobs retried/min		

TABLE 14-1 Project Server Performance Counters in Performance Monitor (`perfmon`)

PART IV

Scaling Your Environment

Typically an organization's initial server deployment entails a single server performing both Web serving and application tier services. As resource demands grow and a second server is considered, the choice becomes whether to break up the application such that the second server is dedicated to serving Web requests while the initial server is dedicated to the application tier, or whether you should simply add another "complete" server that will be used as a load-balanced front end and a load-balanced application server. Although you should make the ultimate decision by analyzing the proportion of PWA users to Project Professional users (noting that both options will add performance capacity to your environment), it has been found that adding complete servers reduces the complexity of design and provides more overall value when scaling your EPM environment.

In this chapter, we discussed the main components that affect end-user experience in an EPM environment, the tools to diagnose them objectively, and some ways to proactively resolve the issues that may occur. EPM has a number of moving parts that individually have a great impact on end-user experience. Although adjusting an end user's subjective assessment may be left to the expertise of an experienced neurosurgeon or psychotherapist, by implementing the suggestions given in this chapter, you should have the tools for objectively assessing and effectively improving the performance of your EPM environment.

CHAPTER 15

Application/Database Migration from Previous Versions

Migration to Microsoft Office Project Server 2007 can be a very complex process. It involves thorough planning and requires an administrator to assess the business needs of those users involved with the existing Project Server 2003 instance. In addition, the administrator needs to plan for the architecture changes, potentially planning for new hardware in the environment. In this chapter, we will discuss different migration approaches you might take, the tools you'll need to complete the migration, and some best practices to help keep surprises to a minimum. Because you may be working within a variety of scenarios, this chapter provides direction for a commonly used approach: a full migration with Windows SharePoint Server (WSS) to different hardware. Using this approach, you should plan at least three to four weeks for your migration planning, testing, cutover, and cleanup activities.

Migration Approaches

Upgrading Project Server 2003 to Project Server 2007 is not a simple process. It does not involve simply putting in the Project Server 2007 CD/DVD, agreeing to a license, and clicking an Upgrade button. This is primarily because of the fundamental application and database architecture changes in the new release. It truly is a migration, in that there is no "upgrade" of the Project Server 2003 environment. As a result, the process involves a substantial amount of premigration work to prepare your Project Server 2003 environment's data for the actual migration. For the migration approach covered in this chapter, you need an existing Project Server 2003/SQL 2000 environment and a fresh Project Server 2007/SQL 2005 environment installed on separate computers. The approach requires that all of the projects and related information will migrate at the same time and your Project Server 2003 environment will ultimately be decommissioned.

NOTE *Regardless of your migration approach, it is important to test your migration to familiarize yourself with the processes and potential issues before performing the live cutover. Microsoft has developed a great deal of information regarding different migration scenarios, including gradual migrations and instructions for different topologies and database version combinations. This document can be found at the following link: http://technet2.microsoft.com/Office/en-us/library/4b407257-04eb-4d48-9d97-f5b0fe3cead81033.mspx.*

Migration Areas

There are several migration areas that you must consider in your overall migration strategy:

- **Global Environment** This aspect includes the Enterprise Global, Enterprise Resources, and other systemwide settings that you may have made.
- **Windows SharePoint Services Data** These include the documents, issues, and risks stored in the Project Workspaces.
- **The Projects** This includes the plans that are in place in the 2003 environment.
- **Client Tools** These include Microsoft Office Project Professional 2007, ActiveX controls, and the PWA plug-in for Outlook.

Items Not Addressed by the Migration Tool

The Project Server Migration tool handles many of the critical data components of your Enterprise Project Management (EPM) 2003 environment and moves them to your EPM 2007 environment. However, some components are not included in the migration process, including the following:

- Pending Status Updates and Status Update Rules
- Timesheet History
- Status Reports
- To-do lists
- View filters
- Project Versions
- Add-on functionality (including database tables and fields created by third parties)

Premigration Steps

To migrate your existing Project Server environment to Project Server 2007, there are a few things that you must do before you begin. These steps help to ensure that the Project Server 2003 data is compatible with and ready to move to the Project Server 2007 environment:

1. Update your current EPM environment to Project Server 2003 SP2a.
2. Ensure that all of your projects have no pending status updates.
3. Ensure you have no duplicate enterprise resources and that they are formatted correctly.

4. Ensure that no projects (including the Enterprise Global template) are checked out.
5. If you are using Project Server 2003 authentication, develop your plan for these user accounts and decide whether to change them to Windows domain accounts or use forms authentication.

The Starting Point—Project Server 2003 SP2a

To ensure a successful migration, your current EPM environment must be upgraded to Microsoft Office Project Server 2003 SP2a. Although upgrading to a previous version is beyond the scope of this book, a wealth of information can be found on the topic from Microsoft's site or through a quick Internet search.

No Pending Status Updates

If there are any projects in your EPM environment that have pending status updates to be applied, migration of those projects risks failure. There are two ways to determine the state of status updates in your 2003 EPM environment. The first is to run the Migration tool with the `-verify` switch. If there are projects with these updates pending, you will be notified via the Migration tool's log, and through the command line specifying these projects. If you do not see a message in the migration log indicating projects with pending status updates, then no action is required. The second approach for determining the state of status updates is to query the Project Server database directly (using a tool such as SQL Query Analyzer) to find these unresolved status updates. The best way to avoid this situation is to remind your organization's project managers to have all of their status updates resolved and projects published prior to the migration.

No Duplicate Enterprise Resources

If your Project Server 2003 environment has duplicate named resources, your migration may fail. Because you will not be made aware of this risk by opening the Enterprise Resource Pool from Project Professional 2003, you must run the Migration tool with the `-verify` option to find out whether you have duplicate named sources. Options for remediation of this situation can be found in the documentation that Microsoft provides, as noted earlier in this chapter.

No Commas in Enterprise Resource Display Names

In Project Server 2007, enterprise resources cannot have a comma in their display name. Thus, if you currently have Project Server 2003 enterprise resources that include commas in their name, your migration may fail. An easy way to validate that this problem does not exist (and resolve it if it does) is to open the Enterprise Resource Pool from Project Professional 2003 and make changes to the resources if necessary.

Ensure That No Projects Are Checked Out or Have Been Recently Edited Externally

In the Project Server 2003 database, there is an Externally Edited flag that is set to true if a system external to Microsoft Project Professional 2003 (for example, if a third-party add-on or a program with a .PDS extension has modified the project). If this error appears when you run the Migration tool with the `-verify` parameter, the tool will identify which projects are in this state. To resolve such problems, simply open any affected project in Microsoft Project Professional 2003, save it to Project Server 2003, and close it (to check it back in). Likewise, if there are projects in the Project Server 2003 database that are checked out, they will be skipped during the migration. To get the identified projects checked in, work with the corresponding owners of the projects to establish a deadline for them to have their projects checked in. After the deadline, an administrator can force the check-in process on the outstanding projects through the Administration pages of PWA 2003.

Versions

Because the concept of project versions is no longer used in Project Server 2007, there must be a way for organizations to retain the data captured in these project "versions." To accomplish this, the Project Server Migration tool treats every project version as a distinct project. For example, if you had a Project Server 2003 project named Robsproject.Published that was saved after migration with two additional versions, .Target and .WhatIf, there would be three distinct projects: Robsproject_Published, Robsproject_Target, and Robsproject_WhatIf.

Project Server Authenticated Accounts

For several reasons, Microsoft decided to let Project Server authentication go the way of the dodo in the EPM 2007 environment. Among these reasons was the fact that WSS now handles the authentication services for Project Server, thus negating the need to store user credentials in the Project Server data store. Project Server authentication is now replaced with forms authentication for providing access to PWA through Internet Explorer and Microsoft Project Professional 2007. Forms authentication requires additional development effort to create and administration effort to maintain. It does not, however, provide transparent authentication, nor does it participate in the authentication between any Office products and SQL Analysis Services for the Data Analysis views. For these reasons, you should consider making Windows authentication your sole provider of authentication for all users of the EPM environment. The migration of your Project Server 2003 environment to Project Server 2007 may provide the catalyst for this change.

The Migration Tool `verify` Option

An important tool that will help assess how much premigration work you have to do is the Migration tool itself. It can run in verification mode, where most of the preceding issues are assessed in your Project Server 2003 environment. The tool, when run with the `-verify` option, will not change any data in your 2003 environment, migrate any projects or data, nor fix the discovered issues, even if its associated configuration file (P12MIGRATION.ini) is configured to do so. Although there are additional steps to take prior to migration, the `-verify` option of the Migration tool is the main method that you use to identify potential problems, enabling you to resolve them prior to the cutover time.

Migration

After you have resolved the potential migration issues identified in the previous section, you can now start to plan the actual migration of data to your new Project Server 2007 environment. As stated earlier, we will focus on a full migration of data (Enterprise Global, Enterprise Resources, projects, and WSS) from an existing Project Server 2003/WSSv2/SQL 2000 environment to a new environment where Project Server 2007 and SQL 2005 SP1 are installed. It is assumed that the user performing the following steps is an administrator on all of the indicated machines and has administrative access to the management tools and applications therein.

The steps are as follows:

1. Install Project Server 2007 on the new server environment and provision a PWA site. Validate that the new PWA site is functioning normally.
2. Move your associated WSS sites. Because you are moving the data from WSSv2 to WSSv3 en masse, you will take the database migration approach for the WSS data:
   a. Run the WSS pre-upgrade scanning tool. Copy the prescan.exe file from the WSSv3 server to the WSSv2 server. From a command prompt, navigate to the folder where you copied the PRESCAN.EXE file and type **prescan /all**.
   b. Back up the WSSv2 Content database.
   c. Move the WSSv2 Content database backup file to the SQL 2005 server (which supports Project Server 2007/WSSv3).
   d. Through SQL Server 2005 Management Studio, restore the WSSv2 Content database backup to the SQL 2005 instance.
   e. From the console of the machine hosting the Central Administration site for WSS, use the stsadm.exe command-line tool to connect the WSSv2 database to the WSSv3 instance using the `addcontentdb` operation (for example, `stsadm -o addcontentdb -url http://ps2k7 -databaseserver PS2k7 -databasename STS_p11_1`).

   Be patient. This command will take some time, depending on how much data you had in your WSSv2 database. The operation is mostly silent, in that the command prompt window provides little feedback.

NOTE *By running the* `stsadm -o addcontentdb` *operation, your associated Project Workspaces will be upgraded to WSSv3, but they will not be linked to any projects. The linkage between projects and their associated workspaces is handled by the P12MigrationTool, discussed later in this chapter.*

   f. After this process completes, verify that the content database was added successfully through the Application Management page in your WSSv3 Central Administration. Depending on your space requirements and capacity, you also may want to limit the number of sites that this database can contain. (If you set this limit to the current number of sites, all new sites will be created in the original WSS_content database.)

g. Depending on the user accounts that were used for the WSSv2 installation, you may receive an "access denied" message for a newly migrated workspace (that is, http://ps2k7/sites/projectserver_101). You might need to modify the site collection administrators (through Central Administration | Application Management) of the Project Workspaces to ensure smooth access and linkage during the next phase of migration.

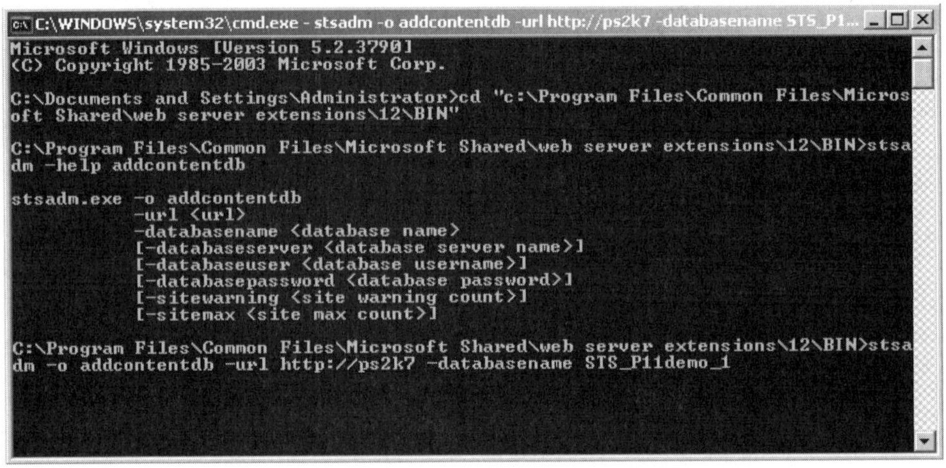

NOTE *The process of migrating Project Server 2003 global data happens only once. For this reason, before you begin to migrate Project Server data, you should back up your four Project Server 2007 databases of the PWA site. If the migration fails at any one point, you will be forced to "reset" your Project Server 2007 site in preparation for your next attempt. Restoring the ProjectServer_Published, ProjectServer_Draft, ProjectServer_Archive, and ProjectServer_Reporting databases accomplishes this task.*

3. Verify Project Server 2003 data as follows:

   a. From your SQL Server 2000 instance (which supports Project Server 2003), back up the ProjectServer database.

   b. Move the ProjectServer database backup file (.bak) to the SQL 2005 Server.

   c. Restore the ProjectServer database to the SQL 2005 instance.

   d. Modify the P12MIGRATION.ini sample file with the appropriate information for your environment. (Configuration options of the P12MIGRATION.ini file are found later in this chapter.)

   e. From a command prompt, run the P12MIGRATIONTOOL, indicating the configuration file and the `-verify` switch. (Regardless of the information indicated in the P12MIGRATION.ini file, if you indicate the `-verify` switch when running the Migration tool, no data will be migrated.)

   f. Using the output log from the P12MIGRATIONTOOL, go into your Project Server 2003 environment and correct any problems using the suggestions provided if they adversely affect your migration and are warranted in your environment. After correction, restart your migration at step 3a (backing up the database).

4. Perform the migration. For this example, you are migrating all the projects at once, so you will have already communicated to your project managers that they must have accepted all status updates and published and checked in their projects prior to migration time.
   a. Ensure the P12MIGRATION.ini file is configured correctly for your migration.
   b. From a command prompt, run the P12MIGRATIONTOOL.exe. Indicate where the configuration file (P12MIGRATION.ini) is by using the `-c` parameter. Press ENTER to run the tool. An example of the tool in action can be found in Figure 15-1.

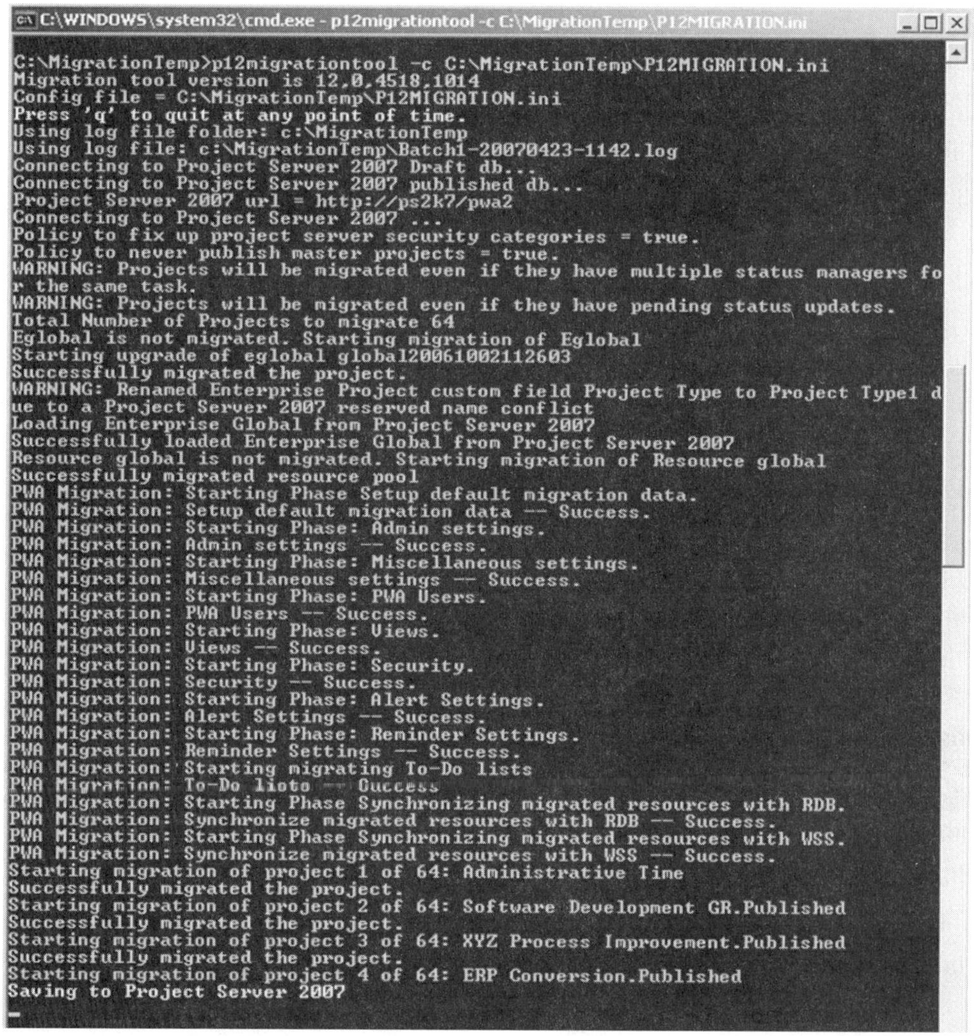

FIGURE 15-1 P12MIGRATIONTOOL.exe in action

The P12MIGRATIONTOOl.exe

The Project Server 2007 Migration tool is the main utility that you will use to migrate your Project Server 2003 data to the Project Server 2007 environment. It is located on the Project Professional 2007 installation media and is installed as an optional component. You can install this component through the Control Panel's Add/Remove Programs page (Programs and Features in Vista) then "Change" your Microsoft Office Project Professional 2007 installation. Once installed, along with its configuration file, P12MIGRATION.ini is located by default in the C:\Program Files\Microsoft Office\OFFICE12 folder.

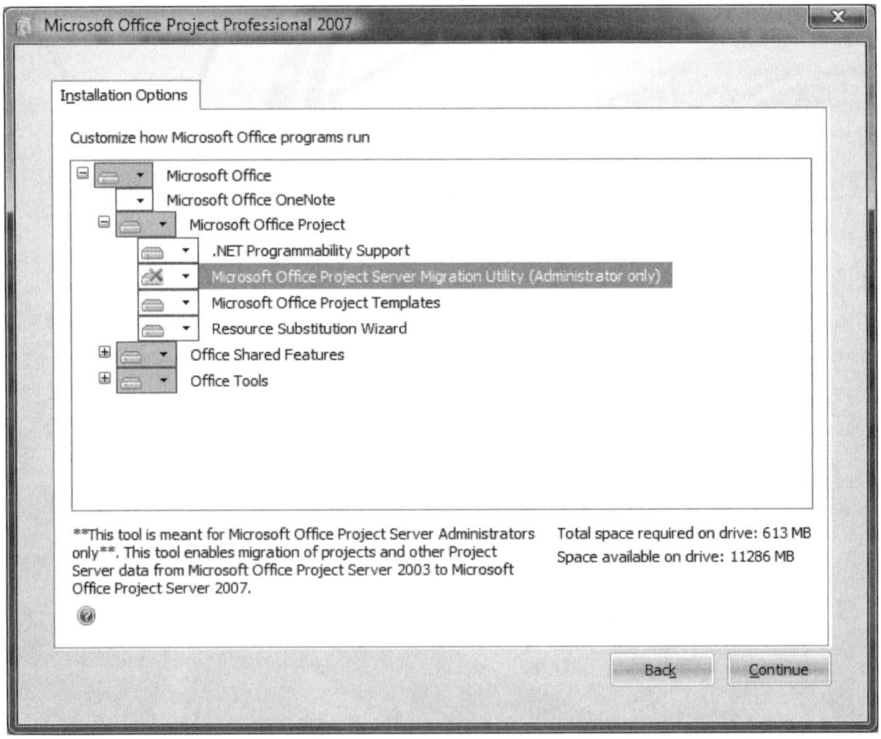

Configuration Settings in P12MIGRATION.ini

The P12MIGRATIONTOOL.ini file is the configuration file for the Migration tool. In it, you configure various parameters and functions that the P12MIGRATIONTOOL.exe performs, including the following:

- `LogFilePath=(`*`path`*`)` This function indicates where the log file will be written.
- `LogFileNamePrefix(`*`prefix`*`)` Using this function, you can identify a prefix for the log file. Though each log file will have a unique name (based on a timestamp), it might be useful to modify this name if you are taking a gradual migration approach.

- **MigrateAll (Save/Publish)** This parameter enables you to indicate that you want to migrate all of the projects in the Project Server 2003 database. The two switches are `-Save`, which migrates and saves the projects to Project Server 2007, and `-Publish`, which attempts to save and then publish all projects to Project Server 2007.

NOTE *If you intend to migrate all projects in Project Server 2003, remember to remove any specific project names from the "Project Names to Save and Publish" and "Project Names to Save" sections.*

- **FixUpSecurityCategories (yes/no)** This parameter automatically adds the migrated projects to security categories. It is recommended that you use the `yes` switch so that your projects have similar security categories applied after migration.
- **StopProjectMigrationIfStatusUpdatesPending(yes/no)** If this switch is set to `yes`, then projects with pending status updates will be skipped during the migration. At times you might want the Migration tool to overlook these issues and migrate the project regardless of the state of the status updates. You will become aware of these issues during the verification run and will subsequently be able to bring them over by using the `no` switch.
- **NeverPublishMasterProjects (yes/no)** If this switch is set to `yes`, the master projects that were saved in Project Server 2003 will be migrated to Project Server 2007, but they will not be published regardless of their presence in the "Project Names to Save and Publish" or inclusion by the "Migrate All" section. Because Microsoft has greatly improved Project Server's support for publishing master projects, doing so is a viable option in this version of the EPM toolset.
- **ResetStatusManagerToOwnerOnConflict (yes/no)** In Project Server 2007, all assignments in a task must have the same status manager. If this property's switch is set to `no` and a task is found with multiple status managers, the project will not migrate. It is recommended to use the `yes` switch for this property.
- **Project Names to Save (*project name list*)** If you are using the `Migrate All=yes` setting, you would leave this section blank. However, if you wish to migrate projects but not save them, you could add their names (such as Project1.published) in this section.
- **Project Names to Save and Publish (*project name list*)** If you are using the `Migrate All=yes` setting, you would leave this section blank. However, if you want the Migration tool to save and then publish your projects, you would add their names to this section.
- **Excluded Project Names (*project name list*)** If you are using the `Migrate All=yes` setting, you can indicate here which projects should be excluded from the migration.
- **Project Server 2007 (*subparameter*)** This parameter assumes that you have restored the Project Server 2003 database to the SQL instance servicing Project Server 2007. The subparameters available include the following:
  - `Project2007PWAServer= (`*`url`*`)`, where *`url`* is the address of your New PWA site.

PART IV

- `Project2007SQLServer= (machinename)`, where *machinename* is the name of your SQL Server and instance if you are not using the default.
- `DraftDB=(draftdbname)`, where *draftdbname* is the name of Draft database of your Project Server 2007 PWA site. The default name is ProjectServer_Draft.
- `PublishedDB=(pubdbname)`, where *pubdbname* is the name of the Published database of your Project Server 2007 PWA site. The default name is ProjectServer_Published.

- **`Project Server 2003 (subsection)`** If, in your Project Server 2003 instance, you have split the project tables from the Web tables, you can identify the following databases; otherwise, you must indicate the same database for both of the following sections:
    - `Project2003ProjectTablesDB=(PS2003dbname)`, where *PS2003dbname* is the name of your restored Project Server 2003 database where the project tables reside.
    - `Project2003WebTablesDB=(PS2003dbname)`, where *PS2003dbname* is the name of your restored Project Server 2003 database where the Web tables reside.

The P12MIGRATION.ini may have the .sample suffix attached to the name. You can safely rename this file by removing this suffix. In addition, you will see many semicolons throughout the file. These are used as comment indicators, so that the tool ignores characters on the lines on which they reside. You can safely add comments to this file, perhaps to leave notes for yourself or other administrators regarding modifications to a particular migration run.

Processing of the P12MIGRATIONTOOL.exe

The Migration tool begins its process with the migration of the Enterprise Global template. It then migrates the Enterprise Resource Pool. After the Enterprise Global template is successfully migrated, it will not be migrated again on subsequent attempts. This has some ramifications. First, if you find that the lookup tables and fields that were created (and possibly modified) in Project Server 2007 are unacceptable, you may need to make changes in the Project Server 2003 environment, restore your four PWA databases, and attempt the migration again. Second, because the Enterprise Global template is migrated only once, any changes you make to your Project Server 2003 environment will not be migrated in subsequent attempts, and if any are needed in Project Server 2007, they will have to be made on the Project Server 2007 environment manually.

Postmigration Tasks

If all goes well, most of your postmigration cleanup will occur in your migration testing phase, and you will be able to resolve any problems in your EPM 2003 environment prior to your production migration. Regardless, after you think that you have successfully migrated your data to Project Server 2007, it is important to test all of the functionality in the Project Server 2007 environment.

Example postmigration testing might include the following steps:

- Open a freshly migrated project, add freshly migrated Enterprise resources, assign tasks, and publish.
- Create a new project, add freshly migrated Enterprise resources, assign tasks, and publish.
- Ensure that resources can log on to PWA.
- Have a resource send status updates, have the project manager accept or reject status updates, and publish.
- Verify Project Workspace functionality by associating risks, issues, and documents with a project's task.
- Through Project Professional's Build Team from Enterprise tool and PWA's Resource Center, view freshly migrated resource availability.
- Check the ability to build Analysis Services cubes from freshly migrated projects.
- Compare the security groups and categories with those in Project Server 2003 to ensure that membership is appropriate.
- Check the PWA, global, and category permissions to ensure that they are appropriate.
- Consider merging or deleting the duplicate groups, categories, and security templates.
- Check the views to ensure that the display is consistent with those in the EPM 2003 environment. (Pay special attention to the grouping and filtering settings in the views.)

NOTE *After migration from Project Server 2003, migrated groups and categories and the out-of-the-box groups and categories are renamed due to conflicts among the names. For example, Team Members Group in Project 2007 becomes Team Members 2007 and the Project 2003 Group now becomes Team Members.*

PART IV

Migrating WSS

After migration, if you wish to use automatic workspace provisioning, you can specify this setting in the Automatic Provisioning section of the Project Workspace Provisioning Settings page found in Server Settings. Also, for the sites that were migrated over in the initial migration steps using the database migration of WSS, you will find that the migrated Project Workspaces have a different URL format than the workspaces created natively in Project Server 2007. As a result, the breadcrumb navigation (shown in the top-left corner of the Project Workspace screen) shows the Project Workspace as the top level rather than the PWA site to which it should belong. Although the breadcrumb navigation and some aesthetic features of the Project Workspace are the only WSS casualties of the migration, you can still use the issues, risks, and documents with full fidelity and connectivity to the parent PWA site.

Enabling Project Server Authenticated Users to Log In

During migration, the users who used Project Server authentication in Project Server 2003 are migrated to the Project Server 2007 environment as resources. Because those users did not have Windows Domain accounts associated with them, Project Server treats them as forms-authenticated resources who cannot log in to PWA. This state is not workable for the long term, so an administrator needs to take the following action to allow the user to log in:

1. Associate a Windows user account with the resource. In the new instance of PWA containing your newly migrated users and projects, navigate to Resource Center, select the checkbox next to the resource's name, and click Edit Details.
2. In the Identification Information section, select the Resource Can Logon to Project Server checkbox.
3. In the User Authentication section that appears after completing step 2, either select the Windows authentication information in the format *DOMAIN\username* (which is recommended), or provide a valid forms authentication–based username in the format *MembershipProvider:UserAccount*.

NOTE *For information regarding the setup of forms-based user accounts, refer to the Microsoft TechNet article "Project Server 2007 Authentication" at http://technet2.microsoft.com/office/en-us/library/559cc03c-56f7-4399-ad28-15ac35e8723d1033.mspx.*

Upgrading Client Tools

Upgrading the client tools is your final step in the migration of your Project Server 2003 environment. Although both Project Professional 2003 and Project Professional 2007 can coexist on the same operating system, Project Professional 2003 cannot connect to a Project 2007 PWA site, and Project Professional 2007 cannot connect to a Project Server 2003 PWA site.

The client tools involved are the following:

- The Project Professional Client
- The PWA plug-in for Outlook
- The ActiveX controls
- The Office Web Components (OWC)

Of these client tools, only the first three must be upgraded. The 2003 version of OWC is the most recent version of this technology and will be the last, as Microsoft plans to replace the components with the functionality offered through Excel Calculation Services in Microsoft Office SharePoint Server.

NOTE *For Information about administratively installing the ActiveX controls onto client computers, see Chapter 8. For information about Microsoft's plans for OWC, see http://blogs.msdn.com/excel/archive/2006/07/17/668544.aspx. For information about cross-platform compatibility, see the Project Server Tech Center at http://www.microsoft.com/technet/prodtechnol/office/project/default.mspx.*

Migrating Project Server 2003 to Project Server 2007 is a daunting project. It is filled with "gotchas" and caveats that will likely force you to test your migration more than once. Through thorough planning, testing, and using an approach that meets your organization's needs, you will minimize the hassles and downtime that can be encountered. In addition, the migration provides you and your organization an opportunity to modify your EPM environment to improve user access, security, and performance.

CHAPTER 16

Techniques and Solutions for New Project Requests

In most cases, an organization that implements Project Server 2007 has established processes for project initiation, planning, execution, controlling, and closure. Likewise, this organization will likely have a central core of project management wisdom that manages, participates in, and modifies these processes when needed. Out of the box, the Project Server 2007 toolset provides an environment to manage planning, execution, monitoring, and closure. Organizations regularly wrestle with many questions: What is a project? Who approves it? When does the Enterprise Project Management (EPM) toolset know when the project starts? This is where initiation processes come into play, and where it can get confusing for people implementing EPM as to which products and approaches to use and when. In this chapter, we'll discuss some typical project initiation processes, existing tools that Microsoft provides to support them, and some custom approaches that companies have chosen to help get their project initiation process into an efficient, effective, repeatable, and stable state.

Initiation Processes

People start work. Sometimes it's initiated by a phone call, sometimes by e-mail, sometimes by a brainstorming session, or possibly by someone storming into your office screaming "I can't print!" but an idea ultimately turns into work. Defining the work (scope, objectives, and deliverables) is a major component of the initiating process, and one frequently overlooked. Work approval is ultimately the point at which initiation ends and planning begins.

Larger organizations normally have very strict guidelines over what is considered a "project." Some consider one threshold of becoming a "project" any effort consuming more than 40 hours of work. Other thresholds may include the number of required resources involved, or the number of external departments affected by the work. Proposed activities that do not reach these thresholds are often considered maintenance, support, or administrative tasks. The intended end result of all of these sometimes intricate processes is the standardization of tools that informed workers use to make important decisions for the organization.

If a company does not have a formal method or process for initiating projects, the venue for project evaluation simply does not exist to evaluate the project for organizational value before it begins. As a result, what seemed like a great idea to the requester and the group fulfilling it, may have very little benefit toward the organization's objectives as a whole. Among other things, the tools described in this chapter help to take the subjectivity out and provide an "objectivity spyglass" for the project initiation process.

Role of the Steering Committee

Organizations that have progressed in their project management standardization efforts normally have a group of decision makers, called the steering committee, that determines a work effort's viability, priority, and alignment with the organization's strategic objectives. This group has ultimate decision-making authority for the "go/no go" regarding projects, as well as guidelines to use when prioritizing projects. The following are examples of these prioritization guidelines:

- There can only be three active "Priority 1" projects at any given time.
- Projects that remain stagnant at "Low Priority" for six months are shelved.
- The decisions of project priority rest solely on the steering committee.

Members of the steering committee require tools to assess potential and ongoing projects objectively. Although political dynamics will likely come into play in the committee's prioritization/approval process, the tools described in this chapter help to standardize the new project request process, provide visibility into the outcome of the steering committee meetings, and objectively assess each new project request based on organizational value.

Tools

Of the various ways that organizations start new projects, there has to be an artifact that triggers the initiation for a given piece of work. We'll look at three products/approaches to managing these artifacts from the following perspectives:

- Flexibility of the system
- Integration with the existing EPM toolset
- Cost—both in monetary terms and in process/development work

The Proposals Feature in Project Server 2007

The Proposals feature in Project Server provides the application the "project management light" functionality of Microsoft Office SharePoint Server (MOSS). It is the function for which the Proposal Reviewers PWA security group was created. The idea is that any EPM user, by default, can create a new proposal. The user can create a summarized overview of the proposal and can enter specific task details. After this is done, a user from the Proposal Reviewers PWA security group can view the proposal and perform certain actions. These include modifying the proposal's summary or specific tasks, creating a resource plan for the proposal, changing the owner of the proposal, building the team for the proposal, changing the state of the proposal from proposed to approved or rejected, publishing the proposal, or converting the proposal to an enterprise project managed through Microsoft Office Project Professional 2007.

Creating the Proposal

When a user clicks the Proposals and Activities link from the Quick Launch Bar, a screen appears that shows all of the proposals to which that user has access, as shown in Figure 16-1. This is a contextually sensitive view that depends on the current user's category, defined by the resource breakdown structure (RBS). The user can click New and then Proposal and give high-level information about the project, enter details if he or she has them, and provide project-level enterprise field values to the proposal owner. After clicking the Save button, the user waits for a member of the Proposal Reviewers group to take action on the proposal. The user can check the status of the status of the proposal by returning to the Proposals and Activities page.

Awaiting the Proposal Reviewers' Approval

After the proposal is created (or possibly while it is being created, based on the creator's rights), a member of the Proposal Reviewers PWA security group can build the team for the project and create a resource plan for the proposal. If you have installed MOSS 2007 in the same farm as Project Server 2007, you can take advantage of the additional workflow capabilities that Office SharePoint Server 2007 provides. If the proposal is approved for promotion to a recognized project in the organization, the Proposal Reviewers group can convert the proposal to a project, indicating the approval and commencement of the piece of work.

Integrating with the Existing Toolset

Because the Proposals and Activities functionality is available by default with any new PWA site creation, there is no additional cost to enable this functionality. Although there are some potential drawbacks to using this approach, you may find that because there is no additional development or implementation effort required, this functionality supports your project initiation processes.

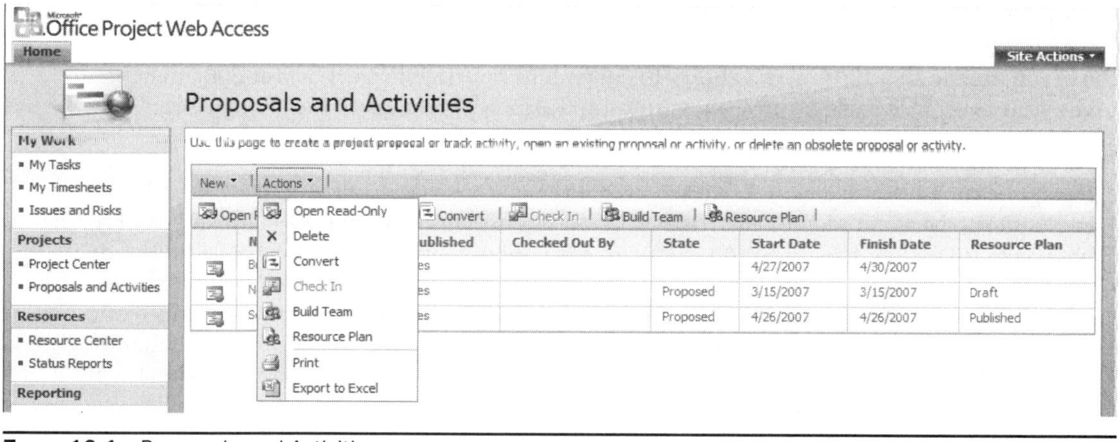

Figure 16-1 Proposals and Activities page

NOTE *The only custom fields that you can use at this stage of proposal creation are project-level custom fields. Likewise, if you have defined required project-level enterprise custom fields, they will force the user to provide values for them before saving the proposal. This has been an impediment for some companies, as they often require additional information that is specific to making the decision to approve the proposal, but gathering this information is frequently different than grouping information for the ongoing tracking of the project. In addition, by creating a proposal and assigning resources to it, the resources' availability will be affected regardless of the project's current state. Because the proposal can be converted to an enterprise project and there is no way to create a template for proposals, there is no way to enforce standardization of the proposals from the resource utilization or work breakdown structure (WBS) perspectives. The result is that these companies forego the use of the Proposals feature in favor of an existing or custom-built project initiation system.*

Project Portfolio Server 2007

If you are currently using Project Server 2003 and enjoy such features as the Portfolio Analyzer views or the Portfolio Modeler, you may be surprised to notice that in Project Server 2007 the word "Portfolio" is notably absent from all features and views. For example, the Portfolio Analyzer views have now been renamed to Data Analyzer views. Additionally, the Portfolio Modeler is no longer available in Project Server 2007. The reason is that the term "Portfolio" is being reserved to refer to the features and functionality available in Microsoft Office Project Portfolio Server 2007. Project Portfolio Server 2007 (now a member of the Office EPM family) is software that Microsoft purchased from UMT in January 2006 to help round out the portfolio management capabilities of the EPM toolset.

The easiest way to explain the differences between Project Server 2007 and Portfolio Server 2007 is this: Where Project Server 2007 helps you to do the projects *right,* Portfolio Server 2007 helps you do the *right* projects. Because the initiation and prioritization processes are usually rampant with subjectivity, Project Portfolio Server 2007 helps to remove the emotion and force objectivity in these two critical processes. It helps you achieve this by capturing metrics of critical budgetary, resource, and organizational strategy for measuring the value of each project. Through the Project Server Gateway, Portfolio Server 2007 maintains a tight, bidirectional connection with Project Server 2007 to provide advanced analytical assessment, modeling (what-if scenarios that provide a superset of the 2003 Portfolio Modeler), resource/ budget forecasting, and strategic alignment for projects across the organization. In addition, the ability to connect to multiple Project Server 2007 instances gives your executive team a single view into the various portfolios of the enterprise.

Cost of Project Portfolio Server

Licensing is similar to Project Server 2007, in that there is a Server License and a Client Access License (CAL)–based model for each user to access the server through Project Portfolio Server Web Access (PPSWA). This PPSWA CAL provides connectivity with Internet Explorer and other Office 2007 client applications. Although the cost of Microsoft Office Project Portfolio Server will depend on multiple factors, such as the type of organization that acquires it and the licensing agreement that you have with Microsoft, it is roughly equal in price to that of Microsoft Office Project Server 2007. In addition, there are significant adoption and maturity components involved to an implementation.

Custom Solution

In certain situations, a company may find itself in a situation where it needs more flexibility than the Proposals and Activities feature in Project Server 2007 provides, but does not require the mass of functionality provided by Microsoft Office Project Portfolio Server 2007. It needs a place where users can submit ideas and steering committees can evaluate each idea based on standardized criteria that the organization defines.

WSS to the Rescue

Because of the flexibility of the Windows SharePoint Services (WSS) platform, organizations can create an additional Web site that is focused on all things related to project management. This site would contain things like sample charter documents, project management process documentation, a glossary that is specific to the organization, a contact list for the project management office (PMO), and a new project request form. Whether it is a subsite of your PWA site (as shown in Figure 16-2) or a site of its own, WSS offers you extreme flexibility to craft a solution that fits to the way your users work and your PMO operates.

New Project Request Form

The portion of WSS that relates to the initiation processes can be a custom list that can capture new project requests from your organization in a standardized way using familiar tools. WSS supports the creation and application of workflow to make this capability a logic-driven tool for facilitating work requests across your organization. If the workflow capabilities don't raise the hairs on the back of your neck, you can utilize the built-in alerting functionality and Really Simple Syndication (RSS) capabilities of WSS to ensure that the right people know when changes happen to the list of new project requests, as shown in Figure 16-2.

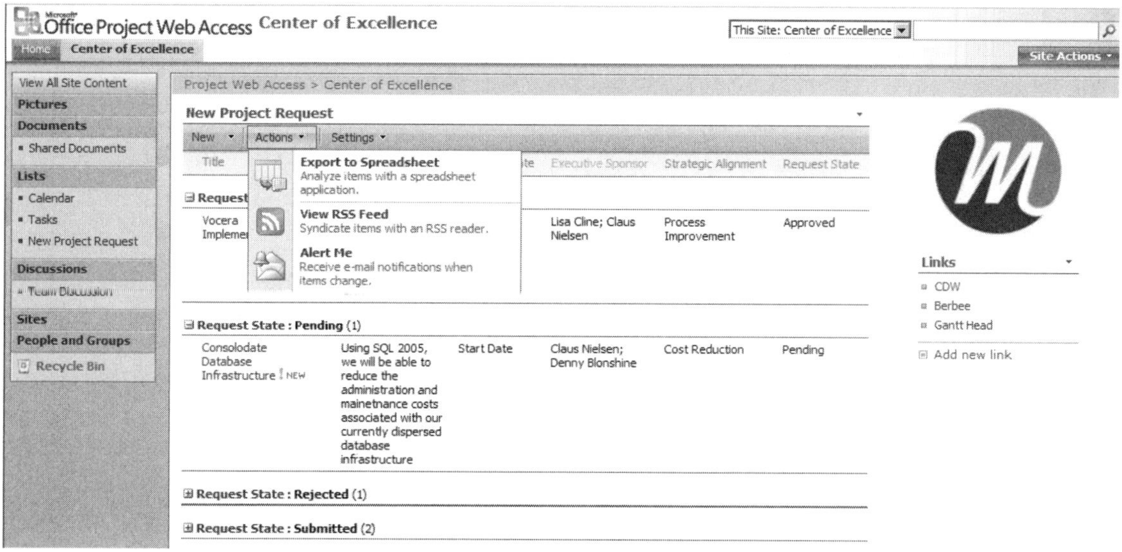

FIGURE 16-2 New project request form and Center of Excellence site

There is a detailed look at one way to execute this process in Chapter 27.

In this chapter, we've reviewed different approaches for handling new project requests within the Project Server 2007 toolset. Whereas the Proposals feature of Project Server 2007 is tightly integrated from the resource capacity and Project Server integration perspective, Microsoft Project Portfolio Server or a custom WSS site can provide a great deal of flexibility and customization to fit your organization's needs.

As you can see from the comparison chart in Table 16-1, each of the solutions discussed has its strong points to help you achieve operational efficiency when turning ideas into projects that help you work toward your organization's overall success.

	Relative Flexibility	Integration with Business Logic of Project Server 2007	Relative Development/ Implementation Costs
Built-in Proposals and Activities Feature	Low	High	Low
Project Portfolio Server 2007	High	High	High
Custom WSS List	High	Low	Low-Med

TABLE 16-1 Comparison Chart of New Project Request Solutions

CHAPTER 17

Integrating Project Server 2007 with External Systems

With the release of Project Server 2007, Microsoft has gone to great lengths to emphasize and promote the deep support for and capability to integrate with external systems. As a result, a number of organizations (including Microsoft) have built "connectors" for interoperability with Project Server 2007. These prebuilt connectors integrate with other Microsoft products such as Project Portfolio Server (PPS), Office SharePoint Server, and Visual Studio Team System. To integrate with other software vendors' products where a prebuilt connector does not exist, one is directed to the Project 2007 software development kit (SDK) provided by Microsoft. The SDK, located at http://msdn2.microsoft.com/en-us/library/ms512767.aspx, provides a wealth of information for integrating third-party applications with Project Server 2007. For example, if you wanted to share resource information between SAP and Project Server 2007, you would start with the SDK to become familiar with the Project Server Interface (PSI) calls and methods, and then work toward developing a solution that fits your specific organizational needs using your software development methodology.

Project Portfolio Server 2007

PPS 2007, a companion product of Project Server 2007, facilitates the objective analysis of investments as they relate to your organization's strategies. For integration with Project Server 2007, the Project Server Gateway is the connector that provides a bidirectional link to expose resource, schedule, and custom field information. In addition, the Project Portfolio Server Interface (PPSI) is the provided read-only application program interface (API) for exposing PPS 2007 information to third-party applications. Although it does connect to the Project Server 2007 PSI, PPS 2007 and the Project Server Gateway do not integrate with Project Server 2003 and its associated API. In addition, PPS 2007 does not integrate with the Enterprise Resource Planning (ERP) component of proposals and activity plans. More information about PPS can be found at http://office.microsoft.com/en-us/portfolioserver.

Project Server 2007 Visual Studio Team System Connector

The Microsoft Visual Studio Team System (VSTS) is a set of integrated software development tools that groups of developers can use to manage complex software projects. Traditionally, VSTS was able to integrate with the Microsoft Office Project Standard or Project Professional clients directly. In late 2006, driven by customer demand, Avanade created a connector that gained quite a lot of popularity. This connector enabled synchronization between Project Server 2003 and VSTS. The usage model was that software development teams work within VSTS, whereas project managers work within Microsoft Office Project Professional. The connector allowed these users to continue to work within their preferred applications, but offered the added advantage of utilizing the task management and control, resource availability, project rollup, and reporting of those projects through Enterprise Project Management (EPM). Although this tool provided the much needed functionality of software development and oversight entities, the setup and maintenance proved challenging.

In mid-2007, the VSTS Rangers, Microsoft Consulting, and the Project Product Team released the Project Server 2007 VSTS Connector. This new solution has the same model for use as its predecessor, but it was specifically designed for Project Server 2007. The installation and documentation for this release are much improved and can be found at http://www.codeplex.com/pstfsconnector.

Microsoft Project Client Add-Ins

In the previous sections, we discussed some of the tools used to integrate with Microsoft Office Project Server 2007. These tools generally connect to the PSI via Web service calls to perform some action within Project Server. In addition to these server-side capabilities, there are add-ins to the Microsoft Project client that have been built (mostly) by third parties that extend the capabilities of this already very capable tool. The functions of these add-in tools range from integration with ERP or financial applications to helping generate advanced reports and extreme analysis of your project data through Project Professional. A frequently updated list of these Microsoft Project companion products can be found at http://project.mvps.org/comprods.htm.

Developing custom integration solutions for your instance of Project Server 2007 will usually begin with the Project Developer Portal, the SDK, and the Project programmability blog found at http://msdn2.microsoft.com. In these places, you'll find detailed how-to articles, programming references, and code samples for customizing your Project Server environment to meet your specified design goals. Along with these resources, there are links to expert developers' blogs that provide detailed solution examples for customizing your EPM environment.

NOTE *Managing software development projects can be a challenging task, and if you use Project Server and Project Web Access for tracking the work being done to customize Project Server functionality, at some point you may find the effect similar to walking into a hall of mirrors (where you use a tool to track the work that is being done on the tool that you use to track the work that is done on the tool). When these situations occur, the developer should increase his or her Mountain Dew/blood ratio (MD/B) and be reminded that development and testing should never be done on your production EPM environment.*

If you use an RSS reader, such as Microsoft Office Outlook 2007, or the free Web-based RSS reader on Live.com, you will be able to import a list of EPM-specific RSS feeds so that you can stay up to date on the latest EPM happenings at http://blogs.msdn.com/project/archive/2007/02/01/so-many-blogs-so-little-time.aspx. You can find the Project Developer Portal at http://msdn2.microsoft.com/en-us/office/aa905469.aspx, and the Project Programmability Blog at http://blogs.msdn.com/project_programmability.

In addition, there is a large pool of consulting organizations that specialize in Project Server development. A list of partners with EPM competencies in your geographical region can be found at http://directory.microsoft.com.

PART V

Project Server in Action

CHAPTER 18

Time Tracking and Task Updates

Time and task entry is where the resources in your organization will likely spend the majority of their time when logged on to the system. The consistency and accuracy of the resource's input determine the consistency and accuracy of the reports that will be consumed by the resource managers, project managers, and executives. Knowing this, you should put considerable thought into how the resources in your organization will provide these data in a consistent, accurate, repeatable, and (perhaps the most important for your initial proof of concept [PoC] or pilot) uncomplicated way. In this chapter, we'll briefly discuss Enterprise Project Management's (EPM) history of time tracking, some features and options that you have for implementing it in Project Server 2007, and the roles which play a large part in the time and task entry process. Along the way, we'll keep an eye on the Holy Grail of the PoC (and your initial stabs at EPM implementation): simplicity.

How Task-Time Entry Has Evolved

In previous versions of Project Server, when a company wanted to implement a timesheet-like function for users of Project Web Access (PWA), it applied something called Managed Time Periods. These Managed Time Periods enabled an administrator to define and ultimately lock down time periods after they had passed, facilitating the requirements of data consistency for historical record and for integrating with external systems. This model posed several problems; for example, a project manager modifying actual work on time when its period had closed would create inconsistencies. Perhaps the summary of the problem was the overall inflexibility of the task updating and timesheet functionality. For example, if an assignment was originally scheduled for 10 hours and the resource worked for one day on the task and completed it (by marking it 100 percent complete), the logic of Project Server equates 100 percent of a 10-hour task to 10 hours of actual work by the resource. If an approval system was in place that involved the resource's manager (via the resource breakdown structure [RBS]), the discrepancy became consistently unbearable. The system required more flexibility.

The Divorce of Task Status and Timesheets

As a result of this limitation (and many requests to the product team), timesheets and task status functionality were separated at the birth of Project Server 2007. Now these two related mechanisms require the resource's deliberate attention. Whereas task status is used by the project manager to understand the project's schedule based on the resource's input, timesheets are used by the resource's manager for accountability and potential integration with third-party payroll or accounting systems.

Process Options

Because of the flexibility in the EPM 2007 system as it relates to task updates and timesheets, organizations have many options to configure, and several factors will determine these settings. Given that the task updates are the life blood of your EPM system (that is, the task updates are the channel by which information is communicated between the project manager and the resource), you have some options for the timesheet integration:

- **Linking task status to timesheets** By administratively linking the task status to the timesheet functionality, you are in effect removing the possibility that what is entered in a user's timesheet will differ from what is sent to a project manager for task status. Users will be able to modify only what is in their timesheet and will be forced to import the timesheet to provide their project manager status on their tasks. There are some drawbacks to this approach, such as the inability of a resource to

Timesheets vs. Task Updates

Although these two mechanisms for capturing resource time seem similar, each has its own purpose as it relates to the scope and the type of activity being reported:

- **Timesheets**
  - Capture all of a resource's work
  - Can use different classifications, for different billing rate, or applying work around a task (such as travel time associated with a task)
  - Ensure that input by the resource has no effect on that resource's capacity (this is explained later in this chapter)
  - Play the communication role between the resource and his or her functional (resource) manager
- **Task updates**
  - Capture the resource's project-based work
  - Capture task-level information such as remaining work
  - Capture information related to a task, such as linked issues, risks, or supporting documents
  - Play the communication role between the resource and a project manager

report a modified Remaining Work value to the project manager. This is often a dealbreaker in organizations with advanced time reporting requirements.

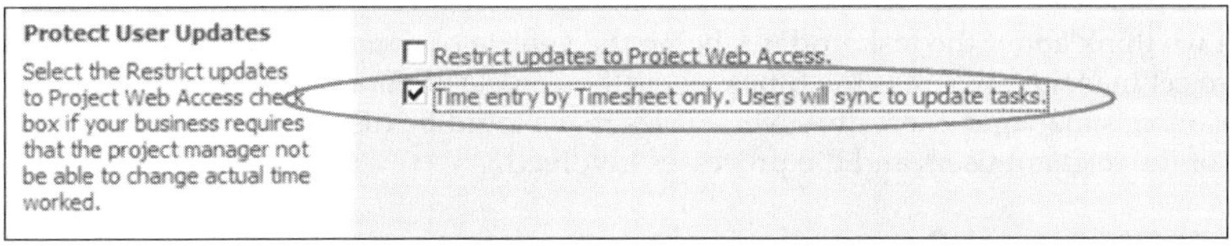

- **Updating task throughout the week and creating and submitting timesheets at the end of the week** Resources fill out and submit their task updates on a daily basis, and then at the end of the week create and submit their timesheet, which is prepopulated with the tasks and their actuals.
- **Using both timesheets and task updates independently** In this instance, the resource manually fills out each, and has a weekly (or possibly monthly) deadline by which they are submitted.
- **Update the timesheets daily and submitting the timesheets weekly (almost always the appropriate time window)** This is immediately followed by importing the Project related time entries into the task updates and submitting them to the Project Manager.
- **Using the task updates much like they did in previous versions of PWA** That is, resources use the timesheets mechanism only for capturing administrative or nonworking time.

The following are some questions that you may ask to help determine the method of reporting and the tools used:

1. Is Project Server 2007 intended to replace an existing timesheet or time card system?
2. Do you need to capture all time that a resource spends at work?
3. Do you want to involve the process by which a resource requests vacation time from his or her manager? And if that vacation time is approved, do you want to automatically create a calendar exception for that resource across all of the projects and tasks to which he or she is assigned?
4. Do your project management methodologies dictate that task status be relayed from resource to project manager in the percentage complete, or by actual hours worked?

NOTE *Although there are a number of reporting options in Project Server for exposing timesheet information (including a cube in Analysis Services that is devoted to it), the information available from the task updates is naturally tied to projects and resources and flows through the majority of the reports available in Project Server 2007.*

Different Roles Associated with the Task Update and Timesheet Processes

When we think about the task updates being the vehicle of data sent from the resource to the project manager, whereas the timesheet is the vehicle of data sent from the resource to the resource's manager, there are several roles that should be discussed. Figure 18-1 shows some of the relevant users and the processes involved.

Default Assignment Owner

The default assignment owner, specified in the Resource Detail page, allows you to specify a proxy for this user's assignments. This is helpful when the user is unable to enter his or her time directly in PWA. The default assignment owner will be the target of all tasks assigned to the user. In other words, he or she will be responsible for providing task status for all resources for whom they are designated the default assignment owner.

NOTE *Although the actual hours that the default assignment owner submits will prepopulate the resource's timesheet, the default assignment owner cannot perform the Import Timesheet function on these tasks, as it will import from his or her timesheet, not the resource's.*

Timesheet Manager

When a resource is first added to a PWA site, that resource is specified as the Timesheet Manager. This simply indicates that there is no timesheet approval process and that all timesheet submissions will be considered automatically approved. In scenarios where timesheet approval is used, the timesheet manager is typically the resource's functional manager or a person who is responsible for ensuring that the resource is working to expected levels of quantity. Although we'll see that there is flexibility in specifying this person, the timesheet approver is typically higher than his or her resources in the RBS.

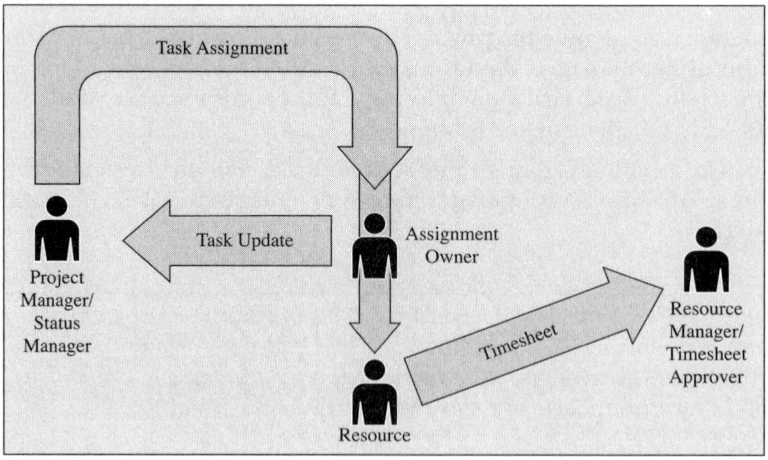

FIGURE 18-1 Assignment, task status, and timesheets

This designation of timesheet manager is made in the properties of the resource whose timesheet is to be approved. A typical scenario is that on Monday morning, the resources are expected to have submitted their timesheets for the previous week. The timesheet manager then validates the timesheets and approves them by Monday afternoon.

There may be instances where a resource's timesheet manager is not available to approve a timesheet. In this case, a user can redirect where the timesheet is sent. It is important to note that for the user to redirect his or her timesheet, the following requirements must be met:

1. Fixed Approval Routing is turned off (this option is discussed later in this chapter).
2. Other users (peers of your regular timesheet approver) in PWA have the Accept Timesheet global permission and the Approve Timesheet category permissions allowed. (These permissions are granted by default via membership in the Resource Managers PWA group.)

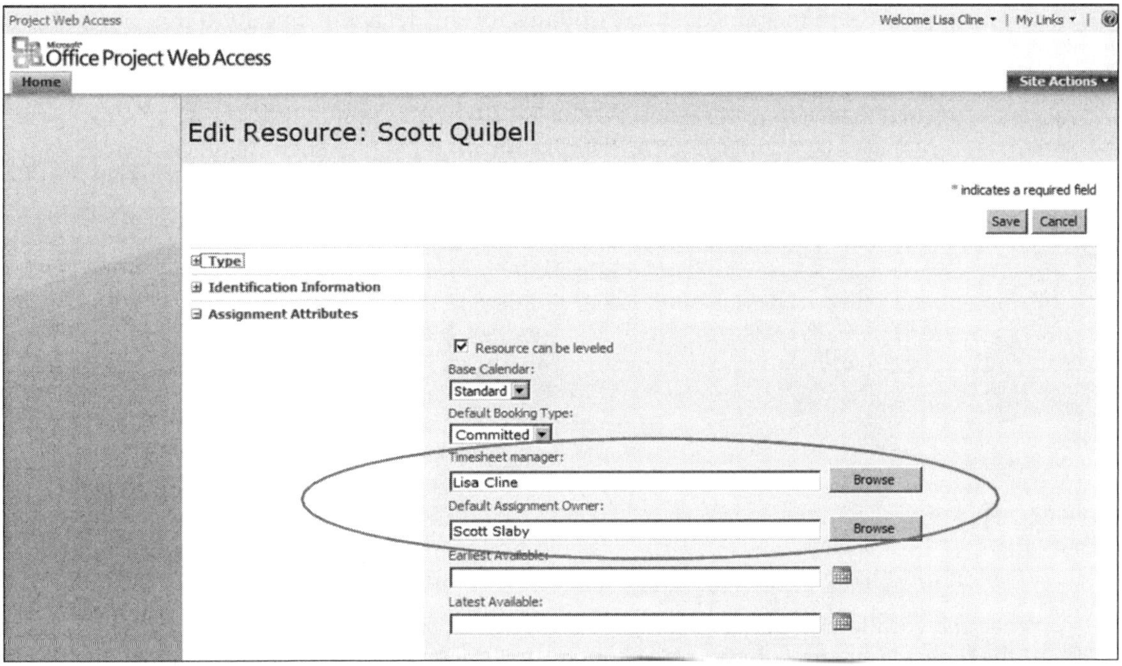

Status Manager

The status manager role in Project Server 2007 is typically played by the project manager for the project. It is represented in the system as a task-level field that by default designates who created the assignment, so the system knows to whom to send the resource's task update. In Project Server 2003, this field was not exposed through Project Professional or PWA and it was unique for the assignment, so if you had multiple resources assigned to the same task (with multiple assignments), it was possible to have multiple status managers for the same task. In Project Server 2007, all assignments for the same task share a single status manager.

PART V

Using the Status Manager Field

The Status Manager field is a very useful tool to use when a project manager goes on vacation. One method of addressing this common scenario is to complete the following steps:

1. After the outgoing project manager addresses all pending status updates, the temporary project manager can open the project, expose the Status Manager column in the project plan, and use the drop-down list for each task to specify himself or herself as the status manager to whom the updates need to be redirected.
2. Upon publishing of the plan, the temporary project manager receives task status updates for the specified tasks.
3. When a resource goes into the details of the task to which he or she has been assigned, that resource will see the new temporary project manager listed as the approval manager. All status updates for this task will be sent to this approval manager.

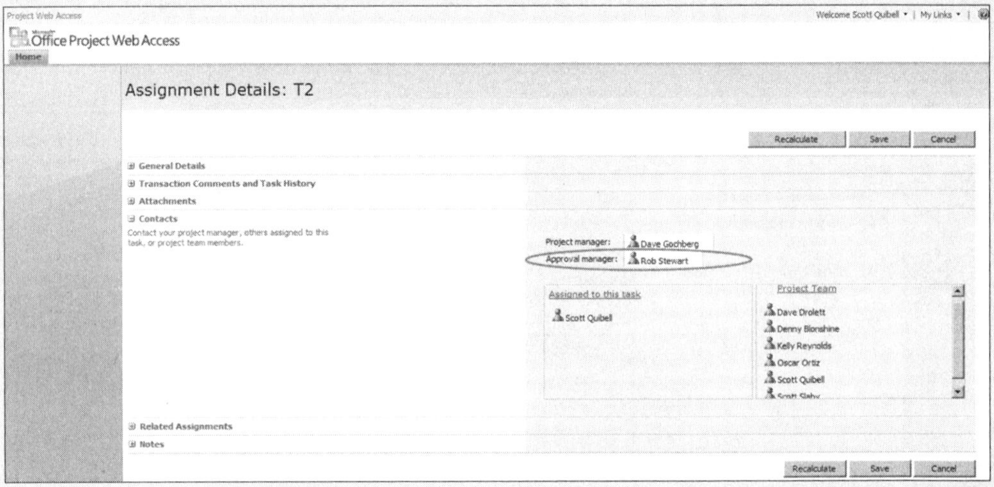

When the vacationing project manager returns, he or she can open the project, insert the Status Manager column, and change all of the tasks' Status Manager fields back to their original state. (See Chapter 21 for more information about the Status Manager macro.)

Features and Pages Related to Time and Task Entry

In PWA, several tools can be configured for your specific organization's needs. (More information on the usage of these timesheet and task entry pages can be found in Chapter 22.)

Fixed Approval Routing

Fixed Approval Routing refers to the timesheet functionality only and determines whether a resource can redirect the approval of his or her timesheet to another resource manager. If Fixed Approval Routing is not enabled, the resource can make this redirection upon clicking Save and Submit from their timesheet. If it is enabled, the timesheet is submitted immediately, without the intermediate step.

My Work

The My Work page is intended to be a single location for resources to interact with their assignments and timesheets in PWA. The page has three tabs, each of which displays information differently:

- **Tasks** As the default view, the Tasks page is nearly identical to the My Tasks page, accessed from the Quick Launch Bar. The My Assignments View is used to display current task assignments for the PWA user.
- **Timesheet** This view takes the user to the current timesheet period to facilitate quick creation and entry of timesheet information. Using this page, you would typically bypass the My Timesheets page, as you will be taken to the current time period and offered the ability to create a new timesheet if one does not already exist.
- **Schedule** This is a view of current tasks in a monthly calendar view.

Notes

Notes, as represented in Project Server 2007, allow a resource to view the notes that the project manager may have associated with the task through Project Professional 2007 or add task-specific information intended for the project manager.

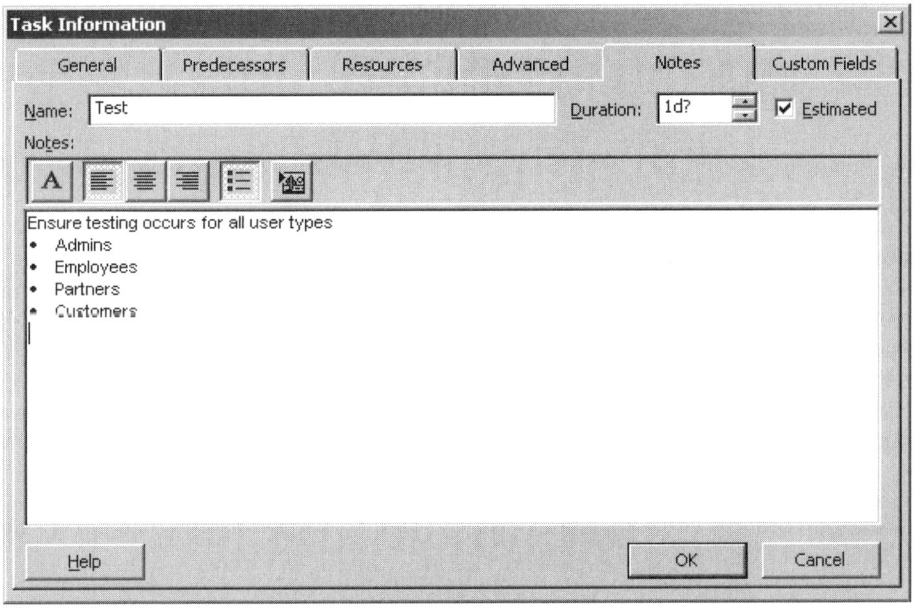

Notes are exposed through PWA in the following places:

- The My Tasks or My Work (Tasks) View in the indicator column
- The Assignment Details page in the Notes section
- The Task Updates approval page

New to this release of Project Server is the resource's append-only rights to the notes associated with his or her PWA tasks.

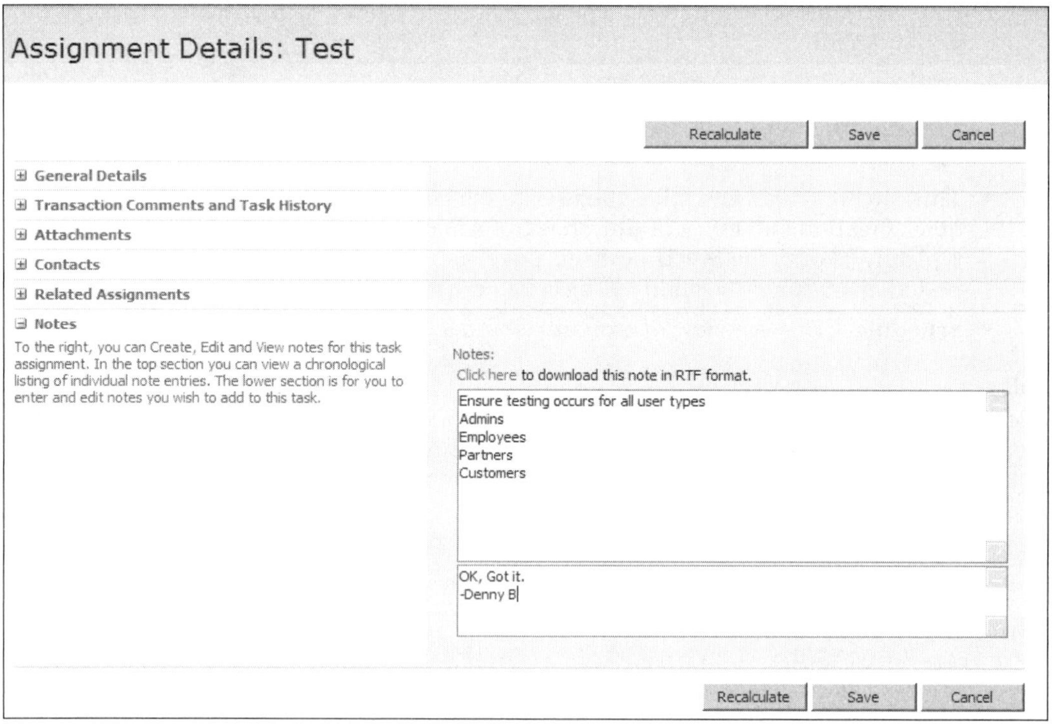

Transaction Comments

Transaction comments come in a few different flavors, but each provides timestamps on actions that happen to the item that a user is submitting (whether it is a task update or a timesheet). The chance to submit transaction comments occurs when resources submit their timesheet or task updates. The project manager can view the task update transaction comments by clicking the name of the task in the Task Updates page prior to accepting or rejecting the updates. The resource can also view the comments from the Assignment Details page in the Transaction Comments and Task History section. (If you submit changes for multiple tasks in a single submittal and provide transaction comments, those comments are then associated with all of the tasks that you are submitting.) For timesheets, the most recent transaction comments are exposed in the My Timesheets View.

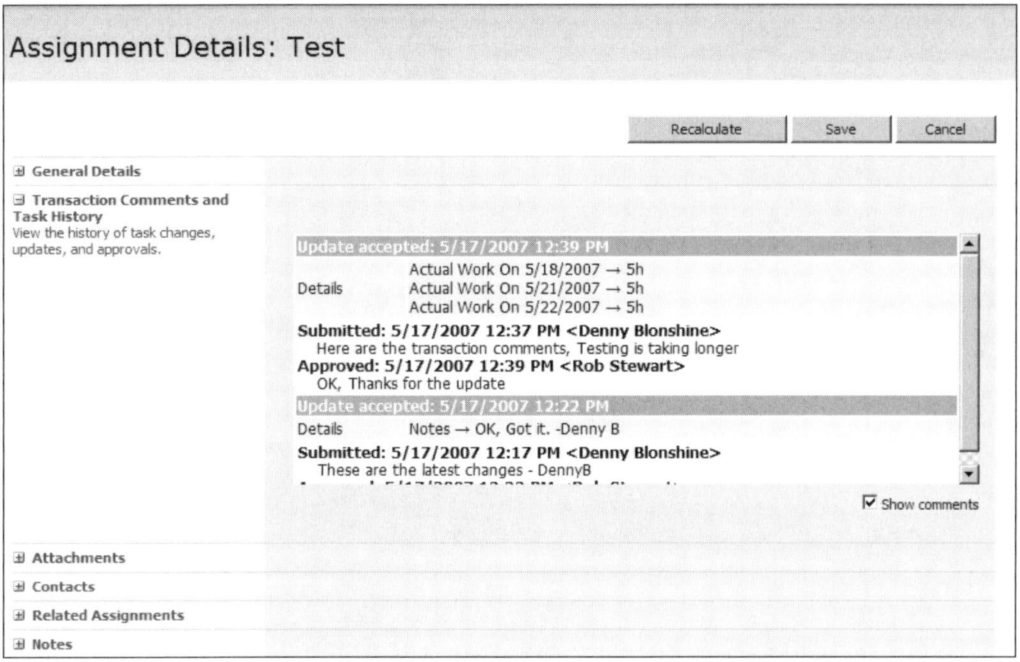

Timesheet Auditing

Project Server 2007 enables timesheet auditing. Although there is no out-of-the-box user interface for accessing this log and the data contained in it, some organizations need to be able to look at a large number of timesheets over a given period to determine whether resources have entered 40 hours of work for the week, or which resources have time entered in their timesheets but haven't submitted them. For this need, we turn to the Project Server Report Pack for SQL Server Reporting Services. To use the Report Pack, you will need to be using at least SQL Server 2005 SP1 with SQL Server Reporting Services 2005. To create or customize reports, you'll also need SQL Server Business Intelligence Development Studio, which is installed with SQL Server along with Microsoft Visual Studio 2005. The Project Server Report Pack is part of the Microsoft Office Project 2007 Software Development Kit (SDK) and can be found at http://msdn2.microsoft.com/en-us/library/bb428831.aspx.

If you were to think of the EPM system as a garden, time tracking and task updates make up the water and sunlight that give it life. Project Server reports are the results of your effort—beautiful plants that consume the water and light—and your standardized project management methodologies are the rows that keep your garden from becoming an unmanageable jungle. It's the maintenance of this EPM ecosystem that will determine whether you can achieve consistent, powerful, high-yield results that the executives will expect from this toolset and your people.

As EPM evolves and the capabilities of the toolset grow, the overall complexity of the system must naturally increase as well. Often overlooked, timesheet and task entry standardization helps to ensure that you are providing your EPM system a balanced diet of normalized data in order to produce the consistent and highly accurate reports that your executives demand.

CHAPTER 19

Reporting and Views

The reporting capabilities in the Enterprise Project Management (EPM) toolset are continually evolving. Whether it is through the deep and flexible Data Analysis views or through the rich reporting interface of the Visual Reports feature of Project Professional, this evolution continues in the 2007 version of this toolset. Whereas in Chapter 11 we discussed what views are available in Project Server 2007, in this chapter we'll dig a little deeper into some of the most commonly used views and the user's motivation for viewing them. Along the way, we'll talk about some specific solutions for extending the reporting capabilities of Project Server 2007.

Types of Views

Rarely will a single person use all the views available within Project Web Access (PWA). This is not to imply that people are inherently lazy, but rather to recognize that because this toolset depends on the participation of several different types of users, there are specific out-of-the-box views that are targeted specifically to specific roles but may not be relevant to others. Our discussion of the different views will begin at the macro level, where an executive might be, with the intent of showing how these views give a holistic view of the organization's progress. We'll then progress to the views that dig deeper into the organization's resources, projects, and tasks, and conclude the chapter with an examination of Project Professional, which can be used to generate powerful reports in conjunction with other members of the Microsoft Office family.

Common PWA View Functions

Several functions are common among most of the PWA views discussed in this chapter. These functions include the ability to export the currently viewed grid to Microsoft Office Excel and to format the currently viewed grid for printing.

Export to Excel

Exporting view grid data to Microsoft Excel can be a very effective way to utilize the sorting and calculation capabilities of this spreadsheet application. This action utilizes an ActiveX control that was likely installed on your first visit to the PWA site to open Microsoft Excel and populate a blank spreadsheet with the data currently exposed in the view. Exporting to

Excel works a bit differently when you perform the action from a Data Analysis View. In this case, Microsoft Excel makes a direct connection to SQL Server Analysis Services and works directly with the cube data. It is important to note that exporting to Excel exports only the table data, not the charts or graphical representations of the data.

Print

When formatting a particular view for printing, you will usually come to a screen where you can choose to add or remove available columns in preparation for printing the data to paper. The exception is when you are viewing resource availability. In this case, the date range units that you specified in the View options will be your columns, with the capacity, availability, and time dedicated to specific projects grouped by resource as the rows in the report.

Data Analysis Views

As perhaps one of the most powerful reporting view types available, the Data Analysis views are a high-impact, self-service, business intelligence reporting tool. When introduced in Project Server 2002, the Portfolio Analyzer views were the first out-of-the-box online analytical processing (OLAP) cube-based reporting tool that Microsoft had offered to that point. Although they were (and still are) read-only, they provide powerful pivot table and pivot chart capabilities exposed through the Office Web Components (OWC). Since that time, the name has changed and capabilities have increased, as not only have the options for cube building increased, but the number of cubes built has increased dramatically as well.

The dynamic nature of a Data Analysis View enables executives and resource managers to create the view they need on the fly. For example, if the executive is looking at the total amount of resource work during the year 2007, he or she can quickly add a dimension to this view to show how that resource work may align with the organization's strategic initiatives during the year. In addition, the ability to create calculated totals or use Microsoft Office Excel to manipulate the view makes this an extremely potent reporting vehicle. Creating some initial Data Analysis views will be one of the administrator's chores during the initial proof of concept (PoC) and pilot phases.

NOTE *Although there is some initial setup for configuring the building of your OLAP cube, after it is complete, the cube will continue to be updated using those settings every time that it is updated. Specifying custom fields for inclusion in the cube building process is covered in more detail in Chapter 12.*

Security of the Data Analysis Views

The Data Analysis views have different layers of user access. First is the access to the OLAP data, which is typically given through membership in a group that has the View OLAP Data permission allowed. This permission has a unique purpose, as users with this permission are given access to the OLAP data via cube role membership when the cube is built or updated. Having this permission also allows users to connect their instance of Microsoft Office Excel directly to the cube to consume all of its data. So in some respects, the security of the OLAP data can be thought of as an all-or-nothing affair, whereas access can be granted in different layers.

The next layer of access is by the categories with which the Data Analysis views are associated. You may find that different types of users consistently use a particular arrangement of dimensions and fact tables with a histogram and pivot table. In this scenario, you might create a number of views that are targeted to a specific executive or resource manager category.

The final layer of access is found in the individual Data Analysis views. As an administrator, you can lock down certain aspects of these views, such as whether you wish to make the Field List or whether the toolbar (from which you can export to Excel) will be viewable.

Resource Center Views

The Resource Center views have taken on some new capabilities in Project Server 2007. In addition to being especially helpful for resource managers and project managers to track the work, capacity, and future availability of the resources in the organization, they are also the method by which a user opens the Enterprise Resource Pool. Although the views display information about the work and assignments in your organization, these views are specifically resource-centric. So suppose, for example, that you know of an upcoming project and you need to assess your team's availability quickly during the proposed timeframe; the Resource Center is where you would start.

Project Server ships with five Resource Center views, all of which enable the user to view the assignments and availability for the selected resources and are contextually sensitive (that is, you see only the resources that you have the right to see). In addition to being able to select the checkbox next to the resources and view their assignments or availability, you have three other options that provide additional capabilities:

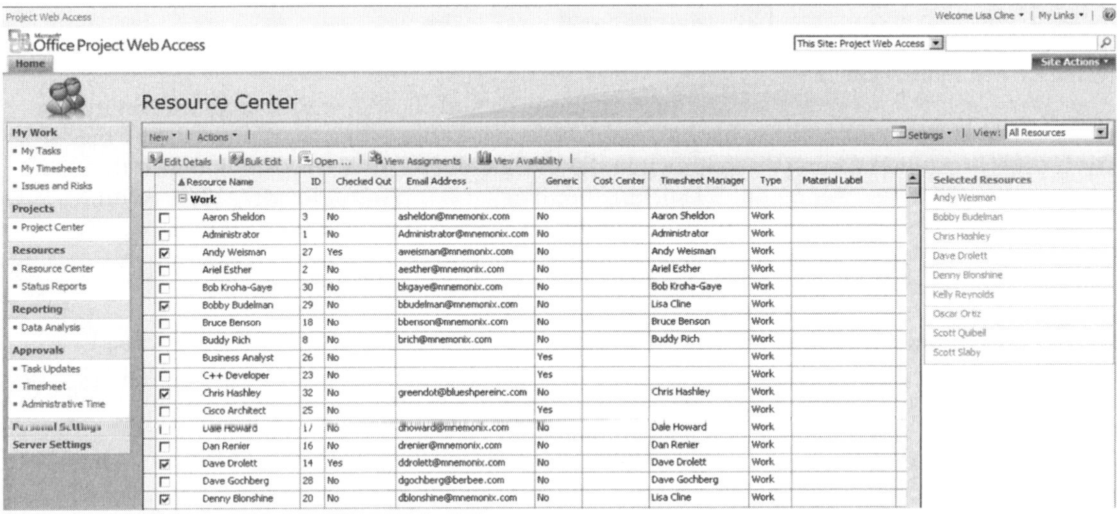

- **Edit Details** If you select a single resource, you will be able to modify a great deal of information about that resource and view even more, including identification information, assignment attributes, the base calendar that the resource uses, any custom resource fields that you may have added to the system, as well as group and team information. If you selected multiple resources and clicked Edit Details, you would be modifying each resource individually, with the ability to save and continue to move to the next resource serially. You might use such functionality when you need to assign an RBS value to a small number of users.

- **Bulk Edit** This function allows you to do just as the name implies: make edits to the group of resources in bulk fashion. Times where you may use this function are when you need to change a large group of users' RBS values to the same value.
- **Open** Performing the Open function is identical to opening the Enterprise Resource Pool, in that a local version of Microsoft Office Project Professional 2007 will open on your desktop (if that version is installed) and the resources will be brought into a resource sheet. You can then perform actions on the resources by taking advantage of Project Pro's sorting, quickly adding columns and quick fill capabilities.

Resource Assignment Views

After you select resources from the Resource Center View and click View Resource Assignments, you are taken to the Summary Resource Assignment View, which is a Gantt type view that shows information about the projects and assignment progress associated with each resource. You can perform several functions from this view, including the following:

- Exporting the list to Excel (as discussed earlier in this chapter)
- Formatting the current view for printing (as discussed earlier in this chapter)

Typically the resource managers use this view when they need to understand the progress that their resources have reported, or view the type of work that is planned for the near future to which their resources have been assigned.

Resource Availability Views

After you select resources from the Resource Center View and click View Resource Availability, you are taken to the Resource Availability page. This page consists of a chart provided by the OWC (likely installed when you first visited the PWA site) and an accompanying grid that supports the chart representation. By clicking Settings, you can select the date range within which you are viewing the availability and assigned work commitments of your resources. You also can include proposed bookings in this view to take those proposed assignments into consideration. There are four default views for resource availability:

- **Assignment Work by Resource** This view allows you to see an overall timephased work view for the resources selected and the timeframe specified. The red Capacity line in the chart is especially helpful, as the resource's capacity will be affected by the resources' individual calendars, their maximum units, and any exceptions that may lie therein (think "nonworking" administrative time categories). Beneath the chart are the details, which are grouped by resource and show the projects to which they have been committed during the timeframe specified. (Although the chart will change dynamically when you select or deselect resources, the Details section will remain static, based on the resources you originally selected from the Resource Center page.)
- **Assignment Work by Project** Just as the name implies, this view will give you a view of to which projects the selected resources are committed. This view can be helpful in assessing the total amount of work as it relates to projects and the project requesters.

- **Remaining Availability** Although this view can be very effective when resources have availability during the timeframe, the best way to show when they are overallocated is either by using the Print command or by using the Assignment Work by Resource or Work Resource Availability views, as the Remaining Availability chart does not represent negative availability values clearly.
- **Work** This is an effective line graph to show how much work the individual users have assigned to them. Each resource is represented by a different colored line and you can toggle each user's line on and off in the graph. The most effective ways to analyze these data is either through the displayed view or by using the Print command, as the Export to Excel function might possibly leave out critical information. (Ensure that your Project Server 2007 environment is updated to the latest Service Pack level.)

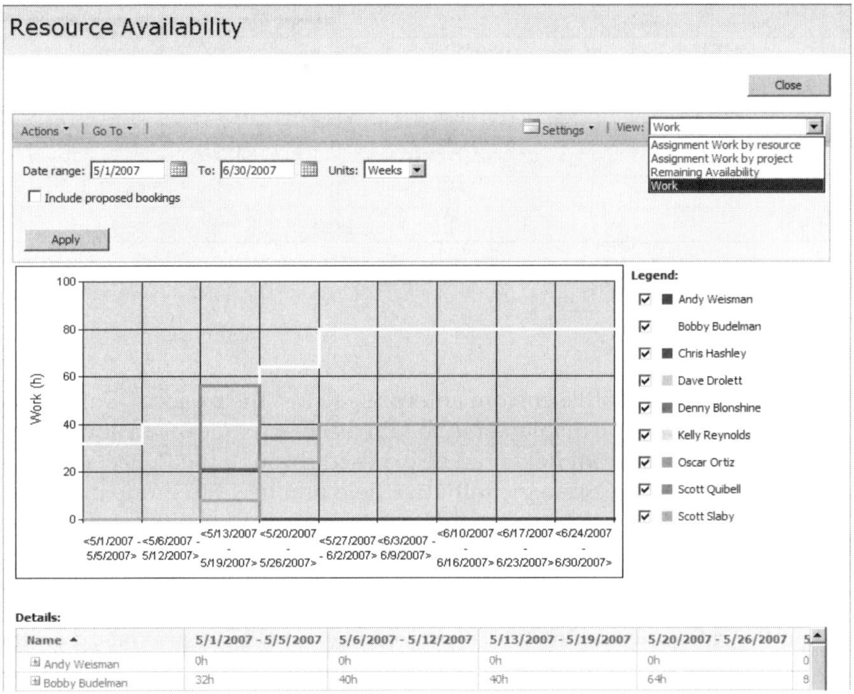

Project Center Views

The Project Center views are intended to give the viewer the overall status of all of the projects with which they are involved in the organization. In project terms, these views display row zero or summary information for each project. The Project Center views by default display information about the whole project—for example, the project's total work and total cost. Although these views specialize in exposing project summary information, there are techniques to make task-level information "bubble up" to these summary views, as shown in Figure 19-1. In this example, each project would have a task named GoLive.

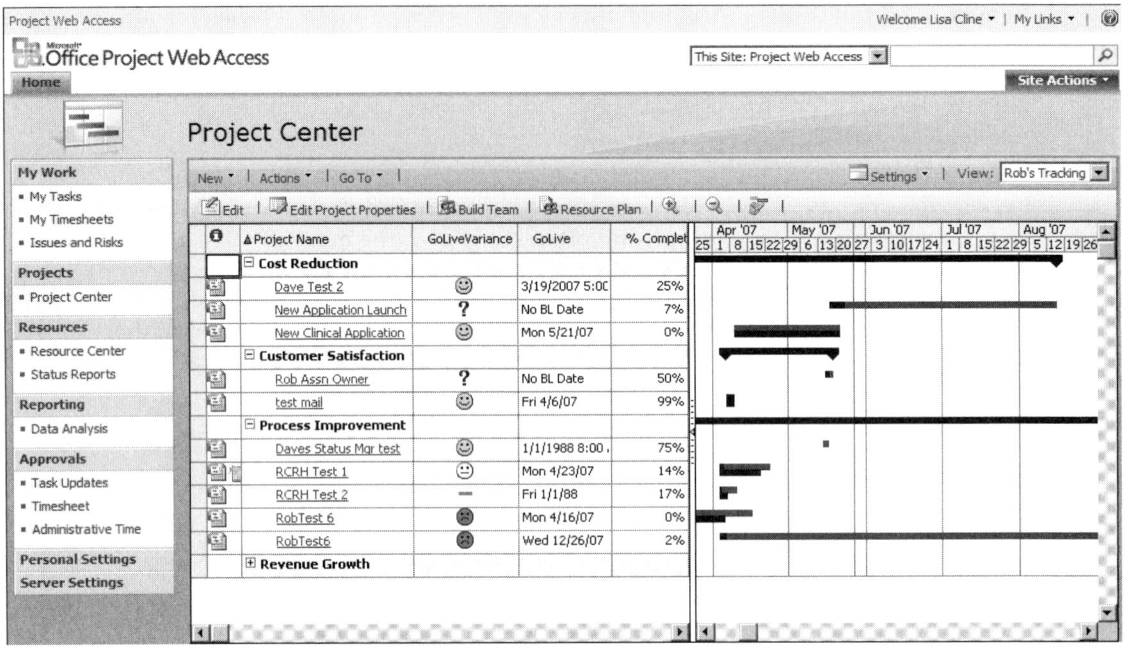

FIGURE 19-1 Project Center View displaying task-level information

Using baselines and a series of five custom enterprise fields, the projects' GoLive task can "bubble up" to row zero and be displayed in the Project Center views. In addition, because all project-level enterprise custom fields can be exposed through the Project Center views, in this view we've exposed the Strategic Initiative field and use it to group our projects.

Security for Project Center Views

By default, members of the My Organization and My Projects categories have access to all of the Project Center views. Because the views are made available by the category association and the categories define which projects the viewer can see (based on their relationship with the project and its resources), by default executives can see all of the projects active in PWA, resource managers can see the projects that involve their resources, project managers can see the projects that they are managing, and team members can see only summary information for the projects with which they are directly involved.

View Options for Project Center Views

When the View options are exposed for Project Center views, you have additional capabilities to specify what types of projects you wish to see and how you want to see them:

- **Show Summary Rollup** By selecting this checkbox, you can see the summary progress of grouped projects.
- **Show Time with Date** This option displays the time of day with the dates exposed.

Displaying Milestones Across Projects

If you have a set of standardized milestones that span projects and you need to expose these milestones in a Project Center View, there are three general tasks you must perform. First, you must create five enterprise custom fields for each milestone that you want to expose. These task- and project-level enterprise custom fields test for the name of a specific milestone, elevate it to the project level, and perform the calculation for variance. Second, you need to create a view that exposes the desired milestone fields. And finally, you must modify your enterprise templates to ensure standardization for new projects being brought into your EPM system. For each project to calculate this variance, there must be baseline data with which to compare.

Five fields are required for each milestone:

- Two task-level Date fields with maximum rollup. These test for the task name for the planned and baseline finish date (for example, GoLiveTask and GoLiveTaskBL):

```
IIf([Name]="GoLive",[Finish],"1/1/1998"
IIf([Name]="GoLive",[Baseline Finish],"1/1/1998"
```

- Two project-level text fields (for example, GoLive and GoLiveBL):

```
IIf([Baseline Finish]>99999, "No BL Date",(GoLiveTask))
IIf([Baseline Finish]>99999, "No BL Date",(GoLiveTaskBL))
```

- One project-level text field that performs the variance calculation and provides the graphical indicator:

```
IIf([Baseline Finish]>99999,"No Baseline", IIF(right[GoLive],2)=88,
"No GoLive Milestone",(ProjDateValue ([GoLive])-ProjDateValue
([GoLiveBL]))))
```

For more detailed instructions on the creation of Project Center views, see Chapter 9.

- **Show Proposals and Activities** This option includes all project proposals and activities in the Project Center View.
- **Show Inserted Subprojects** If you select this checkbox, any project that has been inserted into another project will be visible in the Project Center View; otherwise the user will need to select the Master Project and view its subproject through the Project Details View or other means.

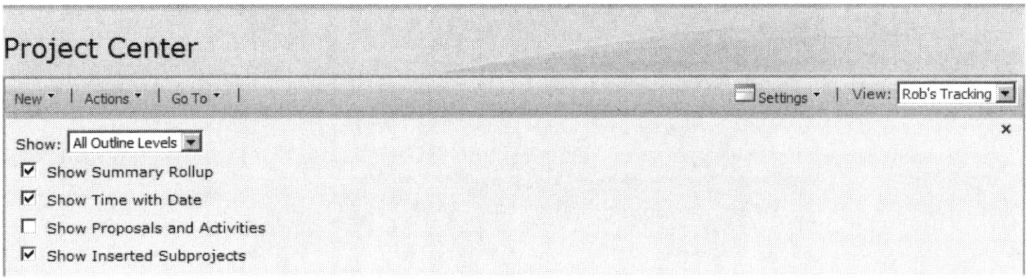

Project Views

Drilling down into the specifics of the work happening in your organization is a shining facet of the EPM system. One of the paths that expose this jewel begins with the Project Center views; then, by clicking on a project's name, you travel to the Project Details View or project views. These Project Details views provide information about each task as it is tracked in PWA. If Master Projects are saved and published to Project Server 2007, the subprojects will be exposed through the Project Details views of the Master Project. As with the Project Center views, the user has a number of options when viewing the Project Details views. The number of Project Details views available to the user is determined by the user's category affiliation, as each of the Project Details views is by default associated with at least one category.

Edit Project Properties

If the project is checked in and the user has the appropriate permissions on it, clicking the Edit Project Properties button allows the user to modify information about the project, including the project name, the project owner, and any lookup table-driven, project-level enterprise custom fields that may have been exposed.

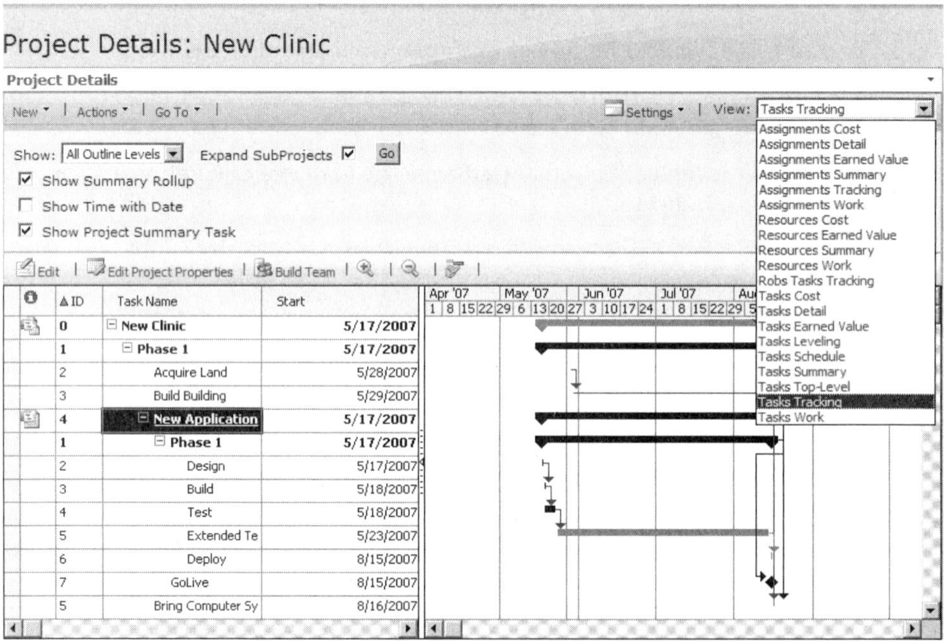

My Work Views

Although the detailed use and interaction with the My Work Views are discussed in Chapter 22, in this chapter we'll discuss how users may use the My Work views to gain insight into the projects they're working on, the tasks they've been assigned therein, and the team members' overall schedule for which they have to account. Because the timesheet functionality has been discussed in detail in other parts of this book, we will focus on the other views from the My Work page.

Tasks

As the My Assignments View allows the user to submit progress for the tasks to which they've been assigned, one often-overlooked ability from this view is for the resource to use the Personal Tasks Gantt View. If the administrator has enabled this view for all resources (by choosing the Task Settings and Display option), then resources will be able to see in a Gantt Chart view the assignments to which they have been committed.

NOTE *Although this view is identical to that which appears when a resource manager selects a single resource from the Resource Center View and clicks View Resource Assignments, when the resource is looking at his or her own information through the Personal Gantt View, any attempt to select Return to Resource Center or View Availability will likely result in a permissions error.*

Schedule

The Schedule page presents resources with a calendar view of the current month, displaying the planned assignments to which they have been committed. They can switch to weekly or daily views. The Schedule page is intended to give resources an overall view of the work they have during the exposed time period. When a resource clicks on the name of a task, the Task Details page appears in which the resource can enter progress information to submit it to the project manager.

Visual Reports in Project Professional

If we were to take Project Server 2007 and PWA out of the equation and focus solely on Project Professional's abilities to report on Project Data, we would certainly be drawn to the new Visual Reports feature of Project Professional 2007. Although it is powerful alone, Visual Reports' capability increases dramatically when matched with Microsoft Excel 2003 or greater and Microsoft Office Visio 2007. This feature allows you to take advantage of templates and graphics provided by the two applications to create visually pleasing reports based on the currently open project(s). In addition, both Microsoft Excel and Visio support the use and generation of personal OLAP cubes, so these reports can create dynamic and compelling representations of your projects' and subprojects' data.

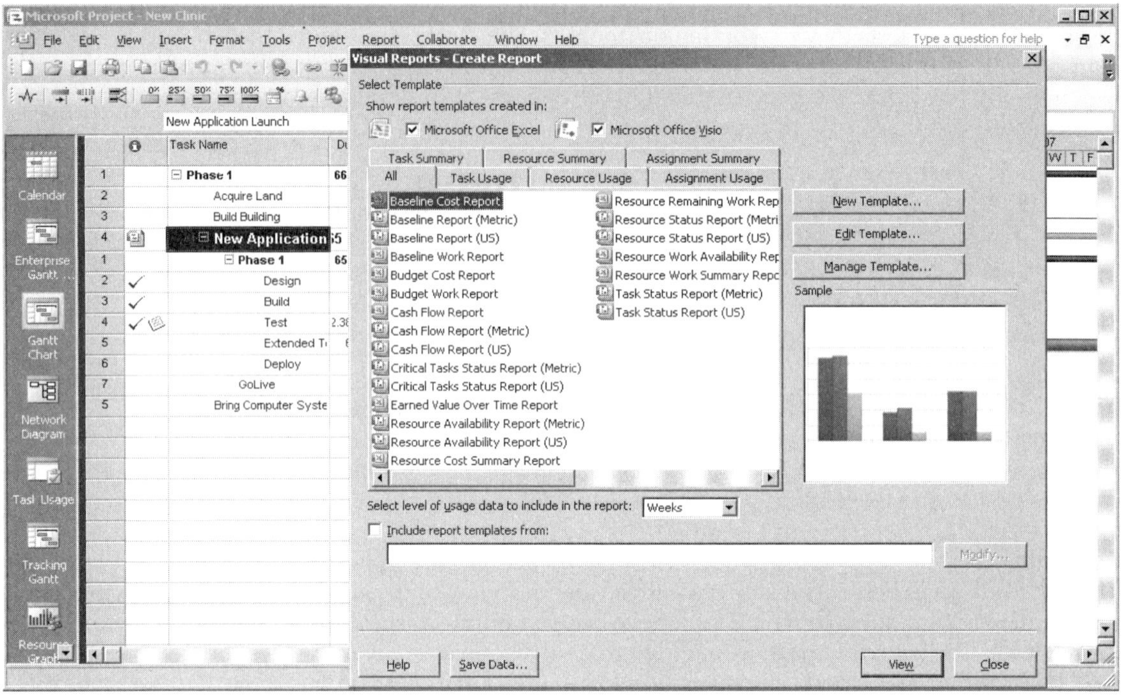

Using the Reporting Features of Project Server 2007 is likely a main reason why you are considering using Project Server 2007. Based on your role in the organization, you are able to get the information that is relevant to you. If you are a resource, you can use the My Work views and the Personal Gantt to achieve a holistic view of the work that you need to accomplish. If you are a project manager, you may use the Visual Reports in Project Professional 2007 to perform an Earned Value analysis of your "hot" projects. If you are a resource manager, you can use the Resource Center views and their components to see what your people are currently working on or to plan overall capacity for the months ahead. And if you are an executive, you may use custom Project Center views to track critical milestones across projects, and the Data Analysis views to slice and dice your organization's effort into views that were simply not possible prior to the introduction of EPM.

In this chapter, we have discussed the capabilities and the features as they relate to reporting in your EPM toolset. Throughout this book, we have stressed the absolute necessity for standardized project management methodologies, because it is the quality and consistency of the data being fed into the system that will determine the quality and consistency of the reports that the system provides. Frequently, it is the power of these reports that is the "purchasing trigger" for the Microsoft EPM toolset. As a result, most of the thought goes to the cart (a powerful report), which has then been placed in front of the horse (how we get data into the system). Recognizing the importance of the front end of this data flow will help you achieve consistency and accuracy in the powerful reporting features of Project Server 2007.

CHAPTER 20

Resource Management

Resource management in a Project Server environment is based on the concept that the goal is to achieve gains in efficiency by using the correct resources with the right skill sets on the appropriate tasks while performing work on optimal projects. Project Server cannot solve resource management issues on its own, but rather provides a set of tools that enable improvement. Some information on resource management has already been discussed earlier in the book, but not in this context.

With the exception of the smallest companies, almost no organization without an Enterprise Project Management (EPM) or similar system can really be sure what work is being performed. The organization cannot normally tell how well projects are tracking, and in particular it cannot determine how staff are allocated. Without a system like Project Server 2007, some resources are overallocated and some need more work to do. Frequently, opportunities are missed because staff in a branch office do not realize that there is a resource in a different branch with the skills that are needed for a project. Other times, the manager of a department full of overworked employees realizes that her team is overburdened, but does not have the justifying proof for adding headcount, nor supporting evidence to reject a new project.

Project Server offers many options for organizations to improve the way that resources are managed. Keep in mind that useful resource data are the result of the data that are input to Project Server (garbage in, garbage out) and that for data to be valid they must meet some key requirements detailed next.

- Resources must be Timephased and leveled (although not automatically leveled) within and across projects. Thus if resources are added to each task in a project or even each project at 100 percent units (that is, the percentage of the resource's available time), then the views and reports will display every resource as overallocated. Timephasing is an absolute requirement to achieve the most useful resource results. It is up to the project manager to execute the timephasing of resources on their projects. (Chapter 21 discusses timephasing in more detail.) Using timephasing is almost always the appropriate way to plan the use of resources who are working across multiple projects. Another option, automatic resource leveling, can also provide assistance in the hands of an expert; however, this feature is very difficult for most project managers to understand and use correctly. In addition to the intricate knowledge of Task Types, a thorough understanding of the scheduling engine of Microsoft Office Project Professional 2007 is required. It is so intricate, in fact, that we cannot recommend its use in most cases.

- If resources need to be categorized for reporting purposes (as they usually do), then custom enterprise resource fields will be required. These fields are attributes that can be assigned to individual resources. They should be based on reporting requirements—that is, things that differentiate one set of resources from another. Keep in mind that when naming these fields, use only letters, numbers and underscores; no other characters should be used. The following are some examples of useful resource fields:
    - **RBS (resource breakdown structure)** The RBS is usually used to define the organizational structure and resources (people and generic users) that are each assigned into one portion of that structure. This field is used for security-related purposes, but is often also used as an attribute for reporting. An example is a Project Web Access (PWA) view that displays assignment data about all resources who report to a particular manager. You will learn more on the RBS in the next section.
    - **Resource Type** This is a built-in field. Each resource must be a work, material, or cost type.
    - **Role** A Role field can be used to establish the primary role for each user. Depending on the organizational requirements, secondary and even tertiary role fields could be used. The primary role field is often a good one to use for the Match function in the Build Team tools (which you will learn more about later in this chapter).
    - **Skills** This could be used to associate many skills with a resource using a single field. You will learn more about this topic later in the chapter.
    - **Team** Project Server uses the Team field to assign a team to a task and to support the assignment team functionality. The field itself is included in the default installation, but the actual lookup (team names) for this field is not, and thus must be built to support this functionality. As noted in Chapter 9 (in the "Correctly Connecting the Team Name Field" section), you should avoid configuring this field until you clearly understand how to use it.
    - **Resource Type or Resource Category** This field can be used in many ways. One example is to indicate whether a resource is a salaried exempt or hourly nonexempt employee for tracking costs. The cost for using nonexempt staff increases directly if they work more hours, whereas an exempt employee's cost will not increase (in most cases). Another way to use such a field is to differentiate between employee and consulting resources.

CAUTION *Resource names should not include any separator characters. Hyphenated names are OK, but be careful not to use the dot (.) character as, for example, a middle initial. As mentioned previously, commas in Project are automatically changed to semicolons if an Active Directory (AD) display name is in the* ***LastName, FirstName*** *format.*

The Resource Breakdown Structure (RBS)

The RBS is a special enterprise custom resource field that comes with Project Server. It includes a lookup table, which should be configured to map to the organization's reporting hierarchy, similar to an "org" chart. Most RBSs are organizationally designed, whereas the most common alternative model is geographically focused. Using the Code Mask functionality that was discussed in Chapter 9, set up the levels as best fits the company. Figure 20-1 shows an example RBS.

In the example shown in Figure 20-1, the corporate executives would be associated at the top-level MNXCorp. You create this association from within Resource Center by selecting Edit Details for the specific users involved. So focusing on information technology (IT), the chief information officer (CIO) would be at this top level. IT directors would be placed at the IT level, the development manager would be placed in Development, and developers would be in Members. This would result in a developer having that following RBS level:

MNXCorp.IT.Development.Members

If there were project managers in Development, it might make sense to add another level between Development and Members. As you learn how the RBS is used in this section, consider why such an additional level could make sense in this instance.

Keep in mind that there is only one RBS field. You should design it with growth in mind. In most organizations, the Project Server deployment starts with a single department. You should assume that it will not remain a departmental solution in the long run, and that the RBS should reflect a structure that allows expansion. In the preceding example, only the IT Department is included, but because the top level is the top of the company, you can expand the RBS hierarchy without having to redesign the RBS.

The RBS has several uses in Project Server.

RBS for Authorization

Authorization (as opposed to authentication) is used to determine whether an identified user is allowed access to a resource. The RBS in Project Server can act in concert with categories and groups to be part of the solution's authorization mechanism. In Chapter 8, this is referred to as contextually sensitive permissions. The RBS is associated with the My Direct Reports category (resources directly below the viewer as defined in the RBS). When a

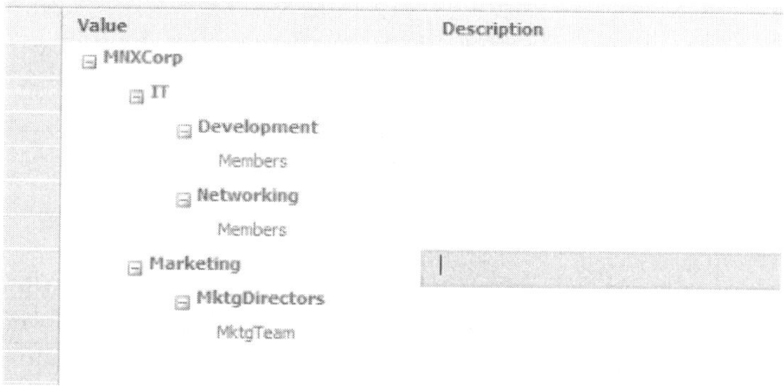

FIGURE 20-1 RBS example

PART V

user or group is associated with this category (remember that it is almost never a good idea to associate permissions to an individual user), the user can have access only to what is directly below him or her in the RBS. What this means at a high level is that if the Resource Managers group is associated with this category (and no other categories), each member of the Resource Managers group will have access to the resources that he or she directly manages and no other resources. Make sure that the RBS includes a level (or node) at the members level. This node is required because someone at a higher node can access only resources below him or her (not those at a parallel level).

The My Resources category is similar, but allows resources to be viewed below the viewer, not just directly below. Note that changing settings within the categories themselves can change how this works. For example, if the My Resources category is changed to allow all current and future resources, the "downhill" restriction will no longer apply. The output from these security settings applies to both PWA and Project Professional.

For a more thorough discussion on Groups, Categories, and the application of contextually sensitive permissions, see Chapter 8.

RBS for Resource View Filtering

Each PWA view must be associated with a category or categories for anyone to actually see any data. Therefore, when an RBS-related category is used with a view, it applies to what each viewer sees. For example, it is possible to limit a Resource View to a single department by using the RBS field for filtering. In this scenario, if a user navigates to Resource Center, this view would not appear as an option from the Views dropdown list. Resource Center views include a special feature for this RBS filtering. Note in Figure 20-2 the checkbox Filter Resources to User's RBS Branch.

As seen in the screenshot, this option can be useful for creating a My Resources View. In other words, a single view can provide data on resources specific to the viewer's RBS branch.

RBS for Reporting

After creating the RBS, you can leverage it in many ways for reporting purposes. Keep in mind that Project Server views act as visual "reports." In addition, most data from Project Server can be exported directly to Excel; the SQL Server or SQL Server Analysis Services, as well as custom reports using queries or a reports tool (such as SQL Reporting Services or Business Objects), can then be accessed from Excel (if permissions allow such access). Here are some examples of how the RBS might be used for reporting:

- A Data Analysis View can be created to view actual work by time period, by RBS, and then by resource. This view would show the viewer how much work had been performed within a specified time period (a month, for example), by RBS level (that is, by the part of the organization that did the work), and by individual. The view could initially be rolled up to the entire organization, and the people analyzing the data could then "drill down" to the specific set of details that they are seeking.
- Using SQL queries and Excel against the Project Server Reporting database (ProjectServer_Reporting), a spreadsheet can display specific time and task detail for each RBS level (team of people) for the team's respective manager. One client did this to verify that time entered into timesheets matched data submitted to project tasks by each team member.
- Project Center views can provide a view into projects relating to a specific RBS level.

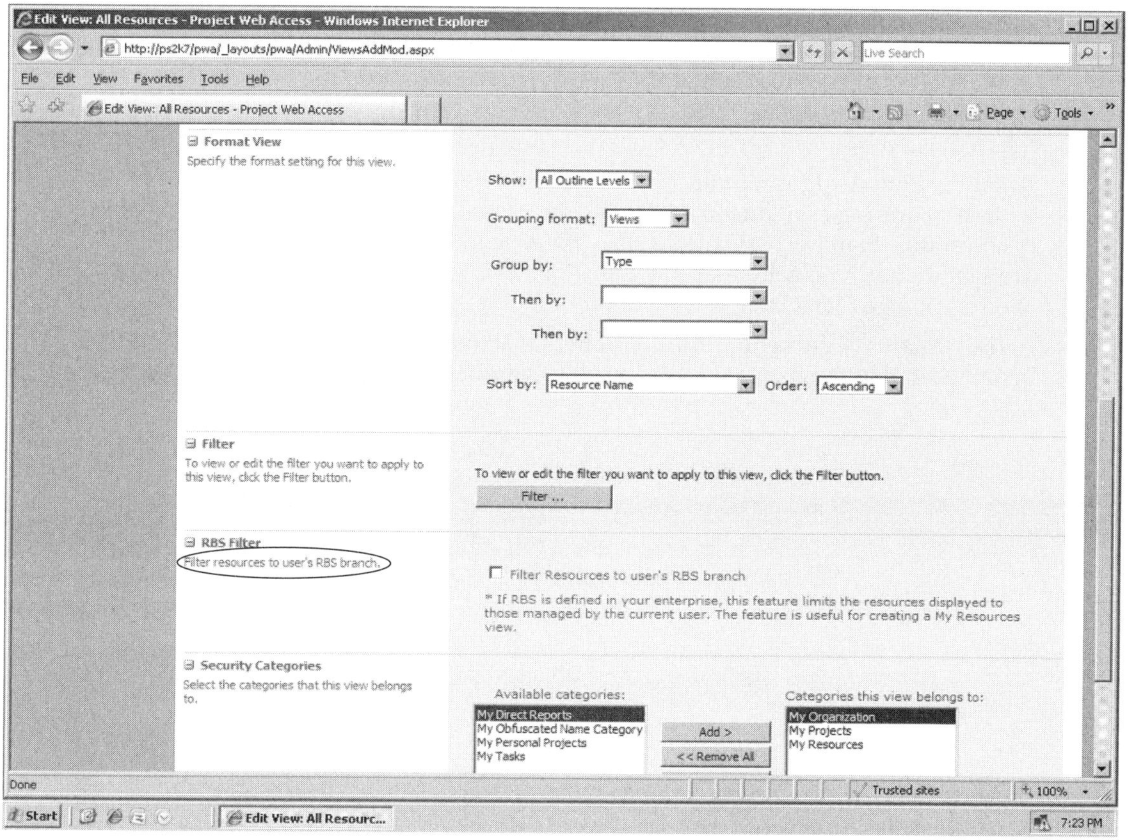

FIGURE 20-2 Filter by RBS branch

Resource Allocation and Capacity

There are many components in a Project/Project Server environment that impact resource usage, capacity, and availability. This section covers them in detail. When planning a Project Server deployment, it is important to understand the effects that each of these components have in order to make appropriate decisions on their use.

- **Proposed and Committed options** Resources can be associated with a project as either committed (the default setting) or proposed. The idea of this feature is to support "soft booking" of a resource for a project. In Project Server 2003, this feature kept the tasks off the team member's timesheet, but that is not the case in Project Server 2007. Microsoft is aware of this problem and a fix should be forthcoming, as the way that the feature works now defeats one of the main benefits. If this feature is working as expected, it should not appear at all for team member Task but should still be viewable in reports. Even with the issue, this feature can be useful. Dave Gochberg was assigned a 100 hour task at 100 percent units as Proposed. When viewing him in Resource Center Availability View, note that if the Include Proposed Bookings option is not selected, no work appears (see Figure 20-3), but when it is selected the viewer can see that he or she is proposed for a task (see Figure 20-4).

- **Resource Plan Assignment option** Resource Plans can block a resource's time without requiring assignment to detailed tasks and projects. If a resource is assigned to a Resource Plan for two hours a day, this assignment reduces the resource's availability by 25 percent (assuming an eight-hour workday). You'll learn more about Resource Plans later in this chapter.
- **Activity plan assignment** Tasks assigned in activity plans work like proposed bookings in that they appear in Resource Center only when the Proposed Bookings

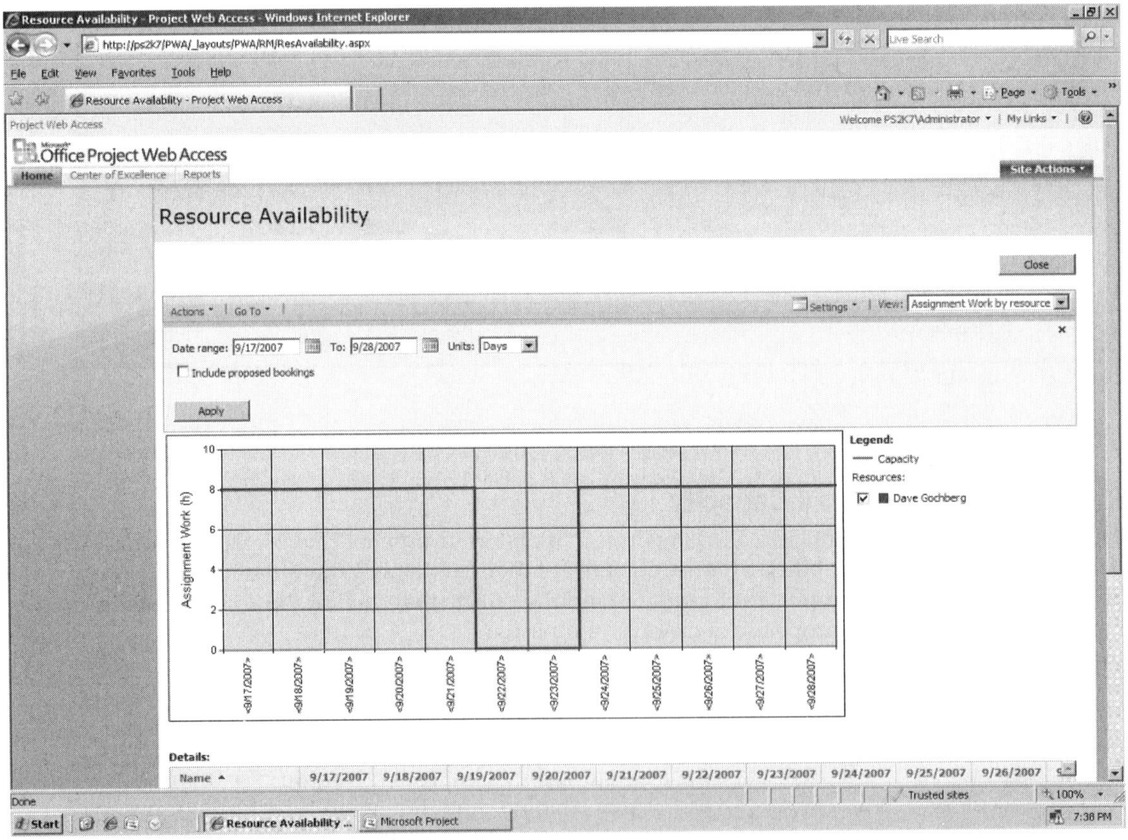

FIGURE 20-3 Availability View (the default setting)

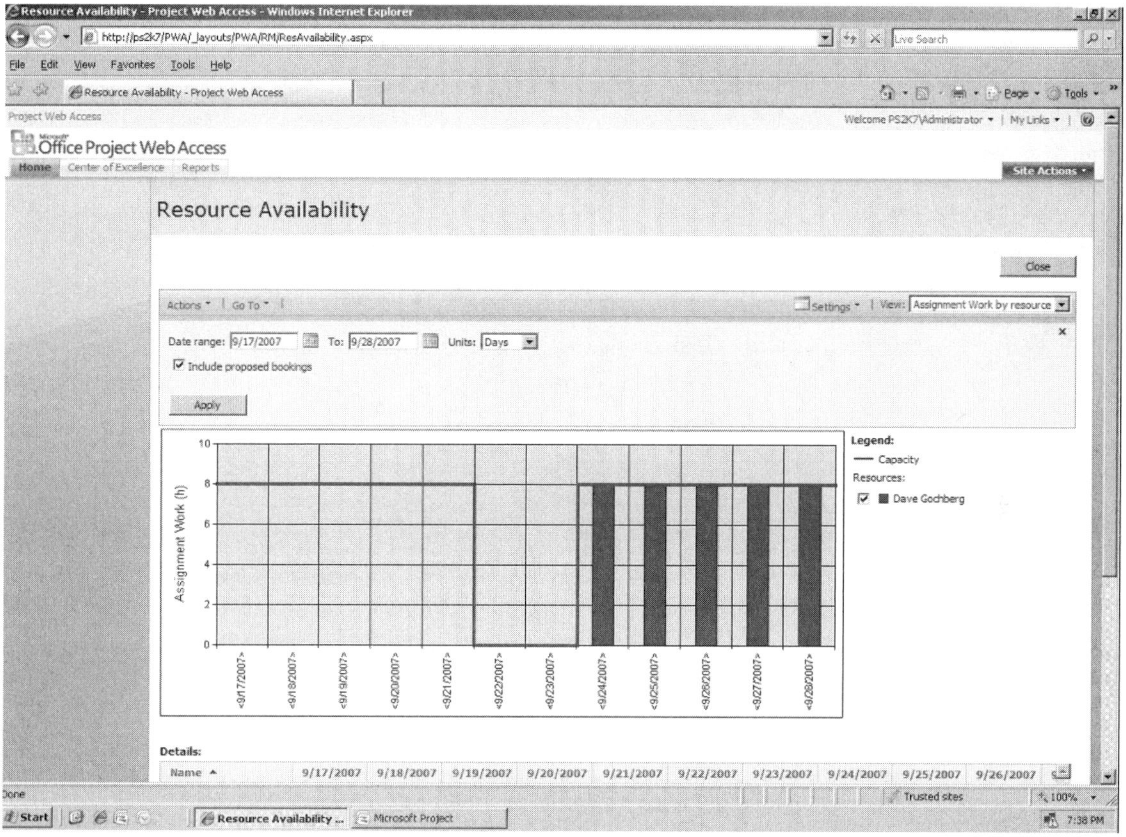

FIGURE 20-4 Availability View including proposed bookings

checkbox is selected. This activity does display in the team member's My Tasks page, as shown in Figure 20-5.

- **Actual project assignments** Actual project task assignments reduce availability. Keep in mind that Project and Project Server calculations will change constantly as projects progress, so availability is always, at least to some degree, a moving target.
- **The calendars (enterprise, resource, and project)** There are three basic calendar types that affect availability. Enterprise calendars are usually set to take into account an organizational calendar. In most cases, this means that company holidays are blocked as nonworking time. You will learn more about enterprise calendars later in this chapter. Calendars can be set at the level of an individual resource. These are most commonly used to define the working time for resources who work nontraditional hours, such as four 10-hour days, job sharing, and part-time work. Only hours set as working and not blocked by nonworking time in an enterprise calendar display as available capacity. Project calendars are also available if a project has a unique calendar. Use of these Project calendars is not encouraged. There is also a place within

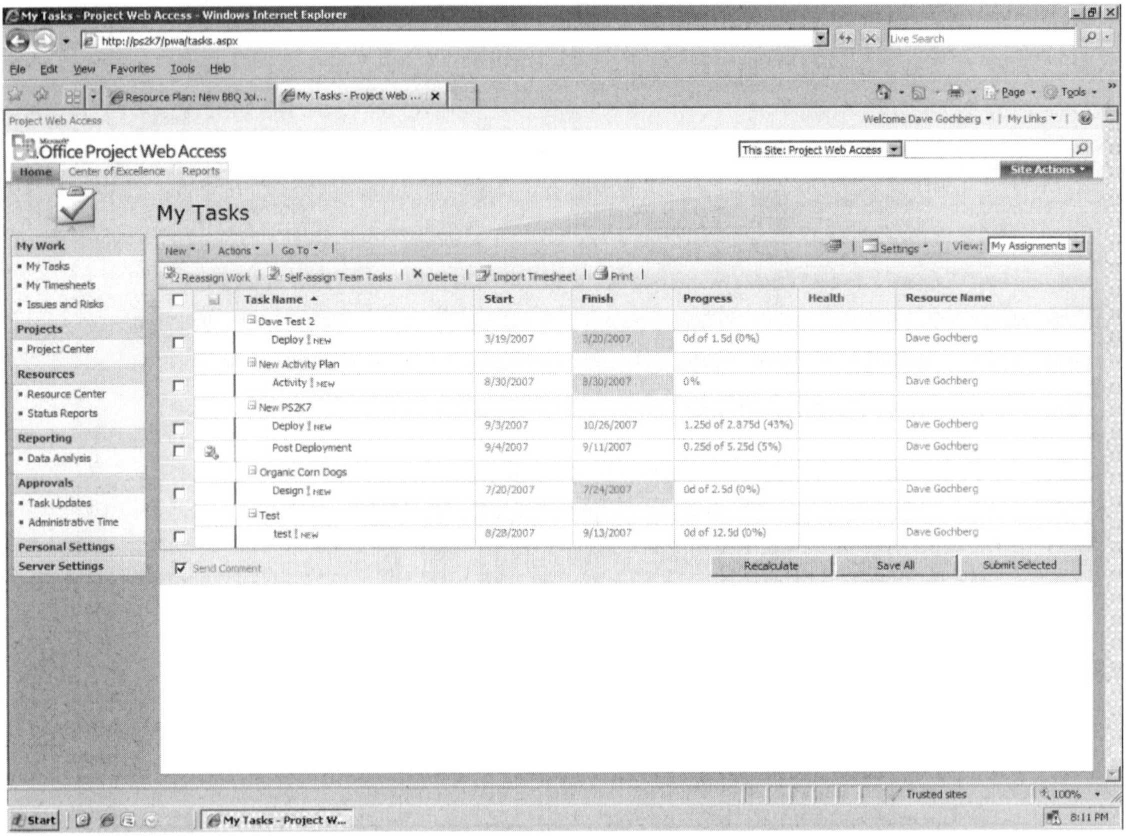

FIGURE 20-5 Activity plan displayed in the My Tasks page

each task to select a task calendar, the options being based on existing enterprise calendars. This feature could be useful in an international situation where a portion of the project is being performed by staff who have a different calendar based on their country of residence or cultural differences. Calendars define when a resource has capacity and are cumulative. Availability is then subtracted from this capacity when other tools (such as project assignments and activity plans) are used to block time.

One key concept should be part of the resource planning process when deciding who should be on which project and assignments. Project managers often "know" which resource they want to use, whereas the resource manager may have made other commitments or have other plans for the resource. A negotiating process often must take place between the resource (functional) manager and the project (or program) manager.

Enterprise Calendars

As discussed earlier in the book, every organization needs to establish at least one enterprise calendar. Enterprise calendars are used to create a standard workday, establish company holidays, and can also be used for things such as shutting down plants. In Wisconsin, entire companies close for a week during deer hunting season (this is not a joke). Other locations close for a week during the year-end holiday season. In support organizations, it may make sense to build a seven-day-a-week enterprise calendar to support weekends as working time.

NOTE *During Packer games, people won't even answer the phone, so you better hope that your project does not require Sunday activity.*

To create a corporate holiday, navigate to the PWA Server Settings page and select the Enterprise Calendars item. From there, select the Standard Calendar and then Edit Calendar from the horizontal bar. Office Project Professional 2007 will then launch and open the Change Working Time dialog. Select a date that is to be set for a holiday from the calendar. For example, for U.S.-based organizations, navigate to July 4. Make sure that the date is shaded in the calendar and then move your mouse to the bottom portion of the page. In the first row, type in the name of the holiday (Independence Day). From there, if you select a different cell by pressing ENTER or TAB, the date fields will fill in with July 4. Clicking OK creates what is called a *calendar exception* and the Fourth of July will be set to a full day of nonworking time. Figure 20-6 shows how this example would appear.

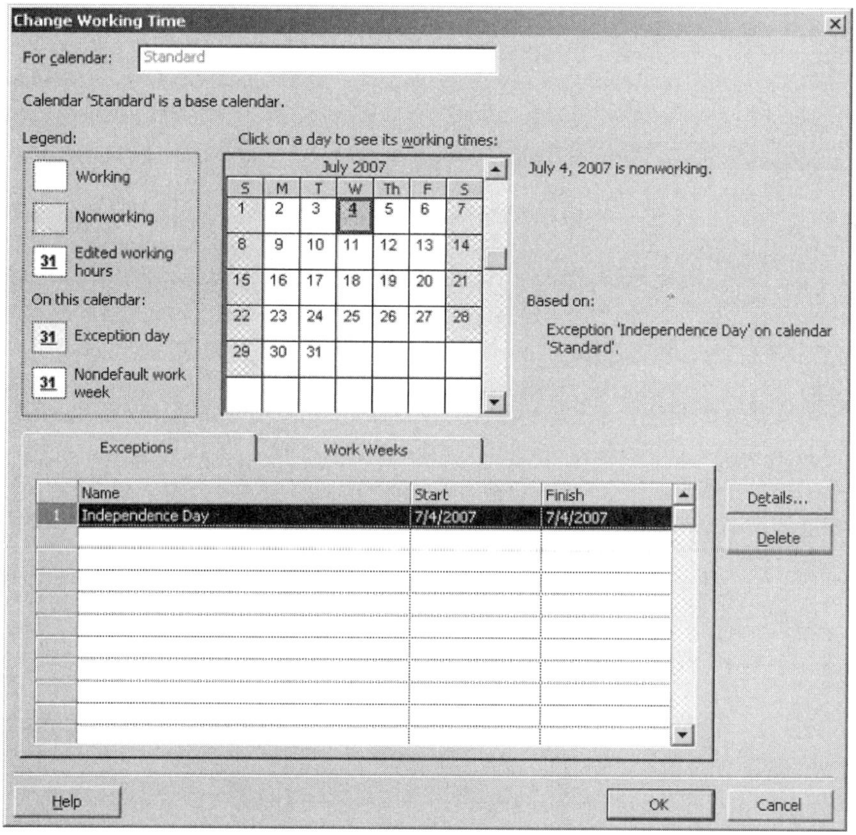

FIGURE 20-6 Change working time for a full day.

PART V

If you need a partial day off at the organizational level, you can create calendar exceptions for partial days from the same dialog. Some organizations have a half-day holiday for New Year's Eve. To implement this example from the Change Working Time dialog, select December 31. As in the previous example, select the first row. Type in a name (New Year's Eve), then press TAB. The date then fills in as in the previous full-day example. To change the hours, make sure that the highlighting remains on this first row and then select the Details button.

The next dialog, which appears as Details for "New Year's Eve" for this example, provides an area for setting the working and nonworking hours. Select the option for Working Times. In most cases, two rows display, as shown in Figure 20-7.

Navigate to row 2 (the afternoon) and press DELETE. The Working Time field then displays a setting of 8:00 A.M. to 12:00 P.M. From this point, click OK, then OK again. This sets a half-day calendar exception for New Year's Eve for a single year. Note that the Details dialog also enables you to set recurrence for calendar exceptions.

This New Year's Eve example is a good candidate for creating a yearly recurrence if the organization always takes this half-day off. Using the recurrence features makes sense for partial and complete days alike, as long as the holidays are date-based. The July 4 example also is a great candidate for setting a recurrence. President's Day is not a good candidate, because the actual date changes from year to year.

Enterprise calendars that include holidays create calendar exceptions for those specific days. Calendars exceptions block time as nonworking time. Nonworking time is time that is not considered in total capacity. In other words, when you are looking at the week of

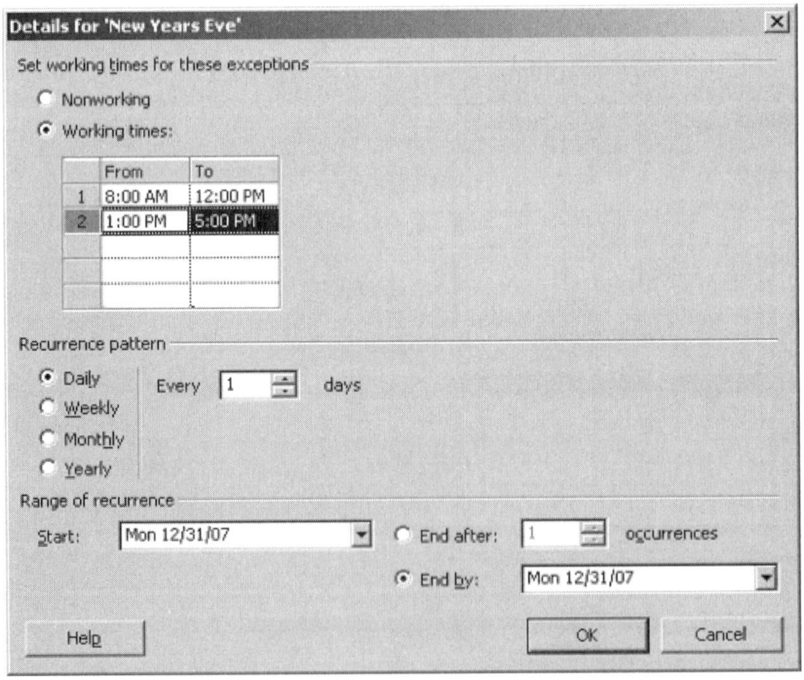

FIGURE 20-7 Breaking down a day into parts for working and nonworking times

Thanksgiving, if the Thursday and Friday of that week are set to be calendar exceptions, each resource in the organization will display only 24 hours of capacity for that week.

Resource Calendars

Setting resource calendars, described in detail in the section "Configuring the Resources" later in this chapter, creates calendar exceptions for resources. These calendar exceptions have the same effect as the enterprise calendar exceptions. Therefore, if a resource has settings created at the individual level that create calendar exceptions, only the working time is considered in capacity calculations.

Max Units

Each resource is set by default to have Max (maximum) units of 100 percent. This means that the system assumes that 100 percent of the resource time can be devoted to projects. Keep in mind that there are other functions that degrade availability that layer on top of Max Units. It also means that when any single project manager assigns a resource to a task in a project, that resource will be assigned at 100 percent units by default. Finally, the Max Units setting is used to calculate when a resource will display as overallocated. The Max Units setting can be changed at the resource level (details are provided in the section "Configuring the Resources" later in this chapter).

NOTE *For resource information to be useful, project managers must examine units for each assignment in each of their project plans. If a project manager assigns a resource to a task without reducing units appropriately, the system will use the default 100 percent setting or whatever other setting was created in the Max Units field. If another project manager assigns this resource to a task in his or her project during the same timeframe, the system will immediately display the resource as overallocated.*

One other important consideration to keep in mind is that project managers cannot set a resource's maximum units on a project-by-project basis. This is one reason that the project manager must look at units on a task-by-task basis.

Resource Plans

Another implement in the resource management toolbox is the Resource Plan. Resource Plans are used when a resource's time needs to be reserved, but there is not a detailed project plan to hold all details of the assignments. Resource Plans can be used on projects, proposals, and activities.

Assignments in Resource Plans impact availability if the resources in the Resource Plans are set to Committed. If they are set to Proposed, this data can be used for future resource planning and capacity planning. In addition, this feature allows flexibility on how the Resource Plan is applied. It can be applied to an entire plan or to a plan after a certain date. This latter option is useful when a project plan's resource planning is more complete for early phases and more unclear later in the project.

To build a Resource Plan for a project, you first must create the project and publish it to Project Server 2007. Then navigate to Project Center in PWA.

Highlight the project and select the Resource Plan button as shown in Figure 20-8. Use the Build Team tool to select the team members, and then fill in the grid with the dates and times for which the Resource Plan is being used to block a user's availability.

Figure 20-8 Resource Plan button in Project Center

Note that to track work, someone (usually a project manager) must add the resource to a project and to tasks. At the time of this writing, an excellent set of examples is available at http://evildoctorporkchop.spaces.live.com/blog/cns!88E61D218103A246!462.entry?_c11_blogpart_blogpart=blogview&_c=blogpart.

Next highlight the row of the target project and click the Resource Plan button. From the Resource Plan page, select Build Team from the horizontal bar. This takes you to the PWA Team Builder. Select the checkboxes next to the resources who are to be assigned to the Resource Plan and then click the Add button. Use the grid shown in Figure 20-9 to place hours to be reserved for each resource on the days that they need to be blocked. After populating the time, save and publish the Resource Plan.

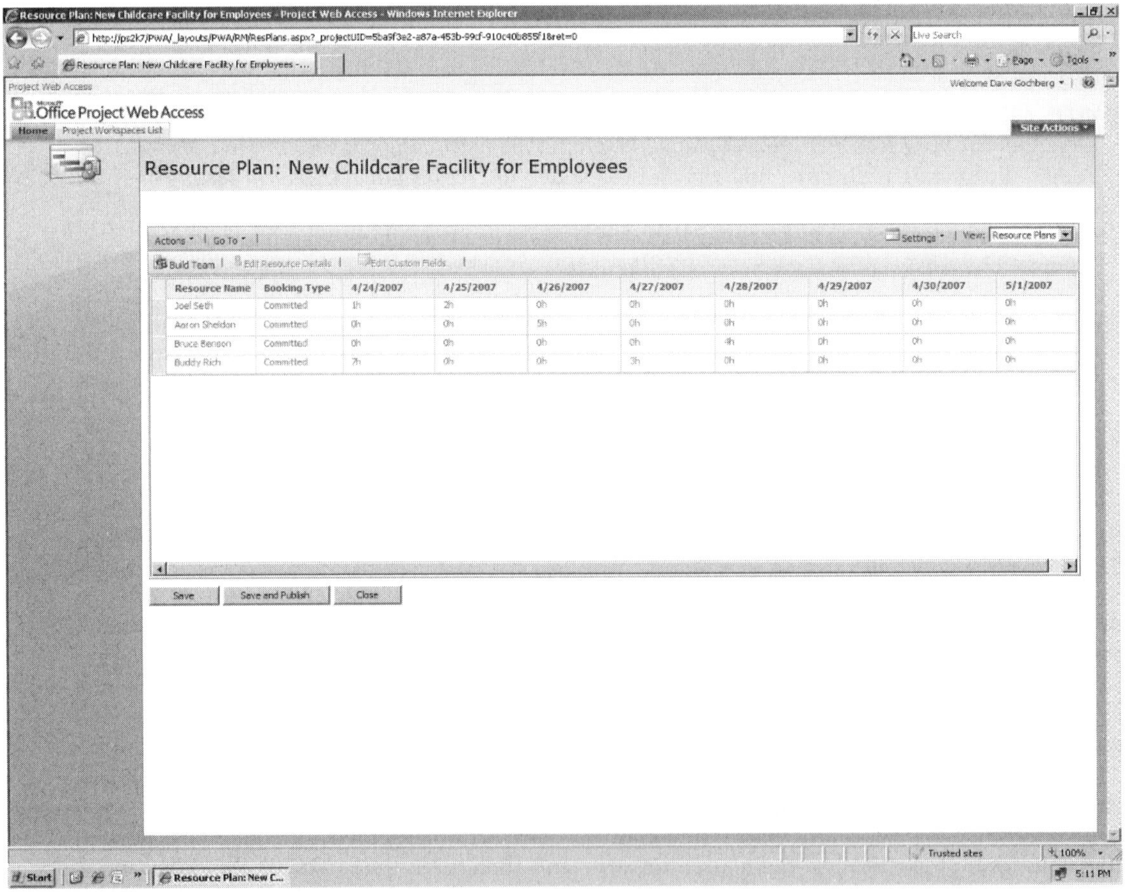

Figure 20-9 Resource Plan team grid

The process is similar for a proposal or an activity. After publishing the proposal or activity, navigate to the Proposals and Activities page in PWA. From there, highlight the row of the specific plan that needs a Resource Plan attached. Click the Resource Plan button, as displayed previously in Figure 20-8, and follow the process as described previously.

Administrative Time

Administrative time is set up in the Server Settings/Time and Task Management area. Administrative Time can be set to working or nonworking time. You should decide carefully how to use administrative time. For example, if the Vacation field is set to nonworking time, that time will not be displayed in total capacity.

By default, there are three categories of administrative time:

- **Administrative** This is working time.
- **Sick** This category is nonwork.
- **Vacation** Vacation is considered nonwork for which preapproval is required.

Although there is an optional built-in process for preapproval of vacation time, for the following example, assume that preapproval was given for a vacation day. The resource reports four hours of administrative time on Monday, four hours of sick time on Tuesday, and the eight-hour vacation day on Friday. The remaining hours were recorded against a single project task assignment. Maximum units remain at the default setting (100 percent). The resource submits his or her timesheet, imports timesheet data into their My Task page, and then submits this update. All submissions are approved.

The results of this example are as follows:

- **Monday** Fours hours of work recorded are against eight hours of capacity.
- **Tuesday** Four hours of work are recorded against four hours of capacity.
- **Wednesday** Eight hours of work are recorded against eight hours of capacity.
- **Thursday** Eight hours of work are recorded against eight hours of capacity.
- **Friday** Zero hours of work are recorded against zero hours of capacity.

Preapproval for Administrative Time One option that is available for administrative time categories is to require approval by the timesheet manager prior to the submission of a timesheet that includes that category (preapproval). Vacation time is set to Approval by default in Project Server 2007.

After a resource has saved time that requires approval, the timesheet manager is sent an approval request. A calendar exception is not put in place until the timesheet manager approves the request.

NOTE *The authors have differing opinions on the use of preapproval. It does add a layer of complication to the timesheet process, which is not usually a good idea, but for certain situations it may make sense. Make sure that, if you are considering the use of preapproval, you include a use case in your planning process.*

Past Reporting Most frequently, administrative time is reported after it has occurred. Examples include sick time ("I was sick on Wednesday") and administrative time ("I performed some nonproject-specific administrative work on Thursday"). This reporting is most useful when aggregated with other types of time and task information when analyzing what has occurred in the past.

Future Planning Vacation time or other future-focused, configurable administrative time categories can be used for future planning. For example, when determining when a project can be executed, you might consider how future planned vacation could affect when a key resource or resources would have time to perform their work. Administrative time creates calendar exceptions after they have been *saved* to the Project Server timesheet. As noted previously, if approval is required, the exception is created when the timesheet manager grants approval. Timesheets do not need to be submitted for a calendar exception to be created.

Future administrative time can be planned by using a different tool. From the My Timesheets page in PWA, click the Plan Administrative Time button. From the newly opened Administrative Time–Web Page dialog, select the administrative time category and the timesheet period. Add the time that needs to be blocked in the future. Then click Save. This function actually creates the future timesheet and then all other rules apply, such as requests requiring approval.

Unique "One-Off" Projects

Organizations can find that none of the out-of-the-box solutions (such as the Resource Plans discussed previously) is the exact match for their organizational needs. It is always better to use the tools that are provided if possible. Substantial planning is required to make sure that the appropriate solutions are put in place. Between activity plans, resources plans, administrative time, calendars, and so on, there is usually a way to meet requirements, no matter what they are. Analyzing the best way to get to the appropriate solution is likely to be a task for which most organizations will require consulting assistance. On occasion, there will be a requirement that calls for a bit more creative thinking.

The following solution is an example of one of these "special" projects.

In this example, a services organization with field resources was using Project Server to manage its internal projects traditionally. The organization needed a way to understand its consultants' availability without burdening them (as these consultants were always out of the office and often had no network access). These resources were never used on internal projects that were being managed in the Project Server environment. In this case, the organization represented each resource in a project:

- The project was named based on the resource name.
- The resource was the only one on the project team.
- Each consulting engagement for the resource was entered as a task in the project, with the start and finish dates used to reflect the beginning and projected end of each engagement.
- Fixed units were set to 100 percent. This made the work equal the duration time of 40 hours per week (except where calendar exceptions were created).
- Actual work was never recorded against the tasks.
- There was a single administrative resource who managed the plan.

The result was that whether the organization was looking at the project details or at the resources in Resource Center, availability and utilization were viewable. It could also view total utilization or timephased utilization by using the Data Analysis views.

NOTE *When managing resources, it is usually best to default to a configuration where 100 percent of a resource's time is allocated to some project or administrative activity. Also, keep in mind that there are many tools available in Project Server for managing resource time. Use the "one-off" solutions like the one just described only if it is not possible to meet the requirements with what is available out of the box.*

Configuring the Resources

As discussed in Chapter 9, there are many ways to configure resources with the appropriate settings. Note that some field settings can only be done through the use of Project Professional. Fields that must be edited from inside Project Professional include individual resource calendars as well as rates and costs for resources. To get to these specific fields, there are two possible methods. To access the first method, select the resources in Resource Center and then click the Open button as shown in Figure 20-10.

The other method is accessed directly through the Project Professional 2007 client. From inside Project while connected to the Project Server, select Tools | Enterprise Options | Open Enterprise Resource Pool. This process opens the PWA Resource Center within the body of the Project client. From that point, follow the same procedure as described next for working from inside Project Professional.

Resource calendars are edited in the following manner. Double-click the name of the resource that requires a calendar change. From the General tab, click the Change Working Time button, as shown in Figure 20-11.

If a single event is to be set for an individual to nonworking time, whether day, week, or month, use the Exceptions tab. Select the date or dates from the calendar at the top of the page. At the bottom half, type in a name. Dates should be as previously selected. When complete, click OK. This action sets the dates as nonworking and displays the resource as not available during the selected days. Time and task updates can still be recorded against these days. This is one of several ways to alter availability and is most likely not the best alternative unless a long period of time is involved (as in the case of a sabbatical, for example). A more useful use of this tool is to set company holidays, which requires an open Enterprise Global template and is usually done annually.

Even though the method just described is not commonly used, this same tool can be used to support part-time schedules, job sharing, four-day work weeks, and other nonstandard work hours. To set a repeating schedule that uses different hours from the standard calendar, you can use the same tool. In the Change Working Time dialog, select the Work Weeks tab. From there select the calendar dates from row 2. From this point, select the start and finish dates required for this individual's calendar. Give this schedule a name. The next step starts with selecting the Details button, as shown in Figure 20-12.

FIGURE 20-10 Open button in Resource Center

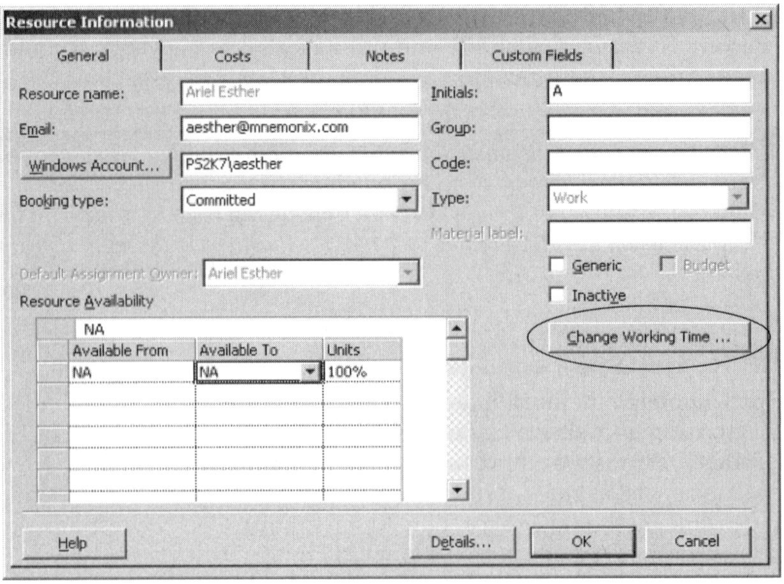

FIGURE 20-11 Change Working Time button on the General tab

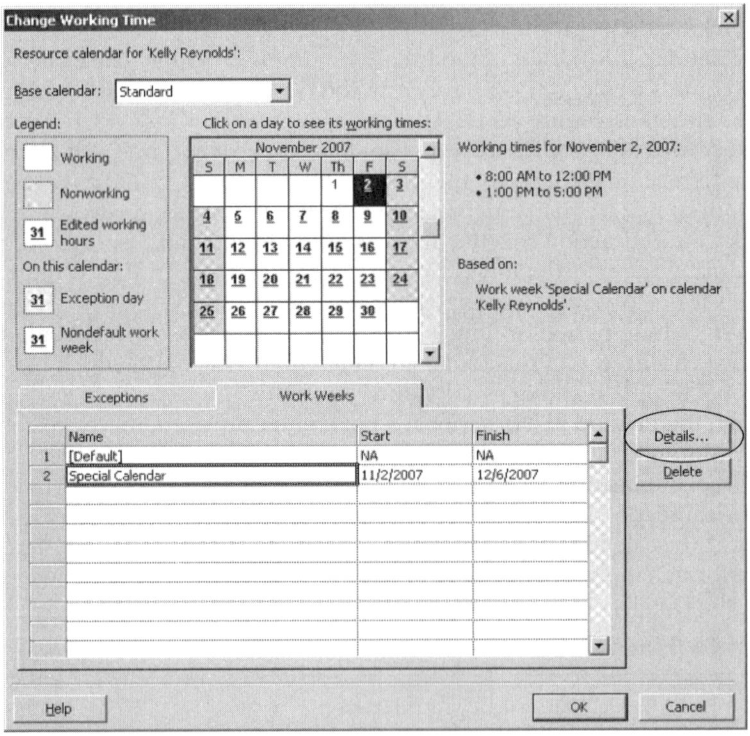

FIGURE 20-12 Change working time using the Details button

After selecting the Details button from the Work Weeks tab, select the Set Day(s) to These Specific Working Times field and start building the schedule. The default display is an 8 A.M. to 5 P.M. workday with a one-hour lunch break, Monday through Friday. Select the first day that does not use the default schedule and enter the From and To times as appropriate. See Figure 20-13 for an example of a split shift.

Resource rate/cost information is set in the Enterprise Resource Pool and can be accessed in a couple different ways. From inside the PWA Resource Center, select any users who need rate modification and then select the Open button, as seen previously in Figure 20-10.

The other way to open the resources for editing is from within Project Professional 2007. Select Tools | Enterprise Options | Open Enterprise Resource Pool. As discussed previously, Resource Center from PWA opens within the Project Professional client. From there, follow the same path as described previously.

By default, the Project Resource Sheet opens with the selected resources, and that view includes rate columns for editing. These are usually all the fields you need to adjust the resource's information.

For a work resource (usually a person), just enter an hourly rate into the Standard Rate field. It is not recommended to use an actual resource-loaded cost in this field as anyone with Project Professional will have access to these data. If appropriate, enter an overtime rate.

Some organizations do not consider the cost of an internal resource an actual project cost. It is almost always the incorrect approach to EPM not to enter a standard rate. If the organization really believes that measuring resource cost is not valuable to understanding its project landscape, then at minimum assign a rate of $1.00 to resources.

NOTE *Understanding resource costs is critical to understanding how much value a project has for the organization. How can a company decide which projects to execute without understanding their respective value? We recommend using some type of blended rate system for determining resource rates. We would happily debate any decision maker who does not believe that measuring internal resources costs on projects is valuable.*

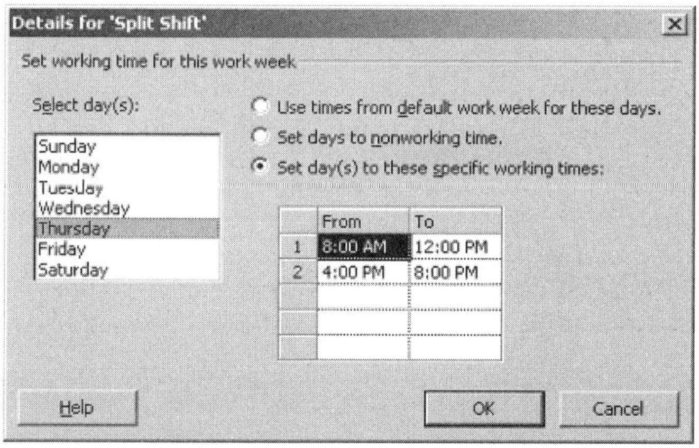

FIGURE 20-13 Changing specific daily details

If more complex rate information is required for work resources, such as different rates for different date ranges, Project and Project Server support this as well. To set resource rate date ranges, double-click the resource from inside the Resource Sheet. Navigate to the Costs tab as shown in Figure 20-14.

From there, start on the A (Default) tab and enter the standard rate and overtime rates (cost per use will be discussed later in this chapter). Each tab is a rate table. Each resource can have up to five rate tables associated, so that if there are project assignments that need to use different rates, it is supported. If there is already a rate entered in the Resource Sheet, tab A will open prepopulated with that information.

Continuing with tab A (Default), if rates must change as of a certain date, move to the second row and select the effective date for the new rate. To set the new rate, use the date picker that is available from the dropdown menu. The new rates can be set either by entering a new value or by entering a percentage, such as 5 percent to represent a 5 percent increase in rate. Service companies have been known to make rate increase decisions on a regular basis (yearly, for example), and this is a way to make those changes without having an effect on previous cost calculations. See Figure 20-15 for a A (Default) tab rate table.

Using different rate tables makes sense if resource rates change from assignment to assignment. To set a second rate table, navigate from the same Resource Information dialog to tab B. The first row is populated with the standard rate but can be changed to a different rate. In addition, the top-level rate can be changed on a certain date as previously described. This can be repeated for tabs C, D, and E if required.

Implementing multiple rate tables in a project is done by the Project Manager in most cases. The rates applied by default are the ones set in the standard A (Default) tab rate table.

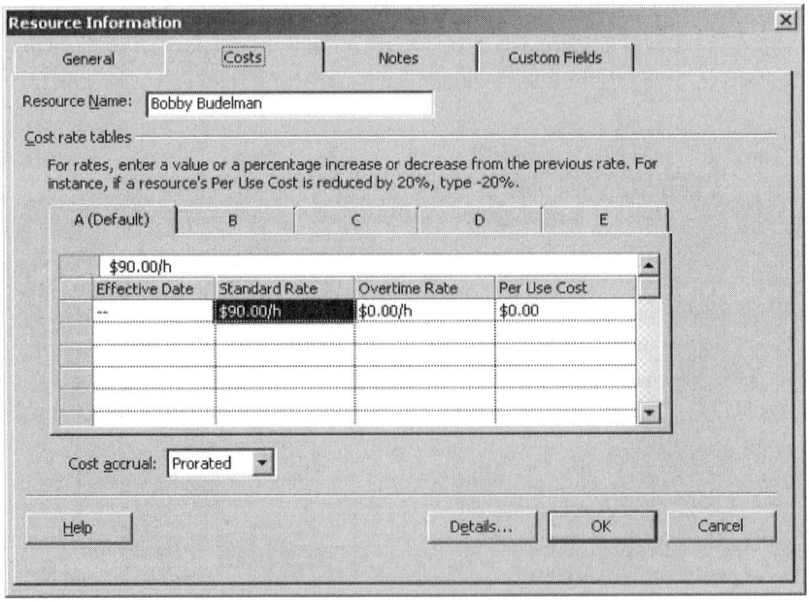

FIGURE 20-14 Resource Information dialog's Costs tab

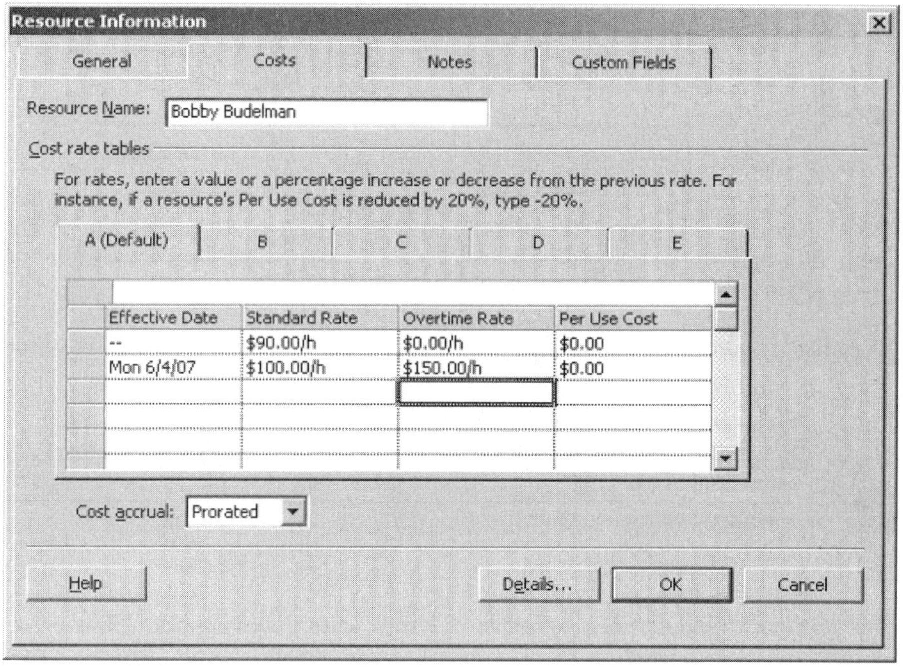

FIGURE 20-15 A (Default) tab rate table with a rate change

To change a rate for an assignment, the project manager should navigate in Project Professional to a Resource View such as Resource Usage. From there, the PM double-clicks the assignment to open the Assignment Information dialog as shown in Figure 20-16.

From there, the project manager can select which rate table to use on that specific assignment (A, B, C, D, or E). For that single assignment, a selection of a different rate table would apply. By pressing CTRL or SHIFT, the project manager can select multiple assignments. To make a rate table change on those multiselected assignments, right-click, select Assignment Information, and changes that are made in the Assignment Information dialog are reflected in each of the previously highlighted assignments.

The Units field in the Assignment Information dialog is used to set the maximum number that a resource is used over time. The classic example of a 100 percent maximum unit resource is that of a full-time, eight-to-five, hour-lunch-break, five-day-a-week employee. This means that the employee's maximum capacity is 40 hours per week. Some organizations lower this number because they realize that no one works 100 percent of the time that they are at the office; others reduce this number to reflect how nonproject work has an effect on people's availability for project work; and many leave this field at 100 percent and use other methods to deal with capacity, work, reporting, and so on. Later in this chapter, you will learn more about the many ways that allocation and availability can be viewed.

Material resources are a type of resource that can be included in the Enterprise Resource Pool. These represent whatever material might be used in projects that could have an effect

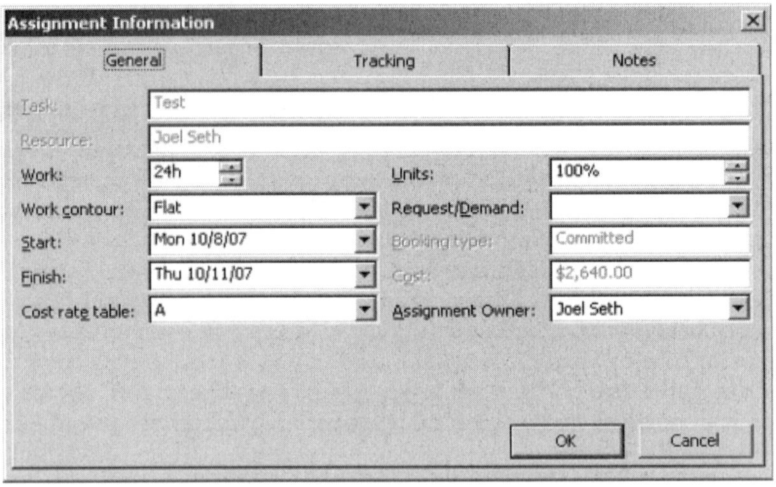

FIGURE 20-16 Assignment Information dialog

on cost, are not work-related, and are not *ad hoc* (such as travel expenses). Here are some examples of material resources:

- Servers (computer)
- Lumber
- Wire
- Test tubes
- Repeatable lease costs
- Desktop software

Note that these items use different types of measurements. Servers are probably measured in servers. Lumber might be measured in board feet. Wire could be measured in feet, yards, meter, or spools. Test tubes might be measured on a by-tube or by-case basis. Finally, desktop software might be measured in client access licenses or packages. These differences are all supported by Project and Project Server.

To create a new material resource and set the unit of measure, open the Enterprise Resource Pool, as discussed earlier in this chapter, without any resources having been selected. From the empty Resource Sheet, double-click on a row. The Resource Information dialog appears. Fill in the name of the resource (in this case, Flux Capacitors Sleeves) and select Material Resource from the Type dropdown list. Next type in the material label to represent the unit of measurement. Figure 20-17 shows where all these fields are located.

Click OK, then enter a standard rate for the material resource in the Resource Sheet that is open. Save the Enterprise Resource Pool and close it.

Project managers or resource managers who want to add a generic resource to a project team can simply follow the same processes that are always followed (resource managers

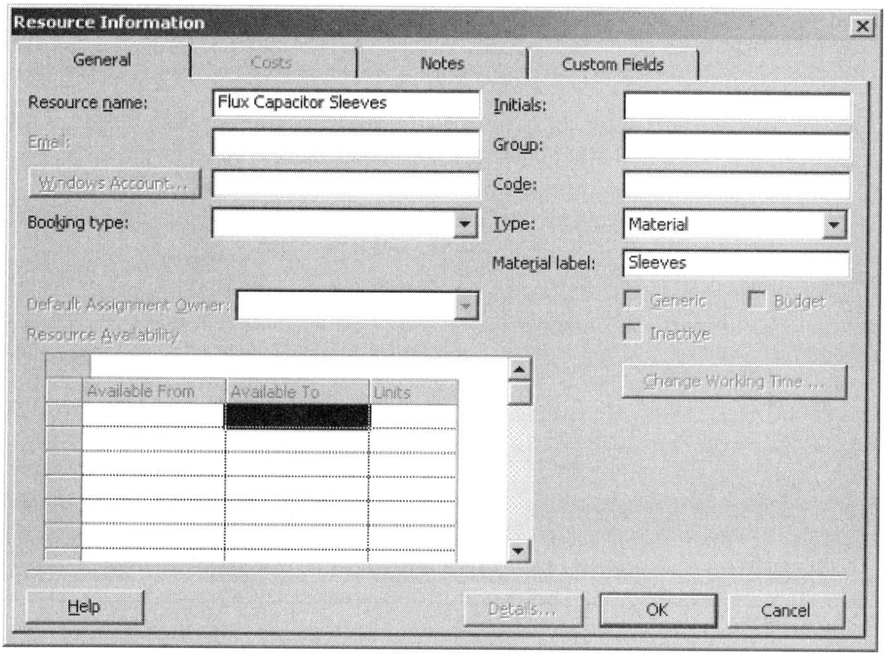

FIGURE 20-17 Creating a new material resource in the Resource Information dialog

often will use the PWA Build Team tool described later in this chapter). To add the material resource to a task (assignment), a project manager can use one of the standard methods (by double-clicking the task and using the Resources tab, by splitting the view in Project by right-clicking in the Gantt area and selecting Split, or by using the Assign Resources function (pressing ALT + F10 or clicking the Assign Resources button). Set the units to the quantity required (in this case, the number of flux capacitor sleeves) and the material costs will be calculated in the project once it is made available on the server.

Cost resources are new to Project Server 2007 and are used for tracking project expenses such as hotels, warehousing charges, meals, and conference room rentals. The process for setting up cost resources is similar to that for material resources. From the Enterprise Resource Pool, double-click a blank row and add the title of the cost resource (for example, Meals and Entertainment). Next select Cost from the Type dropdown list, and finally save and close the Enterprise Resource Pool.

To include a cost resource in a project, the resource is added to the team as usual. From there, the project manager assigns the cost resource to a task and manually enters the cost of the expense. In this way, the project manager can capture these somewhat unpredictable costs as part of a project's overall cost. Figure 20-18 shows where to set the expense for a cost resource within Task Details, which is available by double-clicking on a Task from any Task view in Project Professional.

PART V

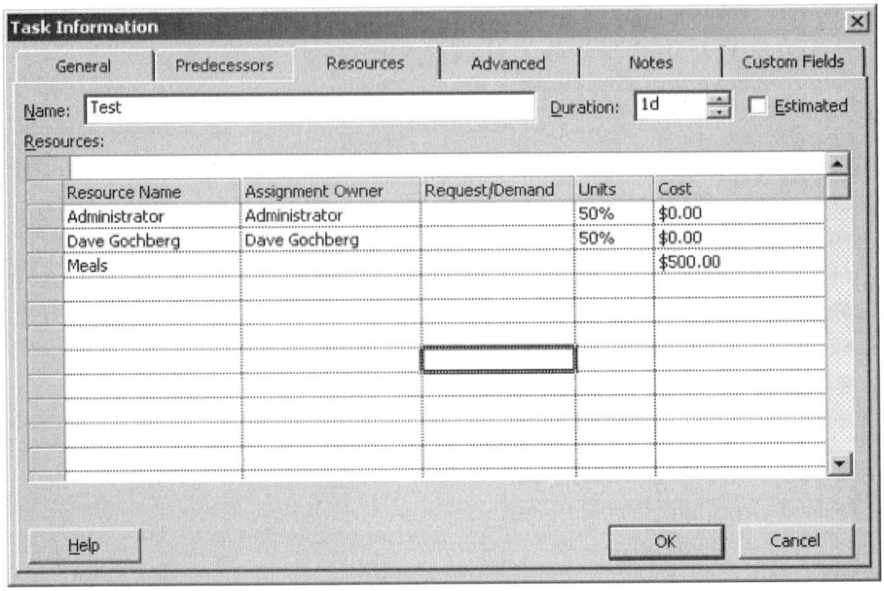

FIGURE 20-18 Expense setting for cost resources

Budget Resources

Budget resources are used to establish a project budget for work and cost. This can be very useful as a means of tracing how a project is tracking to its budget and is a new feature of Project Professional and Project Server 2007. You can create budget resources as part of the Enterprise Resource Pool. Consider starting with a single resource for budget cost and another for budget work. Later add more for categorization purposes, such as Budget_Travel_Lodging, Budget_InHouseLabor, or Budget_Consulting. These detailed fields will roll up to the project budget for cost and work, but can be used later for more detailed reporting.

Budget resources are created in the Enterprise Resource Pool in the following manner. Go to Resource Center and click the Open Project button with no resources selected. This opens the Enterprise Resource Pool. From the empty Resource Sheet, type in the name of the new budget resource and then double-click on that name to open the Resource Information dialog. Select one of the options (Work, Material, or Cost) and then click the Budget checkbox as shown in Figure 20-19.

Save the Enterprise Resource Pool.

To add the budget resource to a project, use the Build Team tool either from PWA or from within Project Professional. The next step is to make sure that the Project Summary Task is displayed. It is not displayed by default in Project Professional. Navigate within Project Professional to Tools | Options. On the View tab, select Show Project Summary Task. This action displays a task in row 0 that represents the name of the project. If it is not yet saved, it will say Project1 in bold type.

After a Project Summary Task is displayed, go to the Task Usage View in Project Professional to make the assignments. To do this, insert the columns Budget Work and

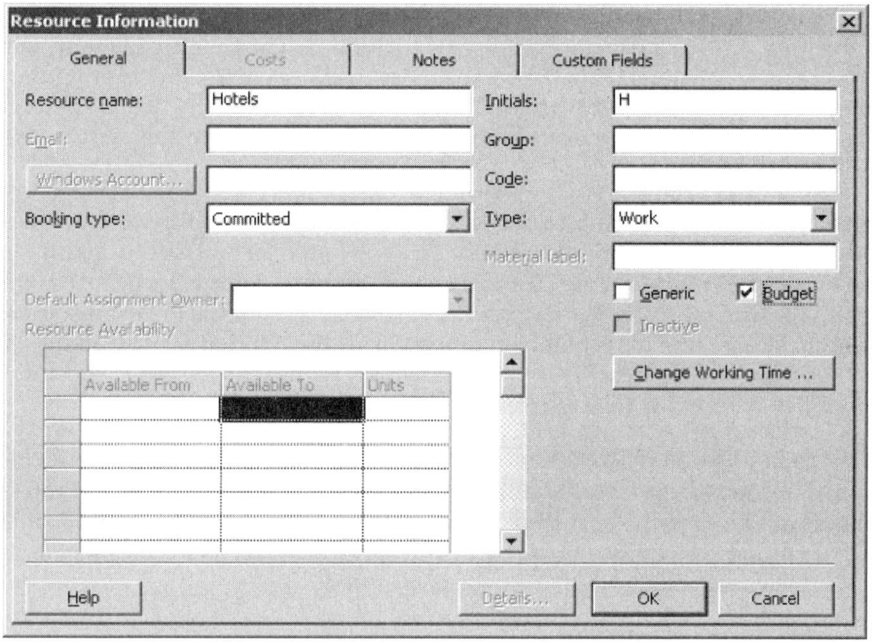

FIGURE 20-19 Creating budget resources in the Resource Information dialog

Budget Cost by right-clicking the column names on the left side of the screen and select Insert Column. After displaying these columns, enter the budget cost and or work in the respective columns on the Project Summary Task row. You can enter only currency into the Budget Cost and Work in Budget Work columns. This process creates the project budget, and after a baseline is set for the project, it establishes the project baselines for these fields.

NOTE *The project manager, rather than the resource manager, must execute top-down budgeting work if typical settings are used.*

Other Resource Settings Set in Project Professional

There are other resource settings that are configured only from the view of the Enterprise Resource Pool from inside Project Professional. They are Max Units and Accrual Method.

Max Units As described previously, Max Units is the percentage of a resource's total capacity that is used for project time and is also the threshold that Project and Project Server use for determining overallocation. To set this field, navigate to the Enterprise Resource Pool either from PWA or Project as described earlier. From inside the Resource Sheet in Project Professional, change the Max Units field to whatever amount is required. For a person, this would normally be either left at the default of 100 percent or reduced. There are, however, occasions when raising the Max Units setting to greater than 100 percent is necessary.

For example, one of the authors managed a very large project that involved 300 users who did nothing on the project except take a one-week class. They were not even connecting to the Project Server to interact, but the cost of these resources' utilization during the class period needed to be tracked to the project budget. Using 30 resources at 1000 percent was easier than creating 300 resources. It would also be possible to do this with a single resource at 30,000 percent.

Accrual Method There are three possible ways to accrue costs. Usually work accrues the related cost as the tasks in a project progress. This method (Accrual) is the default. In some cases, work resources might accrue cost at the start (Start) or completion (End) of the work.

Start and/or End settings are more commonly used for material or cost resources as these are more likely to occur as points in time. You set the Accrual method in the same way as you set the Max units as described previously from within the Resource Sheet in Project Professional that is accessed through Resource Center.

Other Settings Configured from Multiple Locations

Most resource settings are accessible from PWA or the Resource Pool/Project Professional views. Others can be set only from PWA. Some of these settings are discussed in this section and vary depending on whether any custom enterprise resource fields are created. In every case, these are the resource fields that can be configured:

- **Identification Information**
  - **Display Name** In most situations, this field is populated through the use of an Active Directory synchronization and should be left as autopopulated in that case. If users are not synchronized but Windows authentication is used, the display name is entered manually from PWA.
  - **E-Mail Address** If the e-mail address is populated in Active Directory, synchronization pulls it in here. The setting can also be entered manually.
  - **RBS** The resource breakdown structure is defined for each organization. Setting each resource to belong to the right location in the RBS is required.
  - **Initials** This field is autopopulated with the resource's first initial. If there is any requirement for the use of initials, the initial field should be changed and should be based on a data dictionary (a separate data location that lists all the initials to make sure that initials are not used by more than one user). This data dictionary is not something that is part of the Project Server environment, but can easily be done in a SharePoint list (which you will learn more about in Chapter 25) or in an Excel spreadsheet.
  - **Hyperlink Name** This setting is rarely used, but using it might make sense for a service organization to connect the user's resume to its ID in Project Server.
  - **Hyperlink URL** This concept is the same as Hyperlink Name.
  - **Account Status** This setting can be used to change whether a resource account is active. It is recommended that you use Active Directory rather than this setting when you need to disable a user's account.

- **User Authentication (PWA Only)**
  - **Authentication Type** If AD synchronization is used, this field is prepopulated with Windows authentication set. For non-Windows users, such as nonemployees, the system could be set to use forms authentication or other options. Note that there are limitations for accounts that use forms authentication, especially if these users need access to Data Analysis views.
  - **Synchronization** There is a checkbox that can be selected to prevent an account from using AD synchronization. Keep in mind that the AD synchronization process will remove users from Project Server if they are removed from AD, therefore it is usually advisable not to set this option to yes.
- **Assignment Attributes**
  - **Resource Leveling Allowed (PWA Only)** Resource leveling allows project managers to use Project Professional to perform complex calculations to balance (level) resources so that they are not overallocated within a project. To some degree, resource leveling can also be used across projects. Generally this setting is left on, although leveling is not commonly used, as it is both complex to understand and takes a very high level of experience to get expected results.
  - **Base Calendar** If organizations set up more than just a single enterprise calendar (for example, for different holidays in different countries and cultures), this field is where the appropriate base calendar is set for the resource.
  - **Default Booking Type** This field can be set to Committed or Proposed. By default, it is set to Committed and should usually be left that way. This setting determines whether a resource is definitely going to be assigned to a team or task, and therefore assignments reduce their availability (Committed), or the resource is only being considered (Proposed). Proposed bookings can be used for future resource planning without creating calendar exceptions or tasks appearing on user Time and Task pages.
  - **Timesheet Manager** The timesheet manager should usually be set to each resource's manager. If this field is left at its default setting, the user will be able to approve his or her own timesheets.
  - **Default Assignment Owner** By default, this field is set to the resource (for example, Lenny Bernstein is his own default assignment owner) and should be left that way. It can be changed if there is a resource whose assignments should be owned by someone else.
  - **Earliest Available** This field and the one to follow are used for instances when a resource will be available only for a limited time. You can set this field to a date when a resource will become available, such as the start date for a new employee's job or the first day that a consultant will be on site.
  - **Latest Available** This field can be used to set an employee's last day on the job or the last day for a consultant. This field and its predecessor can be used for other scenarios as well.
- **Resource Custom Fields** These fields can be defined for things such as roles and/or skills that can be set at the resource level.

- **Security Categories** These fields are rarely used at the resource level.
- **Global Permissions** These fields are rarely used at the resource level.
- **Group Fields** These fields are included with minimal or no out-of-the-box functionality, but can be used if an organization chooses. If the fields are used, the setting for each resource can then be configured using the tools discussed in this chapter.
  - **Group** The Group field is included by default, but there are no guidelines for its use nor does it have a particular function in the system. Use it as an attribute in any way that makes sense for your organization.
  - **Code** As with the Group field, use this field in any way that makes sense for the company.
  - **Cost Center** As with the previous two fields, there is no preset way to use this field. Use it as you like.
  - **Cost Type** This is a prebuilt field with a lookup table that can be modified from within the Enterprise Custom Fields area in Server Settings, but the lookup table is not populated with any types.
- **Team Details** Teams are configured in the Enterprise Custom Fields area. Inexplicably, there is a Team Name field out of the box, but no lookup table is included. This lookup table is required to use the resource team features of Project Server. This area of the system requires planning, as each resource can be assigned only to a single team.
- **System Identification Data** This area includes the following fields in display-only mode (with the exception of External ID):
  - **GUID** This field sets the resource's unique ID from the database perspective and is useful for deep troubleshooting.
  - **External ID** This is the only writable field in this section and can be used to link a resource to its corresponding ID in an external system, such as one used for enterprise resource planning or invoicing.
  - **Date Created** This field specifies the date that the resource was created.
  - **Date Last Updated** This field specifies the date that the resource was last modified.
  - **Checked Out By** This field identifies the individual who performs the checkout.
  - **Checkout Date** This field specifies the date on which checkout is to occur.

Build Team from PWA

Some organizations prefer to give the Build Team permission to resource managers in addition to or instead of project managers. Others may allow the project manager to build the team, but only if the team is using resources underneath them in the RBS hierarchy. If the resource managers have the Build Team permission and they are not also project managers, this process would be done through the PWA-based Build Team as opposed to the one in the Project Professional 2007 desktop client. The Assign Resource to Team permission is required to support this feature.

To build a project team from PWA, navigate to Project Center, highlight the row in which the project is located, and select Build Team. The screen shown in Figure 20-20 is displayed. From this page, the following options are available:

- Select resources from the left side by selecting the checkboxes and adding them to the project team.
- Select resources from the right side and remove them from the team. If they have actuals already recorded on the project, they are dimmed.
- Use the Match feature (which you will learn about later in this chapter).
- Use the Replace feature to replace a resource on every task in a project plan. This option is most useful when you are replacing a generic resource with an actual person.

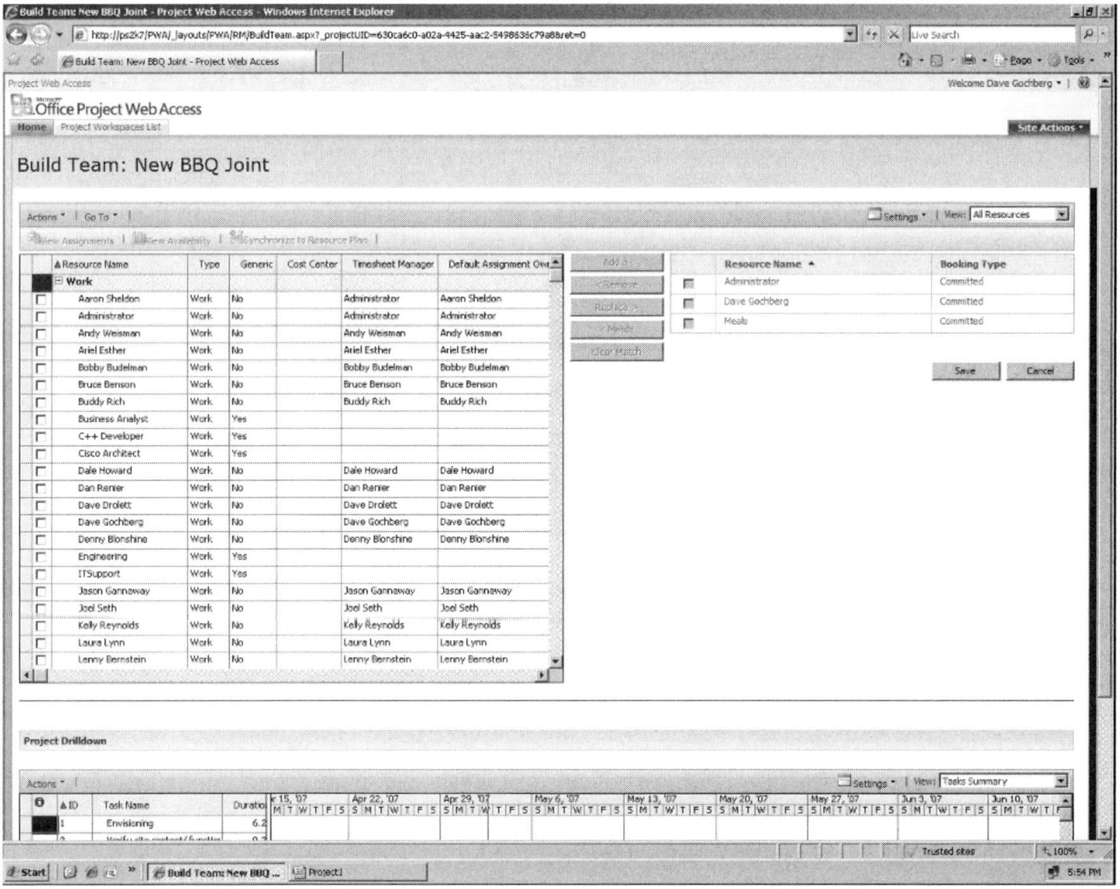

FIGURE 20-20 Build Team in PWA

Other tools for resource management are available from this page. Besides the default All Resources View, there are views for cost resources, material resources, and work resources. In addition, there are some other functions under Settings:

- **View Options** This function changes outline levels.
- **Filter** This option comes with a set of prebuilt filters for *ad hoc* filtering.
- **Search** This is a quick internal Search tool that is especially useful in large organizations.
- **Grouping** This option enables you to view resources by attribute, such as Timesheet Manager, as shown in Figure 20-21.

The resource manager can use this page to navigate to View Assignments or View Availability of the selected resources or to synchronize to a Resource Plan (Resource Plans were discussed earlier in this chapter).

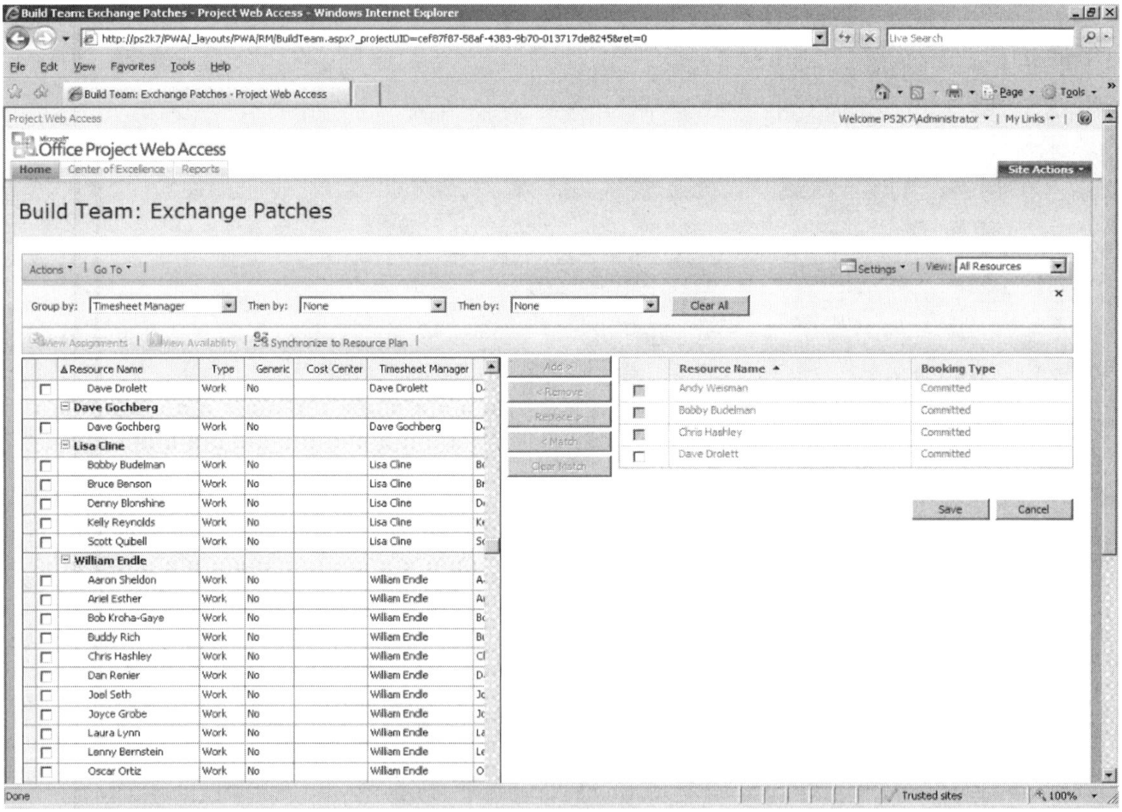

FIGURE 20-21 Resources grouped by timesheet manager

Surrogate Timesheets

If a resource is not available to complete a required timesheet, Project Server provides a way to complete a timesheet for someone else. The Surrogate Timesheet function normally is available only for use on a timesheet manager's resources. To perform this action, navigate to the My Timesheets page and select the Surrogate Timesheet button. See Figure 20-22 for the Surrogate Timesheet page.

Using this page, first browse to the name of the resource. Next, select one of the following settings:

- **Create with Default Setting** The Default setting is made inside the Timesheet Settings and Defaults page from Server Settings and can be set to one of three settings:
  - **Current Task Assignments** (This is usually the option that makes the most sense.)
  - **Current Projects**
  - **No Prepopulation**

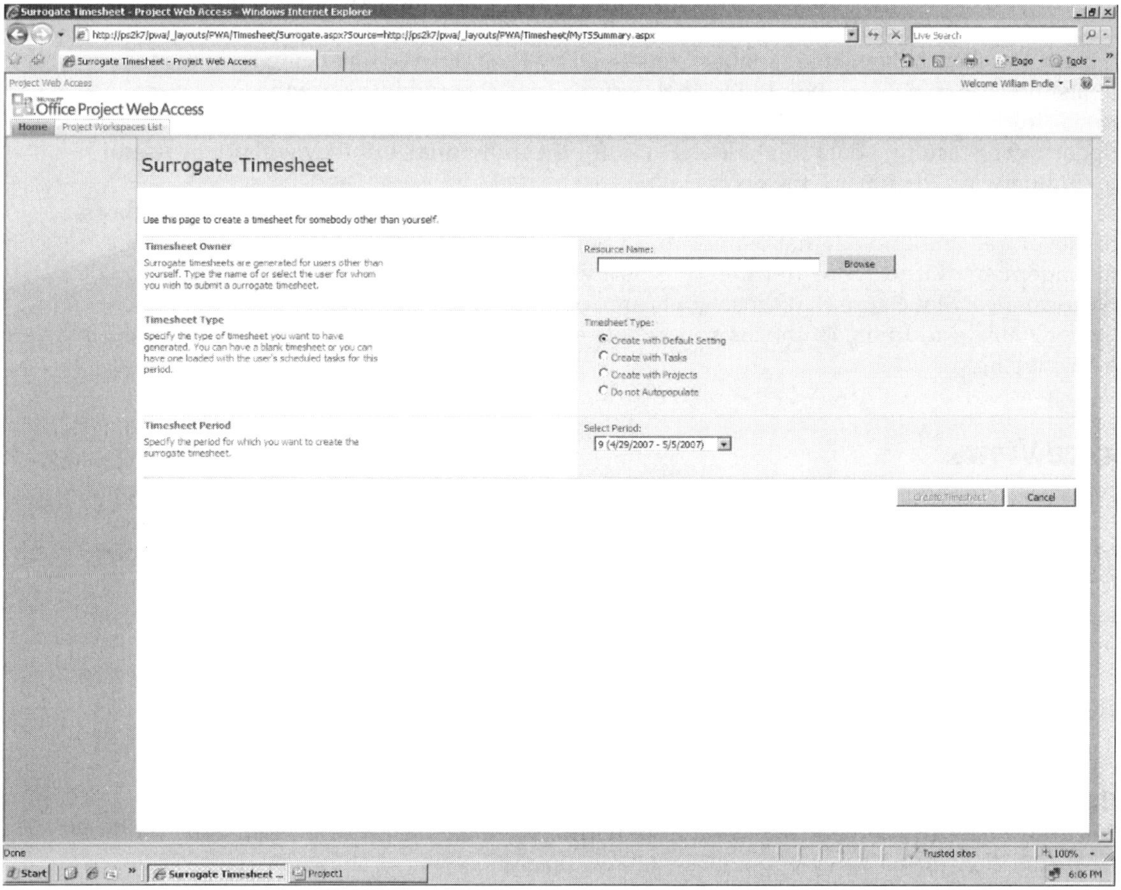

FIGURE 20-22 Surrogate Timesheet page

- **Create with Tasks** Use this or one of the next two options if it makes sense to use a format other than the default format.
- **Create with Projects** This option imports Tasks from all current projects.
- **Do Not Autopopulate** No prefilled task items are included.

After selecting the Tmesheet Type, select the Timesheet Period for which a timesheet is needed and select Create Timesheet. This timesheet can then be completed and submitted.

Using Resource Information

Organizations are always seeking ways to use data to improve their staff. These data can be generated through a combination of built-in and Custom Enterprise Resource fields, actual data from project task updates, and PWA views. Start by considering how the information is to be used. This is a very important consideration because if it used in certain ways, the behavior of the organization's team members could be influenced in ways that were not anticipated.

Here is an example. A resource manager brings data from Project Server into a resource's performance review. The resource manager asks bluntly why the individual's project tasks required 25 percent more work than estimated. There could be many causes for the overrun. If team members believe that numbers generated by Project Server are being used to make unjustified judgments on their individual performance, it could influence the team members to start fudging the numbers that they enter into Project Server from their timesheet and task updates. The resulting data might look better for the individual, but they will not be useful in finding ways to improve the organization.

EPM tools can be used as part of a performance management infrastructure. The authors, however, recommend against using Project Server as a tool for individual performance management. Rather, consider the tools as a way to improve overall organizational performance. Make sure that those goals are communicated to the people using Project Server 2007. In addition, let the team members know that their honest input is considered in a positive light.

Resource Views

A useful set of built-in views is available for support of resource management in Project Server. Almost certainly, however, none of these views will be the exact fit for any particular organization, and resource managers should be part of the project team and provide their input for what these views should include. They are easy to modify. Often the more difficult job is deciding what they should display rather than modifying that display once requirements are set.

Resource Center Top Level

The Resource Center page displays a list of resources to which the viewer has permission.

Built-in Resource Views

There are some great built-in views for resource management. Start by navigating to Resource Center. A View dropdown menu appears on the top-right corner as shown in Figure 20-23.

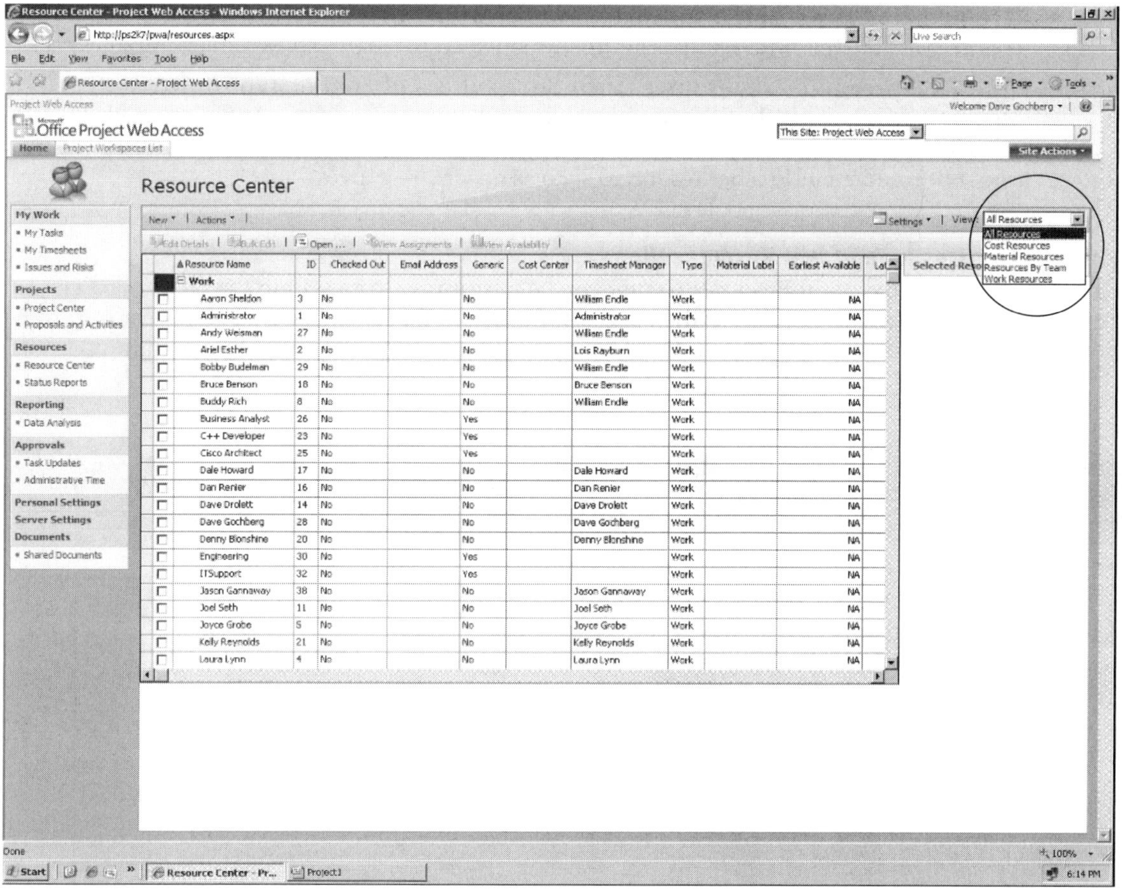

FIGURE 20-23 Resource Center's View dropdown menu

Five views are available from the menu:

- **All Resources** These resources are grouped by resource type (Work, Cost, and Material) and this view includes a large, interesting set of resource information.
- **Cost Resources** This view displays only cost resources (examples might include lodging, airfare, other project-related travel costs, lease costs, storage space rental, and so on).
- **Material Resources** This view includes information about material resources and can include items such as computer purchase cost, raw materials such as lumber in board feet, rolled-up costs for items such as a power pole (as opposed to the metal, wires, and so on that comprise the total pole), specialized facilities such as an x-ray suite or a special robotics facility, and many other possibilities.

- **Resources by Team** This distinctive view displays resource information for resources associated with team assignment pools. Figure 20-24 shows an example.
- **Work Resources** Work resources include resources filtered on type 0 (work resources). In other words, this view shows only resources that are set to be assigned to work on a task. Usually these resources are the actual people who work on project tasks, but could include other resources such as generic resources.

Possible Changes in Top-Level Resource Views

Changing Views in the main Resource Center can be performed from within the Server Settings area of Project Server 2007 if the user has the required permissions. Changes can be simple, such as removing a column that is not needed or reordering the columns that

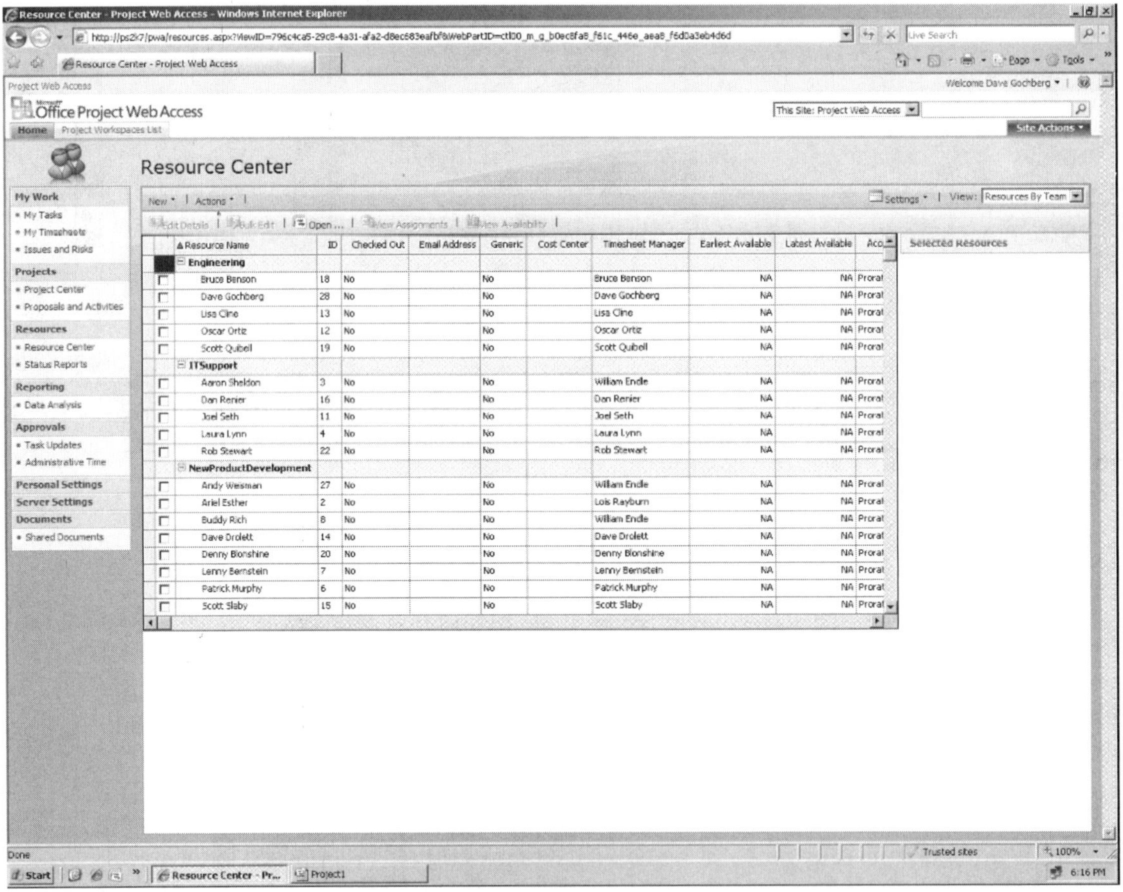

FIGURE 22-24 Resources by Team View in Resource Center

are displayed. Resource views do not generally require complex formulas, but do tend to need "personalization."

Personalization in this context refers to using the same data source to provide the appropriate subset of data depending on who is viewing the system. For example, some organizations allow team members to view only their own data, resource managers to view the information for those over whom they have supervisory responsibility, and the program management office (PMO) staff to see all resource information. These differences would normally be set using security categories.

It is also possible to display different information in a custom view. Such a view might make sense, for example, when resource managers in the Information Technology (IT) Department are interested in different columns altogether from the managers in the Marketing or New Product Development departments. Consider all these possibilities when planning the EPM project requirements.

Assignment Views

Assignment and Availability views are two very powerful assets in understanding what resources are working on and what openings there may be in their availability. To select the resources for which assignment information is sought, use the checkboxes to the left of each name. Notice how the right side of the page displays any resources that have been selected. These selections are remembered the next time that the user navigates to Resource Center. Select All and Clear All options are available when you click the Actions button. After choosing the correct resources, select the View Assignments button, as shown in Figure 20-25.

This displays a screen in which you can view the individual resource assignments. The out-of-the-box Summary View groups the assignments by resource, then project, then assignment, and includes Work, Remaining Work, Start, Finish, % Work Complete, and Resource Name fields. Figure 20-26 shows how this information is displayed.

By default, a single Summary View is available. It is organized by resource, then project, then summary task, then task assignment levels. More views that contain different data can be built to meet the organization's needs.

As Chapter 9 describes, you can control how the data are displayed by using the Settings button.

Availability Views

The availability views that launch from Resource Center in PWA are among the most valuable tools for resource management. They do, however, require that the data be accurately gathered. If project managers do not appropriately build their project plans, or if the task updating process is allowed to slip, the data will be invalid. For resource management to be successful, process adoption is absolutely critical.

FIGURE 20-25 View Assignments button

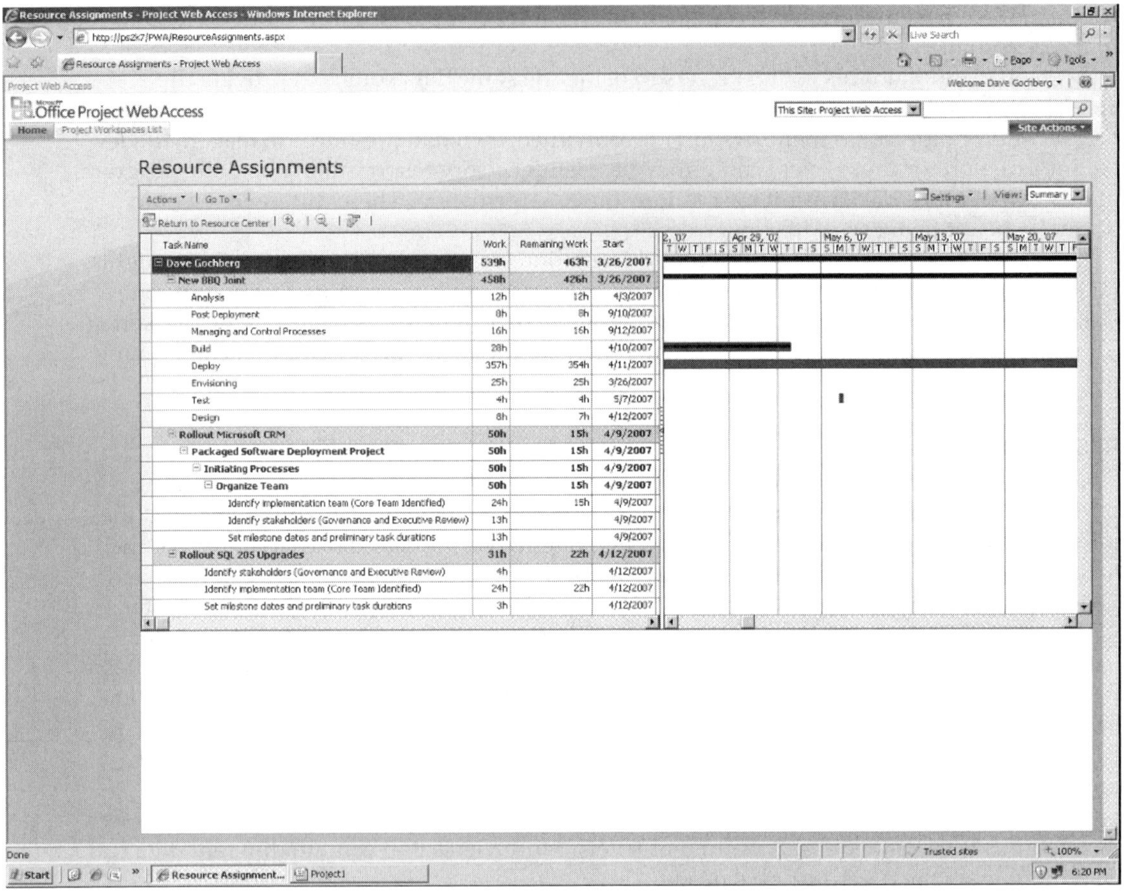

FIGURE 20-26 Resource Assignments Summary View

To view resource availability views, start at the Resource Center, then select the resources that are part of the particular set of required information that is sought. Next select the View Availability button, as shown in Figure 20-27.

Four different out-of-the-box views are available from the dropdown menu on the top-right of the horizontal bar:

- **Assignment Work by Resource** The top of this page is a bar chart that shows the combined assignment work, with each resource displayed as a separate color. The red line represents the total capacity for the selected resources. To the right of

FIGURE 20-27 View Availability button

the bar chart, each resource is listed with a checkbox next to its name. You can modify the view to see one resource or a subset of the originally selected resources. At the bottom of the page is a table that lists each resource with separate rows indicating their availability and capacity, and a row for each project to which they are assigned. All the numbers are displayed. If you click the Settings button and select View Options, you can include proposed bookings and control the date range that you are viewing. Figure 20-28 shows this view.

- **Assignment Work by Project** This view displays a bar chart that shows combined hours for the resources that have been selected, with each color in the bar representing a single project. The legend on the right side includes checkboxes that can be used to reduce the number of projects that are being viewed. Capacity is represented by the dark red line. The bottom of the page lists each project, then each

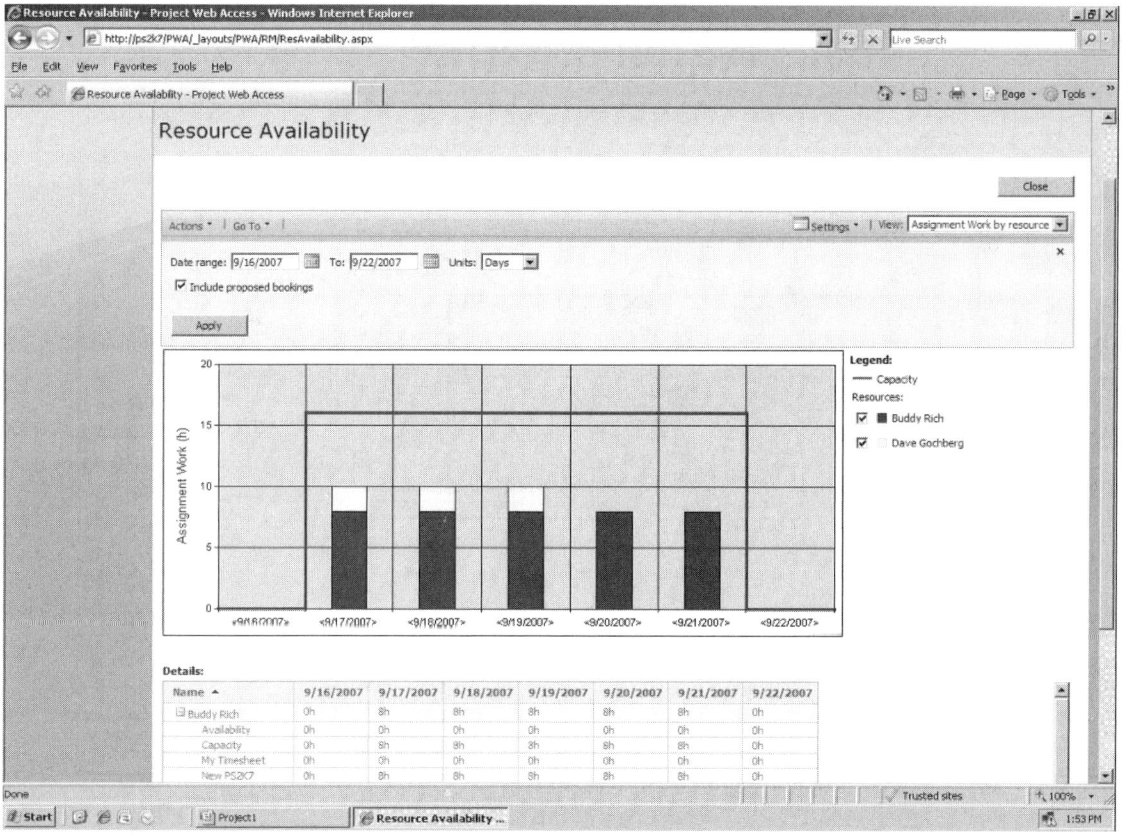

FIGURE 20-28 Assignment Work by Resource View

resource, and then the amount of work within each period. Periods can be defined by selecting Settings | View Options, changing the date range and units (days, weeks, months, or years), and clicking the Apply button. There is also an Include Proposed Bookings checkbox. Figure 20-29 shows this view.

- **Remaining Availability** This view displays the remaining availability of the previously selected resources. The legend allows for deselection to reduce the scope of the view to fewer resources. Each resource is represented by a single color. The most useful part of this view is near the bottom of the page, the Details section, where the grid indicates whether each resource has remaining availability. Just as with the Assignment by Work View, you can reduce or expand periods by selecting

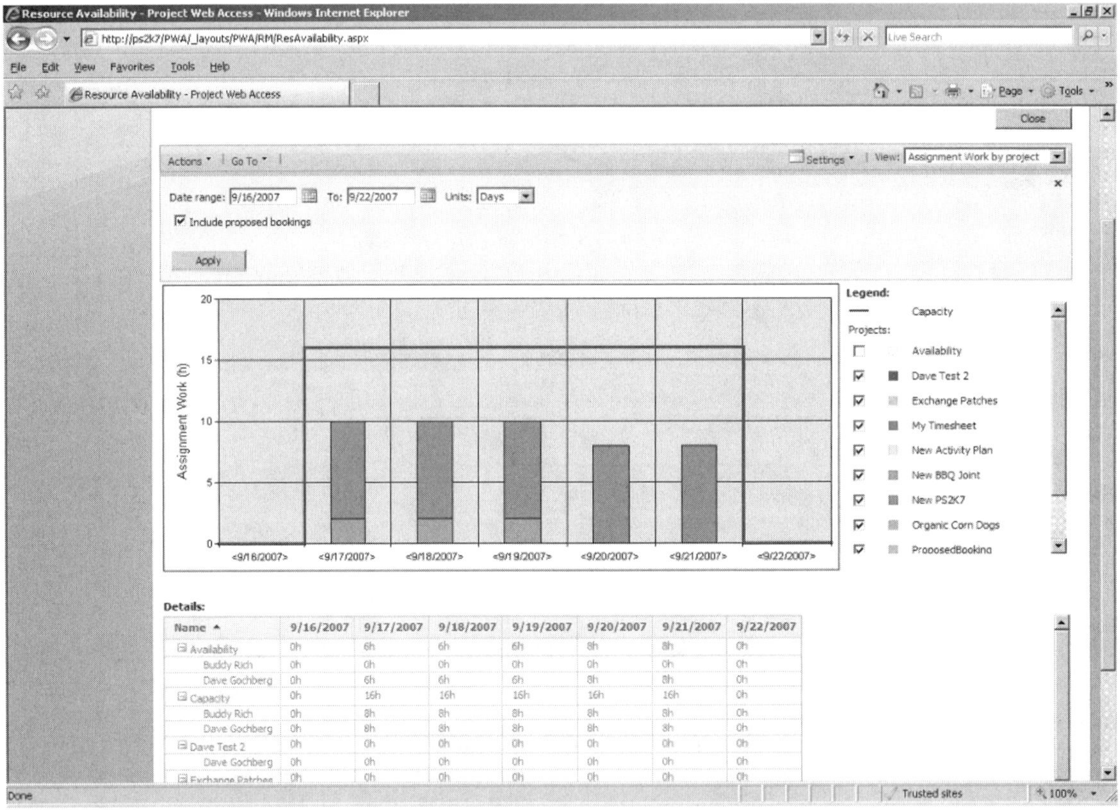

FIGURE 20-29 Assignment Work by Project View

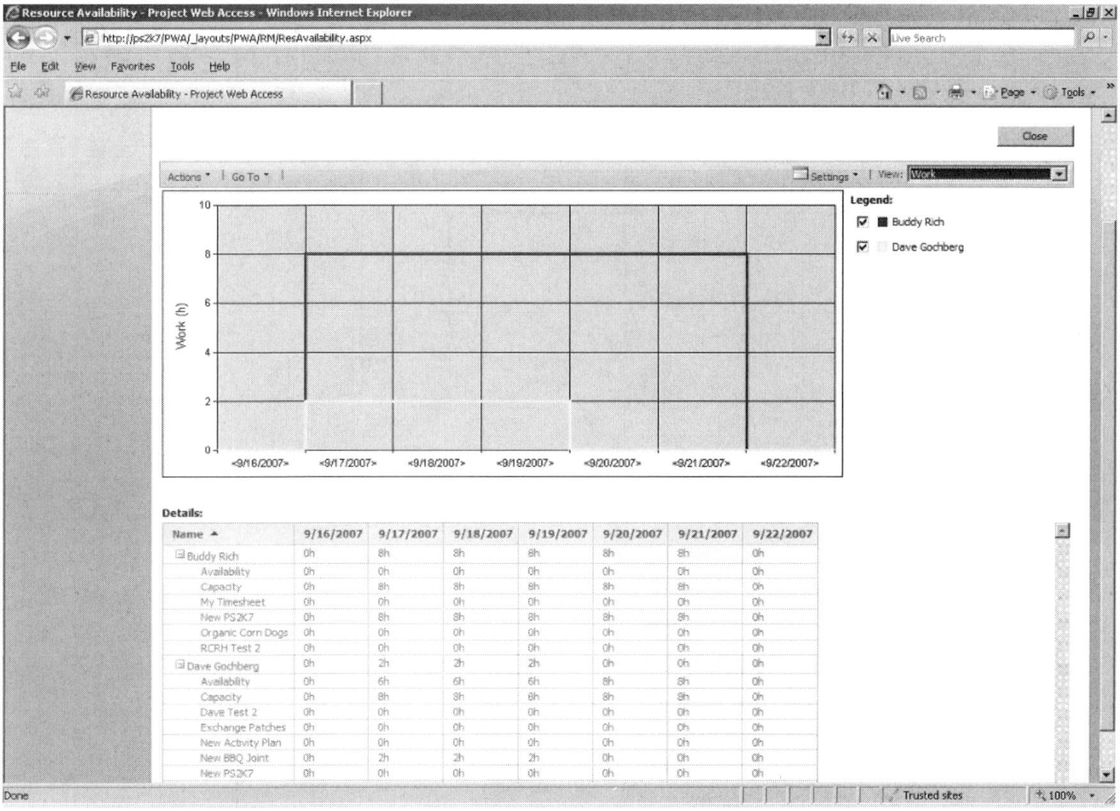

FIGURE 20-30 Remaining Availability View

Settings | View Options, changing the date range and units (days, weeks, months, and years), and then clicking the Apply button. There is also an Include Proposed Bookings checkbox. Figure 20-30 shows an example of the Remaining Availability View.

- **Work** This view displays work by resource over a specified timeframe. Like the Remaining Availability View, Work View enables you to change unit scale as described previously. Note that this is another view where the table at the bottom is more useful than the chart at the top. The Details section is organized by resource, then by project, and includes availability and capacity numbers. Note that this view also displays hours saved in timesheets. Figure 20-31 shows the Work View.

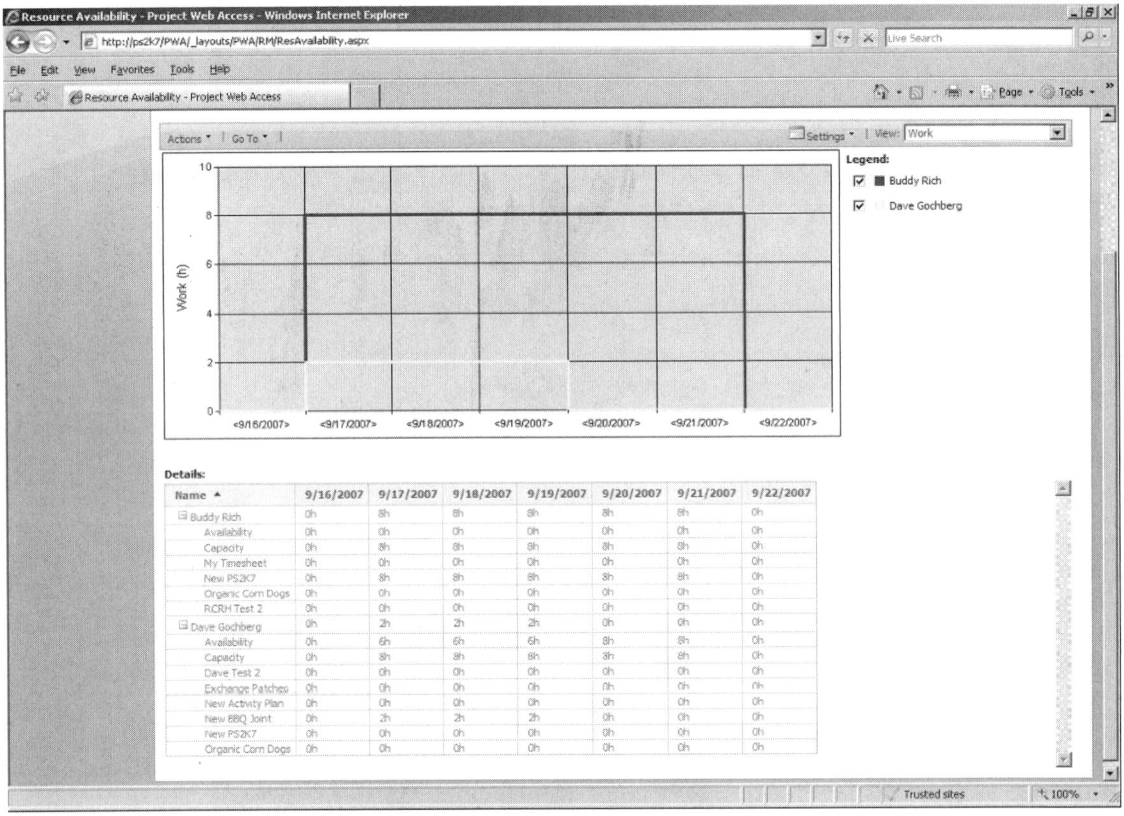

FIGURE 20-31 Work View from within Resource Center View Availability

Use of Generic Resources

Project Server 2007 and Project Professional 2007 include a feature called generic resources. Generic resources are built through the same tools as other resources. They represent a placeholder, usually based on a role that can be applied to projects or enterprise project templates, to assist in several ways:

- **Capacity planning** Generic resources assist with capacity planning without assigning specific resources to tasks. An example would be using a generic resource called DBA to plan how much DBA capacity will be required in the months ahead.
- **Templates** If you assign a generic resource to specific tasks in an enterprise project template, the project manager will be able to use it while constructing a plan based on one of the templates. If a task is staffed with the generic resource DBA, the project manager knows to look for an actual DBA when seeking the appropriate actual person. You'll learn more about this topic in the "Resource Skills" section later in this chapter.

- **Matching** Using generic resources for matching is discussed in the "Matching Resources" section later in this chapter.

At the time of the writing of this chapter, there is one issue that exists with using generic resources assigned to specific tasks in a template. Whoever builds the template and posts it to Project Server will take on the role of default assignment owner for that assignment. This is expected, but what is not expected is that after an actual project is created, this assignment owner stays with the template builder rather than being transferred to the new status manager (the project manager). Thus, as long as there is a generic resource on any plan built with the template, the task will appear in the original template publisher's Task pages.

Matching Resources

While you are creating a custom enterprise resource field, there is a setting that is used for matching. The matching function is part of the Build Team from Enterprise tool in Project Professional and the Build Team options in PWA. When the setting is enabled on a custom enterprise resource field, a resource is selected from the existing project team (the right side) and the Match button is selected, the available resources (the left side) are filtered to display only those resources that are an exact match to the resource on the project.

Keep in mind that the resource on the project team could be a generic resource, which is a common and powerful way to use this feature. Assume that there is an enterprise custom resource field created that is called Role and each resource has a single role associated with its ID. In the DBA generic resource example, if the generic DBA assigned to a project team is selected from the right when the Match button is selected, only people who are DBAs will display. Another possible use is for matching to resource skills. You'll learn about this use in the following section.

Resource Skills

Skills-based resourcing is an important and somewhat lofty goal for most EPM implementations. Most organizations aspire to achieve this objective, but don't know where to start. In a nutshell, the organization must go through a process that is similar to the following:

1. Establish what skills matter to an organization. These skills should not be narrowly defined; for example, they should not be limited to only technical skills. Often included in addition to technical skills are the languages that resources speak and their subject matter expertise (HIPAA, Sarbanes-Oxley compliance, customer service, communications, marketing, six sigma, intellectual property law, human resources, and so on).
2. Decide whether to include level of skills. Does an organization need to understand whether a resource is a Mandarin speaker or does it need to know how well the resource speaks Mandarin (beginner, moderate, or fluent)? If skills-based resource management is required, it is important to understand that this is a difficult process to accomplish effectively and that it requires substantial planning and executive support.

3. Assess the skills of the company's resources. This is difficult. There are several approaches for getting this information. Although many larger organizations use systems that store this type of information, the information is rarely of high quality. For smaller companies, after defining which skills are important, try surveying the users to ask them to assess their own skills. This is a good start, but often resources will say they have a skill even though their skill level is not high enough to be useful (rather than having years of experience, for example, perhaps they took a four-hour class three years ago). The opposite can also be true. After the resources assess their skills, ask each manager to review and adjust the resource's input. This is not a perfect process, but it is a good start.
4. Decide whether to use this field for matching, keeping in mind that the Match feature displays only an *exact match.*
5. Assign each resource's skills to the individual resources.

TIP *When planning the EPM project, there should be a discussion about the strategy and approach for handling skills, roles, generic resources, and teams due to overlap in some functionality. This discussion can be complex and often requires consulting assistance for assessment objectivity.*

A Word on Local Resources

The idea of the Enterprise Resource Pool is that all resources are being drawn from a single database to support the ability to view all resource data across projects, locations, and departments. It is possible to assign a resource that is not part of the Enterprise Resource Pool to a project team, and resources can be assigned to tasks.

Local resources are identified by a dark head graphic in a Project Professional Resource Sheet and in other Resource views in Project Professional.

Using Local Resources is strongly discouraged. It can only cause problems with an organization's understanding of what is actually occurring and there are some technical considerations. Just say no to using local resources.

The resource management features within Project Server can provide organizations with substantial improvements in their resource efficiency and visibility into capacity. It is vital to the success of an EPM project that use of these features is carefully planned. In addition, make sure that it is understood that deep resource management functionality will not be achieved in early iterations, as many other aspects of the project must be put into place before the organization receives the value from using these tools. The next chapter covers the role of the project manager in a Project Server environment.

CHAPTER 21

How the Project Manager Interacts with Project Server

This chapter describes the way that the project manager interacts with the components of Microsoft Office Project Server 2007. Other tomes on this topic have tended to include everything that might be possible, depending on configuration decisions. Instead of taking that tack, this chapter is based on the author's experience of what the more common interactions are likely to be, and makes substantial assumptions about the system settings.

Project managers tend to assume that using Project Server will make their jobs easier. That assumption is reasonable from the perspective of increasing the percentage of successful projects, their ability to get better information about progress or project tasks, better team collaboration, and improved communications, risk management, issue management, scope management, and so on. Using Project Server will not, however, reduce the amount of time that the project manager will need to spend actively managing projects. It *could*, in fact, increase the project manager's work load. In the long term, the benefits outweigh the work for the project manager. In addition, organizationwide improvements will be clear if Project Server is implemented effectively and is married to continual improvement in project management maturity and process development.

The project manager role in any Enterprise Project Management (EPM) environment is the most complex. This is also true for Project Server 2007.

Project Manager Basic Lifecycle

This section describes the project manager's view on the project lifecycle from the basic perspective. Plans are built and published from Project Professional with resources applied from the Project Server Enterprise Resource Pool. Team members are notified of assignments and record their task updates to Project Web Access (PWA). Project managers approve (or reject) the updates, and the project plan is then synchronized back to Project Professional. Along the way, Project Workspaces are provisioned, allowing for project teams to collaborate using powerful tools for document management (check-out, check-in, versioning, rollback, Recycle Bin, and more). Projects are tracked and become visible in the context of programs, portfolios, or just in general with the use of PWA views and, to a lesser extent, Project Professional Reports.

Connecting to Microsoft Office Project Server 2007 from the Project 2007 Client

Some organizations have processes for proposing projects that are used to determine which projects should be executed. This book covers that topic in a separate chapter. For now, the assumption is that the project has the "green light" and that the project manager is now tasked with building and then executing the project.

The project manager starts by opening Microsoft Office Project Professional 2007 (assuming that he or she has the correct permissions and has had the Project client configured to connect to the Project Server). If presented with the dialog shown in Figure 21-1, the project manager selects OK without making any other changes. (The authors prefer the manual connection setting. This connection to Project Server can be set to fully connect without this dialog being presented if the connection is set to automatically connect.)

Either start building a project manually or start the project by using an Enterprise Project template (as described in the next section).

Using Enterprise Templates

Project Server can be used to support continual growth in project management maturity. A part of that Project Server support is in its ability to house Enterprise Project templates that can be accessed by project managers across the organization. These templates usually start with a base set of included items, such as a work breakdown structure (WBS) to support the specific methodology of the company, and may include generic resources (see Chapter 20) applied to tasks in the template to support the Project Server Build Team tool Match and Replace functions (you will learn more about these topics later in this chapter).

Over time, more templates are developed that are targeted at specific repeatable projects. This makes sense where organizations have gathered knowledge about details of the specific project type and can eventually include task estimates that are reasonably accurate based on historical data.

These templates are valuable for several reasons:

- They reduce the project manager's time for building new project plans.
- They assist in keeping project plans consistent with organizational methodology and project standards.

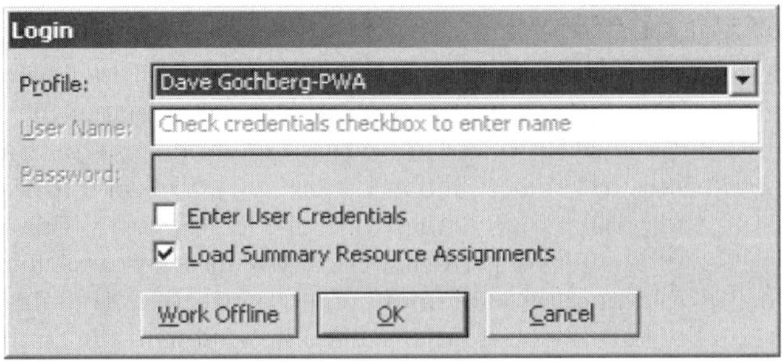

FIGURE 21-1 Login to Project Server

- Using generic resources or using actual resources set to Proposed rather than to Committed provides information that can be used for resource projections if future potential projects are published as part of a portfolio process.

These templates are generally posted by a closely held group of people, such as a project management office (PMO) or Project Server administrator. These templates are made available to all project managers. To start a project by using an Enterprise template, follow the process described next.

For a new project, click File | New as shown in Figure 21-2.

Next select On Computer. Then click the Enterprise Templates tab and select the project template that is most appropriate as shown in Figure 21-3.

The project should now open prepopulated with a predetermined set of tasks and resources.

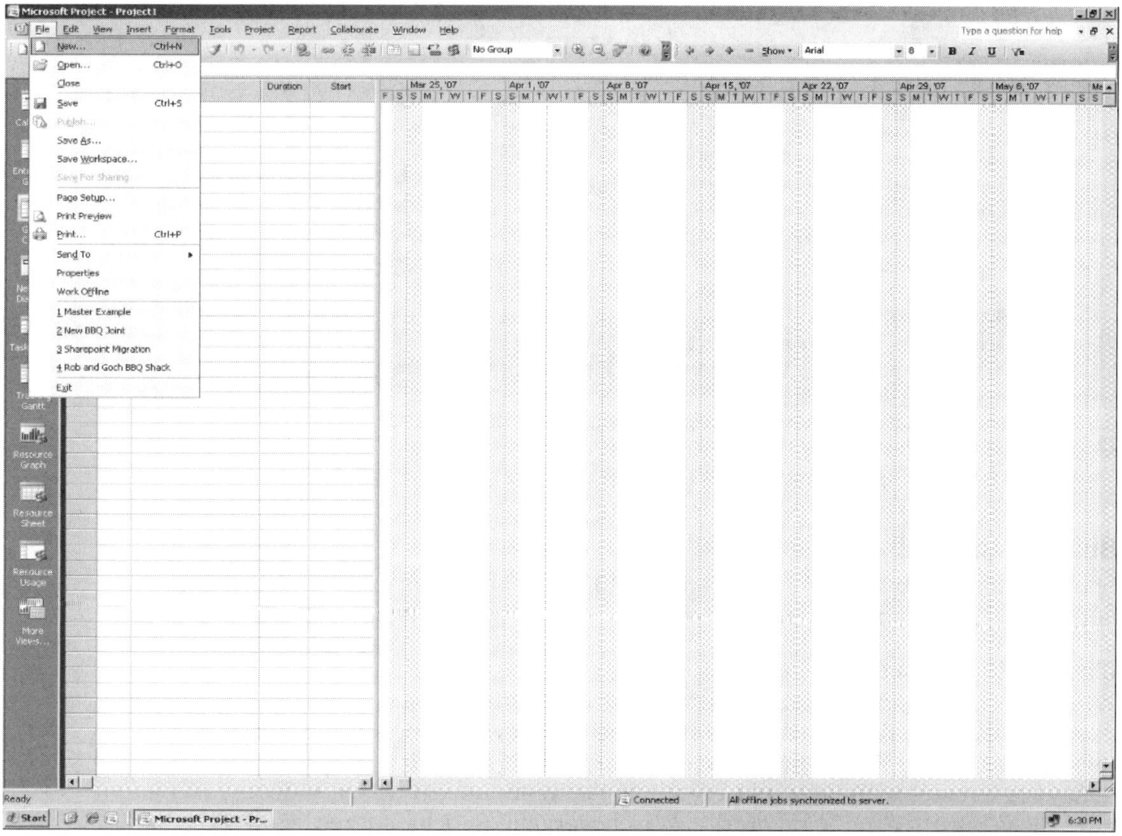

FIGURE 21-2 New project selection

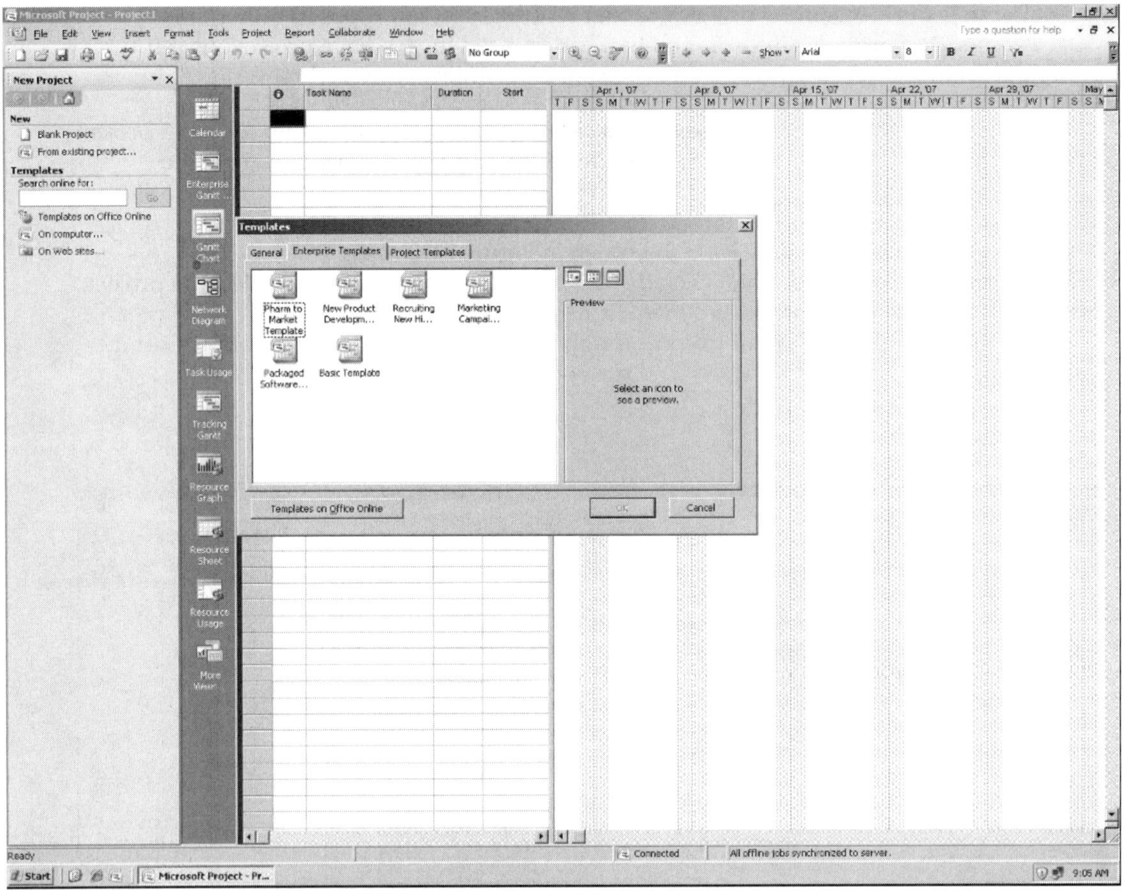

FIGURE 21-3 Enterprise templates

Building the Plan

The next step is to build out the Project Plan to reflect how the project will be executed. As noted above, the plan may be built from scratch or by using a template.

Changing the Project Start Date

Whether you are using an Enterprise template or starting a brand new project, change the project start date to the date that you think the project will start. Select Project | Project Information and set the date with the calendar tools. If the plan is built from scratch, it will default to Today. A template will have a date that reflects what was included when the template was posted to the Enterprise. Whichever date is included, see Figure 21-4 for setting a different project start date.

The next section describes how to change the status manager, a key function when using Enterprise templates.

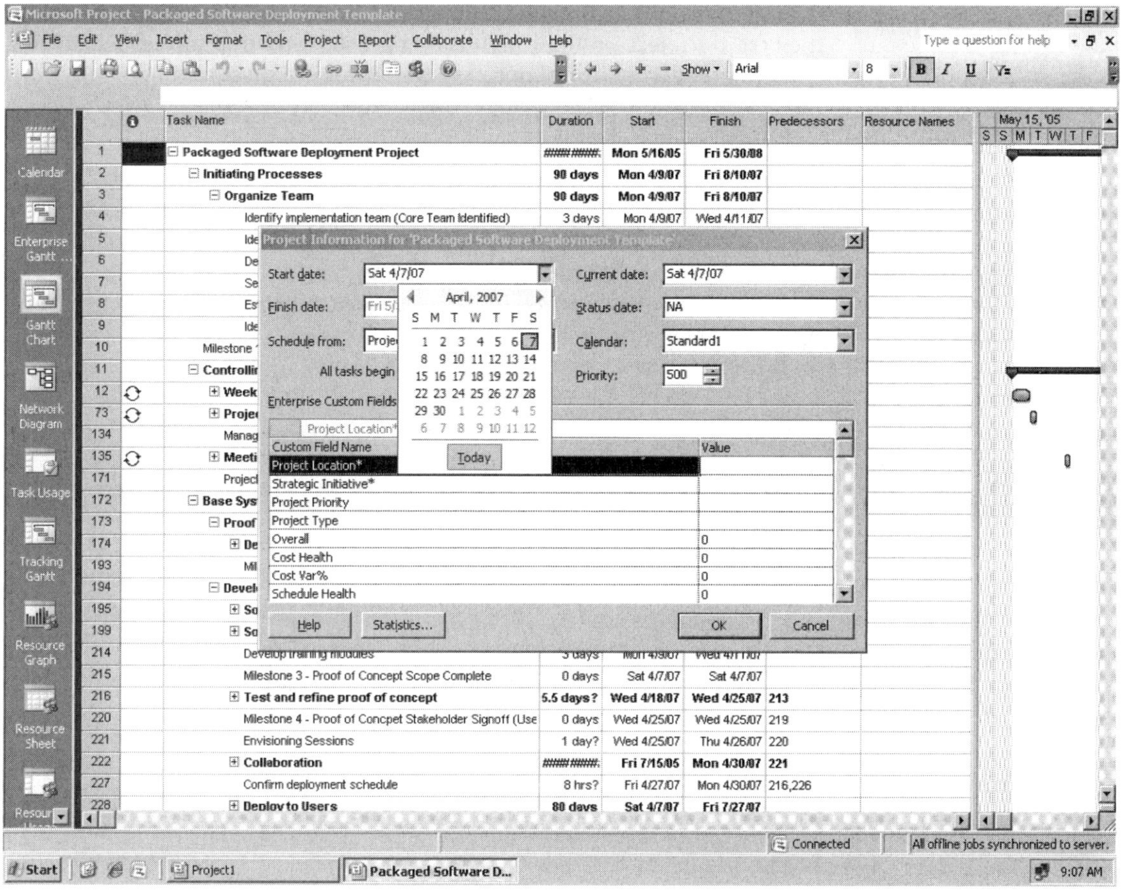

FIGURE 21-4 Set Project Start

Changing the Status Manager

In Project Server 2007, the status manager is the resource in charge of managing a particular task. This feature can be leveraged when more than one project manager is involved in a single project, but most of the time it specifies the person who receives task status updates for approval, which is normally one person per project.

There is a known issue with the Microsoft 2007 EPM environment that each project manager must address in his or her plan when using Enterprise Project templates. If a template is working as it should, once it is opened, it automatically changes the status manager to the person who opens it and then saves the project under its real project name. Unfortunately, although this process correctly changes the summary tasks, the detailed tasks retain the name of whoever posted the template. Here is a workaround in the form of the UpdateStatusManager macro.

For example, to work, this macro assumes that the Enterprise Gantt Chart View (one of the Views available out of the box in Project Professional) is being used, and in that view the Status Manager field has been added as a column (later in this chapter is a discussion on how to add a column). In the example, the DATE AND NAME text could be replaced by an organization's developer, or it could just be deleted.

The Status Manager Macro

Many thanks to Claus Nielson at Microsoft, with whom we had the opportunity to work, for creating the original macro!

Start the code below

```
Sub UpdateStatusManager()
' Macro UpdateStatusManager
' Macro Recorded  DATE AND NAME
On Error GoTo Err_Catch

    Dim objActiveProject As Project
    Dim i As Integer
    Set objActiveProject = ActiveProject
    ViewApply Name:="Enterprise Gantt Chart"
    If objActiveProject.Tasks.Count > 0 Then
        SelectTaskField Row:=0, Column:="Status Manager",
RowRelative:=False
        EditCopy
        For i = 1 To objActiveProject.Tasks.Count

            SelectTaskField Row:=i, Column:="Status Manager",
RowRelative:=False
            EditPaste
        Next i
        SelectTaskField Row:=0, Column:="Indicators",
RowRelative:=False
    End If

Err_Resume:
    'Error catching
    Set objActiveProject = Nothing
    Exit Sub

Err_Catch:
    MsgBox Err.Description
    Resume Err_Resume

End Sub
```

That ends the macro code

The plan must allow macros in order for this one to run. To set macro security, navigate to Tools | Options | Security | Macro Security and set the security level to Medium or Low, as shown in Figure 21-5. Note also that all tasks must be expanded (that is, they cannot be rolled up).

The plan must also display the Project Summary Task (task 0). If there is no task 0, select File | Options, click the View tab, then fill in the field as shown in Figure 21-6.

Once installed, the UpdateStatusManager macro is available via Tools | Macro | Macros, which displays the Macros dialog shown in the Figure 21-7.

In the Macros dialog, select the macro and run it. It will place your name throughout the project as status manager. To see the macro actually run, you must be in the Enterprise Gantt View (in this example). It is recommended that you include this macro in the Enterprise Global template and that you place a button for running the macro on one of the toolbars.

NOTE *We expect a fix for the status macro issue to be released soon. It still provides value, however, as a utility for use when changing ownership of a complete project. In that case, the new PM would open the project and run the macro. Changing owners also requires changing the owner from within the PWA Project Center | Edit Project Properties feature.*

Building the Team

The next step is often to create your project team. The other option would be to choose to build the WBS (or modify the Enterprise template) of the project first. Assuming that the

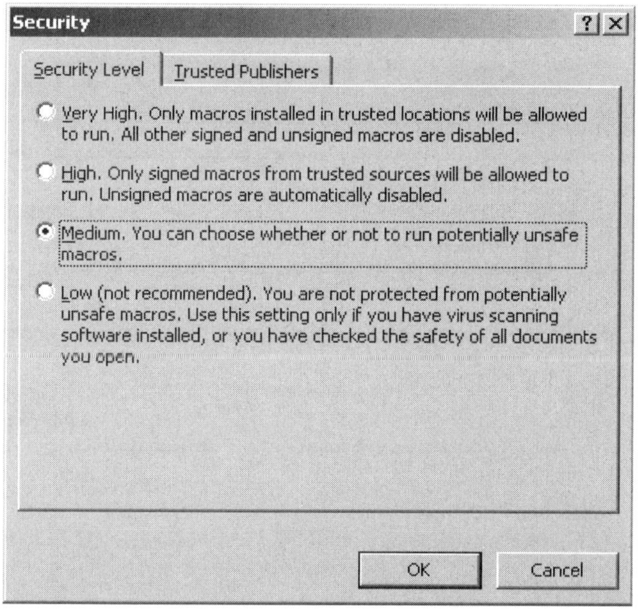

FIGURE 21-5 Macro security settings

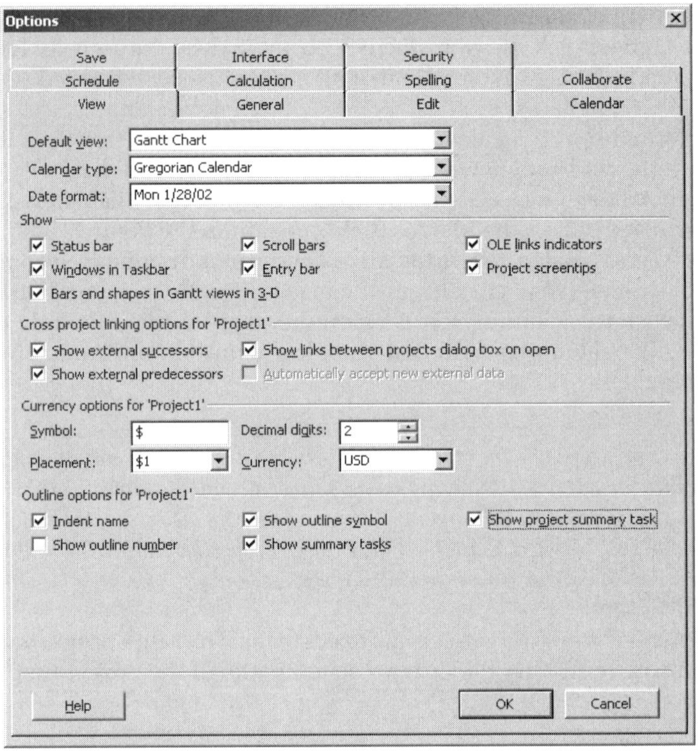

FIGURE 21-6 Project Summary Task

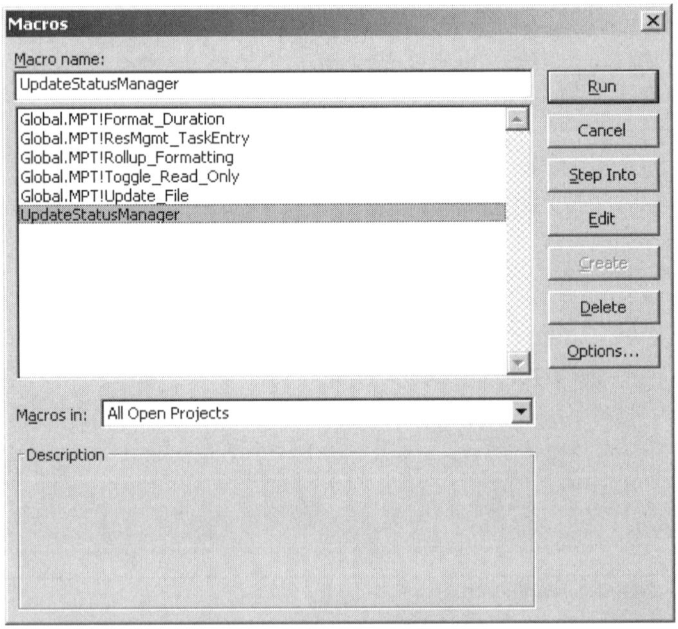

FIGURE 21-7 Locating the macro

resources will be populated first, choose Tools | Build Team from Enterprise as shown in Figure 21-8.

This feature provides a view displaying all the resources to which you have permission. These resources are populated on the left side of the window. This is the most basic view that the tool offers, as you can accomplish much more with it. (You will learn more about the Build Team tool later in this chapter.)

Select your team by highlighting who you want and selecting the Add button. (Note that you can use the CTRL key to select more than one resource at a time.) Notice in Figure 21-9 that after the user has added three resources, they now appear on the right side of the page and are dimmed on the left side. If you have your team set, select OK.

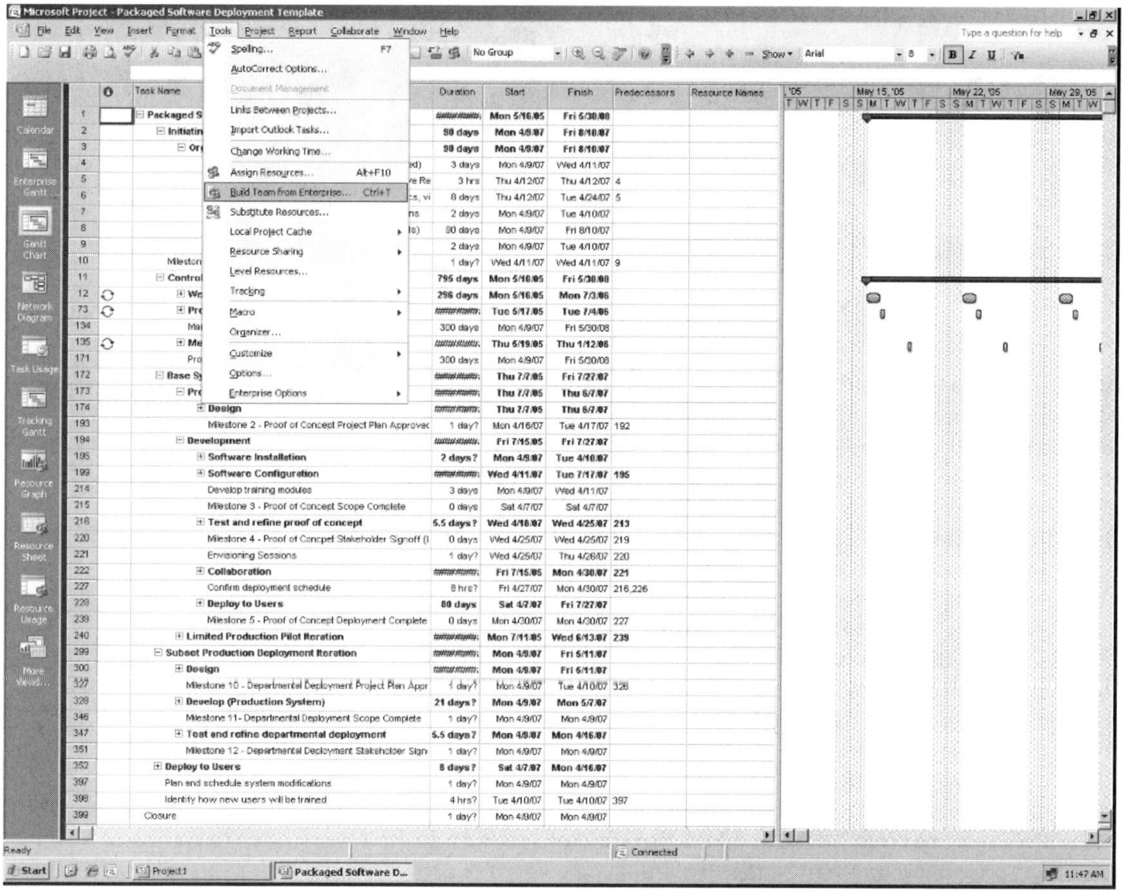

FIGURE 21-8 Select Tools | Build Team from Enterprise

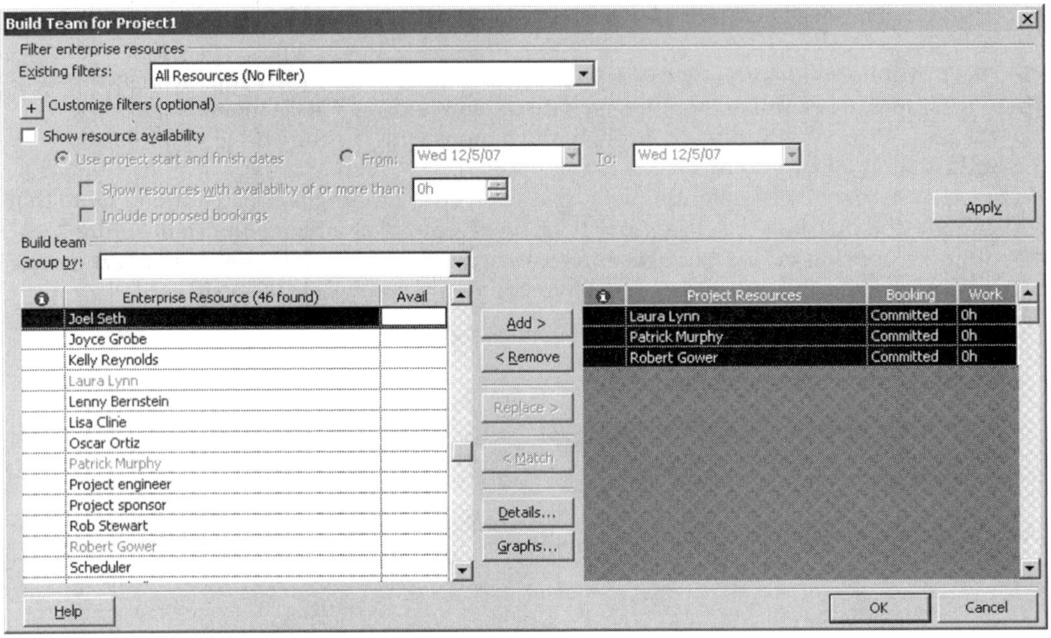

FIGURE 21-9 Select resources from the Build Team tool

Assigning Resources and Making Task Modifications

Now your team is assigned to the project. The next step is to start modifying the plan. There are several methods for each of the functions described in this section that you will learn over time, but the preferred method is as follows: Position your cursor in the white (Gantt Chart) area of the page and right-click. Select Split. From there, you have options for several views at the bottom of the page. To see the options, just right-click on the large gray area on the bottom right. In the example shown in Figure 21-10, we have selected our favorite called Resource Work. Next select a single task and populate the resource(s) as shown in Figure 21-10. Note that each resource must be entered on a separate row.

Also, from the bottom half of the split screen, you can change the task type, set units (the percentage of the resource's availability), and define how much work (effort, not duration) that the task will take. Usually, it is best to leave the Duration setting alone and allow the tool to calculate it for you as seen in Figure 21-10. Notice that Buddy Rich was allocated 25 percent of his time to work on this task and Lenny Bernstein was set to 50 percent. Also set in the example were the specific work hours expected for each resource. After OK was selected, the tool determined that it would take a duration of seven and a half work days to complete the task. Note that many parameters are in play during this process and the results will vary depending on each variable.

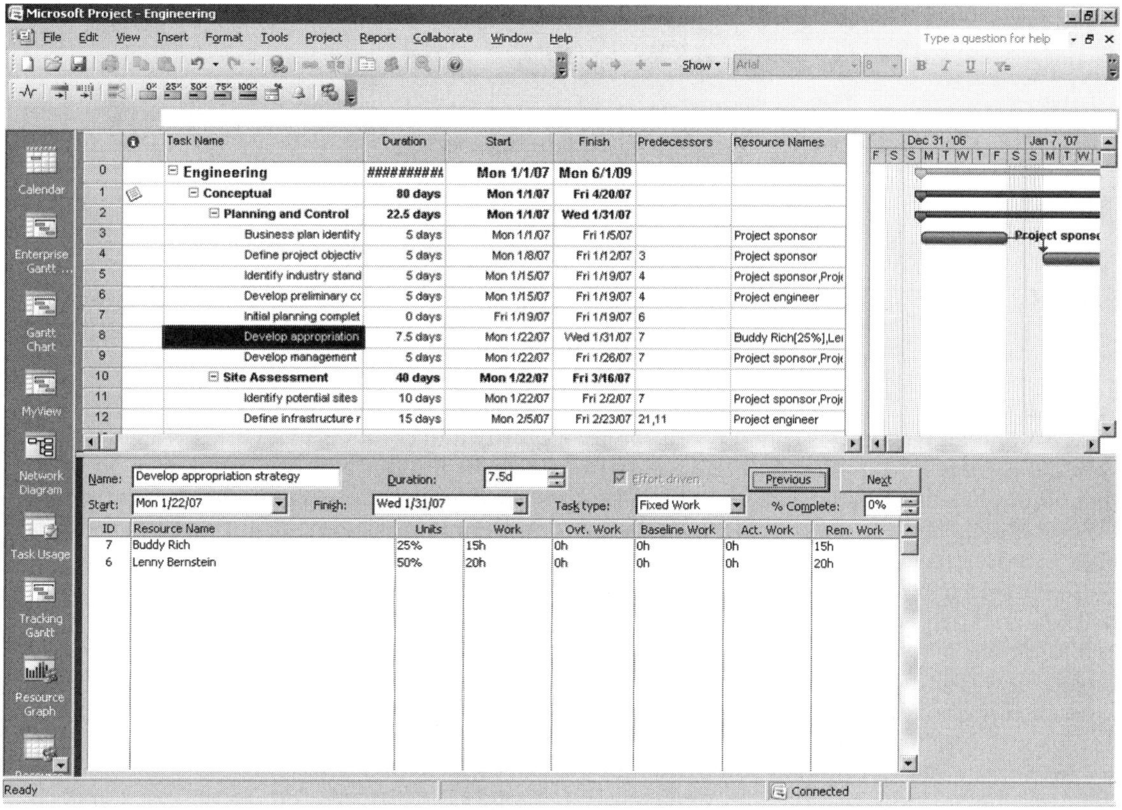

FIGURE 21-10 Adding a resource in a split view

When you select OK, the Previous and Next buttons appear and you can navigate to the rest of your plan's tasks.

You can remove the split by right-clicking in the same white Gantt Chart area and selecting Remove Split. Note that there are several prebuilt views that allow access to different information in your plan and that are easily accessed from the View Bar. If you don't see the View Bar, select Views | View Bar and it will appear. The most commonly used views include Enterprise Gantt, Tracking Gantt, and Resource Sheet, but the correct choice is very organization-specific.

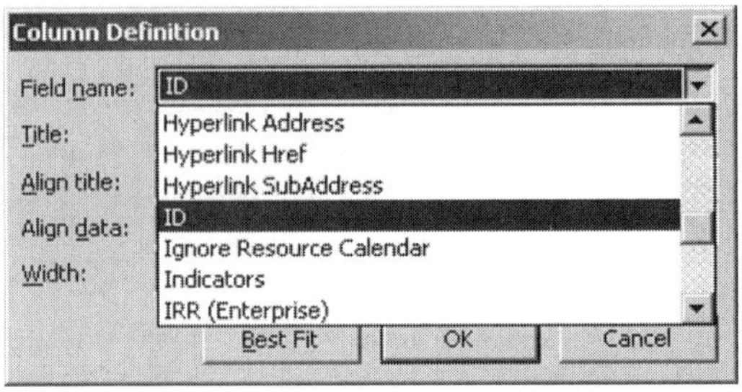

FIGURE 21-11 Column options

Adding a Column

As mentioned earlier in this chapter, you can temporarily add columns to a view if you would like more information on a temporary basis. To perform this addition, right-click on the column heading (on the actual name of the item, such as Duration), then select Insert Column. Many choices are possible from the Column Definition dialog that appears (see Figure 21-11). (Fields were discussed in detail Chapter 9.)

After selecting a new column, you will see the dialog displayed in Figure 21-12. This dialog is to be expected, as the views are set to standards in the Enterprise Global template and cannot be permanently changed by most staff (you'll learn more about creating custom Project views for individuals later in this chapter). Just select OK and the column will be available for use during the session. You can hide a column by right-clicking on the column header and selecting Hide Column.

In the example shown in Figure 21-13, the Actual Work column was added.

After making any changes, notice the blue highlighted cells. The coloring indicates that the tasks have changed. This is very useful for managing a project, because a single change can impact other tasks if the plan has been built (correctly) to include predecessor/successor relationships.

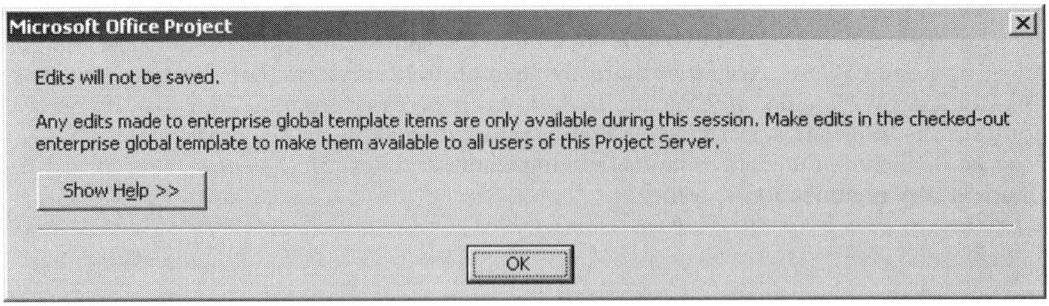

FIGURE 21-12 Dialog warning that changes will not be saved

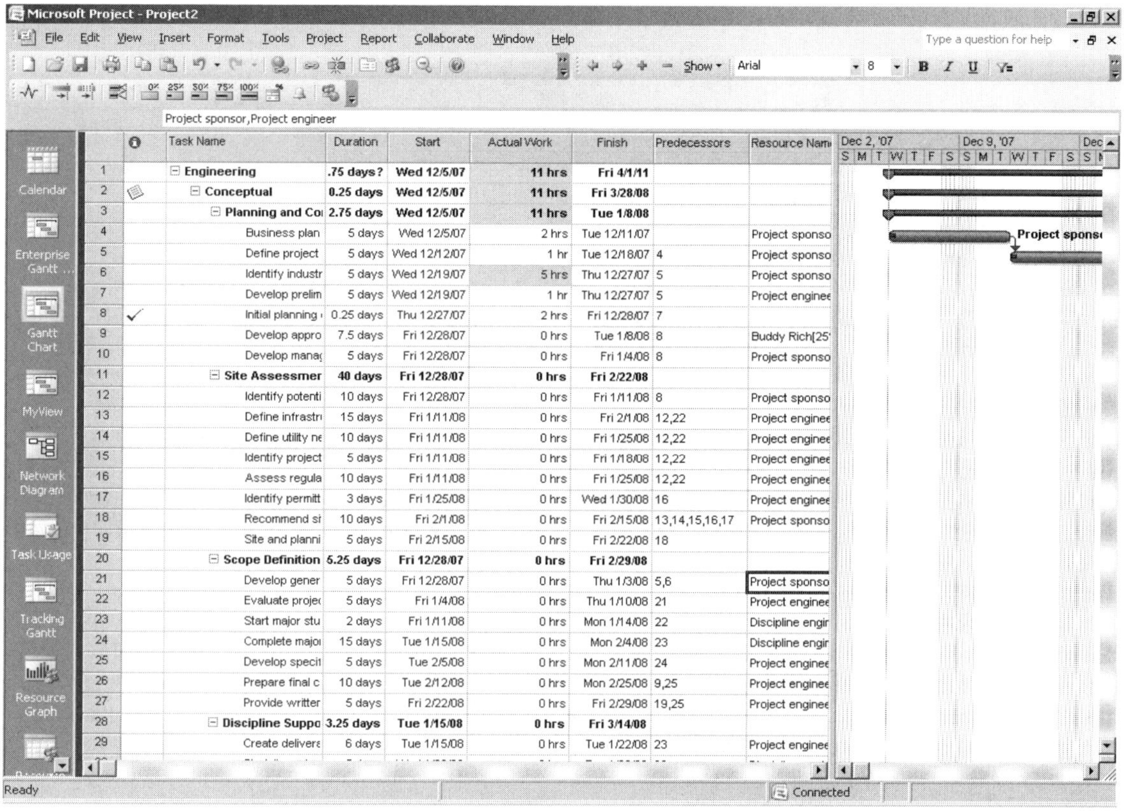

FIGURE 21-13 Actual Work column inserted into a view

Building the WBS

Build the tasks in the project using a WBS format. A WBS is a hierarchical view of the project. A very high-level example might look like the following planning project for a leased-space buildout:

0 New Martial Arts School Buildout Planning
1 Plan
1.1 Overall Layout
1.1.1 Office Layout
1.1.2 Intro Room Layout
1.1.3 Waiting Area Layout
1.1.4 Electrical and Audio Plan
1.2 Mirrors
1.3 Floor Layout
1.4 Equipment
2 Design and Blueprints

2.1	Office Design
2.2	Intro Room Design
2.3	Waiting Room Design
2.4	Audio
2.5	Electrical Design
2.6	Start Equipment List
2.7	Blueprint Signoff Milestone

There are many places to learn more about using WBS. One helpful description can be found at http://en.wikipedia.org/wiki/Work_breakdown_structure. Note that building plans with WBS is generally considered to be a best practice, so project managers should learn this technique if they do not already use it.

Timephasing

If Project Server data are to mean anything, it is vitally important that project managers timephase their projects. When assigning resources to their individual task responsibilities, check that the units are set for each assignment (percentage of overall capacity). Make sure that the estimated number of units considers not just the specific project being built, but other projects where this resource may be already booked. Make sure that the work is assigned over the appropriate timeframe.

If a resource is committed to a task full-time, this process is easy, but that is rarely how it works in real life. The project manager is responsible for building the plan to reflect the actual state of the project as it is going to run in the enterprise. For example, if a resource has only 50 percent capacity to work on a 40-hour task, it must be spread over two weeks, not just added at 100 percent and 40 hours. It should be the goal of the project manager to get every task on every project to reflect reality as of the date when the project plan is being reviewed.

It should also be expected that project managers in the EPM environment will attain at least a moderate level of skill with Microsoft Project with the goal of becoming experts. Becoming an expert in using Project Professional would require mastery of far more detail than this book can possibly cover, plus a lot of experience. Get the organization's project managers the training that they need to get the most out of this system.

The Task Type is one of the most important fields in a Project or Project Server environment. There are three Task Types and in every task one of them must be set to Fixed. The types are Duration, Work, and Units (the percentage of the resource's availability; for example, if there are eight hours available for a resource in a day and units are set to 25 percent, then that resource could work on that task for two hours per day). Project managers must understand this field in order to work successfully within the EPM environment. The setting chosen for this field will affect every task and thus all project data. Each project manager can specify a default setting for Task Type from within the Project Professional client and individual tasks can use the default or be modified on a task level. Identifying this field's setting is a key part of the training process for project managers. The authors suggest that an organization new to these tools should provide all project managers with something similar to Table 21-1, perhaps on a laminated card, to keep in front of them while they work.

Project managers should experiment with these settings extensively until they gain a solid understanding of what these constraints do. Fixed Duration is not recommended as the default Task Type setting in most scenarios. There is debate about whether to set it at

Task Type	If Units Are Modified	If Duration Is Modified	If Work Is Modified
Fixed Units	Duration recalculates	Work recalculates	Duration recalculates
Fixed Work	Duration recalculates	Units recalculate	Duration recalculates
Fixed Duration	Work recalculates	Work recalculates	Units recalculate

TABLE 21-1 Task Types

Fixed Work or Fixed Units. In more mature organizations, we generally see Fixed Work set as the standard.

Saving the Project

When you are ready, you can save the project to the Project Server. Note that when you save a plan, nothing else occurs. The action does not make some of the other functions available; it simply makes the plan available from the server.

NOTE *A saved plan is stored in the Drafts database. Over time, it is likely that PMs will become aware of how plans are managed by the "back end."*

The plan won't appear, for example, in views, nor will team members be notified of assignments. It is still a work in progress. A saved plan will, however, reduce resources' availability if default settings are used. This reduction will not occur if the resources are set to Proposed rather than the default setting of Committed. If it makes sense to use Proposed Bookings, insert the Booking Type column within the Resource Sheet View and change the booking to Proposed, as shown in Figure 21-14.

To save the plan, select File | Save. Give it a name following whatever naming convention your organization follows.

Project names cannot exceed 200 characters and cannot contain the following characters:

- . (period)
- \ (backslash)
- " (quotes)
- / (forward slash)
- : (colon)
- ; (semicolon)
- | (bar)
- ? (question mark)
- ' (apostrophe)
- < (less-than inequality)
- > (greater-than inequality)

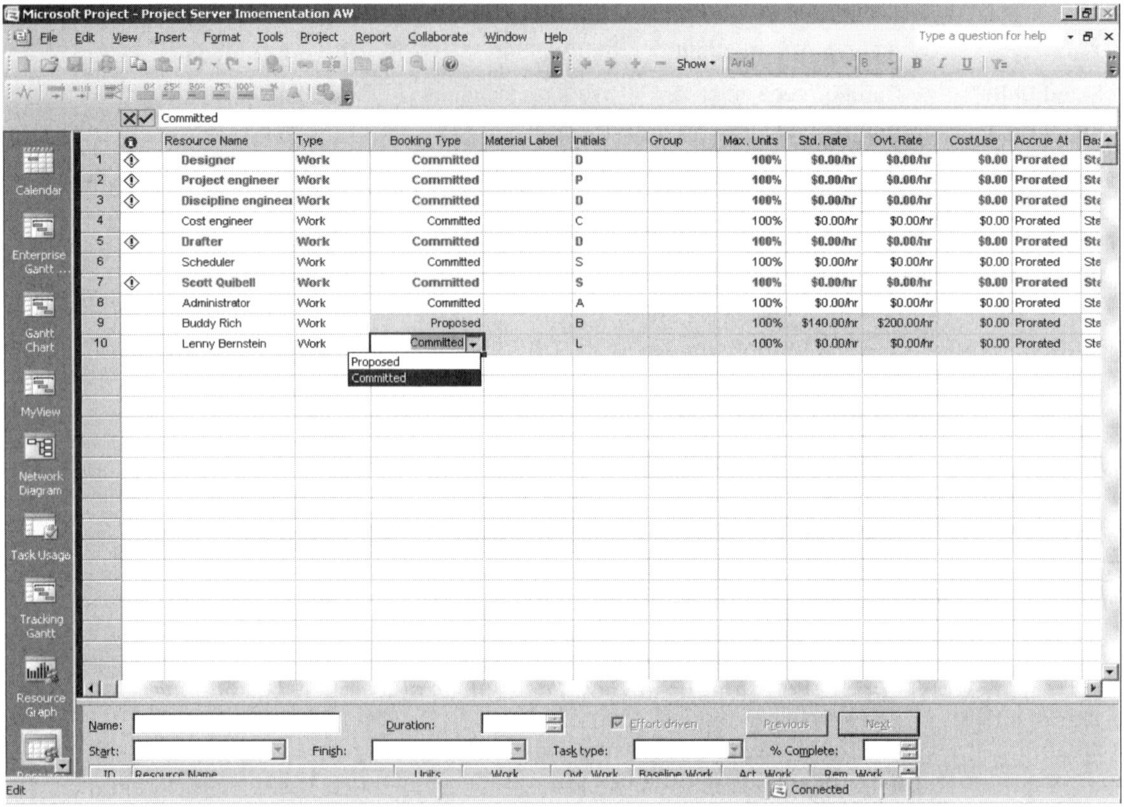

FIGURE 21-14 Proposed versus committed resources

- * (asterisk)
- # (pound)

The authors have read several different versions of what characters are considered "illegal." The preceding list was provided to the authors directly from the Microsoft Project Product Team. Note in particular that hyphens are legal.

Assuming that the system has some required enterprise project fields (as is likely), if you attempt to save your project before completing these, you will receive the error dialog shown in Figure 21-15.

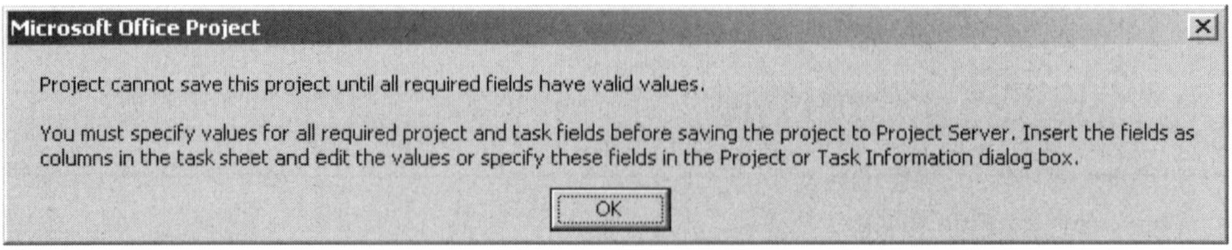

FIGURE 21-15 Results of required fields that have been left incomplete

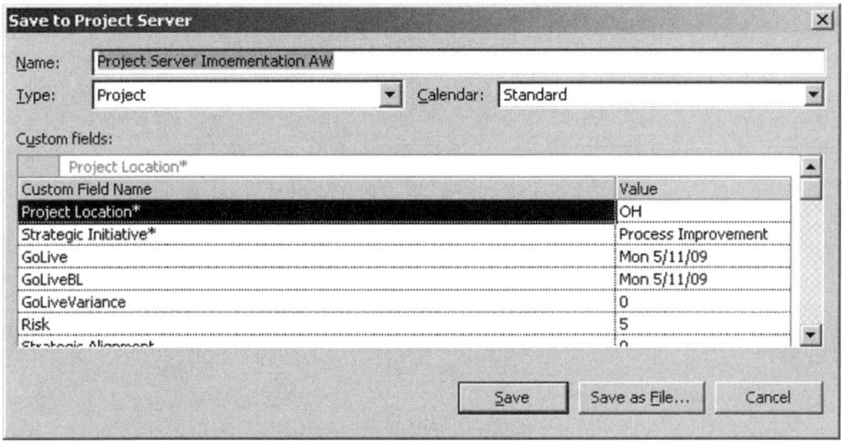

FIGURE 21-16 Save to Project Server dialog with required fields

You must complete the required fields in the custom fields at the bottom of the Save to Project Server dialog (see Figure 21-16) prior to saving. The required items are marked with an asterisk. To set the items, the Value column will contain either dropdown menus or free text fields for entry. You can also modify these settings by choosing Project | Project Information.

When all this is set, select Save. When you are ready to move on to something else, you *must* check in the project. To perform a check-in, select File | Close and then select Yes from the dialog displayed in Figure 21-17.

CAUTION *Do not close your Project Professional session without checking in your open projects. Do* not *click on the X (the close button) at the top-right of the window as shown in Figure 21-18.*

The next section describes how to open a project that has been saved to Project Server 2007.

Opening a Project from Project Server

To open a project, select File | Open. This displays the Open dialog shown in Figure 21-19, which presents a list of projects that are saved in the local cache. You can select your project from the list. Note that the cache may include projects that are no longer active. They may be even deleted, as some of the ones in the example are. To get a current list, select Retrieve the List of All Projects from Project Server. (You will learn more on the Project Cache later in this chapter.)

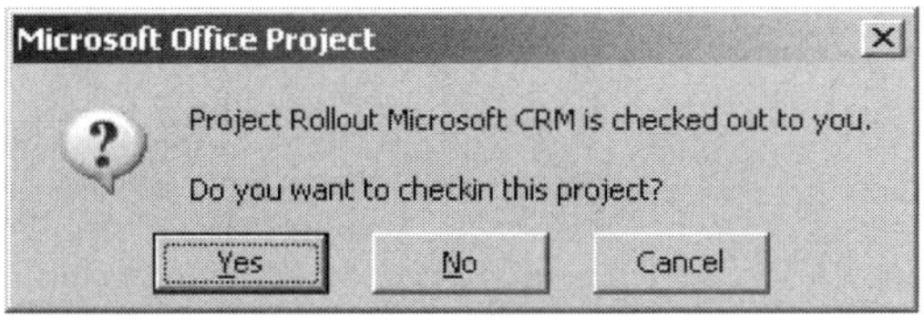

FIGURE 21-17 Check-in dialog (simple)

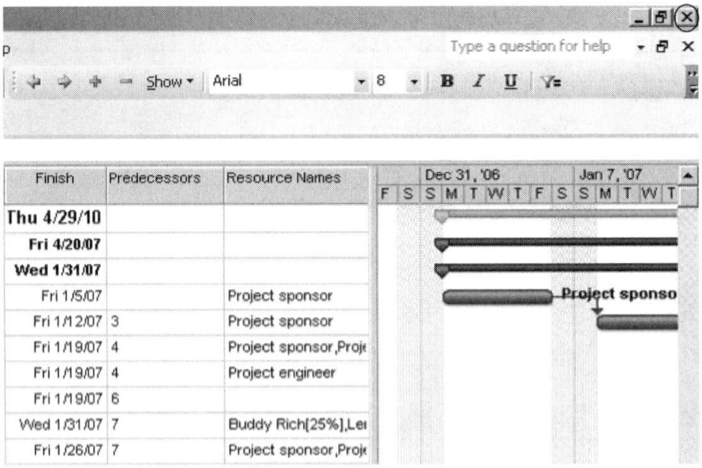

FIGURE 21-18 Don't select the X button!

The dialog that appears next displays the current projects on the server, as shown in Figure 21-20. To open a project, double-click it or highlight it and select Open.

From here the project manager can make changes to the plan as appropriate. The project manager might add new tasks or resources, adjust timelines, build a deeper WBS, or make other changes.

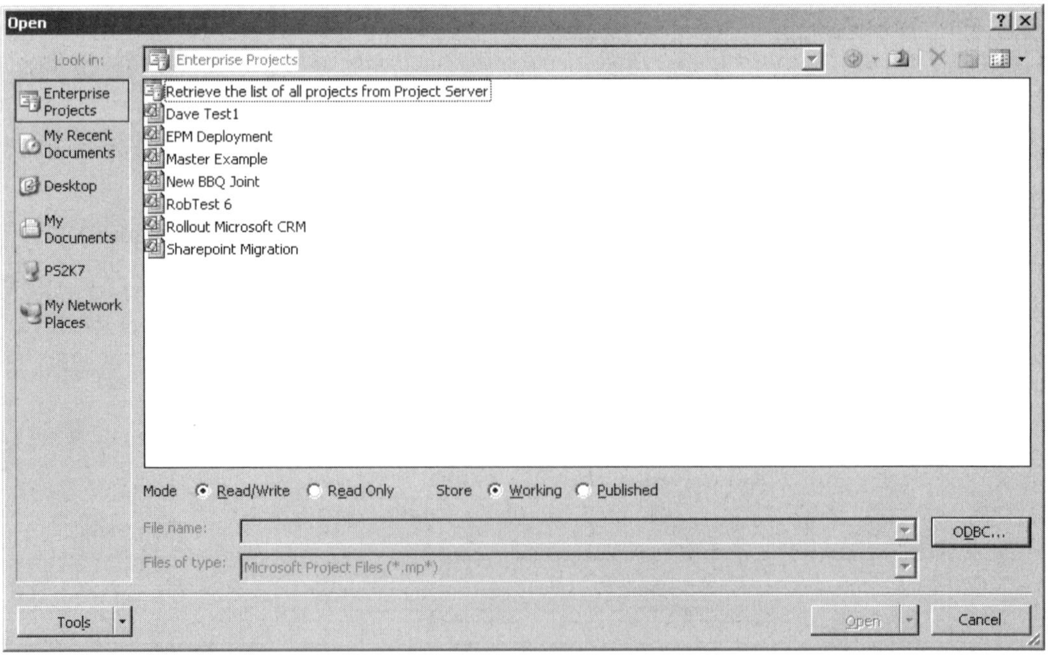

FIGURE 21-19 Open dialog

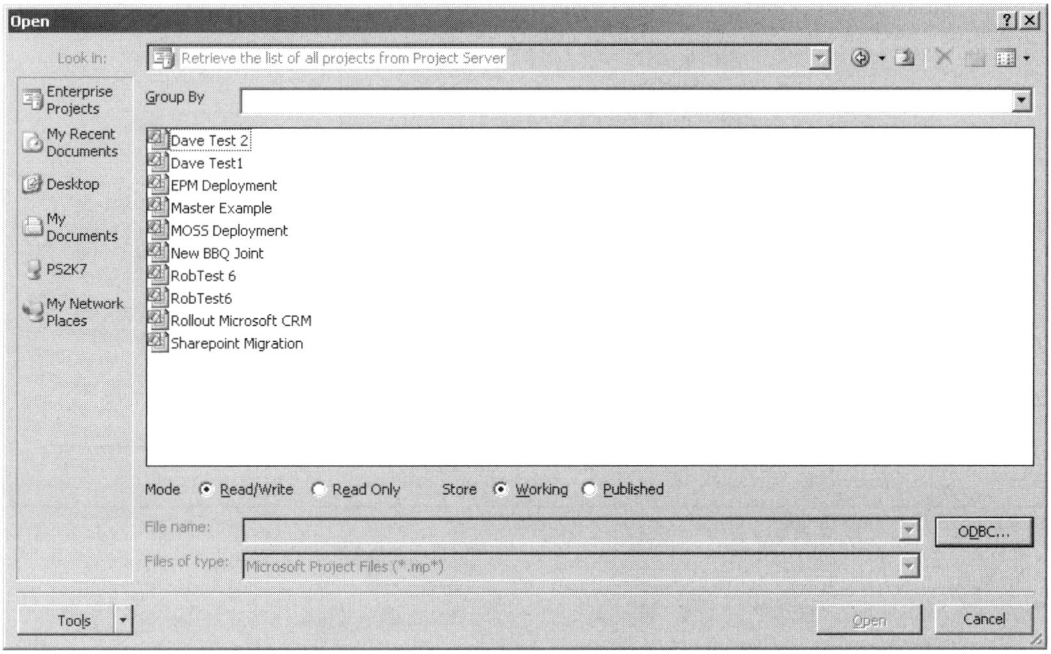

FIGURE 21-20 List of projects on the server

Setting the Project Baseline

A baseline is used to set a point in time from which comparisons can be made during the execution of a project. For example, to compare the expected cost of a project to the actual cost, a baseline is required. Setting a baseline for each project in this environment is very important. When using the baseline feature in Project, everything is baselined, not just duration. This includes work, specific resource assignments and their relative work, duration, dates, costs, and so on. Almost every project should include a baseline. When you are ready to publish the project, at least to publish a version of the project that the team is committed to execute against, a baseline should already have been established. To set the baseline, select Tools | Tracking | Set Baseline to display the dialog shown in Figure 21-21. Just select OK to establish your baseline along with the date it was set. The next section discusses publishing a project for the first time.

Publishing a Project for the First Time

Initially publishing a project is the start of the interaction among all the different resources involved in the project. This includes the people assigned to tasks in the plan, their respective managers, others who might have visibility to the information, and the project manager. When a plan is published for the first time, each person with assignments will receive an e-mail notification, a Project Workspace will be provisioned, and the project will begin to appear in PWA. People with assignments will have items appearing on their respective PWA Home Page as shown in Figure 21-22.

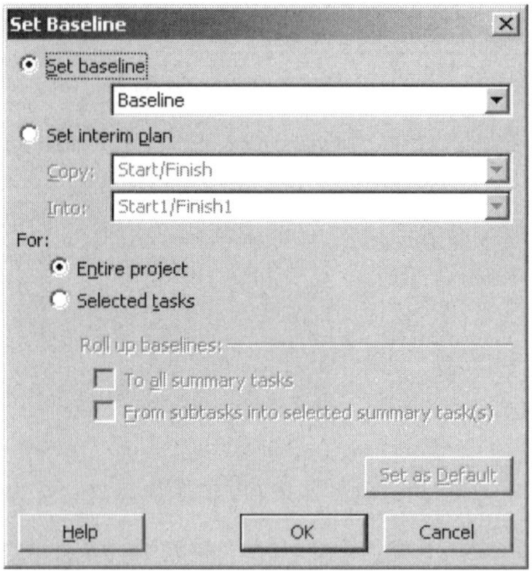

FIGURE 21-21 Set Baseline dialog

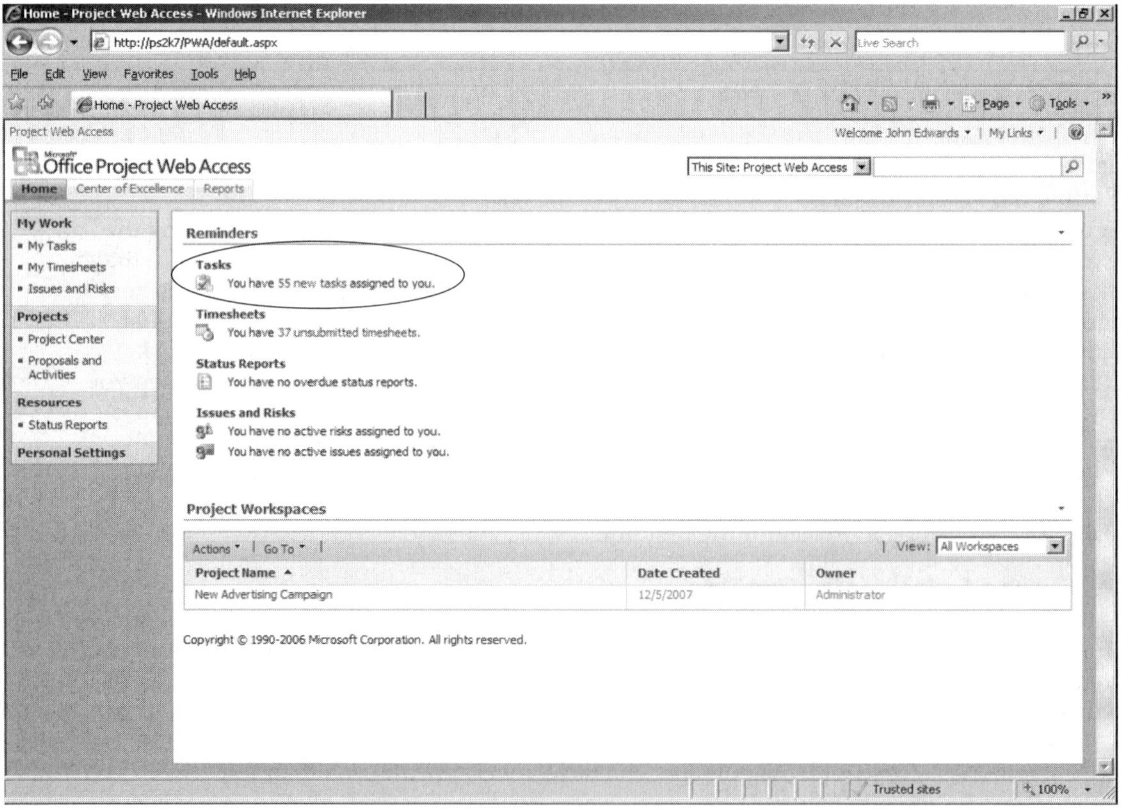

FIGURE 21-22 New tasks on the PWA Home Page

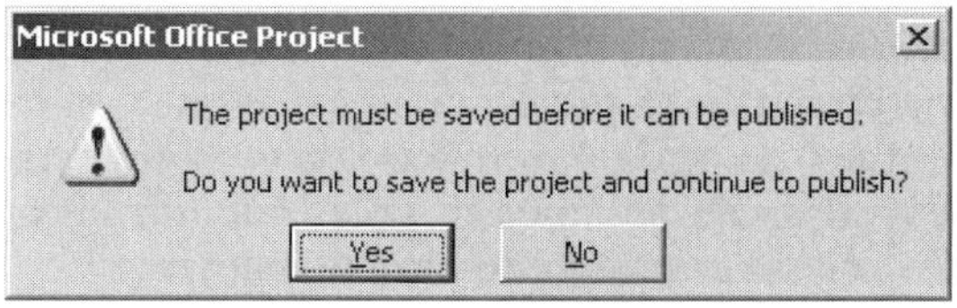

Figure 21-23 Dialog warning that the project must be saved

Tasks will also appear for these assignments in the user's Tasks page. To publish the project, select File | Publish. If the project has not just been saved, the dialog shown in Figure 21-23 will appear. Select Yes.

If settings are configured to always provision a Project Workspace, the Project Workspace provisioning process will ask for interaction (see Figure 21-24). The project manager will be asked whether a Project Workspace subsite is needed (for use in a program of projects, for example). In most cases, such a subsite is not required. If the settings are configured in the other alternative setting, "Allow users to manually create project workspaces in Project Server," the tool will enable the user to create a Project Workspace. For most environments and most projects, creating the Project Workspace is a good idea. Select Publish. Others may disagree, but the authors strongly recommend use of the Project Workspace features.

It is best to wait until the publish process has completed as shown in the status bar at the button of the Project Professional window (the chrome frame all the way at the bottom). When the publish status is Publish Completed Successfully, close Project Professional by selecting File | Close and check in the project. Remember not to select the X at the top-right of the window; use the File menu's Close command instead.

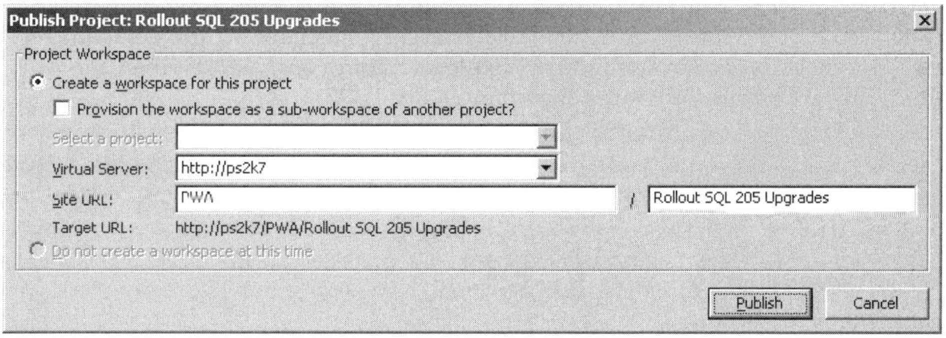

Figure 21-24 Provisioning a Project Workspace

Managing the Plan

This section covers the activities that a project manager is likely to execute while a project is ongoing. It starts with the first update from a project resource as submitted from the Tasks area of PWA. When a resource assigned to a plan submits his or her task updates, the project manager is notified via an e-mail similar to the following:

> The following assignments have been updated by resources.
>
> Reported to: Jo Ellen Amato
>
> Project Name: Example for Doc
> Task Name: Gather business requirements
> Assigned to: John Edwards
> Start: Thursday, February 22, 2007 Finish: Friday, March 02, 2007 Work: 48h
> Remaining Work: 45h % Completion: 6
> Comment:
> To turn off these notifications…
>
> Microsoft Office Project Server

Getting Task Approval from PWA

There are a couple ways to approve task updates: from within Project Professional or from PWA. In general, if you are doing review and approval for multiple projects, the preferred method is to perform the work updates from PWA. The process of approving a single project is nicely handled from within Project Professional.

To follow the PWA approval process, type in the address bar http://*YourServerName/YourPWAInstanceName* (for example, http://grumpy1/pwa) and press Enter. It is recommended that the resources using Project Server, especially the project managers, create an Internet Favorite inside Internet Explorer. From your PWA Home Page, you should see any approvals for you, as shown in Figure 21-25.

FIGURE 21-25 Approvals waiting

Select the link (four task updates from resources) or just select the Approvals item on the Quick Launch Bar (left navigation). Figure 21-26 shows how a single task update would appear if default settings are configured for the page.

As you can see, if the project manager received many updates from people on multiple projects, the Task Updates page would become a very long. This page is actually quite flexible. Start by locating the Settings dropdown list, as shown in Figure 21-27.

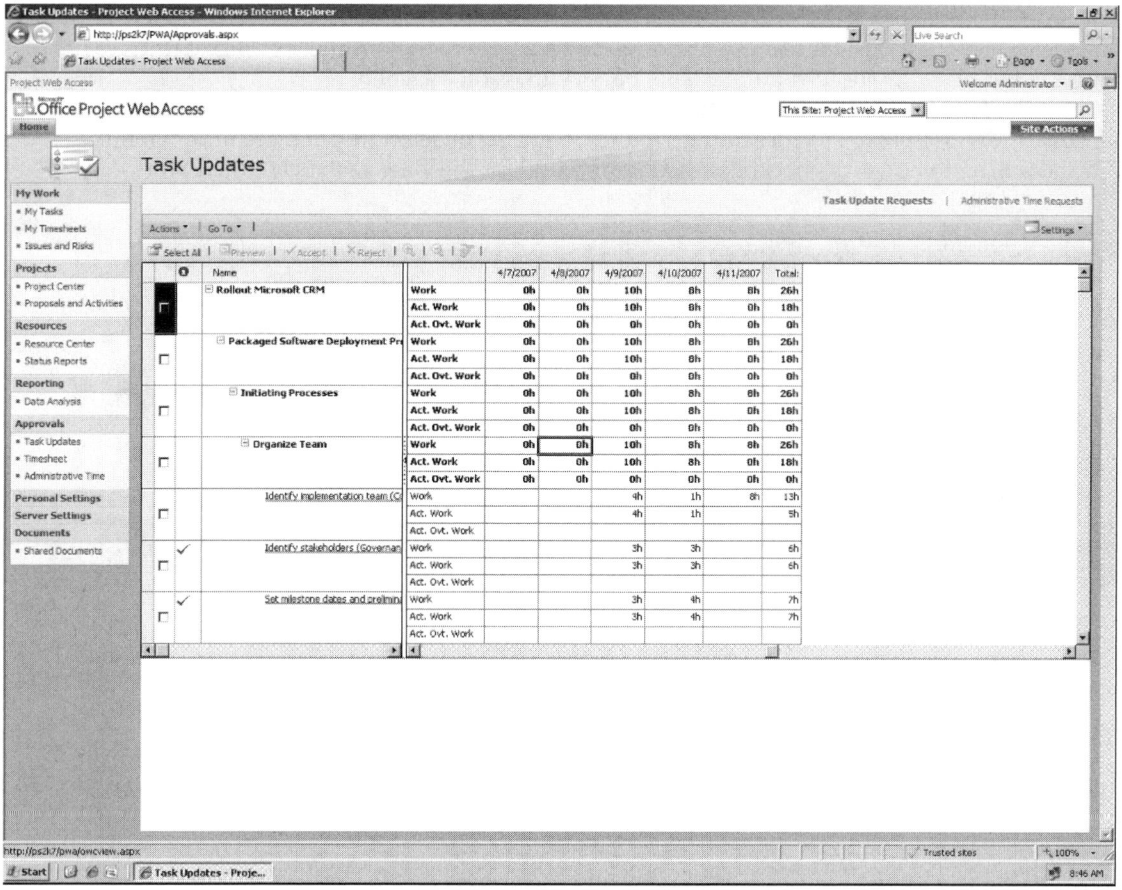

FIGURE 21-26 Task Updates page

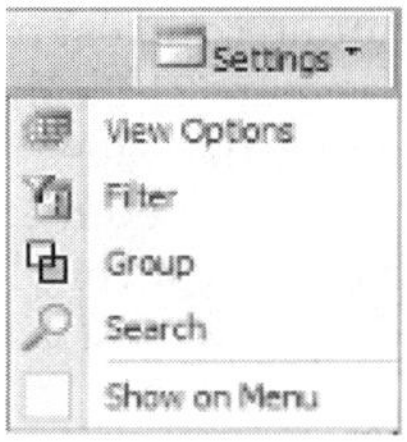

FIGURE 21-27 Settings dropdown menu

Select View Options. Figure 21-28 shows the view where the outline level is set to 1, whereas Figure 21-29 shows you the same page with outline level 0.

These settings allow the project manager to view information rolled up with drilldown flexibility. It is also possible to deselect (to reduce the page) or select (to get more information) the Show Scheduled Work checkbox (see Figure 21-30 for the view with Scheduled Work).

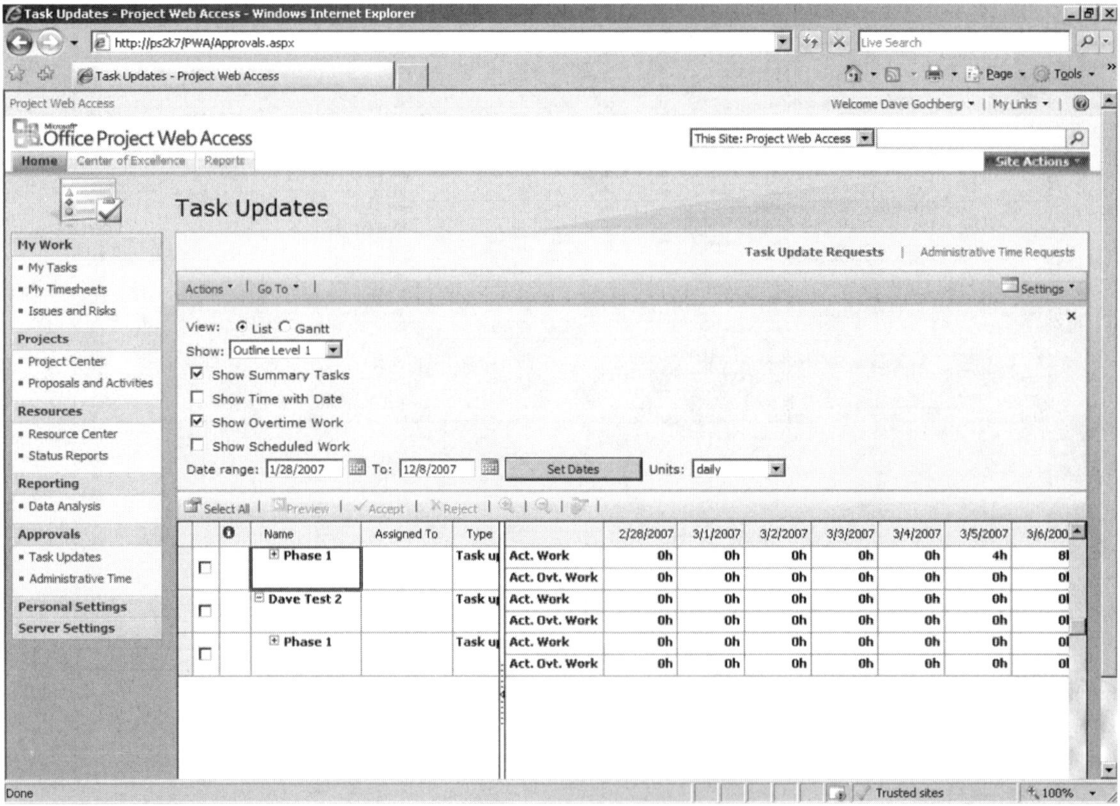

FIGURE 21-28 Outline level 1

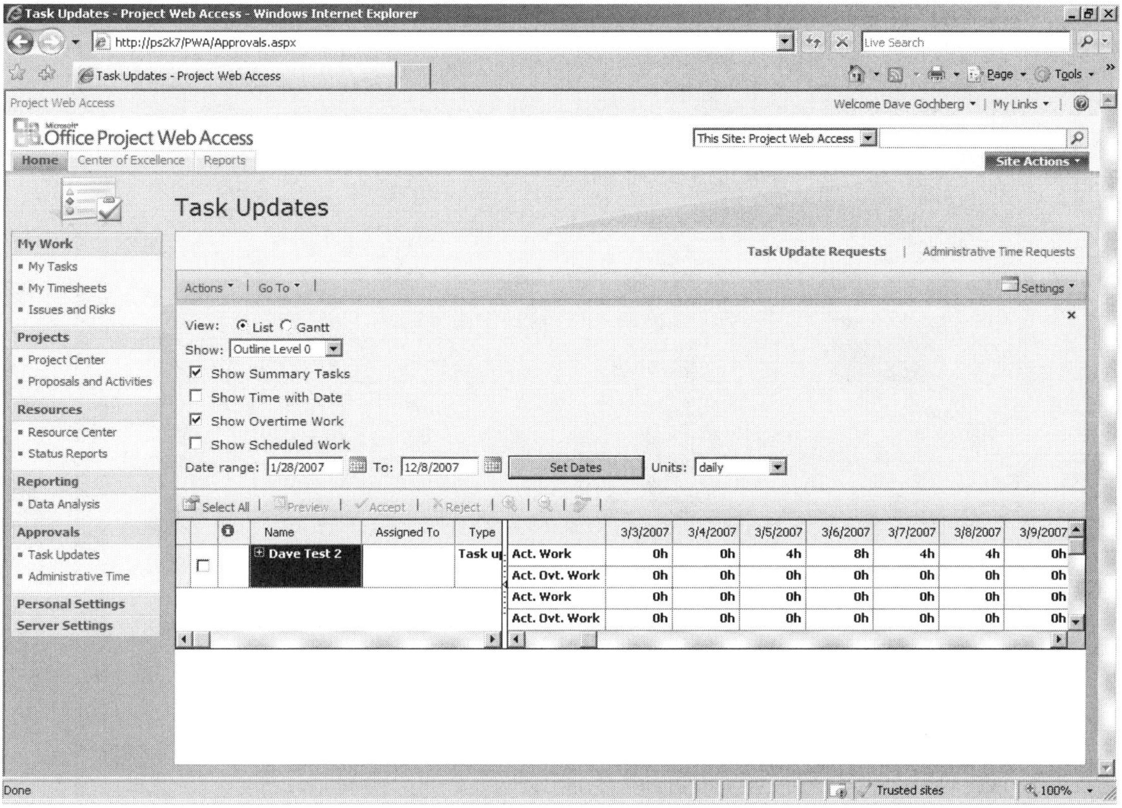

FIGURE 21-29 Outline level 0

You can also change the view by using the Filter and Group options from the Settings dropdown menu. Note that you can attach a note to a task update at the task level, which appears as a yellow icon. When selected, the contents of the note are shown as a yellow sticky icon in the Indicators column.

When the project manager is ready to accept the updates, he or she must select which items merit approval. Then the project manager should select the Accept button. A comment can be sent to team members (see Figure 21-31) and a preview is available.

Any items approved show up in the preview as links. When selected, these links show the history of the task. To see a preview of the changes just accepted, select the Preview button. Note that the tasks where updates were just accepted display as links. The links can be clicked to get the transaction detail. Note that changes to the plan display in blue.

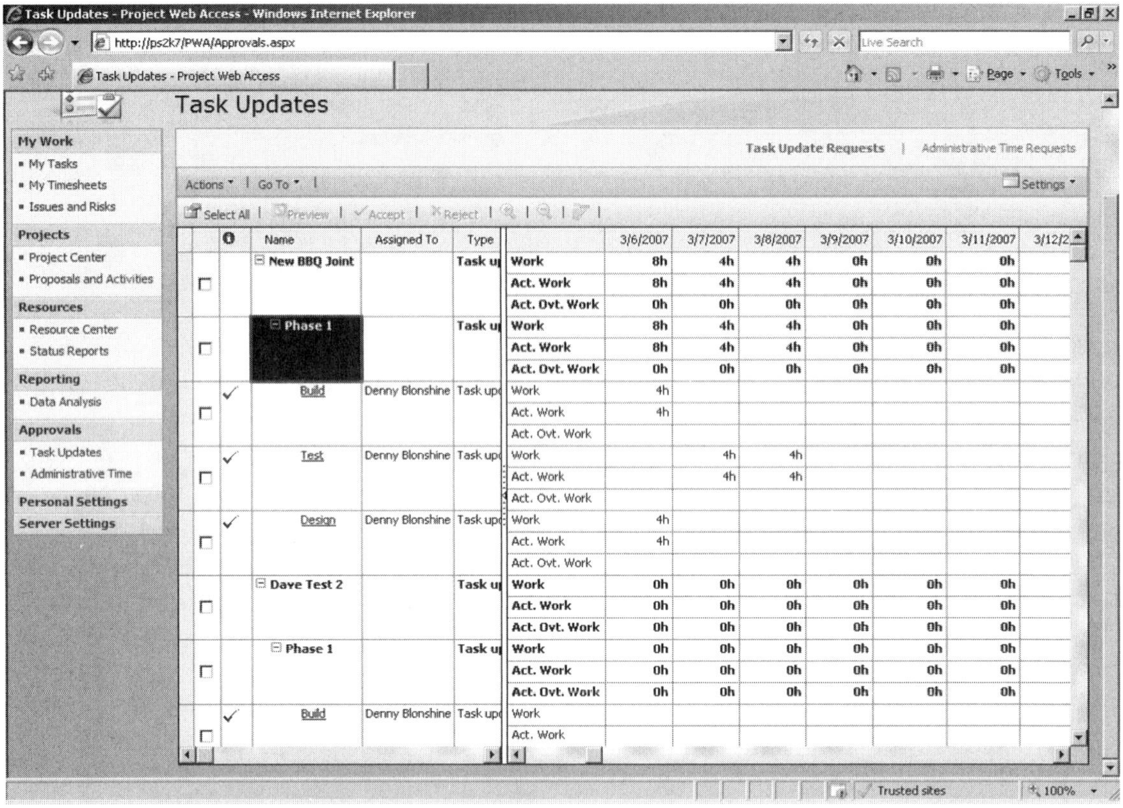

Figure 21-30 Show Scheduled Work option selected

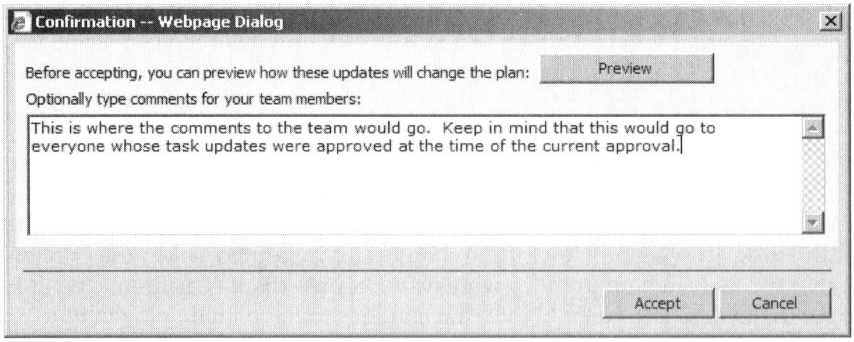

Figure 21-31 Comments

After the Accept button has been selected, the update has been completed from the server perspective. There is one more step needed, however, to complete the update process.

Syncing Updates to Microsoft Project from PWA

There are a couple of ways to bring the updates into line from PWA to Project Professional 2007, a step that is required to get all the data in sync. To complete the cycle, select the name of the project that needs to be synchronized by clicking on the vertical bar next to the name of the project, then select Edit from the button bar (see Figure 21-32).

The plan should then open in Microsoft Project Professional with the updates included. Make sure that you check whether any tasks have slipped due to inactivity and move them appropriately if needed. Once that is done or if no additional changes are required, select Save | Publish | Close and Check In. Remember not to close the plan by selecting that close button in your Project Professional window (the X in the top-right corner).

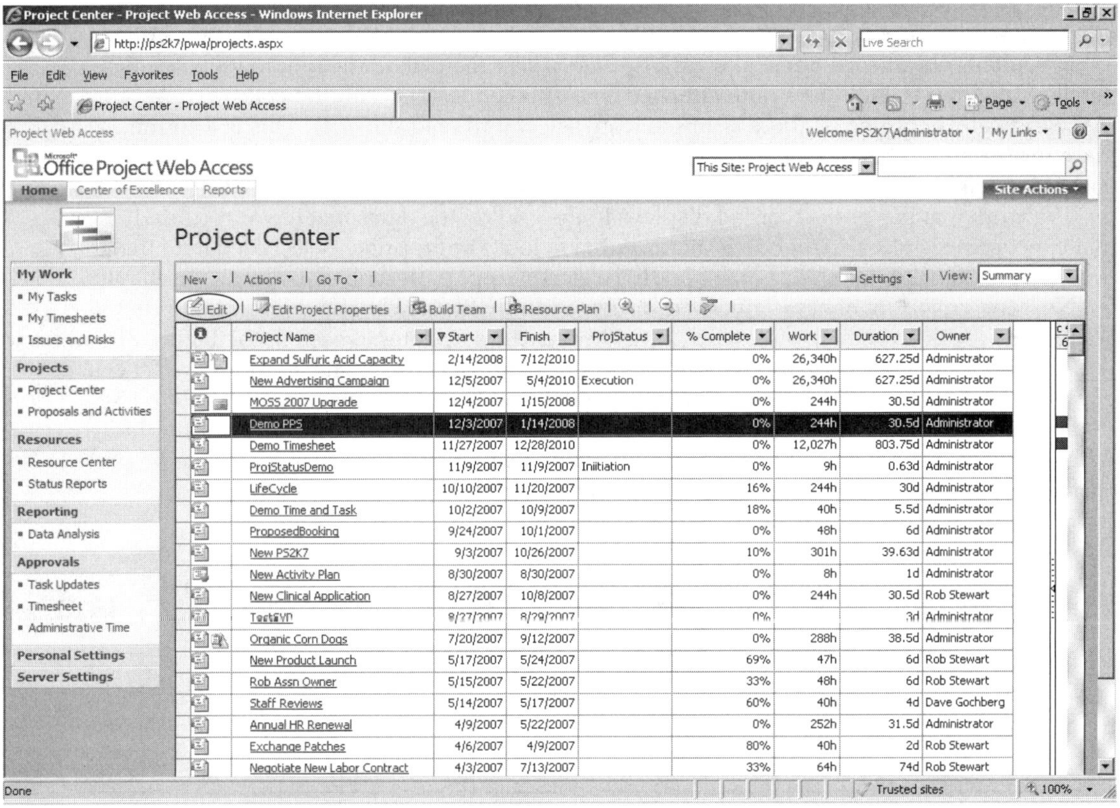

FIGURE 21-32 Selecting the project from Project Center

Your plan is now in sync. Another way to approve task updates is to perform them from Project Professional, which is the next topic.

Approval from within Project Professional

Project managers can approve task updates from within Project Professional 2007. This method makes sense if the goal is to approve and sync time for a single project or if the project manager just happens to open a project after an update has been submitted. It could be argued that this method is preferable because it is more likely that task updates will be accepted to the plan, reviewed appropriately, and republished all at once. Also, it makes more sense for a PM to review a single project as opposed to the significant possibility that the mass approvals described in the previously discussed method will lead to a selection of "approve all" without any review at all. From Microsoft Office Project Professional 2007, open the project file from the Project Server using the method described earlier in this chapter. If tasks have been updated, a dialog will alert you that there are task updates, as shown in Figure 21-33.

To review the updates and perform the approval, select Yes. The Task Updates page that normally would appear in PWA opens within the Project client, as shown in Figure 21-34.

For details about each particular task update, select the task name link to view the details. Take care to look for a note attached as displayed to you with the yellow sticky icon in the Indicators column. If there is a note icon, select it to read the note. This is a common place for team members to inform the project manager about information relating to a particular task, such as that it is running late or that it has completed ahead of schedule.

The work that has been recorded displays in the grid on the dates that it was recorded (daily recording is recommended). If the submission looks appropriate, select each item that needs approval using the checkboxes and then select Accept as described earlier in the chapter.

Next the project manager is given the option to apply the newly approved updates to the plan. Select the link on the words "click here" to apply the updates as seen in the Figure 21-35.

Another dialog then appears asking the project manager if he or she would like to check out the project. In most cases, the answer should be yes. The project now opens with the new updates, and any tasks that have changed based on the updates are highlighted in blue within Project Professional. Take the time to review the project, make changes, make progress changes to the project tasks as appropriate, and save, publish, and check in the project.

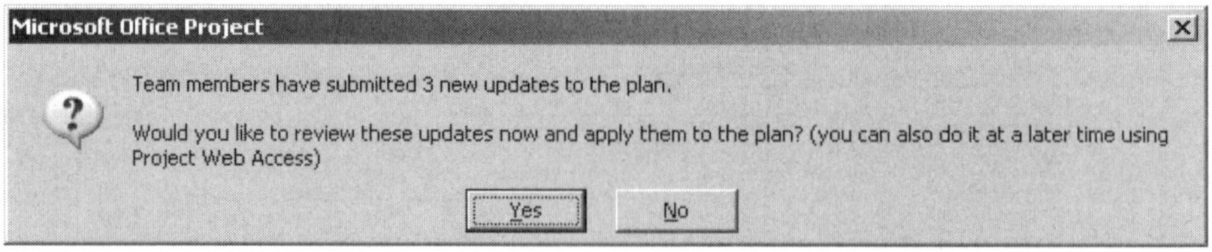

FIGURE 21-33 Task Update dialog

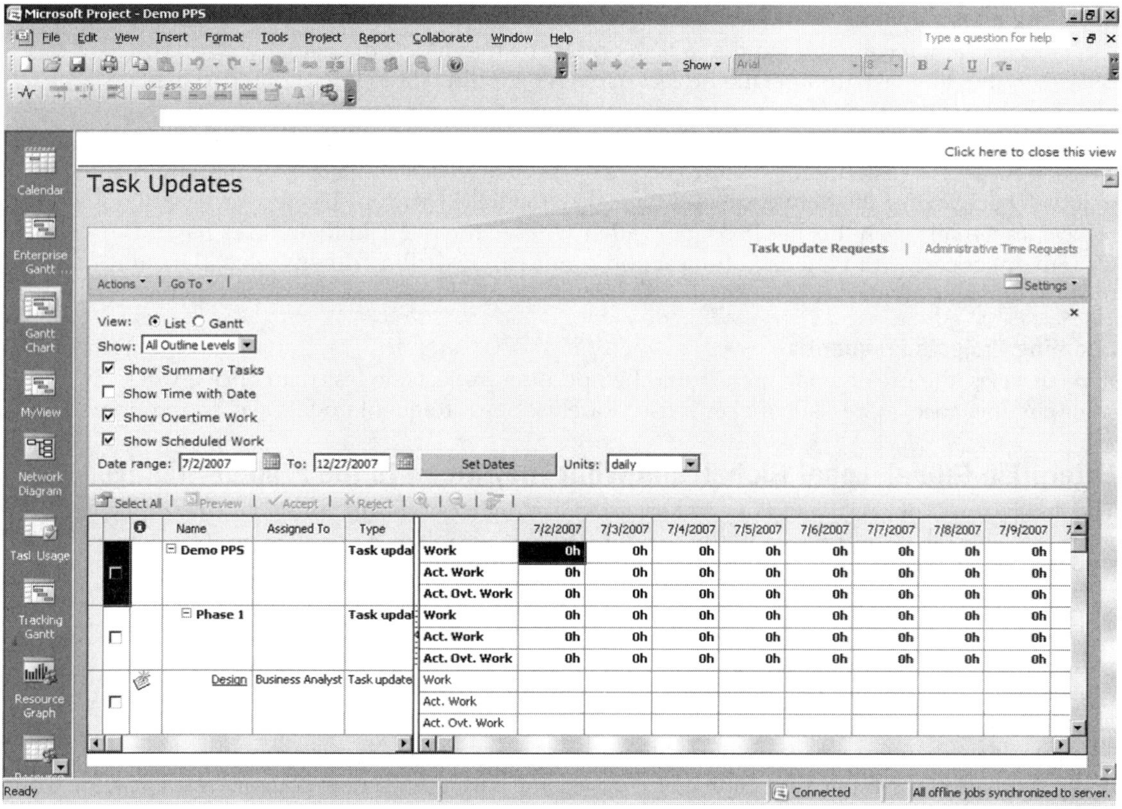

FIGURE 21-34 Task updates inside Project Pro

TIP *Here is a tip that is also a potential pitfall. In order to avoid leaving scheduled work in the past, Project professional provides a way to progress tasks using automation in Project. Select Tools | Tracking | Update Project. Then, select Reschedule Uncompleted Work to Start After with the current date. Next select OK. This moves everything that was scheduled previously that has not completed forward to the current date. You can also do this on specific tasks by selecting them before going to the Update Project tool. This technique has potential to make things easier; however, it is almost guaranteed to create overallocations, especially with other projects, so be careful.*

FIGURE 21-35 "Click here"

Rejecting a Task Update

It is not generally recommended that a task update be rejected. If there are questions or issues relating to a task update, the project manager should talk to the resource to explain any concerns. If it still makes sense to make a change, the team member/resource should make the change in the Tasks page and send in the revised version. Finally, if there is still a reason to reject a task update, the project manager should select the task by making sure that the checkbox for the item is set and then click the Reject button. The resources will not receive an e-mail when this happens, but rather will see the red *X* in their Tasks page. The team member can see an attached transaction comment by drilling down (select the name of the task to drill down).

Updating Projects Frequently

In most cases, the project manager should be updating projects no less than once a week. In some circumstance, more often makes sense. Rarely is a less frequent update cycle appropriate.

Enterprise Global, Local Global, and What They Mean to the Project Manager

The Enterprise Global is a template that is stored in Project Server that provides the settings for things like tables and views in the default new project when you are using Project in a Project Server environment. There is also a local file on the local PC called the Global template (global.mpt) that stores information that is local to the specific user or machine. This file contains items such as the settings configured by the individual project manager within the Tools | Options settings in Project Professional, such as date format and how calculation is set. (It is not recommended to disable autocalculation in an EPM environment.)

The Enterprise Global template is used as the foundation for enterprise templates. For example, if a macro is written to change the project status manager (as discussed previously) and it is a part of the Enterprise Global, it will become part of each new plan or template. On the other hand, the macro security level setting (which you configure by choosing Tools | Options | Security | Macro Security) is stored in the local global.mpt file.

If a project manager wants a personalized view—with different columns displayed, for example–this would not be allowed in the Enterprise Global, but rather would require that changes be stored locally. The result of creating the local view would not provide visibility to that view for any other user.

Here are a few examples of working with the Enterprise Global:

- **Add or hide a column** If you add a column (by right-clicking the column name, inserting the column, then selecting the column), the insertion will be there for the specific Project session, but will not appear the next time that Project is launched. A hidden column would reappear once a new session is started.
- **Move a column** If the project manager moves a column in Project (by selecting a column, then dragging the column to a different location), this column will appear in its original position once Project is closed and reopened.
- **Modify a toolbar** Any toolbar changes revert to their Global settings upon a restart of Project.
- **Record or save a macro** New macros cannot be recorded or saved.

Local Project Views

Project managers can create views specific to their needs by using the Organizer. In the following example, the project manager will create a modified Enterprise Gantt View that adds the Actual Work and Baseline Work columns and removes Duration.

To start this process, the project manager navigates to View | Table | More Tables from within Project Professional. This opens the More Tables dialog. Next the table named Entry is highlighted and the Copy button is selected.

A new name is entered into the Name field, in this case MyEGantt. Using the Cut, Copy, Paste, Insert Row, and Delete Row functions, the project manager adds the Actual Work and Remaining Work fields and deletes the Duration field. Note that other settings, such as column and title alignment, can also be made from this tool, as shown in Figure 21-36.

After creating a new table and applying it to a view, the project manager can make most changes directly from the view without having to go into the modify view mode. View/table changes are automatically saved with the underlying table. However, specific settings are easier to control if they are made using the table edit dialog as just described.

Once everything is in order, the project manager selects OK. The More Tables dialog should remain open. The next step is to push this new table into the local global file. To do this, select Organizer from the More Tables dialog. The Organizer appears as shown in Figure 21-37.

Next select the new table from the right side of the Organizer's Tables tab and then select Copy to move a copy to the left side of the dialog (Global [+ non-cached Enterprise]). Close the Organizer, select the new table, and then select the Apply button.

Select Views | More Views. While the Enterprise Gantt item is highlighted, select Copy, then name the new view. Confirm that the Table dropdown list is populated with the newly

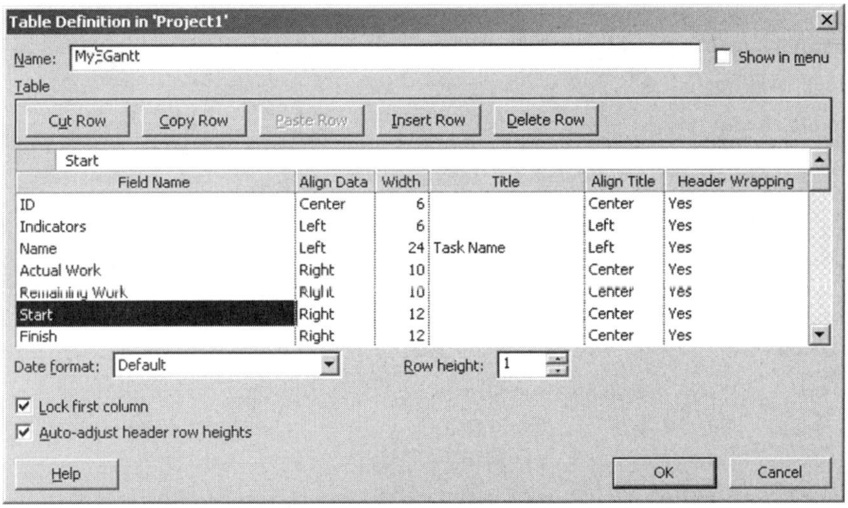

FIGURE 21-36 Name, Add, Delete, and other options

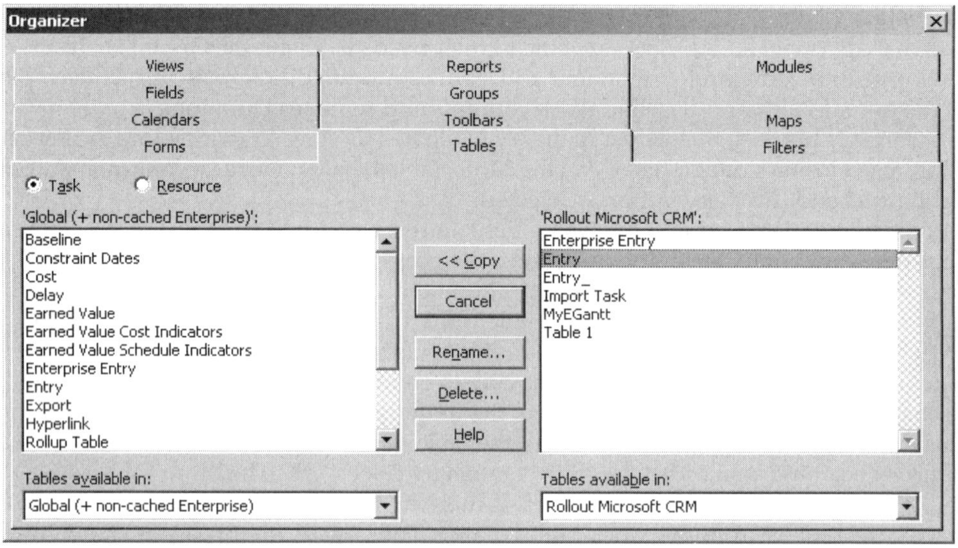

FIGURE 21-37 Organizer for tables

created table, select No Group from the Group dropdown list, select All Tasks for the Filter dropdown menu. If the new field is to display in the menu or icons in the View Bar (rather than in the More Views menu), select that checkbox. Select OK. The displayed icons are usually reserved for the views that are most commonly used.

Next select Organizer from the More Views dialog. As in the previous process for the table, select and copy the new view from right to left as shown in Figure 21-38.

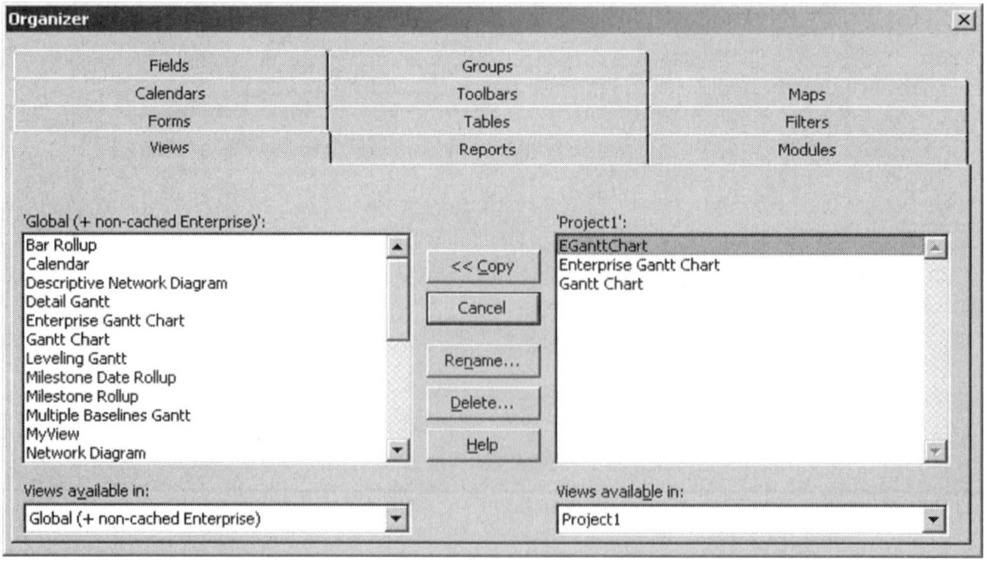

FIGURE 21-38 Organizer for views

Close the Organizer dialog, highlight the new view, and select Apply. The next time that Project is restarted, this view will be ready to use.

More Options in Project Professional

Within Project Professional are many options that you can configure. To start, navigate to Tools | Options. From the Options dialog, there are 11 tabs. The vast majority of settings are set appropriately out of the box or are useful only for running in a non-Project Server environment. Some useful tips include the following:

- **View** This tab includes many options. In most cases, you should leave these alone. However, the following are some items that might be worth consider modifiying:
  - **Default View** This setting defaults to Gantt, but other views, especially a custom view, could be considered. One of our clients created a Planning View with items tied to initial project planning work.
  - **Date Format** The date format should provide the information that is needed, but should use as few characters as possible because of how dates affect column width. An example of the default format is Mon 1/28/08. Consider using 1/28/08 (dropping the "Mon").
  - **Currency** Change this if you are not using "USD" or the dollar sign ($).
  - **Show Project Summary Task** Select this checkbox. Note that this field is saved only on a project-by-project basis. It can also be made a part of an Enterprise Project template.
- **General** In this tab, consider increasing the number of entries in the recently used file list. The default is four. This represents the list of projects that appear at the bottom of the page when selecting File | Open.
- **Schedule** One option worth considering is whether new tasks should start on the project start date (which is the default setting) or the current date.
- **Calculation** The authors recommend that you *not* change the calculation mode to manual. Many project managers have done so in non-EPM projects. Turning off autocalculate defeats the idea behind an enterprise system.
- **Interface** You may consider using the Project Guide, a feature that walks the project manager through the steps of creating and staffing a project. Note that it is possible for an organization to create a custom Project Guide to follow its own methodology. This tab includes a set of check boxes for how the individual PM uses the feature, if at all.
- **Security** It is often true that the default settings for macro security are too restrictive.

The Collaboration menu is another area where the project manager can leverage tools. The project manager will be allowed to access only those menu items for which he or she has permissions. Most of the options allow the project manager to open parts of PWA directly within the Project client. Other options include the following:

- **Request Progress Information** This tool allows the project manager to request progress updates from the team via e-mail and enables the project manager to edit the e-mail itself. The e-mail can be sent to all resources, tasks, or selected items.

- **Manage Deliverables** This can be used to create deliverables and associate them with specific tasks. This can be useful when you are using deliverables-based planning techniques. When you create a deliverable and link it to a task, it displays a Indicator icon in Project Professional ("This Task Is Linked to a Deliverable").
- **Manage Dependencies on Deliverables** This feature allows connections between dependencies in the current project and dependencies on other projects. This can be useful when managing programs, and loosely coupled interproject dependencies. You'll learn more about programs in Chapter 26.
- **Collaboration Options** This feature takes the project manager to the Collaboration Options tab under Tools | Options. Changes there are rarely required.

Looking for Resources

The process of selecting the resources for a project team can differ dramatically depending on settings, but in most cases project managers will have permission to build a team. That is the assumption here. In any case, however, the process of populating a project team usually starts with a negotiation between the project manager who is charged with the successful delivery of the project and the resource manager or managers who have responsibility for resources. Information can be located in several ways.

Assessing Resources from Resource Center in PWA

The PWA Resource Center contains a list of all resources in the Enterprise Resource Pool that the project manager has permission to see. In small-to-midsize companies, this list could consist of all resources, but it could also be a subset based on security settings. For example, if you are using a resource breakdown structure (RBS) and the My Direct Reports category, this list may contain only resources who work under the project manager. Larger organizations usually do not allow access to all resources for both security and usability reasons (imagine a page with 5,000 names).

Whatever is visible, the project manager or resource manager can select the resources of interest and then select the View Availability button from inside Resource Center on the horizontal bar. The Resource Availability page displays as shown in Figure 21-39.

Additional filtering is possible based on whatever fields have been displayed. It is common, for example, to include a Roles or Skills custom field to narrow the view. Here is one scenario.

The project manager needs a database administrator (DBA) who can speak Japanese. Using filters on the Role and Skills fields reduces the list to only those who have both DBA and Japanese speaking attributes. Then when the View Availability button is selected, a much smaller list will be presented for comparison.

As mentioned above, the resource manager and the project manager then have a discussion and reach an agreement on the appropriate resource for the job. Note that in most organizations the process of making resource decisions is usually a negotiation. Purely technical solutions rarely are the best options for resource selection.

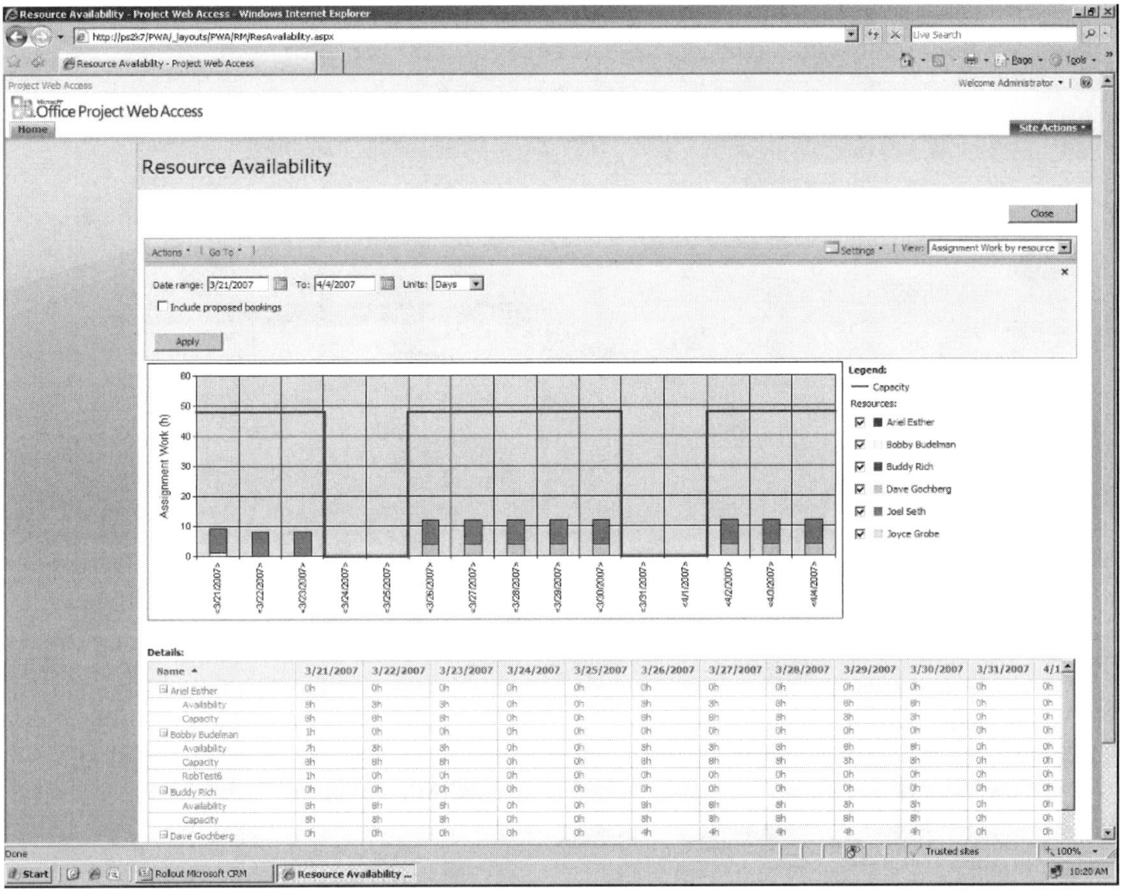

FIGURE 21-39 Resource Availability view

Using the Project Professional Build Team Tool to Search for a Resource

Project managers use the Build Team from Enterprise tool within Microsoft Office Project Professional 2007 to select resources for the projects that they are managing. One commonly used feature from this Build Team tool is to view resource availability for a certain window of time. To do that, select the Show Resource Availability checkbox and select and change the dates in the From and To fields. When you have set these, then select Apply. You can see the results as shown in Figure 21-40.

As with the Resource Center, it is possible to filter on resources from the Build Team from Enterprise tool. A set of prebuilt filters can be found under the Existing Filters dropdown list as shown in Figure 21-41.

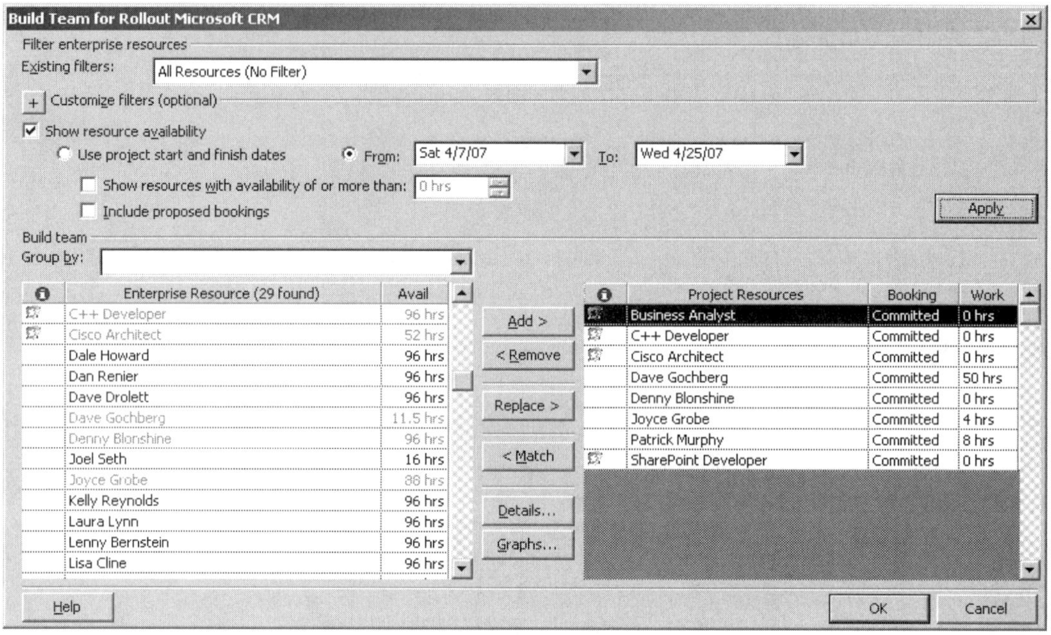

FIGURE 21-40 Resource availability added to the Build Team tool

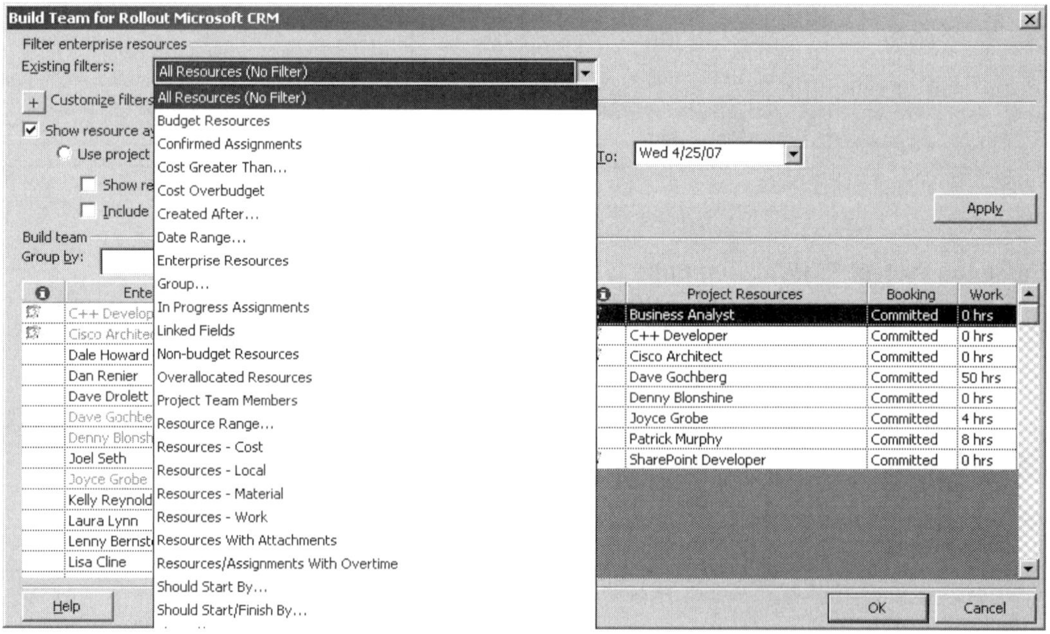

FIGURE 21-41 Existing Filters dropdown list

Custom filters can also be used to replicate functionality as was previously described in the discussion about finding resources in Resource Center. To apply a custom filter, select the Customize Filters (optional). Populate the Field Name (for example, Role), select the Test (equals, contains, and so on), and then set the value for testing (DBA for this example). Using the And/Or option, add a second filter such as Skill. Finally, select Apply.

Using Advanced Features of the Build Team Tool

The Build Team tool supports some really advanced features for searching for resources.

- **Match** When custom enterprise resource fields (attributes) are created, there is a setting called Use This Field for Matching Generic Resources that can be enabled for the field. Fields that have this enabled are used when the Build Team tool is looking for a real enterprise resource to replace a generic one—for example, in an Enterprise Project template. To use this function, highlight the resource that is on the right side of the Build Team tool, then select the Match button as shown in Figure 21-42.

  The resource list will be reduced to those resources who are an exact match for the generic resource based on whichever fields have the Match feature enabled. Because it requires an exact match, the more complex the attribute used (such as a skills, outline code, or multivalue field), the less likely it is that a match will be located. In many cases, it is easier to use a simpler field such as Primary Role, where outline codes or multivalue components are not required to find a match.

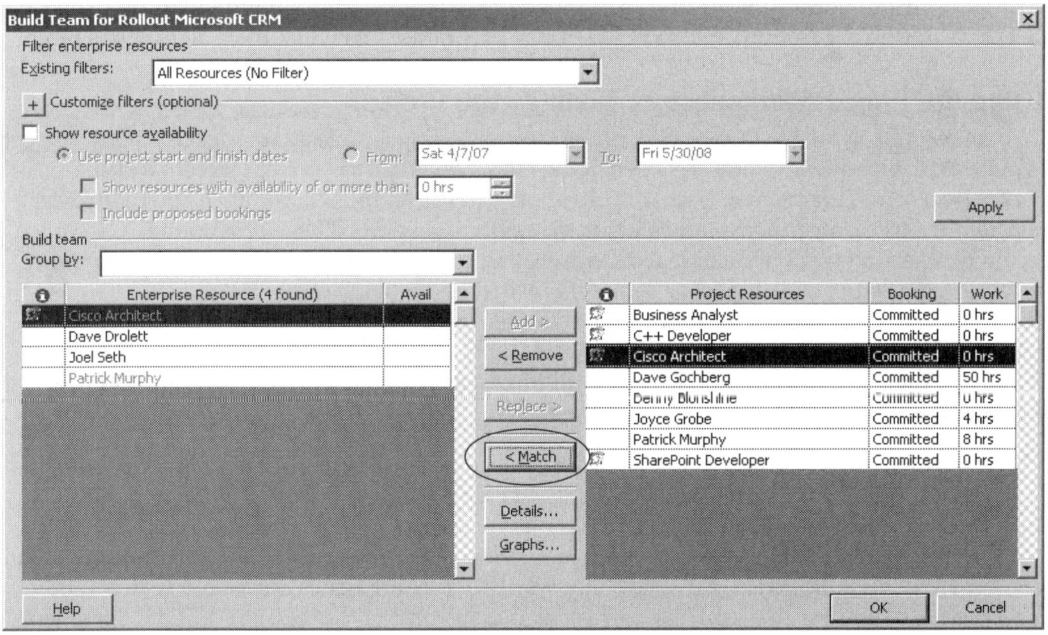

FIGURE 21-42 Matching

- **Replace** This function allows the project manager to replace a resource everywhere that the resource appears in a project plan as long as that resource has no actual work recorded. It is commonly used to replace a generic resource from an Enterprise Project template. To replace a resource, select the existing resource from the right side, select the replacement from the left side, and then select the Replace button.

A common process might start with a project template, a Match operation performed to produce a reduced list of possible resources, application of date and time parameters, and use of the Availability feature. After the right match is found and availability is confirmed, a Replace operation can occur to populate the tasks in the project.

These features can help the project manager use the tool much more efficiently. They are strongly recommended.

Keeping the Project Current

It is important that the project manager keep an eye on the impact of task updates on the plan. One great feature of Project Professional 2007 is that if a task is affected by a change in a predecessor, it shows the changes with blue background shading. It is recommended that the project manager take a look at the changed tasks to see whether they create overallocations, to assess resource constraints, and to make changes if needed.

Another thing that the project manager should examine is whether tasks that have started or that were scheduled to start are progressing at the expected pace. For example, work that was assigned in the past but which is not executing will remain scheduled in the past. This backlogged work needs review and in many cases needs to be rescheduled into current or future periods. It is also recommended that the Autocalculation feature always be selected. To find this setting, click Project Tools | Options, then click the Calculations tab.

Using the Project Workspace to Manage the Project

Two settings are available in Project Server for provisioning a Project Workspace when a project is published. No matter which is chosen at the global level, provisioning Project Workspaces is a very powerful feature that is used to support project team collaboration. Many project consultants discounted this feature's value in previous versions. They were wrong.

In this section we will discuss the features that are available out of the box. Many more features can easily be enabled and they will be discussed in Chapter 25.

The Project Workspace is based on a single template. The template can be modified at the global level, but there is only one template for the enterprise. Out of the box, the template contains the following features, all of which can be useful to the project manager. The most useful features are marked with an asterisk.

- **Issues*** The project team can post project issues. The team members can assign, categorize, and prioritize the issues, change their status (to Active, Postponed, or Closed), and more. In addition, the project team can associate the issue with a project task or tasks. If this is done, when a user views the project from within a Project View in PWA, an indicator icon displays that warns "There are issues associated with this task." Upon selecting this icon, the user is taken to the project's issues. In addition, documents can be attached. Resources with issues assigned have visibility to those assignments from their PWA Home Page, as well as the Issues and Risks item that can be located under the My Work area of the Quick Launch Bar. Version history can be enabled.

- **Risks*** The Risks component is a great feature for recording and managing project risks. Although not perfect for everyone (yes, it can be modified), it does include critical items such as probability and impact, cost if risk occurs, mitigation, contingency, triggers, and assignments. Note that documents can also be attached. Resources with risks assigned can see those risks from their PWA Home Page, as well as the Issues and Risks item that can be located under the My Work area of the Quick Launch Bar. These also can be associated with specific project tasks and that association is reflected in the Project views for the project in the Indicator column. Version history can be enabled.
- **Deliverables** This new feature supports deliverables-based planning. Deliverables are entered into this feature and they can be used with project dependencies across projects.
- **Tasks** This is not a favorite feature, as normally tasks are kept as part of the project plan. This function does not have a relationship to the plan, but simply keeps a list of tasks.
- **Documents*** The document features available are very useful for storing and managing project documentation. Document libraries include support for check-out and check-in, including an option to force the document to be checked out for editing. There is an option for version history including a choice between major versions only (1, 2, 3, and 4) or a combination of minor versions (1.2, 1.2, and 1.3) and major versions. There are even features that require that new versions receive approval before the team members can view them.
- **Discussion** Threaded discussions are supported out of the box.
- **Announcements*** This useful feature allows the posting of project announcements.
- **Recycle Bin*** Any user with the Delete permission will see a Recycle Bin in the Project Workspace allowing them to "undelete" an item.
- **Calendar** The Calendar Web Part is located on the Project Workspace Home Page and can be used to display a project calendar in either list or boxes (calendar format).
- **Links** The Links Web Part is located on the right side of the Project Workspace and can be populated with links that are important to the project.

PART V

How Project Server Handles Resources Who Are Not Available as Expected

One great feature is the ability the system has for dealing with resources who are no longer available—for example, those who have left the company. When a resource has been assigned work in a project plan and becomes unavailable (deleted from synchronized Active Directory, deleted from Project Server, and made inactive in Project Server), when the project manager opens a project, a notification appears as shown in Figure 21-43, alerting the project manager of the issue.

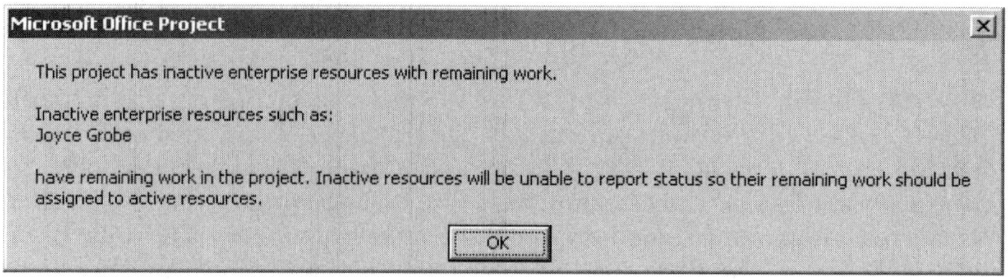

FIGURE 21-43 Resources have left the building

Master Projects

For a long time, Microsoft Project has included the ability to create Master Projects with subprojects. This was a popular feature for managing programs and keeping track of a set of small-effort projects such as support and for a variety of other purposes. Many organizations assumed that when they moved to Project Server, this feature would be one of the expanded set of tools available as it had been in previous versions of Project Server. Alas, this was not the case. This function caused severe problems with resource data as the assignment hours were counted twice for resources included in these Master Projects and subprojects.

We are pleased to report that Master Projects work well in the Project and Project Server 2007 environment. In fact, the setting that allows the publishing of Master Projects (the one where consultants always advised their clients, "No matter what, don't check this box") is now set on by default.

To create a Master Project, first create the subprojects that will be part of the master. Next, while connected to the Project Server, open an empty project. Then select Insert | Project.

The first subproject will then appear in a single row in the master as it is displayed fully rolled up. To see more detail in the subproject, select the plus sign to drill down.

Add any additional subprojects following the same method as before until your subprojects are all in the Master Project. You can then link tasks between the subprojects, often a valuable and necessary capability. There are a couple of ways to create the cross-project links. The first method (the easy way) is to select the predecessor task and then the successor task while holding down the CTRL key. This should highlight both tasks. Then press the Link button from the Standard Toolbar as shown in Figure 21-44.

The second method is to select the predecessor cell in the successor task. Then type in the name of the predecessor task using the following naming convention:

```
<>\(Name of project that includes the predecessor task)\(task number of
predecessor task)
```

An example follows:

```
<>\Rollout Microsoft CRM\35
```

No matter which method you use, repeat the process until the links are ready to go. Next, save the master. A new dialog then appears asking whether you want to save the subprojects as well. If you are sure about the changes that you made, select Yes to All.

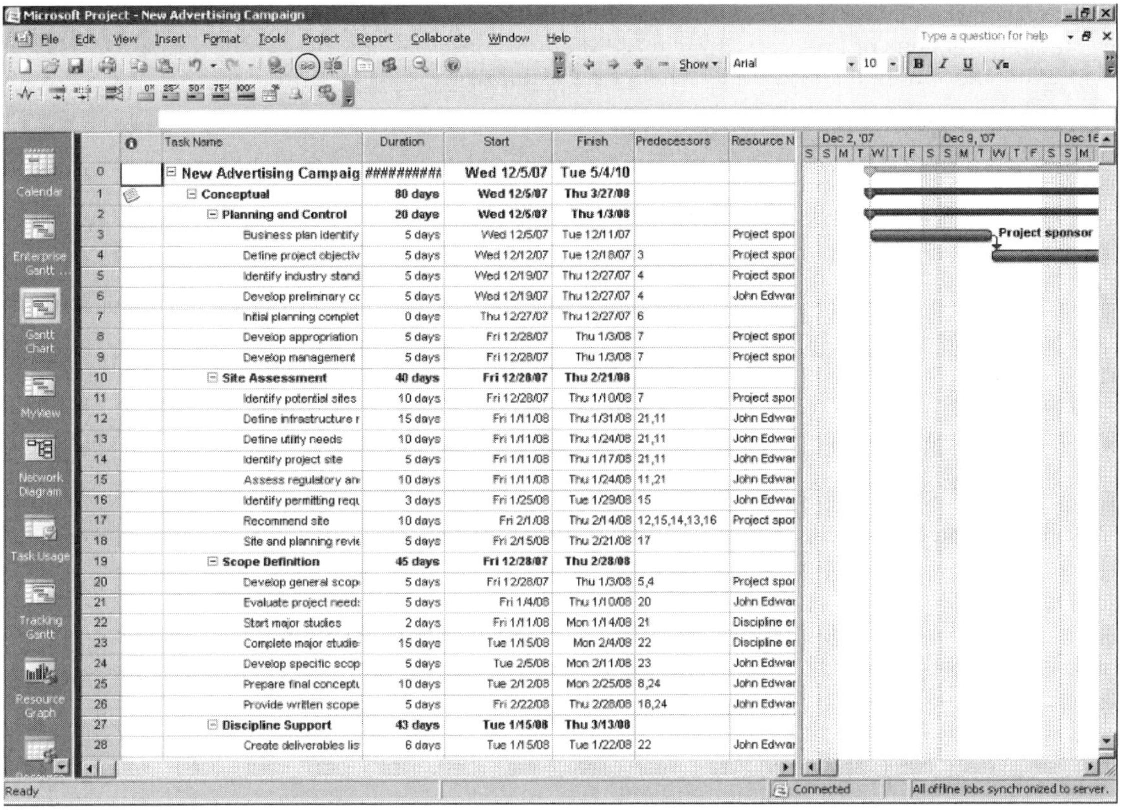

FIGURE 21-44 Link button

Then publish the Master Project (and then subprojects) and create a Project Workspace for the master. Once the Master Project Workspace is created, sub-projects can either be at the same level as the Master Workspace or be provisioned as sub-sites of the Master.

Cross-Project Task Dependencies (outside of Master Projects)

It is possible to link tasks between projects without the use of a Master Project. To do this, follow the same processes as were used to create the Master Project cross-project dependencies.

Start with a blank project while connected to Project Server. Next insert the projects that are going to include cross-project links. Then, using one of the two methods described in the preceding section, create the links. Next, select File | Close. In the dialog that appears, select Discard Changes. From the next dialog, select Yes to All. This command saves the established cross-project dependencies without creating a Master Project.

Project Reports and Visual Reports

In previous versions of Project, within an EPM environment or not, project-level reports were available. Out of the box, Project includes the following:

- Overview with the following reports:
  - Project summary
  - Top-level tasks
  - Critical tasks
  - Milestones
  - Working days
- Current activities reports, including the following:
  - Unstarted tasks
  - Tasks starting soon
  - Tasks in progress
  - Completed tasks
  - Tasks that should have started
  - Slipping tasks
- Costs reports, including the following:
  - Cash flow
  - Budget
  - Overbudget tasks
  - Overbudget resources
  - Earned value
- Assignments reports such as the following:
  - Who does what
  - Who does what when
  - To-do list
  - Overallocated resources
- Workload reports:
  - Task usage
  - Resource usage

In addition, Project continues to enable the user to create custom project reports using the Custom Reports tool shown in Figure 21-45.

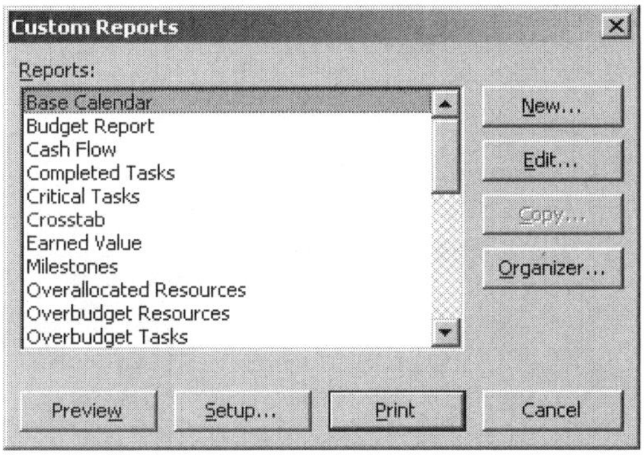

FIGURE 21-45 Custom project report building

These out-of-the-box reports were useful, especially when Project was being used as a stand-alone application, but they were rarely the best option in a Project Server environment. This is similarly true with the Project Server 2007 version.

A more powerful set of project report functionality called Visual Reports exists today. These reports, which can be viewed in Excel or Visio, are a combination of data for the project that are based on online analytical processing (OLAP) cubes. These reports provide views in pivot chart and table form, and are definitely far more useful than the standard project reports in Project Professional (or Standard Edition, where they are also available in 2007). Keep in mind that if your system is connected to Project Server when you are using this feature, data from multiple projects are used. If a single project-based Visual Report is desired, you can build the report while working offline.

To navigate to Visual Reports, select Report | Visual Reports from the Project Professional main menu bar. A dialog appears with many options. From this dialog, the project manager can create reports that include pivot charts based on templates that either come with Project out of the box or using customized templates. To see what is available out of the box, navigate through the tabs to see the specific views and a preview of the style of the chart in the Sample window on the right (see Figure 21-46).

The following are the data types available in these reports:

- Task usage
- Resource usage
- Assignment usage
- Task summary
- Resource summary
- Assignment summary

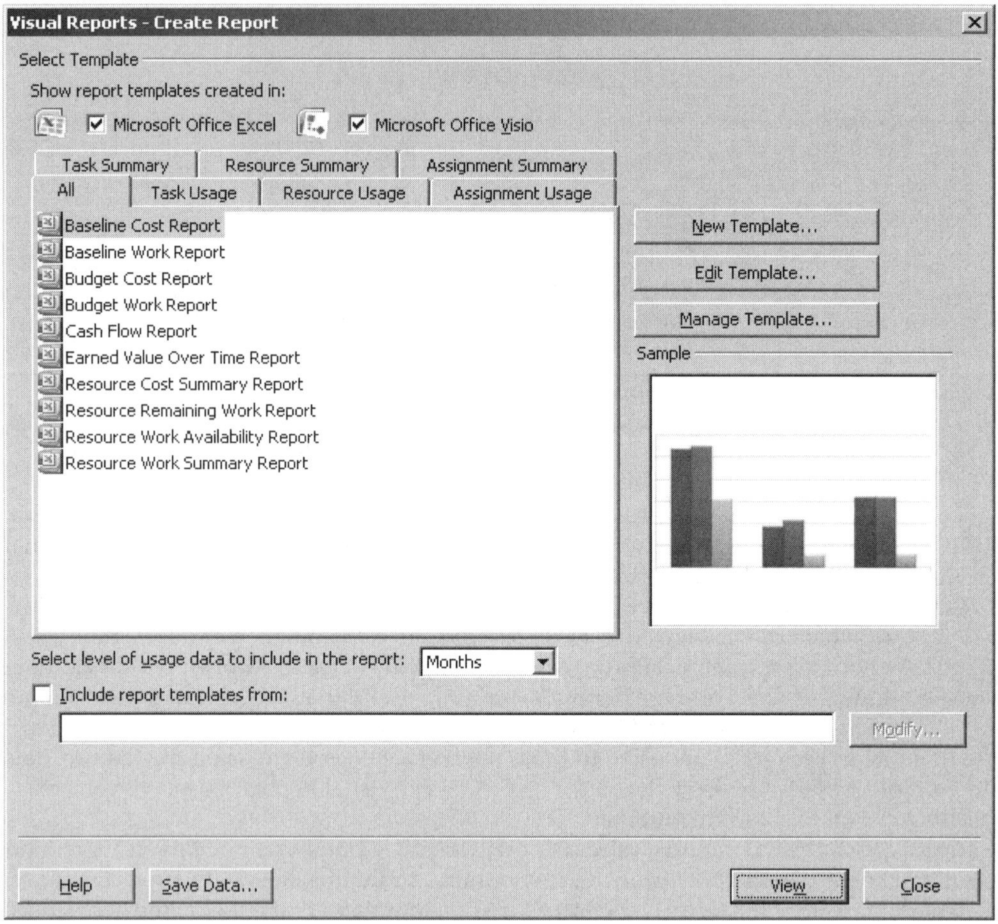

FIGURE 21-46 Sample window

Note that there is no data type for viewing and sorting project-level data. Figure 21-47 shows an example Visual Report.

Note that if the actual graphic is double-clicked, a toolbar appears on the right that enables the user to modify the data displayed in the chart. Finally, the data are displayed in table form on the second worksheet in the report.

Project reports and Visual Reports have their uses, but the most useful reports in the opinion of the authors are the views available via PWA. The next section discusses PWA views that the project manager can leverage.

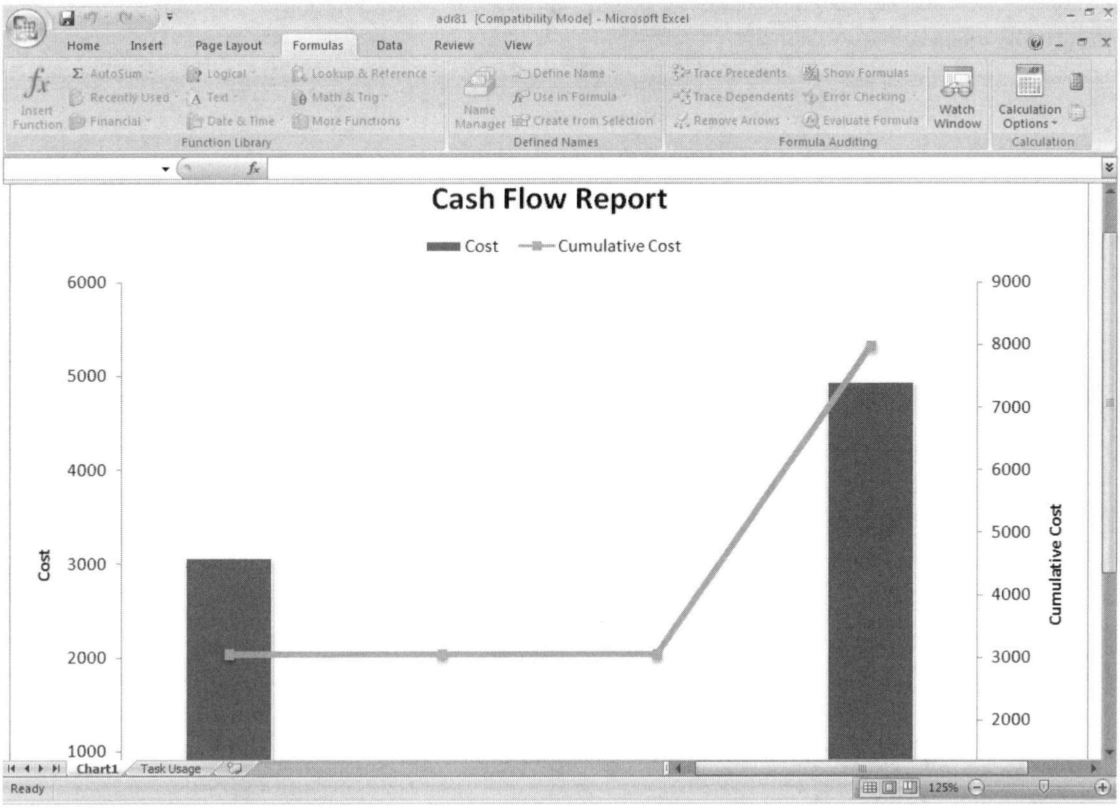

FIGURE 21-47 Example Visual Report

Status Reporting

Project Server includes built-in support for status reports. This functionality can be used by anyone with permission, but is most commonly used by project managers. Thus this section will focus on how the project manager can use the built-in status report functionality. Status reports can be located by selecting the Status Reports item on the Quick Launch Bar in the Resources section. Remember that everything is based on permissions, so that if there is no Status Reports item, it is because the permission is not enabled.

After selecting the Status Reports item, you will be on the Status Reports page. There are two sections: Requests and Responses.

Status Report Requests

To build a status report request, select New | New Request from the horizontal bar under Requests. To locate it, see Figure 21-48.

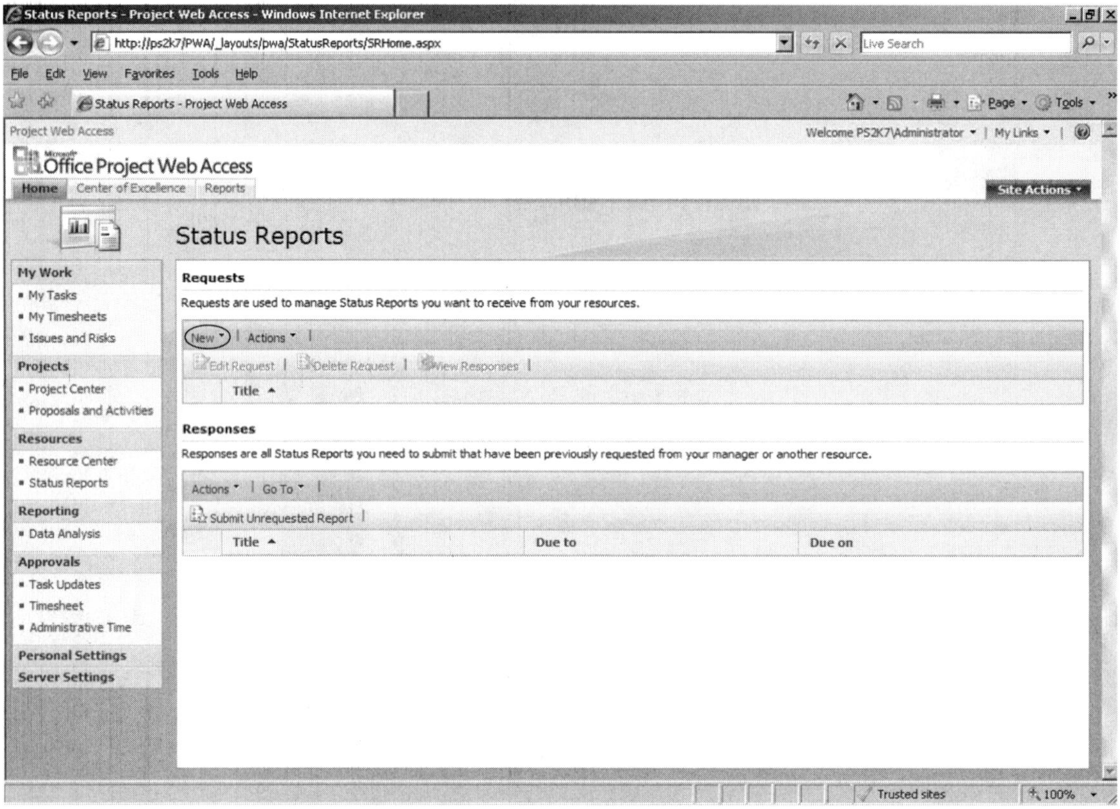

FIGURE 21-48 New status report request button

Start at the top by giving the report a name. If it is for a departmental team, consider naming the report after the team name. After naming the status report, select the frequency that the report should be completed by the team. Frankly, although options exist for monthly and yearly frequency, the only practical option is weekly. The next item in the Frequency part of the page allows for biweekly or other less frequently used options. Once again, although there may be some roles that would seek a less frequent status report, such a frequency is probably not appropriate for the project manager. Finally, in the next part of the page are a set of checkboxes for the days of the week when the report or reports are required. On rare occasions, when a high visibility or priority project is in "crunch time," it could make sense to seek status reports more frequently than weekly, but remember that completing the report takes time. See Figure 21-49 for a common setting for Status Report frequency.

The next step is to select the team that is being asked to complete the status report. Move the resources from left to right in the Resources section of the page. Multiselect is enabled in this feature, so use the CTRL or SHIFT keys as appropriate. After selecting the resources, click the Add button.

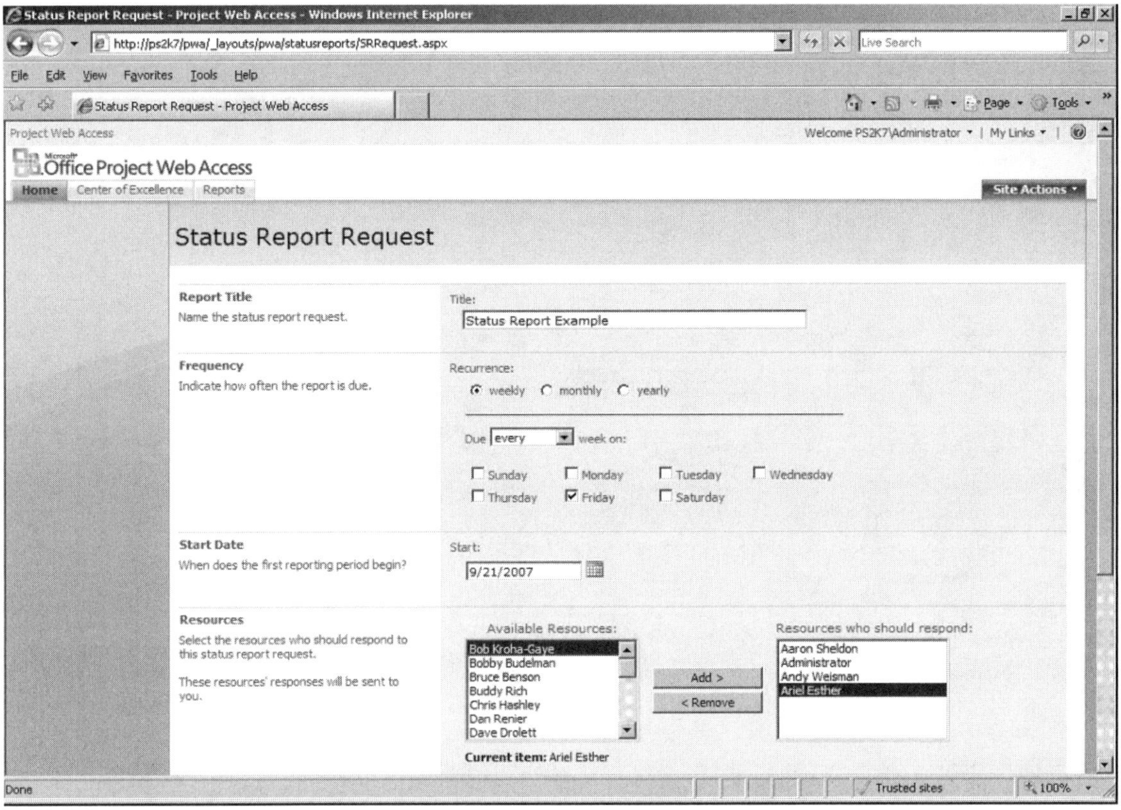

FIGURE 21-49 Status report frequency settings

The last section of the page allows the requester to determine the content of the status report. In following classic status report basics, Microsoft provides the following sections to start the status report:

- Major Accomplishments
- Objectives for the Next Period
- Hot Issues

These sections are just a starting point; you can change and delete them as necessary. To delete a section, highlight the row, as shown in Figure 21-50, and select the Delete Section button.

New sections can be added as well. Once the status report request is ready, select the Send button and the recurring status report will be enabled. The people who were selected each

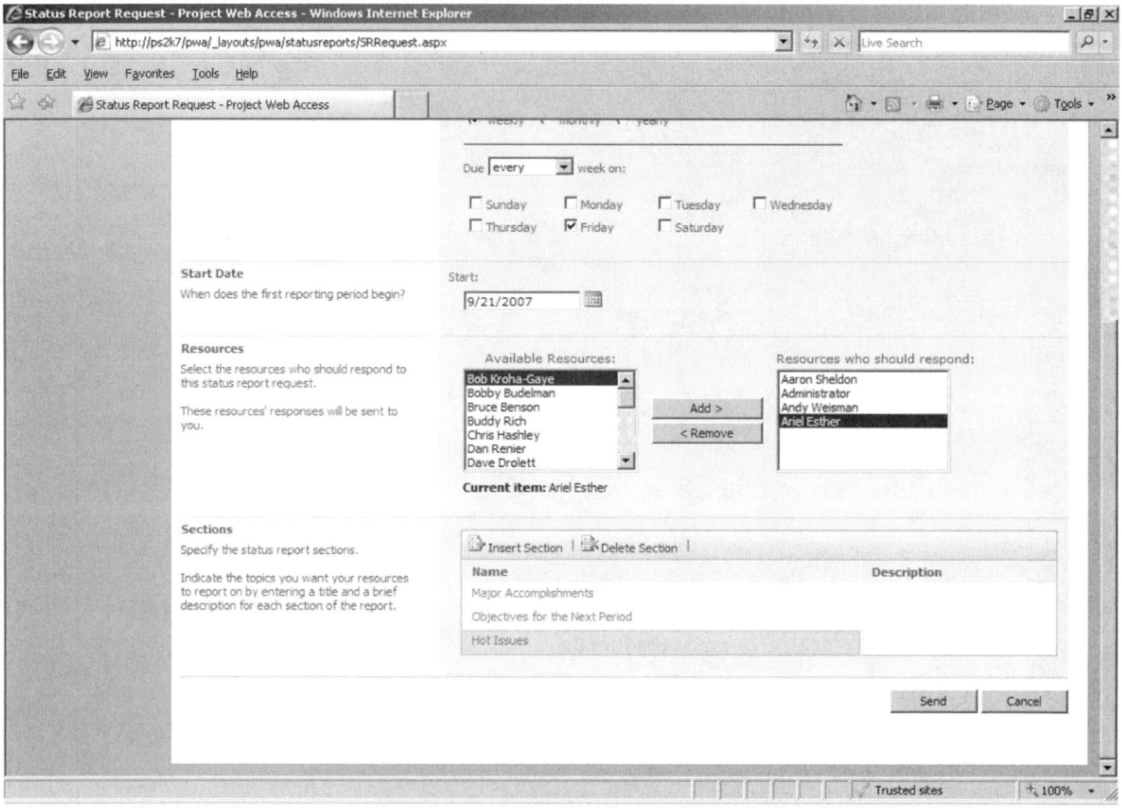

FIGURE 21-50 Status report sections

receive an e-mail notification. In addition, they can individually add personal alerts if they so choose. Finally, if a status report is late, the PWA Home Page displays a notice for the user.

When status reports are submitted to the requester, a useful set of features is available. Select the title of the requested report to see the details of any responses. You can view any individual response by highlighting the paper indicator and then selecting the Open button. To see an aggregated team report (a great feature), select the row header (the date range of the report), then select Open. Figure 21-51 shows how this aggregated report appears.

Notice that each section of the status report includes all of the team's respective responses. Each response includes a date stamp to reflect the day that the report was submitted.

In previous versions of Project Server, there was no practical way to print a status report. Although the authors prefer to work in electronic views in most cases (including this one), some organizations or individuals prefer to print the reports. The PWA status report can be exported to Microsoft Word 2003–2007, where printing is easy.

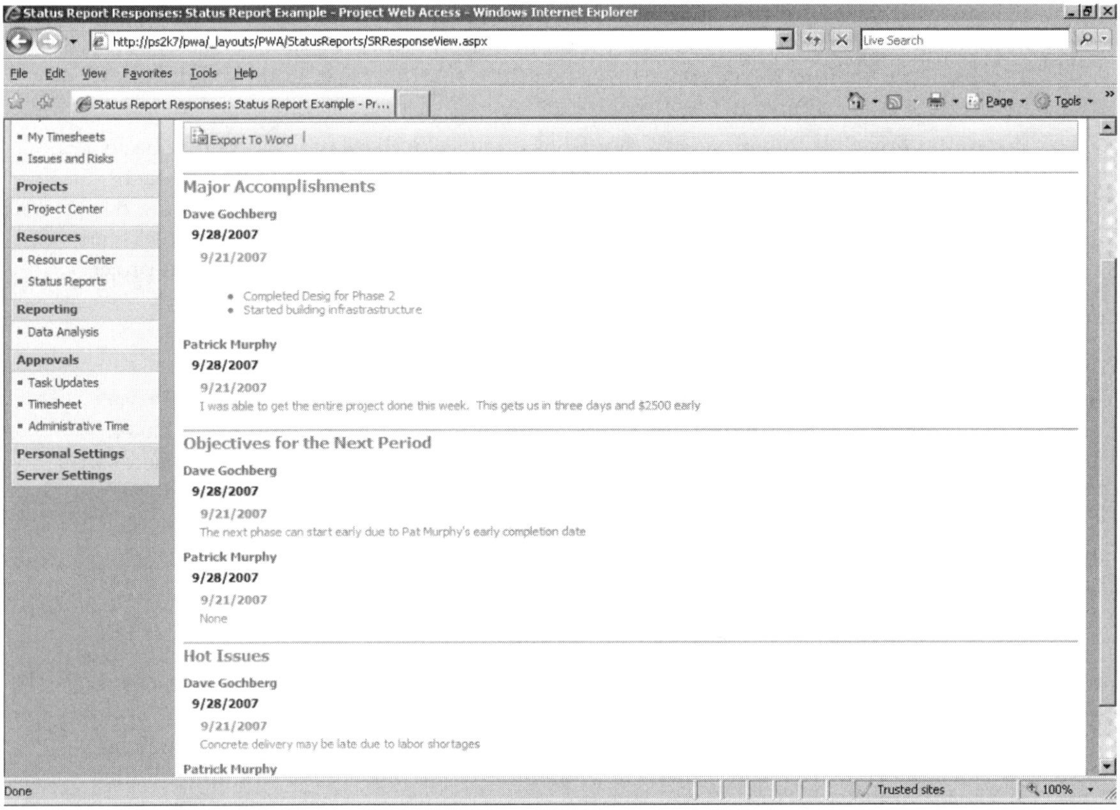

FIGURE 21-51 Aggregated status report

PWA Views

Although project managers do the bulk of their work from within Project Professional and the Project Workspaces, there are some great things that can be done with views in PWA, as discussed in Chapter 11. Depending on the level of organizational maturity and the preferred methods for tracking projects, here are some useful views.

Project Center Views

Subcategories of Project Center views include the following:

- **Progress views** Progress "dashboards" are always good, especially for a project manager with multiple projects. They could include things like red-green-yellow indicators for SV (schedule variance), CV or CV% (Cost Variance/Cost Variance Percentage), and work variance fields to indicate project progress.

- **Earned Value views** If the organization is mature enough to use earned value (EV) fields, this type of view can provide even more useful tracking data. Once again, graphics give the user a quick survey or the projects so that exceptions (red or yellow, for example) can be quickly identified for action.
- **Program views** If the organization wishes, views can display projects that have common elements as a program. This allows a group of people visibility to each portion of the larger program. For example, if project manager Bob is working on a large program managed by Susan along with three other project managers, each can view the entire program. Such a view can be especially useful if there are cross-project dependencies.

Project Views

The Project views include the detail level of the individual project as selected from Project Center. A ton of views come out of the box, including task, assignment, and timephased views, although there is nothing in these views that could not be done locally inside Microsoft Office Project Professional. It is possible, however, to have a Project View that may include certain corporate metrics without requiring a local Project View.

Data Analysis Views

These views may be provided to project managers depending on organizational decisions. The reason that they are not always available is that opening the data for these views involves providing access to OLAP cubes from SQL Analysis Services. This access, from the security perspective, is a bit like all-or-nothing access (for reading the data).

If access to OLAP and data analysis is provided, project managers can use Data Analysis views to get historical data that can be used in preparation for a project. For example, similar projects can be assessed to see how long tasks actually took in order to get a better perspective on how much time those same tasks will require in the current project.

In one actual case, an organization used a custom resource field to apply an attribute to consulting resources. By creating a Data Analyzer View that used cost (rate), time (months), projects, and resource names, the organization was able to validate whether invoices that were received from consulting companies matched the amount of time charged for the project(s) to which the consultants were billing. If a project manager is managing both in-house and consulting resources, this type of view can be useful.

A Word on the Project Cache

The new architecture of Microsoft's EPM solution includes a local Project Cache for each user per machine. There are some known issues at the time of the authoring of this book.

Projects can become stuck in a situation where the server has the project checked in and the cache shows it as checked out or "Pending Checkin." To resolve the problem, first attempt to clear the cache by navigating to Tools | Local Project Cache and then clearing the project (or even all the projects). Restart Project Professional. If that does not work, close Project

Professional, open My Computer, and navigate to C:\Documents and Settings\Administrator\Application Data\Microsoft\MS Project\Cache. From there, delete all the files. Reopen Project and the problem should be resolved.

Another issue occurs when the project fields become jumbled. These fields are available from with the Project | Project Information dialog, or from within the Save dialog for a first-time Save. The symptom is that the fields that have dropdown menus include items that don't belong in the specific dropdown (perhaps from a different dropdown in the dialog), or might not allow the use of portions of hierarchical fields. The procedure discussed in the previous paragraph will resolve this issue as well.

This chapter has covered the interaction with Project Server and Project Professional from the project manager's perspective. In the next chapter, the discussion focuses on how team members typically interact with Project Server 2007.

CHAPTER 22

How the Team Member Interacts with Project Server

In Project Server 2007, team members represent the majority of the system users. They are not project managers charged with guiding projects to successful conclusions. They usually don't have staff who report to them and they are not corporate executives who look at summary information for organizational trends. Team members are assigned tasks, perform those tasks, and report time to their managers and task progress to their project managers.

In many ways, a significant goal of the Enterprise Project Management (EPM) project team is to configure the system so that team members' interaction with it is limited, for reasons of ease of use, security, and time efficiency. After all, if the people working on a project are spending all their time using Project Server, there will never be any actual work performed.

This chapter describes the processes that are performed by the team member under general circumstances. As with the previous chapter that covered the project manager role, there is no intent here to cover every possible configuration scenario. Instead, this chapter makes assumptions about how many organizations choose to operate in the Project Server environment. Critical assumptions include the following:

- The system is configured for time to be recorded in hours.
- The Hours of Work Done Per Period setting is set to Resources Report Their Hours Worked on Each Task Per Period.
- Time periods are each one week.
- Team members are required to use timesheets rather than only using task-updating functions. (Timesheets are not always needed.)

Team Member at Work

The team member in Project Server 2007 does not have the Microsoft Office Project Professional client installed on his or her desktop. All actions occur through Internet Explorer. Note that Project Web Access requires the use of ActiveX controls, so alternative browsers are not supported.

E-Mail Notifications

From the technical perspective, team members first interact with the system when they receive an e-mail informing them that they have been assigned to tasks in a project. Note that, is not generally a best practice to assign someone to a task in a project that he or she has not been informed of in some other way, but alas, it has been known to happen.

The e-mail includes all the tasks on a single project, as opposed to many separate e-mails, as in the following example:

> Project: New Soy Bean Packaging
>
> Below are the latest schedule changes. Contact your project manager if there are any problems with the changes.
>
> Your work assignments below have changed.
>
> Task Name: Test
>
> Start: Friday, August 17, 2007 Finish: Tuesday, August 21, 2007 Work: 24h Remaining Work: 24h % Completion: 0
>
> Task Name: Integrate
>
> Start: Friday, August 10, 2007 Finish: Thursday, August 16, 2007 Work: 40h Remaining Work: 40h % Completion: 0
>
> To turn off these notifications, go to Project Web Access, click Personal Settings on the left menu, and then click Manage My Alerts and Reminders.
>
> From this page, you can clear the checkbox for those notifications you no longer want to receive.
>
> Microsoft Office Project Server

The team member will next navigate to the Project Web Access Home Page (http://*servername/instancename*); for example, http://SERVER12/pwa.

Project Web Access Home Page

The Project Web Access (PWA) Home Page is a personalized, permission-based set of information specifically for the user who is logged in. Typically, the team member is logged in automatically based on how that user has logged in to his or her desktop. In the top-right corner, there will be a personal welcome (for example, "Welcome Aaron Sheldon").

Reminders

There is a Reminders Web Part that is the primary tool for the team member to see what he or she needs to know about his or her Project Server activities. This Web Part fills the top of the Body section of the page, as shown in Figure 22-1.

Included in the Reminders area are the following:

- **Tasks** This portion lets the team member know how many new assignments he or she has received.

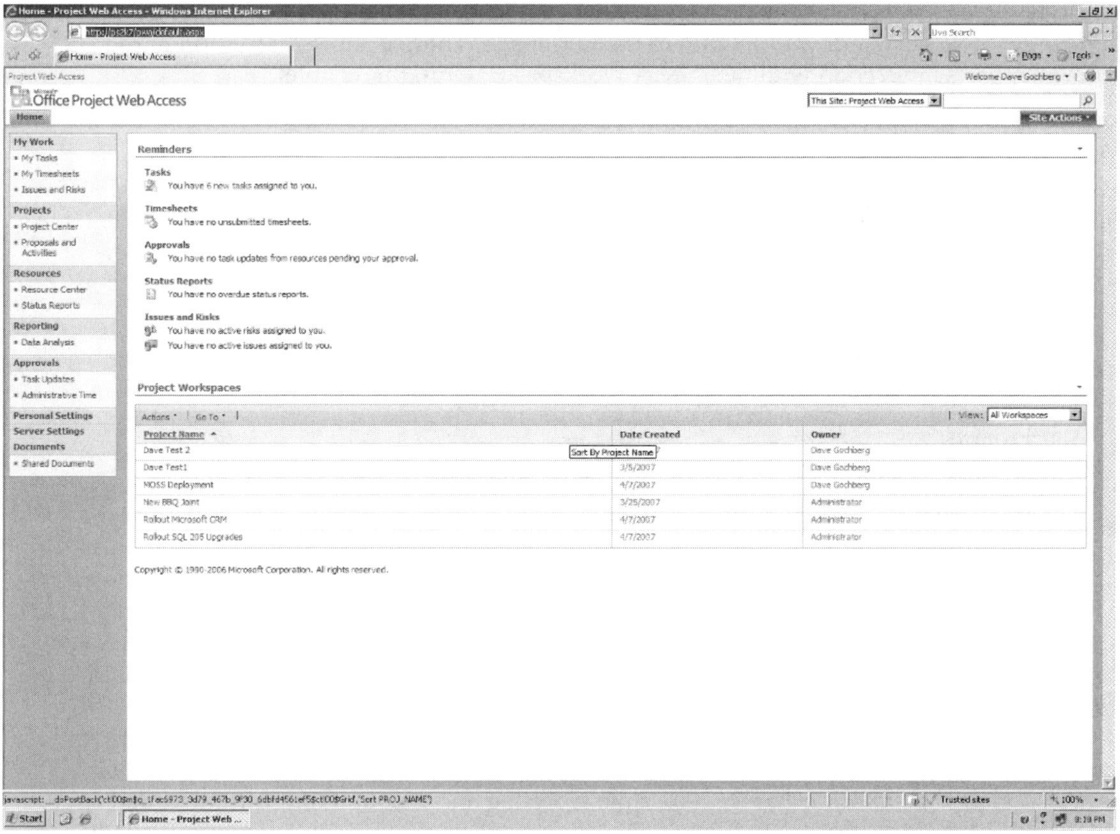

FIGURE 22-1 PWA Home Page, with reminders front and center

- **Timesheets** This row alerts the team member of any overdue timesheets (typically, one timesheet is due per week).
- **Status Reports** Often, project managers or functional managers (resource managers in Project Server) seek recurring status reports on a weekly basis. This feature lets the team member know of late status reports and of those that are soon coming due.
- **Issues and Risks** If the team member has been assigned any issues or risks, these two rows display those that are in active status.

Project Workspaces Web Part

The bottom half of the page body includes a list of Project Workspaces to which the team member has permission. Note that there is a filter dropdown list in the top-right corner that could be set to Owned Workspaces, but for which a typical team member will be completely blank. If you change the setting to All Workspaces, the team member will see all the spaces to which he or she has access.

To navigate to a Project Workspace, just select the name of the project from this Web Part and a new browser window will open in the target site. There is more discussion of the team member's interaction with the Project Workspace later in this chapter.

Navigation

There can be top navigation from the PWA Home Page, but typically all the navigation is done from the Quick Launch Bar along the page's left side. For the team member, the following options are usually displayed:

- My Work
  - My Tasks
  - My Timesheets
- Issues and Risks
- Projects
  - Project Center
- Resources
  - Resource Center
  - Status Reports
- Personal Settings

Team Member Assignment and Reporting Process

After the team member receives task notification and navigates to PWA, the time and task updating process begins. This section covers the typical way that team members report their progress. Note that in Project Server 2007, time reporting and task updating are two different things, and that for the team member to report time to his or her timesheet manager (usually the functional manager) and to update the project manager of task progress, a multistage process is required.

Timesheet

Team members use the timesheet to record time. It is usually the first step in the reporting process for team members.

Creating a Timesheet Typically the next step is to create a timesheet. To do so, navigate to the My Timesheets page from the Quick Launch Bar. Usually the dropdown menu on the top-right is set to Current + Last 3 Months, as shown in Figure 22-2.

Find the current week and if it displays a status of Not Yet Created, select Click to Create. From there, the system goes to the timesheet for the user who created it. Under most configurations, it will pre-populate the timesheet with any assignments that are scheduled for the week of the timesheet created. In addition, at the bottom of the timesheet is a list of Administrative Time categories, such as Vacation or Sick Time.

In some cases, organizations may choose timesheet options other than the prepopulate option. Other possibilities include not pre-populating the timesheet at all, or instead populating it based on projects rather than current task items.

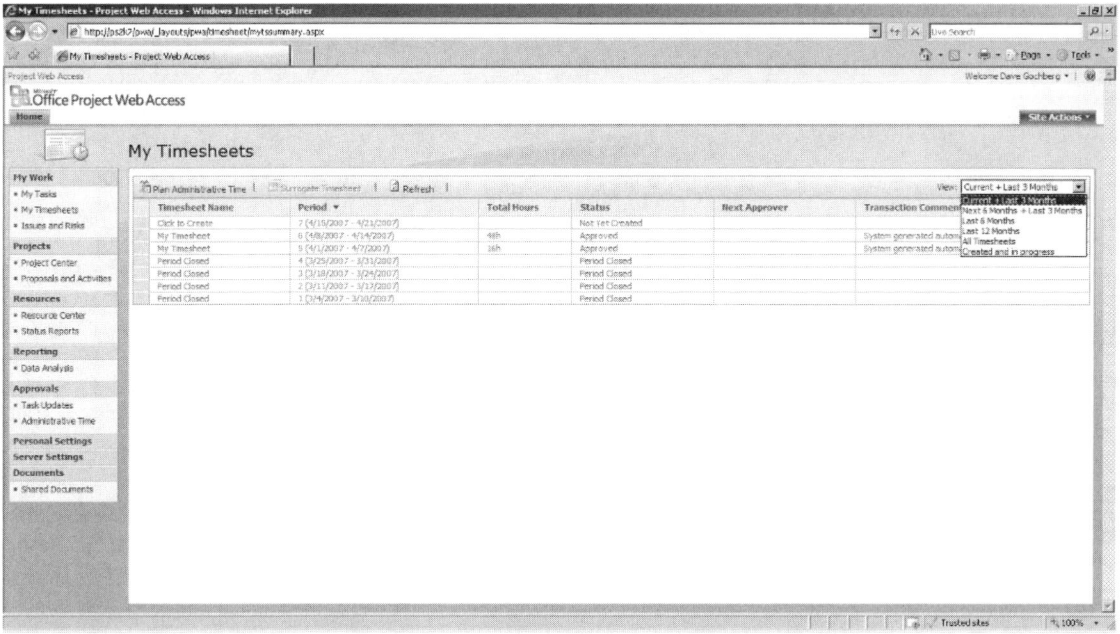

FIGURE 22-2 Dropdown menu on My Timesheets page

The user records time by entering in the timesheet the hours worked. A good practice is for the user to enter time daily and save it, but not submit the timesheet on the day that the user performed the work. Enter the time in the timesheet, as shown in Figure 22-3.

After entering time into the timesheet, the team member should save the entries by selecting the Save button from the bottom of the page. Saving the timesheet does not submit the time to the timesheet manager (who is normally the team member's boss). Rather, it just saves it for further activity (such as later in the week).

There is another way to navigate to the timesheet that may be a better option after the working timesheet has been created. If the team member navigates to the My Work page from the PWA tag page, it takes them to a combination view featuring three different views: Tasks, Timesheet, and Schedule. By selecting the Timesheet option from the top-right corner, as shown in Figure 22-4, the team member has a different way to get to the timesheet. This method is preferable in cases where the timesheet is known to have already been created. The reason is that the timesheet and the Tasks page are often used during the same session for time and task reporting (you will learn more about this topic later in this chapter). Even after team members have been informed of this navigational path, they often choose to select My Timesheet and then select the current week's timesheet because the label in the navigation My Timesheet is a more obvious tag for locating the timesheet. Either path works fine, but the recommended path from a usability perspective is to travel through the My Work page.

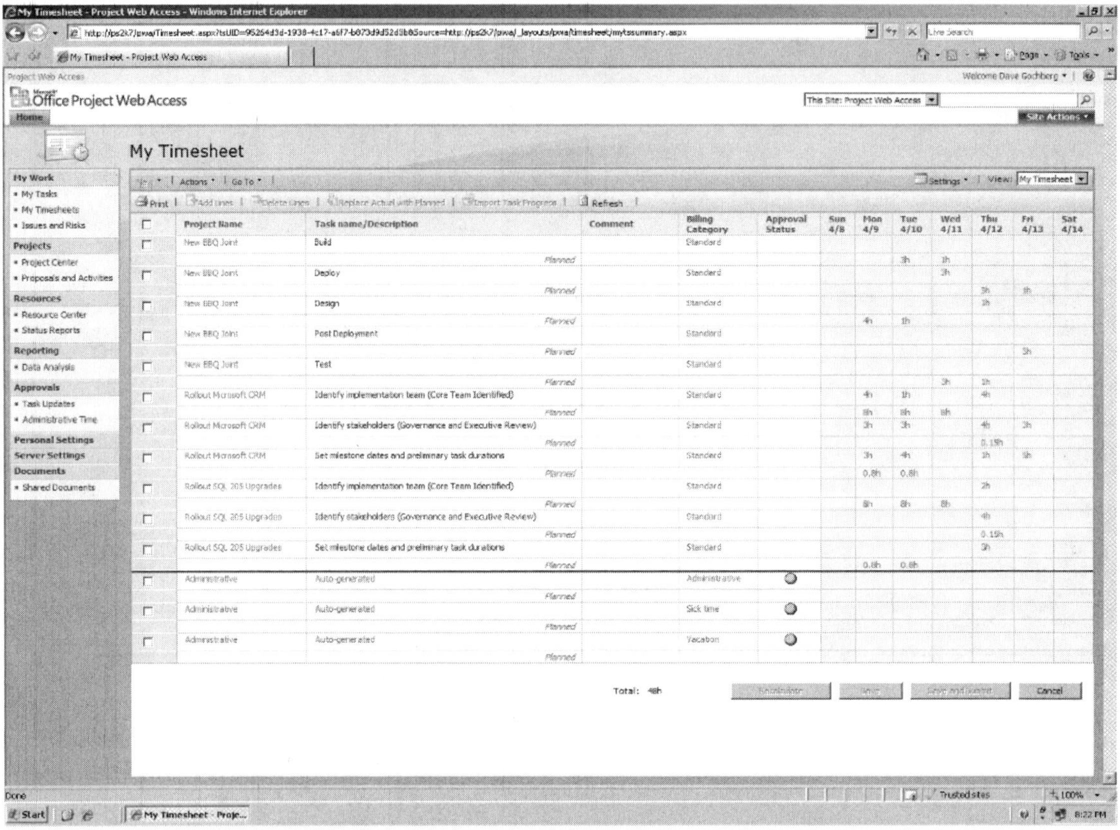

FIGURE 22-3 Timesheet with some time entered

From either view of the timesheet, there are other key features available for the team member. Under the Settings button, if timesheet header data are displayed, the window is added to the timesheet for changing dates and date ranges as shown in Figure 22-5.

For the team member to scroll back a week at a time or forward the same way, there are graphics available that support the previous and next functions, as shown in Figure 22-6.

The team member can also use the Go To button to navigate to the My Timesheets page, where he or she can locate other timesheets or create new ones. There are other features in the Timesheet View. The timesheet is normally pre-populated with whatever tasks are assigned for the time period. However, in many organizations, the timesheet is created first thing in the week. If new tasks are assigned after creation of the timesheet, they do not automatically appear in the already-created timesheet. Rather, the team member needs to add the new

FIGURE 22-4 My Work page multiple page options controls

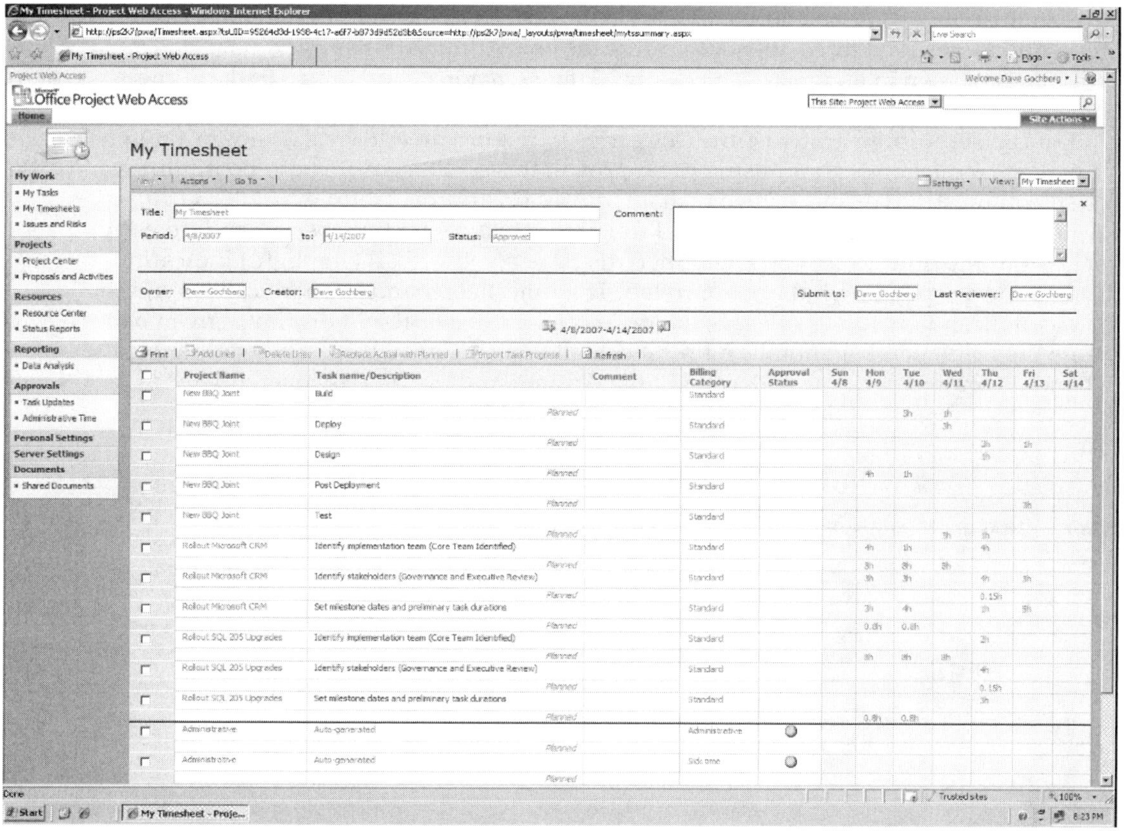

FIGURE 22-5 Timesheet with header data

tasks by using the Add Lines feature. To add lines, select the Add Lines button, then in the displayed dialog, select the tasks to include on the timesheet. The team member can add any task to which he or she is assigned. This feature also allows a team member to bring assigned tasks into the future if he or she has an opportunity to start work early on those tasks.

NOTE *There are a couple things to keep in mind when using the Add Lines feature. If a team member adds a line to the timesheet, he or she must save the timesheet to ensure that the added line remains after the team member navigates from the timesheet. Also, the Add Lines feature allows the use of the* CTRL *and* SHIFT *keys for making multiple selections; however, if the selection includes* any *task that already appears in the timesheet, the entire Add Lines process fails. In that case, the user must repeat the process without the offending tasks.*

FIGURE 22-6 Previous and next functions from the timesheet header data

Administrative Time categories appear on the bottom of the timesheet in most cases. Microsoft has included three categories out of the box: Administrative, Sick Time, and Vacation. As shown in Figure 22-7, a thick black line separates the Administrative Time categories from regular time.

You can set Administrative Time categories to require preapproval or not. Although we have mixed feelings about using preapproval, this section covers both possibilities. For an Administrative Time category that requires preapproval—for example, a future vacation—the team member should add the time into a future time period and save (but not submit) the time. The Status field then displays a yellow ball (stoplight) indicating that a request is pending but not approved. The timesheet manager receives the request for vacation, and on approval the Status field on the timesheet will display a green ball. Before the team member submits a timesheet, all the balls must be green. Another way to handle required preapproval, called Plan Administrative Time is covered later in this chapter.

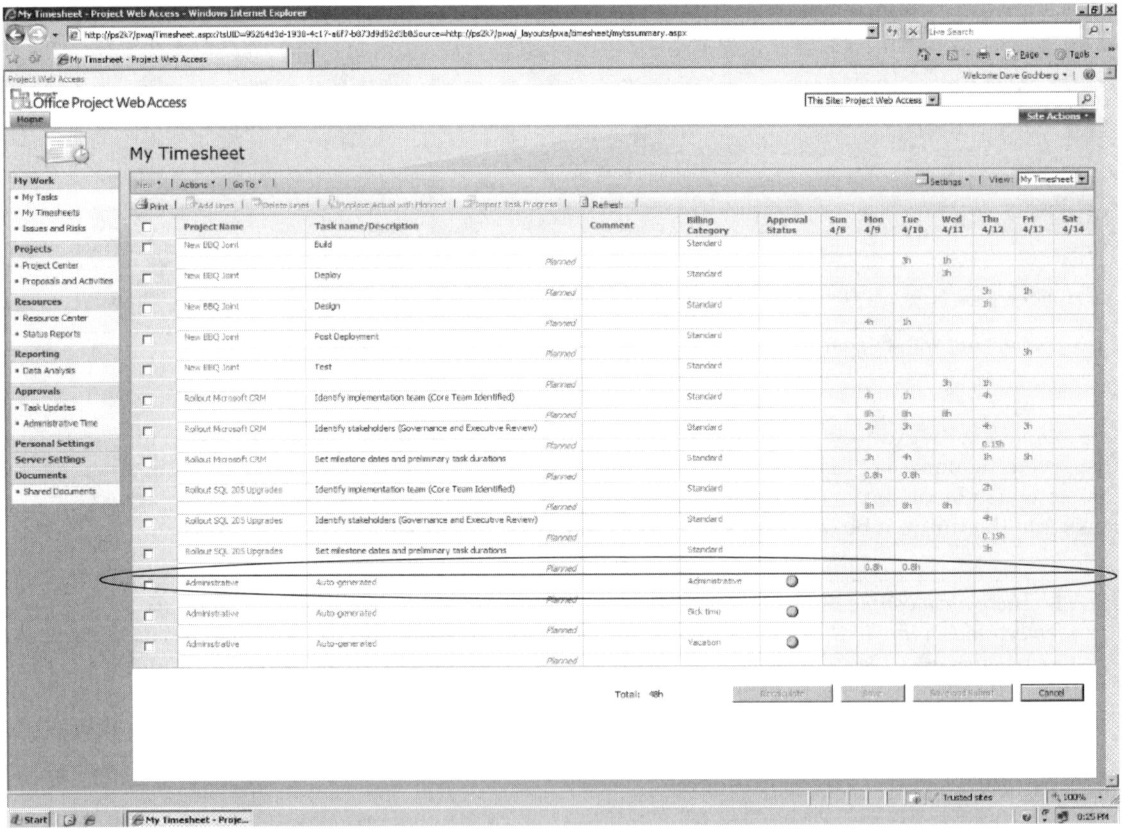

FIGURE 22-7 Separator line for Administrative categories

NOTE *As mentioned earlier preapproval requires several additional steps for Team members and Timesheet Managers. The Timesheets require approval even without the extra steps in pre-approval. Is the extra step really needed? Make sure that the Project Team considers this during the planning of your implementation.*

After all the Administrative Time balls are green and time has been entered for the week, the team member can submit his or her time to the timesheet manager for approval. The team member does so either by selecting specific items (the boxes are normally under the print icon button) to submit, or by submitting all items (even the ones where nothing was recorded). To submit specific items, select the checkbox to the left of the task rows, as shown in Figure 22-8.

After selecting the items to submit, select Save and Submit. The timesheet is then submitted to the team member's timesheet manager for approval. The team member can attach a comment. Note that if the team member is also the timesheet manager (for example, if a manager is reporting time, but there is no higher approval authority), the timesheet is auto-approved.

Timesheets cannot be edited when they are in the submitted state. If changes are required, the team member must recall the timesheet. To recall a timesheet, click the Timesheet Actions button from the My Timesheet page and select Recall Timesheet, as shown in Figure 22-9.

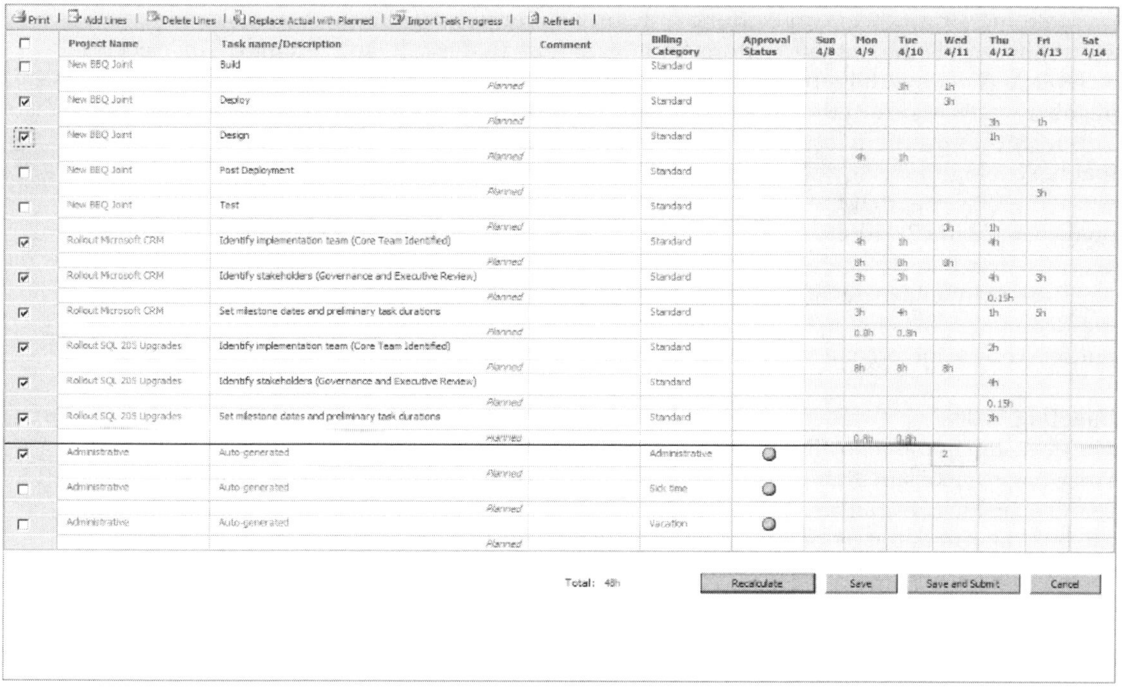

FIGURE 22-8 Selecting specific items to submit from the timesheet

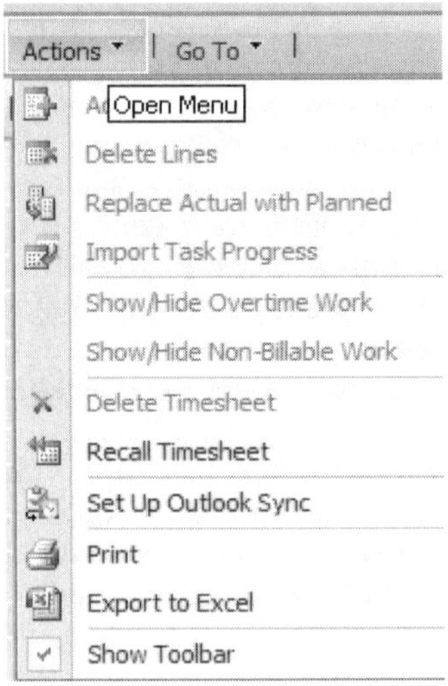

FIGURE 22-9 Recall Timesheet option

Deleting a timesheet can be done only on unsubmitted Timesheets. This can be accomplished via the Actions button. Another feature that is available from the Timesheet is Replace Actual with Planned. This fills in the time for reporting purposes if the team member wants to record the same amount of time as was planned by the project manager. This feature is useful in less mature organizations, but is not the ideal fit for companies that have a high level (or even a moderate level) of project management maturity, as it would be very rare that the time actually performed would be identical to that which was predicted. Figure 22-10 shows the location of the Replace Actual with Planned and Import Task Progress features.

The team member can also import into the timesheet work progress already entered in the Tasks page (which you'll learn more about shortly) by clicking the Import Task Progress button. This is not as commonly used.

Updating Tasks

The next step in the reporting process is to update progress on assigned tasks. From the My Work page, make sure that the View field is set to Tasks. From there, the team member will see all active tasks or all current tasks (the default setting). The period that defines "current" can be configured, but by default is set to 10 days. Thus the Tasks page will display any tasks that are scheduled to start within the next 10 working days, as well as any tasks that have been started but not completed.

On the Tasks page, the team member can import the time that was entered and saved in the timesheet by selecting Import Timesheet. After selecting the Import Timesheet

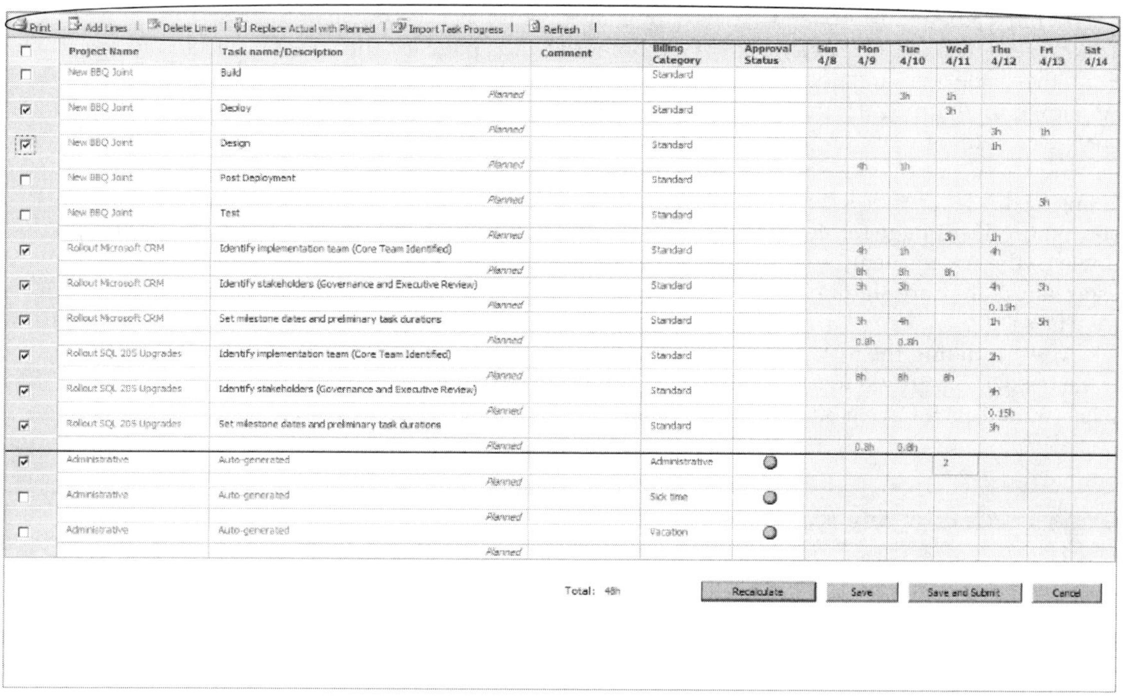

FIGURE 22-10 Locations in My Timesheet for the Replace Actual with Planned and Import Task Progress features

button, select the timesheet period to import and then select the Import button. The next page displays a preview of what is being imported, which can then be imported or canceled.

From this point, the time that was entered in the timesheet is applied to the task progress. In most cases, there is more work to do prior to submitting the task updates to the project manager(s).

By default, the Task page includes a Progress column that displays how a task is progressing in number of days and by percentage. Often, configuration also includes a Remaining Work column. It is very important for the team member to assess the Remaining Work column and change it if appropriate. This will let the project manager know whether tasks will require more effort or finish ahead of schedule. These critical pieces of information can have a profound effect on the success of a project. Unfortunately, the Remaining Work column on the Tasks page displays in days instead of the (preferable) hour units. To change the Remaining Work column of the Tasks page, type in the Remaining Work field either in parts of days (.5 for 4 hours), or by explicitly typing in hours (4h). If you type a 4 without the *h*, the system assumes that you mean four days.

Perhaps a better approach to reviewing a task is to select the name of the task from the Task page. This takes the user to the Assignment Details page for the specific selected item. From there, the team member has more control over what is submitted to the project manager. As shown in Figure 22-11, the Assignment Details page allows the user to add actual work; change remaining work (in hours); modify the start and finish dates (although we recommend leaving these alone); view attachments, history, and related assignments; and add a note. Going to this level of task depth can be time consuming, so the recommended approach is to stay on the Tasks page for items that do not need modification after time was applied. Drilling down to the Assignment Details page makes sense when additional modifications are needed, especially if they are significant (such as adding 50 percent more time to what was planned for a task).

After updating the tasks, make sure that they are saved by clicking the Save All button. If the tasks have grown to a point where there are more than can be displayed on a single page (which each have a 30 row limit), make sure that each page is saved.

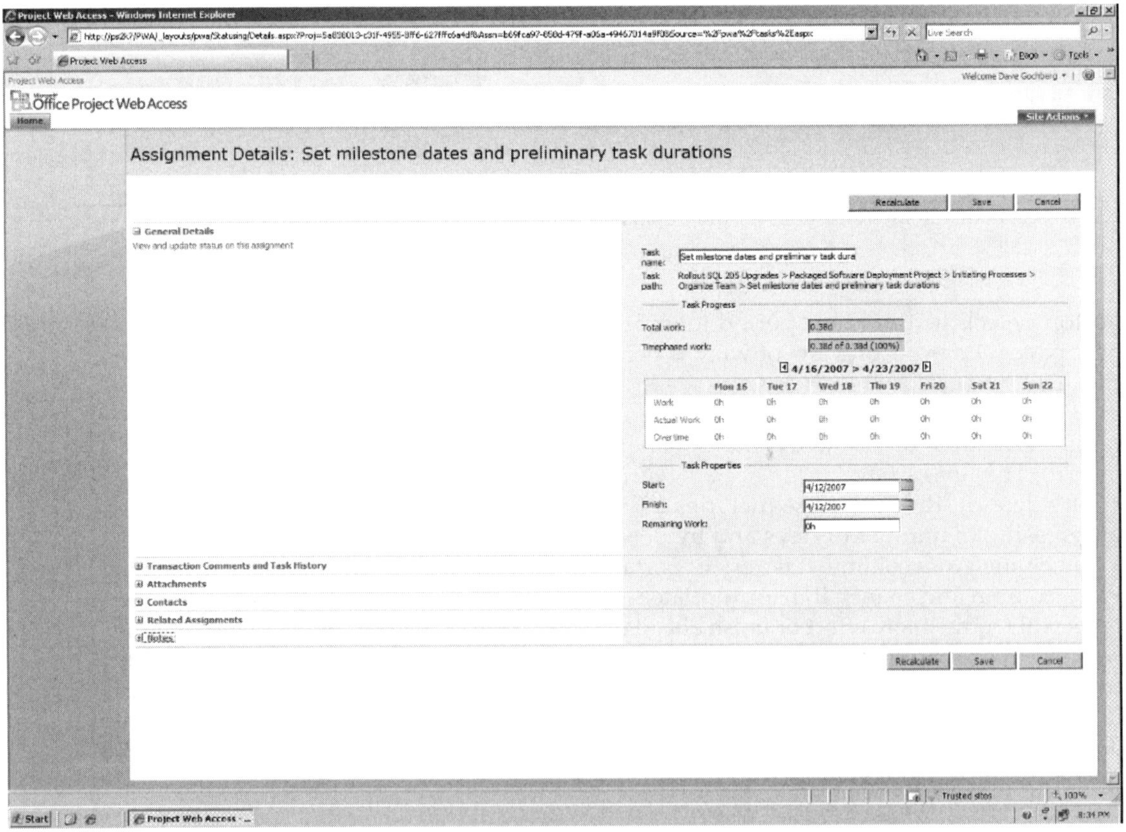

FIGURE 22-11 Assignment Details page

To submit the task updates, make sure that the checkboxes are selected on the left side of each task being updated and click the Submit Selected button. Notice the checkbox at the top of the page that selects all rows. Use this if appropriate; however, note that for multipage task lists, you will have to select this checkbox on each page.

The Task page includes a set of visual clues. Table 22-1 describes each graphical hint. The finish cells are color-coded. If the cell is pink, the finish date has already passed. If it is peach (the author's best guess at the color), it means the finish date is imminent (within a week). Indicator icons include those displayed in Table 22-1.

There are also other color-coded hints using some vertical bars. These bars only reinforce the items in Table 22-1 and have no independent meaning. For example, the little green bar only appears on tasks that also have the New icon. Kudos to Microsoft for considering accessibility and making sure that there are no clues that rely on color only.

Note that on the My Work page, the View | Schedule option is all the way to the top-right. As shown in Figure 22-12, the Schedule View displays the team member's tasks in a calendar format.

Selecting a task from the Schedule View takes the team member to that task's Assignment Details View (which you'll learn more about later in this chapter) for possible action. Otherwise, team members commonly use this view just to see how their assignments fall in the calendar.

Visual Clues in the Task Page		
Indicator Icon	**Meaning**	**Action**
	This green icon means that the task was added since the last time that the user viewed it.	
	The submitted task data were rejected by the project manager.	Seek input from the project manager, resolve, and resubmit.
	The assignment was changed since the user last saved its status. Any changes made by the user were overwritten with those made by the project manager.	Examine what has changed and take action with the project manager if required.
	This amber-colored exclamation means that the user has made task changes, but has not submitted them.	Submit the changes when appropriate based on process and policy of organization.
	There is a note on the task	View the note by clicking on the icon.
	The task has an associated document or documents.	Select the task, then select the document(s).
	The task has an associated risk or risks.	Select the task, then select the risk(s).
	The task has an associated issue or issues	Select the task, then select the issue(s).

Table 22-1 Visual Clues in the Task Page

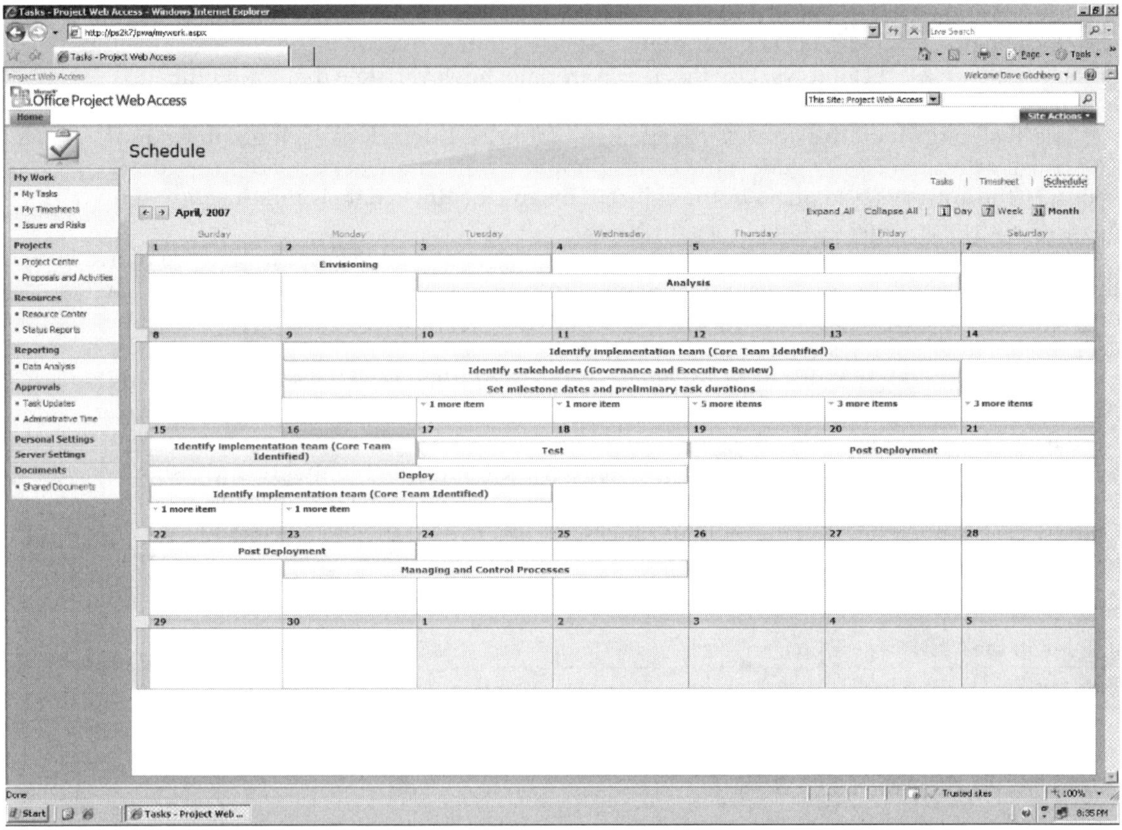

Figure 22-12 Schedule View from the My Work page

Additional PWA Updating Features

There are a few additional updating features worth a look, even though they are not used in the basic updating process:

- **Plan Administrative Time** This button, which appears on the My Timesheets page (the place where timesheets are created), displays the Administrative Time dialog shown in Figure 22-13. This dialog enables the team member to schedule future administrative time such as vacations without requiring the creation of timesheets. After saving these data, the team member creates a *calendar exception*, thereby blocking the time from the availability perspective.
- **Surrogate Timesheet** Depending on the user's permissions, he or she may be able to create and complete a timesheet for another resource. In most cases, Team Members don't have this permission, but we have seen exceptions. This option may be useful for several reasons:

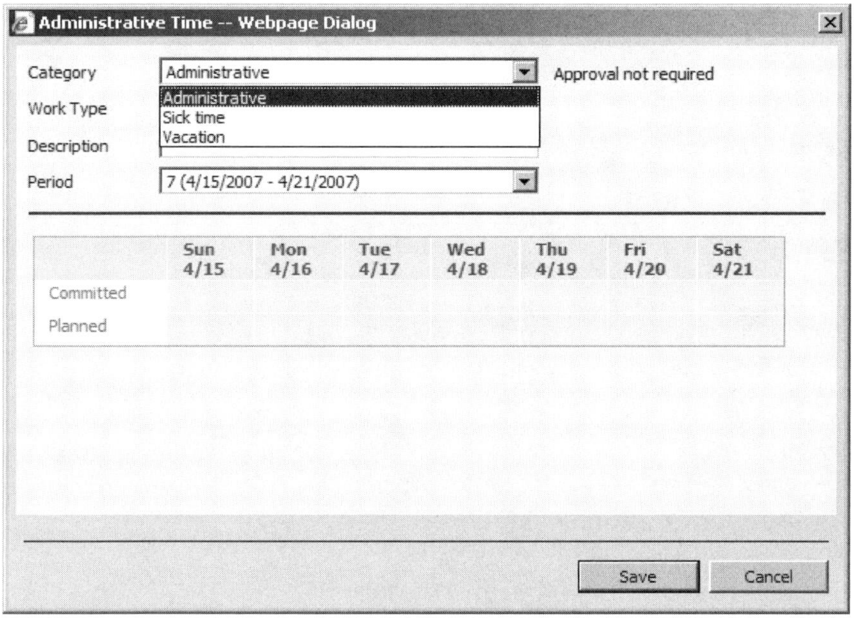

FIGURE 22-13 Administrative Time dialog

- To add time for a nonemployee or an employee who does not have access to the system
- To enable an administrative assistant to complete a timesheet for a manager
- To complete a timesheet for a resource who forgot to do so before taking off for vacation or for an employee who has left the company

To create a surrogate timesheet, select the Surrogate Timesheet button from the My Timesheets page to display the Surrogate Timesheet dialog shown in Figure 22-14. Select the resource from the browse button, select the timesheet type (Create with Default Setting, Create with Tasks, Create with Projects, or Do Not Autopopulate). Then select the time period and finally select Create Timesheet.

Self-Assignment to Team Tasks Team members may be part of an assignment team that has been assigned to a task. This new Project Server 2007 feature is most commonly used for maintenance and support activities. For example, suppose that Company X has built a project plan that will be used to hold support items such as help desk requests. Instead of adding the new request as a task with a particular resource assigned, the owner of the support plan may assign a team of people to the task instead.

A team task requires each user to navigate to the Self-Assign Team Tasks page from his or her own Tasks page in PWA. From there, a list of available team tasks appears. After the team member selects an item and then clicks the Assign Task to Me button, the task appears

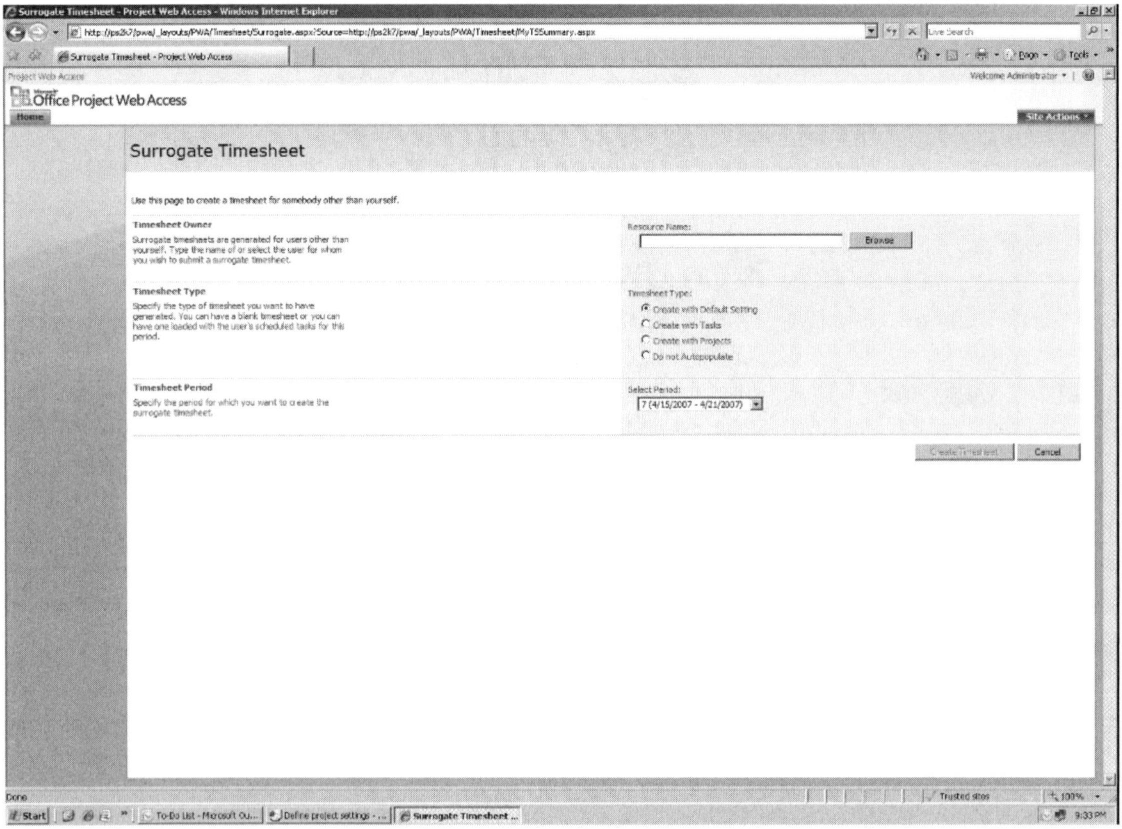

FIGURE 22-14 Surrogate Timesheet dialog

in the team member's Task page to report progress. This final assignment does not occur until after the project manager approves the assignment. After a resource self-assigns a team task on a project, Project Server removes the possibility of others self-assigning to the same team task.

Activity Plans It is also possible for a team member to self-assign a team task on an activity plan following the same process. Others can also assign themselves to the same activity plan. Note that under an activity plan, after any progress is reported on the team task, no one who has not already self-assigned the team task can record against it.

Updating Tasks from Outlook 2007

Team members using Outlook 2007 can use the Outlook client to update their Project Server tasks. To download the Outlook add-in, team members can navigate to Personal settings from the Quick Launch Bar. The next step is to select Setup Outlook Sync. From the Synchronize Your Task with Outlook page, shown in Figure 22-15, click the Download Now button.

Clicking the Download Now button displays the File Download dialog shown in Figure 22-16. Make sure that Outlook is closed. From the dialog, click either Save and then Run or just Run.

Once the download is installed, a help window will display the next time that Outlook is launched. Read it or read what is needed later, then close the help window. You will notice that there is now a new toolbar in Outlook, as shown in Figure 22-17.

Select the Import New Assignments option and they will import. A screen showing the progress of the action appears (see Figure 22-18).

A confirmation window appears. From there, go ahead and import. The Outlook Tasks page now displays the Project Server tasks. After you select a task, a rich, full-featured Task Update page is displayed as shown in Figure 22-19.

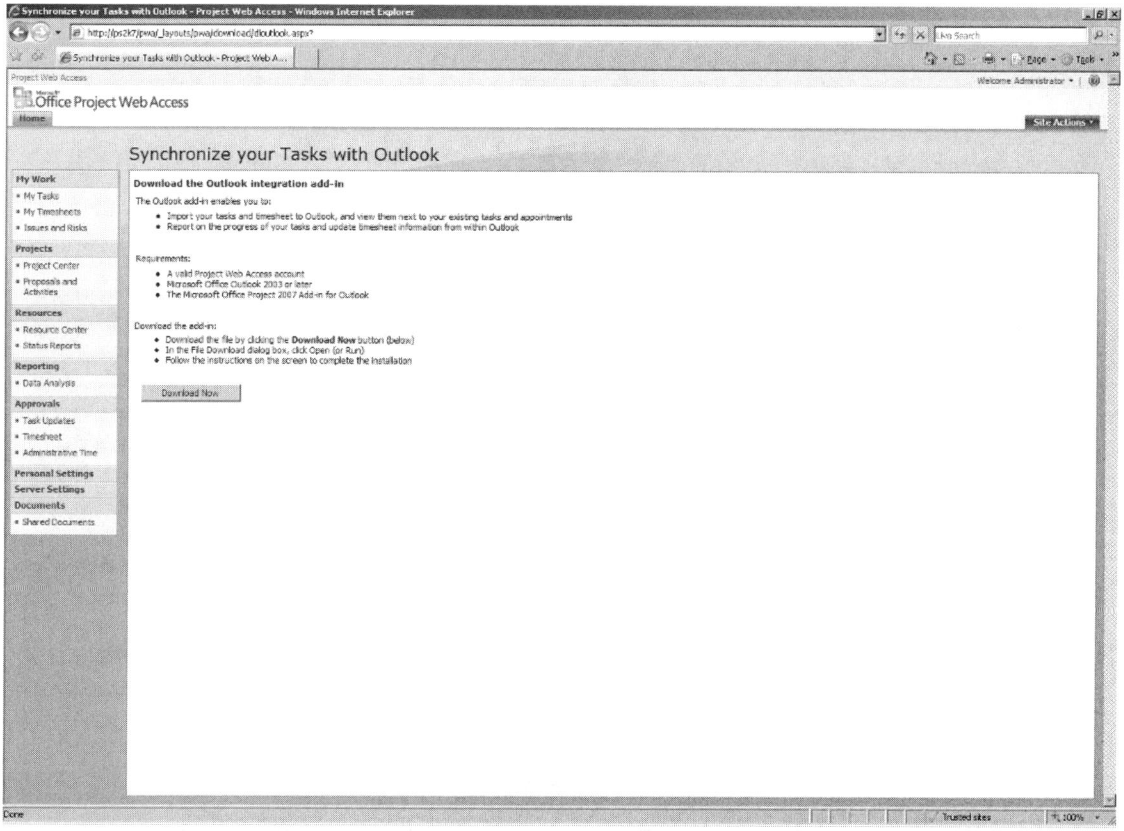

FIGURE 22-15 Synchronize Your Tasks with Outlook page.

PART V

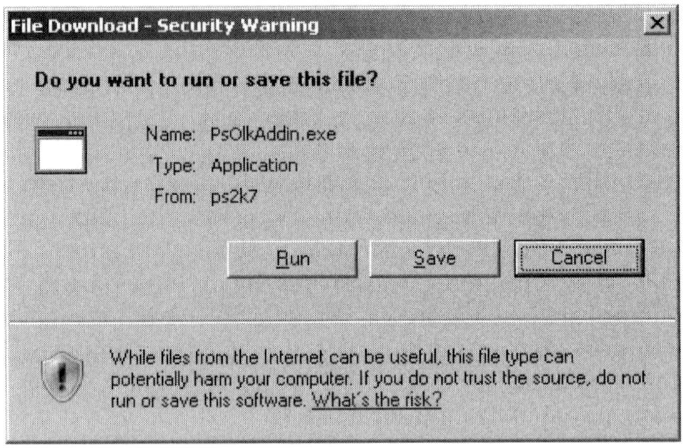

FIGURE 22-16 File Download dialog

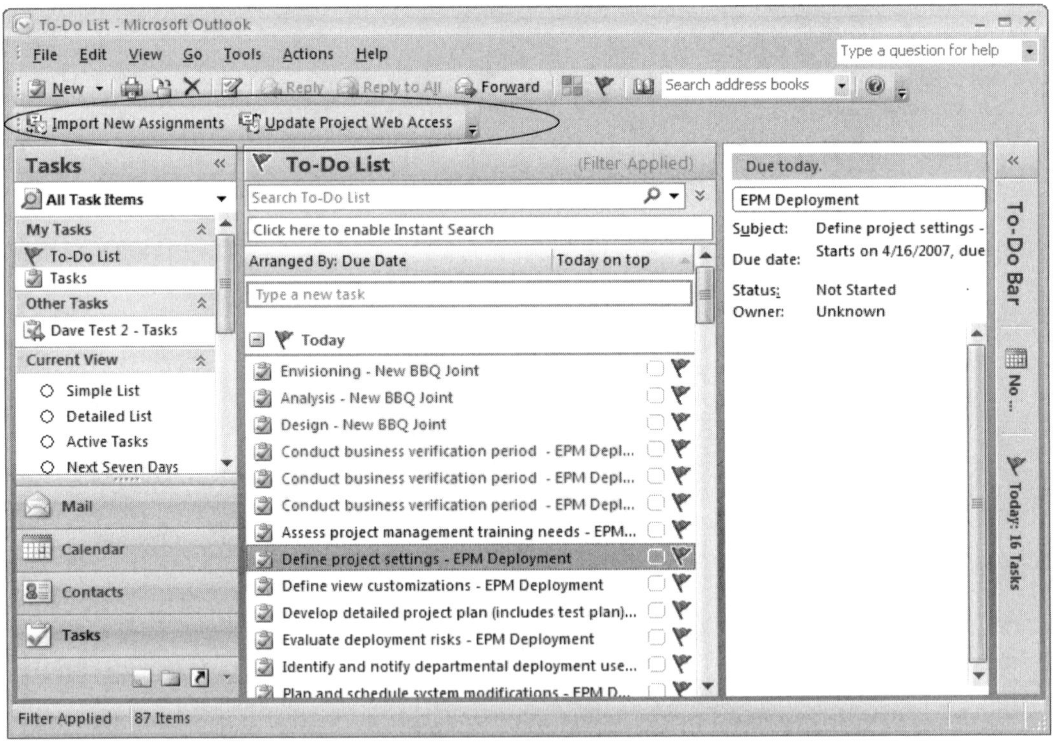

FIGURE 22-17 New Outlook toolbar

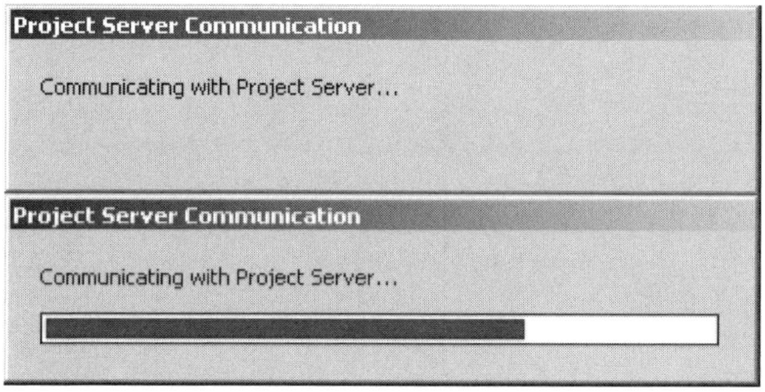

FIGURE 22-18 Importing information progress

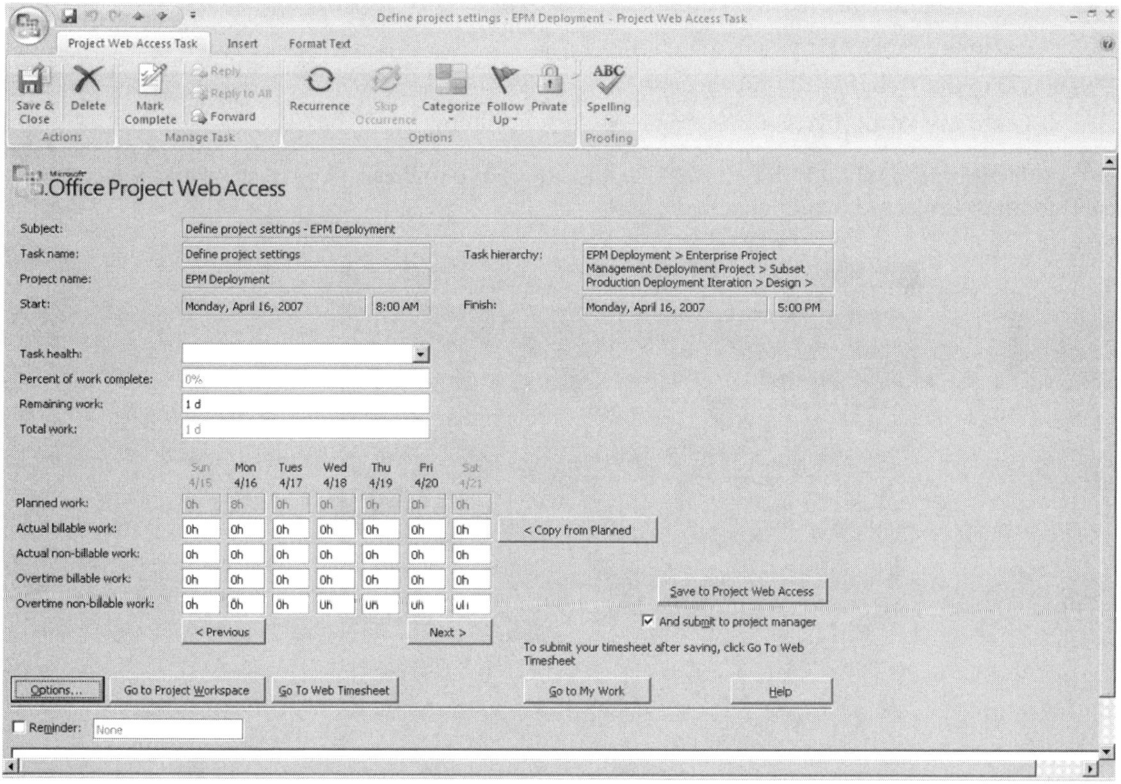

FIGURE 22-19 Outlook task details

From there the user can work on many items:

- Set the task health:
  - Not specified
  - On schedule
  - Late
  - Early
  - Blocked
  - Completed
- Apply actual work:
  - Enter on days in current week
  - Go to past or next week
- Copy from the planned work to actual (for project management reasons, this option is not recommended)
- Go to the Project Workspace
- Go to the Web (PWA) timesheet
- Go to My Work (PWA) for more global task updating

Set the options as shown in Figure 22-20 and click Save to Project Web Access and select the Submit to Project Manager checkbox.

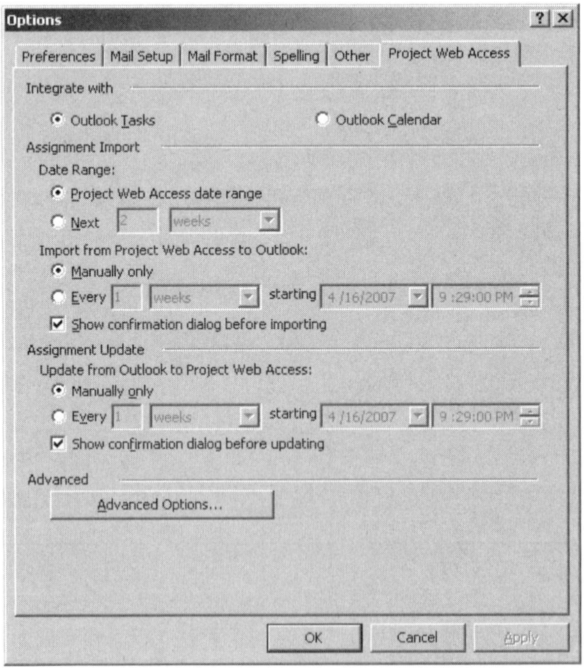

FIGURE 22-20 Options for syncing with Outlook

PWA Views

Project managers have the Project Professional desktop client, but team members do everything from PWA. Therefore, it is important for team members to understand that PWA offers views that enable them to see the context of the tasks to which they have been assigned.

Project Center Views

Typically Project Center views enable the team member to see into the combined set of organizational projects or, in larger organizations, to view projects by department. These views usually include summary project information rather than a lot of detailed progress tracking data. Other PWA views may include tracking detail to provide additional context, but only for the projects to which the specific team member is assigned. Some organizations that have a more open philosophy may decide to display more information. That is usually OK until the sheer size gets unwieldy (think 2,000 rows, one per project).

Project Views

Detailed project views are often displayed to team members but only for the projects for which they hold assignments. These views are very important to allow the team member to see the context of his or her specific tasks, so in almost every organization the views should be made available. In addition to weekly project status meetings and reports, the team member can use these views to see how others affect his or her assignments, and how what they are working on will shape other work.

Issues and Risks

In addition to viewing the Reminders Web Part on the PWA Home Page discussed earlier, team members can quickly see the total picture of their issues and risks by selecting Issues and Risks from the Quick Launch Bar. From that link, a page displays that shows all issues and all risks by project and the respective status of those items. By selecting the project name from this page, the user is directed to the appropriate risk or issue list hosted in the Project Workspaces (discussed later in this chapter).

Resource Center Views

Many organizations choose not to provide any access to Resource Center for team members. A strong alternative is to provide team members with access to view only their own information. If that latter approach is used, individual team members can see items such as their future assignments and availability.

In smaller or more open environments, team members can use these views to see other resources' information. An example would include allowing access for peers. This should never be allowed if cost information is included in the Resource Center unless "blended" costs are used.

Status Reports

The project manager or resource manager (or both) may ask team members to provide status information. If a team member has been added to a status report request, he or she will receive an e-mail notification. In addition, overdue status reports appear in the Reminders Web Part.

It is possible for team members to submit an unrequested status report. This option is rarely used, but it is available. See Chapter 21 for more on Status Reports.

Collaborating with the Project Team (Project Workspace)

As discussed previously, the Project Workspaces provide a strong platform to support project team communication around project documents, issues, risks and deliverables. Chapter 25 focuses on that topic. Team members should be active in Project Workspace use, as their understanding of the project's big picture is valuable in the effort to achieve successful results. In addition, no one wants to work in the dark. As we have done in earlier parts of the book, the most useful features for Team Members are highlighted with asterisks. Some other rarely used features are omitted.

- **Issues*** As discussed in Chapter 21, the project team can place issues on the Project Workspace. Team members can assign issues, categorize them (including status), prioritize them, and more. Issues can be linked to specific tasks, specific risks, documents, and other issues which then display as icons in the project view with the tool tip such as "There are issues associated with this task." Team members should be instructed in the use of issue features.
- **Risks** Team members may have assigned risks and may be part of the team that identifies project risk. In such instances, team members should use the Risks area, especially if they are charged with specific risk avoidance, which is a type of risk management technique.
- **Documents*** Team members can use the strong document features in the Project Workspaces to post, edit, and especially review project documentation. For example, a construction site foreman can review specifications that are shared from a Project Workspace. We have seen an internal project team sharing new product workflow diagrams, technical specifications and requirements, documented regulatory material, completed project methodology documents, parts lists, and much more.
- **Discussion** The team can use these threaded discussions to communicate when there is no urgency.
- **Announcements*** Team members can check announcements, depending on how the project manager has decided to use the feature.
- **Recycle Bin*** If team members have the Delete permission, they will see a Recycle Bin in the Project Workspace allowing them to "undelete" an item.
- **Links*** The Links Web Part is located on the right side of the Project Workspace and can be populated with links that are important to the project.
- **Deliverables*** This is a new concept in Project Server 2007 which facilitates loosely-coupled interproject dependencies.

This chapter has focused on the Team Member role. While the Team Member is the one that spends the least amount of time using Project Web Access in many cases (other times it is the Executive), they are a lynchpin to project success. If the data is entered incorrectly you'll end up with fancy reports and views with incorrect data. Focus your efforts on making the Team Member role as easy as possible. In an ideal Project Server environment, the Time and Task process should average only about five to ten minutes a day after a period of adjustment. The time and task process is also one of the major potential stumbling blocks in the project because timely entry is very important and time entry is no one's favorite activity. Gain Team Member buy-in by showing them the value to the organization. Reward people for time entry compliance if possible (happy hour for whichever department has the highest compliance percentage perhaps). In some organizations, executive mandates are required to force compliance. Each organization will know the best way to make compliance happen based on culture. Remember that communication failures are a leading cause of project failures. The next chapter focuses on the role of the Resource Manager in Project Server 2007.

23

CHAPTER

How the Resource Manager Interacts with Project Server

Microsoft Office Project Server 2007 considers the resource manager (RM) the person who manages the resources within his or her purview, whether those resources are people, material resources, or, in some cases, cost resources (see Chapter 20). The role of the resource manager in Project Server 2007 depends greatly on the way that the system is configured. In some cases, the resource manager is reduced almost to the role of interested spectator. On the other end of the spectrum, configuration can result in the resource manager having a relatively active role in the system. Note that some of the content in this chapter has already been covered elsewhere in the book, but in a different context.

As was done in the chapters for project managers and team members, the chapter makes assumptions on how this role is likely to be configured based on the authors' experiences. The first major consideration in configuration is whether to use timesheets in Project Server at all. Timesheets make sense for an organization when it needs a way to keep track of all hours (40 hours/week, for example) including project hours worked, vacations, sick time, nonproject work, and so on. They are also valuable when using hours tracked in Project Server to send data to an outside system, such as payroll and/or invoicing. For the sake of this discussion, the assumption is that timesheets are being used. Note that in a situation where timesheets are not used, resource managers have *no* part in the approval of work unless they are also acting in the role of project manager.

As mentioned earlier in the book, for resource managers to have accurate information about their resources' work and availability, the project managers first must build good project plans. All assignments must be timephased and the units (the percentage of the resource's time) must be set appropriately. The project managers must understand the meaning of fixed units, fixed work, and fixed duration and must understand the effects of these settings. These things may sound simple, but often getting this level of skill in line for project managers is a critical obstacle to success.

Building Project Teams

Depending on the organization, resource managers may be given access to Build Team on Project and/or View Team Builder. This access might be restricted to just team building for their direct reports or might be more global. In some cases, the task of assigning resources to project teams is performed only by project managers. Other times, the Build Team function is assigned only to the program management office (PMO) staff. In a situation that we have encountered multiple times, the resource manager could assign people as long as those resources were their direct reports. If they were not their own staff, the PMO took charge of all other resource team building. From a process perspective, no matter how the system is configured, the decision making about appropriate resource assignments is almost always a discussion/negotiation between the resource manager and the project manager. Note that no system in the world can fully automate such decision making. Tools can't do everything.

Resource managers use the Team Builder tool in Project Web Access (PWA) for this job. All of the discussion herein also applies to resource plans, proposals, activities, and projects (details of all aforementioned planning tools are covered in Chapter 20). To build a project team from PWA, find way to the Project Center, select the row in which the project name appears, and then click on the Build Team button. The Build Team screen appears in PWA.

From this page, the following options are available:

- Resource managers can select resources from the left table by filling the checkboxes for the appropriate resources and then selecting Add. They can also remove the resources from the team by using the Remove button. Notice that on the bottom of the page, displayed in Figure 23-1, is a project details–level view of the project that is currently being populated with resources.
- If the system is using role- or skills-based custom fields (described in Chapter 20), the resource manager can use the Match feature. Remember that matching on fields displays only *exact* matches.
- They can also use the Replace feature to replace a resource on every task in a project plan. Generally, this feature is best left to project managers unless the project is just getting off the ground. There are times when it makes sense for the resource manager to replace a resource mid-project. It is often used for replacing placeholder generic resources in Enterprise Project templates.

From this page, some other features are available. The dropdown menu in the top-right corner offers several views that include filters that are useful to the resource manager. The default view is All Resources; other views include the following:

- **Cost Resources** Cost resources are expenses such as mileage, hotels, meals, and one-time fees. You can associate these expenses with a project to capture the project's cost.
- **Material Resources** Material resources are set up for use when materials such as computer hardware (desktop is one cost, small server another), raw materials (steel, concrete), manufactured material (widgets), or even special facilities (such as a room with special robotics that has a cost and is used multiple times) need to be tracked on projects. The Material Resources View displays only these material resources.

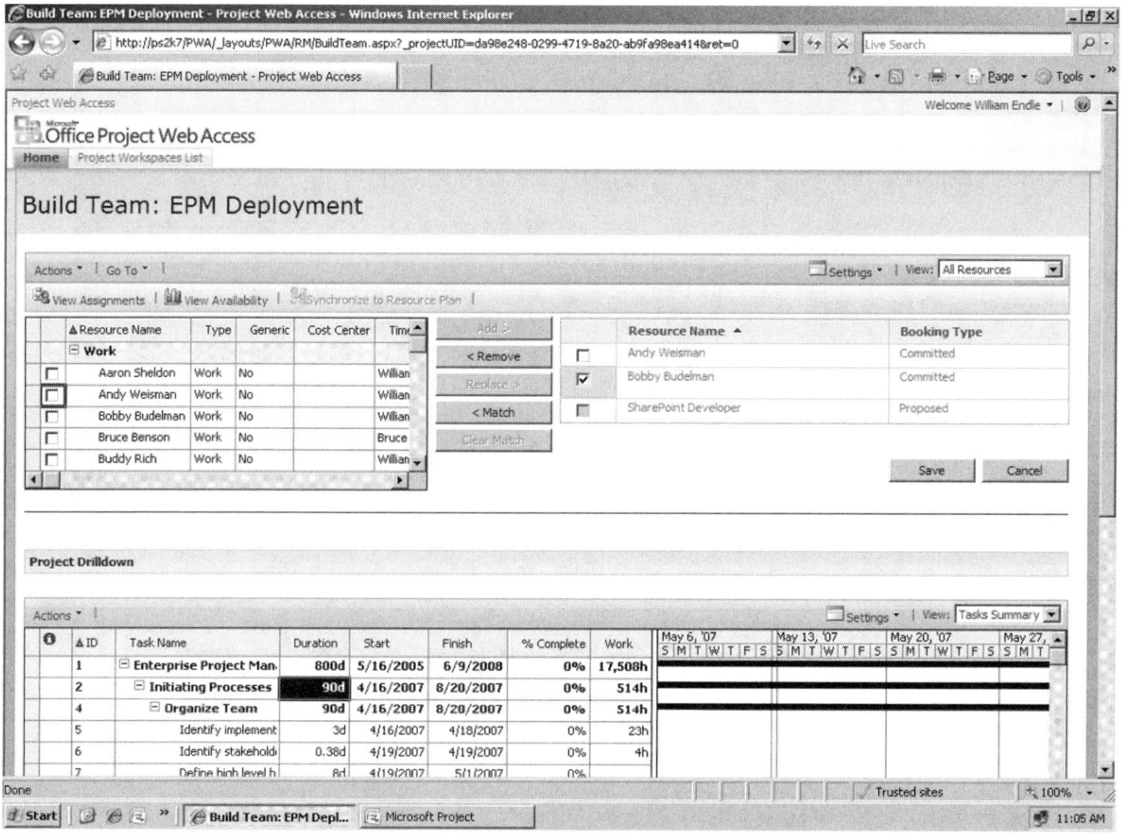

FIGURE 23-1 Build Team page includes buttons for adding and removing resources.

- **Work Resources** Work resources are usually people. This view can also be used for objects or spaces that have a cost and also require the use of resource-level calendars. An example would be the robotics room described for the Material Resources View that required scheduling of use as well as scheduled downtime, perhaps for maintenance.

A Settings button on the top-right corner allows other configuration of the views on the page. These options allow for sorting and locating specific resources or information about them:

- **View Options** These options allow for changing outline levels. If the view is set to Outline Level 0 (zero), then material, cost, and work resources would roll up, as shown in Figure 23-2. Other outline levels show the same list of all resources unless additional hierarchical work has been done for resources (which is not likely to come up).

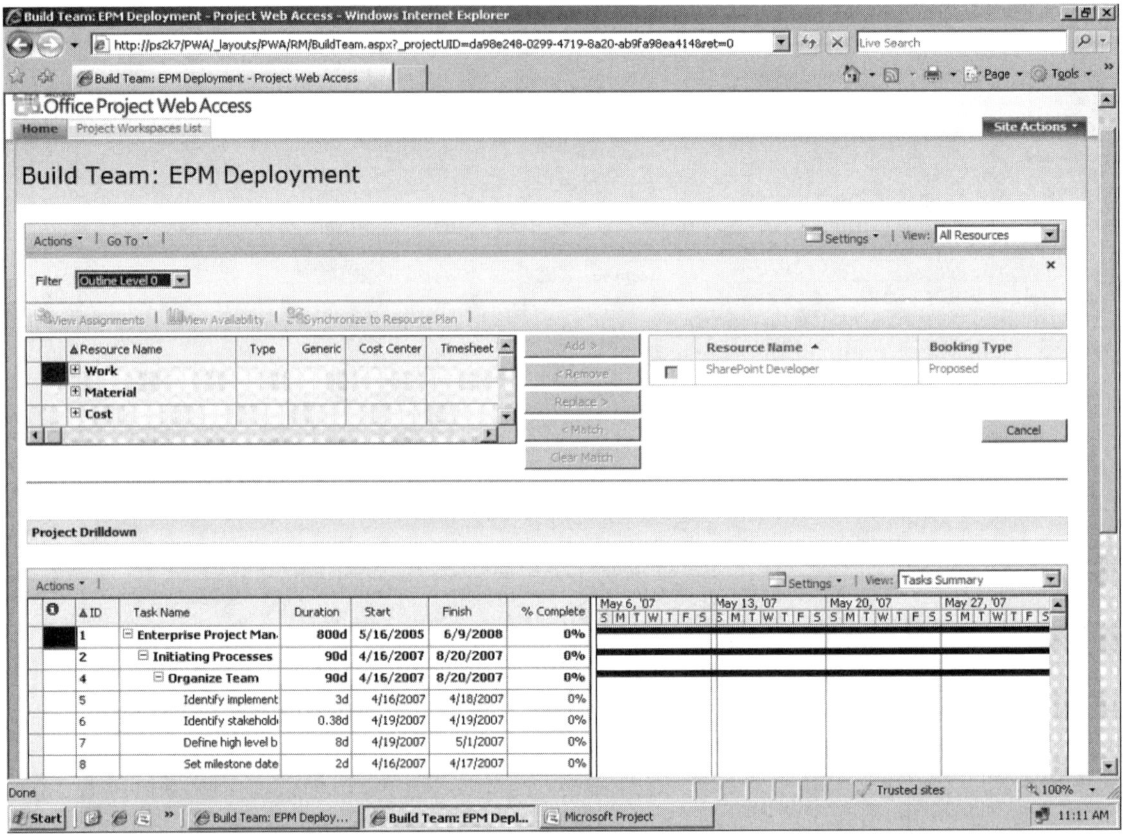

FIGURE 23-2 Rolled-up build team in All Resources View

- **Filter** The prebuilt filters can be very useful. They include the following:
  - All Resources (the default)
  - Generic Resources
  - Budget Resources
  - Non-Budget Resources
  - Resources with In-Progress Assignments
  - Overallocated Resources

  Custom filters are also supported

- **Search** Simple search of this page only
- **Grouping** This filter can be used to group by field and can support up to a three-level grouping, as shown in Figure 23-3.

The resource manager can also navigate to view assignments or availability of the selected resources or synchronize to a resource plan.

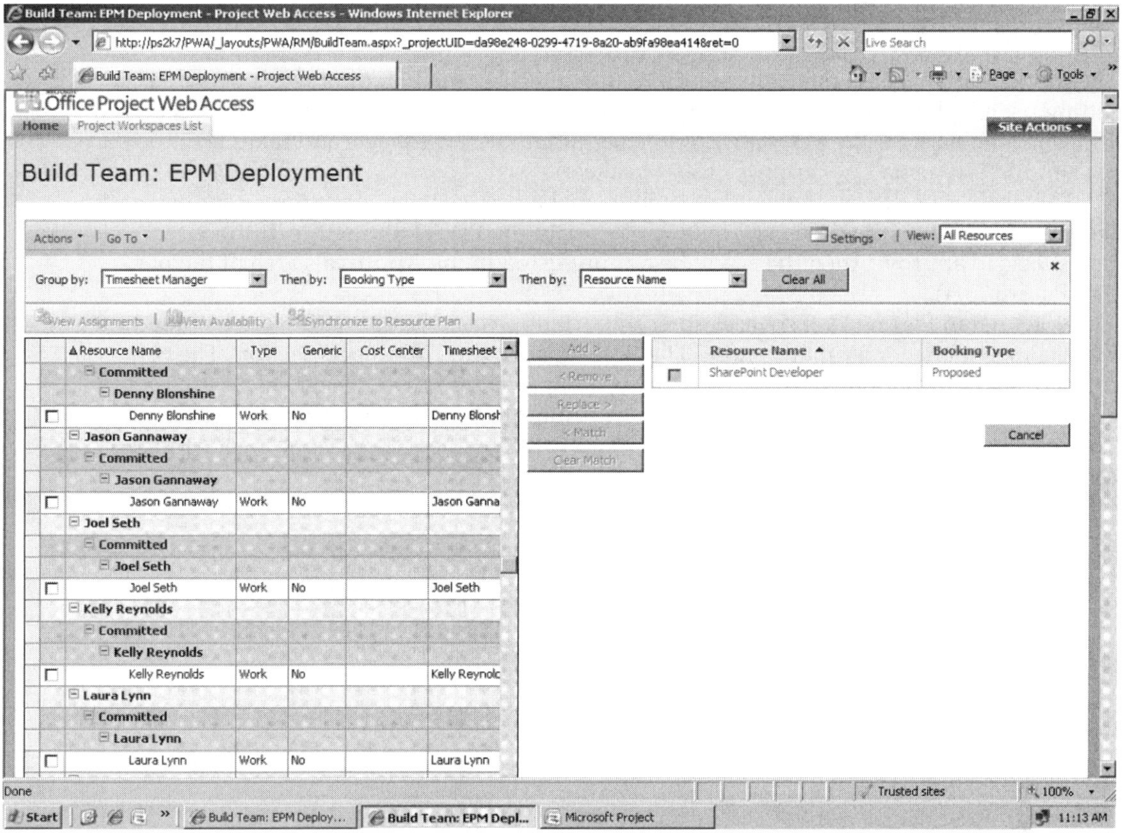

FIGURE 23-3 Setting a three-level grouping

Surrogate Timesheets

The resource manager is normally set up as the timesheet manager for the people they supervise. Sometimes the resource cannot complete a timesheet and the timesheet manager must do it instead. The timesheet manager, under a typical configuration, can complete a surrogate timesheet only for their own resources. To do this, click on the My Timesheets link from the Quick Launch Bar and left-click the Surrogate Timesheet button.

In the next page, first browse to the name of the resource. Next select one of the following settings:

- **Create with Default Setting** The default setting is usually Current Tasks, which makes the most sense in most cases.
- **Create with Projects**
- **Do Not Autopopulate**

Next, select the timesheet period and then click Create Timesheet. You can then complete and submit the timesheet.

Timesheet Management

The resource manager is normally set up as the timesheet manager in Project Server. The setting itself is done through the Enterprise Resource Pool or User Settings (Security). The Timesheet manager is the person who reviews submitted timesheets and takes action on the submission (usually to approve the timesheet).

The process itself starts when the resource manager (for this discussion, assume that the resource manager is the timesheet manager) goes to the PWA Home Page. If there are timesheets to approve, then there will be a count listed in the Approvals area of the page (see Figure 23-4).

Note that in Figure 23-4, several other important pieces of information are included for the resource manager, William Endle. The first is under the Timesheets section. The count of unsubmitted timesheets is displayed. During what is commonly a weekly cycle, this count can be used to track whether all time has been submitted. To get to more detail, select the You Have *x* Unsubmitted Timesheets link. From there, the next page, Timesheet Approvals, displays the details (see Figure 23-5).

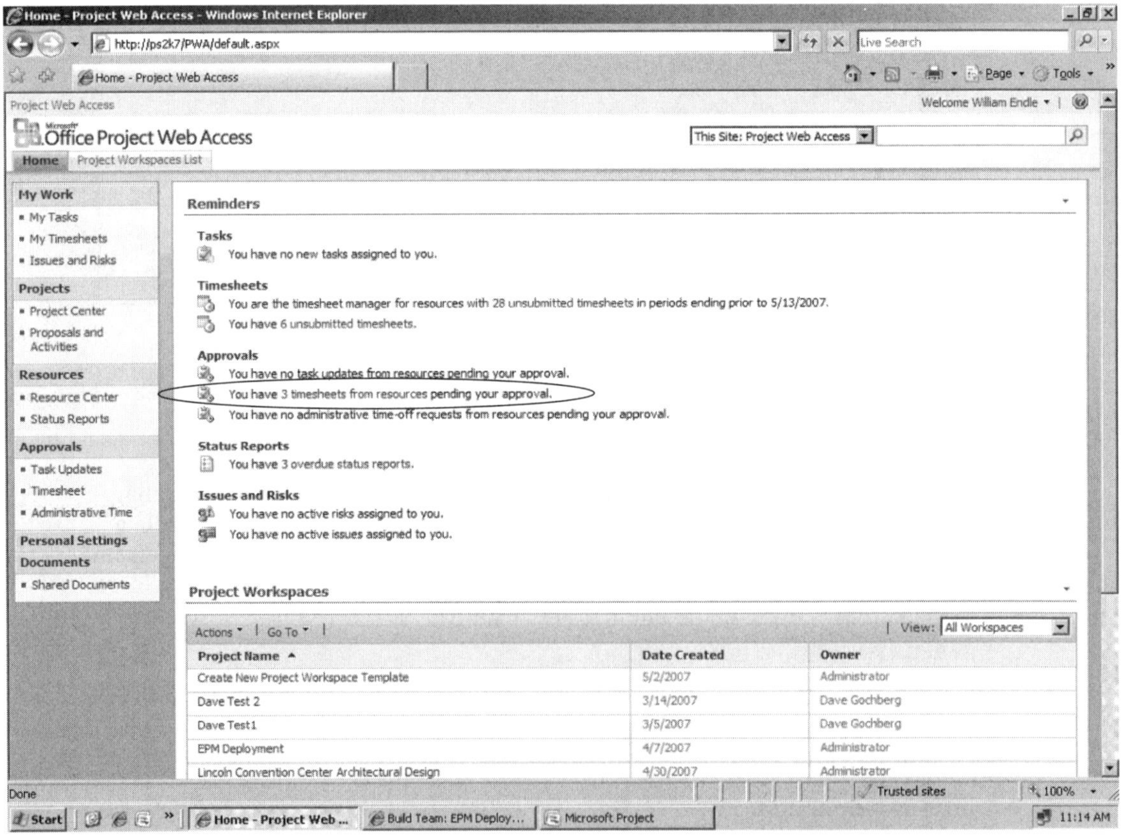

FIGURE 23-4 PWA Home Page with timesheet counts

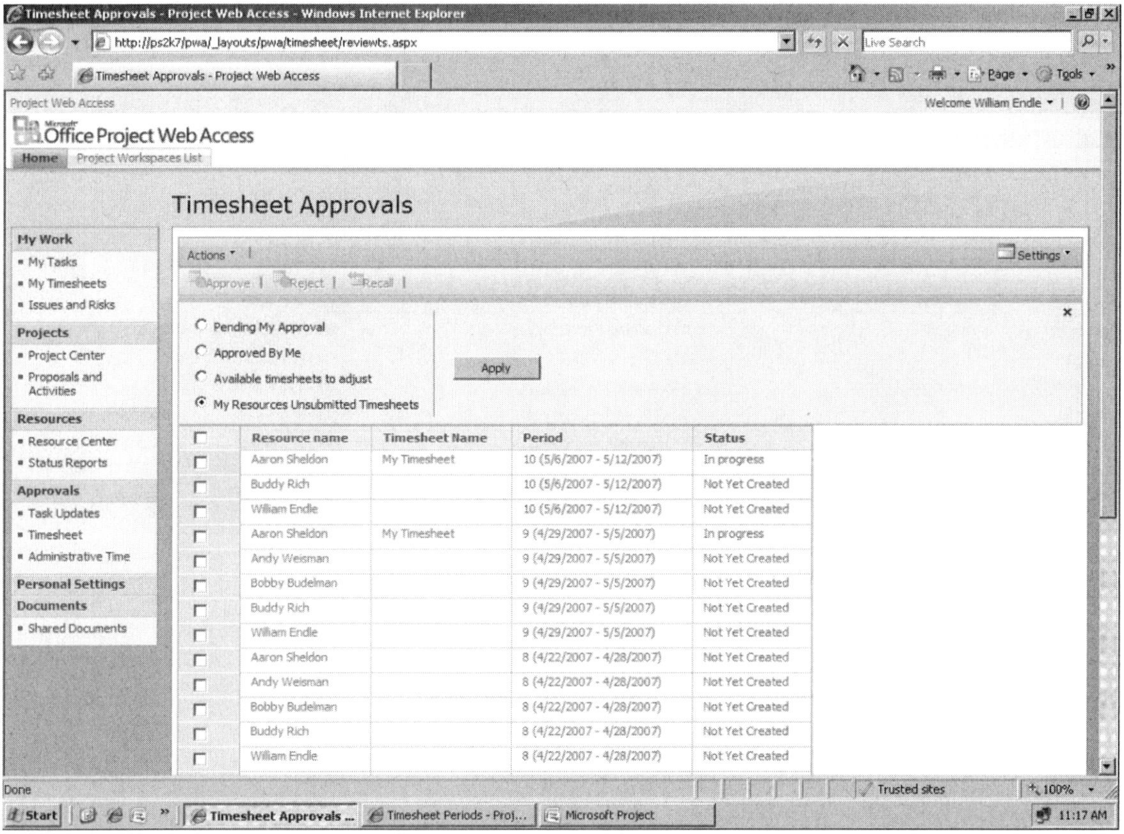

FIGURE 23-5 Unsubmitted timesheets

Notice that this view displays the timesheets that are both in-progress and those that have not yet been created. Also note that this view allows navigation to view timesheets in other states:

- Pending My Approval
- Approved by Me
- Available Timesheets to Adjust (you will learn more about this option shortly)

You can export this page to Excel or send it to a printable grid by clicking the Actions button. The resource manager can use this printable grid as a check list of sorts while he or she checks the timesheet completion status (see Figure 23-6).

Approval of Administrative Time Requests

The other pieces of information on the PWA Home Page that are important from the resource manager perspective can be found under the Approvals section in the middle of the Reminders Web Part (the top section). If the Administrative Time Approvals

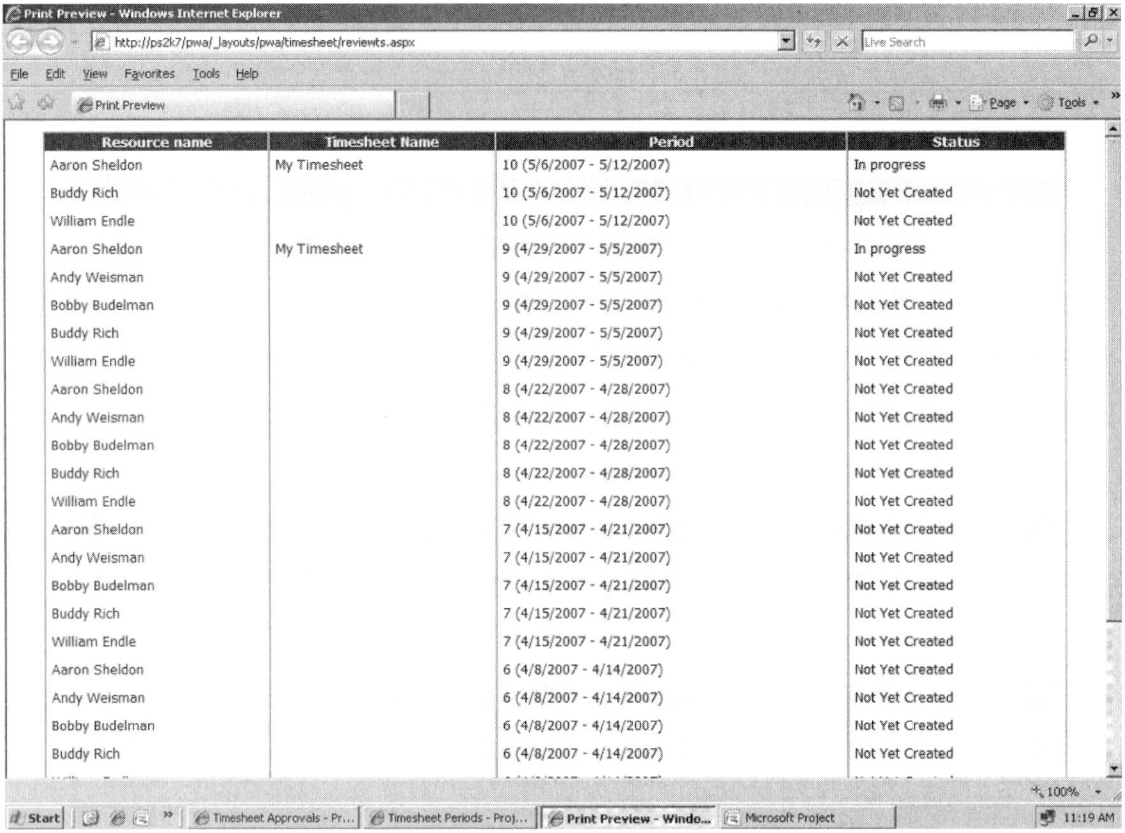

Resource name	Timesheet Name	Period	Status
Aaron Sheldon	My Timesheet	10 (5/6/2007 - 5/12/2007)	In progress
Buddy Rich		10 (5/6/2007 - 5/12/2007)	Not Yet Created
William Endle		10 (5/6/2007 - 5/12/2007)	Not Yet Created
Aaron Sheldon	My Timesheet	9 (4/29/2007 - 5/5/2007)	In progress
Andy Weisman		9 (4/29/2007 - 5/5/2007)	Not Yet Created
Bobby Budelman		9 (4/29/2007 - 5/5/2007)	Not Yet Created
Buddy Rich		9 (4/29/2007 - 5/5/2007)	Not Yet Created
William Endle		9 (4/29/2007 - 5/5/2007)	Not Yet Created
Aaron Sheldon		8 (4/22/2007 - 4/28/2007)	Not Yet Created
Andy Weisman		8 (4/22/2007 - 4/28/2007)	Not Yet Created
Bobby Budelman		8 (4/22/2007 - 4/28/2007)	Not Yet Created
Buddy Rich		8 (4/22/2007 - 4/28/2007)	Not Yet Created
William Endle		8 (4/22/2007 - 4/28/2007)	Not Yet Created
Aaron Sheldon		7 (4/15/2007 - 4/21/2007)	Not Yet Created
Andy Weisman		7 (4/15/2007 - 4/21/2007)	Not Yet Created
Bobby Budelman		7 (4/15/2007 - 4/21/2007)	Not Yet Created
Buddy Rich		7 (4/15/2007 - 4/21/2007)	Not Yet Created
William Endle		7 (4/15/2007 - 4/21/2007)	Not Yet Created
Aaron Sheldon		6 (4/8/2007 - 4/14/2007)	Not Yet Created
Andy Weisman		6 (4/8/2007 - 4/14/2007)	Not Yet Created
Bobby Budelman		6 (4/8/2007 - 4/14/2007)	Not Yet Created
Buddy Rich		6 (4/8/2007 - 4/14/2007)	Not Yet Created

FIGURE 23-6 Printable grid of unsubmitted timesheets

setting is enabled and time requiring such preapproval has been submitted, that link will include a count of all the requests that require preapproval. It is important to remember that a timesheet with this type of administrative time included cannot be submitted at all without action being taken by the resource manager on the items requiring approval.

To make decisions on these requests, navigate to the Administrative Time page by selecting either the link You Have *x* Administrative Time-Off Requests from Resources Pending Your Approval, or by selecting the Administrative Time link from the Quick Launch Bar. Select the items for approval, then select the Accept button shown in Figure 23-7.

The other option is to reject the request. Note that it is not a recommended practice simply to press the Reject button. Instead, pick up the phone to speak to the resource to explain why there is a rejection (of that vacation for which the resource has been saving for years and already purchased his or her nonrefundable airfare). Seriously, it is better to communicate this type of news verbally. Next the discussion will be on approving and/or rejecting timesheets.

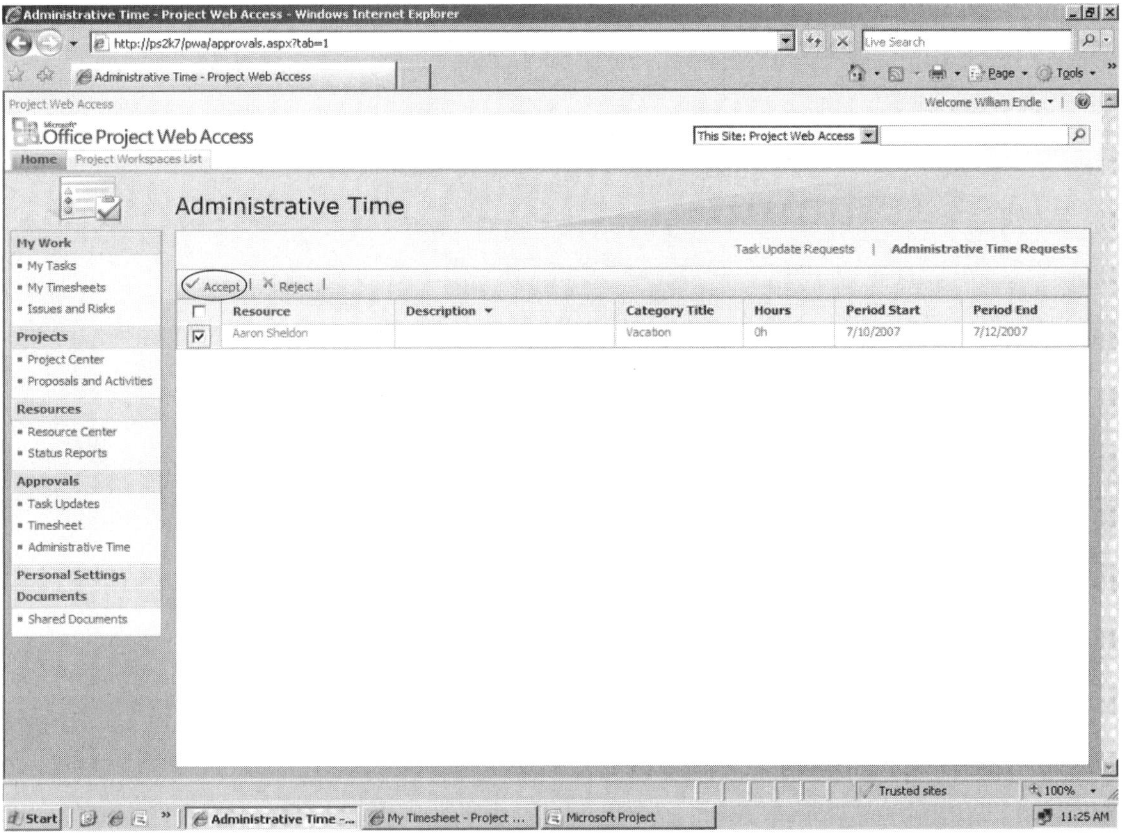

FIGURE 23-7 Accept button

Approval and Rejection of Timesheets

Now that the resource manager has approved the administrative requests, the resource can complete the submission of his or her timesheet(s). The resource manager can manage the submitted timesheets by navigating to the Timesheet Approval page from either the Timesheet option on the Quick Launch Bar (under Approvals) or from the You Have x Timesheets from Resources Pending Your Approval just above the Administrative Time option as described in the preceding section. See the Timesheet Approvals page in Figure 23-8.

In addition to the My Resources Unsubmitted Timesheets View, which was discussed earlier, there are three other views possible from this page. The one that is the most commonly used is the Pending My Approval View shown in Figure 23-8. From this page, the timesheet review and approval process begins. To see the details of an individual timesheet, select My Timesheet between the name and the date of the specific timesheet.

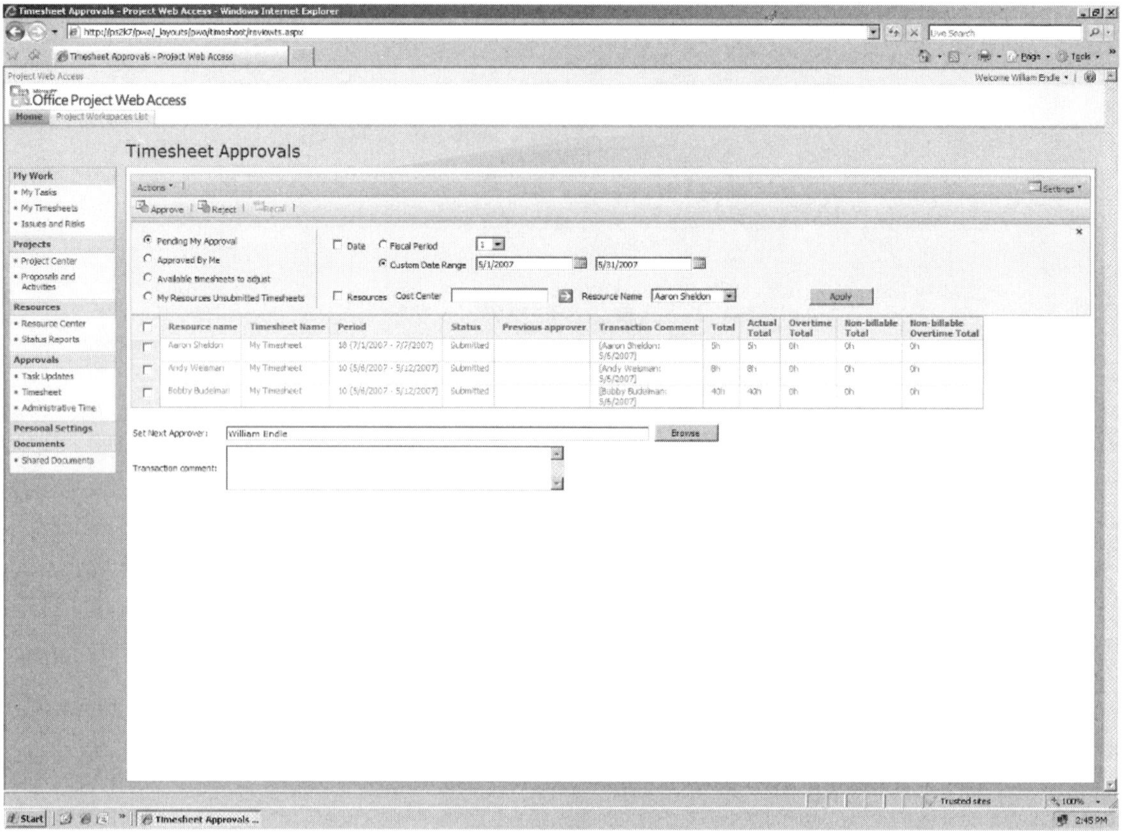

FIGURE 23-8 Timesheet Approvals page

The specific timesheet appears next for review. The timesheet may have included a comment from the individual resource, but no comment is required. Hours are displayed on the days (assuming that daily reporting is configured—the best practice) that they were entered by the resource, and administrative time always appears at the bottom as shown in Figure 23-9.

From this page, the resource manager can approve or reject entries by selecting the items and the appropriate button. At the time of the writing of this content, if detailed task information is sought, selecting the link that is the Task Name does not work in any of the environments tested. Note that the system allows the user to resubmit a rejected timesheet without changes. Consider contacting the resource some other way prior to rejecting his or her timesheet. To select all items, check the box next to Project Name at the top of the screen, as shown in Figure 23-10.

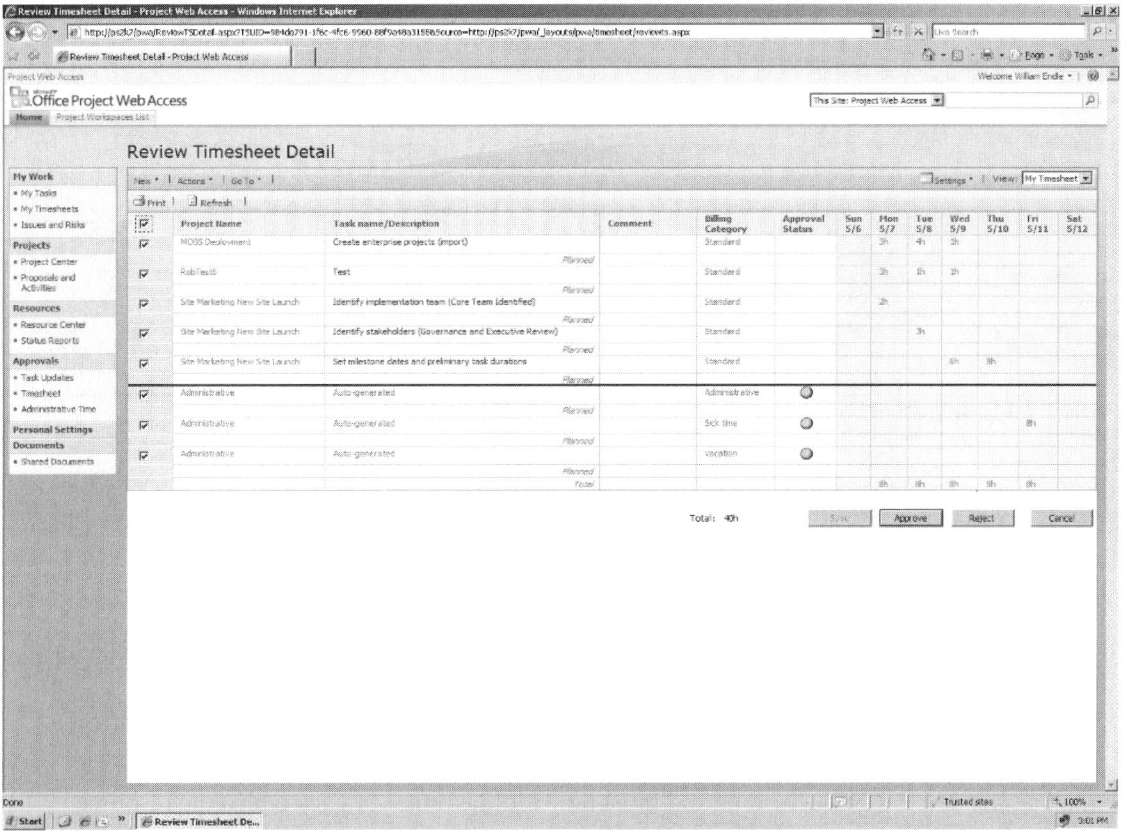

FIGURE 23-9 Individual timesheet pending approval

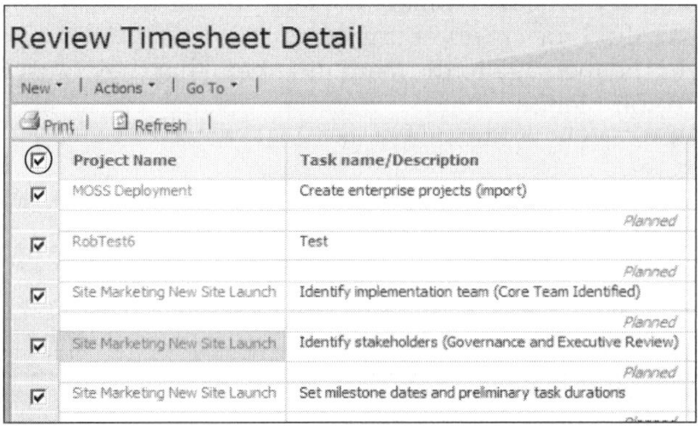

FIGURE 23-10 Select all items

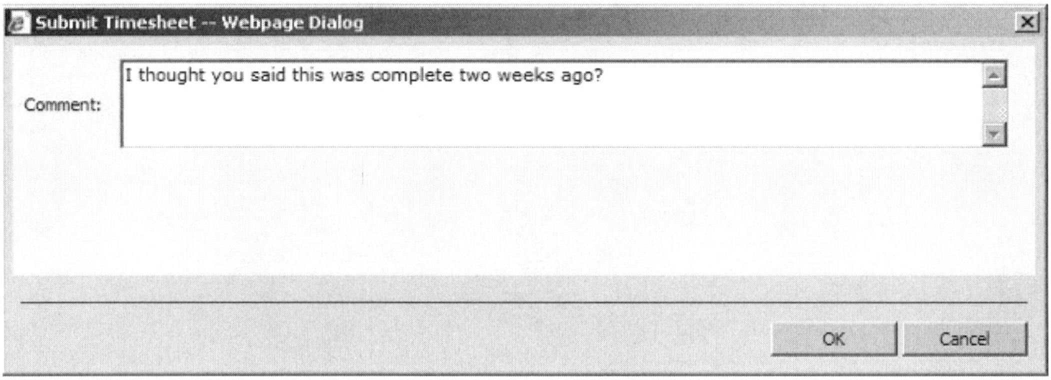

FIGURE 23-11 Comment box

After making the appropriate selections, take action by selecting the Approve button. For an approval, the dialog shown in Figure 23-11 allows a comment to be stored with the transaction.

A slightly different comment box appears when rejecting an entry (selecting the Reject button) that goes to the resource who made the submission. The resource will see this comment from his or her My Timesheets page (see Figure 23-12).

If the resource manager would like to review previously approved timesheets, all he or she needs to do is select Approved by Me from the Timesheet Approvals page and then select Apply. From there, the resource manager can review any timesheets from the past. Note that the date range or fiscal period must be set to the timeframe for which the resource manager is interested in examining timesheets.

Note that the Timesheet Approvals page also allows the resource manager to adjust timesheets for those resources to which the resource manager has permission. Although there are many possible reasons for making a timesheet adjustment, such adjustments should not be required often. Work with the team to get their timesheets right the first time. The adoption of the time entry process is one of the key process hurdles that must be overcome to have a successful Project Server implementation. It is very important that the resource manager deliver the message to the team members that they must complete the timesheet on time and to completion.

Timesheet Name	Period ▼	Total Hours	Status	Next Approver	Transaction Comment
My Timesheet	10 (5/6/2007 - 5/12/2007)	40h	Rejected		[William Endle: 5/6/2007] I thought you said this was complete two weeks ago?

FIGURE 23-12 My Timesheets comment to team member for rejected time

Status Reporting

As noted in Chapter 21, Project Server includes built-in support for status reports. Although to many this feature seems more valuable to project managers, it could be argued that given the wealth of specific project and task information available to the project manager, resource managers and their respective teams will find the status report feature even more useful. Details of how this functionality works are included in Chapter 21.

Views and Reports

In a typical environment, resources managers have access to Resource Center views at least to view the team members who are under their supervision. If the configuration includes use of the resource breakdown structure (RBS), the resource managers will have access to these views. Some of the views were covered in depth in Chapter 20, but this section will cover what is normally part of the resource manager's toolkit. In addition, there will be some discussion on use of Data Analysis views by resource managers. These views are not as common for use by resource managers, but can be valuable.

Resource Center Views

The resource manager has a useful filtered view of resources who are under the resource manager's supervision in the RBS. This dramatically simplifies the resource manager's job, as there is no need to identify the "right" resources. Five views are available at the root of the Resource Center. The one that is most useful for the resource manager is the Work Resources View. This view includes a set of fields that are useful, but also others that are unlikely to be that practical. The following are the out-of-the-box fields, left to right:

- **Resource Name**
- **ID** This is just a number that represents the order in which the resource was created.
- **Checked Out**
- **Email Address**
- **Generic**
- **Cost Center**
- **Timesheet Manager**
- **Earliest Available**
- **Latest Available**
- **Accrue At**
- **Booking Type**
- **Can Level**
- **Windows User Account**
- **Initials**
- **Group**
- **Code Phonetics**

- **Hyperlink**
- **Hyperlink Address**
- **Default Assignment Owner**
- **Unique ID**
- **Last Modified**

The value of these views and the specific fields is somewhat subjective, but the average resource manager is unlikely to find the Unique ID field (for which a typical output is something like 56dbb047-55c6-4423-a5ae-5ea284b11d67) or Phonetics (describing how to pronounce the name) useful on a day-to-day basis. Use imagination and determine what really matters for the resource manager's viewing. Ask the Project Server administrator to get the views that make the resource manager's job easiest. We offer the following alternative for consideration. Note that this alternative requires the creation of Enterprise Custom Resource Fields. Of course, these views would differ for each organization.

- **Resource Name**
- **Resource Location (custom)** This is the branch or city in which the resource works.
- **Standard Rate**
- **Overtime Rate**
- **Role (custom)** This field identifies the resource's primary role at the organization (developer, computer-aided design [CAD] designer, advertising specialist, and so on).
- **Primary Skill (custom)** Avoiding the complex possibilities of a field with many values, identify the resource's primary skill (for example, a developer might require proficiency in .NET, CICS, Java, and so on).
- **Max Units**
- **Billable (custom—Yes or No)** For service companies, this can be a valuable field.
- **Employee Type (custom)** This field might identify whether the resource is exempt or nonexempt, employee or consultant, and so on.

The views in Resource Center have some flexibility. Use the Settings button to change the view. Options include the following:

- **View Options** Usually these should just be left as is.
- **Outline Levels** This option is useful only if resources are hierarchical, which is rare.
- **Show Time with Date** This option is turned off by default.
- **Show/Hide Selected List** By default, this option shows the list.
- **Filter** This option enables the user to create *ad hoc* filters. More valuable, however, is a checkbox to enable autofiltering by column heading. Figure 23-13 shows how the autofiltering works.
- **Group** This feature allows up to three levels of grouping, such as by location, role, then primary skill or in any other combination of the displayed fields.

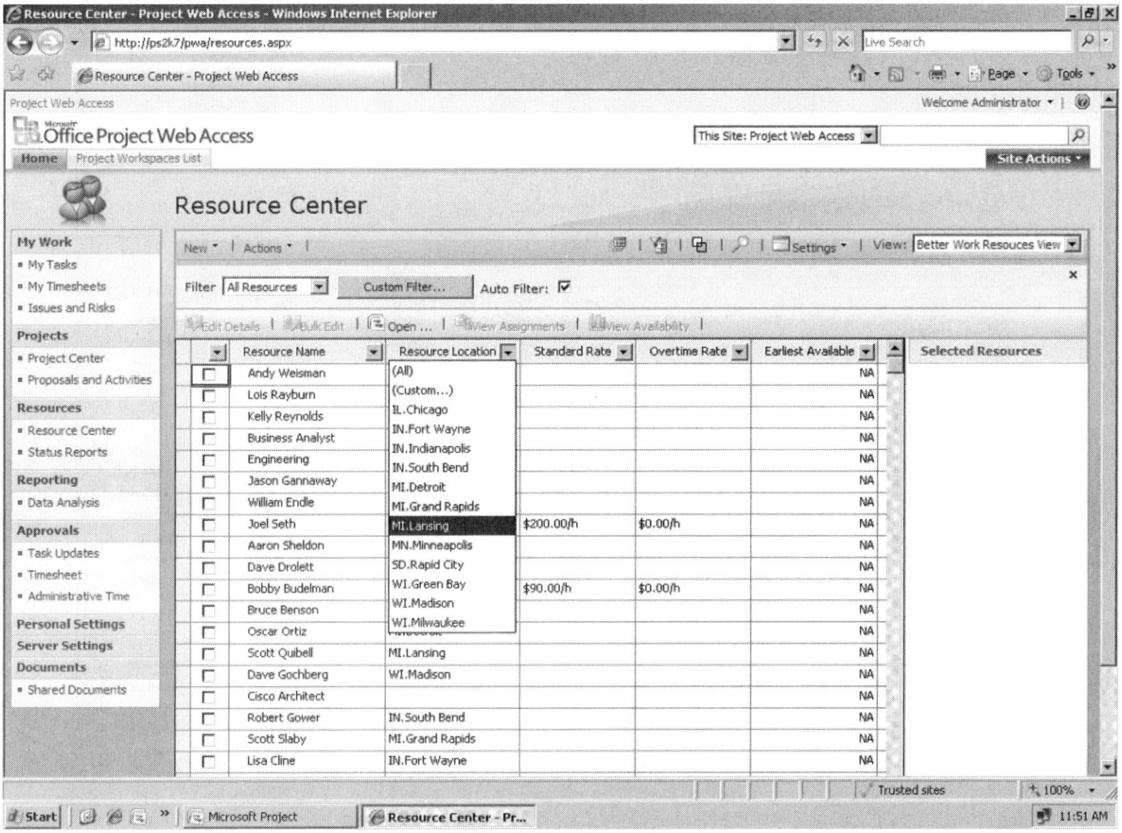

FIGURE 23-13 Autofilters turned on in Resource Center

- **Search** If you are looking for a detail among the list of resources, this feature is helpful.
- **Show on Menu** This option displays buttons for View Options, Filter, Group, and Search on the horizontal bar.

Select the resources for which you need more information by clicking the checkboxes to the left of the resource names. From this point, a variety of views are available under two buttons: View Assignments and View Availability.

View Assignments

The View Assignments view (shown in Figure 23-14) displays each resource that was selected from the Resource Center, as well as the resource's projects and tasks. The table's columns display work, remaining work, start date, finish date, the percentage of work completed, and comments. There is also a Gantt (bar) chart view to the right with a separator bar in between that can be dragged as needed. The view includes one additional, useful field, Actual Work.

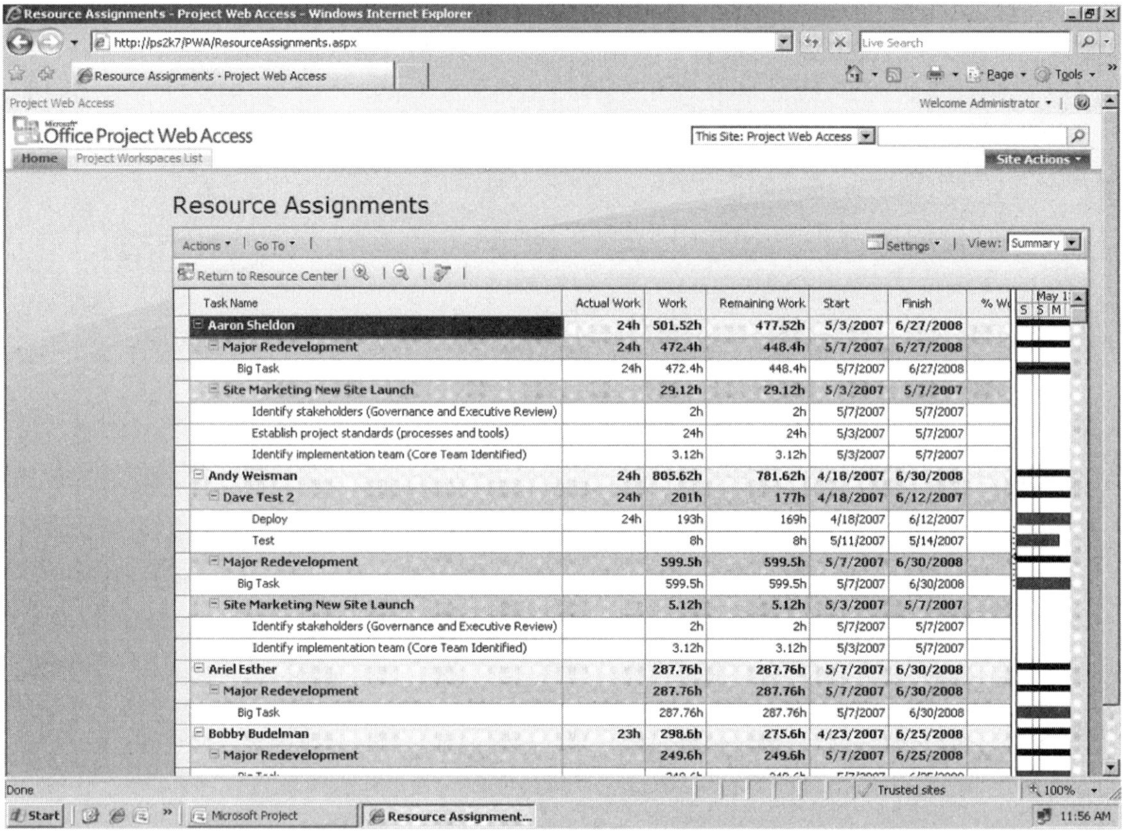

FIGURE 23-14 View Assignments page

Although it is often difficult to come to a consensus about what each view should contain, the tool offers great flexibility, so adding the Actual Work field should take a Project Server administrator only a few seconds. Other fields can also be added if they fit a company's requirements.

View Availability Views

To get to these views, select the View Availability button after selecting the resources from Resource Center. There are four different views that can be accessed from there. You cannot modify these views (at least not by using the tool). Each of these views provides the following viewing options:

- Under Settings | View Options, the date range can be set for this view. In addition, detail can be set at the day, week, month, or year level. You can also include proposed bookings within this pane by selecting the appropriate checkbox. See the View Options pane shown in Figure 23-15.

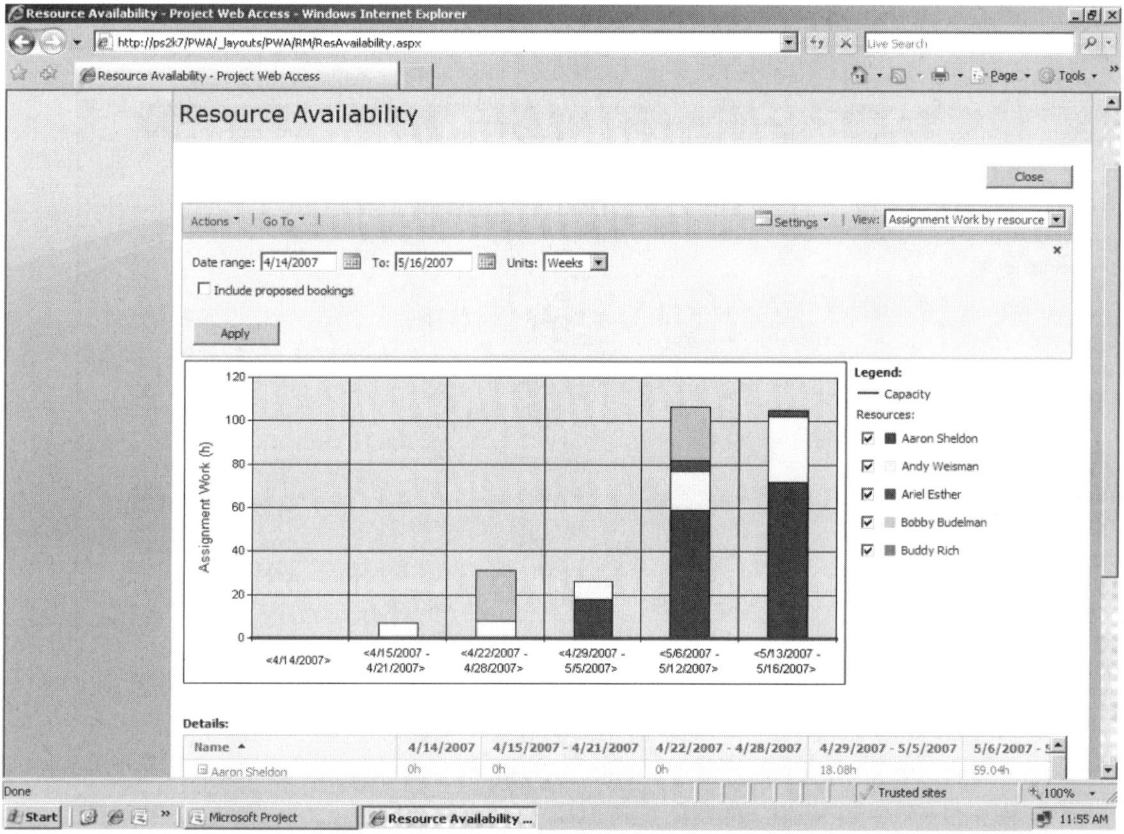

FIGURE 23-15 View options in View Availability views

- Under Actions, the resource manager can export to Excel or send to a printable view. In some cases, the print previews are not ideal, but in this case, they are quite usable. See Figure 23-16 for an example.
- The Go To button allows for navigating to resource assignments or returning to the Resource Center.

The following are the four different views:

- **Assignment Work by Resource** This view is among the most useful to the resource manager. It displays each of the resources selected, along with detail on what they are working on and when. It includes data for each selected resource that includes availability, capacity, and timesheet data, as well as each project to which the resource is assigned. In addition, a graph displays each resource as a different color for each period as defined in the View Options pane described previously.

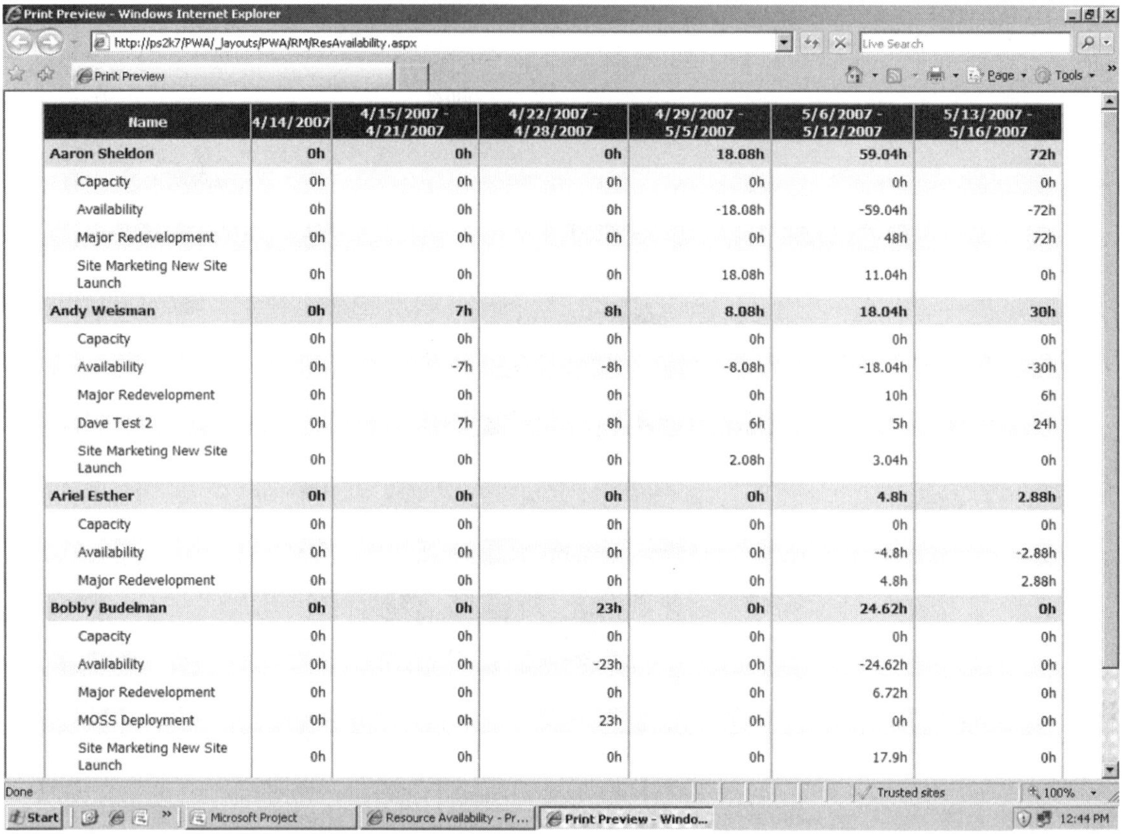

Name	4/14/2007	4/15/2007 - 4/21/2007	4/22/2007 - 4/28/2007	4/29/2007 - 5/5/2007	5/6/2007 - 5/12/2007	5/13/2007 - 5/16/2007
Aaron Sheldon	**0h**	**0h**	**0h**	**18.08h**	**59.04h**	**72h**
Capacity	0h	0h	0h	0h	0h	0h
Availability	0h	0h	0h	-18.08h	-59.04h	-72h
Major Redevelopment	0h	0h	0h	0h	48h	72h
Site Marketing New Site Launch	0h	0h	0h	18.08h	11.04h	0h
Andy Weisman	**0h**	**7h**	**8h**	**8.08h**	**18.04h**	**30h**
Capacity	0h	0h	0h	0h	0h	0h
Availability	0h	-7h	-8h	-8.08h	-18.04h	-30h
Major Redevelopment	0h	0h	0h	0h	10h	6h
Dave Test 2	0h	7h	8h	6h	5h	24h
Site Marketing New Site Launch	0h	0h	0h	2.08h	3.04h	0h
Ariel Esther	**0h**	**0h**	**0h**	**0h**	**4.8h**	**2.88h**
Capacity	0h	0h	0h	0h	0h	0h
Availability	0h	0h	0h	0h	-4.8h	-2.88h
Major Redevelopment	0h	0h	0h	0h	4.8h	2.88h
Bobby Budelman	**0h**	**0h**	**23h**	**0h**	**24.62h**	**0h**
Capacity	0h	0h	0h	0h	0h	0h
Availability	0h	0h	-23h	0h	-24.62h	0h
Major Redevelopment	0h	0h	0h	0h	6.72h	0h
MOSS Deployment	0h	0h	23h	0h	0h	0h
Site Marketing New Site Launch	0h	0h	0h	0h	17.9h	0h

FIGURE 23-16 Print Preview output

The viewer can change the graph by deselecting one or more resources to narrow down the data output. Note that the dark line in the graph represents the total capacity of all the selected resources (see Figure 23-17).

- **Assignment Work by Project** This view reverses the reporting perspective from the Assignment Work by Resource View described previously. Instead of displaying an Assignment and then Project output, it displays a Project and then Assignment point of view. The capacity line is also present in this view.
- **Remaining Availability** The table in this view is far more useful than the chart, as colored lines used in the chart are marginally readable. The table is additionally useful, however, in helping reveal when resources are available. Although this tool is valuable for planning, remember that the data are only as valid as the quality of the input from project managers and the team members who record their work in the system. Using the example view in Figure 23-18, try to envision the crossing resource lines being multiple colors that sometimes overlap and cross.

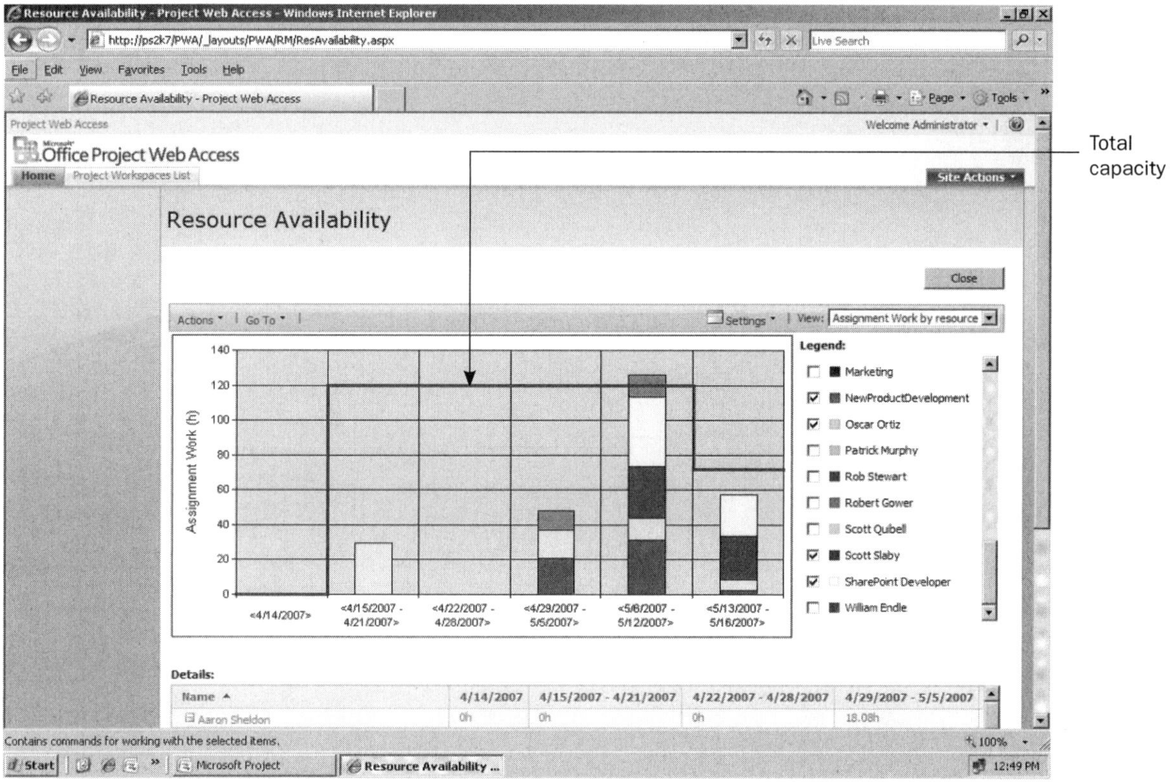

Figure 23-17 Capacity demarcation

- **Work** This view displays availability, capacity, and all the projects and the assigned work for each selected resource. In this view, as in the Remaining Availability View, the Details table is much more useful than the chart.

Data Analysis Views

One set of possible views in Project Server is not enabled by default for resource managers. These views are extremely flexible and are based on online analytical processing (OLAP) cubes. These cubes allow combinations of data from multiple sources with Project Server. This combined data can not otherwise be viewed together in one place without creating custom reports with other tools, such as SQL Reporting Services. In addition, the views based on these data can enable the viewer to change the contents of the views on the fly with very fast responses to those changes.

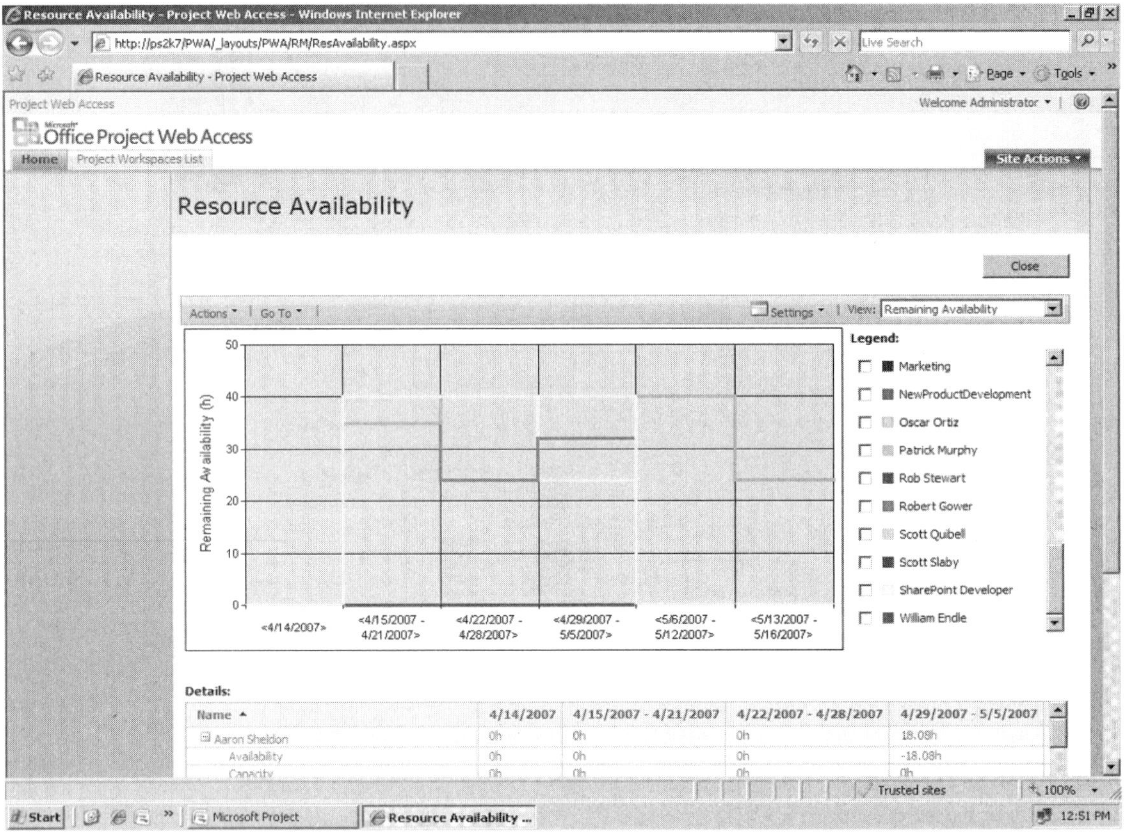

FIGURE 23-18 Remaining Availability View

The issue with these views is that the decision to make the data that supports them available is an all-or-nothing proposition. After access is provided to the OLAP cubes, the person with the permission can see any data in those views. For this reason, many organizations keep these views in the hands of a small number of people, such as the PMO or specific data analysts.

Resource data can be put together in just about any way that makes sense with these views, but the resource manager may need to acquire these data indirectly. An example where a resource manager might find such a view useful would be in a view that displays the number of hours recorded by individuals in a team detailed by week to ensure that each team member recorded his or her required 40 hours. Figure 23-19 shows such a view; note that there are some missing hours.

Remember that Data Analysis views may not be available to the resource manager. Among other possibilities, if allowed, would be a Data Analysis view that focuses on future resource demand by role and time period. Such a view could be used for future capacity planning.

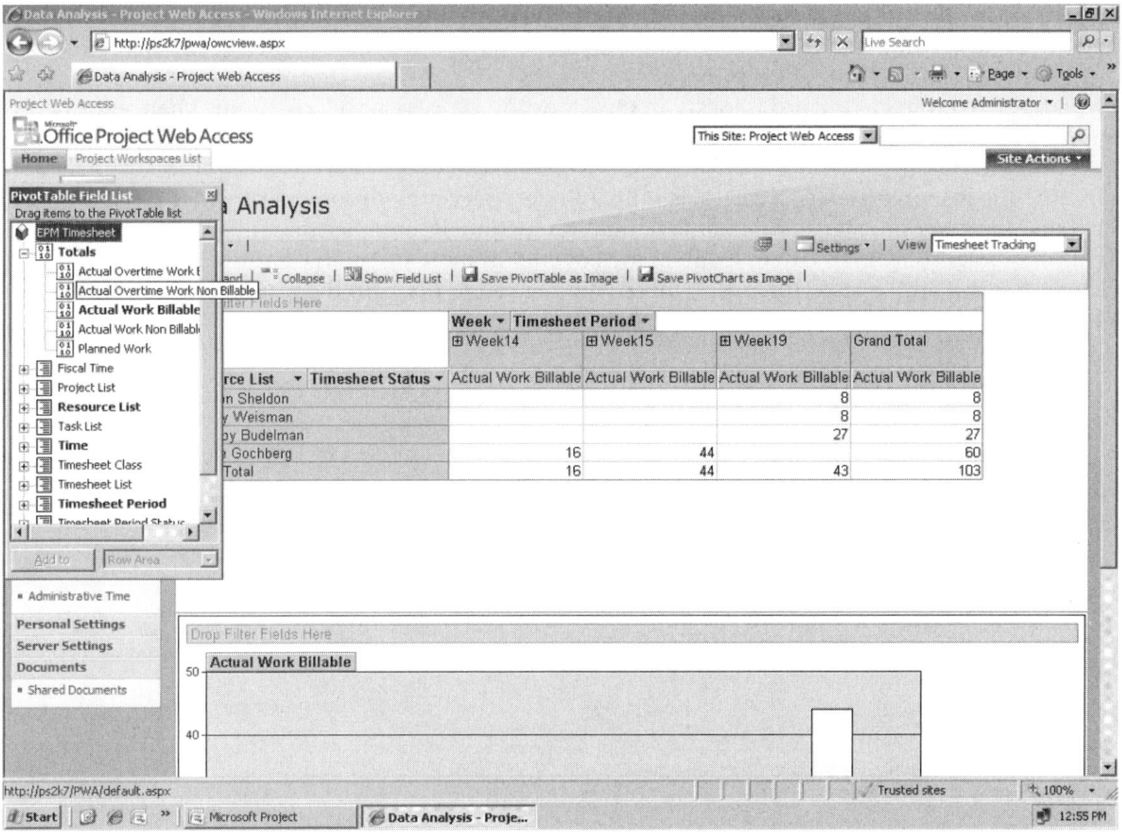

FIGURE 23-19 Timesheet by Team Data Analysis View

Resource Information

Unless you have started reading the book with this chapter, the following advice will sound familiar: It is not a recommended practice to use Project Server 2007 as a tool for individual performance management. In other words, it is probably not wise to use data that are output from Project Server when conducting performance management activities or when deciding who should receive a salary increase or who should be let go. If people believe that the data in this system are used to determine their salary increase or that they play a significant role in their annual review, they can easily manipulate the data that they input to get a (false) positive result.

A better use of Project Server data is to identify trends that can be translated into an environment of continuous improvement. For example, if there is a trend showing tasks running over the estimated work or duration, seek the cause. Keep in mind that in most cases people want to do a good job if given the chance. One very possible cause is that projects are built and published without getting the buy-in from those who are expected to do the work. Another possibility is that project managers are not examining resource availability when building their projects.

Support your team, reward honesty in the reporting process, and look for the chance to improve as a team. These "soft" factors can influence the likelihood of success in your Project Server deployment.

How the resource manager interacts with a Project Server environment can vary greatly. This chapter described key components of that interaction. Remember that much of the "nuts and bolts" of resource management are covered in more detail in Chapter 20. The next chapter focuses on the team members, those being asked to perform the project's work and keep the data in the system accurate and up to date.

24

CHAPTER

The Executive and Miscellaneous Roles

After the resource manager has decided who should be assigned to projects, the project manager builds the plan and assigns resources to tasks. Team members submit timesheets and task updates to their respective resource and project managers. Projects progress and tracking begins. These are the building blocks for all the impressive output scenarios that appear as views, reports, dashboards, and so on. These building blocks as well as the people, processes, and technology needed to make them function are all required to support real improvements in project and resource management for the organization. Finally, there are ways to view, analyze, and track projects and progress is being made against baselines. In the end, though, the success of an Enterprise Project Management (EPM) project requires executive buy-in (remember that the project sponsor should be an executive Or at least someone whose authority is at least as large as the deployment's impact). Executives' perspective of the success or failure of Project Server is often determined by whether they have access to the right set of data filtered in exactly the right way with the correct level of detail. The primary focus of this chapter is the executive. A brief discussion of other built-in roles is saved until later in the chapter.

Executives usually want broad but not deep access to the entire set of ongoing projects (or at least those over a certain size). They seek easy paths to quickly ascertain which projects might require them to take action, and have less interest in all the projects that are going well. Executives seek exception-based reports, not complete reports. In other words, executives are busy and do not have the time for details. Instead, they want to get the information needed to make timely fact-based decisions. Executives should be part of the planning team; ensuring that the planning team considers their reporting and tracking needs. Planning and executing the custom enterprise fields (as detailed in Chapter 8) are important steps toward making sure that when there are enough data to perform analysis (Data Analyzer views are discussed later in this chapter), the data will already have the correct attributes.

Project Center Views

Certain Project Center views can be targeted at executive viewers. Project Center views are valuable because they display everything about a project at a summary level. If the project is over budget or if the project's baseline finish date has slipped, these facts can be displayed. They also can be displayed in different ways. For example, the cost variance of the project can be shown as currency, perhaps using earned value, to give the viewer a feel for value to date. Project Center views display these outputs using graphical indicators to represent the cost variance within certain thresholds. Finally, numbers or "stoplights" can be used to display the percentage of variance, rather than just the raw differences between baseline and actual data.

Graphical indicators are great for reporting by exception. If a set of fields is green for 100 rows and 3 columns, except for 3 that are yellow and 2 that are red, the executive's eyes track to the items that are not green. Decisions can then be made on whether these "red projects" need intervention.

Each organization must determine which views make the most sense for its use. This section presents a few examples of Project Center views that could be valuable to the executive. The first view (shown in Figure 24-1) is based on the standard Project Web Access (PWA) Project Center Summary View, but has an additional column based on a subjective custom enterprise field that allows the project manager to display the overall health of the project.

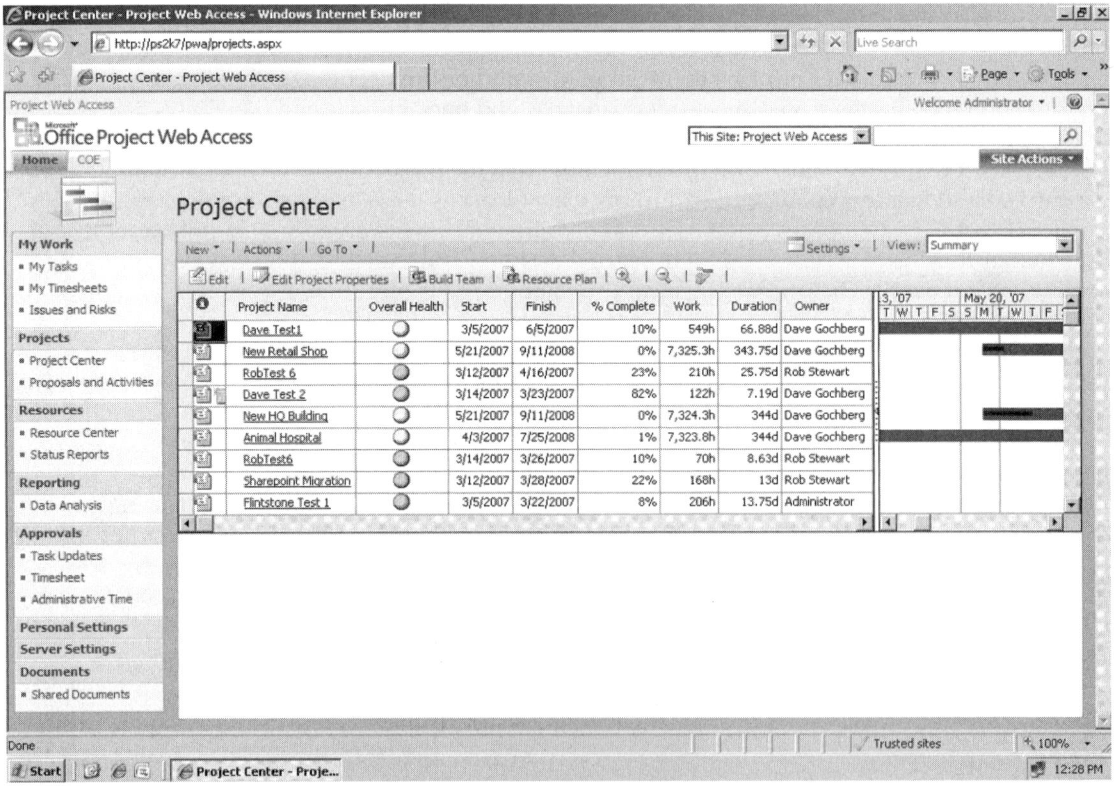

FIGURE 24-1 Summary View with a subjective overall health stoplight

NOTE *Even more can be done to develop exception reports if the Project Server is in a Microsoft Office SharePoint Server environment (which you will learn more about in Chapter 25).*

This first example view is very simple but provides a single, fast perspective for decision making. However, although the view is simple to use, it provides only minimal actual value. If that subjective field were married to a calculated, earned value indicator (or two or three), a more complete set of data points would result. This next example (see Figure 24-2) starts with the built-in Earned Value View. This view provides a wealth of valuable information for examining projects from the value perspective. For an executive, however, it is too busy. Determine exactly what is of value to the executive and then narrow the view, perhaps by including some graphical indicators. See Figure 24-2 for an example of an Executive Earned Value View.

Another critical Project Center view that is commonly used is a type of executive "dashboard." There are a few different ways to approach building such a view, but however this view is built it can also be the basis of a portion of Windows SharePoint Services–based

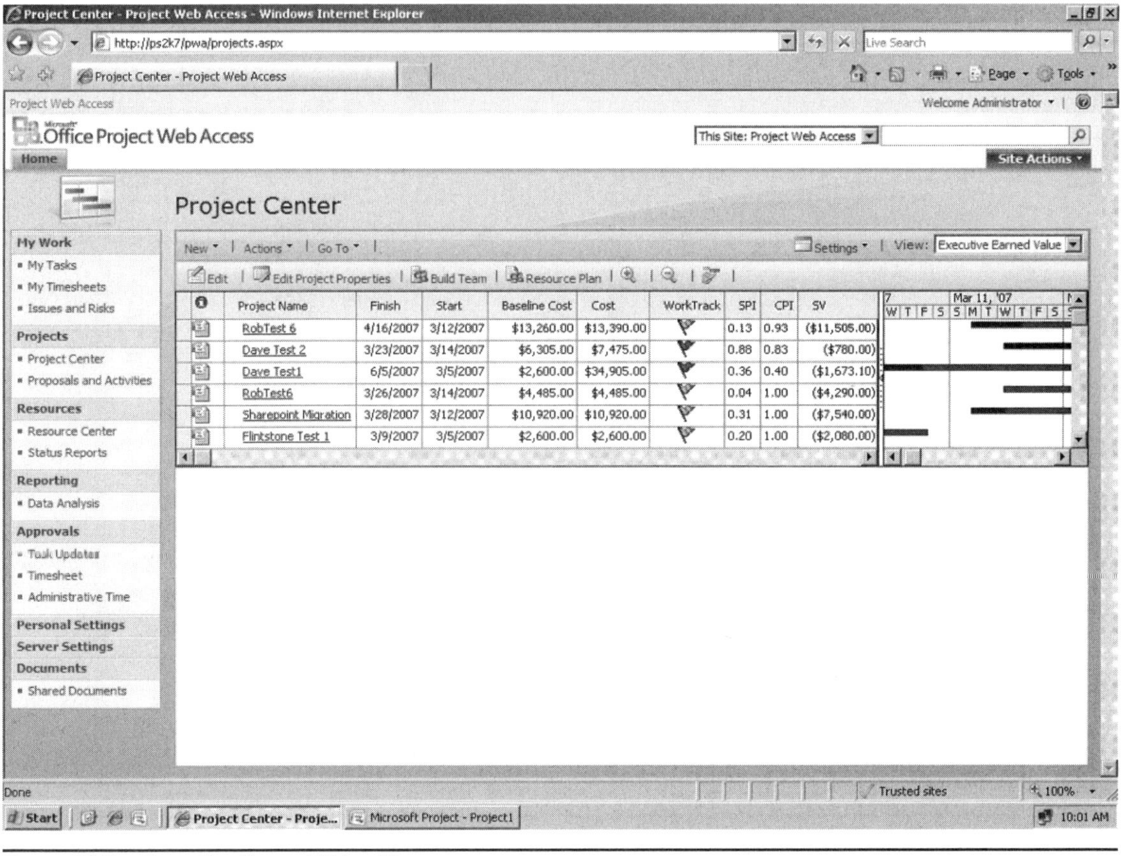

FIGURE 24-2 Executive Earned Value View

dashboard solutions (which you will learn more about later in this chapter). See Figure 24-3 for one example of this type of view.

There are many ways that Project Center views can be used for the executive. Another idea is to display strategic projects over 200 hours of work (or some other number). See Figure 24-4 for an example.

The view in Figure 24-4 uses filters to display only projects that have strategic alignment as based on an enterprise custom field. It displays the corporate strategy to which it is aligned, as well as its alignment value score. In addition, the view is filtered to display only projects over 200 hours, using the following fields:

- Field Name – Work
- Test – Is Greater Than
- Value – 200h

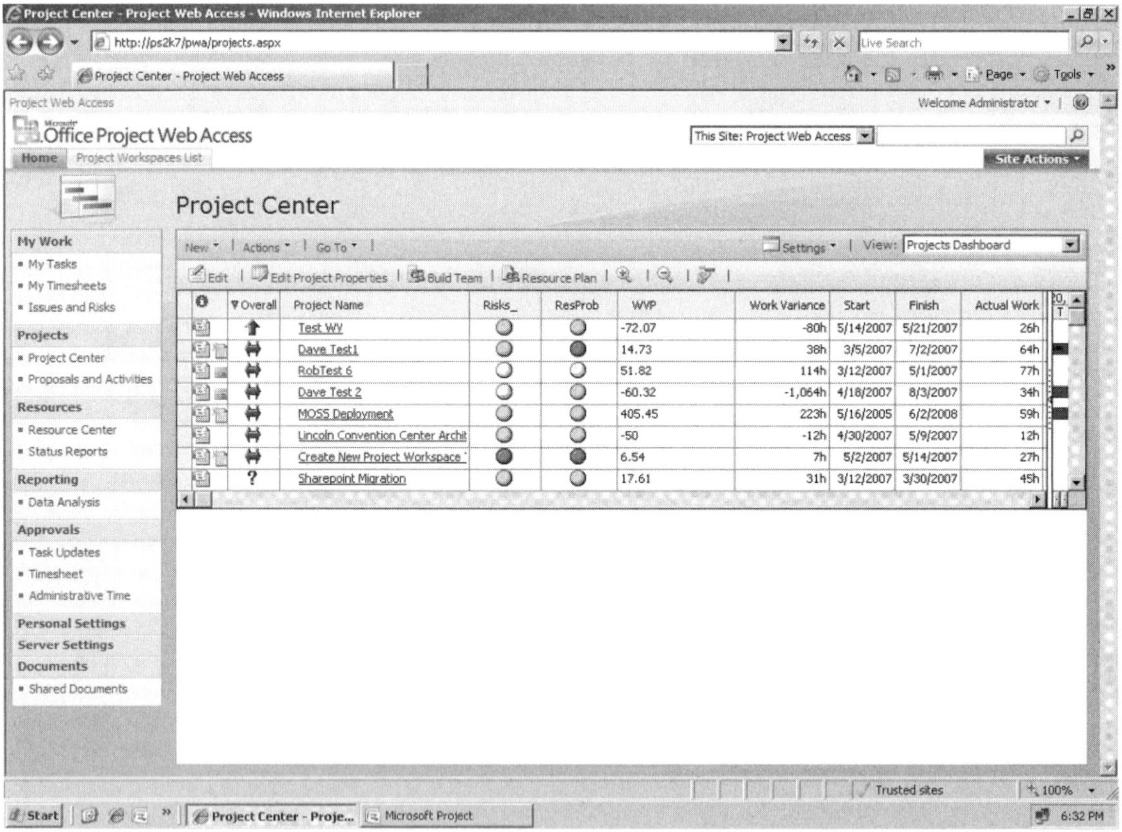

FIGURE 24-3 Executive project dashboard

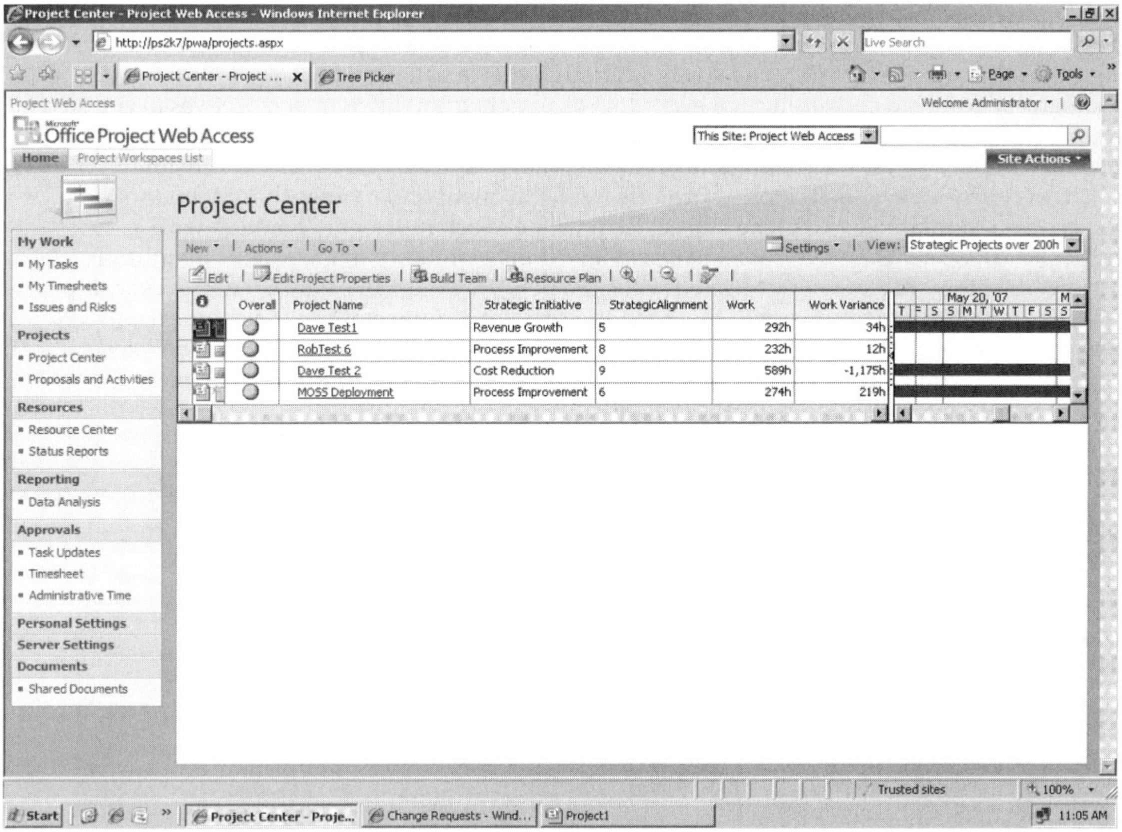

FIGURE 24-4 Strategic projects over 200 hours

The tools provide a basis for displaying almost anything that the executive requires. Project Center is a critical tool for executive management use. Use imagination to provide valuable information that the busy decision maker can view and absorb quickly.

Project Center views are best used on screen rather than in hard copy. Although there are tools for printing, print output is not as powerful as the on-screen presentation. Even exporting to Excel, which offers a very usable output, will not display graphical indicators unless you add some custom code. However, many executives like to use printed reports. Project Server provides a much improved set of tools for getting printed output. In general, though, the words "report" and "view" are synonymous, and PWA, rather than paper, is the primary medium for presenting information. Try to get the executives used to using EPM via the screen (bring a projector to meetings).

Data Analysis Views

In some circumstances, the best way for an executive to get the required information is to use Data Analysis views. The complex nature of these views makes them somewhat time consuming, so the best solution is often for the executive to delegate the work to someone else. ("Please get me a report that shows all the projects that were more than 25 percent over baseline, summed by department.") In other cases, however, executives find these views so useful that they use them extensively (although this is usually not the case in large companies). Some executives like to be able to look at data from different perspectives to get a complete understanding of what the numbers mean. With Data Analyzer views, this is possible. Build the views with the goal of making the executive's job as easy as possible.

If an executive wants to look at projects by department and by month for a total of the amount of planned work (the Project field called Work represents planned work), he or she can do so using the Data Analysis View. If instead they want to look at months of total work with a breakdown by location (a custom field), it would take only a few moves with a mouse to modify the same view that held the first set of information. If a comparison between baseline cost, actual cost, and cost by quarter is needed, creating a Data Analyzer View for that would be a snap for the administrator, or possibly the portfolio manager of Project Server. Figure 24-5 shows that example.

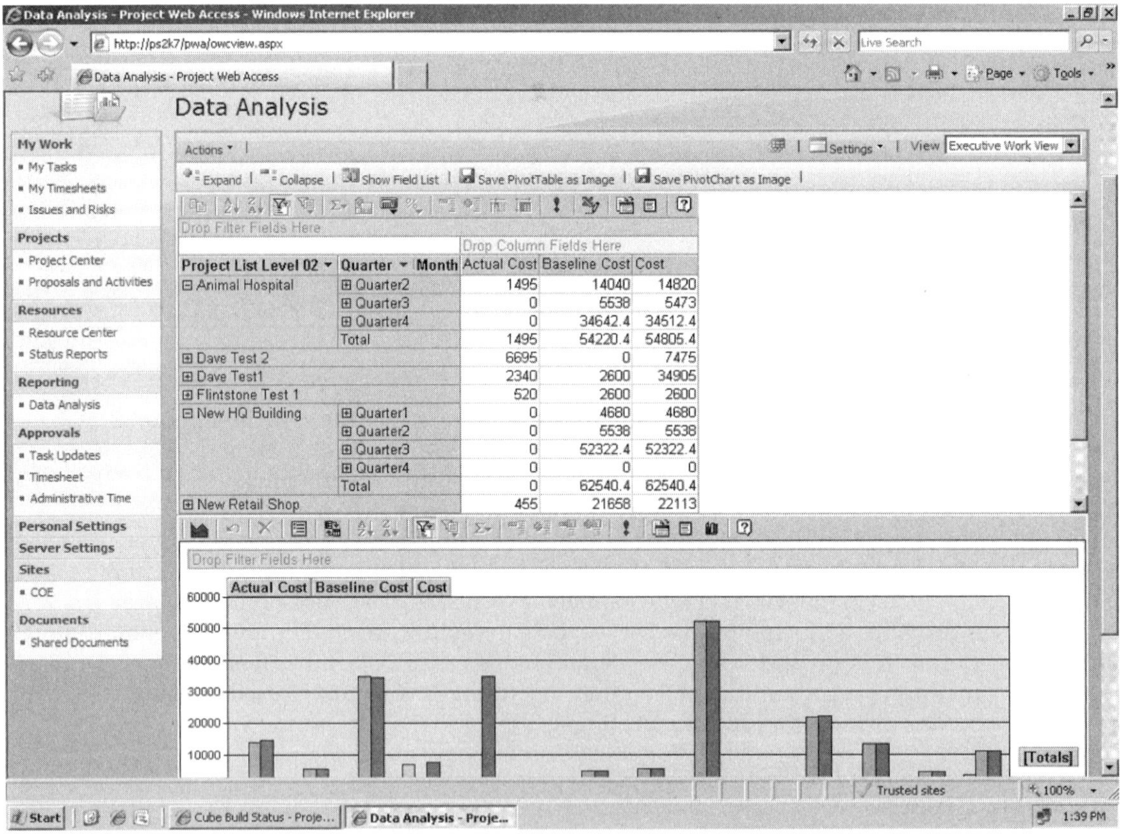

FIGURE 24-5 Data Analyzer cost by quarter

Once that view is built, the executives themselves can change the view to weeks or even days very easily (if the view settings allow them to do so). See Figure 24-6 for the result of simply dragging the quarters off the page and adding the Weeks field from the Chart Field tool to the location after projects.

As mentioned previously, it is even possible to view these data by the day. Figure 24-7 shows the tool that makes such a view possible.

Suppose that one executive has asked for a Data Analysis View that can show performance for projects by category. Specifically, she has requested a way to categorize projects by type (using a custom enterprise project field). She wants to look at baseline cost, actual cost, baseline work, actual work, and CVP (Cost Variance Percentage).

The first thing that is required for this is view creation of a new custom enterprise project text field for the category of Project. In this case, using a technology services model, the field called IT_Type includes the following:

- Applications
- Back Office

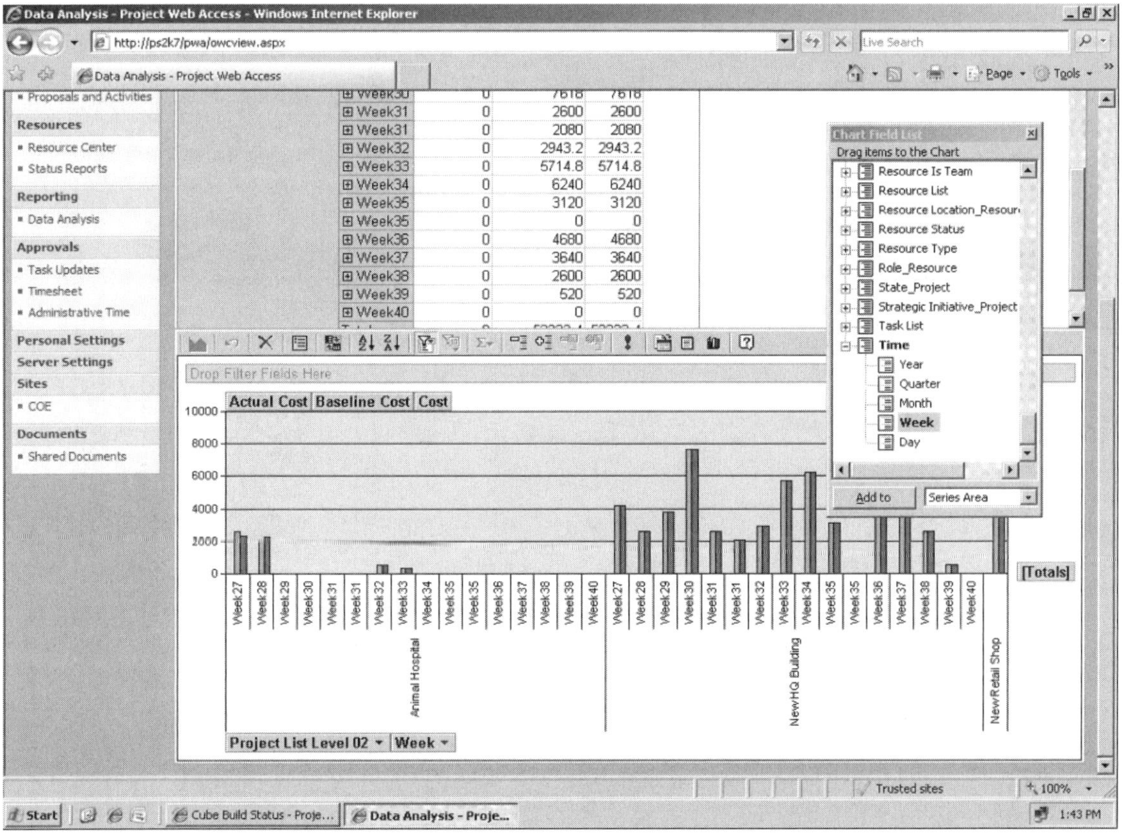

FIGURE 24-6 Data Analyzer cost by week

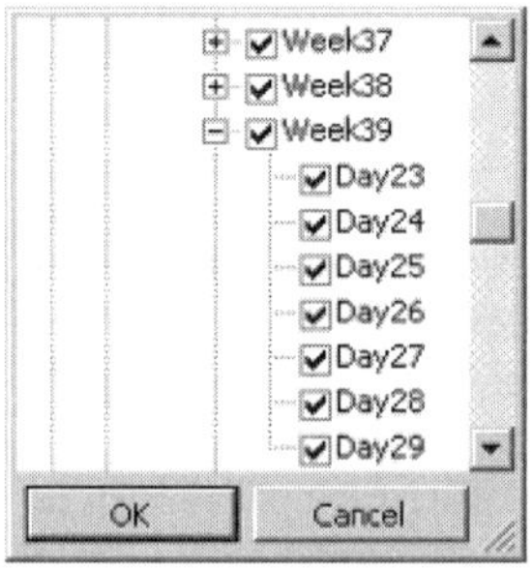

Figure 24-7 Picking the days

- Infrastructure
- Office

Next, a Data Analysis View must be created. Figure 24-8 shows the outcome. These examples just scratch the surface of possibilities.

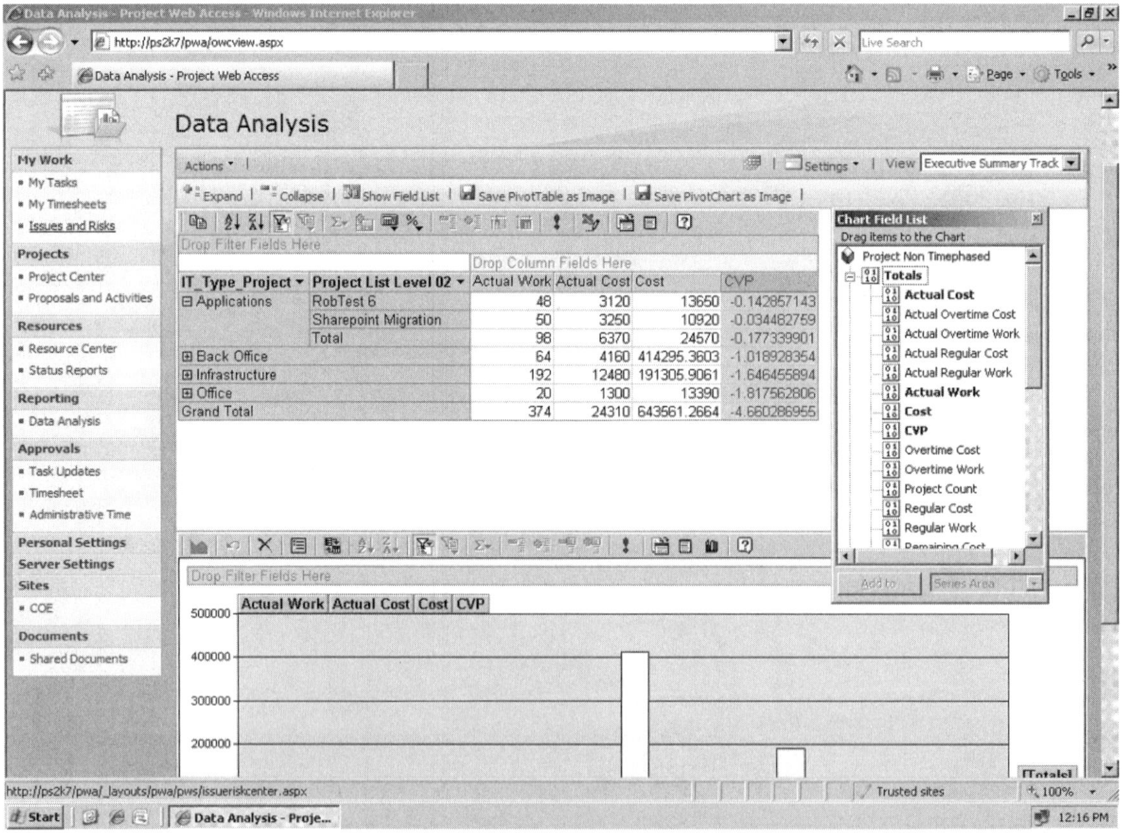

Figure 24-8 Executive Summary View by IT_Type

Excel

Excel has always been a very powerful application and the 2007 version is better than ever. Once again, the spreadsheet work could be delegated, but the authors have met quite a few executives who are very comfortable using Excel for analysis. This is true for analysis of raw data, for example, from the Project Server database. It is also possible to use Excel to pivot on data in an online analytical programming (OLAP) cube by connecting Excel to Analysis Services. Such pivot functionality can be quite useful.

To connect to the Project Server cube from inside Microsoft Office Excel 2007, first select the Data menu item just above the new Office 2007 ribbon on top of the spreadsheet. From there, select From Other Sources | From Analysis Services. See Figure 24-9 for this navigation.

Next enter into the Data Connection Wizard (see Figure 24-10), which is the next page, the name of the server where SQL Server Analysis Services is housed. Then select Next.

Next select the specific database for connection and then select the cube from the list that is displayed. In the example shown in Figure 24-11, the MSP_Portfolio_Analyzer is selected. Click Next.

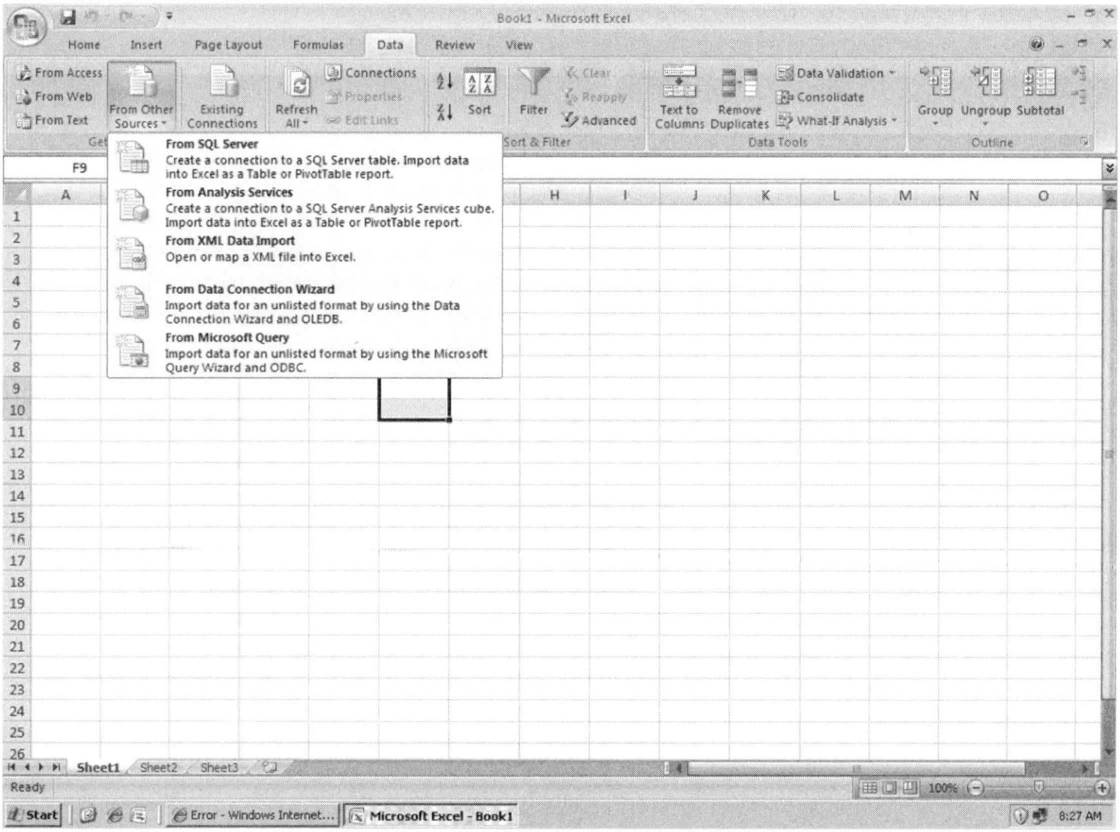

FIGURE 24-9 Navigate to Analysis Services

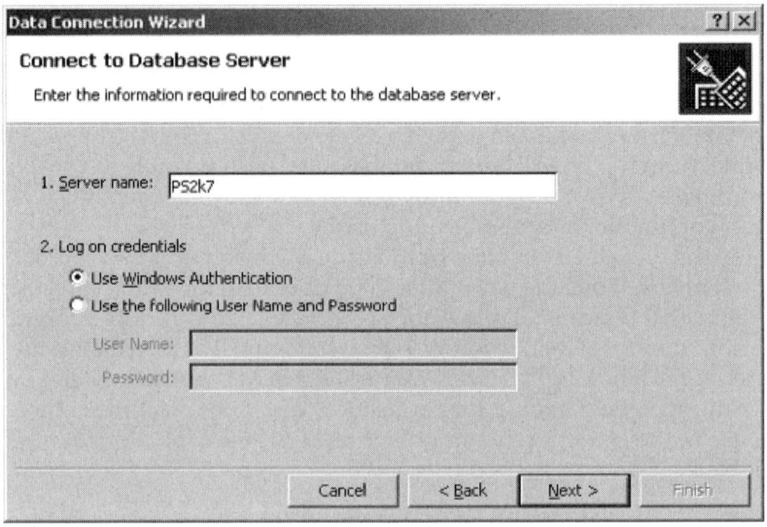

FIGURE 24-10 Data Connection Wizard's Connect to Database Server dialog

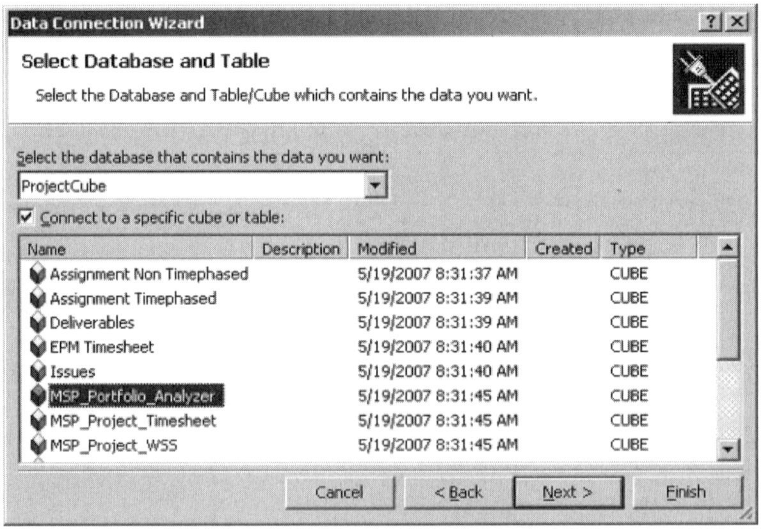

FIGURE 24-11 Select a cube.

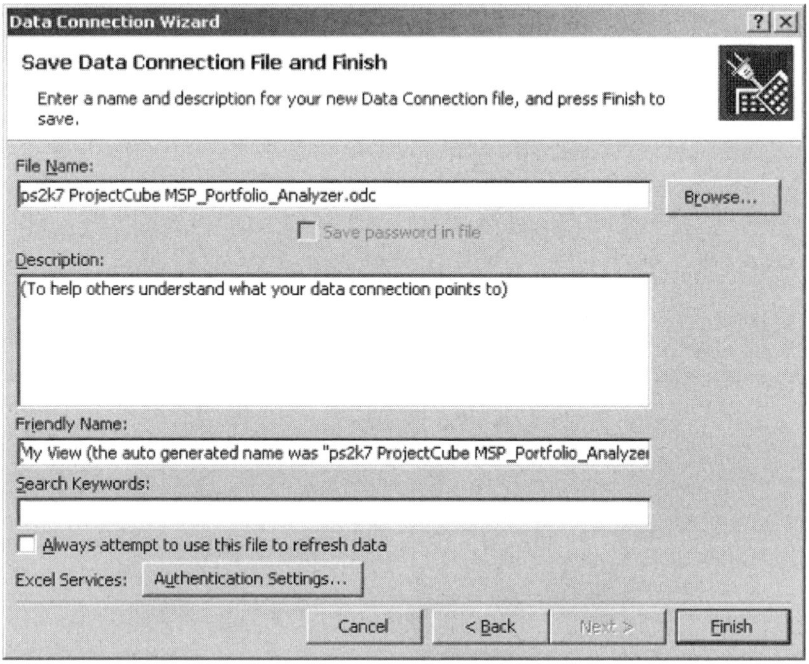

FIGURE 24-12 Save Data Connection File and Finish dialog

This process creates an Office Data Connection (ODC), a new feature in Microsoft Office 2007. In the screen in Figure 24-12, the wizard offers options to give your connection a friendly name and/or include a search. Note that in the screen shown in Figure 24-12, the Excel Services options are available only if you are using Microsoft Office SharePoint Server 2007 (MOSS) Enterprise (you will learn more about Excel Services in the MOSS environment in Chapter 25).

The next dialog asks you in which cell it should place the pivot and enables you to select a chart and/or table. The Properties button takes you to some display options such as Font Size. Quite a few other configuration options are available in the Properties pages, but the executive will rarely need to use them.

From this point, the executive is presented with a wealth of possibilities. See Figure 24-13 for how the screen looks before the executive makes any selections.

From this point, the executive (or the executive's designee) can build the pivot with the fields that are required. In the following example, the following fields have been selected:

- Work
- Project List

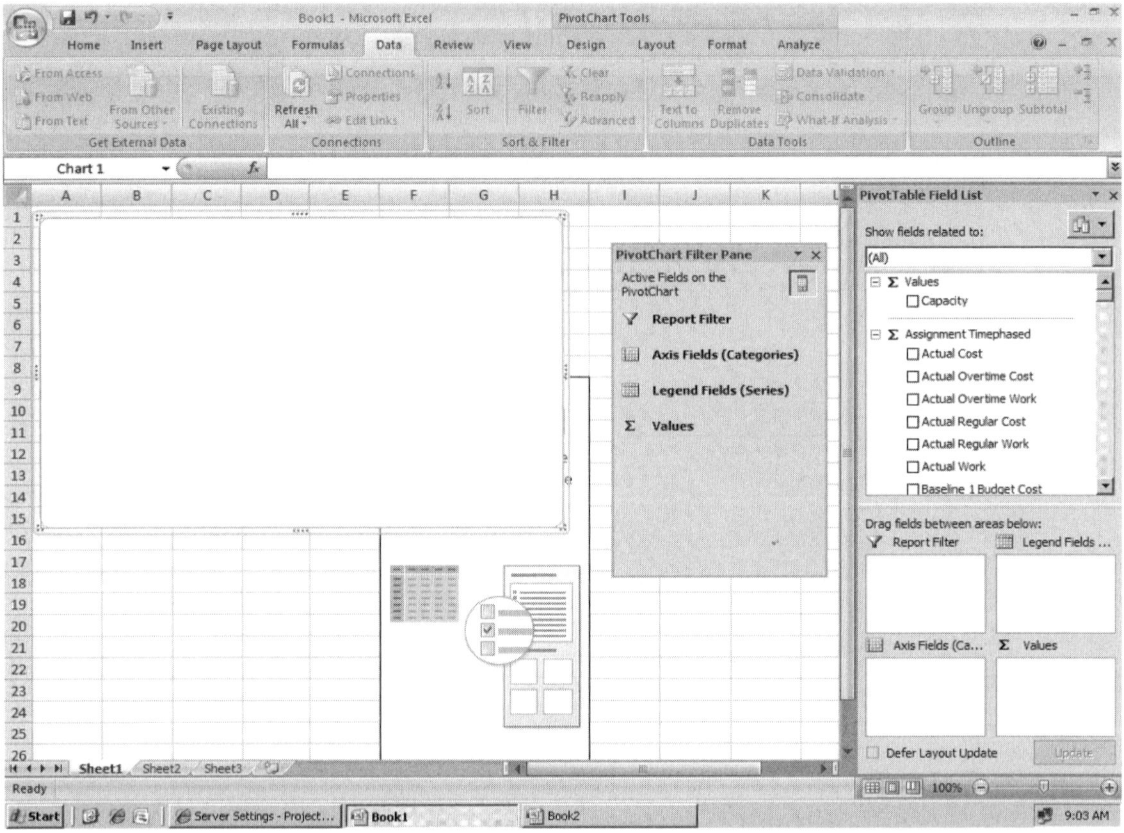

FIGURE 24-13 Pivot without configuration

- Project Location_Project (a custom field)
- Time

The goal is to build a pivot that shows work by project and location and that can be filtered on time. Use the tools on the right to select the desired fields. Note that these can be set to different levels from here. In the example shown in Figure 24-14, the Project Location_Project field is filtered on certain states in the Midwest.

You can filter the pivot shown in Figure 24-14 to specific time windows by changing the time from All to whatever time window is required. Note that this filtering can go from an individual day to a year or years. One nice feature of using Excel is the flexibility available for printing the results. In fact, the best way to print from the PWA Data Analyzer views is to export to Excel.

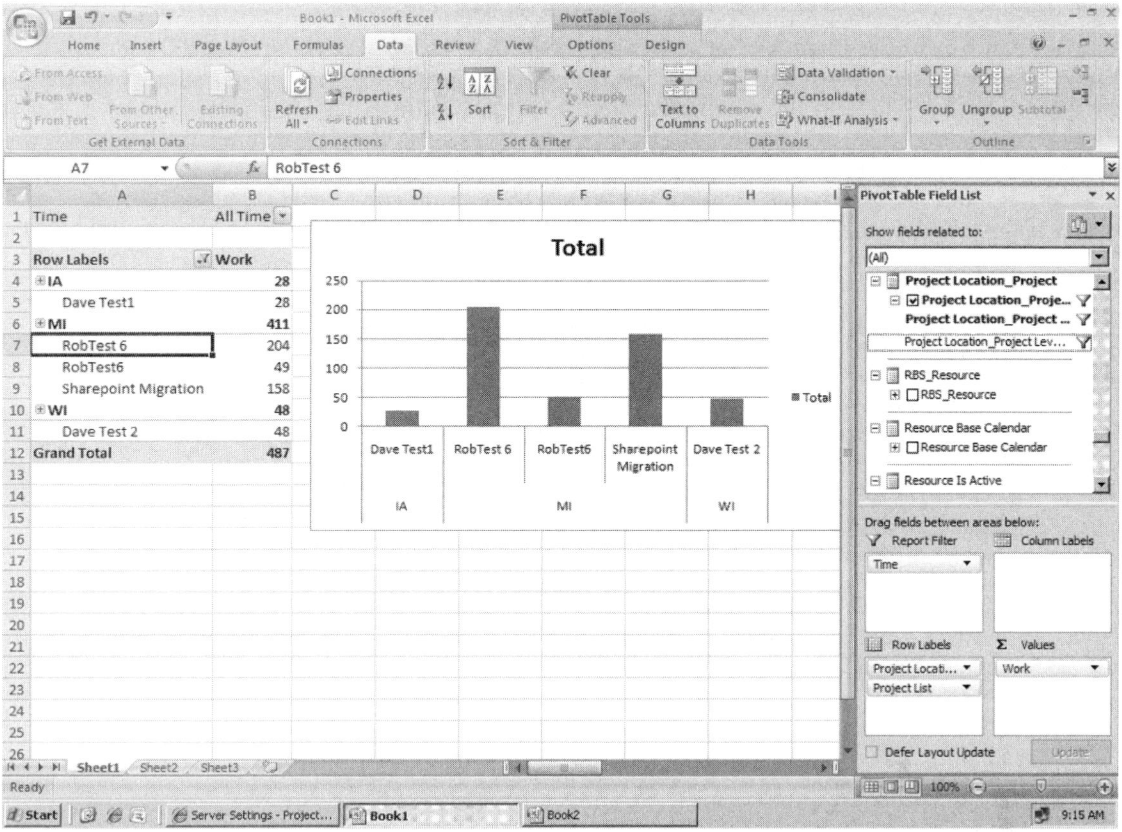

FIGURE 24-14 Pivot filtered for All Time

SQL Reporting Services Reports

If there are staff available with SQL Reporting Services skills, custom reports can be created using SQL Reporting Services. The executive then can get exactly what is required in a format that can be viewed directly from SQL Reporting Services, via the Web, in a Project Workspace or other SharePoint site. It also can be built to be print-centric. As discussed earlier, PWA and Project Server are not primarily designed to be output to hard copy, so SQL Reporting Services can be a lifesaver in print-centric organizations. An example SQL Server Reporting services report is displayed near the end of Chapter 25 as a Sharepoint reports "dashboard."

Hybrid Views in Windows SharePoint Services 3.0

The next chapter provides details on how to use the Microsoft Windows SharePoint Services (WSS) 3.0 platform on which PWA resides. At the conceptual level, one of the critical strengths of the WSS platform is the ability to aggregate information from multiple sources.

The executive can access information from Project Server alongside information from other sources. As an example, imagine that an executive wants to see a view of the Project Center View, "Strategic Projects over 200 Hours," as discussed earlier in this chapter, in a single page with his or her Exchange In-Box, Outlook Calendar, and revenue data from an Enterprise Resource Planning (ERP) system. All of this is possible with a WSS Web Part page, and only the revenue data may need any custom code.

Does it make sense to use the Project Server's WSS to build such a view? Perhaps not. It might make more sense for organizations to deploy MOSS 2007. This powerful set of tools provides amazing functionality that makes MOSS a difficult platform to resist, especially for Microsoft-centric shops. (You will learn more about MOSS in the next chapter.)

With just the tools that come with Project Server and WSS, the executive can usually achieve his or her desired results. The aggregated view in WSS shown in Figure 24-15 includes announcements, a Web Part displaying an executive-focused Project Center View, and the PWA reminders, also in a Web Part.

Chapter 25 discusses the SharePoint tools in more detail.

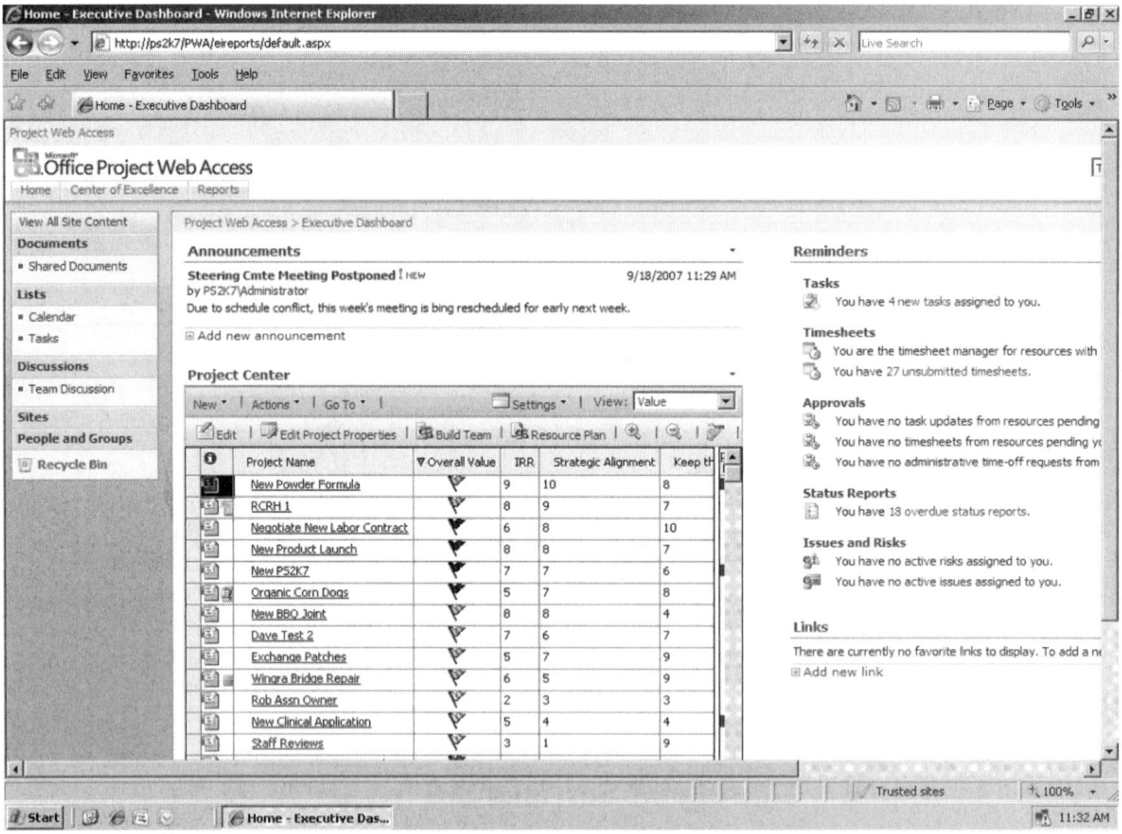

FIGURE 24-15 Aggregated WSS site

Miscellaneous Roles

There are other groups in addition to those detailed in this book, each with narrow roles. Using them may make sense in some cases. In addition, it can often make sense to create new roles. For example, in a recent project, a new group called Security was created along with a category, My Security. This role was used for adding and removing users, changing permissions, and so on. Additional out-of-the-box roles include the following:

- **Portfolio managers** This role has a combination of permissions allowing project management, as well as some resource management permissions. In addition, it provides control of the tools for building OLAP cubes and views.
- **Proposal reviewers** This role has many project manager permissions but is focused on items using the new proposals feature.
- **Team leads** This role is just slightly more than a team member, in that it can request a status report.

Although executives usually spend only a small amount of time in PWA, getting them what is required is an important component of making the deployment of Project Server a success. This chapter described some ways to get there, while briefly touching on other roles that Microsoft provides in the system out of the box. Keep in mind that you can modify all of these roles to include whatever levels of access make sense for your organization.

25

CHAPTER

Project Server 2007—Doing More for Collaboration and Communications

Especially with the improved functionality that is available in Project Server 2007, more organizations understand managing projects as stand-alone activities is an incomplete approach. Which projects are executed should be based on their relative value to the entire organization (Project Portfolio Management) and managed as collections of projects that have things in common (Program Management). Project staffing choices should be made by taking advantage of resources in the most efficient way, keeping people busy but not overwhelmed by work.

Using Enterprise Project Management (EPM) (Project Server) and Project Portfolio Management (PPM) concepts and technology (such as Project Portfolio Server), systems can go a long way toward supporting improvement in all these areas when married to an effort to improve people and processes in an organization.

Communications and collaboration considerations are often the last things on which organizations focus when implementing improvements that use EPM systems. These are the very areas, however, where breakdowns can often spell doom for projects. It is fundamental that communications and collaborative solutions be a part of every EPM endeavor. There are many ways to deal with team communications and collaboration, but with the Microsoft solution, there is a powerful set of tools at hand.

Project Server 2003 used Windows SharePoint Services (WSS) 2003 to provide Project Workspaces where project teams could collaborate on project-related items. Especially powerful were the connections between three critical parts of project communications: issues, risks, and project-related documents. Many other features could be extended or built to extend those workspaces, but 2003 features pale in comparison with the powerful possibilities in Project Server 2007 and WSS 3.0.

The first section of this chapter will focus on the out-of-the-box features that are built into Project Server 2007. Later on, the focus will shift to the nearly endless possibilities for extending the communications and collaboration environment within the tools. Finally, this chapter will delve into an even more powerful set of solutions that can be had when Project Server 2007 is part of a Microsoft Office SharePoint Server (MOSS) 2007 environment.

Built-In Features

There are a host of out-of-the-box features to support project communication and collaboration in the Project Workspaces feature of Project Server 2007. Built on the WSS 3.0 platform, these features offer a great starting point for organizational improvement in the way teams work together on their projects.

There are several ways to find the Project Workspaces for a Project Server–based project:

- In the lower half of the default Project Web Access (PWA) Home Page, there is a Project Workspace Web Part. In the top-right corner of the Web Part is a dropdown menu that displays either all Project Workspaces (assuming the user has permission to them) or only "owned" Workspaces. The owner of a Project Workspace is the resource who is the project owner when the project is first published.
- Another way to get to a Project Workspace is to highlight the project in the PWA Project Center and select Go To | Project Workspace.
- Some pieces of the Project Workspace can be opened from within the Collaborate menu in Microsoft Office Project Professional 2007. Figure 25-1 shows an example. Other items that can be viewed in the same manner include Risks, Documents, Project Center, Resource Center, and Status Reports. Deliverables are also managed from this menu.
- Finally, from any Project View in PWA (Project Details not Project Center), select Go To | Project Workspace.

Issues

Issue management can be the first collaborative feature used during Project Server deployments when the Project Workspaces feature is rolled out as part of the iterative deployment plan. One useful built-in feature allows project issues to be posted into the Project Workspace and connected to the project plan/schedule.

To post a new issue after navigating to the Issues link on the Quick Launch Bar (left navigation), select New. This form (called a *list* in SharePoint-speak) can be extended, but it offers a useful set of features even without modifications. It includes the following fields:

- **Title** This is where you should name the issue.
- **Owner** This field includes a feature that checks names against system users. The name checker is used for the All Issues Owned by Me View (which you will learn more about shortly).

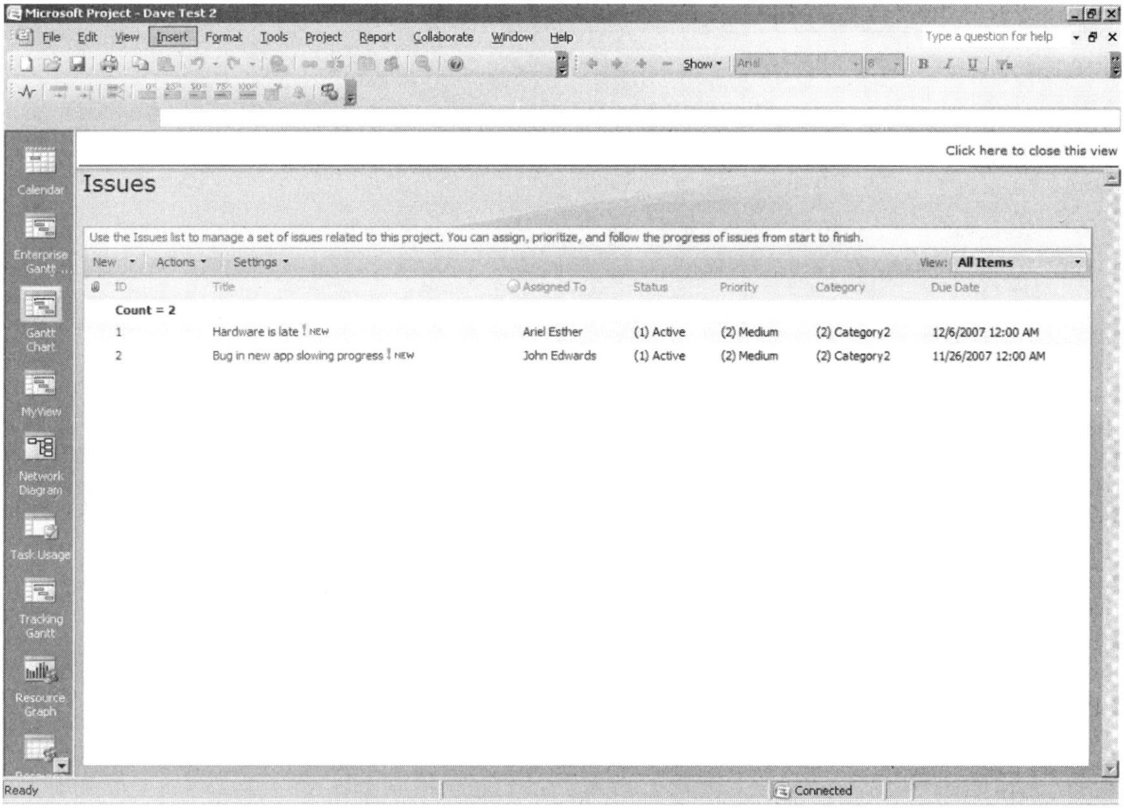

FIGURE 25-1 Issues within Project Professional

- **Assigned To** This field also includes the name checker to support the All Issues Assigned to Me View and the issues on the PWA Home Page display (for example, in Figure 25-2, the Home Page alerts you that you have one active issue assigned to you) as well as an e-mail notification.
- **Status** This can be either Active, Postponed, or Closed.
- **Priority** This is set to Low, Medium, or High.
- **Category** This field is set to Category 1, Category 2, or Category 3 (this is the first candidate for modification).
- **Due Date** This field offers a date-picker tool.
- **Discussion** This rich text field supports color, bullets, bold, italics, and more.
- **Resolution** This is another rich text field.

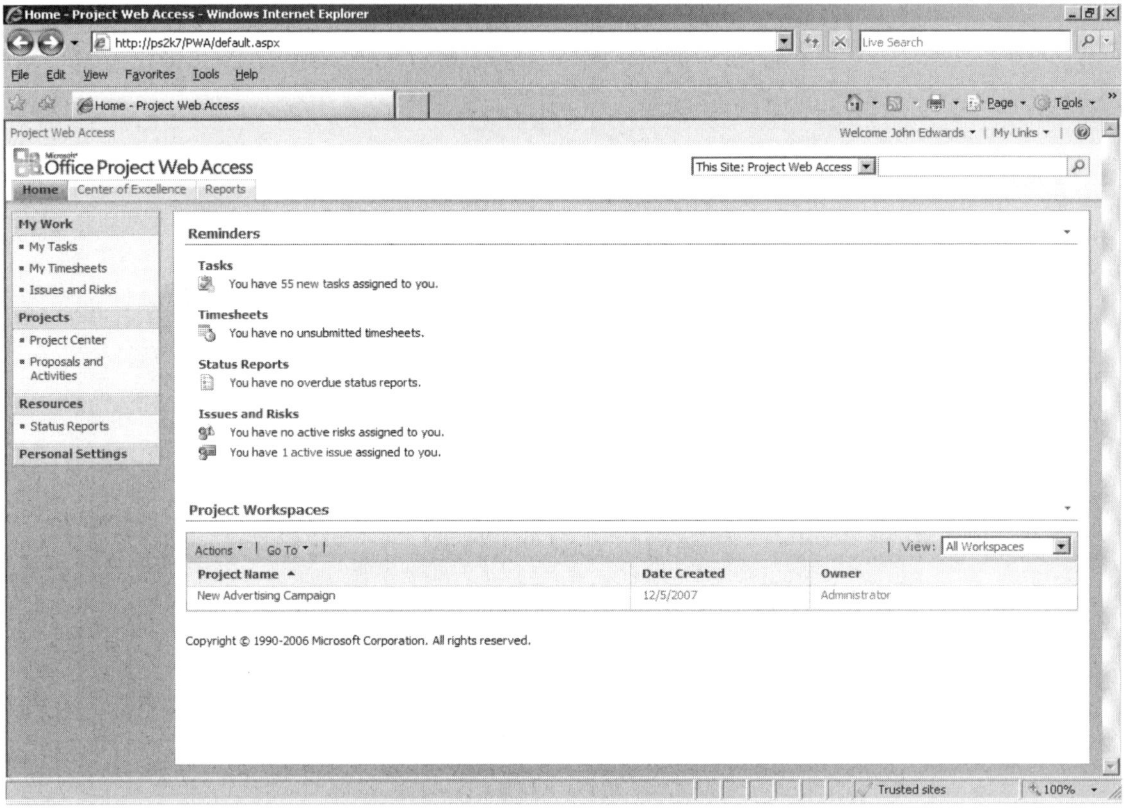

FIGURE 25-2 Issue display on PWA Home Page

Documents can be attached to an issue. Perhaps the most useful feature is the ability to link a project issue to a specific project task or to specific project tasks, other issues, and project risks. This linkage displays in PWA's Project Center (which alerts you that there are issues associated with this task) and within Project (details) views (which also warns you that there are issues associated with this task).To set a link, select Link Items from the horizontal toolbar within the issue.

The dialog that appears offers a list of project tasks that can be viewed either in an All Tasks or MyTasks perspective. Select the box or boxes next to the tasks to be linked, as shown in Figure 25-3. Links can also be established to project risks, other issues, and project documents from within this dialog. After you have set your links, select OK. The indicator

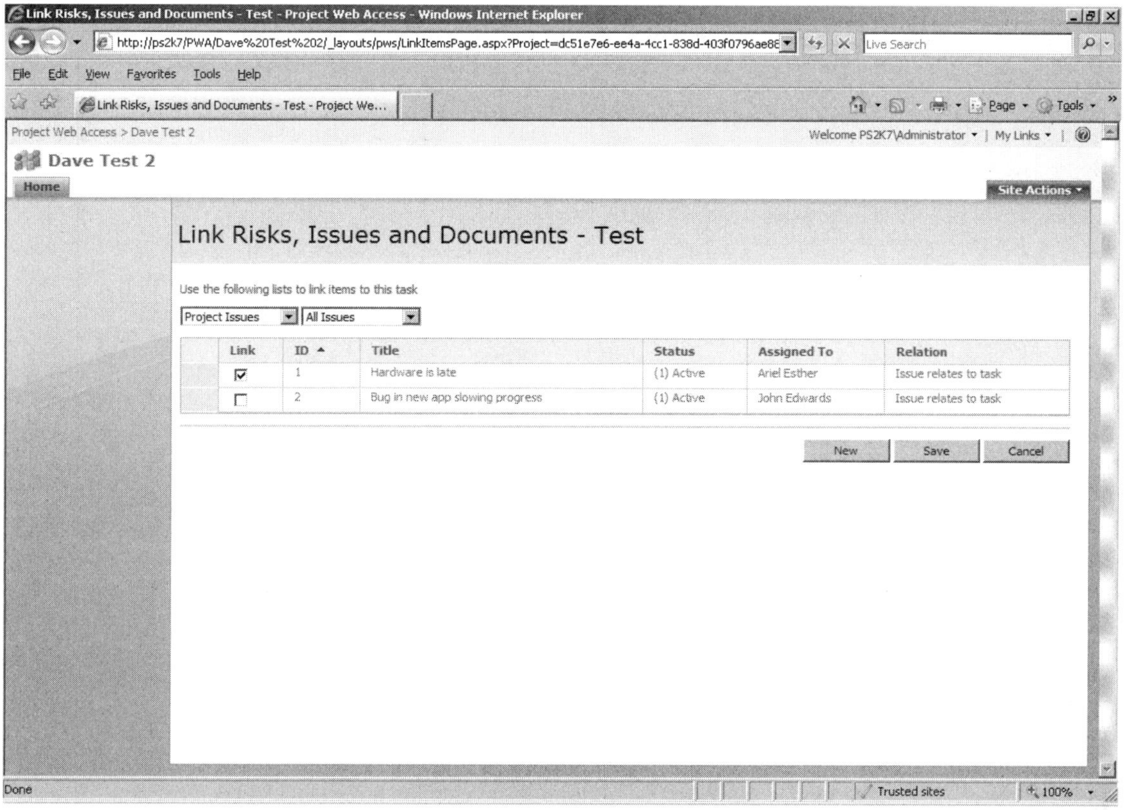

FIGURE 25-3 Link Items button

icons that display in PWA are actionable (they are links to the issues). Figure 25-4 shows how an icon is displayed.

When the icon is selected, the issue itself is displayed along with any other issues for that particular project, as shown in Figure 25-5.

Several actions can be performed from the Issues page. The entire list can be edited in Datasheet View, a handy tool for mass editing. The data can be exported to an Excel 2007 spreadsheet (older versions can also be used to a point). There is an RSS feed option available from the Actions menu, but it is not really appropriate for issues. There is a spellcheck feature in lists in Project Server 2007, a useful new element. Finally, the Issues list supports SharePoint alerts functionality (Alert Me) at the list or item level (you will learn more on alerts later in this chapter).

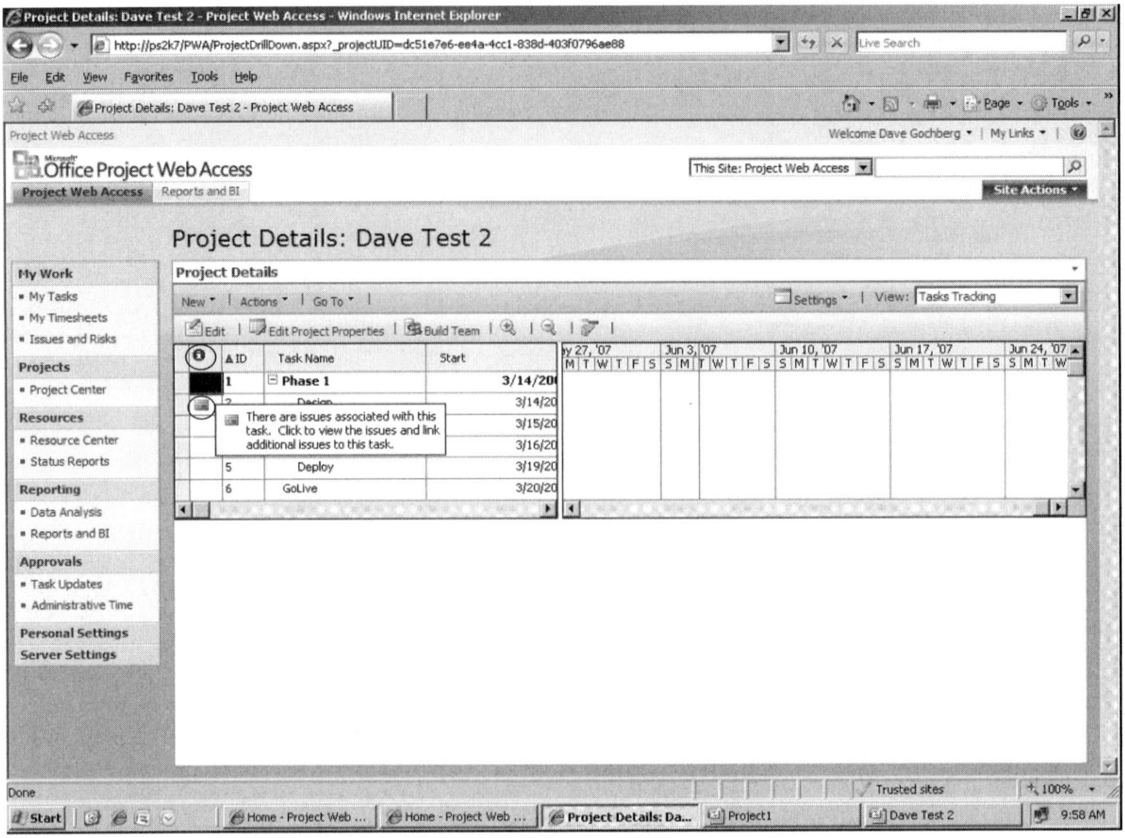

FIGURE 25-4 Indicator icon for issues

Among other settings, List settings include the following Versioning options that are included but not enabled by default:

- Require content approval for submitted items
- Create a version each time you edit an item in this list
- The number of versions to be stored
- The number of draft versions to be kept for approved versions (this option is enabled only if approval is enabled)
- Control over draft version security if using approvals
  - Any user who can read items
  - Only users who can edit items
  - Only users who can approve items (and the author of the item)

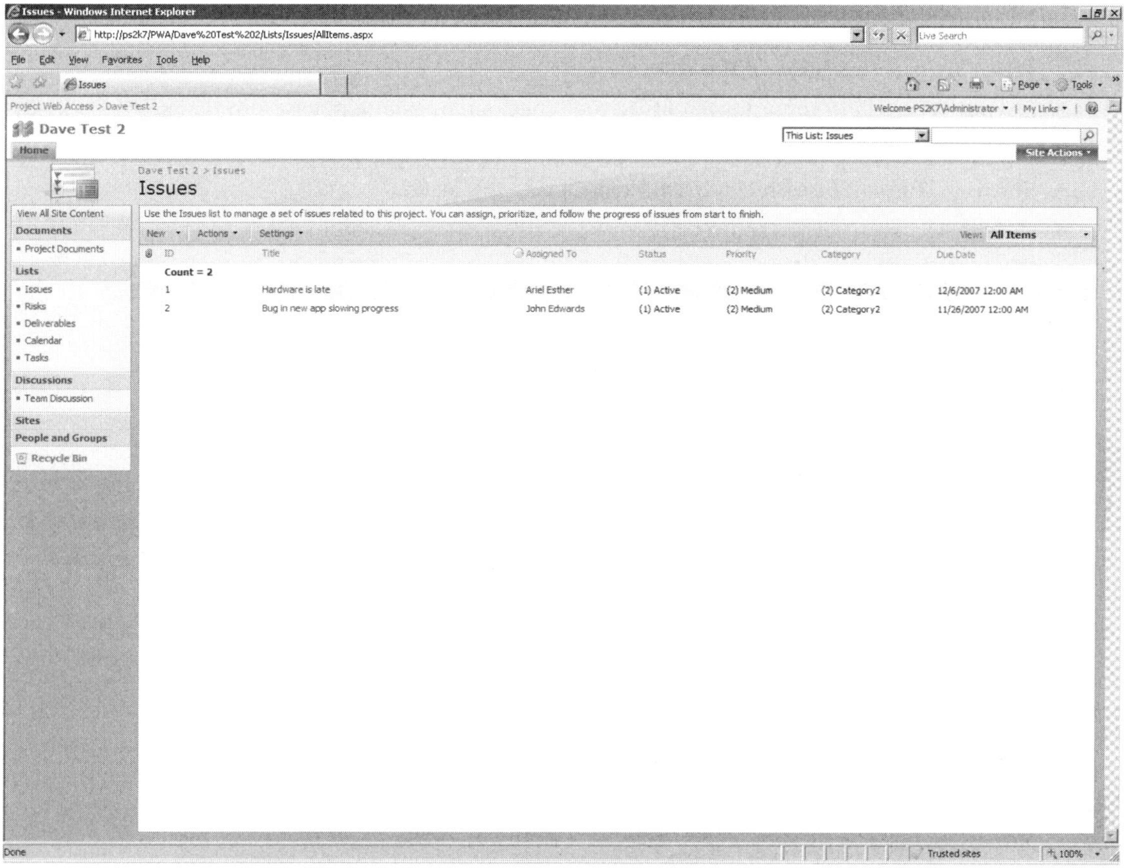

FIGURE 25-5 Issues display from the indicator icon

There will be more discussion on Versioning later in this chapter. Other settings affect audience targeting, content types, and item level permissions, or determine whether attachments are allowed or not, whether the New Folder option is displayed, and whether the list items should be displayed in search results. In most cases, these settings should be left alone on all the out-of-the-box features. Customized additions to the Issues list (new columns/form fields) can be made into issues if needed to support a specific process. This is also true for risks (discussed in the next section).

Risks

Risk management is inherently more complex than issue management, as risk management involves planning for risk mitigation and avoidance. Issues are not predicted, so no planning for mitigation is required. But since risks can be foreseen, the technology to support risk management includes more features.

The form itself includes the following:

- **Title** This is the name of the risk.
- **Owner** This field includes a feature that checks names against system users.
- **Assigned to** This field also includes the name checker.
- **Status** This can be either Active, Postponed, or Closed.
- **Category** This field is set to Category 1, Category 2, or Category 3.
- **Due Date** This field offers a date-picker tool.
- **Probability** This field is presented in percentages.
- **Impact** This is set from 1 to 10.
- **Cost**
- **Description** This is a rich text field.
- **Mitigation Plan** This is also a rich text field.
- **Contingency Plan** This is another rich text field.
- **Trigger Description** This also is a rich text field.
- **Trigger** Possible settings include Date, Exposure over Threshold, Tasks Not Completed, Other, or Specify Your Own Value.

As with issues, risks can have documents attached and they can be associated with specific project tasks, etc. Also, the same set of Actions are available as discussed in the "Issues" section. The same options apply.

Documents and Document Libraries

Project documents can be stored in the Project Workspaces. When first installed, the Project Workspace template includes a single Project Documents library. A subfolder hierarchy can be defined and this area is commonly used to store the project's collateral in an organized way. Every organization has different ways of handling the organization of folders in document libraries. The Project Documents library starts without any content.

Alerts

A great feature available in the WSS platform that is included in Project Workspaces is the alerts functionality. Alerts allow an end user to set an Alert Me option in any list (such as the Issues list) or document library.

These alerts can be set for the entire list or library. The idea of alerts is for a user to be notified if something he or she is interested in has changes applied. Project managers would often want to receive an alert if a new issue is posted on a project that they are managing.

If a user wants to set an alert for the Issues list on a specific Project Workspace, that user would start by navigating to the Issues list from the Quick Launch Bar. From there, the user would select Actions | Alert Me. Next the user is offered several options. Depending on permissions, the user could be provided an opportunity to alert other people. Most users won't have this option, but instead will only be able to set the alert for themselves. As shown in Figure 25-6, the next option, Change Type, specifies the type of changes that will elicit an alert. The options include All Changes, When New Lines Are Added, When Existing Items

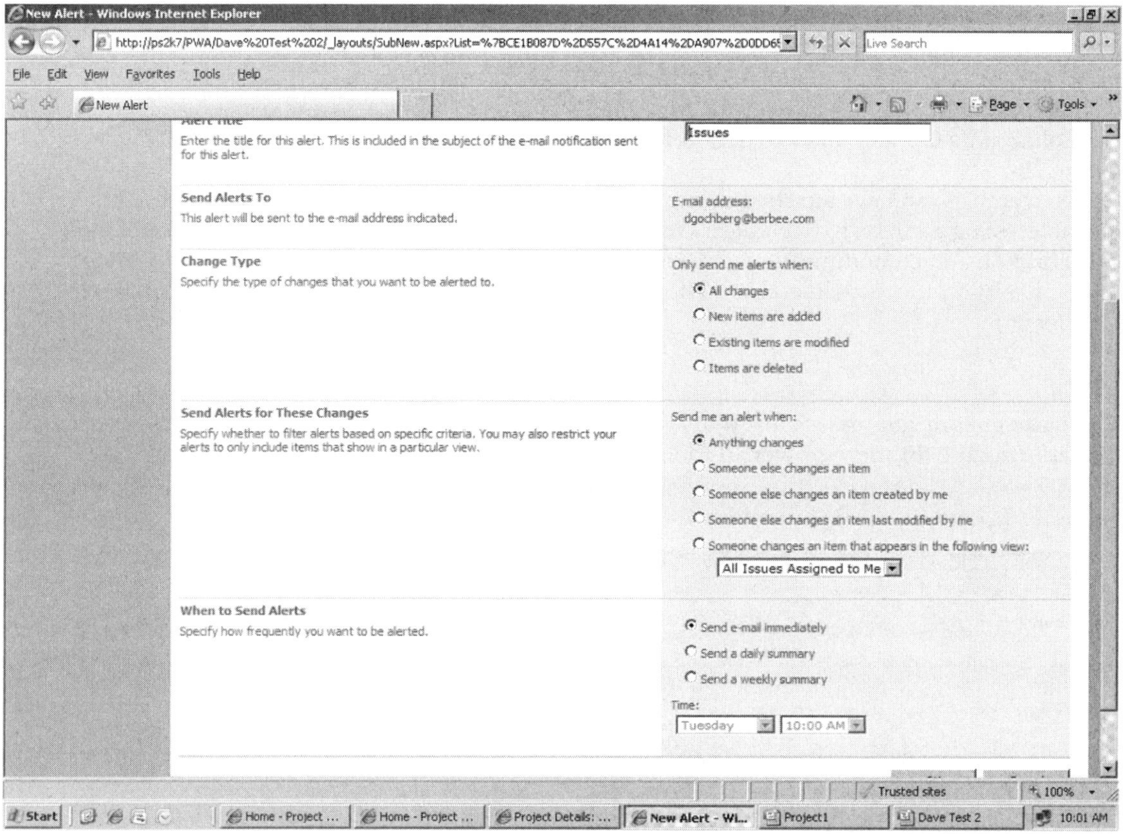

FIGURE 25-6 Setting alerts

Are Modified, and If Items Are Deleted. The next section, Send Alerts for These Changes, enables the user to specify the circumstances under which alerts will be sent. The options are Anything Changes, Someone Else Changes an Item, Someone Else Changes an Item Created by Me, Someone Else Changes an Item Last Modified by Me, and Someone Changes an Item That Appears in the Following View. The section includes a dropdown menu from which the user can pick the view (you'll learn more about views later in this chapter).

Finally, the user can set the frequency and timing of the alerts.

In addition to setting an alert for an entire list or library, a user may want to be notified of a change to a specific item within the list or library. To set an item-level alert, hover over the name of the item until a dropdown arrow appears, select the arrow, and then select Alert Me. This process will limit the alerts to that specific item.

Deliverables

The Deliverables feature provides a vehicle for posting project deliverables in this special list type. Deliverables can be mapped to specific project tasks in the current project. In addition, the contents of this list can be set as loose dependencies (the successor task will not move automatically, but rather an indicator will display when the predecessor is late) for tasks in projects other than the current workspace-connected project (cross-project deliverable dependencies) through the use of the Manage Dependencies on Deliverables option from the Collaborate On menu in Project Professional. Take a look at this Deliverables list in Figure 25-7.

Deliverables can have attached documents and have alerts set. Although this functionality is an interesting addition to the Project Workspace default features, it is not a crucial piece of the collaboration and communications framework. It can, however, be useful for communicating milestones and process deliverables within programs (you'll learn more about this feature in Chapter 26).

Tasks

The Tasks feature comprises a list that is included in the default Project Workspace template. Considering the far more powerful tools available for task management in the PWA and

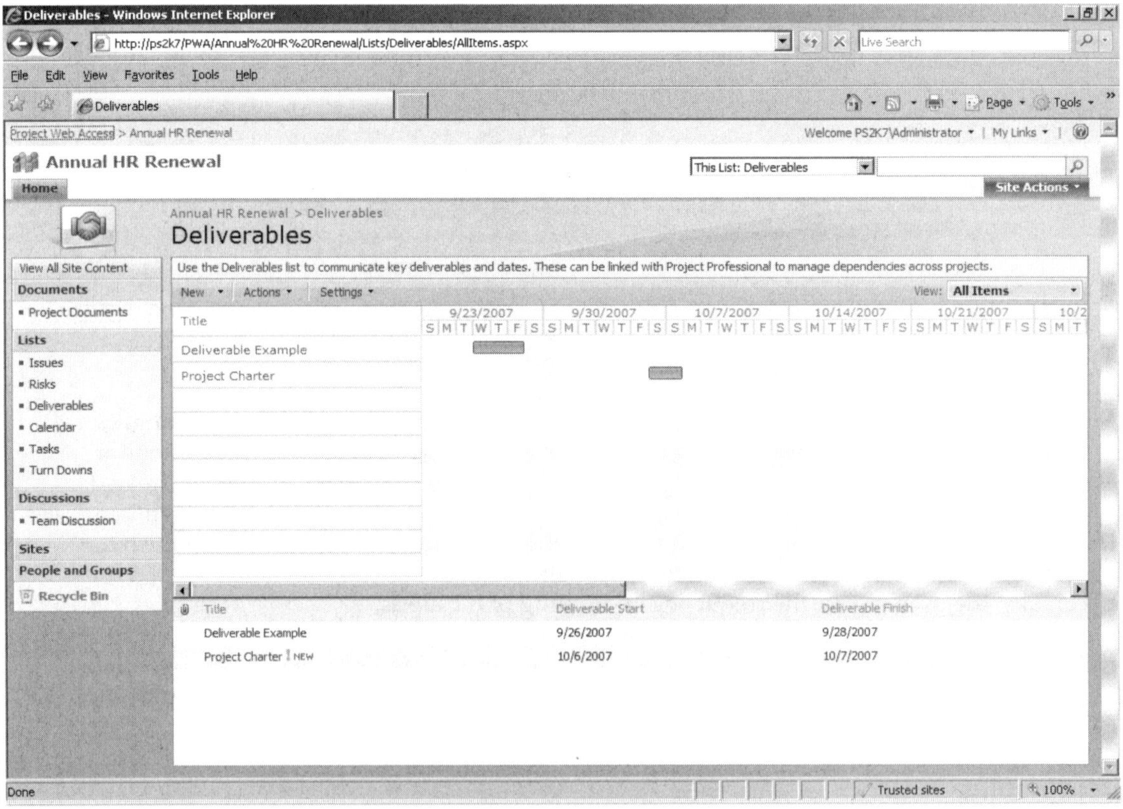

Figure 25-7 Deliverables list

Project Professional areas of the solution, perhaps this should have been more accurately titled the To Do List. The following are the fields in the task list:

- **Title**
- **Priority** The settings are High, Normal, and Low.
- **Status** This field can be set to Not Started, In Progress, Completed, Deferred, or Waiting on Someone Else.
- **% Complete**
- **Assigned to** This field includes name checking.
- **Description** This is a rich text field.
- **Start Date** This field provides a date picker.
- **End Date** This field also offers the date picker.

Documents can be attached, there is a spellchecker, and alerts can be set. One of the best features is that these tasks can be linked to Outlook 2007 tasks.

Announcements

The Announcement list is built into the Project Workspace template. The list's critical use, however, is via the Announcements Web Part that displays on the Project Workspace as shown in Figure 25-8.

Using the Announcements Web Part is often an appropriate and valuable way to communicate to the project team. You can add an announcement directly from the Web Part by selecting the Add New Announcement link. As shown in Figure 25-9, the Title field is used for the main (short version) announcement, a rich text field is provided for detailed information, documents can be attached, and the announcement can be set to expire. That would be a nice feature for at least one of the three announcements shown. See Figure 25-8 for an example of using the expiration setting.

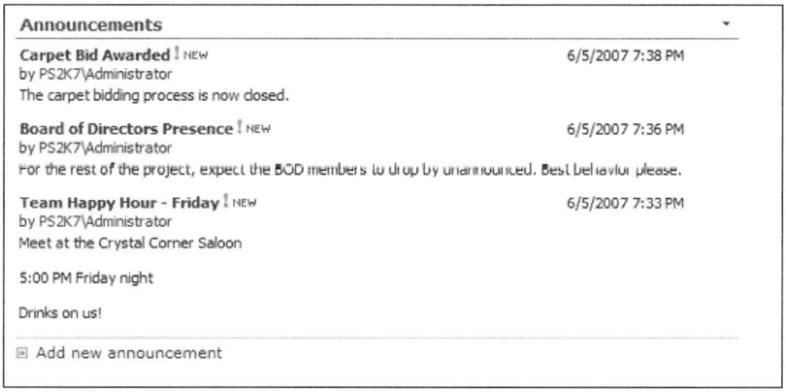

FIGURE 25-8 Announcements Web Part

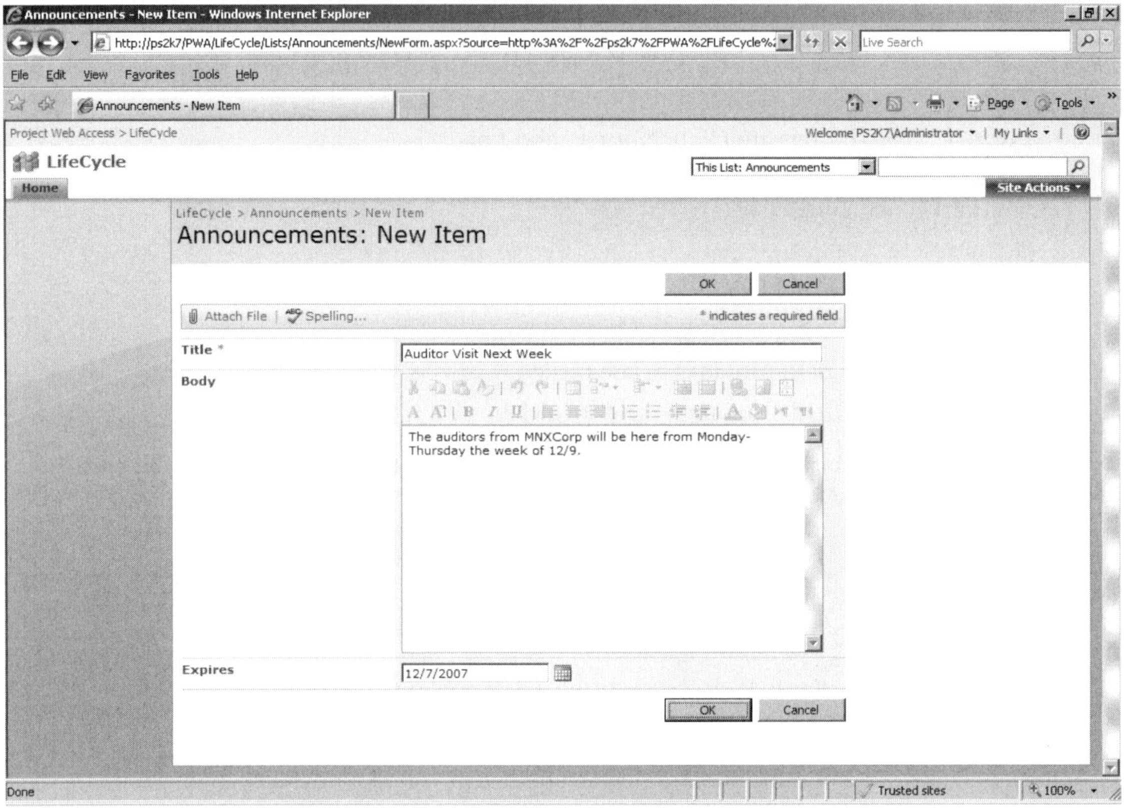

FIGURE 25-9 Creating an Announcement page with content expiration

Announcements can be modified to support versioning and other WSS features (you will learn more about these later in this chapter), but these settings are all usually configured at the most basic level in the default template.

Discussion

Team discussions are built into the template out of the box. This special list type supports threaded or flat discussions and under certain circumstances can be a useful form of nonurgent communication. Figure 25-10 shows an example.

These discussions can be synchronized with Outlook folders, an extremely powerful function to support communications. Because Outlook is open on most users' desktops all day long, this functionality puts the discussion at the fingertips of the user community. At the time of this writing, alerts do not function as expected on discussion lists.

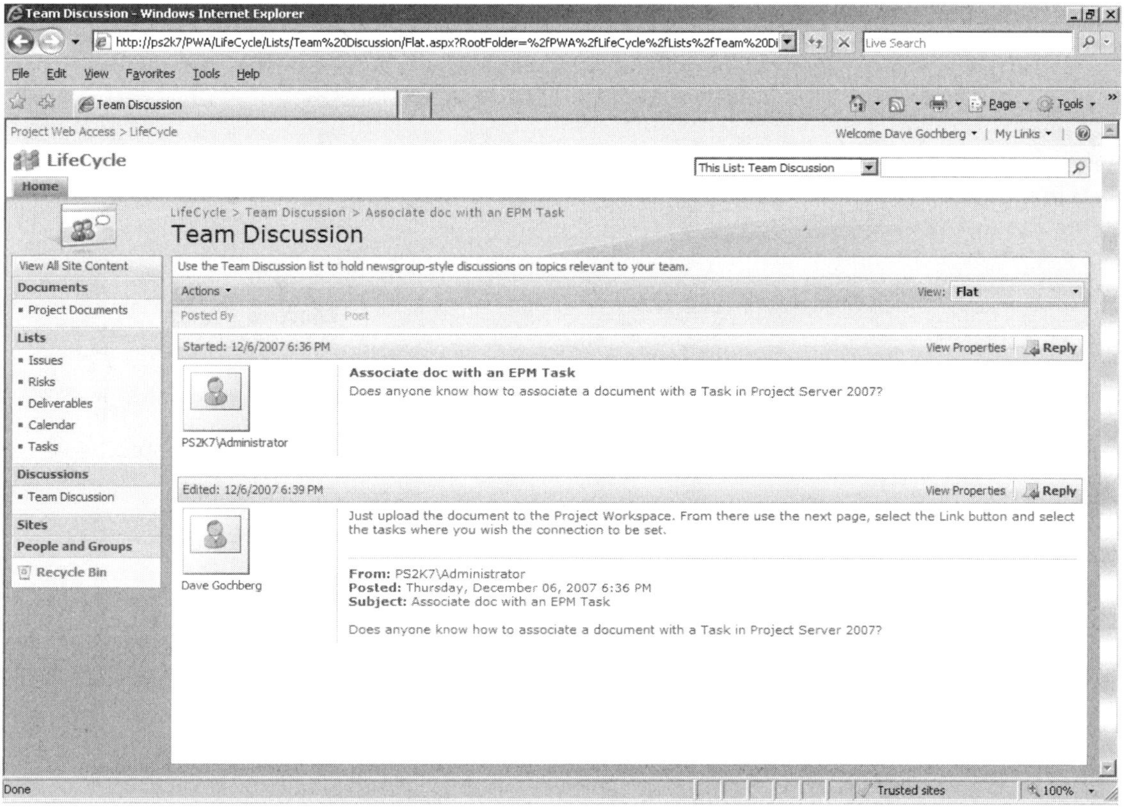

FIGURE 25-10 Discussion board thread

Links

The Links list and its Web Part can be used to give team members easy access to project-specific locations. These can be displayed as plain text rather than in hyperlink format for ease of use. Note that more can be done with this list and Web Part through a custom Project Workspace template. Figure 25-11 shows how the links Web Part displays on the default Project Workspace.

Personal Views

WSS 3.0 allows the possibility for each viewer to establish his or her own personal view. There are controls at the disposal of administrative resources to configure how and where these personal views can be used. Assuming that permissions allow a particular viewer to set a personal view, he or she starts by selecting his or her name as displayed in the top-right

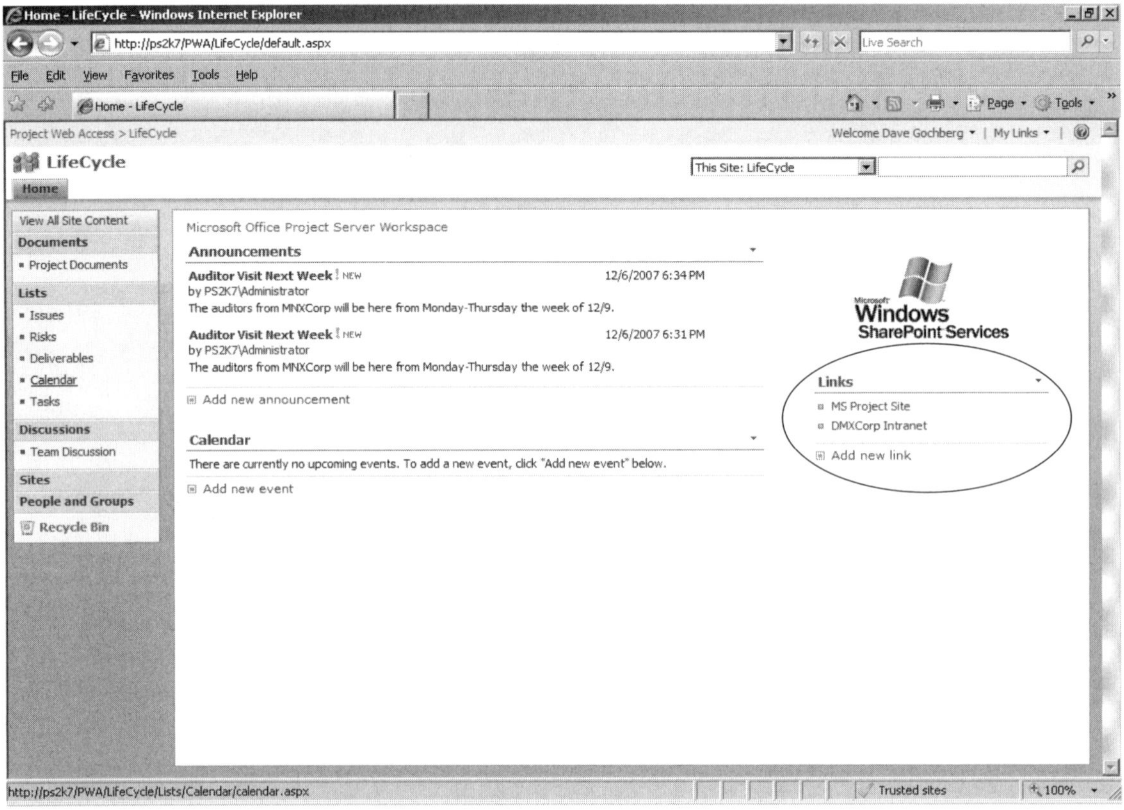

FIGURE 25-11 Links Web Part

corner of the Project Workspace or other WSS site. Next, the user selects the Personalize This Page option as shown in Figure 25-12.

Note that if the user is personalizing a view, the text "Version: You are editing the Personal Version of this page," displays just under the tab (top navigation). It is important to make sure that if the user intends to modify a personal view, it does not display the alternative message, "Version: You are editing the Shared Version of this page." The Shared Version of the page is the one that affects all users who have access to the page, so be careful to understand what you are editing. Using personal views allows viewers to control such customizations as which Web Parts are displayed and how they display specifically. The following section provides more detail on how these customizations can be made.

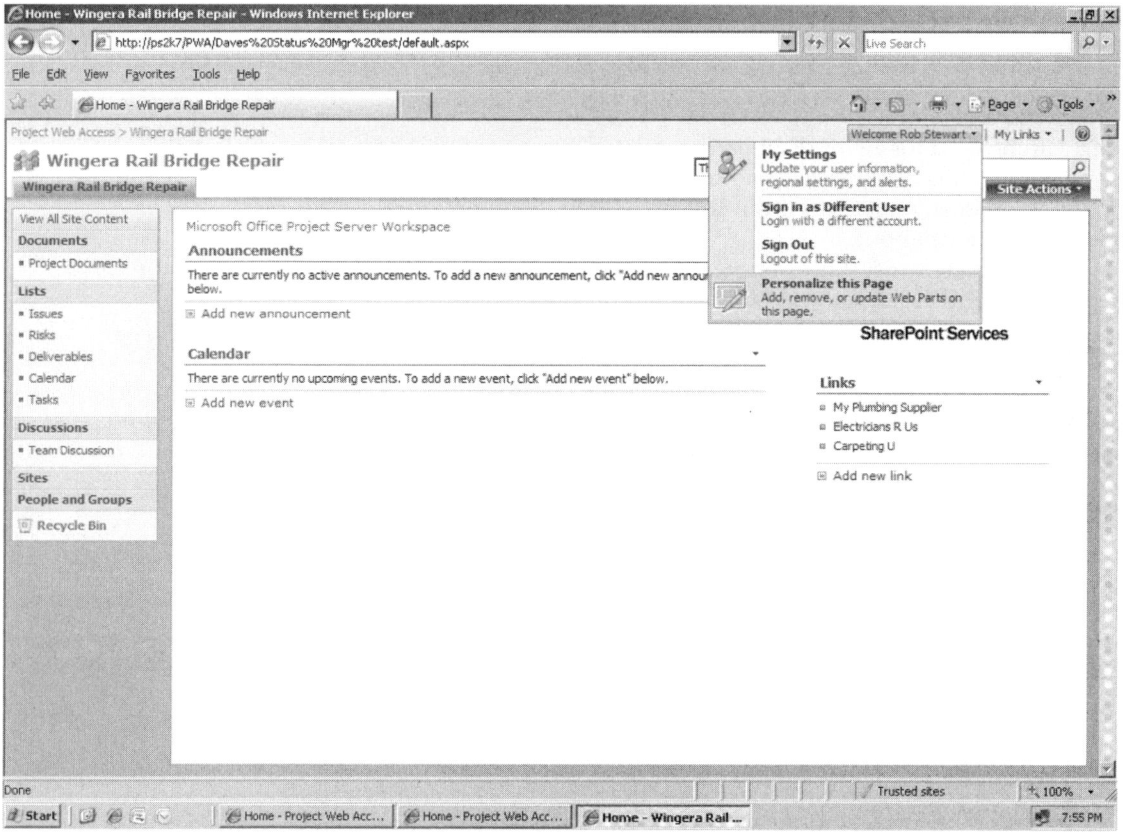

FIGURE 25-12 Personalize This Page option from Welcome dropdown list

Extending the Environment

The supporting WSS 3.0 platform can be extended in many ways. In this section, discussion will focus on some of them—modifying individual sites and pages, customizing the Project Workspace, building a project management center of excellence, and finally, leveraging the power of Project Server in a MOSS 2007 environment.

Modifying a Site

There are many ways to modify a Project Workspace. Take care, however, when working with the following components, as it is possible to break all or some of the parts of the functionality as applied to Project Server:

- Issues
- Risks

- Deliverables
- Project documents

Creating a List

Lists can be used for all kinds of project-related uses, such as change requests, travel requests, meeting agendas and minutes, and new project requests, as described earlier in the book. As seen with the built-in lists, they are a combination of a form and a view or views of the form input.

To create a new list (for example, Meeting Minutes), select Site Actions from the top-right and then select Create, as shown in Figure 25-13.

Next select Custom List from the Custom Lists section of the page. Then name the list (Meeting Minutes). There is an option to display this list on the Quick Launch Bar, with radio buttons for Yes or No. Remember that the Quick Launch Bar is the left-side navigation. If Yes is selected, the Meeting Minutes item will display on the Quick Launch Bar throughout the site. When you are ready to proceed, select Create.

This action creates the new list with only the Title field. Note that the Title field is required. The process then creates the following fields for a basic Meeting Notes list:

- Date of Meeting
- Attendees
- Topics
- Meeting Content
- To-Dos and Assignments
- Next Meeting Date

To create the form, you must create columns. To start, select Settings | Create Column and then create the first column as shown in Figure 25-14.

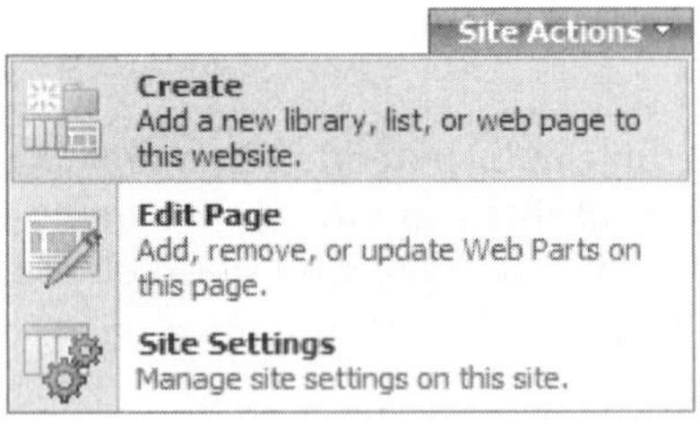

FIGURE 25-13 Site Actions menu and the Create option

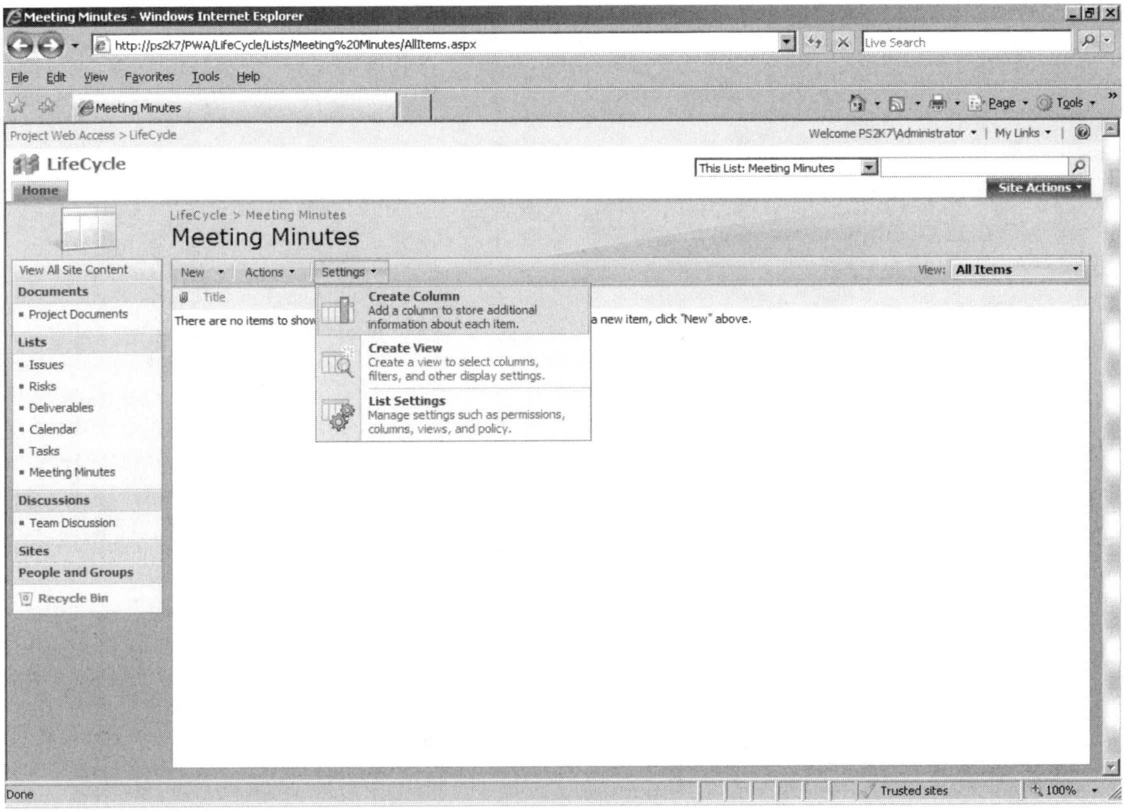

FIGURE 25-14 Settings menu and the Create Column option

Date of Meeting Following the preceding field list, name the column Date of Meeting. Then select Date and Time as shown in Figure 25-15.

Type a description if you like. This description will display next to the field to assist users in understanding the purpose of the field or what content is expected. Using the radio buttons, choose whether the field is to be required (for this example, it is). Decide whether to use Date Only or Date and Time (Date Only is selected in Figure 25-16) and make the appropriate selection. The next step is to decide whether to use a default for this field. In this case, the list will use Today's Date. Finally, decide whether to add to this column

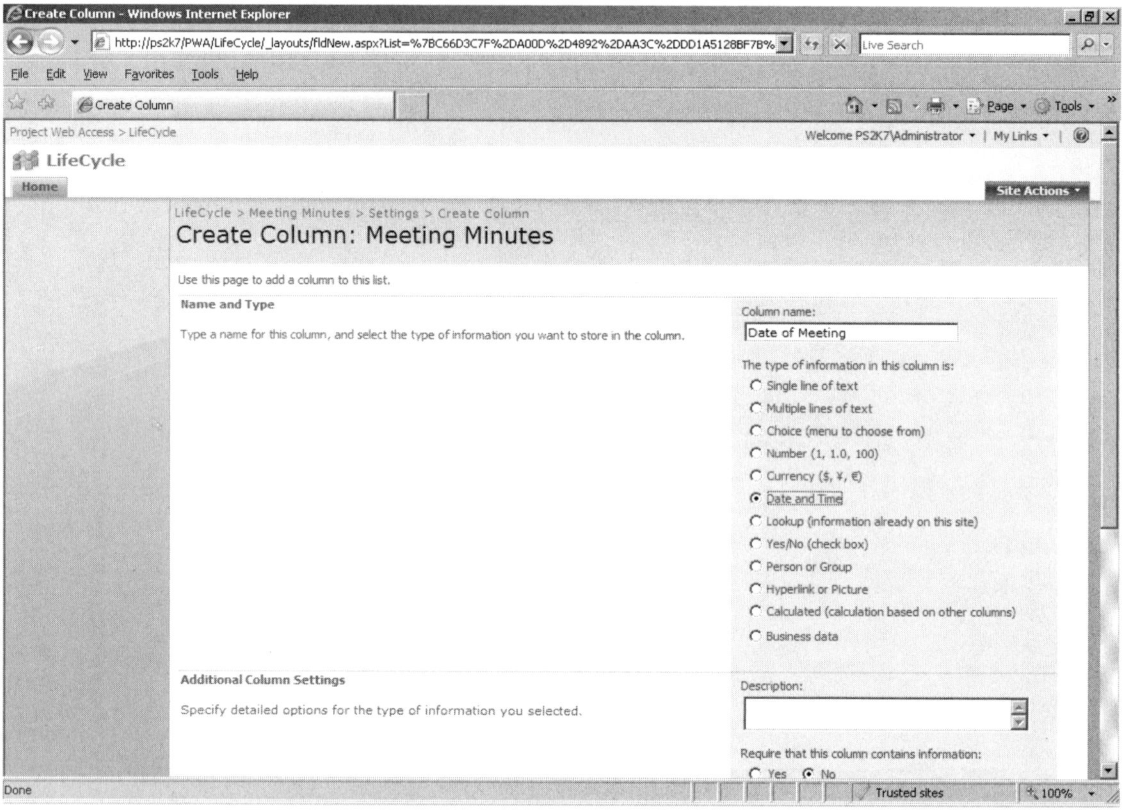

FIGURE 25-15 Selecting the Date and Time field type

default the view. The default view is the one that shows the items that users have added by using the form. In this example, that means that each meeting will appear on a list or view and each item in that view will hold minutes from a single meeting. So the question then is whether the meeting date should be displayed on that view. In this case, the right answer is almost certainly yes. Figure 25-16 shows how this page looks while you are building the column. Then when you are ready, select OK.

From this point the process repeats using different field types.

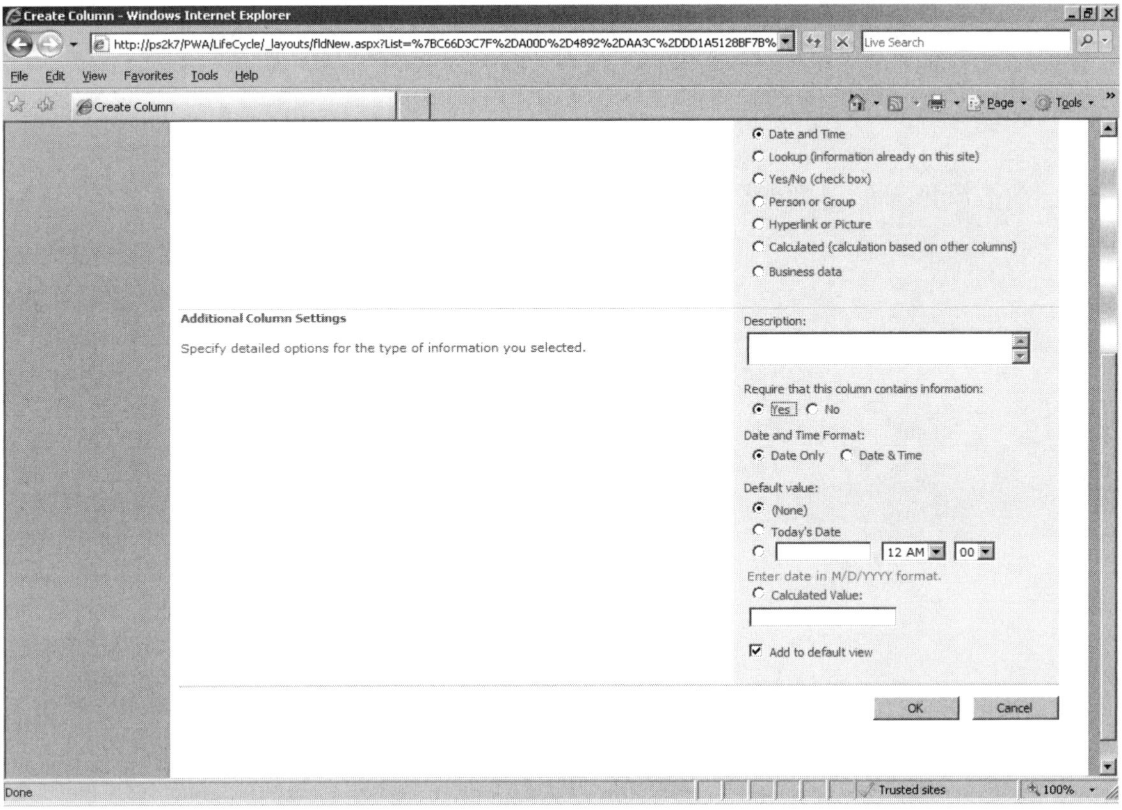

FIGURE 25-16 Bottom half of the Create Column page

Attendees For this field, once again select Settings | Create Column. Then enter the name Attendees and select Person or Group from the radio buttons. Type a description if necessary. For the field Require That This Column Contains Information, choose Yes, and for the field Multiple Selections, choose Yes. For the Allow Selection Of field, select People Only. In the Choose From field, All Users, and in the Show Field setting, select Name (or Name with Presence if you are using any presence-aware applications). Deselect the Add to Default View option, then finally click OK. Figure 25-17 shows these settings.

Topics Once again, start with Create Column. Enter the title, (Topics) then in the field The Type of Information in This Column Is, select Multiple Lines of Text. Add a description and

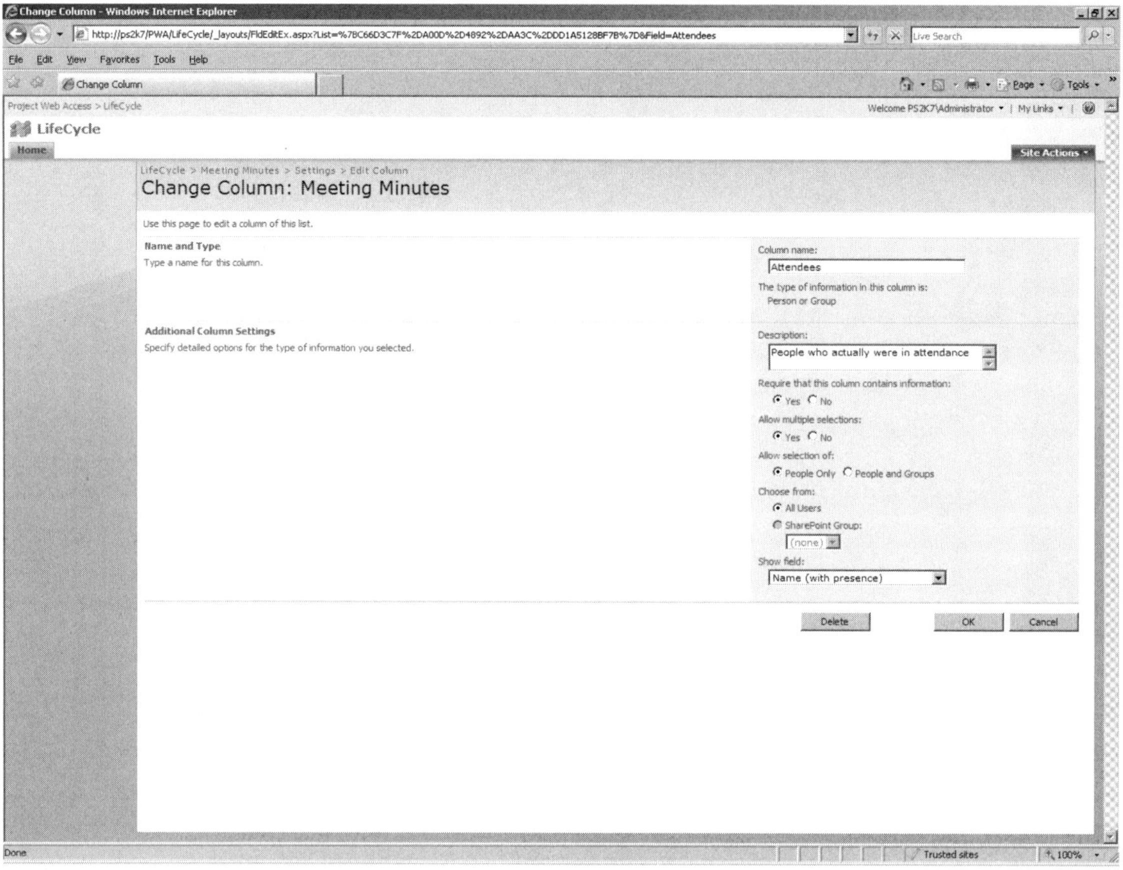

FIGURE 25-17 Creating the Attendees column

decide how many lines should be displayed. (Note that if the contents exceed the number of lines, a scroll bar appears and the field will allow more content than will fit in the preset number.) Select Rich Text from the next set of options. Decide whether to use appending or not, then choose whether to display the field in the Default View. When you are finished, select OK. Figure 25-18 shows these settings in the Create Column form builder tool.

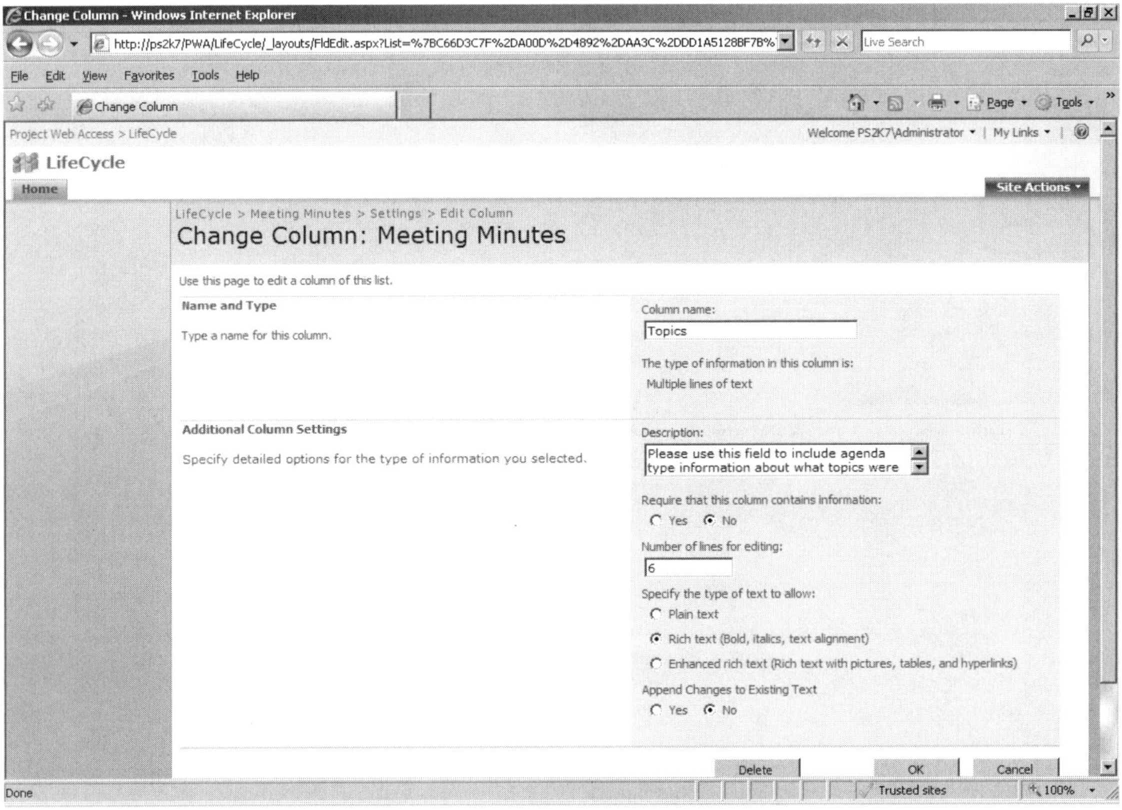

FIGURE 25-18 Create Topics column

Meeting Content Meeting Content is also a Multiple Lines of Text field; you set it following the same process previously described. Notice in Figure 25-19 that for Meeting Content you are not entering anything in the Description field.

To-Dos and Assignments Use the same settings as for the preceding list, only use a different title.

Next Meeting Date Create this Date and Time field the same way as the Date of Meeting field. In this case, however, include the time of the next meeting and do not make it required (see Figure 25-20).

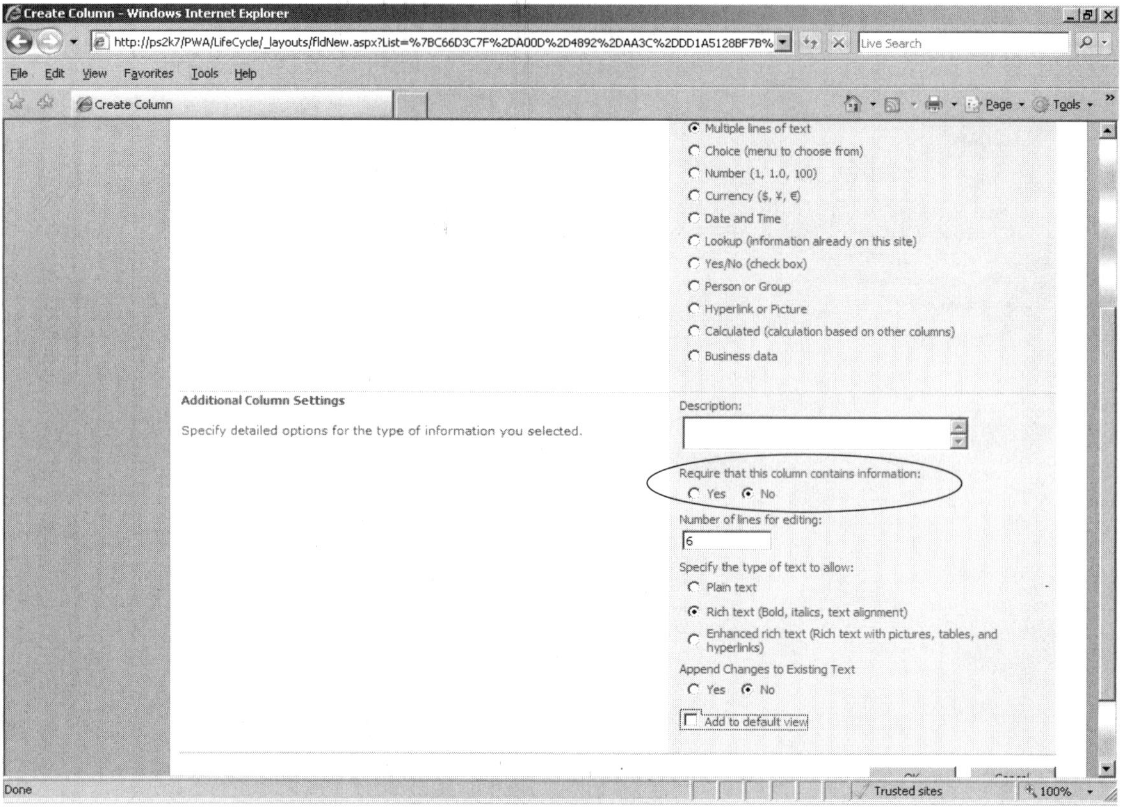

Figure 25-19 Meeting Content column

Completed Form The completed form is shown in Figure 25-21.

The next thing is to examine how the user completes this list form. Most of the fields are pretty obvious, but not all of them. Enter the short description or title in the Title field. Set the date or use the prefilled default of the current date.

Populate the Attendees field. Note that name checking is part of this, so users don't just type in Liz or Jo Ellen. If the attendee's Windows login is known, this can be entered manually. If you select the icon shown in Figure 25-22 with the head and checkmark, the name will be validated (or not). Using this process, the login name must match the attendee's name exactly.

The other way to add an attendee is to use the lookup tool by selecting the icon that looks like a book (see Figure 25-23). Select the magnifying glass icon then type in a name.

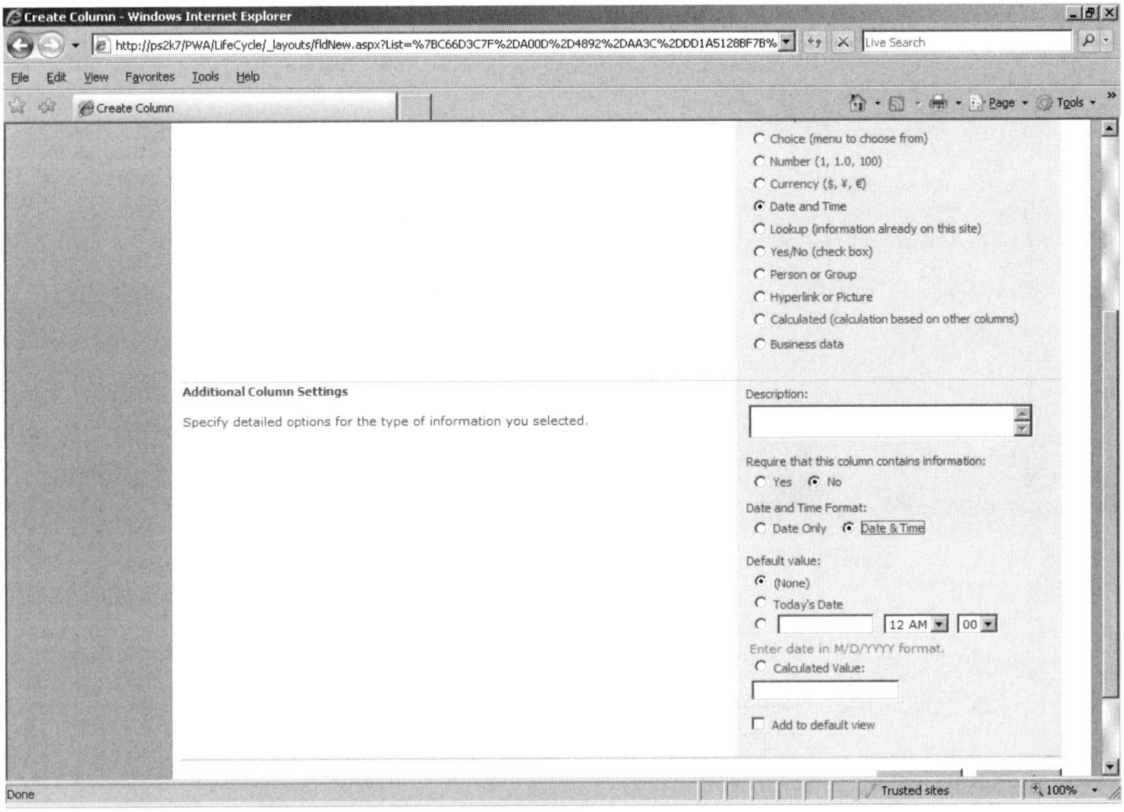

FIGURE 25-20 Next Meeting column

If the process finds the name, highlight it and select the Add button. Follow the same process and keep adding names until the Attendees list is complete. Figure 25-24 shows the dialog used for selecting resources using the lookup functionality just described. This is the way that all people lookups work in WSS.

Complete the rest of the form as appropriate. Figure 25-25 shows the completed form. Note that a document can be attached and spellcheck is available from the top bar.

Another More Complex Form That was a simple list. Following is a more complex list that will be used as the basis for different custom views later in this chapter.

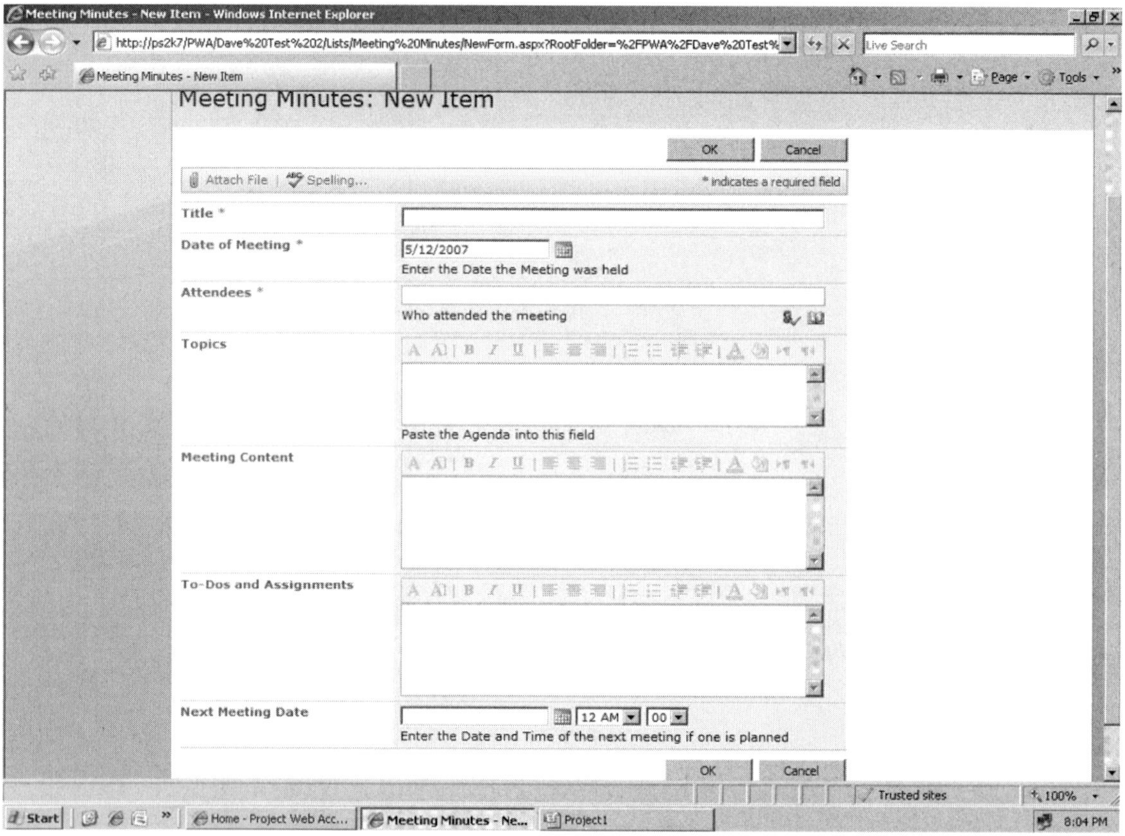

FIGURE 25-21 Completed new list form

This list is used to manage change requests. The list will include the following:

- Title (name of request)
- Date required
- Requestor
- Change type
- Reason for request
- Detailed description

FIGURE 25-22 Check Names icon

FIGURE 25-23 Lookup button

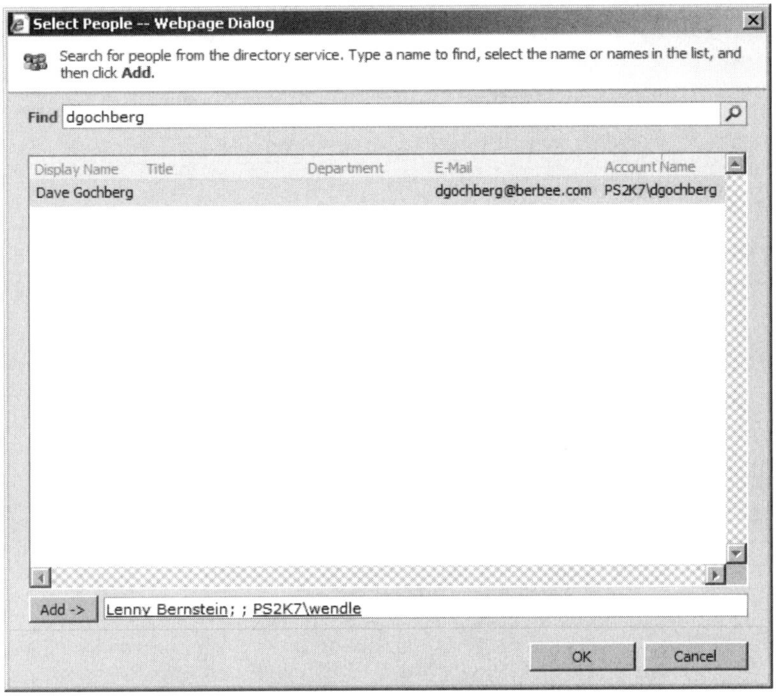

FIGURE 25-24 Select People dialog

- Expected result of not changing
- Assessment approved by
- Estimated cost of assessment
- Assessor
- Results of assessment
- Cost impact
- Functional impact
- Technical impact
- Schedule impact
- Recommendations
- Request approved?
- Sponsor approval date
- Sponsor name

PART V

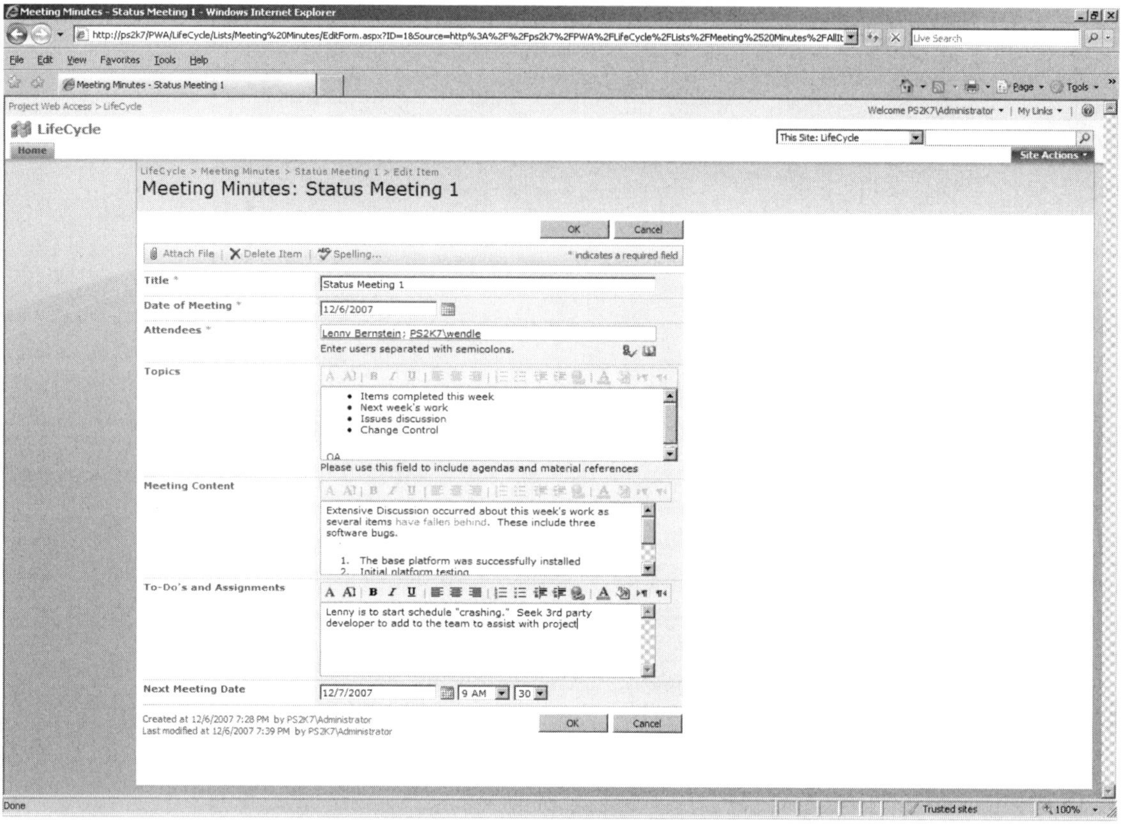

FIGURE 25-25 Completed Meeting Form

Let's see how to build such a list. Remember that this list can use whatever change management process is in place for a specific company. To start, once again select Site Actions | Create | Custom List, name the list, and select Save.

Title (Name of Request) This is the built-in Title field; just use it as is. This can hold the name of the request. Next follow the new column process as described previously.

Date Required Select the Date and Time field type and add a description if needed. Next choose whether to use the date and time or just the date and decide whether the field is required. Decide where there should be a default, perhaps today's date. Finally set the Add to Default View option as desired. Figure 25-26 shows the way the authors would set this up.

Requestor Using the Person or Group type, set the Person or Group to Person only. Next decide whether the field should allow multiple selections and whether it should be required. Select the field to show Name or Name with Presence. Choose whether to set to display in default view and select OK.

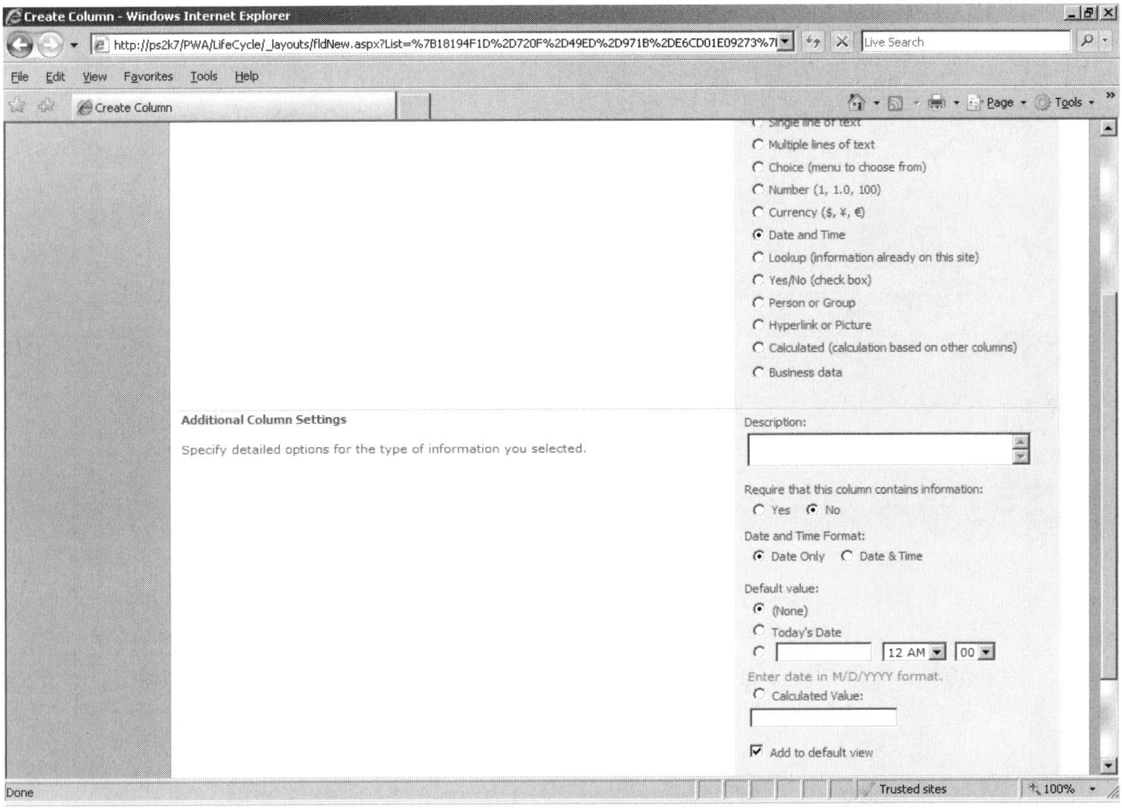

Figure 25-26 Date Required column setup

Type of Change Keeping in mind that this list is just an example, create this new column. This list will use the Choice field type. Once the Choice type has been selected, the screen will change slightly for the appropriate options. In this case, the intent is to build a multiselect set of checkboxes. To do that, enter the choices that are available in the Type Each Choice on a Separate Line section of the screen. Type the options required, in this case Scope, Cost, Schedule, and Quality.

From this point, use the radio buttons to choose Checkboxes (Allow Multiple Selections). Decide whether to allow choices other than those in the form and choose a default option. Note that a form always has a default option unless the person building the form manually deletes the one that prefills the screen. Do not choose to display this field in default view as the multiselect can be a mess in a List View. Finally select OK. See Figure 25-27 for the completed column settings.

Reason for Request Select the Multiple Lines of Text type. Then choose the options that fit the requirements best (the form is self-explanatory).

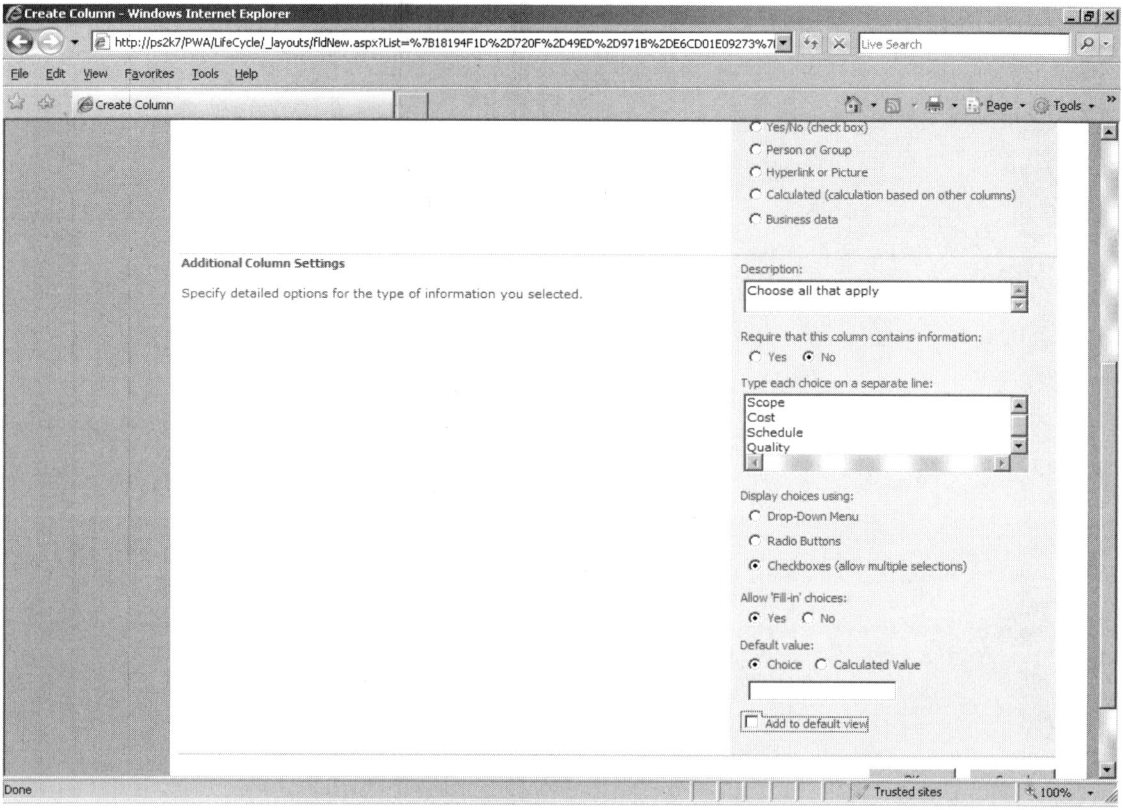

Figure 25-27 Type of Change column settings

Detailed Description Select the Multiple Lines of Text type. Then choose the options that fit the requirements best (the form is self-explanatory).

Expected Result of Not Changing Select the Multiple Lines of Text type. Then choose the options that fit the requirements best (the form is self-explanatory).

Assessment Approved By Use the Person or Group type and set it to Person only. Don't make it required, as it is unknown at the time that the form is first created. Also, it is probably not a good idea from a general project management maturity perspective to allow multiple selections. Decide whether to display in the default view and select OK.

Est. Cost of Assessment Select Currency as the field type. In addition to including the usual fields, this field type also provides fields for setting the minimum and maximum range, the number of decimal places, and the currency format. See the Currency dropdown list in Figure 25-28.

FIGURE 25-28 Currency dropdown

Assessor Use the Person or Group type for this. This represents the person who is charged with reviewing the request, researching impact, and providing a recommendation as to whether the request should be accepted.

Results of Assessment The assessor will provide the overall results in this Multiple Lines of Text field. More detailed results follow in the next few fields.

Cost Impact This field uses the Currency type and is used to record how much the change will cost if executed.

Functional Impact There are several ways to approach this type of field. In this case, we use a Choice field with dropdown menu for High, Medium, or Low Impact.

Tech Impact This field uses the same type of field as for Functional Impact.

Schedule Impact This field also uses the same type of field as for Functional Impact.

Recommendations This could be a text field, but instead this example uses a Choice field. The options available are as follows:

- Approve the Change
- Deny the Change
- More Information Required

Request Approved? This field could use either the Yes/No or a choice field type. In this case, the Choice field was chosen include a Decision Pending option.

Sponsor Approval Date This field uses a simple Date field type.

Sponsor Name Finally, the Sponsor Name field is a Person or Group field set to Person Only. Figure 25-29 shows the top half of the completed form.

After completing the form and saving it, items that were set to display in default view will appear as shown in Figure 25-30. Other items require the user to drill down by hovering the cursor over the name of the item and selecting Edit Item from the available options.

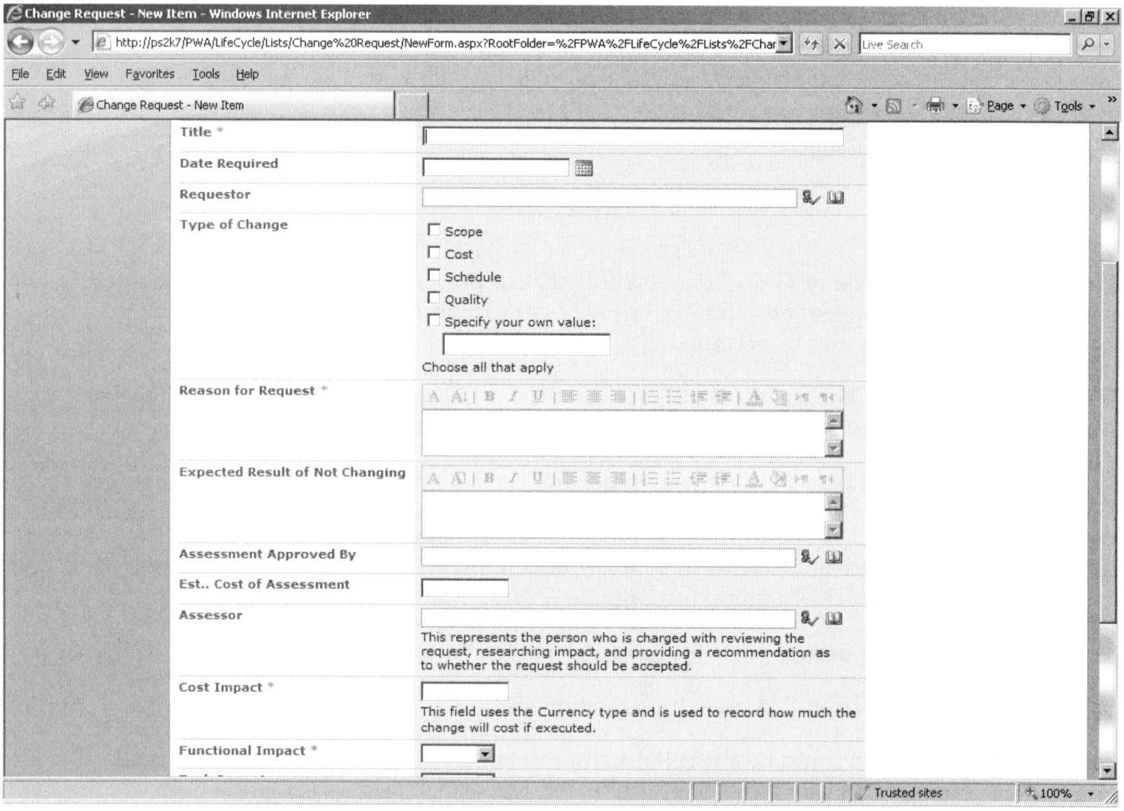

FIGURE 25-29 Change Requests form

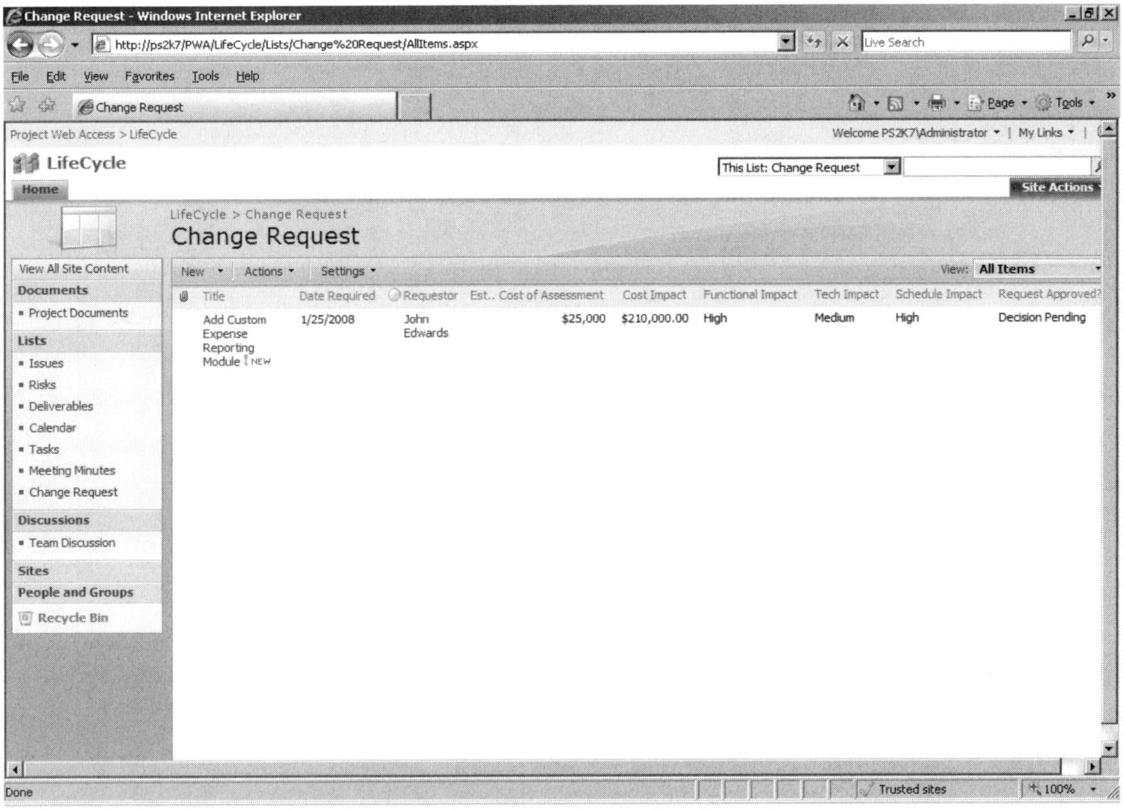

FIGURE 25-30 Default All Items view

Creating a View

One of the great features of WSS is the ability to use the data gathered in libraries and lists to view only specific subsets of that information. It is of great use in the standard lists such as a view like All Issues Assigned to Me.

Using the example of the Change Request described previously, this section describes how to create custom views in WSS 3.0 and particularly in the Project Workspaces. Start by navigating to the list itself, in this case the Change Request list. Next select Settings | Create View as shown in Figure 25-31.

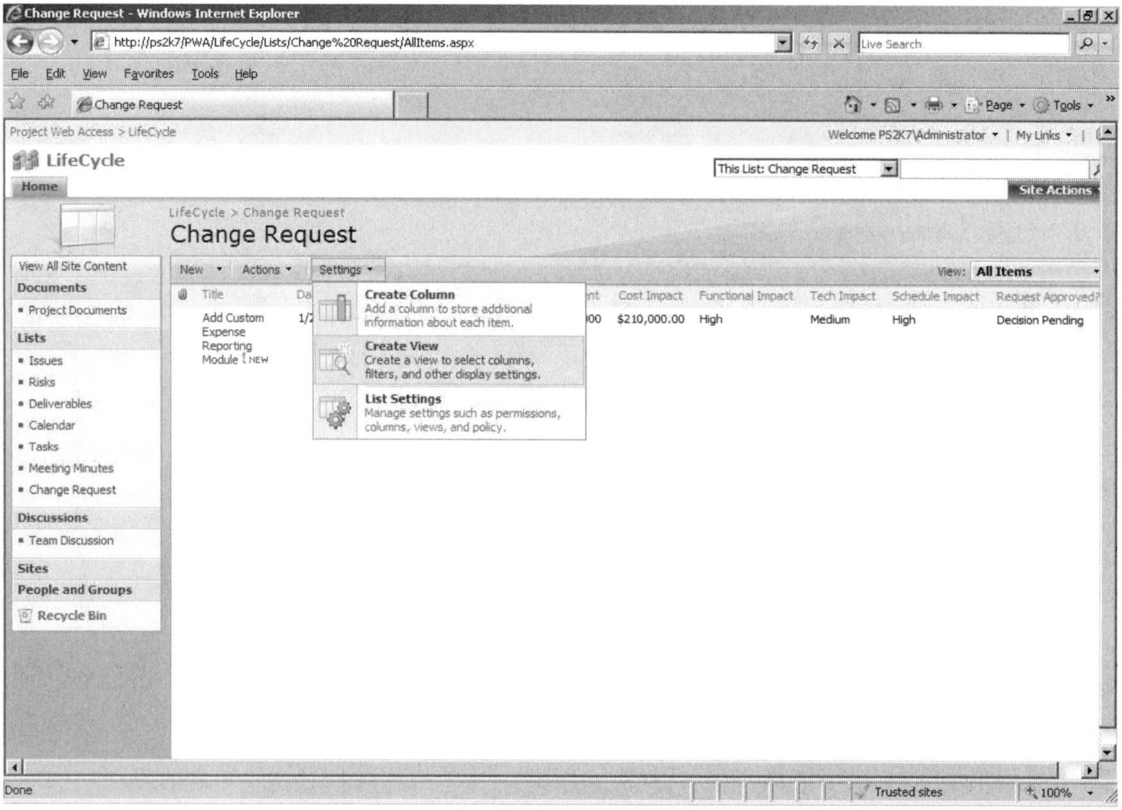

FIGURE 25-31 Create View option

There are other ways to navigate to Create View. One is to select the dropdown list on the top-right that by default displays All Items and then click Create View. Another way is to create a view from the List Settings page that can be found by selecting Settings | List Settings. Whichever way was used for navigation, the result will be a page that looks like Figure 25-32.

Select a view format. Usually, the Standard View is best. Next give the new view a name. Decide whether the view is to be set as the default view. In most cases, it makes sense to leave the default view at the All Items settings.

If settings allow, individual users could create a Personal View, but for now the focus will stay global (Public View). The next step is to select which fields to display in the view. All available fields will be on the list, including those that were part of the creation of columns

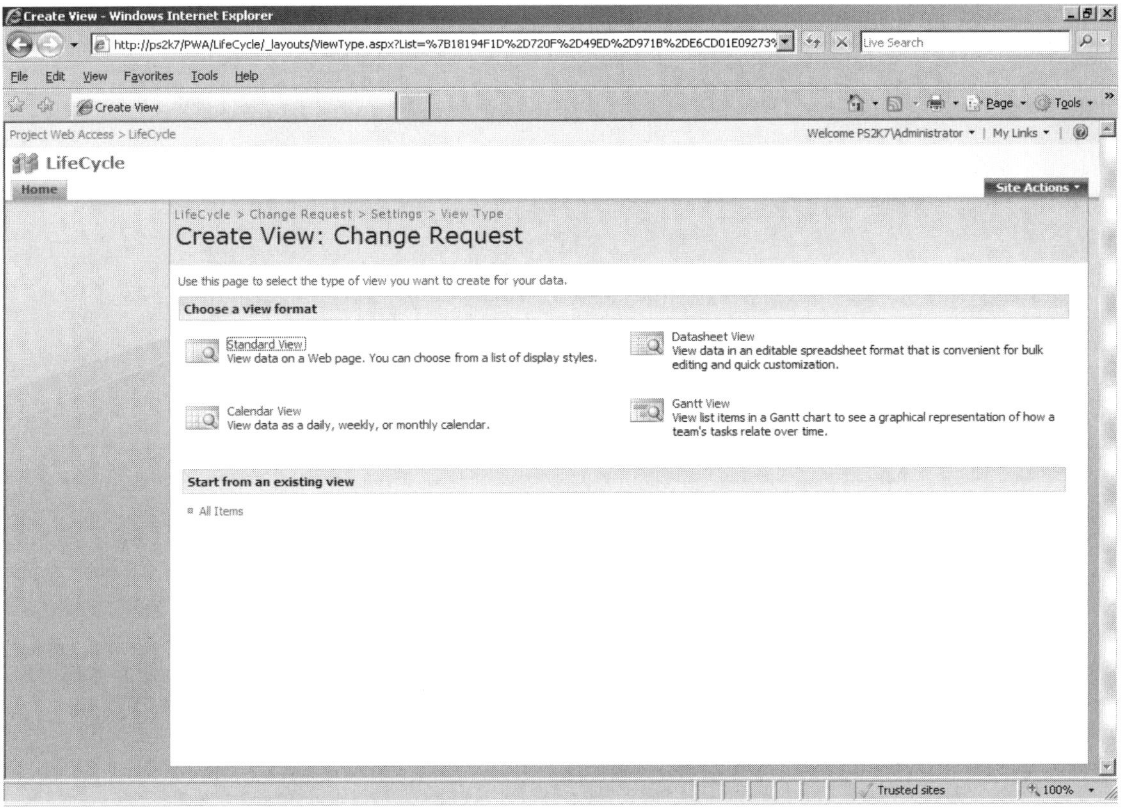

FIGURE 25-32 Create View page

done for the form and out-of-the-box fields such as Created By. Figure 25-33 shows how that appears in the tool.

Use the checkboxes to decide the fields that are appropriate, and use the dropdowns to the right of the field names to set the order in which the fields should appear. In this example, the new view is called the Cost Impact View. The idea is to make a view that displays only those forms that include a cost impact and to sort those by cost. To build this view, use the Sorting feature to sort by the Cost Impact field as shown in Figure 25-34.

Also notice that the view is being filtered so that if the Cost Impact field is left blank, that particular item will not display in the view. There are an amazing number of options available when creating a view that are not detailed (that detail is in someone's SharePoint book), but they include the ability to group list items, keep totals for configurable criteria,

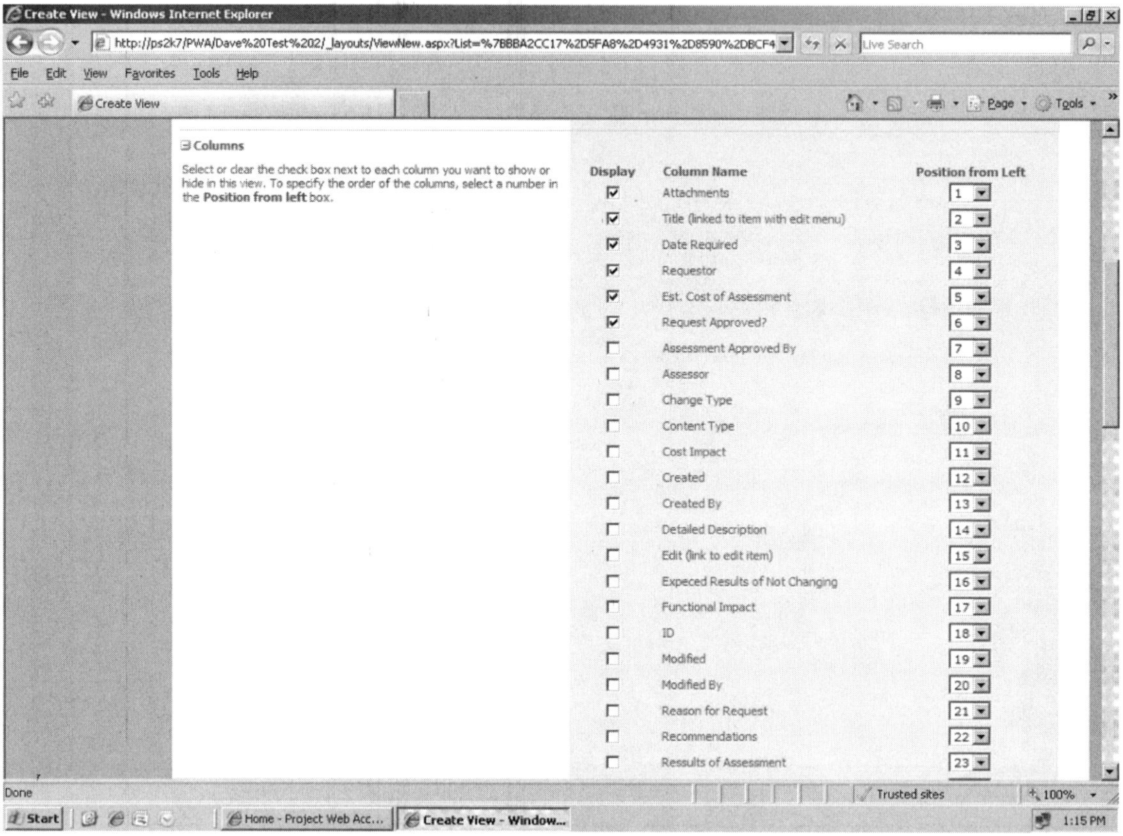

FIGURE 25-33 Create View fields to display

change styles (shaded is attractive for this type of use), view with or without folders, place a limit on the number of items, and even to make the view available via mobile devices.

Adding Web Parts (and Removing Them)

One of the best features of the SharePoint platform is how easy it is to change the types of data displayed on a page. Keep in mind that in a Project Server environment, all these SharePoint features are available even inside of PWA. The little boxes that are within the body of Project Workspaces are called Web Parts. These are similar to what other technologies call portlets or modules. If permissions allow, these can be added and removed easily, as the following description indicates.

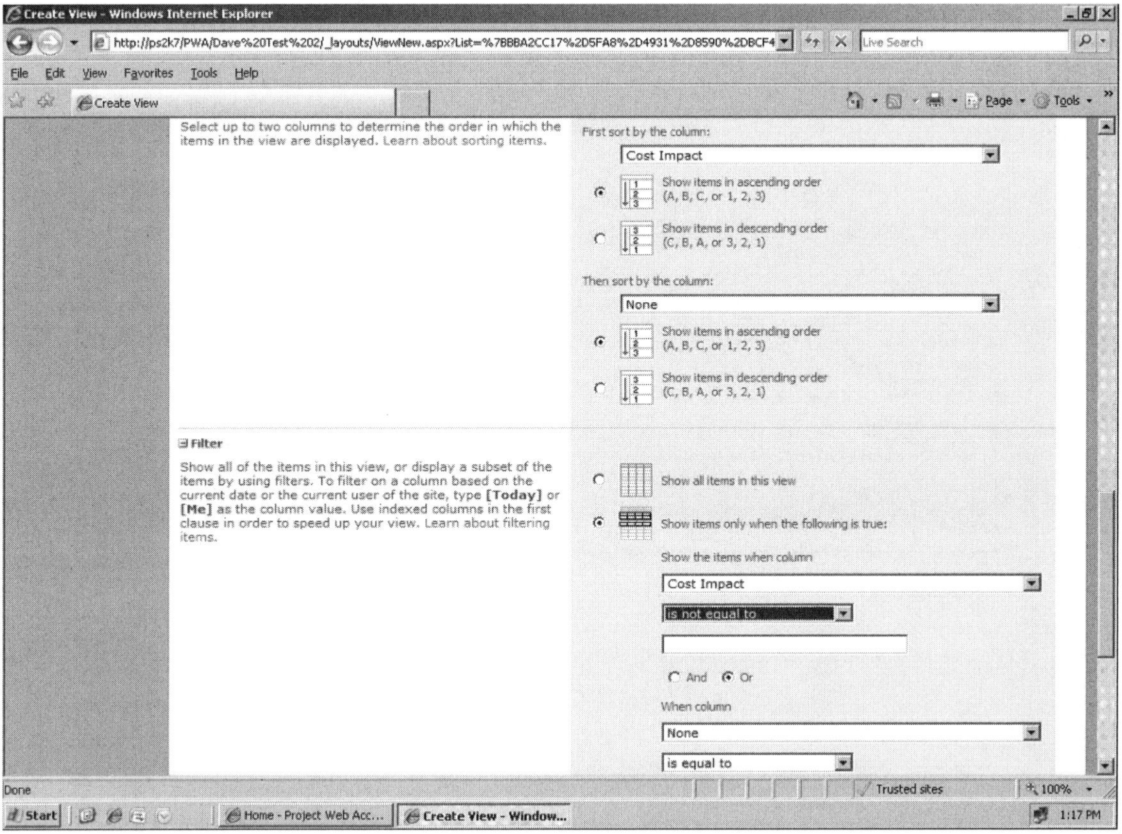

FIGURE 25-34 Sorting and filtering

You can start at the Home Page of any Project Workspace. Next select Site Actions (from the top-right menu), then Edit Page. The result will appear as shown in Figure 25-35.

As noted earlier, the Calendar Web Part is a candidate for removal. Just click on the X in the top-right corner of the Calendar Web Part, then select Exit Edit Mode to remove the Web Part for all users.

To add a Web Part, once again select Site Actions | Edit Page | Add a Web Part (see Figure 25-36).

The next dialog lists all the available Web Parts. Select one or more of them and then select Add. The Web Part(s) then appear on the page, still in Edit mode. The Web Parts can be moved, by dragging them to the location desired. Note that when a Web Part is in a

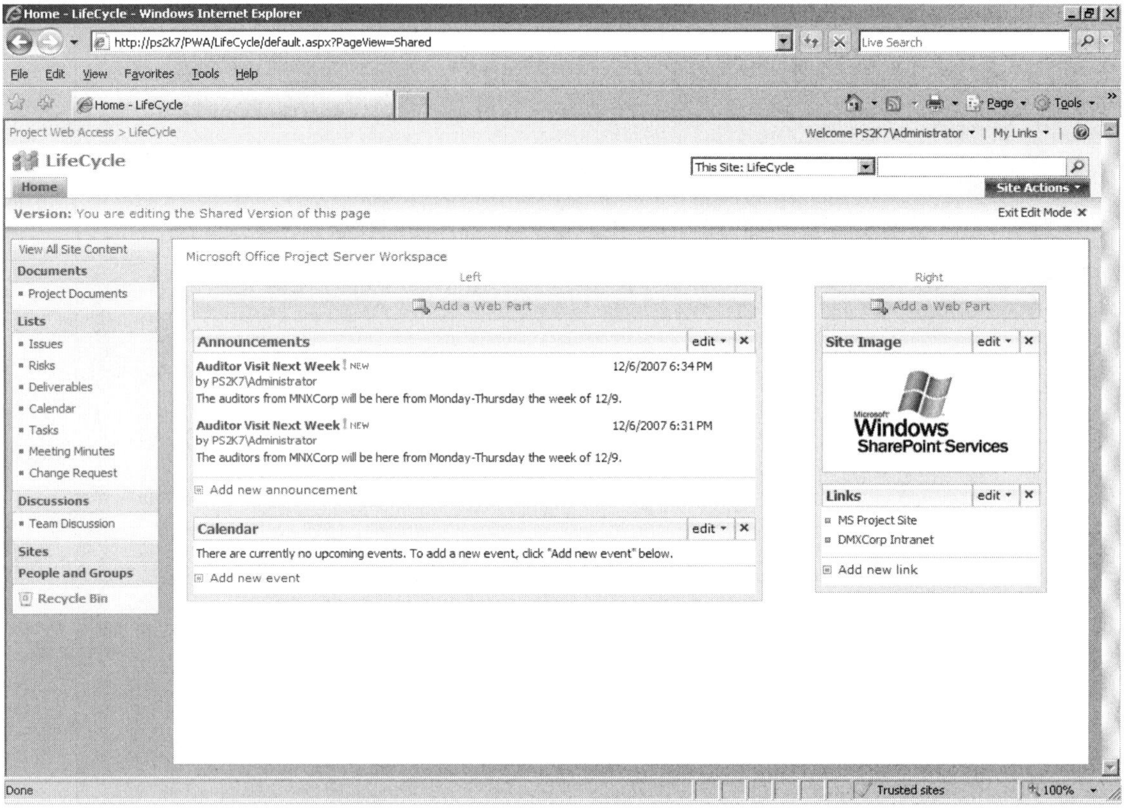

FIGURE 25-35 Home Page in Edit mode

position to drop into the desired spot, a red line appears. Be aware that there are some great Web Parts out of the box with Project Server. Other Web Parts can be added. They can be found from Microsoft and third-party sources. In addition, custom-developed Web Parts can provide stunning solutions. There is a discussion about dashboards using Project Server and other Web Parts in Chapter 24.

FIGURE 25-36 Add a Web Part bar

Modifying a Web Part

Web Parts each have tools to allow for modification. These modifications include some that are standard across all Web Parts, as well as configuration for some specific Web Parts. To modify a Web Part, select the small dropdown arrow at the top-right corner of the Web Part that you want to modify. Then select Modify Shared Web Part, as shown in Figure 25-37.

Choosing this option opens a tool pane on the right side of the screen. In this pane, you can see view options if there are multiple views from which to choose. The next option is to set a toolbar type. Figures 25-38 and 25-39 show examples of how this setting can work.

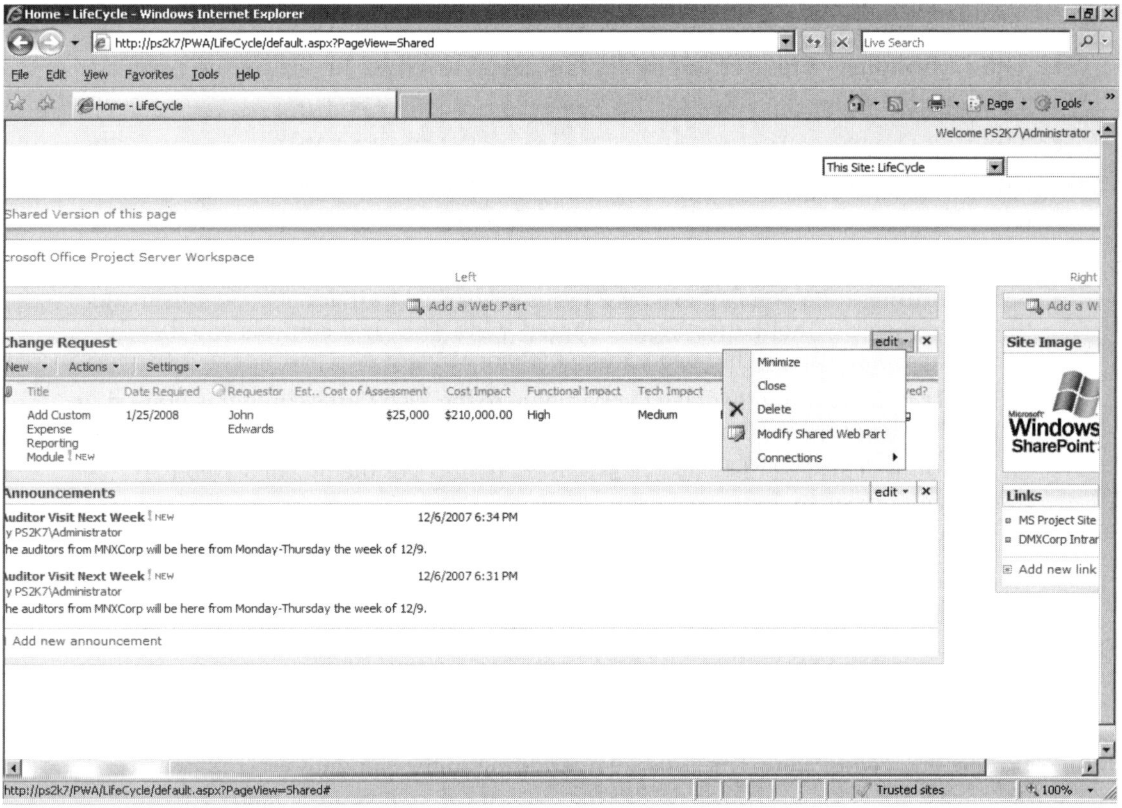

FIGURE 25-37 Modifying a Web Part navigation

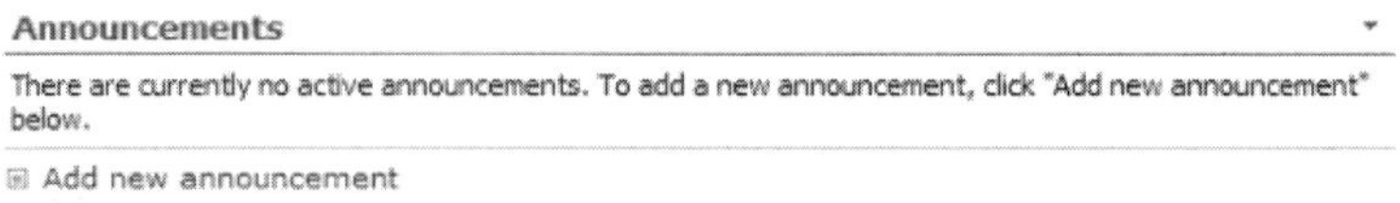

FIGURE 25-38 Summary toolbar

The next section is Appearance. From this part of the tool pane, you can set height and width. The Chrome type is the border and labeling of the Web Part. Layout includes controls for direction, zone (columns on page), and zone index (where in the zone order the Web Part appears when there are multiple Web Parts).

In the Advanced section, the following fields can be modified:

- **Allow Minimize** This setting enables the viewer to reduce the size of the Web Part.
- **Allow Close** This field enables the viewer to close the Web Part.
- **Allow Hide** This setting enables the viewer to hide the Web Part.
- **Allow Zone Change** This field determines whether the Web Part can be relocated to a different part of the page.
- **Allow Connections** This setting allows connections to the Internet.
- **Allow Editing in Personal View** As discussed earlier, individual users can create their own views without affecting the Shared View. This field controls whether the specific Web Part can be changed within a Personal View.
- **Title URL** This setting displays the path where the Web Part's content is housed. It is usually a bad idea to change this setting.
- **Description** This text displays when a user hovers over the title of a Web Part, much like a classic tooltip.
- **Help URL** This field provides a path to the help if any exists.
- **Help Mode** This field offers Modeless, Modal, or Navigate options.
- **Catalog Icon Image URL** This setting is used for the icon that appears next to the name of the Web Part in the Web Part list.
- **Title Icon Image URL** This field can be used to place a small graphic next to the title of the Web Part.
- **Import Error Message** This field allows editing of the standard error message.
- **Target Audiences** By selecting a group using this name-checker field, you can target the Web Part toward a specific audience.

FIGURE 25-39 Full toolbar

Using the Web Parts Available from Project Server and WSS

Web Parts are used to display data that actually reside in a different location. For example, the Project Center Web Part displays data from Project Server, whereas the Project Documents Web Part displays documents that have been uploaded into the Project Workspace Project Documents Document Library. One very useful feature is that when new content is created, such as the Change Request List described previously, a new Web Part is automatically created. This section lists the Web Parts that come with Project Server and its base WSS 3.0 platform and describes their usage:

- **Announcements** Post announcements for a Project Team. One nice feature in this Web Part (and its base list) is that announcements can be set to expire.
- **Calendar** This Web Part is used to display events. It can be set to display in an actual calendar grid or as a list of events with associated dates.
- **Deliverables** The Deliverables Web Part displays items from within the Project Workspace's Deliverables list.
- **Issues** This Web Part displays issues from the Project Workspace's issues list. Note that multiple views are possible using the Edit features (which you'll learn more about later).
- **Links** Add and display relevant links. One helpful feature is a built-in link tester.
- **Project Documents** This Web Part displays documents from within the current project's workspace.
- **Risks** The Risks Web Part displays risks for the current project as added to the Risks list. Each of the filtered views available in the Risks list (for example, All Risks Assigned to Me) can be chosen for this Web Part.
- **Tasks** This Web Part is not related to tasks in Project Server and therefore not a commonly-used option in an EPM environment.
- **Team Discussion** The Team Discussion Web Part displays content from the Project Workspace's list. Although the list itself can be useful, the Web Part is not necessarily of use.
- **Content Editor** This Web Part includes a rich text editor that can be used for WYSIWYG (what you see is what you get) editing. It includes tables, bullets, and colors. It allows for adding a picture or hyperlink, and includes tools for fonts, alignment, and more. In addition, there is a source editor that can be used to insert and edit Hypertext Markup Language (HTML) source.
- **Data Analysis** This can be used to display Data Analysis views from the Project Server Analysis Services–based online analytical processing (OLAP) cubes. Even from inside the Web Part, the data can be "sliced and diced" using pivot functionality.
- **Form** This Web Part basically is a blank form field with a submit button and includes the source editor to build a basic entry to apply to other Web Parts.
- **Image** The Image Web Part is just a placeholder for a Web-ready image. It is used, for example, to post the default WSS logo graphics on Project Workspaces.

- **My Queued Jobs** This Web Part displays any queued jobs on a personalized basis. Few users are likely to use this Web Part.
- **My Schedule** This displays a personalized calendar view of the individual's Project Server tasks. The Web Part is based on the same functionality that is displayed in the My Work page in Project Server, where the Schedule tab is one of the three tabs available.
- **My Tasks** This Web Part displays a personalized view of the user's assignments as seen from the My Tasks page in PWA.
- **My Timesheet** This is a personalized PWA timesheet.
- **Page Viewer** This interesting Web Part can be configured to display any Web page to which permission is available. In the PWA environment, that could be any internal Web page. One example of that would be the output of a SQL Reporting Services Report. It is even possible to point this Web Part at public facing Web sites, possibly one that includes topical or project management–related content.
- **Project Center** This Web Part displays the PWA Project Center and enables users to select any Project Center View to which they have permission.
- **Project Details** As with the preceding Web Part, the Project Details Web Part displays the project detail level and enables users to switch between views.
- **Project Workspaces** This Web Part that is part of the default PWA Home Page can also be displayed anywhere in the environment.
- **Reminders** This is the Web Part that is the top of the body within the PWA Home Page. Under certain circumstances, it might make sense to display it elsewhere. It acts in a personalized manner, so whoever is viewing it will see information that is targeted only toward them.
- **Resource Assignments** This Web Part displays the resource assignments to which the user has permission.
- **Resource Center** As with the Project Center and Project Details Web Part, the Resource Center Web Part displays the Resource Center based on the user's permissions.
- **Site Users** This Web Part displays all of the users who have permissions to the current site.
- **Task Update Requests** The Task Update Requests Web Part displays the same information that appears within the PWA task updates (within Approvals). It allows a project manager to approve submissions to the project plans to which tasks are assigned and for which the viewer is the status manager.
- **Team Tasks** This Web Part displays the user's team assignments.
- **User Tasks** The User Tasks Web Part displays personalized assignments.
- **XML Web Part** This Web Part includes Extensible Markup Language (XML) and Extensible Stylesheet Language (XSL) editor tools, as well as linking tools for external XML and XSL content.

Web Part Configuration

Many Web Parts have specific configurable settings. There are far too many to go through here, but this section describes one. After adding the Content Editor Web Part, select the link within the "To add content, open the tool pane and then click Rich Text Editor" text that first appears in the Web Part or use the path previously discussed. From the tool pane, select Rich Text Editor. By adding some text, changing font sizes, and adding a photo to the Rich Text Format (RTF) Editor, the Web Part displays what appears to be regular Web page content. In Figure 25-40, the arrows point to the Add a Picture and Font Size controls. Figure 25-41 shows an example of the type of Web Part content you can provide using the Content Editor Web Part.

Changing Site Styles

It is possible to make major changes in the look and feel of Project Workspaces or any other WSS site. Some of these changes require changes in site templates, which would be a topic for a WSS book. For a simple option of changing the look of a site, select Site Actions | Site Settings. Then select a site theme from the Look and Feel section and choose a style. Finally, use the Preview pane to see what the site looks like. When you are ready, select Apply and the entire site will take on the new theme.

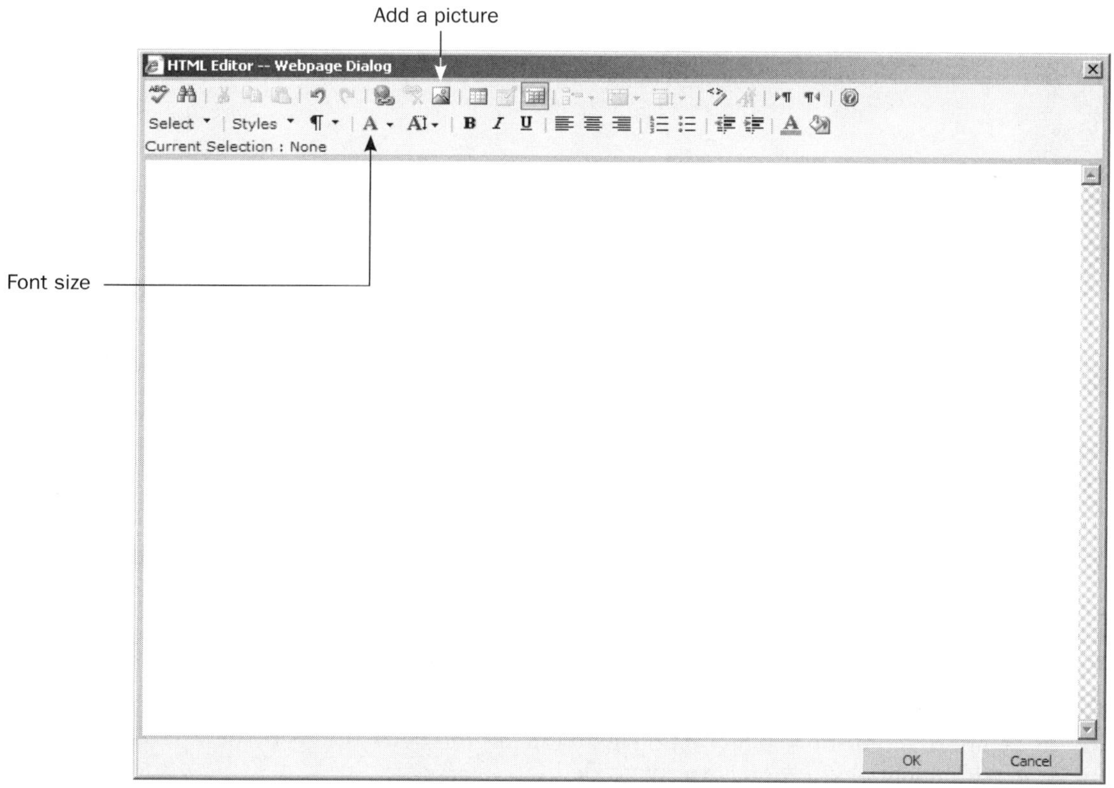

FIGURE 25-40 Toolbar

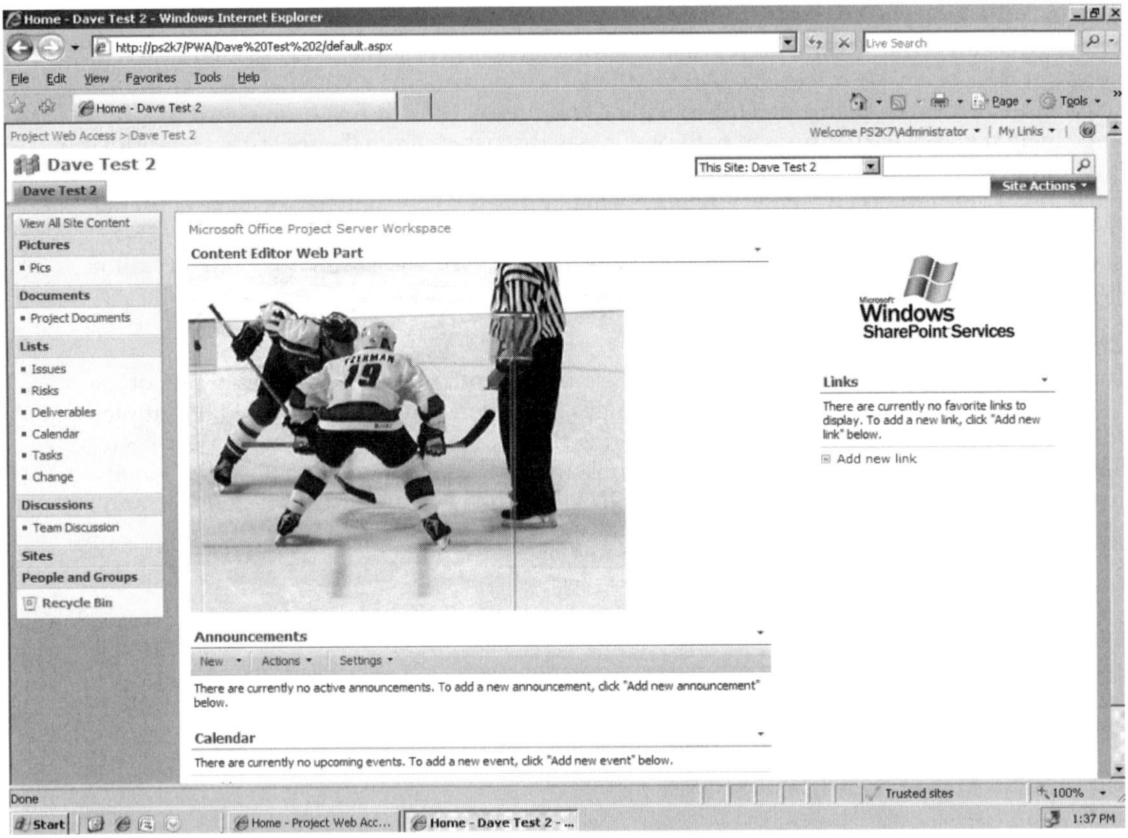

FIGURE 25-41 Content Editor Web Part result

Enabling Versioning

One of the critical features available in WSS is Versioning. By default, no Versioning is enabled in the Project Workspace template. In almost all cases, this feature should be enabled. The best way to make this happen is by setting the Versioning options on the Project Workspace template (creating this template is discussed later in this chapter).

Versioning is set on an individual list and library basis. In the following example, Versioning is enabled in an Issues list. From inside the Issues list, select Settings | List Settings. Next, under General Settings, select Versioning Settings. From the page shown in Figure 25-42, make selections for Versioning.

The following options can be set:

- **Content Approval** This can be set to require that new content in this list must be approved prior to being made available. In the PWA/Project Workspace environment, this option is rarely needed.

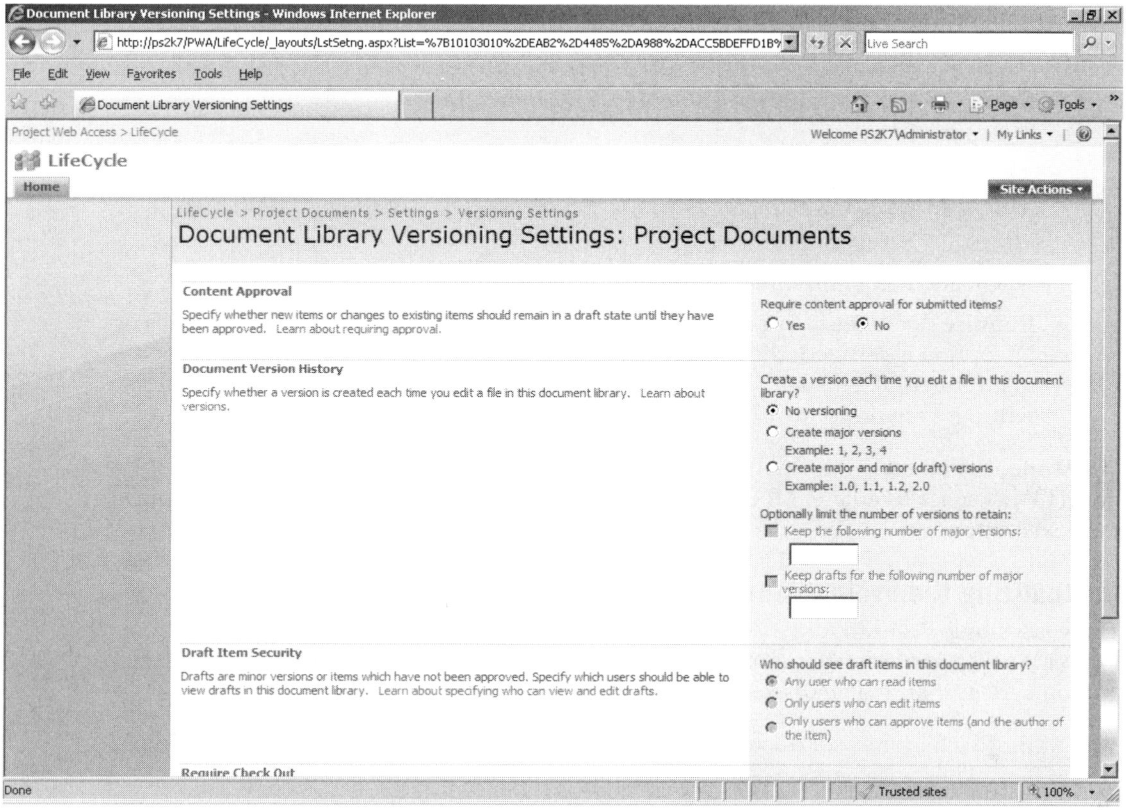

FIGURE 25-42 List Versioning Settings page

- **Item Version History** To enable Versioning, select Yes under Create a Version Each Time You Edit an Item in This List? Next decide whether to limit the number of versions. If you leave this field blank, there will be no limit set. The next option, Keep Drafts for the Following Number of Approved Versions, will be dimmed unless Content Approval has been selected.
- **Draft Item Security** This option will also be dimmed unless Content Approval is enabled and/or when using Major/Minor versions. Using a combination of these two options provides slightly different versions of how draft content with a limited audience can become final content for the broader audience.

Document libraries have a more complex set of configuration settings. To set them up, navigate to the library, then select Settings | Document Library Settings | Versioning Settings.

There are two extra items to configure for a document library. The settings are the same as in the previous example except for the following:

- **Create a version each time you edit a file in this document library?** There are three options:
  - No Versioning
  - Create major versions (Example: 1, 2, 3, 4). This is usually the best option in a Project Server and Project Workspace.
  - Create major and minor (draft) versions (Example: 1.0, 1.1, 1.2, 2.0)
- **Require documents to be checked out before they can be edited?** If this Yes or No option is selected, the user is forced to check out the document formally if it is to be edited. It is usually a good idea to keep people from changing a document without version control.

As mentioned earlier, to enable Versioning in the environment is to make it part of the Project Workspace template. Modifying the template and posting it to PWA is the topic of the next section.

Customizing the Project Workspace

There is a single Project Workspace template that is used for automatically provisioning Project Workspaces. Smart organizations leverage this template in a number of ways. Here are some ideas that will be discussed in the sections ahead:

- Build a hierarchy of document folders to include supporting project methodology templates with version control.
- Create a change management process using custom list functions and workflow.
- Remove lower-value content and Web Parts.
- Reorganize content layout.
- Change the look and feel.
- Add a meeting minutes list.
- Add a communications plan custom list.

Using Project Document Methodology Templates with Version Control

When you are using the WSS document library functions, it can be valuable to include a set of project document templates in an organized set of folders in the Project Workspace template. Several options are worth considering in the library settings. Leave the Document Library General Settings (Settings | Document Library Settings—the leftmost block of settings) as is unless it makes sense to rename the library, or there is a reason to hide the Quick Launch Bar item for the library (which would rarely make sense).

Next navigate to the Document Library Versioning Settings in the Document Library General Settings block as shown in Figure 25-43.

Content Approval defaults to No and that setting generally makes sense for template creation. It is recommended that Versioning is enabled from the top level of the document library. Choose between using only major versions (1, 2, 3, 4, and so on), or major and minor

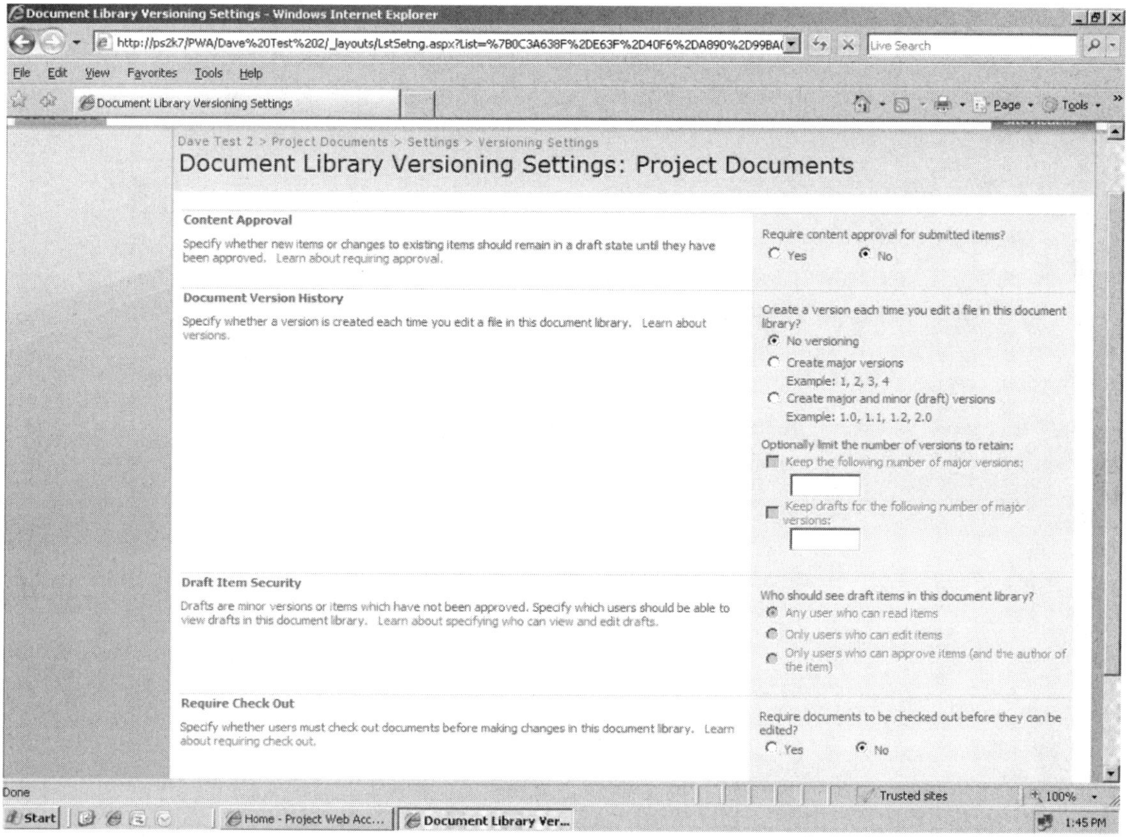

FIGURE 25-43 Document Library Versioning Settings

(2.1, 2.2, 2.3, 3.0, 3.1, and so on). If you choose to use minor versions, consider whether there should be a limit on the number of versions or whether to limit the number of minor versions. Next, select Require Check Out. This feature ensures that people cannot edit the document without the edits resulting in the edited version receiving a new version number. This is a critical feature of the document libraries not previously available. There are more options available for customizing a document library, but those discussed here are a likely combination for use of these settings. Figure 25-44 shows an example of how a document hierarchy might be used.

Removing Lower-Value Content and Web Parts

Decide which Web Parts will not be used in the template and remove them by placing the page into Edit mode (choose Site Actions | Edit Page). Then simply click on the X at the top-right of any unnecessary Web Parts.

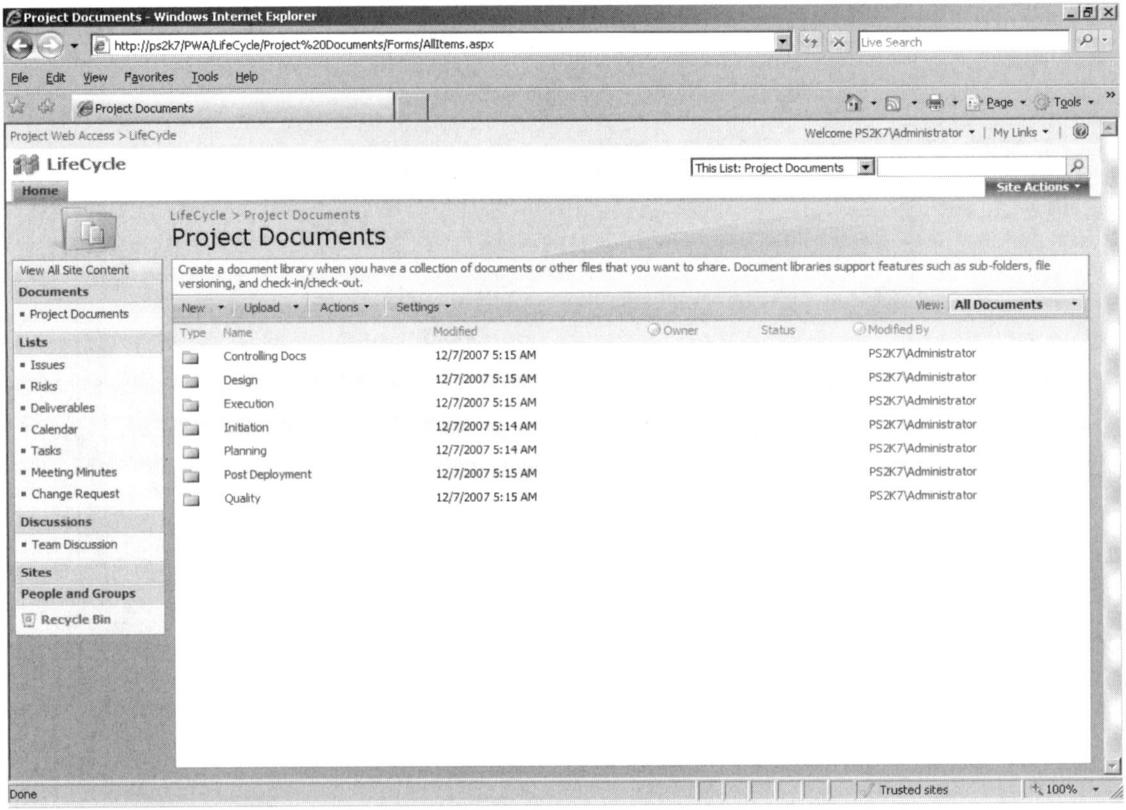

FIGURE 25-44 Document library example

Reorganizing Content Layout

If the layout is not what your organization requires, you can move Web Parts around by dragging and dropping them between zones. Consider adding a Web Part or two. Adding the Issues Web Part is recommended. Others may also be worth adding.

Changing the Look and Feel

Consider replacing the WSS graphic with a company logo. To do this in a single location, go to the server's My Computer icon and navigate to C:\Program Files\Common Files\Microsoft Shared\web server extensions\12\TEMPLATE\IMAGES. Replace homepage.gif with the company logo. Another option is to place a new Web-ready graphic in the same directory with its own name and point the Site Image Web Part to the new file using the tool pane.

Another common option is simply to remove this Web Part to free some screen real estate for other content.

Adding a Meeting Minutes List

As discussed earlier in this chapter, one possible option is to include some new content. The Meeting Minutes list is one possible addition to the Project Workspace template.

Adding a Communications Plan Custom List

This is another option for new content. Use a Communications Plan list to hold and make visible the methods and frequency of project communications (status reports, status meetings, e-mail, and so on).

Considering Other Possibilities

There are many other possibilities that might be considered. Here are a couple ideas:

- **Quality management** Create libraries with quality templates, lists for recording test results, and so on.
- **Defect management** Create a lightweight defect tracking system with lists. Otherwise, if there is an existing defect management system, find or develop a Web Part that allows its inclusion in Project Workspaces as appropriate.

Evaluating Views

Consider whether there are views, either in lists or libraries, that may be needed but are not already available. In addition, evaluate whether the default view is set to the appropriate view for the organization.

Using the New Template Process

This section describes how to change the Project Workspace template that is used by Project Server for autoprovisioning. To build a new Project Workspace template and then apply it, you must work from a nonconnected location. However, the easiest way to make a new template that includes all the advanced features is to use one that was created by Project Server provisioning. There are two ways to accomplish this seemingly conflicting process.

The first way to start this process is with a site provisioned from a different instance of Project Server. This could be the test server, a second instance on the same server, or even a virtual environment supported with VMWare or Microsoft Virtual Server.

The other method to get a site template started is to provision a site from the production environment. Make a note of the URL of the new site (make it a favorite). Next navigate to PWA's Server Settings and select Project Workspaces from the Operation Policies section. Highlight the URL for the site that will be used and then select Edit Site Address. In the Edit

Workspace Address dialog, select the option Remove the URL for the SharePoint Site and click OK (see Figure 25-45).

NOTE *You can also use this page to delete and create sites.*

This disconnection process leaves the site in place, but removes any connections it has with the specific project that was associated with its provisioning.

After modifying a Project Workspace using one of the two methods just described, you are ready to turn the site into a template. Before proceeding, make sure that you have made all the desired changes. Next, from within that site (use that favorite to get back there), navigate to Site Actions | Site Settings. Next select Save Site as Template from within the Look and Feel section of the Site Settings page (see Figure 25-46).

Now designate the filename (it is best not to use spaces) and name the template. Next select the Include Content checkbox if any site content such as documents is to be included with what you have created (see Figure 25-47). Finally, select OK.

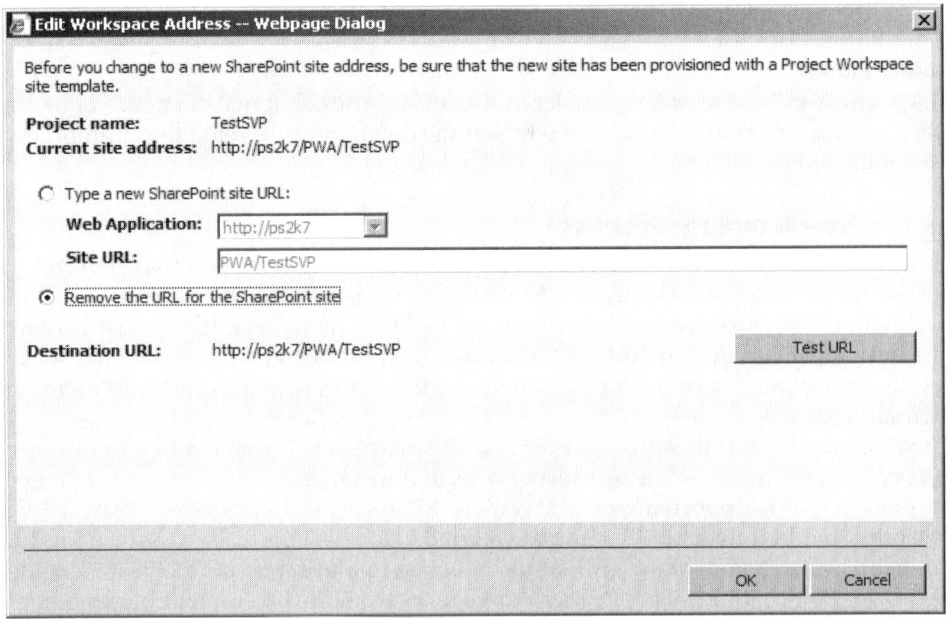

FIGURE 25-45 Edit Workspace Address dialog

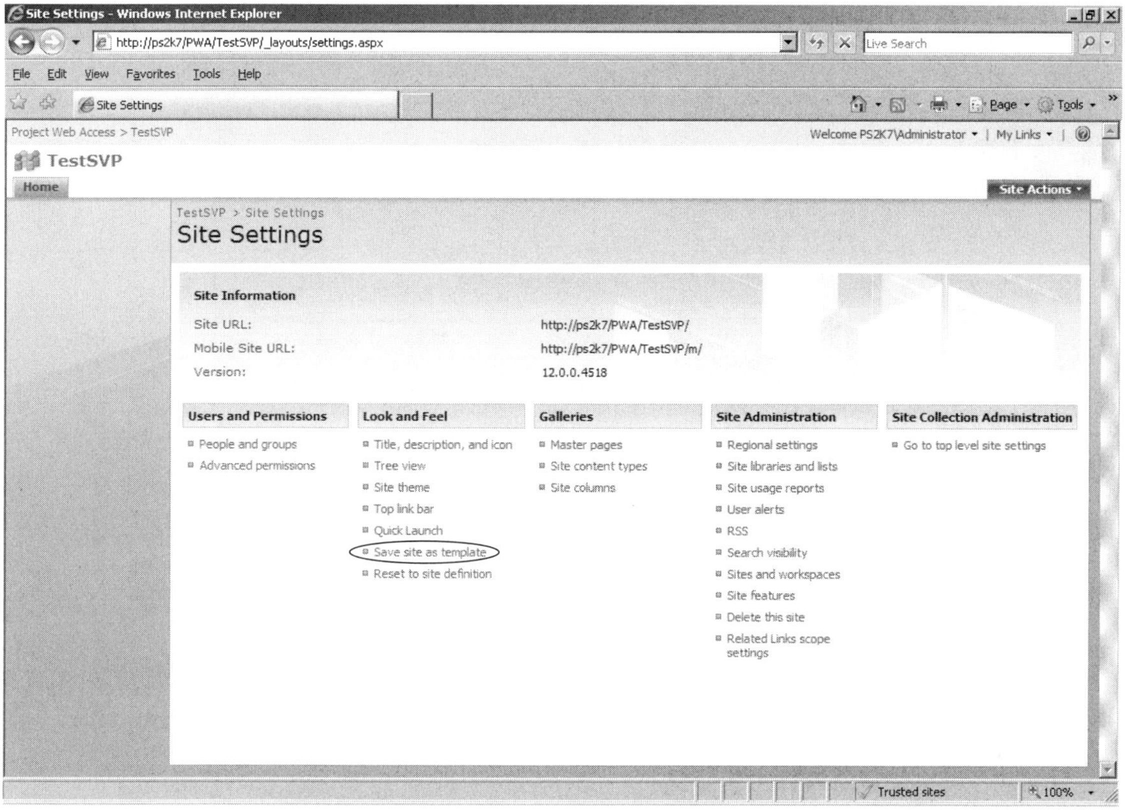

FIGURE 25-46 Save Site as Template option

Saving the Template as a File

Next navigate to the Site Template Gallery. For the location of this gallery, navigate to the instance's PWA Project Web Access Home Page and select Site Actions | Site Settings | Site Template Gallery. Locate the template that was just saved, right-click it, and choose Save Target As to get the actual file to a location from which you can move it into the production environment. Relocate the file to a production instance of PWA and place the new .stp file in Program Files\Common Files\Microsoft Shared\web server extensions\12\BIN.

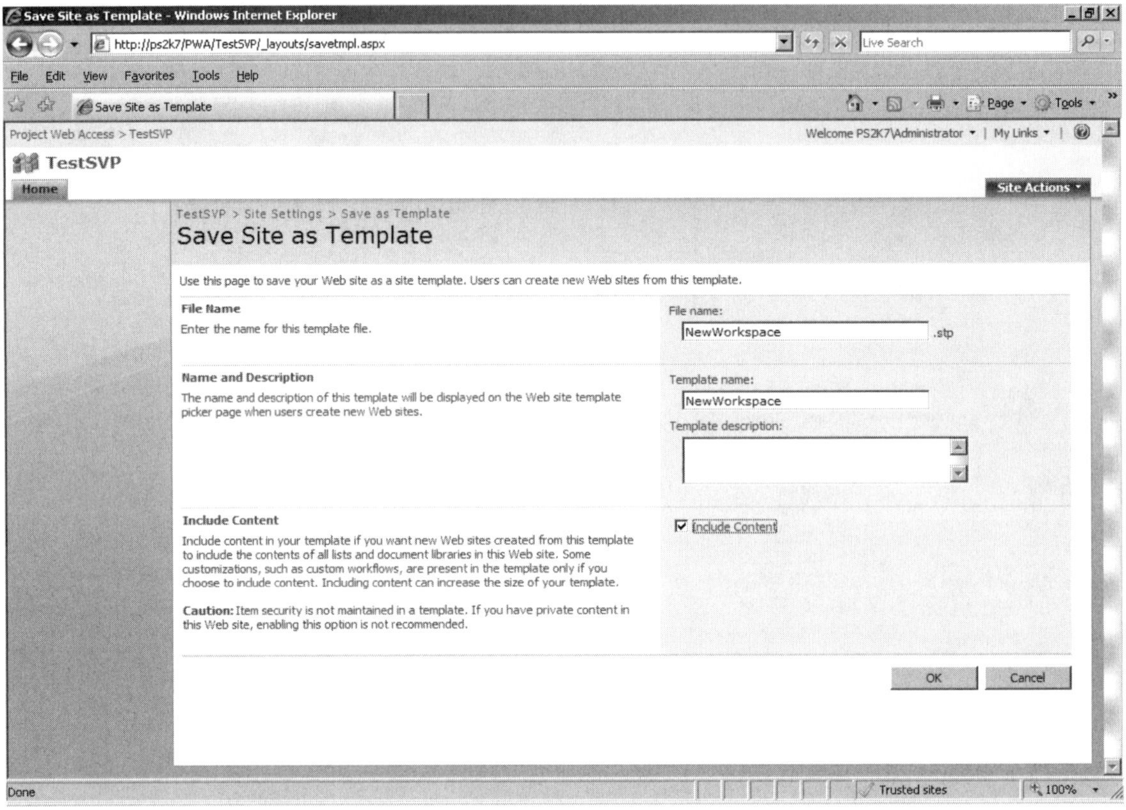

FIGURE 25-47 Template detail

Registering the New Template

From the command prompt (which you can access by choosing Start | Run and then typing cmd), change to the directory listed in the preceding section by typing the following (assuming that Program Files is located on C:\):

```
cd Program Files\Common Files\Microsoft Shared\web server extensions\12\BIN
```

Next type in the following command and press ENTER:

```
stsadm -o addtemplate -filename "template path\MyWorkspaceTemplate.stp"
-title "Workspace Title"
```

Note that if the template were placed in the location ...\BIN, the command would be simpler:

```
stsadm -o addtemplate -filename MyWorkspaceTemplate.stp -title "Workspace Title"
```

If the title does not include any spaces or illegal characters, the quotes are not required.

Next you must restart Internet Information Services (IIS). To do so, type the following from the command line and press ENTER:

```
iisreset
```

Note that the resetting of IIS should not be performed when people are using the system. After IIS restarts, the new workspace will be registered with the server. The next step is to make the new template the default Project Workspace for all new Project Workspaces.

Changing the Default Workspace Template in Project Server

After registering the template, go to the Server Settings on the production PWA instance. Select the Project Workspace Provisioning Settings link. Then change the Default Project Workspace Template setting to the new option that appears in the dropdown menu. Leave all other settings as is and click Save. All new projects will take on this template.

NOTE *There is a known issue with the List View Web Part, where changes made do not "stick" in the Project Workspace template. There is a reference to this at http://support.microsoft.com/kb/926284.*

Building Workflows

It is possible to build workflows into Project Workspaces. Complex workflows require the use of Visual Studio.NET and the skills of a .NET developer. More straightforward workflows, however, can be created using the Microsoft Office SharePoint Designer 2007. The skills involved in this type of work more closely resemble those required of someone with deep Microsoft Office FrontPage experience. SharePoint Designer is very similar to FrontPage and, in fact, has replaced it for sharepoint modifications.

In the following example, an e-mail workflow will be added to a custom New Project Request form. Start by launching Microsoft Office SharePoint Designer 2007. Next open the site by choosing File | Open Site and entering the URL of the site address—in this case, http://ps2k7/PWA/RS/NewProj. Next navigate to the New Project Request List All Items View, as shown in Figure 25-48, and double-click on the All Items link from the left pane.

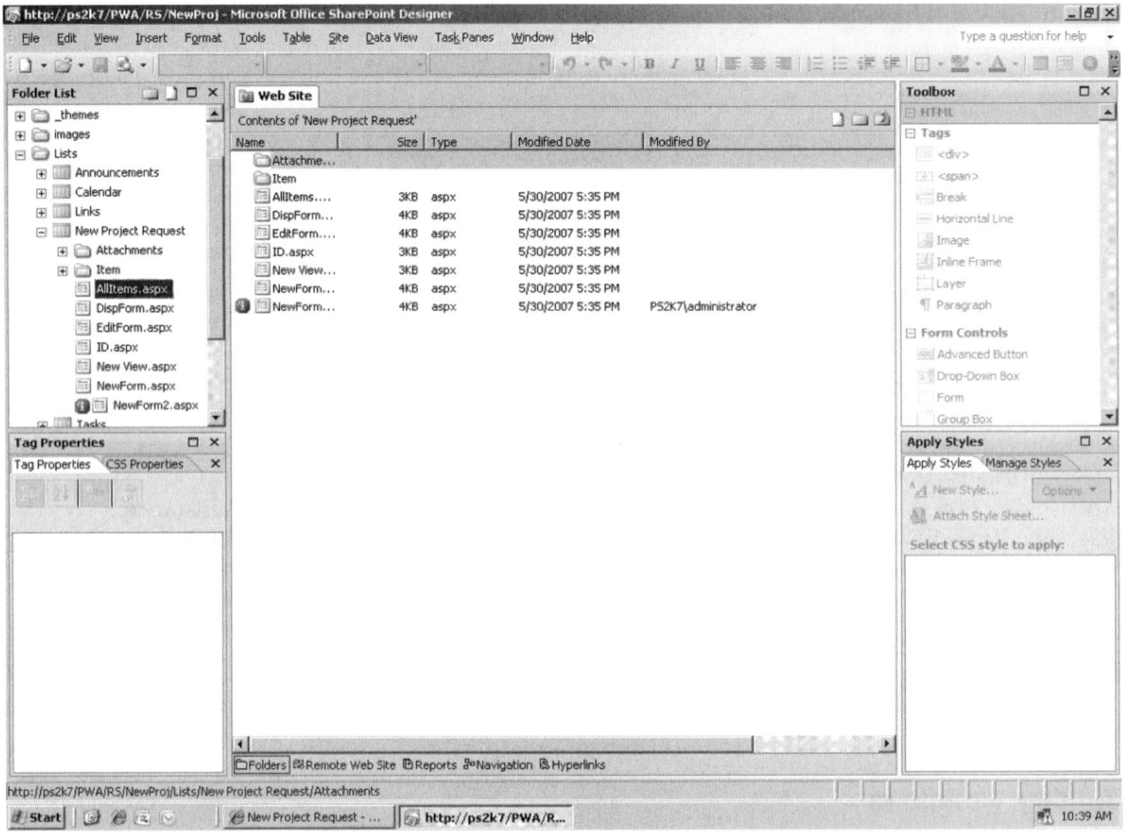

FIGURE 25-48 Navigating to the New Project Request list through SharePoint Designer

Then choose File | New. Using the right-pointing arrow, select Workflow, as shown in Figure 25-49.

Name the new workflow. In this case, we will name it Workflow 2. There are some decisions to be made right away. The workflow can be set to be launched in any combination of one or more of the following:

- Manually
- Upon creation of the item
- Upon item change

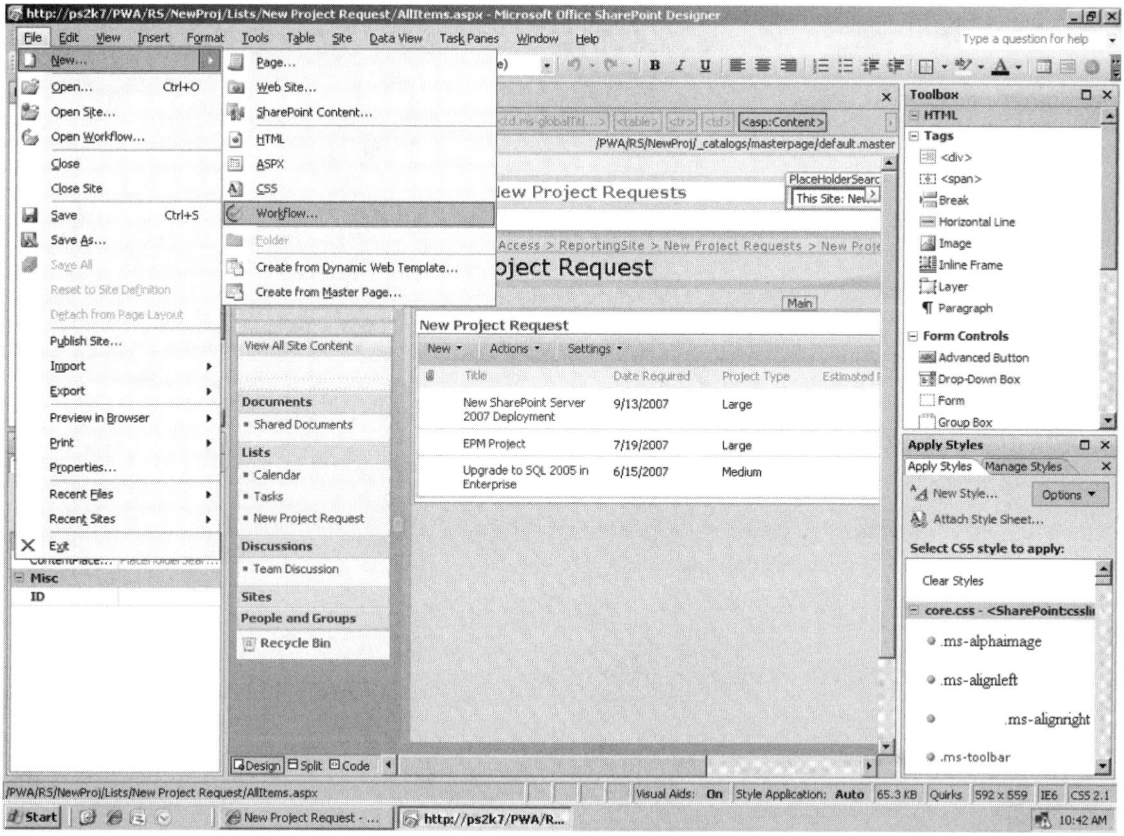

FIGURE 25-49 New workflow

In this case, it is set to Manual only. See Figure 25-50 for the completed first step in the Wizard. When you are ready, select Next.

The next step is to set up the workflow that will send an e-mail to a specific person who is the requester's departmental project management office (PMO) contact. The e-mail must include the title of the request and the project size, as well as some informational text from the Detailed Description field in the form.

Now choose Conditions | Compare New Project Request Field. Then select PMO Rep from the field link and Is Not Empty from the equals link (see Figure 25-51).

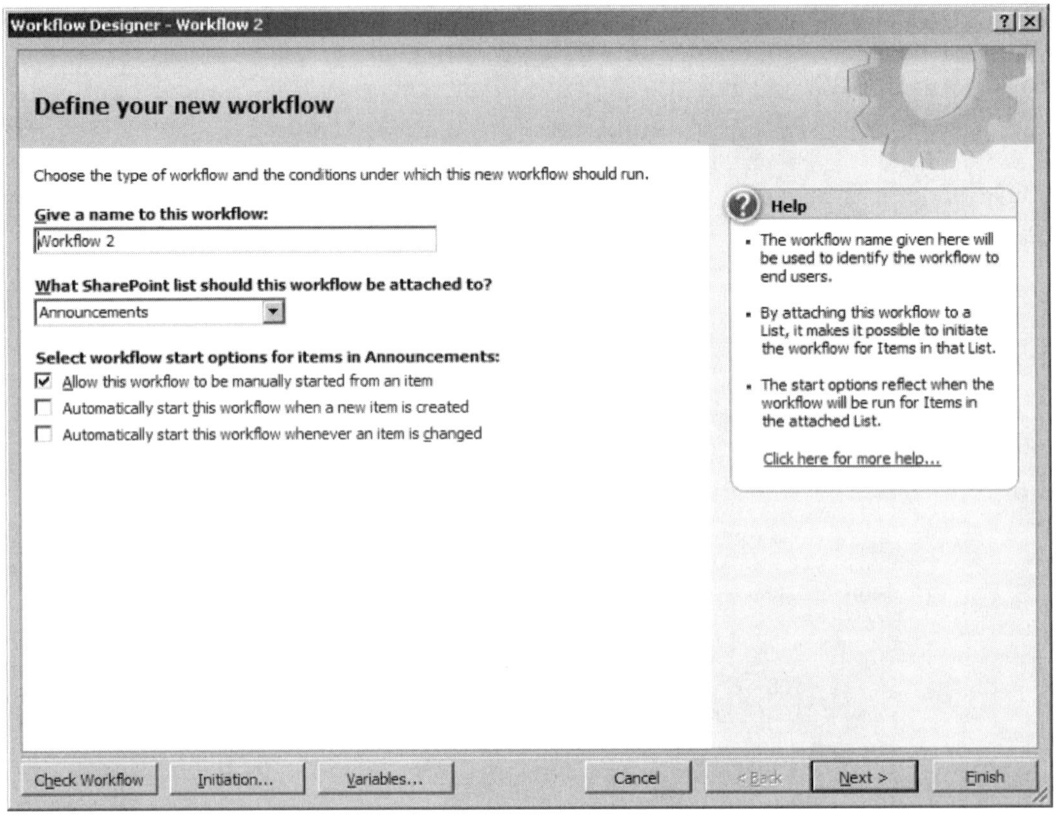

FIGURE 25-50 Define your new workflow

Next select Actions | Send an E-Mail. Then select "this message" from the Email options that appear. Next to the To field, select the Address Book icon and then choose Workflow Lookup as shown in the Figure 25-52.

In the next dialog, fill in the Source and Field information as shown in Figure 25-53. Select OK. The Define Email Message dialog appears. In the Subject field, fill in some informational text. Next use the Add Lookup to Body button to fill in information that is dynamically generated from the form (Current Item). The completed Define Email Message dialog is shown in Figure 25-54.

When you are ready, select OK. This takes the designer back to the main Workflow Designer page. From there, select Check Workflow to make sure that no errors were made during creation. Assuming all is well, select Finish. Finally, save and close the site in SharePoint Designer. If the Site Definition warning appears when you click Save, select Yes.

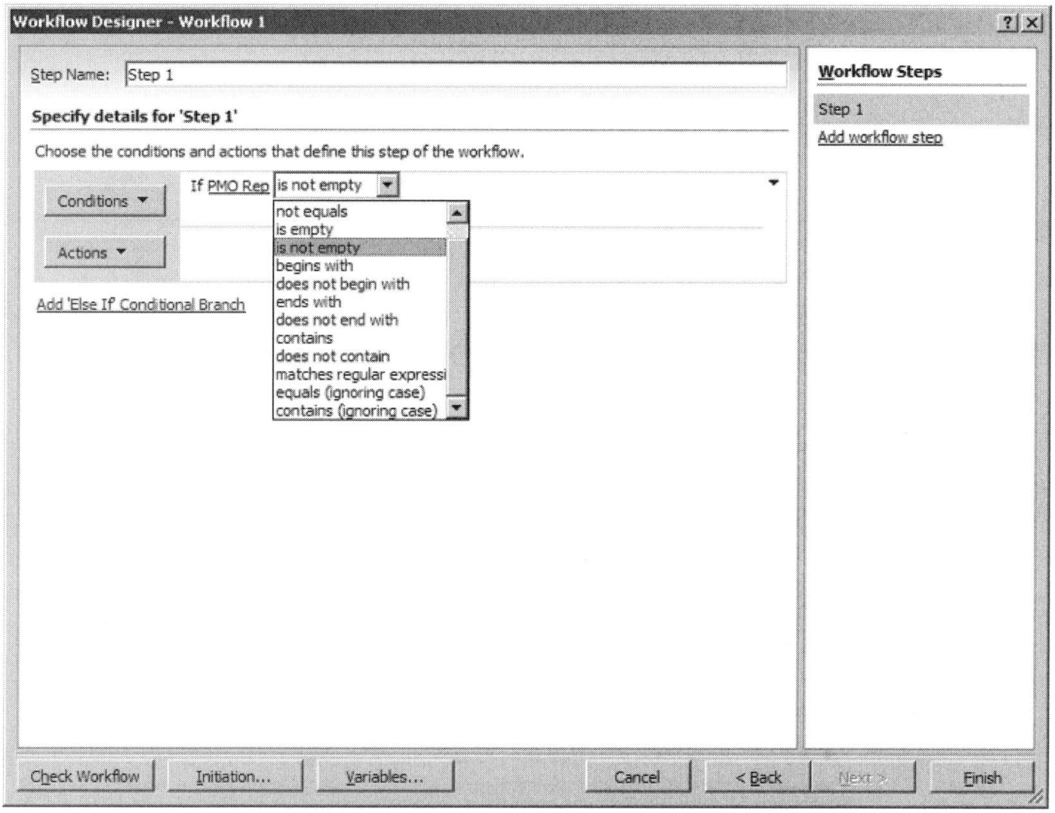

FIGURE 25-51 Selecting the option for Is Not Empty

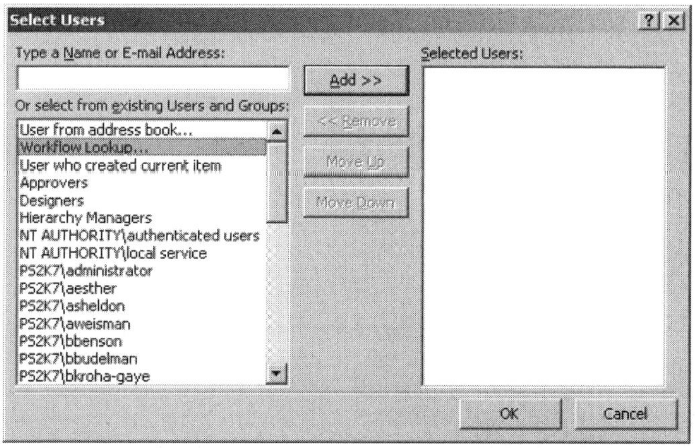

FIGURE 25-52 Workflow Lookup

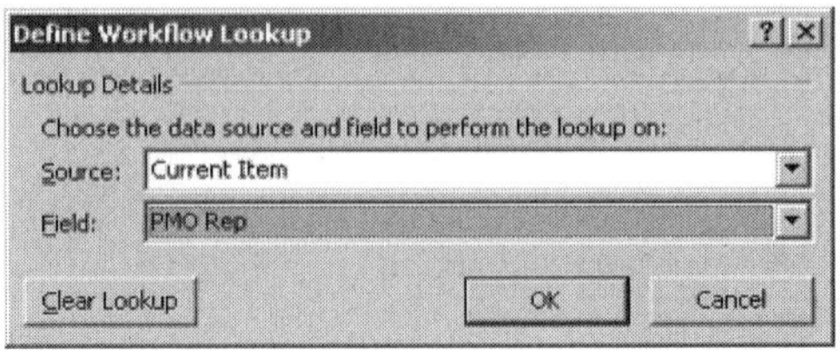

FIGURE 25-53 Specify the source and field

To launch the workflow (remember that you can set this workflow to launch automatically), hover over the item in the New Project Request list. Select Workflows from the dropdown menu. Select the name of the workflow (in this case, Workflow 1) and then click Start to execute the workflow. The workflow's status appears in the view as shown in Figure 25-55.

NOTE *The ability of users to launch a workflow is based on the permissions that they have on the site. These custom workflows can also be used in the MOSS environment.*

Creating Subpages and Sites

From within any Project Workspace, new subsites or subpages can be created. To create a new subsite, select Actions | Create from within the site. Under Web Pages, select Sites and Workspaces. Then give the site a title and designate a URL. Select the type of site from the

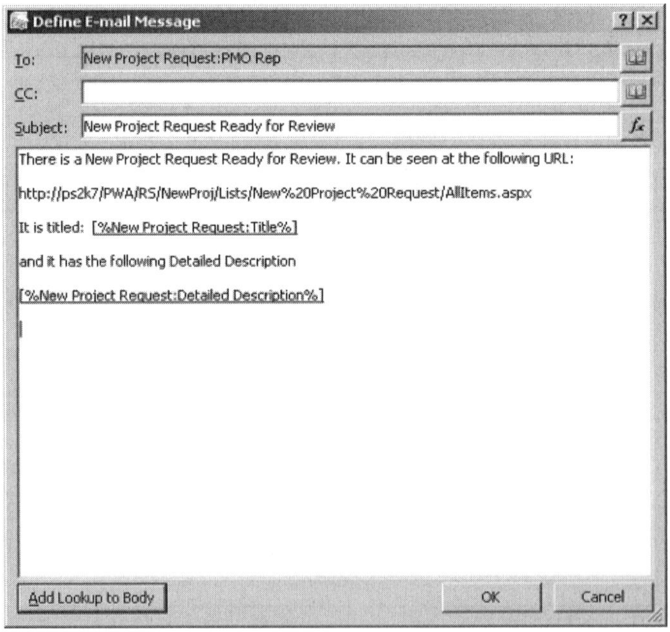

FIGURE 25-54 Define Email Message dialog

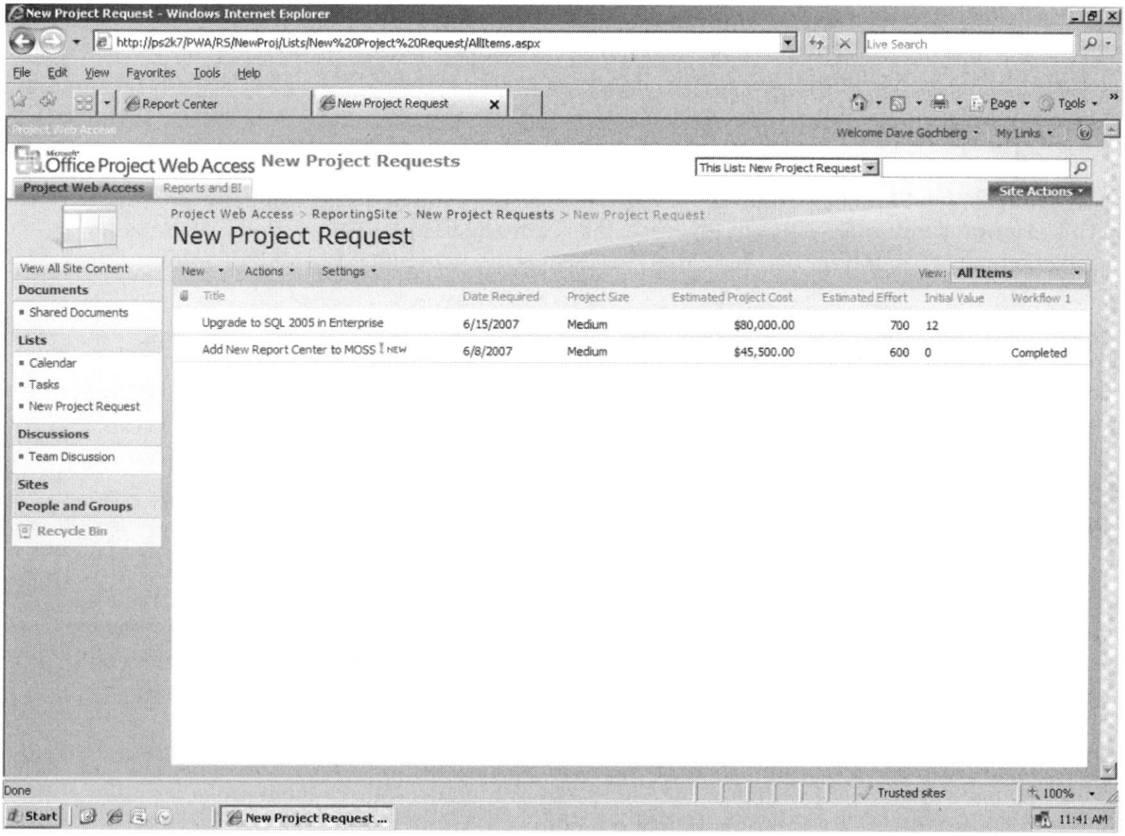

FIGURE 25-55 Workflow status complete

many options available. Note that as possible sites are highlighted, a description is available. For example, when Wiki site is highlighted, the description says "A site for a community to brainstorm and share ideas. It provides Web pages that can be quickly edited to record information and then linked together through keywords." Navigation can also be set from this page as it relates to the subsite's navigational relationship to the parent. More detail about sites and site templates are beyond the scope of this book.

Subpages can also be created from the same Create page. In most cases, the correct option is Web Part Page. The type of layout can be selected (the number of zones and locations and so on). As you are highlighting different options, a visual of the layout appears to the left.

Project Management Center of Excellence

Separate sites can also be created in the WSS platform that supports Project Server. Usually, it is not the best idea to start using the WSS environment for all types of collaboration just because it is there (thanks to a Project Server initiative). There is one type of site that does make sense and many Project Server deployments that have involved the authors included one special site. This site is dedicated to project management generally and Project Server specifically as is used in the organization. Call it the PMO site, the Project Center of Excellence, or whatever else fits. This site can be very valuable to the improvement of project management maturity.

Decide where to place this site. In this case, it will be placed at the level just under the PWA Home Page. From Site Actions | Create | Sites and Workspaces. Name the site (COE, in this example) and set its URL. In this case, the Team Site template is selected. All the other settings remain at their defaults. Note that this creates the navigation desired, including a top link bar item.

Configure the site as a central location for "all things project management." Consider including things like frequently asked questions (FAQ), a document library of standard practices and process descriptions, project-focused discussion boards, white papers, quality management information, links to the local meetings and presentations on project management topics, and so on.

Working with MOSS 2007

Project Server 2007 does not require the installation of MOSS. In fact, many organizations will get what they need from the combination of Project Server and WSS. There is an additional cost associated with MOSS, a replacement for what was SharePoint Portal Server. However, it does add a wealth of features that would add value to any environment. In this section, the book discusses the ways that MOSS features are relevant in a Project Server 2007 environment.

Business Intelligence Features

There are some great new features in the MOSS environment. None of them are better than the business intelligence components when it comes to being useful in a Project Server environment.

Excel Services

Chapter 12 included a discussion about how Excel spreadsheets can be displayed as Web pages using the new Excel Calculation Services feature in MOSS 2007. The real value of using Excel to display data in SharePoint is that the spreadsheet gets data directly from the Project Server Reporting database. Even better is that the data are pulled from the Analysis Services Cube.

Cube data can be pulled using the Office Data Connection (ODC), or by using the Business Data Catalog (BDC). The BDC will be described in the next section. Connecting with the ODC requires a very simple connection that can be made from within Excel 2007 under the Data menu. Then follow the Wizard to make the connection. Here are the steps:

1. Choose Data | From Other Sources | From Analysis Services.
2. Type in the server name and then select Next. Select a cube. For a start, use MSP_Portfolio_Analyzer. Then select Next.

3. The next screen offers options in several areas, but when you first trying this, just select Finish.
4. From the Import Data dialog, select OK.
5. Use the Pivot Table List that appears on the right to set up which pieces of data are to be analyzed. Move items in and out or between axes as appropriate.
6. After you have the data that you need, experiment with the possibilities of the powerful new Excel 2007. For the example, in Figure 25-56, try some of the amazing new ways to perform conditional formatting.
7. Upload the Excel document to a SharePoint Report Library. Note that for Excel Services to work properly, the library must be made into a Trusted Excel File Location in the SharePoint Central Administration tool (choose Shared Service Provider | Excel Services Settings | Trusted File Locations).

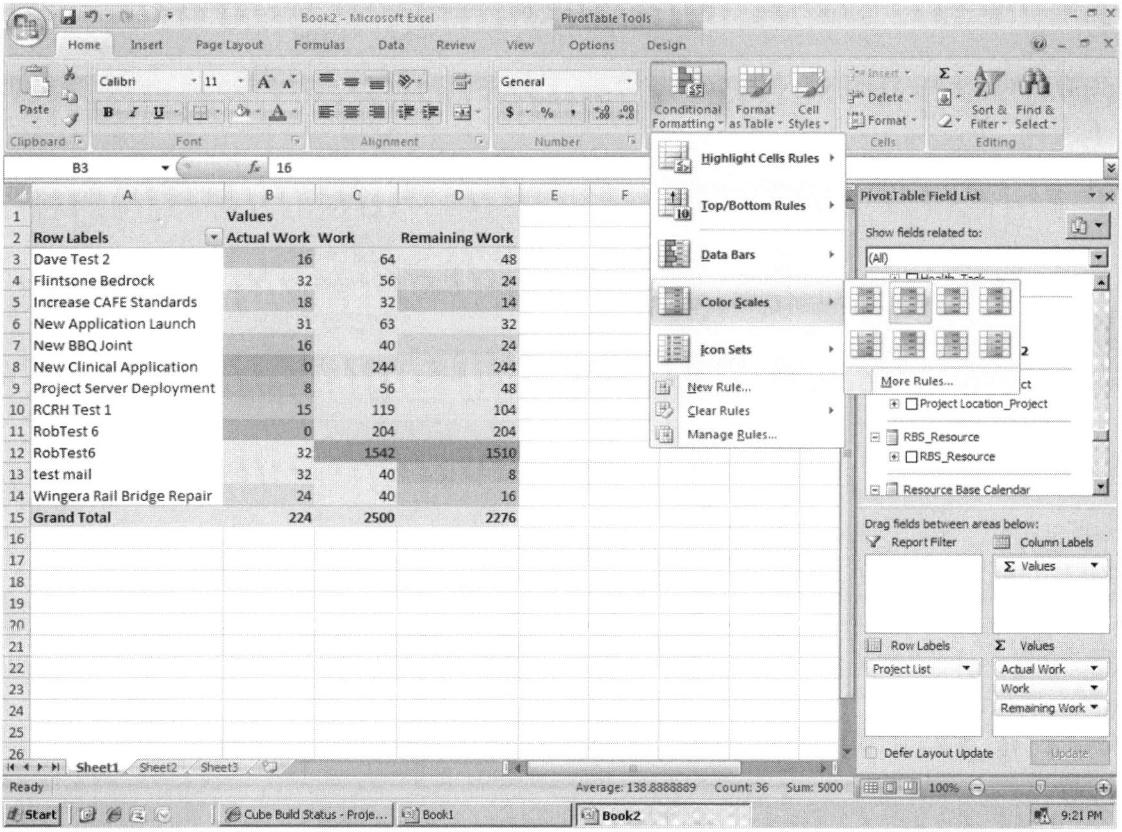

FIGURE 25-56 Conditional formatting

The spreadsheet can be displayed as a Web page directly from the library as shown in Figure 25-57.

An even more interesting use is to display the Excel data in a Web Part, possibly with Key Performance Indicators (KPIs). KPIs are another new feature in MOSS that can leverage data from Project Server as indicators, as shown along with the Excel Services Web Part in Figure 25-58. You'll learn more about KPIs later in this chapter.

Refer back to Chapter 12 for more details. You can accomplish much more with these tools, but the topic is beyond the scope of this book. We encourage you to discover more about Excel Services (in particular, make sure to understand when Kerberos authentication would be required).

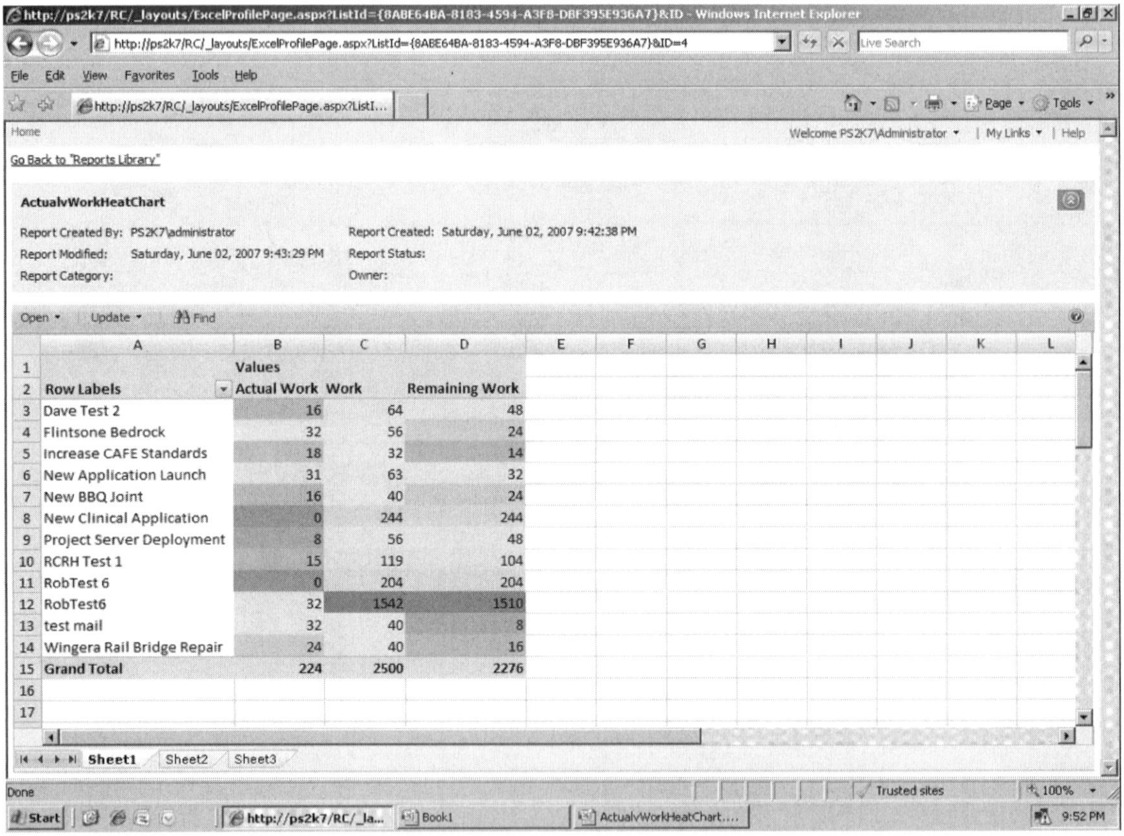

FIGURE 25-57 Spreadsheet displayed as a Web page

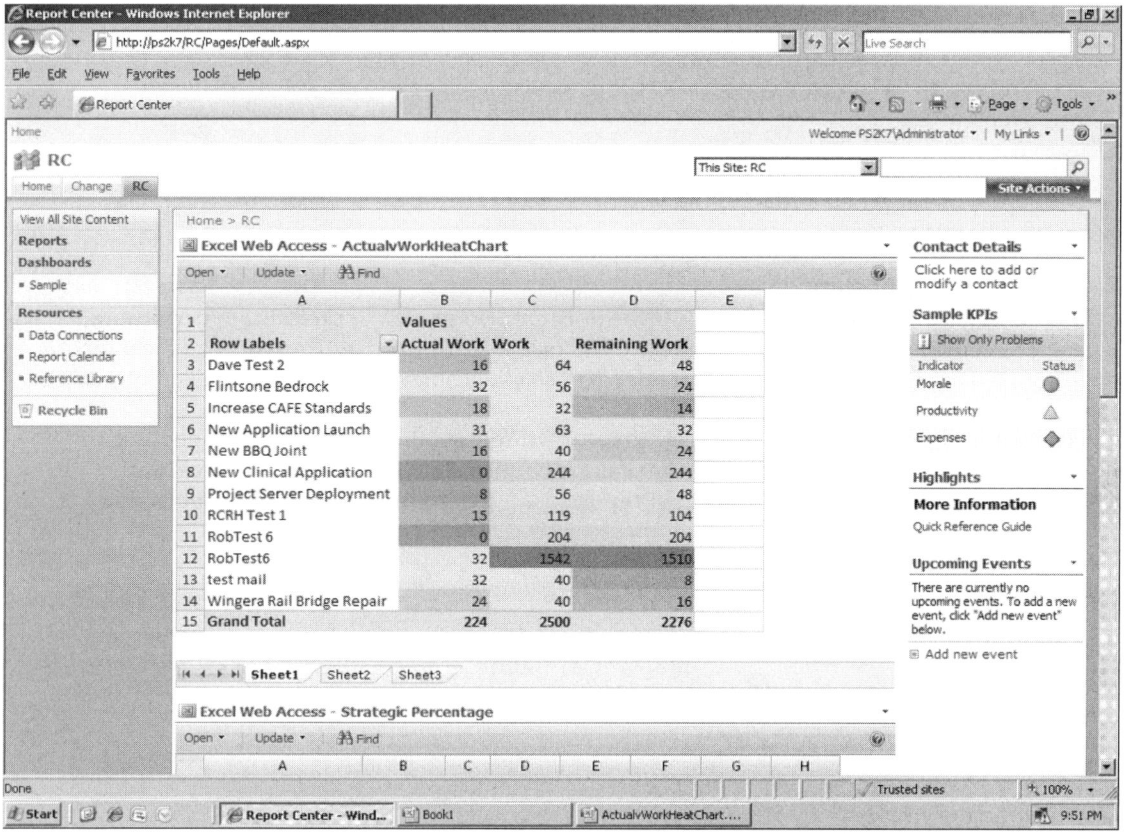

FIGURE 25-58 Excel Services Web Part with KPIs

Business Data Catalog

The Business Data Catalog is a new feature within MOSS Enterprise 2007 that allows connection to back-end systems without the need for composition of complex custom software code. Instead, through the use of an XML file (an example of which is provided by Microsoft), connections can be edited with a text editor. Keep in mind that no connections can function without the proper permissions both on SharePoint and in whatever back-end systems are being read.

Using the BDC presents amazing possibilities. A majority of the value would be realized in an environment where Project data and data from other systems need to be aggregated in a single view (or dashboard). From the Project Server–only perspective, the following uses could be considered:

- **Query Page** The BDC is useful for performing queries that can be displayed in tabular form. If connected to the Project Server Reports Database or an Analysis Services Cube, users can perform ad hoc queries on project data using And/Or logic and get the result displayed directly to a page in tabular form. This can be very useful for reports that are not repeated on a regular basis.

- **Search** If a BDC connection is established, it is possible to set the MOSS search utility to index the data from the external database for search purposes.
- **Web Parts** Data from Project Server Database sources can also be displayed in Web Parts.

On their own, none of the BDC features make moving to MOSS compelling for a Project Server deployment. When added to the other rich MOSS features, however, these represent persuasive bonus features.

Key Performance Indicators

KPIs are a way to graphically display how the portfolio, programs, or projects are performing. It can be based on data pulled through the ODC or the BDC, from an Excel spreadsheet, or even from a manually set SharePoint List item. KPI can be displayed in a list like the out-of-box sample shown in Figure 25-59.

The list in Figure 25-59 allows a user to set the numbers that are then displayed with graphical indicators using thresholds that can be configured very easily in SharePoint. This function can be used in a Project Server–focused environment for setting subjective

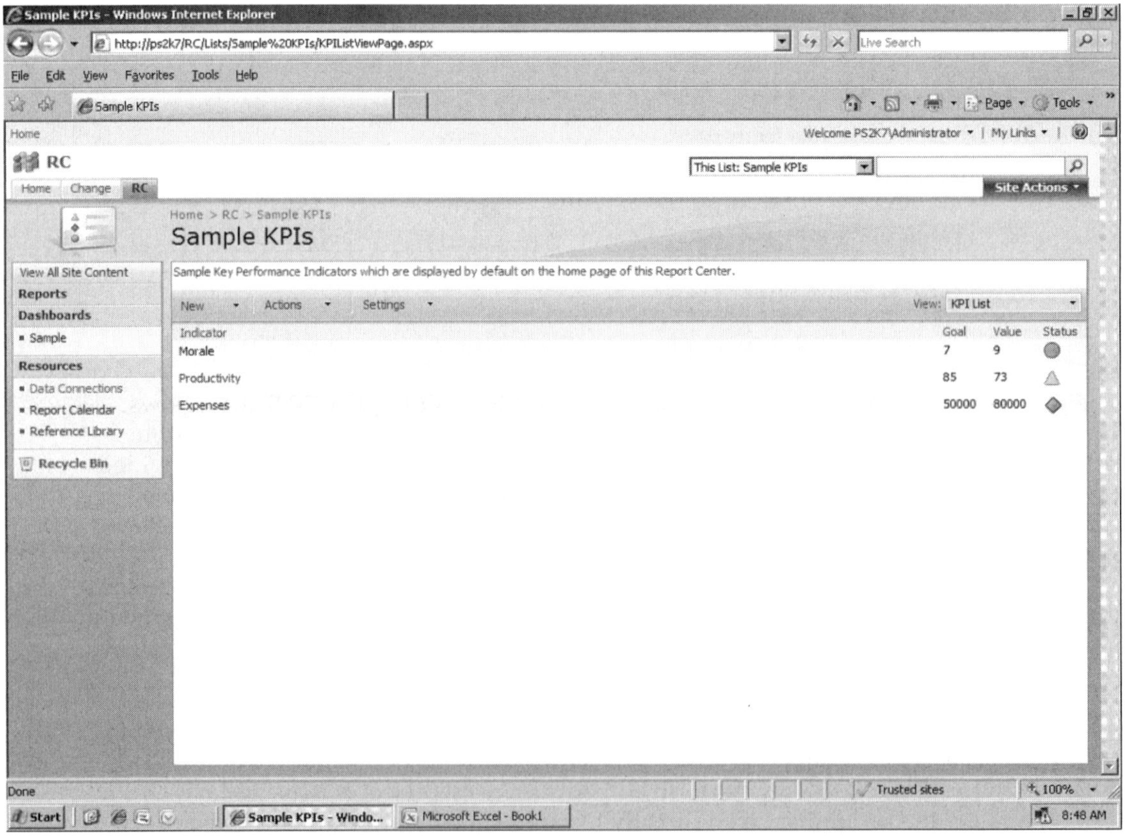

Figure 25-59 KPI list sample

project status. For example, the project manager could set an indicator for overall project health. In the end, though, subjective indicators such as the overall health indicator are only of minimal use. More powerful, especially in a Project-focused environment, is a KPI list that displays data from the Project Server database or the Analysis Services OLAP Cube.

Start with the same Excel spreadsheet that was pulled from the Project Server MSP_Portfolio_Analyzer cube described in the "Excel Services" section earlier in this chapter (adding the Baseline Work field to the Excel file). The next few paragraphs and figures describe the process for using that data in a Project Server/MOSS environment.

Navigate to the site where the KPI list will be housed. In this case, that is a Report Center that was created at a level parallel to the PWA site. Select All Site Content from the Quick Launch Bar (on the top), select Create | KPI List, then name and create your list.

If appropriate, add more information to the spreadsheet. In this case, a simple formula was added to compare baseline work with actual work. For each project, name the KPI and select the spreadsheet by locating it using the graphic next to the Workbook URL field. Select the cell for reporting, in this case the one with the comparison formula. This type of usage is a great match, not so much for a view into all projects, but rather as a window into a group of related projects where the actual projects themselves will be static. See Figure 25-60 for how the output of Excel Services–driven data can display as a KPI list.

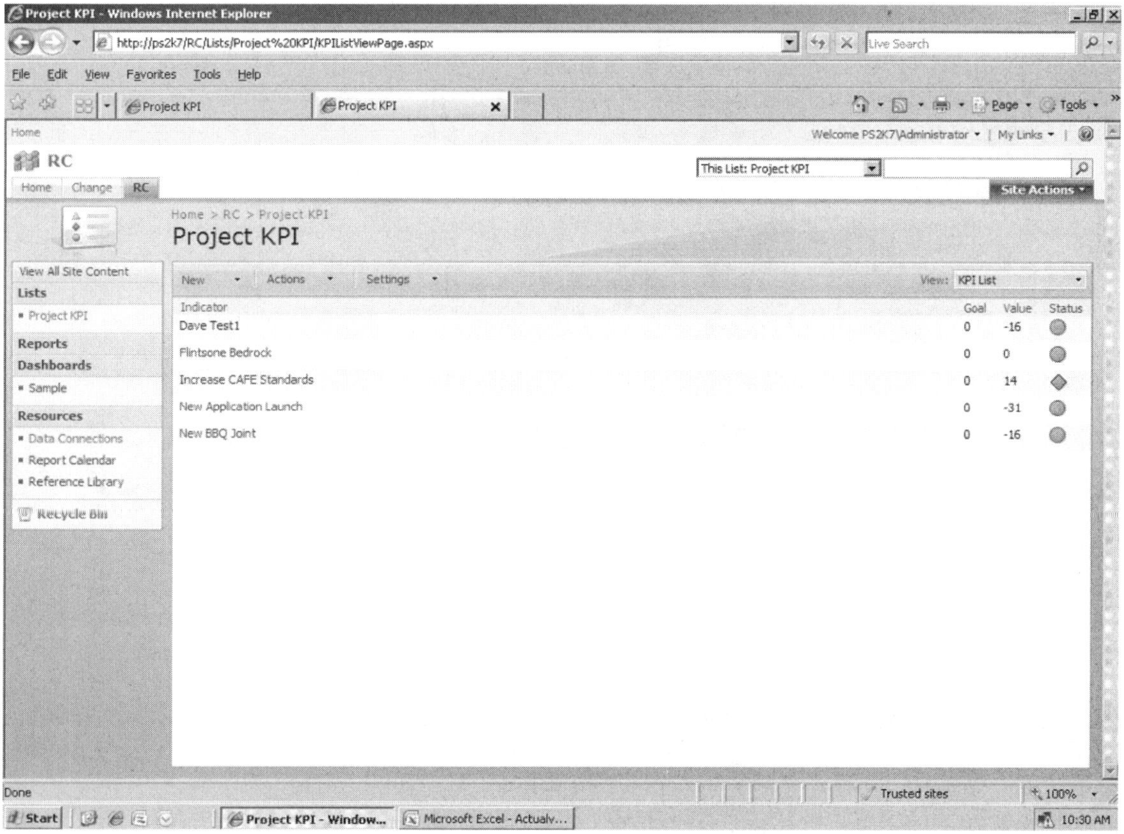

FIGURE 25-60 KPI list from Excel Services

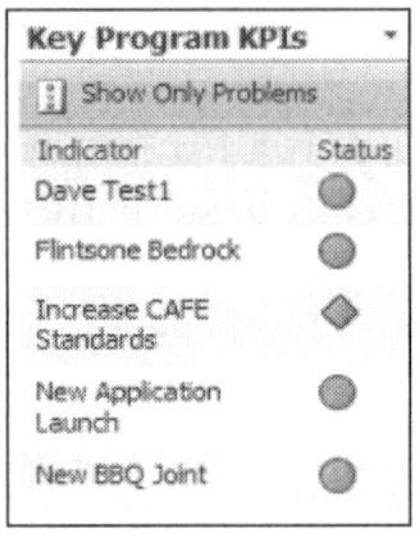

FIGURE 25-61 KPI Web Part

There are two KPI Web Parts that are available with MOSS. The first displays the KPI list, as shown in Figure 25-61. There is also a Web Part called KPI Details where a single large indicator can be used to display overall status based on summary data. Figure 25-62 shows that Web Part in the top-right corner of a page with several different uses of Excel Services for reporting.

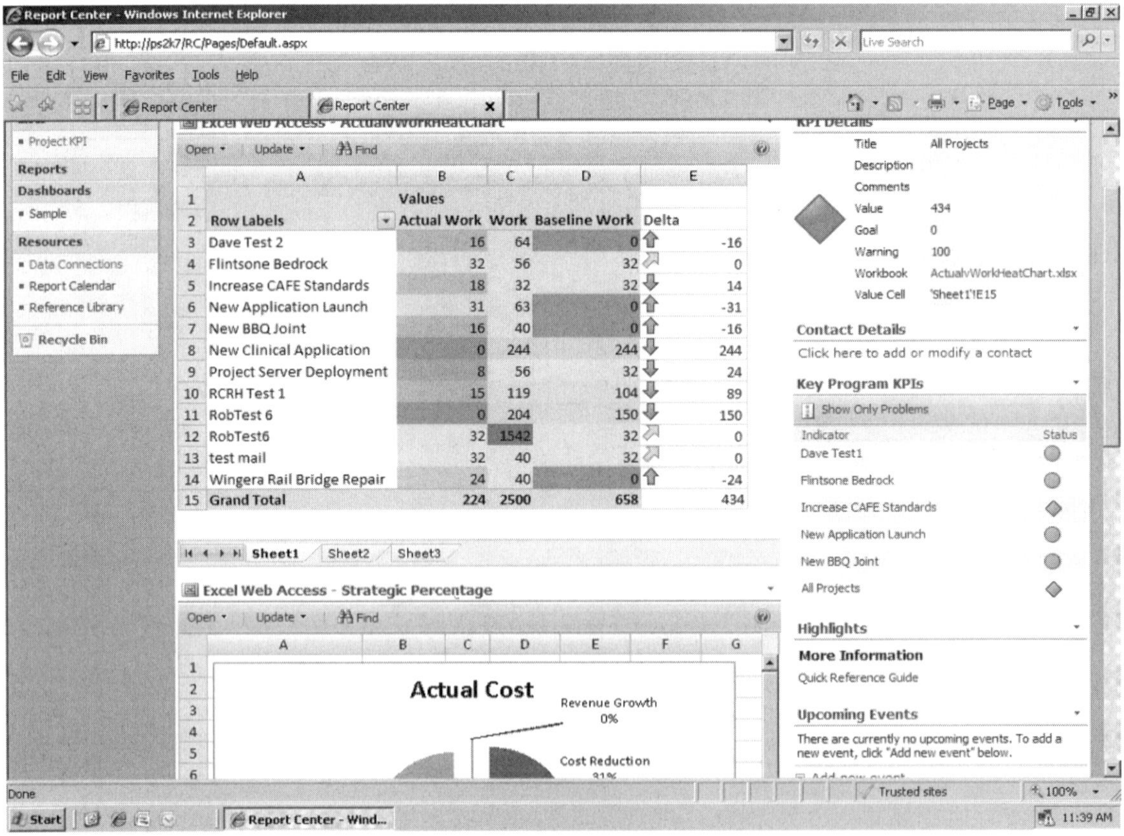

FIGURE 25-62 Reports page with Excel Services Web Parts

Displaying SQL Server Reports

While not part of the Project Server, WSS, or MOSS, SQL Reporting Services 2005 provides a strong report-building platform that can be exposed in SharePoint. These reports can make valuable additions to the Project Server/MOSS Business Intelligence platform we are covering here. Report pages such as seen in Figure 25-63 (supplied by our Technical Editor, Dan Ling) are one method for displaying SQL Reports. Reports can also be displayed in smaller Web Parts as part of an overall BI dashboard.

Forms Services

This new feature of MOSS 2007 Enterprise allows use of forms using Microsoft Office InfoPath 2007 functionality as Web-based tools. In earlier situations, the only way to use the power of InfoPath was for each person who touched a form to use the InfoPath desktop client. Like all client software, there were classic deployment issues and it limited use in the case when non-employees might need to make contact with a form.

In MOSS 2007, forms are designed using the desktop tools and can be published as web forms for use by whomever has access to the particular location in the MOSS environment.

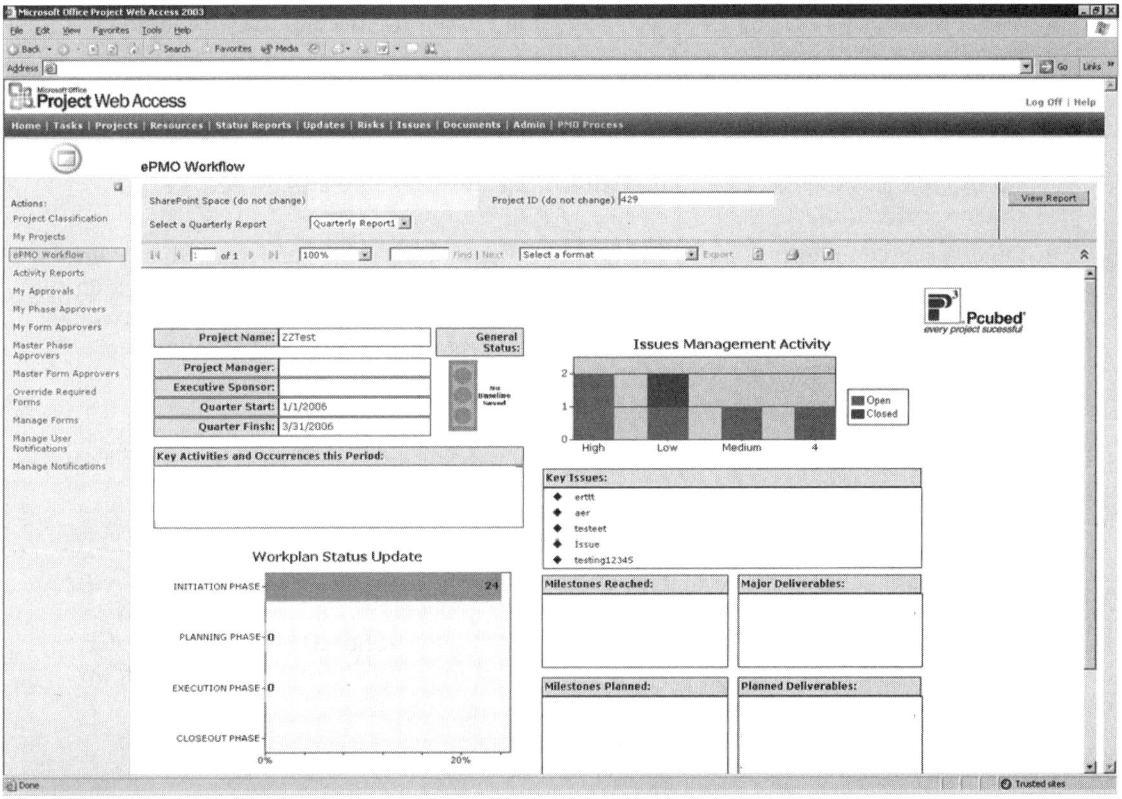

FIGURE 25-63 SQL Reports Page

For a Project Server solution, uses could include New Project Requests, Change Requests, Defect Management, or other possibilities.

Enterprise Search

WSS 3.0, the base platform where Project Server resides, includes a site search tool. This allows indexing and searching from within an individual Project Workspace or other WSS site. It will not search across sites.

The MOSS search utility can provide index and search services across the entire SharePoint infrastructure. In addition, other content sources can be indexed as well. These include exchange folders, Web sites, and back-end systems where a BDC connection has been established. Having this search flexibility can be a powerful usability bonus if the Project Server 2007 environment is in a MOSS environment.

Other SharePoint Ideas for the Project Server Environment

The following are a few ideas that might be useful in specific Project Server environments where SharePoint technologies might be leveraged:

- **Recruiting dashboard** Projects based on an Enterprise template are used to track the progress of the new hiring process. A SharePoint list can be used to track a candidate's resumes, interview results, and hiring status.
- **Defect management** For software or manufacturing, if an external defect management system is in place, the recommendation would be to leverage that investment by integrating it with SharePoint. If not, it would be possible to create a list that tracks the defect and the status of the defect as it relates to a group or a single specific project.
- **Quality management** Quality is a critical portion of the project lifecycle. SharePoint is a great platform for managing test plans, test scripts, and test results for each step of testing. In addition, modern quality systems such as Six Sigma can be supported in SharePoint. For example, a list could be created to track the status of individual training in quality metrics.

The bottom line is that SharePoint technologies are a fantastic potential partner with Project Server beyond the obvious components (documents, issues, and risks). For almost all organizations, it makes sense to extend the Project environment using SharePoint. Specific environments and their requirements dictate the best solutions.

In this chapter we discussed how to use technologies provided by Microsoft as tools for communication and collaboration. There is a lot of room for imaginative uses and we have touched on only a few. We have found that surprising organizational improvements can be enabled with very little technical cost using the tools we discussed here. The last two chapters of the book will touch on how to use Project Server 2007 to support Program and Portfolio management.

PART VI

Program and Portfolio Management

26

CHAPTER

Program Management

In project management methodologies, the term *program* generally refers to a group of projects that have something or things in common. For example, a corporate acquisition could entail integration of human resources departments, information technology (IT) departments, facilities, and more. Each of these could be separate projects. In fact, merging IT departments alone could include many individual projects, all with different project managers. Together, however, they make up the acquisition program.

Project Server generally would treat each of these separate projects as independent of each other. Earlier versions of Project Server provided limited ways to connect these projects into a program. More tools are available in Project Server 2007, and in fact program management is now a capability in Project Server.

Program management does add extra levels of complexity in the tools, especially in the use of cross-project dependencies. Developing appropriate processes for program management is critical to making use of these features, as is developing specific program reports and views.

Custom Program Field

As with any important characteristic that can be used to group projects together, commence by making the attribute a custom enterprise project field. As described earlier in the book, navigate to Server Settings in Project Web Access (PWA). Create a lookup table with a list of the organization's ongoing programs. This lookup table can be changed as programs are added. (It is not a great idea, however, to remove items from this lookup table, as doing so can create data issues. For reporting purposes, it makes more sense to leave each option in place anyway.)

Select New Lookup Table. Give the table a name (in this example, Programs), select Text, and populate the table with the names of programs. In this example, one of the items listed is Acquisition. Next create a custom enterprise project text field. Select the Programs lookup table and decide whether the field should be required. Finally, save the new field.

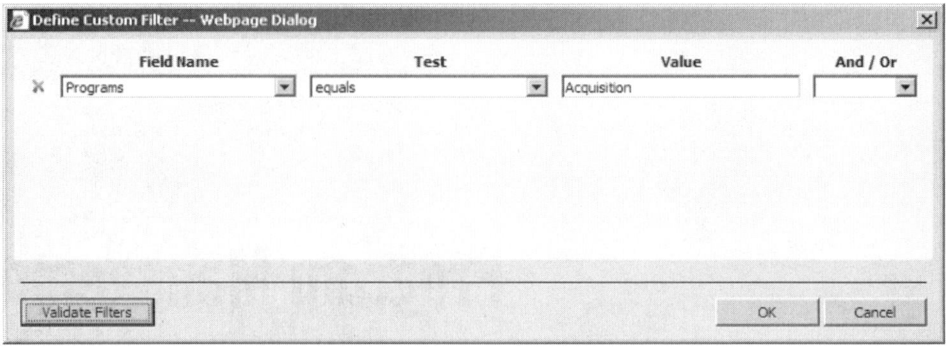

FIGURE 26-1 View filter for an acquisition program

Program View

The next step is to create a new Project Center View that filters on a single Program. From Server Settings, select Manage Views and either create a new view or use the Copy feature on an existing view. In this case, the Project Center Summary View was copied and a filter was added to the new Acquisition View to display only projects where the Programs field is set to Acquisition. Select the Filter button from within the View and use the tool to set the filter that is needed (see Figure 26-1).

Once projects have this new field set, those projects that have the Acquisition Program attribute set will display in the new Acquisitions Project Center View.

Master Projects

As discussed earlier in Chapter 21, Master Projects are supported and functional for the first time in Project Server 2007. By default, the Allow Master Projects setting in Project Server is enabled. Therefore, using a Master Project makes sense in some cases to view details of the projects that are part of a program.

As a reminder, you set up a Master Project by opening a new blank project in Project Professional. This new project will be the future Master Project (If you plan on using the Workspace sub-site feature described later in this chapter, make sure that you Save and Publish the project before moving to the next step). Next select Insert | Project, then select the first project of the program. Repeat this process until you have added each project that is part of the program.

NOTE *It is recommended that Master Projects should be published to the server only if all the subprojects are also saved or published to the Project Server. Don't mix project types.*

The projects start out being displayed completely rolled up, but can be selected so that you can drill down into the details. Cross-project dependencies can be added next. When all of that is ready, set any required project fields. Then save the new project with the subprojects included by selecting the Save button, as shown in Figure 26-2.

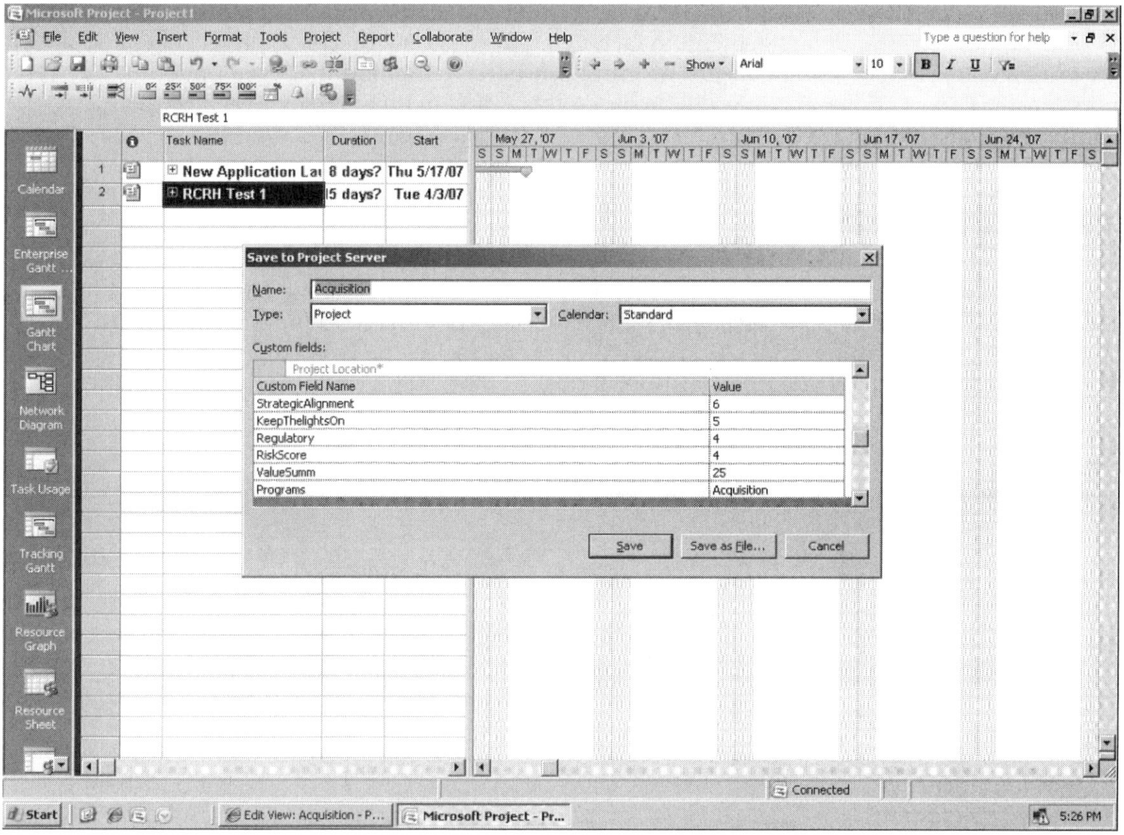

FIGURE 26-2 Saving the master

From this point, a Save dialog appears that supports the Save function across all the individual projects in the program (see Figure 26-3). Select Yes to All.

From this point on, if the program manager wants to see a view of the details of the program and everything in it, he or she need only open the Master Project. It is important to note that inserting an individual project into more than one Master Project can be problematic.

FIGURE 26-3 Saving subprojects

It is not necessarily true that using Master Projects and subprojects represents the best way to support program management. In fact, using the custom enterprise project field and views for each program may make just as much sense. Keep in mind that even under the non–Master Project/subproject paradigm, it is still possible to link tasks between projects, as you will learn in the next section.

Cross-Project Dependencies

To link tasks between projects, follow the same process just described until the projects where cross-project dependencies are to be used are inserted. In the example shown in Figure 26-4, the two small projects are both displayed. Notice the dates of the second project's design task.

Use the CTRL key to select a task from each project, then select the Link button. If you used the example displayed in Figure 26-4, after clicking the Link button, you would notice that the

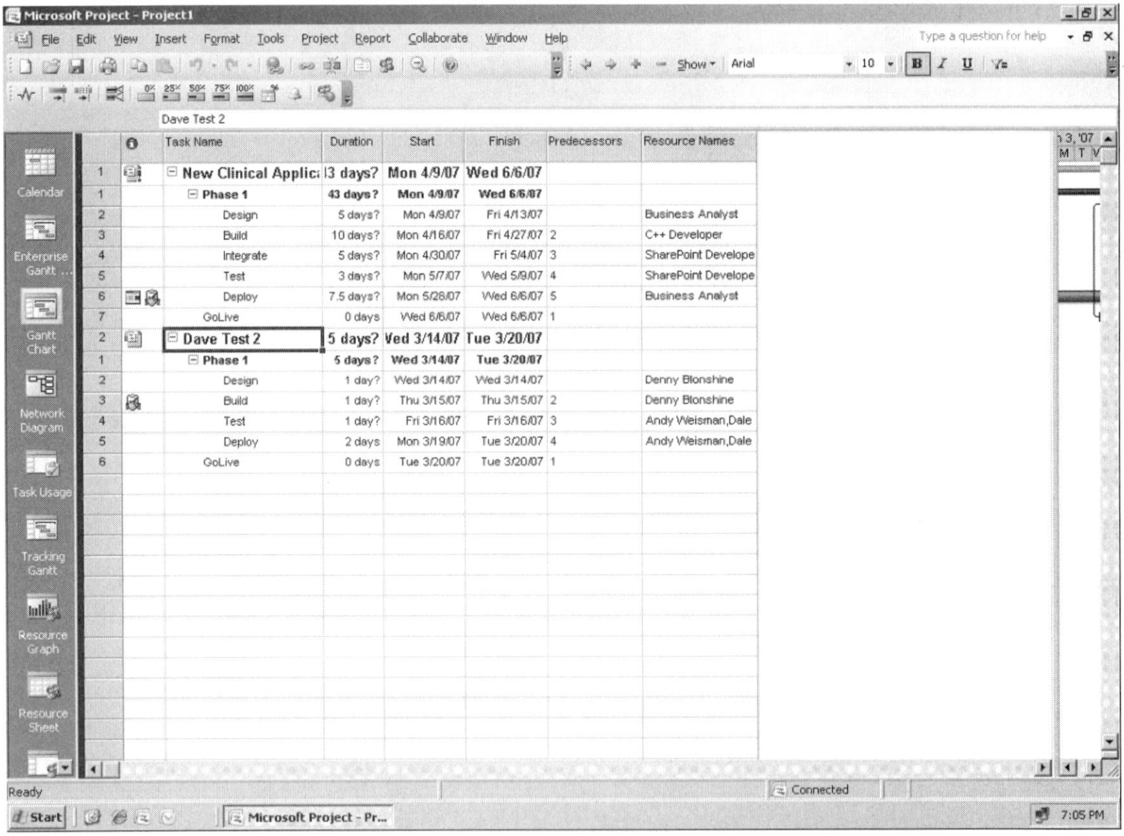

FIGURE 26-4 Two inserted projects

finish date on the successor task was pushed way back. Also notice the information in the Predecessor field. It is possible to save the Master Project with the subprojects that include cross-project dependencies. It is also possible to save only the inserted projects without saving a Master Project. In either case, the links remain in place. Either model can make sense in a program management scenario.

Provision Subworkspaces

Another feature that supports programs is a new ability to provision Project Workspace subsites when a project is first published. For example, suppose that a program-level project called Acquisition Program was published. This project could be a site that was provisioned when a new Master Project was created. In this case, a small project was created and published just for the purpose of creating a top-level workspace for the program.

This top-level site can be used to house information for the program. For example, the Calendar Web Part could be used for program events. Announcements could be valuable. Certainly, a Project Center Web Part that displays information only about the projects within the program can be very useful.

The next step is to create the subprojects. When you are ready to publish the new subprojects go ahead, but when presented with the usual Project Workspace provisioning dialog, instead of selecting Publish right away, select the checkbox Provision the Workspace as a Sub-Workspace of Another Project? Next locate the program-level project from the Select a Project dropdown list (see Figure 26-5). Finally, select Publish and a sub-Workspace will be created underneath the program level.

Once the new sub-Workspace has been created, it will be available from within the Sites and Workspaces page of the top-level site (see Figure 26-6). To get to this page from the top-level site, select Sites from the Quick Launch Bar.

There is no list of links that is automatically generated at the site level. To display the links more visually, use the Summary Link Web Part shown in Figure 26-7.

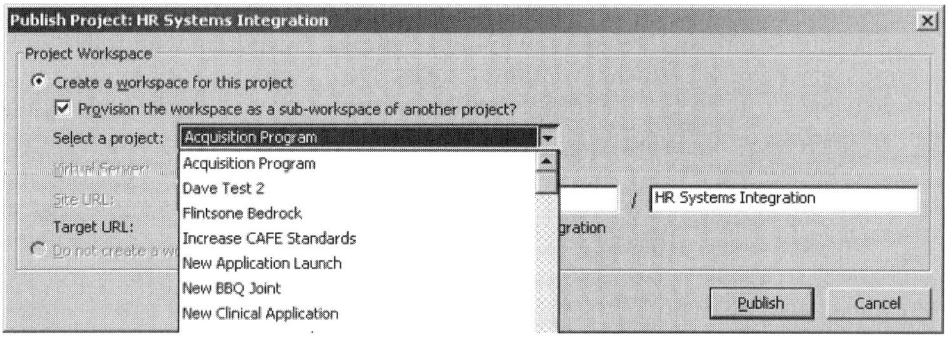

FIGURE 26-5 Provisioning a sub-Workspace

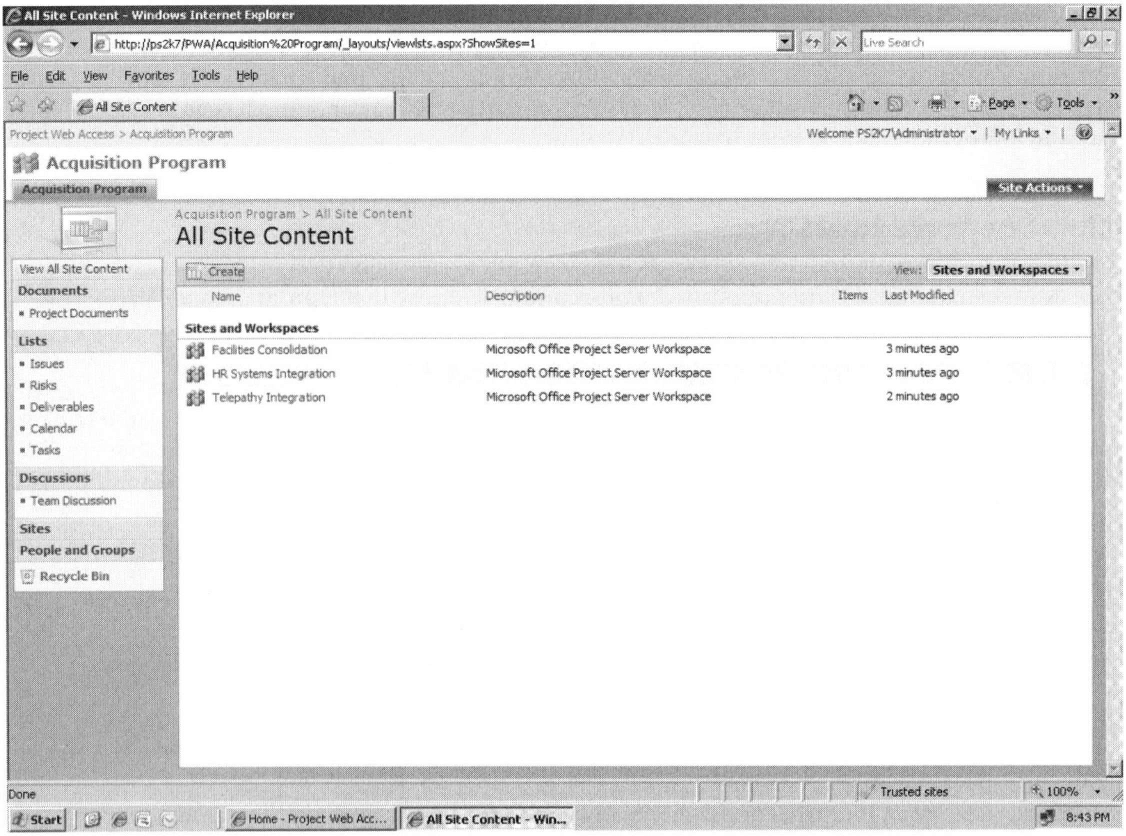

FIGURE 26-6 List of sub-workspaces

Another option is to add the sub-workspaces as items in the Quick Launch Bar. To add a new Quick Launch link, select Site Actions | Site Settings. Next, from within the Look and Feel section, select Quick Launch. From there, select New Link and add the URL and a descriptive name for the item. Finally, decide the new item's location on the Quick Launch Bar by using the Heading dropdown list and click OK.

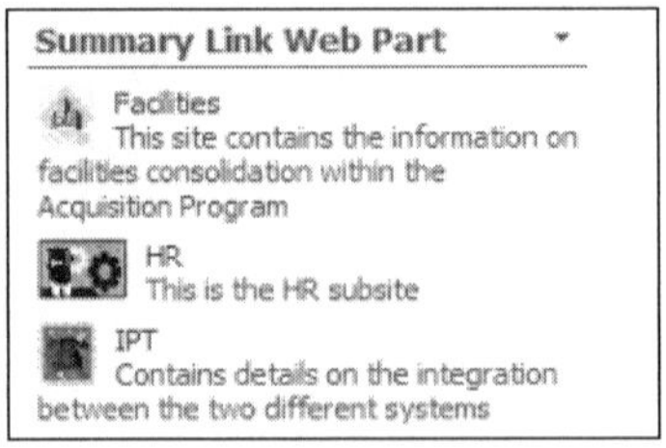

FIGURE 26-7 Summary links of sub-workspaces

If the new link needs to be moved into a different section of the Quick Launch Bar, navigate to Site Actions, Site Settings, and Quick Launch. Then choose Change Order and move the links around as desired.

Deliverables

Deliverables is a new feature in the Project Workspaces. Using cross-project deliverables within a program can be useful in place of hard task links between projects or, in some cases, in addition to them. They create a loose coupling between projects in that if a predecessor deliverable is late, it does not automatically affect the successor's dates. Rather, they are used for informational purposes to allow the PM of the successor project to decide whether action is required. To connect projects via cross-project deliverables, the project (or program) manager starts by creating a deliverable in a Project Workspace (keep in mind that for programs, this Workspace could be a subsite). To create a deliverable, select Deliverables from the Quick Launch Bar in a Project Workspace. Select New and then complete the dialog with the name of the deliverable and start date, as shown in Figure 26-8.

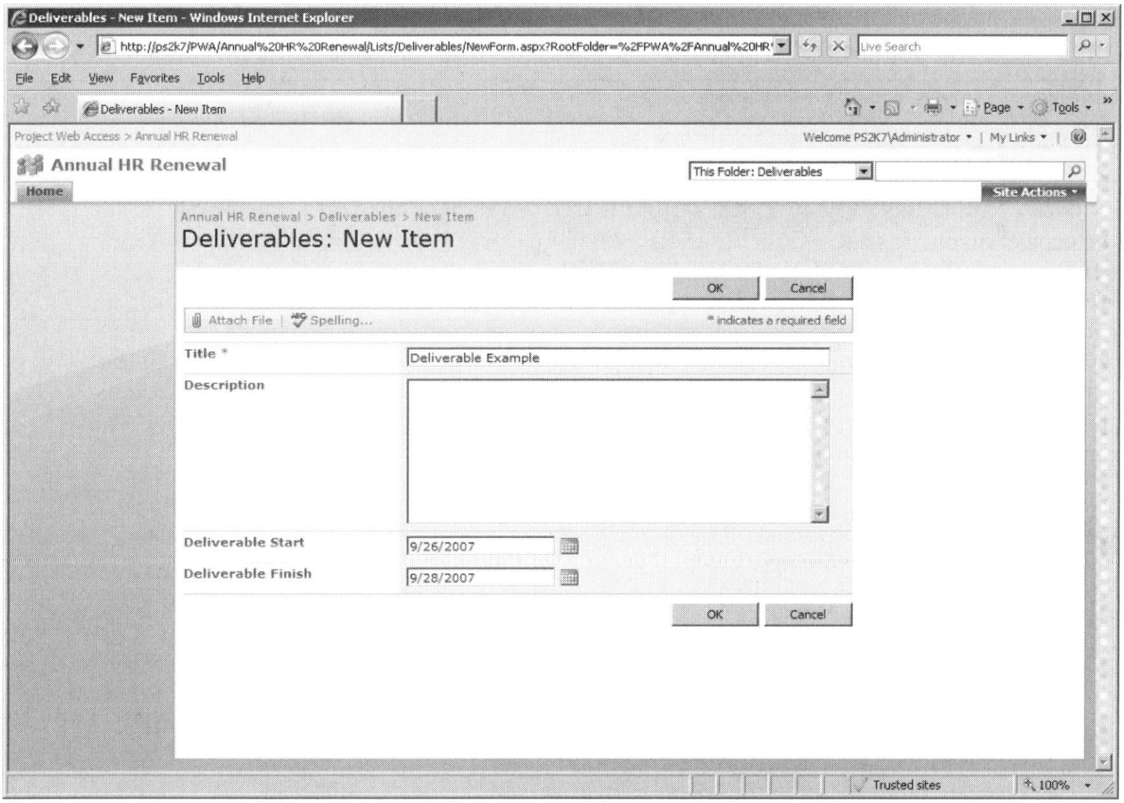

FIGURE 26-8 Building a deliverable

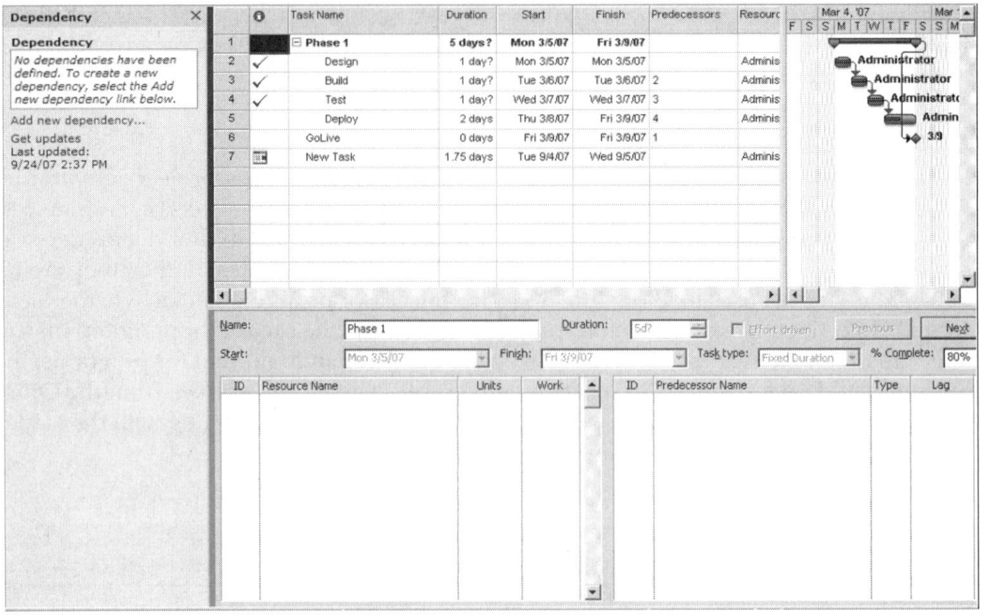

FIGURE 26-9 Dependencies on deliverables

From within one of the program's projects where a dependency on a deliverable exists, the project manager selects Collaboration | Manage Dependencies on Deliverables. A new pane opens in Project Professional, as shown in Figure 26-9.

Next select Add New Dependency and use the dropdown list to select the specific project where the deliverable is located. Highlight the specific deliverable from the list of available deliverables on the selected project. Finally select the task in the current plan that is to be dependent on the selected deliverable, select the Link to Selected Task checkbox, then click Done. An example is shown in Figure 26-10. Notice in Figure 26-11 that there is a new indicator on the task where the dependency was added.

Reporting on Programs

The last piece of program management in the Project Server environment is program reporting. The reporting techniques are the same for program management as they are for other Project Server areas. They include the following:

- **Project Center views** Create Project Center views that include only projects that are within the specified program by filtering on a custom enterprise project field (Programs).
- **Project Details views** In most cases, the standard views will do the trick, but if the projects within a program have different needs, account for the different needs with

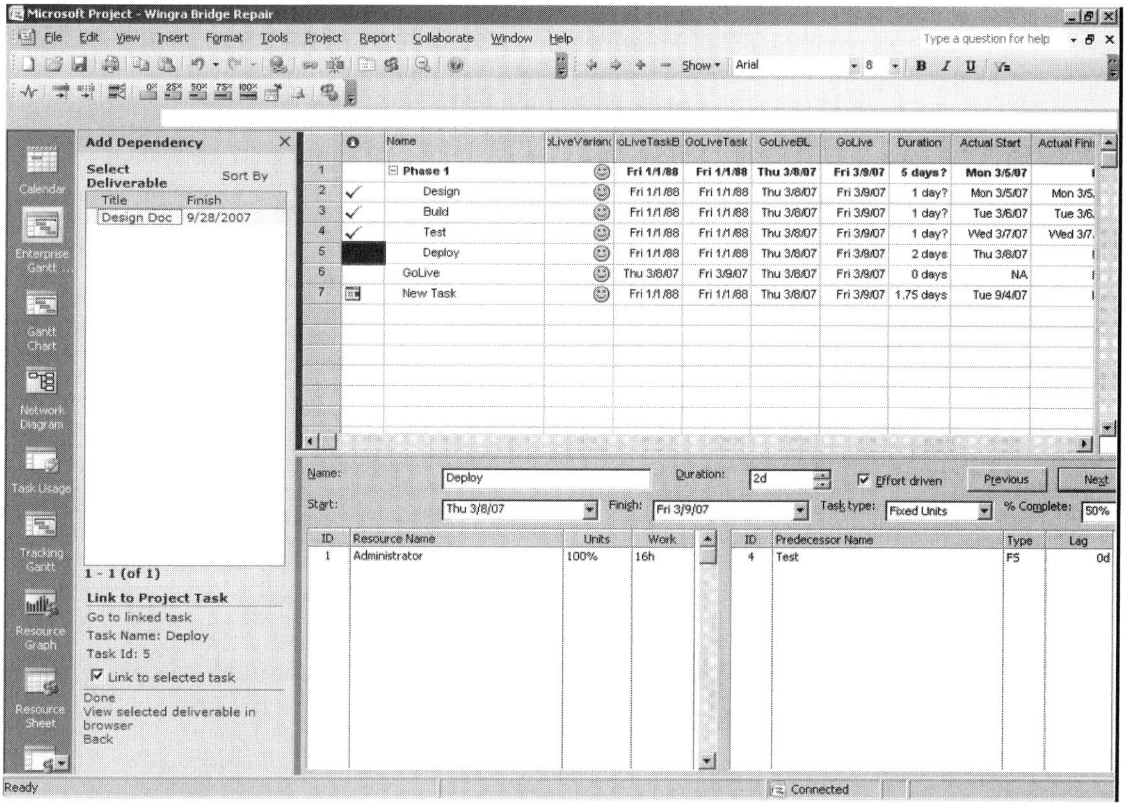

FIGURE 26-10 Example Dependency dialog in Project Professional

new views. For example, if the program has a specific metric that needs to be exposed within each project, create a view that includes this metric.

- **Data Analysis views** Data Analysis views can be filtered using a custom project field such as the attribute discussed earlier. Views can be built just to include the program's projects, or end users can manipulate more inclusive views by using filtering options from the Data Analysis Tool Pane.

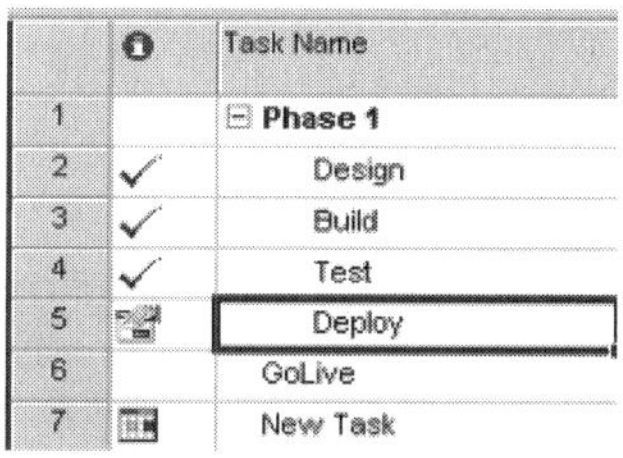

FIGURE 26-11 Dependency indicator associated with "Deploy" task

- **Custom reports** Use any custom reporting tool, such as SQL Server Reporting Services or one of many other reporting options, to get the level of information needed. These can include specific projects in a program, including deliverables and dependencies on deliverables as described in this chapter.

The new Program Management features are a small, but useful addition to the system. There are some caveats, such as the complexity of creating cross-project links as were described in the chapter. When used carefully, these features can add value to your solution. However, they should not be considered a compelling reason to implement, but rather a small piece of a larger solution. We address Project Portfolio Management in the next chapter.

CHAPTER 27

Project Portfolio Management

One of the greatest challenges for companies today is to align projects to an overall business vision. Many executive-level decision makers are unaware of projects that are under way or potential projects that the company could be working on. Business managers may be engaging in projects that do not align with the short- and long-term goals of the company.

Project Portfolio Management (PPM) is a way for organizations to measure the value of proposed projects against a set of strategies and goals. The idea is to execute those projects that will provide the highest value to the company, avoid pursuing suboptimal projects, and use resources in the most efficient way from a global perspective rather than that of a single department. The process generally starts with a New Project Request. This request is evaluated—that is, its value is scored—often by a group of decision makers usually referred to as a steering committee. Establishing the scoring criteria can be a difficult process, but is required in order to make more objective decisions.

Perhaps the most difficult aspect of implementing a PPM process is rebalancing the portfolio. Many companies decide whether projects should continue down the path of implementation based on whether the project is on time, is within budget, or meets other project-specific criteria. PPM adds another dimension. The steering committee should evaluate whether a project is still valuable, whether or not its execution is going well. A dramatic change in market conditions, for example, might lead a steering committee to cancel a project even though it is tracking well.

Microsoft Project Portfolio Server (PPS) is a powerful server-based tool offering companies an opportunity to significantly improve efficiency. Like Project Server, however, Microsoft Portfolio Server is a large and complex toolset that requires a high level of organizational maturity. This maturity must be in more than project management. It also requires experience in project portfolio ranking, balancing, and rebalancing. Portfolio Server offers a way for companies to streamline the project request process. In addition, PPS supports automated governance processes and provides tools for objectively prioritizing projects. It can also be used to measure and track the performance of projects through their complete lifecycle and integrates with Project Server 2007.

Many companies would like to start down the path of PPM but are not prepared to go through the cost and effort of implementing Project Portfolio Server or one of its competitors. In other cases, the organization is looking to implement PPM at an entry level, from which it can grow into a powerful solution over the long run.

NOTE *Also, this is not a book on Project Portfolio Server.*

Project Server 2007 is not designed to be a PPM system. Project Server and its base platform Windows SharePoint Services can, however, provide an effective baseline PPM solution. Imagination is all that is required. The following chapter opens a doorway into PPM and includes a combination of a high-level discussion of the process as well as the technical pieces needed to implement this process. This chapter is not intended to give you a complete end-to-end PPM solution, but it offers a good starting point for implementing a solution that fits your specific environment.

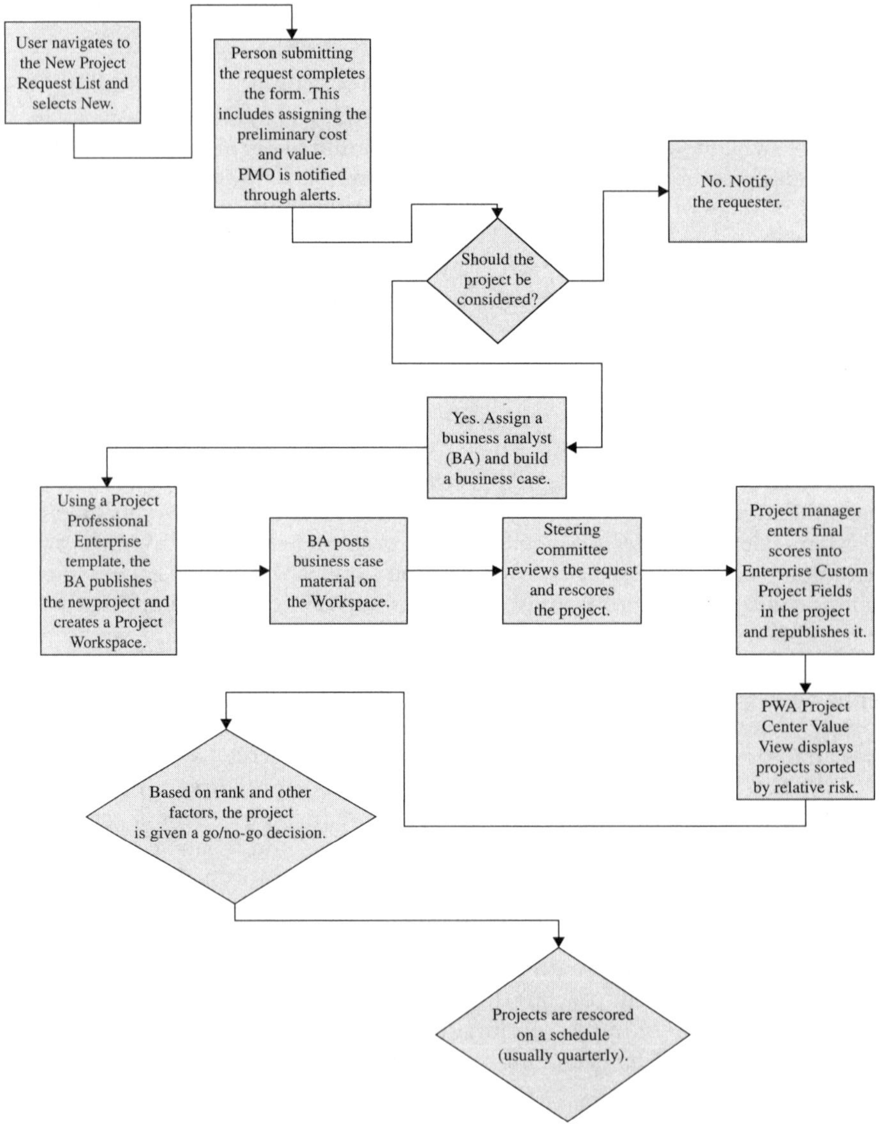

Before you can start the process, you need a way to take in potential projects. As discussed in Chapter 16, there are several ways to go about this. You might use the Proposals feature or InfoPath. For the example discussed in this chapter, the option chosen is to use a SharePoint custom list. (Lists are described in some depth in Chapter 25.)

SharePoint Portfolio Site

It is recommended to create a new Windows SharePoint site to house the New Project Request List. To create a new site, start at the Project Web Access Home Page and select Site Settings | Create. Next, from the bottom-right of the page, select Sites and Workspaces. Stay on the initial tab and choose Team Site. Consider the audience when deciding on permissions for this site. Will everyone need access, or will only certain people involved in PPM need permission? Are there security or other concerns? Keep in mind that you can modify permissions later if necessary.

The next step is to include whatever content is appropriate for an organizational PPM site. Consider a Project Center Web Part (possibly the Value View discussed later in this chapter) and/or a Resource Center Web Part. Remove lower-value Web Parts that will not be used as described in Chapter 25. Changing the look and feel may be appropriate; to do so, navigate to Site Settings | Settings and Site Theme. The next step is to choose the best way to handle incoming project requests. Chapter 16 describes three possible ways to handle these incoming requests. The built-in Proposals feature *might* be the best method for you. In this chapter, however, we will explore a different approach using a custom New Project Request List in Windows SharePoint Services. This is something that we have found useful as an alternative.

New Project Request Details

Consider what fields will be important for scoring the relative value of each potential project. The goal of this form is to get the initial requester's sense of the value of the request. Often corporate cultures initiate projects without giving enough thought to their value. This is especially true when requests are framed within the global corporate value rather than a department, workgroup, or even a single user. Asking the requester to consider worth to the organization is an important cultural step in establishing a value-driven PPM culture.

In this case, the following fields are used:

- **Title** The name of the proposed project. Windows SharePoint Services uses this required field to generate the unique ID in the system.
- **Detailed Description** This is a Rich Text field.
- **Date Required** This is the date and time field.
- **Project Manager** In this case, the choice was to select the project manager from a dropdown list. Under certain circumstances, a Text field would be an option, especially if the possible project manager options change a lot.
- **Cost-Benefit Overview** This is a Rich Text field.
- **Project Type** In this case, the size of the project was the category used for a selection from a dropdown list. It would also make sense to consider a field like this for a different categorization such as Corporate, Departmental, or Customer-Facing. Any number of other possibilities exist.

- **Critical Success Factors** This is a Rich Text field.
- **Estimated Project Cost** This field asks for an actual dollar value and uses the Currency field type.
- **Estimated effort** This is a Number field.
- **Value Scores** Note that in this case, not all the fields have equal ranges of options. In other words, rather than each field being a 1 through 10 list, some are 1 through 5, others are 1 through 10, and some are in between. Thus certain fields have priority when summarizing the total value of the combined scores. These are all Choice fields:
  - Internal Rate of Return
  - Keep the Lights On
  - Regulatory
  - Strategic Alignment
  - Risk

Figures 27-1 and 27-2 show the form detail as described previously for this version of the New Project Request.

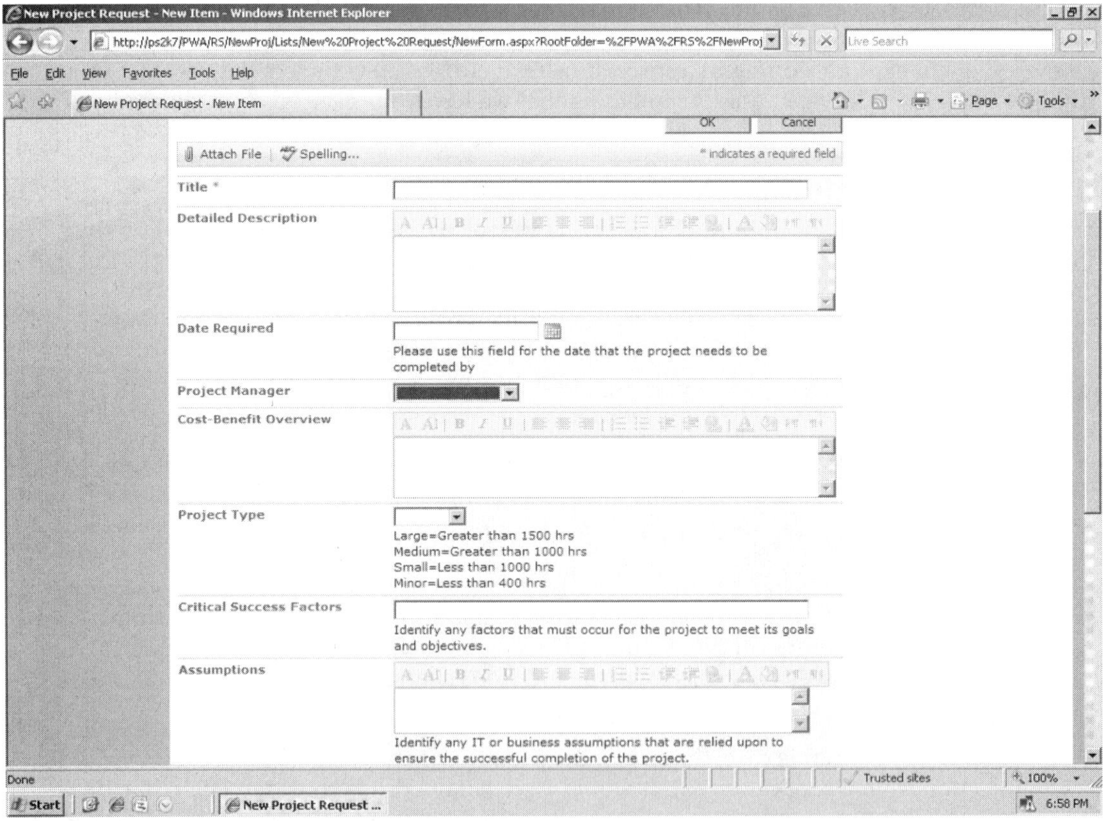

FIGURE 27-1 New Project Request (top)

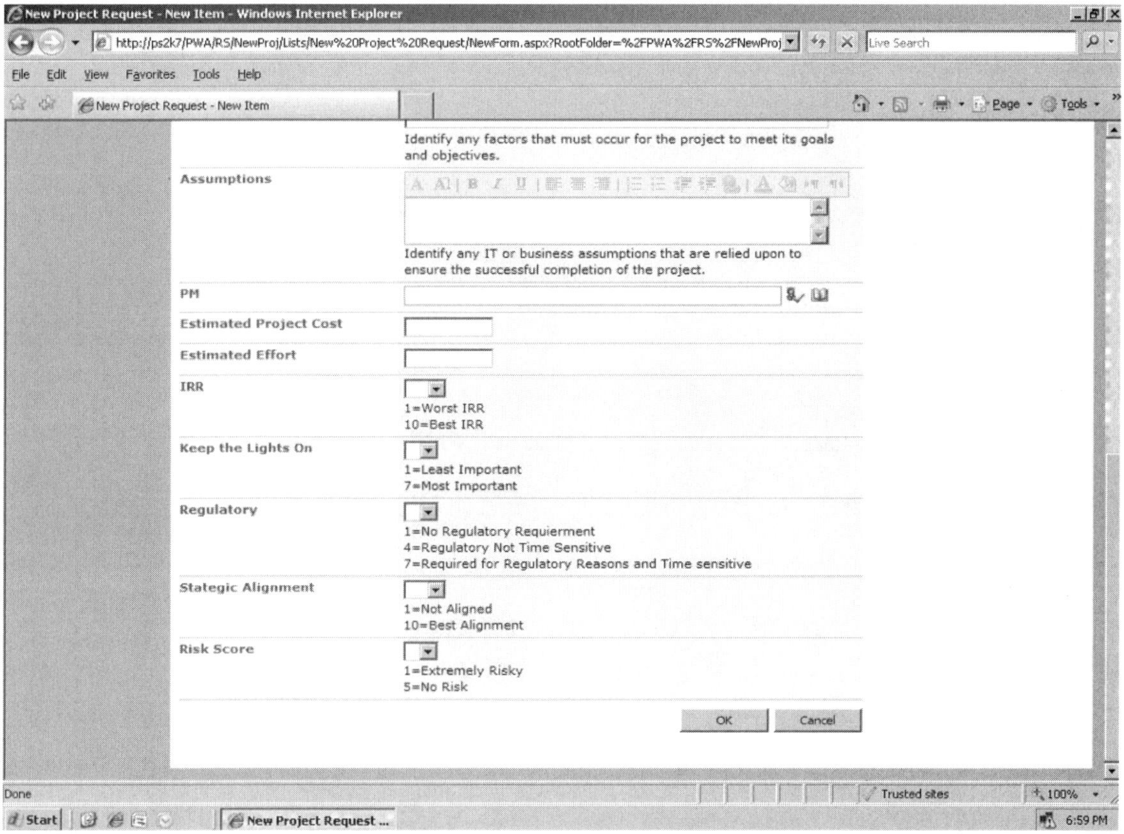

Figure 27-2 New Project Request (bottom)

The list itself can be configured to display an appropriate subset of values from submitted forms. Recall from Chapter 25 that it is generally not a good choice to display Text field types, especially those that can contain multiple lines. In this example, the Default All Items View shows the following:

- **Title**
- **Date Required**
- **Project Type**
- **Estimated Project Cost**
- **Estimated Effort**
- **Initial Value** This field adds the five value scores to display a total. More complex formulas could be used, for example, if the different fields had various weights.

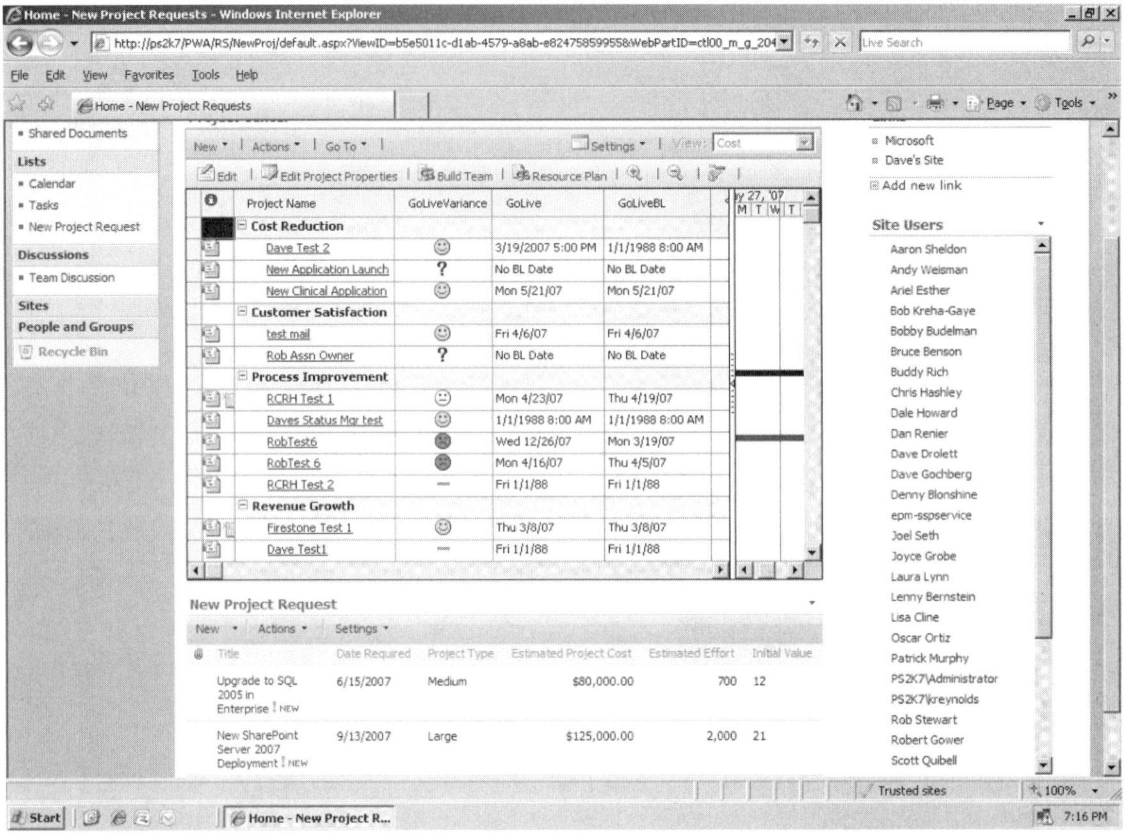

FIGURE 27-3 New Project Requests site with other Web Parts

Keeping in mind that any new content creates a new Web Part (see Chapter 25), add the New Project Request Web Part to the home page for this site. See Figure 27-3 for an example of how the home page of the New Project Requests site could look with Project Center and a New Project Requests Web Parts included.

Designated users can now submit New Project Requests. The next step is to make sure that someone knows about those submissions.

Using Alerts to Notify

Chapter 25 explained how to set alerts. The idea in this process is for the program management office (PMO) team to be alerted when any New Project Request is posted or modified. To do that, each team member must navigate to the New Project Request List and select Actions | Alert Me. From there, options are available, but the default setting probably is the best choice in this case. Another option for notifications that could be considered is using a workflow developed using the SharePoint Designer or Visual Studio.

Initial Evaluation and the Virtual Business Case

The next step is for the PMO or designated group to evaluate whether a request merits more than a cursory evaluation. If a request clearly is not going to result in an approved project, team members can let the requester know that there is not a budget to implement the digital signboard platform boots project at this time. In most cases, however, projects need further appraisal.

From this point, create a project and publish it to Project Server. One of the PMO's project managers can create this project from an Enterprise Custom Project template (based on Project Type, perhaps). The primary goals at this point are to provide the evaluators with a place to record time and work against the evaluation effort and to create a Project Workspace.

The Project Workspace is then used to house any business case or other important project collateral that might be used to make a deeper assessment. From this point, the PMO can assess the smaller requests and rescore the projects. Larger projects, however, go to the project steering committee. Instead of documents being e-mailed or paper being distributed, this Workspace acts as a virtual home for the business case. An advantage of this is that if the project is "green-lighted," these documents stay connected with the actual project plan and all the other project-related information such as risk and issue management.

The project steering committee is usually made up of decision makers who represent all the major stakeholders at the corporate level. One client with whom the authors have worked designated a representative from each department to be included in the steering committee. Normally, a steering committee meets quarterly and scores new projects and also considers whether ongoing projects will continue to be scored and whether they are ranked appropriately. Note that this group might also consider whether any projects should be canceled when they are over budget or have increased risk or when market conditions have changed the project's relative value. Canceling a project due to a change in market circumstances even though the project is otherwise going well can often be one of the most difficult parts of PPM. This revaluation process is not always included in the PPM processes when just starting down the PPM path.

Enterprise Custom Fields and the Value View

The next step is to create enterprise custom fields that match the criteria that were used for scoring in the New Project Request List. Include an extra field that sums all the Value fields just as in the SharePoint list. Next create a Project Center Value View, sorting the projects by the summary of the other fields with most valuable on top.

If the process is targeted at PPM only for incoming new projects, then another field could be created at the project level for the project status (such as Requested, Approved, Executing, Postponed, Canceled, or Complete) that could be used a filter on the view so that only requested projects are displayed and projects in other statuses could be filtered out.

This makes sense for requests, but not if the steering committee plans to evaluate and rescore ongoing projects.

Once the steering committee has reviewed all the business case material, it rescores the project from the enterprise perspective. These updated scores are then entered in the custom fields by the project manager from within Microsoft Office Project Professional 2007 (Project | Project Information), or by anyone with the Edit Project Properties permission from within PWA. Figure 27-4 shows how these fields appear from within the PWA Edit Project Properties window.

The information in the enterprise custom project fields can then be displayed in a sorted by Value View in PWA. Figure 27-5 shows an example of how that view might appear. Note that in this case, the sum of the scores is displayed as graphical indicators based on the range of the score.

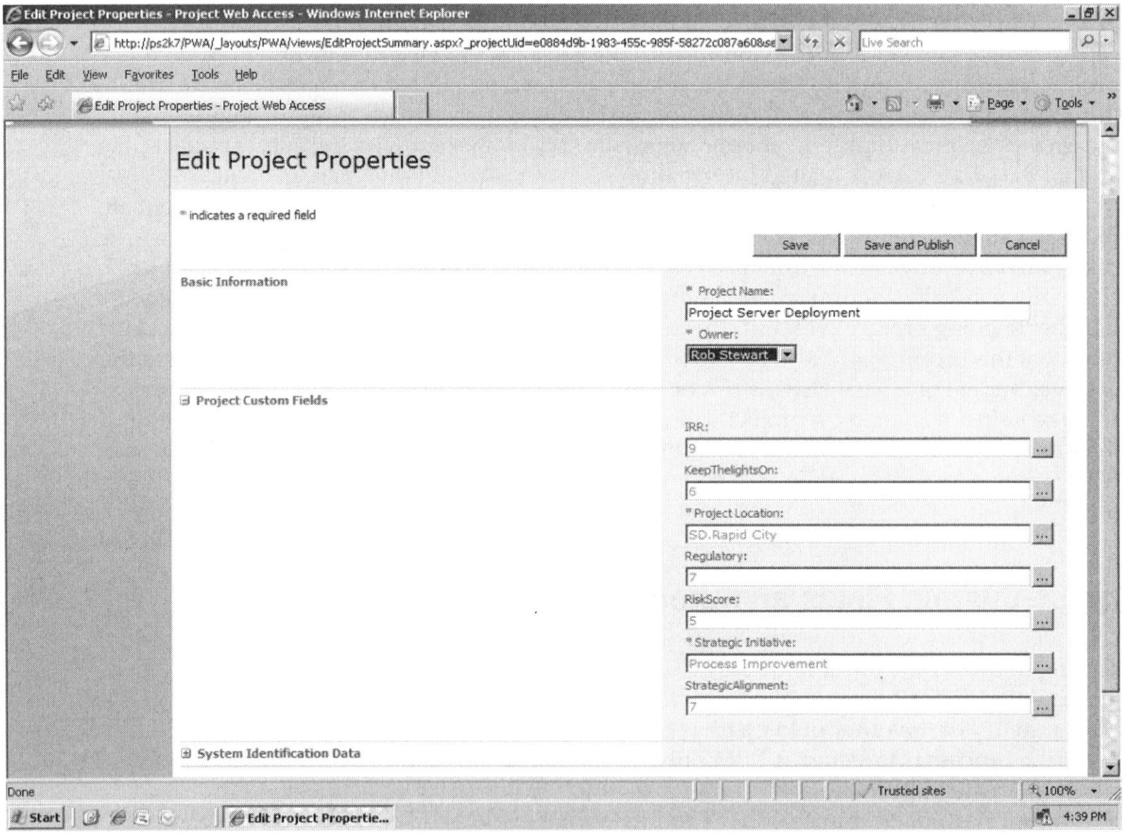

FIGURE 27-4 Edit Project Properties window

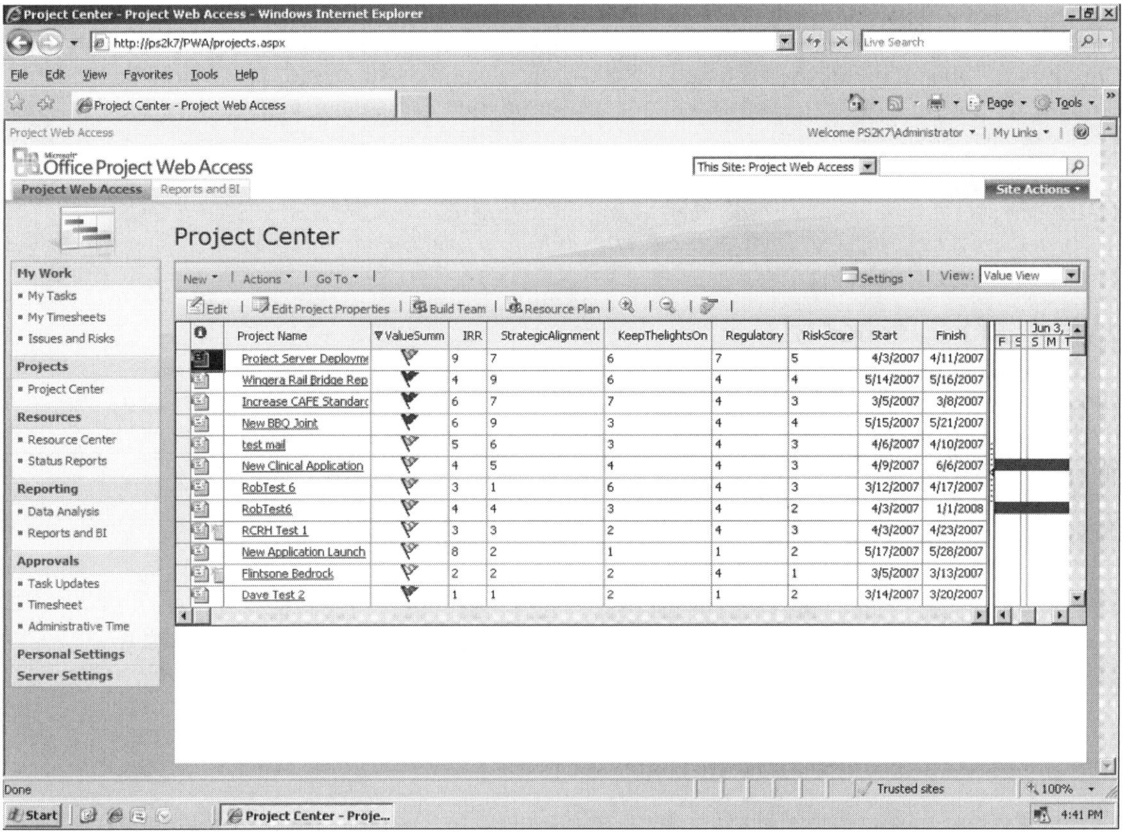

FIGURE 27-5 Value View

Resourcing the Projects

There is one more process component. After the steering committee has prioritized the projects, it must determine when projects can be executed; this involves the consideration of resource capacity. The Project Portfolio Server determines resource capacity very well using resource roles; however, using Project Server requires a more manual process.

Take the projects that were posted to get the Project Workspaces set up to house the business case documents. Use the projects that have already begun to set the steering committee scores. In each project, use the Build Team tool from the Enterprise field to see which resources might have time available. If an Enterprise Custom Resource Role field has been created, filter on resources that match the desired roles needed on the proposed projects.

The steering committee can now execute what-if scenarios by selecting possible resources (or Generic Resources) and setting them to Proposed rather than the default setting, Committed. When the Proposed setting is selected, the potential team members will not be notified and the possible future tasks will not appear on their Tasks page, nor will their time be blocked as unavailable.

CAUTION *At the time of this writing, there is an issue where resources are presented with Tasks even when set to Proposed. Use Generic Resources instead as a work-around.*

Value View and Dashboard

Consider what other fields should be displayed in the Value View. To create the view, choose Server Settings | Manage Views and create a New Project Center View. Just add the fields that make sense. Keep in mind that the field will not be populated until projects are republished.

Referring to Figure 27-5, think of the output this way:

- When the steering committee displays all the scores, there is transparency to the process. Although there may be some grumbling ("Why was my project only given a four for strategic alignment?"), over time the system users will likely begin to understand the type of projects that are likely to be approved and hone their requests appropriately. It can only be considered a positive if the user community matures along with the systems that are being used.
- It will be easy to quickly see whether a project is likely to happen. ("We never do projects unless they are at least light blue.")

Finally, take whatever pieces make sense and aggregate them in a Windows SharePoint Services site that is dedicated to PPM. Perhaps this site would also host the New Project Request List.

As stated at the beginning of this chapter, the example solution described here is not intended to take the place of a more complete PPM solution such as Project Portfolio Server. Rather, it is just a starting point for an organization to begin the path toward becoming a more value-oriented workplace. While PPM ultimately should be done at the top level of an organization, if that top level is not ready for this role (for example if there were no corporate strategic plan with measurable objectives), this process could be executed at the departmental level. For instance, it would add value for new product development or information technology departments. It could also be executed at both the company level for larger initiatives and at a departmental level for departmental strategies. In the case of a department, it often makes sense for the steering committee to meet more frequently because the projects tend to come in at a quicker pace and tend to be smaller. In the end, the mature organization seeks to choose the projects that will add the most value. It then executes those projects and keeps an eye on whether the value is retained during the project life-cycle.

Index

A

D

F

Q

R

U

Y